Plants of Life,
Plants of Death

Plants of Life, Plants of Death

FREDERICK J. SIMOONS

THE UNIVERSITY OF WISCONSIN PRESS

The University of Wisconsin Press
2537 Daniels Street
Madison, Wisconsin 53718

3 Henrietta Street
London WC2E 8LU, England

5   4   3   2   1

Printed in the United States of America

Library of Congress Cataloging-in-Publication Data
Simoons, Frederick J.
    Plants of life, plants of death / Frederick J. Simoons.
    586 pp.   cm.
    Includes bibliographical references and index.
    ISBN 0-299-15900-0 (cloth : alk. paper).
    ISBN 0-299-15904-3   (pbk. : alk. paper)
    1. Plants—Folklore. 2. Medicinal plants—Folklore. 3. Plants—Mythology.
    4. Human-plant relationships. I. Title.
    GR780 1998
    398'.368—dc21   98-9689

To our friends in Wisconsin:
Louise Clark and family, Virginia Emlen,
Ray and Mary Evert,
Ruth Huttenberg and family,
Clarence and Rhea Olmstead,
Charles and Patricia Schrade,
and Thompson and Diana Webb,
and in memory of academic friends
who died recently and too soon:
John Emlen, Norman Kretchmer,
Richard P. Palmieri, James J. Parsons,
and Robert V. Pyle

CONTENTS

ILLUSTRATIONS

Map

Figures

PREFACE

When I was wandering around the ancient ruins at Eleusis in Greece several years ago, I was struck by a carved stone depicting (1) a sheaf of wheat—symbolic of the goddess Demeter, fertility, life, and growth, and (2) a stylized pomegranate flower—symbolic of her daughter Persephone, the underworld, death, and rebirth (Figure 1). As I turned the matter over in my mind, I became aware that, in fact, three articles I had recently completed, as well as the next several articles I planned to do, all related to the themes depicted on the Eleusis stone. Why, I wondered, should I not develop the themes more fully than can be done in a series of articles? The result was further research and writing and, in due time, this book, *Plants of Life, Plants of Death*—inspired by a stone that was probably carved two millennia ago.

I am indebted to the Washington State University and its Department of Anthropology and to Eastern Washington University and its Department of Geography and Anthropology for granting me adjunct appointments which have greatly facilitated my research by providing full access to their library facilities. I am also grateful to Gonzaga University, which has an unusually good collection of materials on religion and the classics, for granting me extended borrowing privileges. Special thanks are also due the following: the excellent staff of the Cooperative Academic Library Services (CALS) of Spokane, who, over the years, have gone out of their

1. Stone at Eleusis with symbols of life and death.

way to assist me in locating and obtaining books and articles; Dr. Antonio Tagarelli of the Istituto di Medicina Sperimentale et Biotecnologie–Consiglio Nazionale delle Ricerche in Mangone (Cosenza), Italy, for making available published and unpublished materials on favism and malaria; Khaled Bloom of the University of California–Davis, who has helped me obtain illustrations from libraries there; Daniel W. Gade for his valuable suggestions for improving the manuscript; Deryck O. Lodrick for similar suggestions; and Robin Whitaker, my editor, who, as before, has made a special effort to see that the manuscript meets her high standard and that of the University of Wisconsin Press. Most of all, I am obligated to my wife, Elizabeth, for her critical, but sympathetic, judgments of my ideas, and for her tolerance of my unusual working hours and repeated trips that have interrupted the normal functioning of our household.

Spokane, Washington   F. J. S.
April 1997

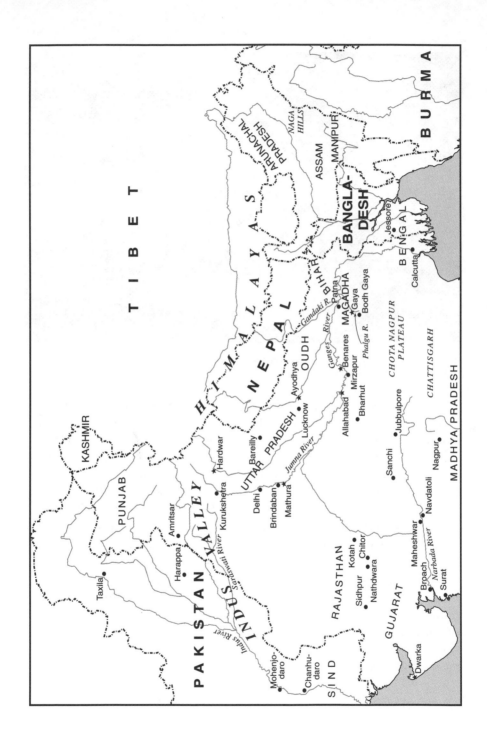

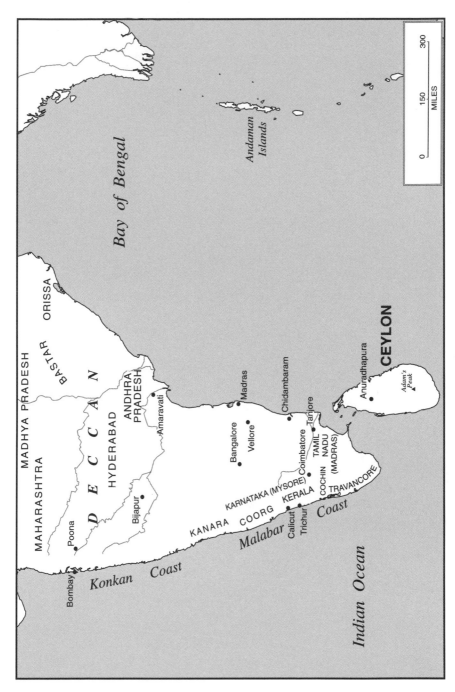

India and its neighbors: place-names mentioned in the text. Each star represents a "sacred city of Hinduism."

MADHYA PRADESH
BASTAR
ORISSA
MAHARASHTRA
DECCAN
HYDERABAD
ANDHRA PRADESH
Amaravati
Poona
Bijapur
Bombay
Konkan Coast
KANARA
COORG
KARNATAKA (MYSORE)
KERALA
COCHIN
TRAVANCORE
Calicut
Trichur
Malabar Coast
Bangalore
Vellore
Coimbatore
TAMIL NADU (MADRAS)
Madras
Chidambaram
Tanjore
CEYLON
Anuradhapura
Adam's Peak
Bay of Bengal
Andaman Islands
Indian Ocean

0   150   300
MILES

Plants of Life,
Plants of Death

1   Introduction

> Voltaire thought it incredible that the Egyptians could ever have
> worshipped onions and other products of their gardens. He always
> jeered at this tradition, and looked upon it as a mere fable. But
> the fact is, in matters of superstition truth is sometimes stranger
> than fiction.
>
> —J.-A. Dubois, *Hindu Manners, Customs, and Ceremonies*

The title of this book may lead certain readers to think that it is one in
plant science. It is not. Nor does it deal with food production or use,
human nutrition, or, except where it relates to my primary interest, with
the medicinal uses of plants. Instead, my focus is on magic, ritual, and
religion as they have shaped the way humans have perceived and used
plants since antiquity,[1] and I write from an ethnographic, geographic,
and culture historical perspective. My primary goal is to tell the stories of
certain plants that, since antiquity, have played unusual roles in ritual in
the areas of high civilization from Europe through the Near East to India
and China. To accomplish this, I have drawn mainly from the literature of
ethnography and cultural anthropology, ethnobotany, folklore, religious
studies, history, and classics. In the chapter on favism, I have also drawn
liberally from biomedical sources so as to understand better a disease
which has been of concern to classicists and historians as well as to physicians, geneticists, biologists, and physical anthropologists.

The plants on which I focus have been associated with ritual purity,
fertility, good health, prosperity, and life, on one hand, or with ritual
impurity, infertility, sickness, ill fate, and death, on the other. Some plants
I consider will be familiar to most contemporary Western readers. Others
will not, because, in selecting plants that have played a vital role in ritual
and religion, I have chosen modern examples largely from non-Western
lands, especially India.

I start with a chapter on an herb or small shrub that, though listed in
seed catalogs and sold here and there by nurseries in the United States,
is little known to the American public. This is *tulsi*, holy basil (*Ocimum
sanctum*), a different species from sweet basil (*Ocimum basilicum*), that flavoring which occupies so important a place in certain Western cuisines. I
chose tulsi because it is widely held to be the most sacred plant of Hindus

today; because it is not only used in temple ritual, but is also a central element in household worship; because it is not just a pretty plant, like our Easter lily, but is also involved in satisfying basic human concerns; because it plays a significant role at critical times of human life, such as birth, marriage, death; because it occupies a major place in Hindu mythology; and because it has powerful ties with leading Hindu deities. Thus not only is tulsi a live, functioning element in present-day Hindu society and culture, but it is also a plant with rich ties with other aspects of Indian culture, one that in ritual importance is surpassed by no other plant.

In my next chapter, I will consider two sacred fig-trees of India—the pipal (*Ficus religiosa*) and the banyan (*Ficus indica*). These two are giant trees that would be hard to ignore, but they are important for more than their size. They enjoy important roles in Hindu ritual and religion today, and they have since prehistoric times. They are also of unusual importance in Buddhist ritual, lore, and history, and play a role among many of India's tribal groups as well. The literature on the pipal and banyan, moreover, is much more extensive than that on India's other sacred trees, and this makes them ideal for opening to the reader the entire realm of sacred trees, which enjoy as rich and varied a role in modern India as they did in the ancient Mediterranean world. India's sacred trees are also important because certain of them are major goals of pilgrimage, and because historical records indicate that their status and affiliations have changed with the rise and decline of Indian religions.

My hope in introducing tulsi and the sacred fig-trees first is that this will make Western readers fully aware of how vital ritual plants can be, even today, in the lives of non-Western peoples. My hope is also that this will prepare them for the chapters that follow, to help them understand and make them sympathetic to similar views of plants that Western peoples possessed in ancient, medieval, and premodern times. I believe that ordering my chapters in this way is called for because, all too often, contemporary Western readers are inclined to dismiss early Western perceptions and ritual uses of plants as bizarre and incomprehensible.

Following the chapters on tulsi and the sacred fig-trees, I will describe the ritual role of mandrake (*Mandragora officinarum* and *M. autumnalis*), a magical plant of great importance in early Europe and the Near East, and will then compare its role with that of ginseng (*Panax ginseng*) in East Asia. I chose mandrake because of the unusual perception humans have had of this plant as a "man-root," a root human in form. As such, mandrake may be as close to humans in its perceived characteristics as it is possible for a plant to be, a likeness that humans took into account traditionally when gathering and using mandrake. Ginseng is considered largely because it, too, is a man-root; because there have been questions regarding what historical links there may have been between mandrake and ginseng; and because ginseng has not experienced the decline in popularity that mandrake has. On the contrary, in recent decades it has gained great popularity in some circles even in the Western world, and one can view it as a success and not merely, as is true of mandrake, a relic of the past.

In my next chapter, I will outline the role of garlic (*Allium sativum*) and its relatives in a belt stretching from Europe to China. I chose garlic because, unlike other plants considered, a significant element in its ritual status is odor. I also chose it because ancient ritual perceptions of the plant persist in the Western world, and because they seem to have evolved into nutritional and medical concerns that are the subject of continuing scientific research.

After garlic, I will turn to certain beans that have long played interesting roles in ritual and magic and are perceived in ways that may extend back to the Indo-European homeland. My first bean chapter focusses on the urd bean (*Vigna mungo*) of India, along with certain other foods, flavorings, and beverages that, in some ritual contexts, have been viewed as impure by Hindus. It is my hope that an understanding of the restrictions on the use of urd in Hindu ritual will prepare the reader for my second and third bean chapters. These focus on ancient bans on fava beans (*Vicia faba*) in the Mediterranean world, especially the ban observed by the noted mathematician Pythagoras and his followers. The question of Pythagoras and beans has long been of interest to classical scholars, and in recent decades has attracted the attention of biomedical researchers—many of whom believe that the ban arose out of Pythagoras's knowledge of and concern with the disease favism, a common disease among Mediterranean and Near Eastern peoples. My first chapter on the fava bean will be written from the perspective of the classical literature and will focus the role of religious beliefs in the origin of the Pythagorean ban on fava beans. My second chapter will be from a biomedical and historical perspective and will weigh the evidence, pro and con, that concern with favism led Pythagoras to ban the eating of fava beans. My final bean chapter, "Pythagoras Lives," is written from the perspective of folklore and folk tradition, and deals with the survival in the modern world of views of beans similar to those of Pythagoras.

In my last chapter, "Further Notes, Elaborations, and Conclusions," I will draw on material presented in previous chapters as well as introduce much new material. Several questions will be of particular concern in this chapter. One is what the characteristics of plants, physical and otherwise, may have been that led them to assume significant roles in ritual and religion. Second is what sorts of relationships humans may have developed with their ritual plants and what role humans may have played in their diffusion around the world. Third is whether the ancients' basic concerns that led them to use plants in ritual and religion are at all similar to concerns important to modern individuals of secular orientation. Fourth is whether the roles of plants in ritual and religion may, as certain present-day scholars are inclined to believe, derive mainly from medical, environmental, and ecological determinants. Westerners have always been ready to accept the view that such material determinants have played a primary position in culture history, and the past 30 years have seen a strong emphasis in anthropology and cultural geography on techno-environmental determinants as they have shaped human life and history. Indeed, some anthropologists and geographers dismiss religious beliefs as mere reflections of the techno-environmental forces that they consider the prime movers. I hope that this book may cast light on that matter and on the question of whether such anthropologists and geographers have become too restrictive in dismissing religious belief as a vital force in human life and history.

2 Tulsi, Holy Basil of the Hindus

With Notes on Sweet Basil in the Mediterranean World

> I adore that Tulasī[1] in whose roots are all the sacred places of pilgrimage, in whose centre are all the deities, and in whose upper branches are all the Vedas.
>
> —common prayer addressed to the tulsi plant, cited by M. Monier-Williams, *Religious Thought and Life in India*

> Nothing on earth can equal the virtues of the *tulasi*.
>
> —Brahmins, quoted by J.-A. Dubois, *Hindu Manners, Customs, and Ceremonies*

> The *Tulsi* (*Ocimum sanctum*) is the most sacred plant in India. No plant in the world commands such . . . universal respect, adoration and worship from the people as does *Tulsi*. It is the plant par excellence.
>
> —K. D. Upadhyaya, "Indian Botanical Folklore."

Tulsi among the Sacred Plants of Hinduism

Since antiquity, Hindus have believed in the sanctity of certain trees and other plants, and even today, it is said, over 30 species are worshipped throughout India.[2] Though they have had rich and varied ties with the Hindu people since antiquity, the stories of these sacred plants, including their ritual roles, remain largely unknown in the Western world.[3] Among the most noted plants, however, are *darbha,* or *kuśa* grass,[4] the sacred fig-tree (*Ficus religiosa*),[5] the banyan tree (*Ficus indica* or *F. bengalensis*),[6] the *neem* tree (*Azadirachta indica* or *Melia azadirachta*),[7] and the *bael* tree (*Aegle marmelos*).[8] These plants often serve together in ritual, as in a wedding among the Kāmi—the blacksmith caste of Nepal—at which the bride's parents may place on the joined hands of the bride and groom some kuśa grass, leaves of tulsi and of the bael tree, and a piece of copper.[9] Copper is a pure metal, an alternate to gold, and its use along with other items of purification and protection is appropriate here.[10]

Despite the holiness and ritual importance of other plants, it is tulsi

(English: holy basil, sacred basil; *Ocimum sanctum* L.) which is considered the most sacred of all Hindu plants. Its importance is revealed in the occurrence of the word *tulsī* in place-names,[11] as well as in family names and given names.[12] It is also revealed in the fact that in the nineteenth century the plant was worshipped by some families in Bengal as their guardian or household deity[13] and that, in a census in British India's North-Western provinces, more than 1,100 people declared themselves not as Hindus, Moslems, Sikhs, or whatever, but as worshippers of the tulsi plant.[14]

Tulsi—Botanic, Geographic, and Historical Background

Ocimum sanctum is one of roughly 60 species of the genus *Ocimum,* the basil genus, which consists of aromatic herbs and shrubs indigenous to tropical regions of Asia, Africa, and the Americas. Various *Ocimum* species provide useful products and may be cultivated in gardens, commonly as medicinals,[15] or as potherbs, condiments, or aromatics to be used in food and drink or for perfume.[16] However, only two species, both under cultivation since antiquity, have produced a range of clearly identifiable cultivars and intermediate forms.[17] One is *O. basilicum* L., sweet basil, widely cultivated around the world and quite diversified genetically (there were 60 named varieties in early nineteenth-century England and France).[18] The second is *O. sanctum,* little known in the Western world but widely cultivated in India.

Both sweet basil and holy basil are believed to have been domesticated in Asia. Nicolai Vavilov[19] placed sweet basil in his Central Asiatic center of plant domestication, which includes northwestern India as well as Afghanistan and adjacent parts of Inner Asia. This fits with the observations that *O. basilicum* grows wild and is native in temperate areas of Central Asia and the Himalayas[20] and that it is indigenous to Iran, the Sind, and the Punjab.[21] It also fits with the ancient tradition that collectors who went with Alexander the Great first introduced sweet basil to Greece.[22] Laufer believes it likely that sweet basil was domesticated in Iran and that the domesticated plant then spread to the Western world, to China, and to India.[23] Indeed, names similar to one of its Persian names, *nāzbō* or *nazbu,* do occur in certain Indian languages (Sindhi, Hindi, Bengali).[24] I wonder, however, whether India itself may have been the place of sweet basil domestication. For early Israel, there is a curious report of a name for sweet basil[25] identical to one of its names in Hindi and certain other modern Indian languages (*sabza, sabzah, sabsa, sabsah, sabja, sabjā, sabjah, sabajhi*).[26] The question of what relationship, if any, the words *sabza* and *nāzbō* or *nazbu* may have is a matter best left to linguists. In recent decades, however, some botanists have placed the domestication of sweet basil, as well as holy basil, in Southeast Asia or Southeast Asia and the Pacific,[27] and thus the matter remains quite uncertain.

Most frequently mentioned among other species of *Ocimum* in the Indian subcontinent are *O. basilicum* (Sanskrit: *munjariki, varvara;* Hindi: *bābui tulsī, kali tulsī, sabsah*); *O. gratissimum* L., shrubby basil (Hindi: *ram tulsī*); and *O. canum* Sims (*O. americanum* L.), hoary or American basil (Hindi: *kala tulsī, manjri*).[28] All these species are recognized in modern India as relatives of *O. sanctum,* and in Hindi and other Indian languages their names often include "tulsī" or "tulasī" (e.g., *kama tulsī, naya tulasī*), and the plants share in the sacredness of *O. sanctum.* This is in keeping with Parlby's observation that Hindus venerate three species of tulsi and that all three are considered sacred.[29]

O. sanctum is an erect annual woody herb or small shrub. It is about one to two feet tall. It has been reported in Asia from Arabia eastwards to Australia and Polynesia. In the Indian subcontinent it is found, cultivated or wild, in lowland areas everywhere, and in the Himalayas at elevations as high as 6,000 feet. It is quite common in waste places. Sanskrit writers identify two varieties of *O. sanctum,* "black" and "white," on the basis of their leaf color.[30] Black (or purple) and white (or green) forms of *O. sanctum* are still found in India.[31] Some botanists consider the purple and green forms (Figure 2) of *O. sanctum* to be distinct varieties,[32] though other observers insist that they hardly deserve to be regarded as such or they call them types or cultivars.[33] In the purple-hued cultivar of *O. sanctum,* that color appears on stems, upper surfaces of leaves, veins, and flowers.[34]

Tulsi's Special Ties with Vaishnavism

General Sketch

In Hindu myth, folklore, and literature, the tulsi plant is perceived as the place where heaven and earth meet. It is said that Brahma, the creator god, lives on its branches; that other gods and goddesses reside on its

2. Young tulsi plants (*Ocimum sanctum*) in a garden.

leaves; and that the sacred Ganges is at its root.[35] Indian folk-songs are bounteous in acclaim for the plant,[36] which is seen as possessing *sattva,* "goodness," and as being capable of bringing on goodness, virtue, and joy in humans.[37]

Above all, the tulsi plant has ties with the god Vishnu and his worship. It is described as a "central sectarian symbol" of Vaishnavism,[38] one that Vishnu worshippers consider "the manifestation of the god in the vegetable kingdom."[39] Vishnu (the preserver), it must be emphasized, is not an ordinary deity, but, along with Brahma (the creator) and Shiva (the destroyer), is one of the three great gods of later Hinduism, the Trimūrti.[40] The origins of the relationship between the tulsi and Vishnu are explained in legend, but, as is so often the case, such legends seem to occur with endless variations. The favorite legend, however, involves an effort by Vishnu to seduce Vṛindā, beautiful and faithful wife of Jalandhar (Jalandhara or Jaladhara), a low-caste man who, because of his wife's fidelity, became a demon so powerful that not even the gods could kill him. Vṛindā resisted Vishnu's advances but was tricked by him when he seduced her by assuming the form of Jalandhar. His invincibility now gone because of his wife's unwitting infidelity, Jalandhar was killed. According to one version of the story, Vṛindā, appalled by Vishnu's deceit and remaining staunchly loyal to her husband, cursed Vishnu and turned him into a stone. This is the *śālagrāma* stone to be mentioned again shortly. Vishnu retaliated by turning her into a tulsi plant. In another version, Vṛindā threw herself on Jalandhar's funeral pyre. Because of his love for Vṛindā, however, Vishnu would not let her go and had her reincarnated as a tulsi plant. By both of the above versions, she became the goddess Tulasī and, over time, Vishnu's beloved.[41] As a result, the tulsi plant is also a goddess, not merely a sacred plant,[42] its special standing revealed in its being called Tulsidev, *dev* or *deva* being a term used both for major Hindu deities and for things or persons who possess innate power.[43] Tulasī the goddess, as Vishnu's great love, shares in the honor accorded that highly respected god. In addition, Hindus respect her in her own right for her loyalty to her husband, Jalandhar. That respect extends to the tulsi plant, which symbolizes the perfect wife and mother. It is thus especially fitting that Hindus sometimes call the tulsi plant *tulsi-mātā* ("mother tulsi"), which is in accord with the way they address the sacred cow as *go-mātā* ("mother cow") and the sacred Ganges River as *Gaṅgā-mātā* ("mother Ganges").[44]

Tradition paints the love affair of Vishnu and the goddess Tulasī as an intense one tied most notably to the Gandaki River of Nepal, where the two practiced love.[45] Stones found in the bed of the Gandaki (śālagrāma) (Figure 3)[46] are said to be the sperm of Vishnu or the deity himself. They serve as an important symbol of Vishnu and are a critical element in Vishnu lore and worship[47]—closely related, as we shall see, to the tulsi plant.

The association between tulsi, the plant, and Vishnu, the preserver, is revealed by Sanskrit terms used for the tulsi plant, *Haripriya*[48] and *Vishnu-priya*, "dear to Lord Vishnu,"[49] and in R. S. Khare's observation, "Where there is tulasi there is Vishnu too."[50] Lakshmī, wife of Vishnu, is identified with the tulsi plant in myth and popular thinking, and the plant is sacred to her, too. Stutley says that it is likely that the goddess Tulasī is identical with Lakshmī.[51] In any case, the plant may be addressed as Lakshmīpriya, "dear to Lakshmī." The tulsi plant is also identified with those other incarnations of Vishnu—Rama and Krishna, playing a major role in the cult of the latter. In addition, it is identified with their wives: Sītā, wife of Rama; and Rukmiṇī, wife of Krishna.[52]

The tulsi's tie with Vishnu is also revealed in the Puranas. One reads there that a light burned for Vishnu with a piece of tulsi wood is the equivalent of burning several hundred thousand other lights in his honor. One also reads that, if a person rubs an ointment made from tulsi leaves on his body and then worships Vishnu for one day, the benefit equals that of a hundred ordinary worships.[53] Vishnu worship commonly involves offering its leaves to the god or his incarnations, but particularly to Rama and Krishna.[54] One reads of a ceremony in one Hindu sacred book in which the performer fasts while a *lākh* (100,000) of tulsi leaves is offered to Krishna one by one.[55] One also reads of offering Vaishnava deities garlands of tulsi leaves and of putting tulsi leaves in holy water offered to them.[56] Without tulsi leaves, it is observed, ceremonies in honor of Vishnu would be incomplete and thus futile.[57] From a food perspective, Khare has noted that, without tulsi, food is simply not acceptable to Vishnu, because the tulsi plant represents Tulasī, his consort, who alters the nature of a food offering from mundane to sacred.[58] One reads that when a Vaishnava offers food to Vishnu, he places a tulsi leaf in it,[59] and that, if a large quantity of food on a single plate is involved, Bengali Vaishnavas sprinkle it with tulsi leaves.[60]

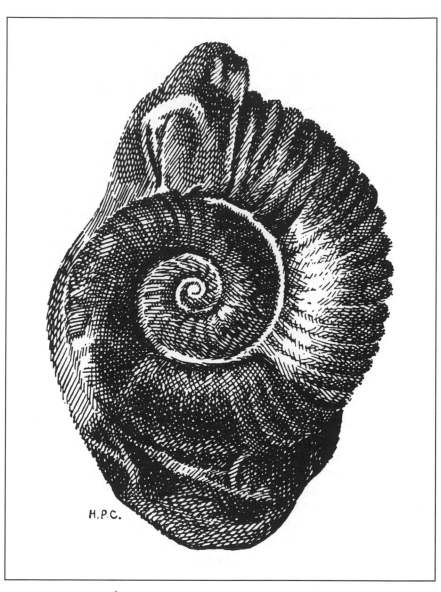

3. Śālagrāma stone of Vishnu (from Havell, 1905).

In view of the above, it is no surprise that one finds, in Ayurvedic writings and popular usage, names for *O. sanctum,* its relatives, and their products that reveal special ties with Vishnu and with his incarnations.[61] Among the terms applied to *O. sanctum,* for example, are *Vaishnavi* ("belonging to Vishnu") and *Vishnu vallabha* ("beloved of Vishnu").[62] "Vishnu tulasī" is one name by which the plant is known in parts of India. The green form of *O. sanctum,* on its part, may be called *Śrī tulsī,* "Śrī" ("fortunate") being one of the names of Vishnu's wife, Lakshmī.[63] The term *Krishna tulsī,* in turn, is commonly used for the dark form of *O. sanctum,* which has darker green leaves or leaves and stems that are purple or dark purple.[64] Krishna, whose name means "black" or "dark," is always shown in paintings with blue, blue-black, or dark skin. With this in mind, some have suggested[65] that tulsi is sacred to Krishna because of its "purplish hue approaching to black."[66] Even the green form of *O. sanctum,* moreover, commonly has small, delicate purplish or purplish-pink flowers, which, in the minds of the devout, might confirm that it, too, has ties with the deity. The plant's pronounced odor, a pleasant and enticing one, may also serve to reinforce that view. In any case, certain devout pilgrims going to the shrine in Dwarka (Dvārakā), Krishna's legendary capital in Gujarat (one of seven sacred Hindu cities[67] and a major goal of pilgrimage),[68] carry tulsi plants in the palms of their hands for the entire pilgrimage.[69]

Tulsi Beads Symbolic of Vaishnavism

A string of beads or necklace (*kanthi* or *mālā*),[70] made from the stems or roots of tulsi plants, is an important symbol of initiation into Vaishnavism, and places an individual in communion with Vishnu or Krishna and under their protection.[71] It also confers merit on its wearer.[72] Vaishnava Brahmins, other Vaishnavas of religious bent, *sādhu*s, or others in India may wear or carry tulsi-bead necklaces, rosaries, or garlands.[73] Indeed, the tulsi is such an integral part of their way of life that followers of Vishnu have long been characterized as ones who "bear the Tulasi round the neck" along with using other symbols of Vishnu or Laksmī and observing cult practices.[74]

By contrast, rosaries and bracelets worn by followers of Shiva are typically made of the polished seeds of the *rudrāksha*[75] tree (*Elaeocarpus ganitrus*) (Figure 4).[76] By one ancient tradition, the rudrāksha tree grew from Shiva's tears, which explains the sanctity of the tree and its berries and

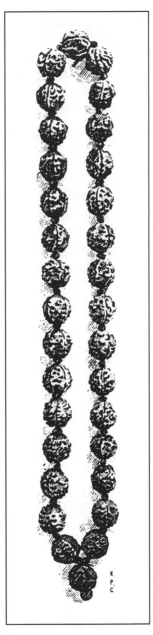

4. A Śaivite rosary (from Havell, 1905).

15

seed. It is widely believed in India that beads made of rudrāksha seeds not only can gain Shiva's good will but are also capable of maintaining the good health of a person wearing them, as well as protecting against the evil eye and turning bad luck aside.[77] The value of the seeds is reflected in their often being set in gold.[78]

Tulsi's Ties with Other Hindu Deities

Despite the unquestioned centrality of tulsi in Vishnu worship and the strength of Vaishnava commitment to the plant, one cannot dismiss tulsi's involvement with Hindu gods and other supernatural beings not associated with Vaishnavism. Clearly it is involved with a broad range of Hindu supernatural beings,[79] as in Orissa, where it represents all local deities and where rituals for a male solar deity and a female deity who are associated with women and their problems are performed in front of a tulsi plant.[80] The Nāyars of Malabar, perhaps surprisingly, have been reported as including tulsi among items offered to an evil spirit.[81]

The tulsi plant's relationship with Shiva, god of terror and destruction, is, however, somewhat unclear. Shiva, who is sometimes called Bilvadanda, "he with a staff of bilva (bael) wood," is associated with the bael tree. Indeed, the bael is regarded as the residence of and the vegetal form of Shiva.[82] Thus, among Hindus the bael tree is tied principally with Śaivism, worship of Shiva, and with Śāktism, worship of Śaktis, female goddesses who generally are consorts of Shiva.[83] The bael tree's trifoliate leaves resemble the trident, symbol of Shiva, and represent the god's three eyes. They also serve in the worship of Shiva. Indeed, Hindus would not think of worshipping Shiva and other Śaivite deities without the bael tree or its leaves, for such worship would not be genuine. Bael leaves to be offered to gods, moreover, become polluted when they touch the earth.[84] All Mondays are considered sacred to Shiva, but on Mondays in Śrāvaṇa (July–August), the god's special month, it is particularly meritorious for Shiva's followers to offer him bael leaves at temples. In northern India on the ninth day of the month of Bhādon (August–September), married girls[85] cast flowers onto the bael tree and anoint its trunk with sandalwood paste in honor of Shiva. Nor, except for Brahmins, would Śaivites use its wood, even that of a fallen tree, as everyday fuel, because of fear of offending Shiva, who resides in the tree.[86] In Kerala, bael fruits are not eaten because they are regarded as Shiva's head.[87]

Shiva is said to be as fond of the leaf of the bael tree as Krishna and Vishnu are of the tulsi leaf.[88] Nevertheless, some writers have observed that the tulsi, too, is sacred to Shiva and his devotees.[89] Indeed, a retired Nair headmaster of a secondary school in Kerala is quoted as saying that, not only is tulsi sacred to Shiva, but also daily worship of tulsi suffices. That is, a person does not have to go elsewhere to worship Shiva.[90] In addition, at a certain time of Shiva worship, the Pārthiva Pūjā, the black earth preferred for making his image, presumably a *linga*,[91] is taken from beneath a tulsi plant.[92] Despite this, Babb, writing of Central India and emphasizing the plant's association with Vishnu, wrote that tulsi is never "to my knowledge found in temples of Shiva" and that its leaves are not offered to Shiva.[93] Beck, on her part, differentiates between Hindu homes where Vishnu is the main god, where a tulsi plant is commonly found growing, and ones where Shiva is the main god, where no precise parallel exists.[94] Other writers say that a tulsi leaf is not offered to a Śakti, for she "is put out of temper" by its very smell, and that, on its part, the leaf of the bael tree is banned to some groups of Vaishnavas who never use it in worship.[95] In addition, it has been noted that pious Vaishnava Hindus will not even mention the name of the bael tree.[96] This suggests a rivalry between deities that requires further investigation.

Places of Tulsi Cultivation

The literature contains many statements, often incomplete or contradictory, about where tulsi is cultivated and by which Hindu groups. Some accounts say simply that a tulsi is found in front of or near Hindu houses, or all, virtually all, or most of them.[97] Some say that a tulsi is cultivated at homes of devout or orthodox Hindus or all, nearly all, or most of them, or at all homes of respectable people.[98] Still others write of tulsi cultivation at or near most Brahmin houses or those of certain Brahmin sections;[99] at houses of Vaishnavas, where it is common,[100] or at all or nearly all houses, or at least at those of all pious or orthodox Vaishnavas;[101] or at those of other groups, such as the Nairs of Kerala, for whom a home without tulsi would be "an anachronism."[102] Tulsi is almost a necessity for household devotions.[103] Its importance is clearly revealed in the observation, "A house with a Tulsi plant in front of it is a place of pilgrimage. . . The wind that carries the aroma of Tulsi spreads purity wherever it blows."[104] Should a person not have a tulsi growing at home, however, other options exist for getting access to tulsi. One, mentioned by Monier-Williams, is of women, likely too impoverished to have tulsi plants of their own, worshipping at the village's tulsi plant grown with a sacred fig-tree on a raised masonry platform in the center of many villages.[105]

Tulsi is also grown at shrines and temples. Some accounts simply say in a general sense that tulsi is cultivated, or is often cultivated, near Hindu shrines or temples, or even that it is cultivated at all Hindu temples.[106] Temple gardens, it is said, commonly feature the cultivation of tulsi plants because their leaves are needed for ritual purposes.[107] Other accounts say that tulsi is found in front of all Vishnu temples.[108] Also mentioned in terms of tulsi cultivation are places of pilgrimage and ritual bathing. Among these are the banks of the Ganges at Benares (Vārāṇasī), that famous holy city; the top of marble steps leading down to a village tank where bathing occurs; a temple pond; and places where Brahmins carry out their ablutions.[109] It may also be cultivated at burial places, for reasons to be elaborated on later.[110]

When cultivated at home, tulsi may be in front of a house. It may be in its courtyard or garden. It may be in other sunny places, inside the house or outside. Sometimes the household tulsi is planted in a clay flowerpot. Such pots, according to Abbott, are always square and are aligned with respect to the cardinal points.[111] They are commonly placed on a small raised structure of earth, plaster, or masonry, which is described as a pedestal or pedestal resembling a tower, a platform, or a small altar. Such structures are sometimes enclosed by a low wall to set aside the sacred space. The structure, according to Abbott, is colored red,[112] apparently as a further mark of auspiciousness. Tulsi may also be cultivated on a brick, earthen, or concrete pillar or stand[113] that is hollow at the top and filled with earth (Figure 5).[114] It has been noted that such stands are so commonly used in Hindu worship that contractors who build a house provide them with as little question as they would garden walls, roof terraces, and well platforms.[115] In one variation, found in front of many houses in Orissa, the pot of tulsi is placed on the stone statue of an Oriya woman who holds the pot on her head.[116] A second variation involves placing images of the deity of greatest importance to a family on all four sides of a household tulsi pedestal.[117] Still another variation may represent an effort to enhance the sanctity of tulsi by associating it with another sacred plant. It involves a pot of tulsi placed on an earthen altar under a sacred fig-tree (pipal).[118]

5. Tulsi plant growing in a household pedestal made of cement (from Smith and Narasimha Chary, 1991).

The place where the tulsi is grown is not merely sacred. It is a center of Hindu daily ritual.[119] It also testifies that a family is religious and seeks to maintain its ritual purity. It certifies further that Vishnu is present and protecting the household[120] by means of the tulsi plant in which his beloved Vṛindā (Tulasī) resides. The association is clearly revealed by names such as "Vṛindāvana"[121] and "Tulsīthara," used for the structures on which tulsi is placed, or for entire sacred enclosures of tulsi,[122] or for groups of 8 or 10 plants grown on a veranda or ground nearby.[123]

Care and Worship of Household Tulsi Plants

General Sketch

The care and worship of tulsi plants have long been regarded as religious duties. Details of how to do this are set down in a special little book identified by Dymock et al. as the *Tulasikavaçam*.[124] Salvation, wrote Dubois, is assured to the person who waters and cares for tulsi daily (Figure 6).[125] Tradition has it, moreover, that even persons who do not worship daily at the tulsi plant but only perform such services as watering and weeding have their sin removed by Vishnu (Hari) and achieve everlasting joy and peace.[126]

The matter of tulsi care is thus of great concern to a traditional Hindu family. It is something carried out with tenderness and diligence.[127] All members of a household may be involved, but the responsibility for tulsi care and worship is that of Hindu women, for Hindu women perform their religious duties separately from their husbands, and commonly their ritual activities relate entirely to the tulsi plant.[128] The primacy of women is aided by the convenience of the plant growing at home and by the simplicity of the rites, which do not usually require participation of formal clergy. It also fits with the role of tulsi as a "symbol of ideal wifehood and motherhood,"[129] mentioned above.

Care and worship of household tulsi are usually done on a daily basis, though Tuesdays and Fridays are said to be especially important.[130] Care and worship may involve such things as watering, cleaning the area around the tulsi with water and cow dung (a ritual purificant),[131] and making offerings of food, flowers, Ganges water, and other gifts to the plant. It may involve drawing designs of deities or saints at the foot of the tulsi. Worship may also involve bowing or prostrating oneself before the plant, walking around (circumambulating) it, chanting mantras, and praying.[132] Worship of the plant may be carried out in the morning and again in the evening, when a small lamp or lamps with ghee (clarified butter) or a candle is lighted and placed by the tulsi for the night.[133]

Though tulsi is worshipped throughout the year, there are times when the plant receives special attention. One is the Hindu month of Vaiśākha

6. Worshipping a tulsi plant (from Thomas, 1961).

(April–May)—an auspicious time for Vaishnavas and a time of Krishna worship, but also a time of worry about the coming monsoon—when special care must to taken to water tulsi plants daily.[134] In Orissa, at a festival held on the first day of Vaiśākha, a small, leaky pot filled with cold drink is suspended from the tulsi plant with support from bamboo rods. The drops that fall from the pot are said to symbolize rain,[135] apparently reflecting the wish that the monsoon rains will arrive in a timely fashion and in sufficient amounts. A similar arrangement is described in general

terms for Hindus. It entails suspending an earthen vessel full of water
above a tulsi plant for that entire month and allowing the water to drip
from a small hole in the vessel.[136] Another time of special note is summer,
when daily worship of tulsi becomes indispensible. Tradition holds that
anyone who provides cool, fragrant water to a tulsi during the summer
will receive eternal bliss, and anyone who protects a tulsi with an umbrella
or carpet will be delivered of all his sins.[137]

By far the leading time of tulsi worship, however, is the month of Kārttika (October–November), when the plant is given unusual attention.[138]
The importance of tulsi during Kārttika is shown by Dubois's observation
that an offer of one of its branches during that month would delight
Vishnu more than an offer 1,000 cows.[139] Kārttika is a time when the
household Vṛindāvana may be cleaned, painted, and garlanded,[140] and
women make special offerings to tulsi plants, such as rice, curd, sweets,
flowers, and Ganges water, and chant mantras and honor tulsi in other
ways.[141] On one day in this month, women may bathe in the Ganges and
then worship the tulsi plant.[142] Kārttika is noted as the month when the
marriage ceremony between the tulsi plant and Vishnu takes place (it is
also the beginning of the Hindu marriage season). At this ceremony,
called Tulasīvivāha, Vishnu is represented by an image—of Vishnu himself or of one of his incarnations, such as Rama or Krishna—or by a śālagrāma stone.[143]

Tulsi's marriage is usually celebrated at home on a modest scale,
though, on occasion, it may be celebrated there in a far more elaborate
manner, with priests brought in to recite, in Sanskrit, mantras that fit
the occasion.[144] The celebration may also be an expensive and impressive
public affair. One reported by Sleeman early in the nineteenth century
involved about 100,000 people as well as a procession of 4,000 horses,
1,200 camels, and 8 elephants, all with riders and ornate coverings and
with the first elephant carrying the śālagrāma stone.[145] On the day of the
wedding, the image or the śālagrāma stone and the tulsi plant may both
be washed with water, or with water and *pañchamṛita*, the five nectars (a
mixture of special sanctity consisting of milk, curds, clarified butter,
honey, and sugar), after which the wedding ceremony, often an involved
affair fascinating in its imagery, proceeds.[146]

Human actions can injure or offend the tulsi plant, and precautions
are taken to avoid such actions lest serious punishment result. Tradition
has it that if people urinate or leave excretions or water from gargling in

areas where tulsi grows, Hari will make them poor and take everything they possess.[147] Related to this is the view that the shadow of a menstruating woman should not fall on a tulsi plant.[148] It is also considered sinful to break the branches of a tulsi.[149] In addition, no gardener will cut or uproot a tulsi plant,[150] for a person who uproots or destroys a tulsi plant is committing a sin that Vishnu will punish by denying him prosperity and taking his wealth, the lives of his children, and even his own life.[151] It is said, moreover, that it is taboo simply to throw a dried tulsi plant away (or a dead tulsi plant of any sort?), that it must be disposed of in a river or pond.[152]

Tulsi leaves are needed for many Hindu religious ceremonies, but there are restrictions on who should pick them and how this should be done. Tulsi leaves, it is said, should not be picked by women.[153] Leaves intended for the gods should not be cut with iron, for iron is impure and inauspicious.[154] Such leaves, moreover, may be picked by day, for there is no sin in that, but not by night, when Vṛindā is thought to reside in the plant.[155] Even in daytime, however, special precautions might be taken. When Brahmins in Orissa pluck tulsi leaves, for example, they pray beforehand and ask the goddess's forgiveness.[156] Dymock et al.[157] quote such a prayer: "Mother Tulasi, who brings joy to the heart of Govindas [a term applied to Krishna], I gather thee for the worship of Narayana [Krishna and Vishnu]; without thee, O blessed one, every work is vain; that is why I pluck thee; O goddess be propitious to me. As I gather thee with care, be merciful to me. O Tulasi, mother of the world, I beseech thee."

It is also said that the picking of tulsi leaves on Sundays and Tuesdays is banned, and that it is an offense to boil tulsi leaves in water, which troubles the soul of the plant.[158] Parlby, apparently referring to areas along the Ganges, noted that, when a tulsi plant dies, it is committed to the sacred river,[159] and Ward, that it is a sacred duty to do so.[160]

Circumambulation of the Tulsi Plant

Of special interest in tulsi worship is the circumambulation of the plant. In Hinduism, circumambulation (*parikramā* or *pradakshiṇa*) involves walking or moving around a person or thing, with the object, if it is sacred, always to one's right.[161] It is usually carried out in order to gain merit for the performer or to benefit the object of the act. Circumambulation is commonly associated with pilgrimage to holy sites. It may involve a pilgrim walking several times around a representation of a deity. It may involve walking around a liṅga (phallus-shaped object revered by Hin-dus)[162] or around a shrine or a temple that ordinarily has a special pas-sage (*pradakshina-patha*) set aside for circumambulation.[163] O'Malley[164] writes that some men circumambulate a temple not by walking but by rolling their bodies as if they were barrels, thereby adding special empha-sis to the circumambulation. With similar intent, a pilgrim to Govar-dhan Mountain near Brindaban has been observed prostrating himself, stretching his hands forward, then crawling forward to place his feet at the point his hands reached, and repeating the process in circumambu-lating the entire mountain, a distance of several miles.[165] Because of a vow, the number of circumambulations may be far above normal, even as many as 100,000. It may, on the other hand, entail a fixed number of circumambulations on each of a specified number of days. A sacred river may be the object of circumambulation, with a devotee following its course on one bank from its headwaters to the sea, and then returning on its opposite bank. Circumambulation of the Ganges may take as long as six years. Other objects of circumambulation are sacred hills and com-munities. The city of Benares has a 36-mile-long circumambulation path with stations along the way, and it takes six days to make the circuit. A holy individual, the tomb of a saint, a portrait of a guru or an image of his footprint, a holy book, an altar, a fire or the household fire pit,[166] the Holi pyre, and even a corpse[167] may be an object of circumambulation.[168] The same is true of the cow, Hinduism's holiest animal,[169] and of sacred trees and plants, including tulsi (Figure 7).[170]

In planting tulsi at home, care may be taken to allow sufficient room for circumambulation.[171] Devout Hindus or Vaishnavas may circumam-bulate and worship the household tulsi plant every morning,[172] for daily circumambulation of a tulsi plant is a virtuous and highly meritorious act.[173] Women are sometimes singled out as performing daily circumam-bulation of the household tulsi, which also entails prayer and offerings, and it is said that this may be the only worship in which many Hindu women engage.[174] At Benares, Parlby observed Hindu devotees circum-ambulating, paying homage, and watering tulsi plants that grew on pil-lars along the Ganges.[175] A devout Nair of Kerala, after he has bathed in the morning, is said to walk seven times around the raised masonry plat-form where the tulsi plant is cultivated.[176] Such circumambulation may also take place on specific days, as in circumambulating a tulsi plant every

7. Women circumambulating a sacred tree at a ghat in Benares (photo by Deryck O. Lodrick).

Saturday, or on a specified moonless day of the month, or for specific purposes, such as curing barrenness or extending the life of a husband.[177] Monier-Williams[178] observed poor women, who had no tulsi plant at home, circumambulating the village tulsi plant.

Benefits Gained from Worship of the Tulsi Plant

General Background

A broad range of benefits may be sought from tulsi (or in rites involving other deities that are held at the tulsi plant), for "she grants children to the childless, wealth to the needy, and opens the gates of heaven to the devout worshipper."[179] Girls may worship the tulsi in order to obtain a good husband, and, appropriately, a tulsi plant may be placed on the marriage altar.[180] Because of the belief that the plant grants fertility and is capable of enabling childless couples to become fruitful,[181] a husband and wife may worship tulsi in the hope of obtaining a male child[182] or of having children (or better children). Tulsi may also be employed to make certain that a pregnant woman will not suffer a miscarriage, which, in popular thinking, is brought on by evil forces. Thus, some tulsi may be tied to a door post of a pregnant woman's house to prevent demons from entering.[183] In an effort to obtain offspring, childless people may also arrange for a marriage ceremony between a tulsi and Vishnu, Krishna, Rama, or other gods.[184] In nineteenth-century Surat, north of Bombay, a childless man might be fearful of dying without offspring and thus not being in a position to carry out a marriage ceremony for a daughter (a highly meritorious act among twice-born castes). In such a case, he might perform a marriage ceremony between a tulsi plant, representing his daughter, and an idol of Krishna.[185] There is a recent report, for Rajasthan, of a man marrying his household tulsi plant to a local god at a time when he celebrated the marriages of his three daughters.[186] In the Punjab, a wealthy but childless couple, in the hope that the wife will bear a child, might sponsor the marriage of a tulsi plant to a Brahmin. Ever after, the Brahmin is regarded as the couple's son-in-law, to his great financial benefit.[187] If, however, such tulsi marriages do not lead to the birth of a child, it is feared that a representative of Yama, lord of the dead, will harass the couple on their journey to the spirit world.[188]

A married woman in the prime of life who has been successful in bearing children may have a somewhat different focus. She may still wish for a fine son or an additional one, but she may also seek material rewards (clothes, ornaments, an abundance of cultivated land) and a healthy, long-lived husband—all hopes that are prominent in the following song of prayer from Orissa:

> I lit a lamp and prayed to Tulasi
> I prayed for golden bangles
> Rich clothes for daily use.
> Reserve of old stock of paddy, never-ending
> A son like [Krishna] on my armpit
> My husband hale and sound
> And he alive till my last breath.[189]

A housewife may request help in ending her sorrows, such as requesting aid for the return of her husband and sons from foreign lands.[190] When a Hindu is ill, a Brahmin may be called to offer, one by one, leaves of tulsi sprinkled with red powder (for driving out demons and curing illness) to a śālagrāma stone while reciting incantations—an affair sometimes involving as many as 100,000 leaves. The sick person is said to recover bit by bit with each leaf offered.[191]

A widow is likely to have greater concern with maintaining her ritual standing and assuring her fate in the afterlife. One problem faced by young widows in retaining high ritual status is that of remaining chaste. Thus, because tulsi seed is thought to quell sexual desires, in some parts of India young widows eat a pinch of tulsi seed, whole or ground.[192] There have also been scientific studies in India that reported that tulsi has antifertility and antispermatogenic effects.[193] Hope has thus been expressed that the plant may serve as a valuable means of birth control in India and other Third World countries.[194]

The month of Kārtikka (October–November) is particularly special for girls and women as a time of tulsi worship.[195] That month, when tulsi (representing Vṛindā) is ritually married to Vishnu, is the most sacred time of year for village widows in Orissa. Widows worship the goddess Brundabati (= Tulasī) during that month by taking an early morning bath, then donning a garland of tulsi beads, decorating a tulsi plant with flowers and its roots with representations of items (lotus,[196] conch shell, discus, and club or mace) associated with Vishnu, then making sounds of joy, presenting gifts, and singing this song of prayer:

O Brundabati, I bow down
And salute at your feet [a] hundred times
Give me good intellect and knowledge
Give me shelter at your feet in heaven after death.
I salute you [a] hundred times.[197]

Tulsi's Ability to Repel Evil and to Purify

In the Puranas, everything associated with the tulsi plant is holy, including water given to it and soil in which it grows, as well as all its parts, among them leaves, flowers, seed, and roots.[198] Tulsi's holiness continues today, and people make use of it to protect against and eliminate evil and impurity.[199] Before a religious rite, for example, a tulsi leaf may be used to sprinkle water to the cardinal directions.[200] Even the air that passes through its branches has antiseptic powers.[201] Thus, it is understandable that Hindu poets say that all people who grow the plant are holy and that it protects them from bad luck and leads them to heaven.[202] Traditional Hindus are convinced that tulsi keeps spirits away from a house, that evil spirits would not risk coming to a place where tulsi is growing, for it would destroy them—which accounts for one of the plant's names, *bhutagni*, "burner of evil spirits" or "destroyer of demons."[203] Because of such convictions, tulsi may be employed in amulets.[204] When evil signs or disasters occur, moreover, a family may perform a ceremony of appeasement that includes offerings of tulsi leaves along with suitable mantras, scriptural readings, and more, depending on the seriousness of things.[205] An eclipse is one inauspicious occasion, a time of impurity when protection must be sought, in much the same way as if the evil eye were involved.[206] Food, for example, is at risk of becoming polluted during eclipses. Therefore, when an eclipse is expected, a housewife may sprinkle Ganges water on tulsi leaves and place them in her containers of drinking water and cooked food in order to keep them pure during the time of the eclipse.[207] An alternative solution is to throw away all water in a house and to throw away or give away all uneaten food. In such cases, however, tulsi leaves may still be used to protect expensive items, such as dairy products, clothes, and books.[208]

Of special note in this regard is the purificatory use of water and earth that have been near or in contact with a tulsi plant.[209] After he has had his morning bath, a devout Nair of Kerala, in atonement for his sins, may drink a few drops of water that have been poured over a tulsi branch. Nairs may also drink water in which a few tulsi leaves have been soaked.[210] In a similar vein is a Tamil story of a gardener who had touched food prepared for a wedding ceremony in the house where he worked, disturbing the bride's mother-in-law, an orthodox woman who feared that the guests might hear of the incident of "touch pollution" and refuse to eat the food. After some thought, she solved the problem by sprinkling tulsi water over the rice, convinced that this would eliminate the impurity.[211] In Orissa, old women and men of religious bent may water a tulsi plant after their daily baths, then sip a bit of the water at its root, and place a small amount of the sacred earth on their foreheads.[212] Earth taken from the base of the tulsi plant may also be smeared on one's forehead to repel Yama, lord of the dead.[213] Some people also apply earth from beneath a tulsi plant or from its enclosure to their bodies when bathing.[214]

Tulsi leaves may be added to pañchamrita, the five nectars offered to deities as food, and then be consumed by devotees as consecrated (*prasāda*).[215] No food offering to a deity, it is said, is acceptable as consecrated unless tulsi leaves have been included.[216] Tulsi leaves may also be offered alone as food for a deity.[217] Tulsi leaves may be added to holy water passed out in temples,[218] as well as serving as a purificant in other ways. Before the water of a new well is used, for example, various things, including tulsi, may be cast into it for purposes of purification (others include cow's milk and butter, cow urine and dung, honey, and Ganges water).[219] Moreover, when a person offers a charitable gift, a tulsi leaf, or a spray or blossom, must also be offered to enhance the gift's value and assure that the donor's intent is achieved.[220] In the Puranas, it says that, just as water is made pure by the addition of Ganges water, firewood is made pure when a small tulsi twig is added to it.[221] One reads further that, after preparing the hearth for a household fire, tulsi leaves are placed on it and, on the leaves, the material to make the fire.[222] Tradition has it that even speaking its name or looking at or touching a tulsi plant is sufficient to eliminate all sin or dispel all impurity.[223] Apparently with this in mind, a man of the Nair castes of Kerala (commonly warrior castes), if taking his morning bath in a temple tank, will wear a small twig of tulsi on his right ear, a consecrated item he obtains at the temple. Even if he does not worship at his local temple in the morning but takes his bath at home, he will wear a few tulsi leaves over his right ear.[224] It is said that tulsi worn over the ear or on the head not only repels evil but also keeps a person from telling a lie.[225]

Of particular interest is the relationship of tulsi, death, and the dead. We have seen that Yama, lord of the dead, dares not go where a tulsi plant is found, and his messengers, too, are unwilling to enter a house where there is a tulsi or a twig of tulsi.[226] Yet when death does occur, tulsi is called upon to protect the dead just as it does the living. In India today, there is a tradition of giving tulsi water to a person who is near death.[227] When a Nair of Malabar is dying, a tiny cup may be fashioned from a tulsi leaf or two and water poured into it. Then members of the family and friends who are at hand, each in his turn, allow a few drops of the liquid to fall into the dying person's mouth while they are holding a gold ring or piece of gold.[228] If a dying man in Gujarat has sufficient strength, he may hold a cow's tail and present it along with a tulsi leaf to a Brahmin.[229] Some observers have written that dried tulsi goes with the dead person on his final journey;[230] that a Hindu dies with a leaf of tulsi on his breast;[231] that a sprig of tulsi is put on the breast of a dead person as a viaticum;[232] that a wreath of leaves is put about the neck of a dying person;[233] that his head is cleansed with water in which there are tulsi leaves and sesame seeds;[234] that his body is washed with tulsi water, which assures his entering heaven, since tulsi is where heaven and earth meet;[235] or that tulsi leaves, or tulsi leaves and Ganges water, are placed in the mouth of a person who is dying or has died.[236] Dubois noted that, when a Brahmin is dying, a tulsi plant is obtained and placed on a pedestal, and homage (*pūjā*) is paid to it. Then its leaves are put on the Brahmin's face, ears, eyes, and chest, and a bit of tulsi root in his mouth. Finally his entire body is sprinkled by using a tulsi twig that has been dipped in Ganges water while his friends chant, "Tulasī! Tulasī! Tulasī!"[237]

One also reads that a dying Hindu may be placed at the foot of a tulsi plant[238] or brought to the shores of the sacred Ganges, where a tulsi branch is planted near his head.[239] Ward observed that mendicant Vaishnavas may be buried along the Ganges, or near a tulsi plant,[240] or with a tulsi planted on the grave. He noted further that they also place tulsi leaves in the corpse's mouth, ears, eyes, and nose; write the name "Krishna" on various parts of its body; and put tulsi beads and a garland of flowers around its neck.[241] After bathing a dead person, members of the Talapada Kōlī caste of Gujarat may place a tulsi leaf and a piece of silver in his or her mouth, with the intent of purifying the body before it goes to the other world.[242] Also in Gujarat, a tulsi leaf may be placed in the mouth of a deceased person along with pieces of silver and gold, and a rosary of 108 tulsi leaves may also be included in the dress of a corpse being readied for a funeral.[243] In addition, Vaishnava rosaries contain 108 tulsi beads.[244] Rosaries of a small number of beads are said not to be good; rosaries of 27 beads, good; of 54 beads, better; and of 108 beads, best.[245] The number 108 is a mystical number that symbolizes the heavens. Thus, one reads not only of 108 beads in rosaries but also of 108 shrines of great sanctity; of bathing 108 times the corpse of a woman who dies in child- birth; of the use of 108 containers of water and 108 leaves of the bael tree in an effort to cure disease; and of circumambulating a tulsi plant or sacred fig-tree 108 times or a temple 108 times for a stated number of days.[246]

Tulsi is one of the fuels used in a Hindu funeral pyre.[247] The Puranas say that even persons guilty of many sins are absolved of sin if they are cremated with tulsi twigs.[248] Ancestral spirits (*pitṛi*) like to receive gifts of tulsi leaves. At rites held after death, therefore, tulsi leaves may be laid on or offered with the balls of rice or barley flour provided for the dead.[249] Tulsi leaves also serve in annual *śrāddha* rites in honor of departed ancestors.[250] One reads further that at certain times of year orthodox Hindus, after their morning bathing, pour water onto tulsi in the expectation that this will assuage the thirst of the ancestral spirits.[251]

Tulsi in Foretelling the Future

Tulsi's divinity, its close association with other deities, and its critical position between the earth and heavens would seem to present humans with a great opportunity for using the plant in divining the future. Nevertheless, I have uncovered only a few suggestions that tulsi may have knowledge of what is to come or that people actually use the plant in divination. I present them here principally to indicate that the subject is deserving of further research.

The possibility of tulsi having foreknowledge of events is suggested by the case of a mother who, on a winter night in 1956, was sitting up and caressing her sick, young son in the hope that he would fall asleep in her lap. While doing this, she became sleepy and, whether in the mist of drowsiness or in a dream, she twice observed that strong gusts of wind caused violent flickering in the flame of the lamp she had placed outside near the tulsi plant at night. Despite her efforts to protect the flame (a symbol of life), a third, even stronger gust extinguished it (an inauspicious event signalling the end of life). This shocked the mother, and at once she became fully awake. She was so disturbed that she woke her husband and told him of the experience, which, however, he dismissed as a reflection of her troubled state of mind. Nevertheless she remained fearful that her child would soon die, that the dying flame was a signal from Rama (i.e., Vishnu), and in truth, the story goes, the child did die three days after her premonition of death. In the mind of the mother, tulsi had successfully protected the child on two occasions (when the first two gusts of wind failed to extinguish the flame), but was unable to do so on the third.[252]

More deliberate efforts to employ tulsi in divination are reported for South India. One involves placing water in half of a broken coconut and then dropping a tulsi leaf into the water. If the leaf turns to the right, it foretells a fine harvest. If it turns to the left, however, disaster is certain.[253] A second case from South India involves a tulsi plant raised by a family at home. After a ceremony on a certain day in Māgha (January-February), they build a fire of cow dung in front of the tulsi plant and boil milk on the fire. Should the milk overflow to the east, an abundant harvest will result. Should it overflow to the west, however, a famine will soon follow.[254]

Tulsi in Oath-taking

Like use of the Bible in oath-taking among Christians, traditional forms of oath-taking among Hindus may involve something sacred, whether water, plant, human, other animal, deity, or some sacred object.[255] Thus, Hindus may take oaths on water from sacred rivers such as the Ganges and Narbada (Narmada), and, it is said, few would dare violate such an oath. They may also take oaths on items associated with the sacred cow, such as a cow's tail, cow dung, or dust from the feet of a cow. Other oaths may involve touching the feet of a Brahmin or taking the oath in front of a temple image. At the turn of this century, it was said that oaths in North India were usually taken on Ganges water; the śālagrāma stone of Vishnu; or, most restraining of all, by laying hands on the head of one's oldest son.[256] In addition, however, oaths were often taken by using the leaves of various sacred plants, and it is thus quite fitting that tulsi, most sacred of all Hindu plants, be involved in this. Abbott writes that Hindus take oaths on the tulsi, which dries up if an oath is violated. He notes further that such an oath may be taken by touching or holding a tulsi plant.[257] Desai writes that an oath may be taken with tulsi leaves in the palms of the oath-taker's hands.[258] Parlby reports that a Hindu may take an oath by placing a sprig of tulsi on a brass water-vessel filled with Ganges water and then swearing by that sacred river.[259] Upadhyaya says that a Hindu who has Ganges water and a tulsi leaf in his hand would not dare to tell a falsehood.[260] Balfour writes of administering an oath to a Hindu while he has some Ganges water and a few tulsi leaves in the hollow of his palm, which he then swallows or chews and swallows.[261] Hutton indicates that such oaths are administered before a caste council (*pañchāyat*).[262] Balfour observes that such oaths were also administered in courts of justice in British India, with a Brahmin placing the tulsi leaves in the oath-taker's hand and repeating the required oath.[263] Several courts of justice in Ceylon (now Sri Lanka) also administered oaths to Hindus with tulsi leaves and Ganges water,[264] which, if the water was actually from the Ganges, involved shipping it a considerable distance. Even in postindependence Indian courts, oath-taking with Ganges water and tulsi is still resorted to in an effort to obtain true statements from an accused or a witness.[265]

Tulsi in Diet and Ayurvedic Medicine

The two standard sources on the history of Indian foods, spices, and flavorings provide little information on early dietary use of holy basil, *O. sanctum,* other than identifying it as tulsi in a list of spices and condiments.[266] Similar studies on early India that I have consulted fail to mention holy basil or tulsi at all, or they identify it as a sacred plant and a drug.[267] Although a few modern sources[268] report food uses for *O. sanctum,* the modern botanic, economic, and ethnographic literature is also largely silent about Hindu use of holy basil in everyday diet. George Watt, an authority noted for his thoroughness, writes of the sweet basil plant, *O. basilicum,* being used as a seasoning, and of its seeds mixed in bread or steeped in water and prepared as a beverage.[269] On the other hand, all that he or Balfour say about food use of holy basil, *O. sanctum,* is that Europeans in India sometimes grow it as a potherb or for flavoring wine, vinegar, and sauces.[270] Other writers identify tulsi as a sacred or medicinal plant rather than a spice or flavoring;[271] and Dymock et al. write that tulsi leaves can be picked only for ritual or medicinal purposes.[272] That its medicinal role far overshadows any role it may have as food and flavoring is confirmed in the argument of one Hindu enthusiast that tulsi cultivation be expanded. His case is based not on concern with diet or nutrition, but on concern with health and disease. It is further confirmed by his observation that Indians should begin to use tulsi "freely in our daily diet to take full advantage of its medicinal properties."[273] Smith and Narasimha Chary are more direct than most observers. They say that, despite the widespread use of herbs, fragrant leaves, and other plant parts by Hindus, they do not use tulsi leaves as a potherb or as a condiment or food flavoring. They explain this by noting that the tulsi plant is greater than "the sum of its parts. It is a sacred presence and must be treated as such."[274]

It is not surprising that holy basil, a plant so central to rituals associated with sanctity, purity, good health, the fertility of women, and birth and death, should come to play an important role in Ayurvedic medicine and enjoy a strong popular following as well. Positive judgments by Indian enthusiasts on the health and therapeutic merits of tulsi are as pronounced as Chinese and East Asian convictions about the merits of ginseng.[275] As with ginseng, practitioners of scientific medicine have been drawn into research on the efficacy of tulsi, and impressive bibliographies can be assembled on the subject.

The central claims made for holy basil, *O. sanctum* (whether the entire plant or leaves, roots, or seeds and their extracts), in the prevention and cure of illness and disease relate to its role in ritual. It is a repellent of dangerous organisms; a purificant, as in purifying the air and cleansing the blood; as well as a strengthening agent. Its reputation as a repellent is reflected in the belief that it can drive away mosquitoes and other insects as well as poisonous reptiles.[276] Holy basil is also considered an antidote to snake bites and scorpion stings. The conviction that holy basil can purify the air has led to its use against respiratory ailments, from colds and coughs to bronchitis and tuberculosis. Holy basil has been found to have antiinflammatory and antistress qualities. It is considered effective against fevers, such as those of malaria and typhoid. In addition, it is regarded as capable of eliminating blood toxins and stimulating and strengthening the heart; of curing problems of the gastrointestinal tract, such as indigestion, vomiting, intestinal gas, diarrhea, dysentery, and intestinal worms; of relieving pain, including the pain of childbirth; of eliminating maggots and worms in wounds and facilitating their healing; of curing chronic skin disease, including leprosy; and much more.[277]

Hinduism, Vaishnavism, and the Spread of Tulsi Sanctity

The spread of Vaishnavism, it is said, has brought tulsi and tulsi worship to every corner of India and into other parts of the world.[278] A good example of this is provided by Sinha, who notes that Vaishnava influence led certain Bhumij tribal people of Chota Nagpur to adopt tulsi worship of the sort found widely among Hindus (a tulsi plant kept on a mud platform in every courtyard, daily worship at the platform by housewives, a lamp placed near the plant at night).[279] It is certain that there have long been similar influences on other tribal peoples as they were drawn into the sphere of Hinduism. What remains uncertain, however, is whether the tulsi may have played a ritual role among tribal groups prior to and independent of Hindu influence. Certain scholars believe that to have been the case, arguing that it was from tribal groups that tulsi worship entered Hinduism.[280] Indeed, the scanty material I have uncovered for tribal groups of India on the role of tulsi in female fertility and abortion shows a clear resemblance to Hinduism. Certain Dosādh of Bihar and Chota Nagpur, for example, hold a festival for their tribal god, Rāhu, during which a priest, believed to personify the god, distributes to the participants tulsi leaves and tulsi flowers. The leaves are thought to heal diseases that cannot be cured in other ways, and the flowers, to enable barren women to bear young.[281] The Kol, a tribal group of Central India, place tulsi leaves on a pregnant woman's abdomen and pray that she remain safe during that time of danger when evil forces can cause a miscarriage.[282] These practices may or may not derive from Hindu influence. Among the Meithei of Manipur, a tribal people of northeastern India who have become Hindus over the past several centuries,[283] that does not seem to have been the case. Among them, tulsi was a sacred plant offered to deities in pre-Hindu times.[284]

In modern Southeast Asia, one also finds striking parallels with Hindu practices relating to *O. sanctum*. Early in the nineteenth century, Crawfurd observed that in Indonesia *Ocimum* (tulsi) is grown specifically for a yearly festival honoring the ancestors, when it is cast on graves.[285] It has also been reported that on Sumatra both *O. basilicum* and *O. sanctum* are grown for ritual offerings to spirits.[286] In Java, *O. gratissimum* is tied especially to the dead, with one variety used in the ritual bathing of corpses, planted around graveyards, and, once each year, cast on graves.[287] In Malacca, too, an *Ocimum* of some type is planted on graves.[288] Furtado observed that in the Malay Peninsula species of *Ocimum* are cultivated mainly for ritual or medicinal purposes or to scent cooked foods.[289] In his book on economic products of the Malay Peninsula, Burkill says that leaves of *O. sanctum* are not added as flavorings to cooked dishes, though they may to a small degree be eaten in salads.[290]

Also of interest are three claims or observations about the basils in Southeast Asia. One is that in the Malay Peninsula *O. sanctum* and other *Ocimum* species are not native but introduced, and that, except for escapees and weeds around areas of human settlement, they are cultivated, not wild.[291] The second claim is that one Malay name for basil (there are many) is *sulasi, solasi, soelasi,* or *selaseh;* that, as with *tulsi* in India, it applies to all species of basil; and that the name derives from the Sanskrit *surasī* or *surasā* (see note 1), while another Malay name, *toelasi, tulasīh,* or *telasih,* comes from the Sanskrit *tulasī*.[292] The third is that the Malay word *selaseh* is the rhyme-equivalent of *kaseh,* "love," and *kekaseh,* "beloved" or "sweetheart," a possible survival of Hindu associations of basil with love and marriage.[293] It is also reminiscent of the Hindu view of tulsi as the beloved of Vishnu. Also of interest is the practice, in Indonesia, of using *O. sanctum* leaves to promote the milk secretion of women who are in childbed.[294] Data such as this have led certain scholars to suggest that one or more species of *Ocimum* (*sanctum, basilicum,* and *gratissimum*) spread from India to the Malay world, an area where Hinduism had a strong cultural presence in antiquity.[295]

The story of tulsi in the Western world has not been told, but at least one form of *O. sanctum* is widely grown in the United States,[296] and one can find both *O. sanctum* seed and seedlings here. A knowledgeable friend bought a seedling for me in Monterey, California, and recommended the catalog of a company[297] from which I obtained seed that grew into sturdy, attractive, and appealing plants.

Parallels between Hindu Perceptions of Tulsi and Perceptions of Sweet Basil in India, Iran, and the Mediterranean Lands

In this chapter, my focus is on the perception and use of holy basil in India, not on the question of sweet basil in Iran and other lands in the Near East and Mediterranean area. Since, however, resemblances have repeatedly been noted, I feel compelled to consider the matter briefly. The existence of such parallels is not surprising when one considers the spread of sweet basil and the likelihood that human perceptions of it accompanied the plant as it was passed from group to group. Laufer, as noted above, thinks it likely that sweet basil reached Greece from Iran.[298] Darrah is more specific in crediting the introduction of sweet basil into Greece to plant collectors who accompanied Alexander the Great in his conquests and who may have obtained the plant in Iran, Afghanistan, or western India.[299]

Whatever the route sweet basil followed in its westward migration, one cannot ignore the striking parallels between India, Iran, and the Mediterranean lands in the association of basil with love and marriage. Reminiscent of the perception of tulsi as an aphrodisiac by followers of Ayurvedic medicine is Pliny's view that sweet basil is an aphrodisiac, for which reason it was given to horses and donkeys at the time of mating.[300] In addition, according to D'Andrea, the ancient Romans viewed basil as a symbol of love, and the ancient Greeks, as a potent love charm.[301] Such associations still survive in Iran, the Mediterranean lands, and elsewhere in Europe. In Iran, for example, there is a belief that a person who consumes a dry mixture of basil and "Bohemian olives" (fruit of the tree *Elaeagnus angustifolia*) is certain to be loved.[302] In Romania and Moldavia, a young woman who wants the love of a young man is believed certain to be successful if she gets him to take a sprig of basil from her.[303] In Italy, basil is a symbol of love, as reflected in its Tuscan name *amorino*, "little love."[304] In Chieti Province in central Italy, the smell of basil is thought to create an instant attraction, which has led it to be called *bacia-nicola*, that is, "kiss me, Nicholas"[305]—an invitation to a young man that his advances are welcome.

Recalling the worship of the tulsi plant by Hindu girls seeking husbands is the Greek and Italian custom of girls employing a pot of basil with similar intent. At one time in Smyrna, a Greek girl would plant a pot of basil in May if she wanted to get married in the year that followed. She would care for the plant until the Epiphany (January 6), when she would exchange her sprig for one the priest had used in blessing holy water. The blessed sprig was then placed in the frame of one of the family icons, after which "the girl waited patiently for her husband, who could not fail to come."[306] In Italy, it is said, a girl who wishes to get married may plant a pot of basil on May 15. If the basil flowers by June 24, she can anticipate being married during the following year.[307] In Sicily and certain mainland areas of southern Italy, a pot of basil on a balcony signals that a family has a daughter of marriageable age for whom they seek a suitor.[308] In a fifteenth-century story by Gentile Sermini, removal of a pot of basil from a window served as a notice to a lover that the coast was clear for a meeting.[309] A pot of basil is also prominent in Boccaccio's story of Lisabetta, who put the head of Lorenzo, her dead lover, in a pot, covered it with earth, and then planted basil and, with care and love, watched it grow, fertilized by her lover's flesh and watered in part by her tears.[310] Marriage does not necessarily end the service of basil in matters of love, for, in Chieti, married women may wear basil on their heads.[311]

Related to the above is the association of basil with the chastity of young women. In Chieti, all young women clip a small sprig of basil and place it on their breasts or in their waistbands, likely as a symbol of chastity, virginity.[312] In the old district of Vogtland in Germany, basil even served in a test of purity, indicating a lack of chastity if a basil plant withered when held in the hands.[313] Such concerns may be behind reports that a young Italian from Chieti or a young Greek who calls on his beloved may have a bit of basil behind his ear, but he is careful not to give it to her, for that would be a sign of contempt.[314]

Recalling the widespread Hindu use of holy basil in connection with death and burials are reports of similar associations for sweet basil in lands to the west. The ancient Greeks regarded basil as a sign of mourning.[315] Early Greek Christians believed that basil had grown on Christ's grave, which may have contributed to its image as a plant of mourning in modern Crete.[316] In medieval England, people would usually take sprigs of basil or some different aromatic herb to a cemetery, where they held them during the burial ceremony.[317] In former times in eastern Europe, it was common to lay a bunch or stalk of basil on a shroud, casket, or grave.[318] In modern Iran, basil is used in funerals and planted on graves, and its growth is described as prolific in graveyards and burial grounds there, expressed in Thomas Moore's poem "Lalla Rookh": ". . . the basil tuft that waves / Its fragrant blossom over graves."[319] In Italy, too, basil is said to be found growing on some tombs,[320] and in modern Egypt women may throw basil flowers on the graves of their dead.[321]

Among Hindus, as we have seen, holy basil is used to protect against Yama, lord of the dead, as well as against evil spirits. It is of special interest, therefore, to read that leaves of basil may be included in charms carried by women in Greece.[322] The matter of the Kallikantzaroi, evil spirits who live in the underworld for most of the year but appear on earth during the time from Christmas to the Epiphany, is quite similar. They are driven away on Epiphany Eve by a Greek priest who dips a cluster of sweet basil (or a cross together with a cluster of basil) into a vessel of holy water and then sprinkles the water about the house. As the Kallikantzaroi depart the world of the living, they whisper to one another: "Let us go, let us go—for here comes the blasted priest—with his sprinkler and holy water."[323] On the island of Lemnos, a sick person or animal is sprinkled 40 times[324] with a bunch of basil dipped into holy water.[325] In a book on the Cyclades, Bent observes that in Greece on St. Basil's Day (January 1, New Year's Day), women bring basil to church to have it sanctified, then take it home and cast some leaves onto the floor to assure good fortune for the coming year. They also eat a bit of basil with their families to assure good health for that period of time, as well as putting basil leaves in a cupboard to safeguard embroideries and silk clothes from moths and rodents.[326] In parts of Greece, New Year's Day is still celebrated on September 1, ancient beginning of the new year and today the beginning of the religious year. Early in the morning of that day on the island of Carpathos (Karpathos) in the Dodecanese, women carry out rites to gain purity, protection, and good fortune somewhat similar to those just mentioned. They sprinkle the floors of their houses with fresh water, then tie sprigs of basil, other flowers, and "wreaths of pomegranate" (fruit?) around the pillars of their houses and leave them there all year long.[327]

One cannot ignore the fact that in the Near East–Mediterranean region and elsewhere in Europe, from antiquity to the present day, basil has also had a sinister image. In a medieval work in Arabic, it is said to be a bad sign if one sees basil in a dream.[328] Basil is also presented as a premonition of evil in a book on dreams—by Achmet, a Byzantine Greek Christian who lived in Asia Minor—that dates from roughly the same period (between A.D. 813 and 1075) but draws on sources from other cultures and times. In a section giving credit to the Persians and Egyptians, Achmet writes that, if an individual dreams that he is given basil by someone else, it will bring on sorrow and anxiety according to the amount received. He also writes that, if the individual knows the giver, he will be oppressed by him or someone like him, or, if he does not know him, by an enemy. Other dreams of basil detailed by Achmet cause worry, agony, suffering, need, sorrow, and weeping to the individual or members of his household.[329] In the matter of basil as sinister, one recalls a Persian legend that, while viewing the plant as a valuable medicinal, nevertheless portrays it as carried by a snake from the underground.[330] Images such as these may derive from basil's ties with death, mourning, and the exorcism of evil spirits. They may relate to the confusion that came to surround its name and that of the basilisk, an evil mythical monster that can kill a person merely with a glance.[331] Views of basil as evil may also relate to widespread notions in the Mediterranean area and elsewhere in Europe— from antiquity onward—that basil was tied to scorpions and other noxious creatures. Among these notions are the following: that scorpions are drawn to basil; that basil can bring on the spontaneous generation of scorpions as well as other creatures, usually nuisances or noxious ones;[332] that if one smells basil frequently, it can cause a scorpion to develop in one's brain; that if a man is bitten by a scorpion on the same day that he has consumed basil, death will result, or, by a different version, that he will suffer no pain at all; that, applied externally, basil is effective against scorpion bites and basilisk venom; and that indeed it can draw out any poison from an organism.[333] As we have seen, in India holy basil is viewed as effective against the bites of scorpions and snakes, and other species of *Ocimum,* including *O. basilicum,* are also so regarded.[334] In addition, sweet basil has been used in the Near East and Mediterranean area for various other medicinal purposes that *O. sanctum* and other *Ocimum* species serve in India.

Careful research should uncover much more on sweet basil in the imagery, ritual, and medicine of Iran and other Near Eastern and Mediterranean lands. Even the above material, however, shows such striking parallels with tulsi in India as to justify again raising the question about possible exchanges of ideas about *Ocimum* between the two regions.

3 Sacred Fig-Trees of India

Young leaves grow green on the banyan twigs,
And red on the peepul tree,
The honey-birds pipe to the budding figs,
And honey-blooms call the bee.

—S. Naidu, "Spring"

There is that ancient tree [fig tree], whose roots grow upward and
whose branches grow downward;—that . . . alone is called
Immortal. All worlds are contained in it, and no one goes beyond.
—*Katha Upanishad* 2.6.1

He then goes to a sacred fig-tree, and with his face towards the
east makes it a profound inclination, repeating the following
prayer the while: "O *aswatta* tree! You are a god! You are the king
of trees! Your roots represent Brahma, your trunk Siva, your
branches Vishnu. Thus are you the emblem of the Trimūrti [the
triad of great Hindu gods just mentioned]. All those who honour
you in this world by performing to you the ceremony of the
upanayana [thread ceremony, an initiation rite symbolizing a boy's
fitness to be given sacred knowledge] or of marriage, by walking
round about you, by adoring you and singing your praises, or by
other similar acts, will obtain remission of their sins in this world
and a home of bliss in the next. Penetrated with the consciousness
of these truths I praise and adore you with all my strength."
—A Brahmin in his daily ritual, quoted by J.-A. Dubois,
Hindu Manners, Customs, and Ceremonies

There is nothing greater than a Brahmin, Tulsi, Peepul tree
[sacred fig-tree], Cow, and the river Ganga [Ganges]. Always seek
association with these five.
—Y. Rai, *Holy Basil*

A pipal tree is as holy as a place of pilgrimage.
—M. Stevenson, *The Rites of the Twice-born*

Introduction

Many fig species are found in India, and people have applied the term
sacred to various of them. In this chapter, however, I focus on two species
that are preeminent in their sanctity. The first, under whose branches
the Buddha received enlightenment (the Bodhi tree), is *Ficus religiosa*, in
English often called the sacred fig-tree of India. In the Sanskrit literature

41

of India, it is the *aśvattha* or *pippala*,[1] and in modern Hindi, *pipal* (often *pīpal*).[2] Among the sacred trees of India, the pipal[3] "comes first on the list" and is the "king" or "sovereign of the trees,"[4] its primacy well expressed in Krishna's declaration, "I am the Himalaya among the . . . mountains . . . the ocean among reservoirs of water . . . the aśvattha among all trees."[5] Our second sacred fig-tree, *F. indica* or *F. bengalensis*, is, in English, the "banyan tree"; in the Sanskrit literature, *nyagrodha* ("growing downward"), later *vaṭa;* and in modern Hindi, *bor, bar, ber,* or *bargat*. The banyan tree was of great importance in Vedic villages. It remains so in modern Hindu villages, where, like the pipal tree, it is thought to possess a degree of immortality and is only slightly less revered than the pipal itself.[6] On one of the seven mythical great insular continents identified in the *Vishṇu Purāṇa,* there was a large pipal tree, whereas on another continent there was a banyan tree (in which Brahma lived).[7] When a mythical flood drowned the entire world, moreover, only the top of a tall banyan tree, with Krishna as a small child in its highest branch, reached above the waters.[8] This reflects the fact that, though members of the genus *Ficus* range in size from shrubs to giant trees, *F. religiosa* and *F. indica* are among the giants.

Geographic Occurrence

The geographic distribution of pipal and banyan trees in a truly wild state in India is limited. Such wild pipal trees occur in the sub-Himalayan forests, in Bengal, and in Central India, but not in Ceylon or southern India, except possibly along its northeastern borders.[9] Wild banyan trees, on their part, are also found in sub-Himalayan forests as well as at lower elevations in certain hill areas of the Deccan Peninsula. The banyan does not, however, appear to be native to Ceylon.[10] Through the agency of man, however, pipal and banyan trees are now cultivated in most parts of the Indian subcontinent, including Ceylon. In the Himalayas, however, the pipal tree, though deciduous or semideciduous—losing its leaves in the cold season—grows only to about 5,000 feet in elevation, and the banyan, which is evergreen, to about 4,000 feet.[11]

The fruit of the true fig-tree (*Ficus carica*) is so well known as a human food, and in some parts of the world as such a major dietary element, that a word of caution may be justified here.[12] Though people eat the small fruits of the pipal and banyan trees, they are of quite minor dietary importance. Indeed, they are consumed mainly by animals such as birds

8. Banyan tree and its many trunks (from Rousselet, 1878).

and monkeys, who are fond of them,[13] or by poor people, especially during times of food scarcity and famine.[14] Thus, the importance of the two trees derives not from their dietary role but from other factors.

Physical Characteristics of the Trees as They Relate to Sanctity and Ritual Role

The physical characteristics most significant for understanding the sanctity of the pipal and banyan trees are size, perceived age, and method of growth. Both trees can become tall, but it is not so much their height as their beauty and massiveness—their thick trunks, wide-spreading branches, and the circumference of the area they shelter—that is telling.

Mature banyan trees reach heights of from 70 to 100 feet, and their principal trunks may be 8 or 9 feet in diameter and reach the first branches at about 25 feet above the ground. The size of the banyan tree is enhanced by its striking method of growth, that of sending down aerial roots from its wide-spreading branches.[15] Each of the roots becomes a new trunk, which adds support to the branches, and they may, over time, number in the hundreds or even thousands (Figure 8).[16] The entire cluster spreads by this means and, with the original trunk and the pillarlike

9. Banyan tree in Lahaina, reputed to be the oldest banyan in the Hawaiian Islands (photo by Edwin B. Allen).

newer ones beneath a canopy of branches, may cover a very large ground surface, with extraordinary trees reported to be as much as 1,500–2,000 feet in circumference (Figure 9).[17] The banyan's many roots led the Portuguese to call it tree of roots (*arvore de ráiz*).[18] They have also been a matter of wonder to Indians, as shown by the writer who likened banyan roots to "heavenly knowledge, descending and taking root on earth."[19] In the Himalayas, there is an interesting and practical use of the banyan's aerial roots. People tie together the aerial roots of trees growing on opposite sides of a stream or gorge. The roots then fuse and thicken to form "living bridges" (Figure 10).[20]

There have been many statements about how many thousands of people specific banyan trees of great size can shelter. Estimates of 5,000–7,000 are not unusual, and there is one of 20,000,[21] and another, however improbable it may seem, of 30,000 men and horses.[22] It is no surprise

10. Living bridge in the Himalayan forest (from Ragozin, 1902).

45

11. Mature pipal tree in Singapore (from Corner, 1952).

that people often highlight the majesty of the banyan tree in their descriptions. Among them are "immense," "of amazing size," "probably the most astounding piece of vegetation on the face of our earth," and "what a noble place to worship."[23]

Though the horizontal dimensions of pipal trees may not be as impressive as those of banyans, Indians consider the pipal to be one of India's most beautiful trees, and it, too, can be very large[24] and provide excellent shelter (Figure 11).[25] An entire village of more than 100 huts in Ceylon is said to be beneath the shade of a single pipal tree.[26] Thus, the pipal is well suited to serve, as it has since antiquity, as the "cosmic tree" of India, a giant tree symbolic of the universe, a tree that was the source of all creation.[27] Another attribute that enhances the pipal's sanctity is its exceptional vitality. When moisture has led pipal seeds to germinate, writes Alabaster, "even in a crack in some lofty tower, they will not die, but forcing the thin air and the hard bricks to nourish them, they will send down their suckers to the earth; and then these suckers, growing into huge roots, will crack and rend the building, shiver and destroy it, and only preserve its memory by the huge fragmentary masses which it will for centuries retain clasped in its embrace."[28]

Birds are agents in the dispersal of pipal and banyan seeds,[29] and commonly both the pipal and banyan start life as epiphytes that grow from seeds that have fallen on another tree such as the palmyra-, or fan, palm (*Borassus flabelliformis*) or date palm (*Phoenix dactylifera* and other species of *Phoenix*), with the "strangler fig" ultimately growing and squeezing to the point that it may kill its host.[30] Not all host trees are killed by strangler figs, however, for if a tree can grow without expanding its girth and competing with the fig that envelops it, it may successfully compete with the fig. More than one palm tree, for example, has been observed growing up through the center of a strangler fig, with its crown in the middle of the fig's crown (Figure 12).[31] Whatever the case, such strangling made an impression on ancient Indians, for in the *Atharva-veda* the pipal tree is called "the displacer" or "the destroyer."[32] In much later times, the emperor of China expressed an awareness of the power of the pipal tree to spread and dominate. In a letter to the court at Ava, capital of Burma, he said: "Everything that occurs in elder brother's empire [China] shall be made known to younger brother. With respect to younger brother's empire [Burma], it is not proper to allow the English, after they have made war and peace has been settled, to remain in the city. They are accustomed to act like the peepul tree [that is, to spread and take such hold that they cannot be eradicated]. Let not younger brother therefore allow the English to remain in the country."[33]

Another oft-noted feature of the pipal tree is that its leaves tremble;[34] "wave . . . in an uncanny way";[35] make "a characteristic fluttering sound";[36] and are subject to a "mysterious quivering and rustling."[37] This, to one foreign observer, sounds like falling rain.[38] Hindu authors, on their part, have sometimes compared the rustling of pipal leaves to the melodious sound of the Indian lute.[39] The association of rustling leaves with the lute goes back to great antiquity, for already in the *Atharva-veda* one reads that celestial nymphs (*apsarās*) live in aśvattha (pipal) and nyagrodha (banyan) trees, in which their lutes and cymbals sound together.[40]

In India, the rustling of the pipal's leaves has been thought to be done by supernatural beings who speak by that means.[41] The concept of the "talking tree," as noted by Coomaraswamy, "is at home in India," and, in a sense, every tree inhabited by a spirit or deity is a talking tree. The concept relates to that of the musical trees mentioned above, to the Vedic

12. Strangler fig-tree growing with a palm tree (from Tennent, 1859). A fig tree, through its strangling habit, may ultimately kill the other tree with which it grows, though palm trees, especially toddy palms (*Borassus flabelliformis*), seem especially well able to survive.

"Tree of Life," in whose branches all creatures sit and "hymn their share of life," and to the "jeweled and resounding Bodhi tree in the Land of Bliss."[42] It also fits with the observation that, when the Buddha went to sit under a pipal tree to seek enlightenment, he was likely expecting a supernatural communication of some sort. It fits even better with a myth of the Kuttia Kond of Orissa in which pipal leaves are directly tied to speech: the creator goddess Nirantali, when forming the first human being, used "the ever-quivering pipal leaf" as a tongue.[43]

Also relevant are the life-spans that Hindus ascribe to certain giant trees, a span—to be considered again later—that can cover thousands of years. This makes such trees witnesses of the past, observers and even participants in the great historical and mythological events that shaped Hinduism and other Indian religions.

Earliest Evidence of Sanctity of the Pipal Tree

Hindu veneration of trees, including fig trees, is shared by many non-Hindu ethnic groups in South and Southeast Asia and more distant parts of the Old World.[44] In the Indian subcontinent, such primitive peoples as the Andaman Islanders are in this category, which seems to add support to Hutton's suggestion that Hindu views of the sanctity of fig trees may go back to the earliest populations of the Indian subcontinent.[45] The pipal tree, for example, was often represented on pots in the borderlands between India and Iran before the time of the Indus Valley civilization.[46]

The first clear indications of sanctity, however, are for the Indus Valley (Harappan) civilization (c. 2500–1700 B.C.). In the Indus Valley script, which is a logo-syllabic system, one sign clearly represents a pipal leaf. In Fairservis's interesting recent effort[47] at Indus script decipherment, which is based on the assumption that the language of the Indus Valley was Dravidian, this sign is assigned the Dravidian stem *ara* and a possible meaning of "head or high superior as in Chief or God," and perhaps, he suggests, it was tied to a female of elevated status. The pipal sign is sometimes joined with an arrow sign (*amb*) to form another sign which Fairservis assigns a Dravidian equivalent of *ambara* or *ambala* and a suggested meaning of "court, open area by a 'temple,' or 'temple' grounds." Fairservis qualifies *temple* because no temples have been identified with certainty in Indus Valley sites so far. I wonder, however, whether the pipal tree itself may have been the temple, the place beneath which worship occurred. In ancient India, it should be noted, there were open-air Buddhist tree-temples, *bodhigharas*, that consisted basically "of a pillared gallery surrounding an umbrella-crowned and garlanded Bodhi-tree" and a seat, throne, or altar.[48] Coomaraswamy insists, moreover, that it is reasonable to believe that the tree-temple is an ancient temple form that preceded Buddhism, that *yakshas* (phantoms, earth spirits, or deities) occupied sacred trees, and that the trees were honored just as if they were their anthropomorphic images. The essential element of a yaksha place of worship, he notes, was a stone table or altar set beneath a tree sacred to the yaksha.[49] What I am suggesting is that a pipal-tree temple was likely in use among people of the Indus Valley civilization.

13. Indus Valley potsherd with a pipal-tree design (from Mackay, 1943).

In any case, Fairservis also notes equivalents to *ambara* in Dravidian languages today, as in Chidambaram, the name of a modern temple city in South India.[50] There is also other evidence—in representations on seals, amulets, and potsherds (Figure 13)—that confirms the fact that the pipal tree played a role in ritual and religion among people of the Indus Valley civilization. Though scholarly interpretations of scenes vary considerably, it appears that, as among Hindus today, a canopy was set up for weddings, and on Indus seals such canopies are made of leaves, usually pipal[51]—perhaps because the pipal was associated with fertility.[52] Prominent in the depictions are animals, such as a unicorn bull, and personalities many consider a male god and a goddess who, on occasion, is pregnant or nursing a baby, and who, on one seal, is standing under a pipal tree while a goat is being brought for sacrifice to her.[53] One scene shows what appears to be a pipal tree emerging from the heads of two animals (unicorns), which suggests to Marshall that they may have been associated with the goddess of the tree, perhaps in the role of a *vāhana*, or vehicle of her will.[54] Other scenes are interpreted as pipal trees, or deities in pipal trees, and their worshippers.[55] On Harappan-level pots at Chanhu-daro, the pipal is the most common plant motif and is represented in natural or conventionalized form.[56] The pipal is depicted as growing on a mound of earth, platform, or altar, as in India today.[57] Certain other plants sacred to modern Hindus also seem to be represented at Chanhu-daro, among them what appears to be the neem (margosa) tree, which, as we shall see, now enjoys a special relationship with the pipal tree. On one Indus Valley amulet, a kneeling man is making offerings to what seems to be a neem tree.[58] In a different scene, a goddess kneels on a neem branch while extending her arm toward a tiger that is looking back at her; in still another, she has come down from the neem tree and is standing behind the tiger,[59] which is looking back at her.[60] The conclusion reached by various authorities is that trees of more than one kind were sacred to people of the Indus Valley civilization (the acacia is often mentioned, too), but that the pipal tree seems to have been venerated more than others, and that such sanctity was expressed in forms surprisingly similar to those found in present-day Hinduism, for example, in ritual practices in South Indian villages, most of whose people are Dravidian. It may also be relevant that after a child is born, the Brahui, Dravidian-speaking Moslems who live in the hills west of the Indus Valley of Pakistan and are the last surviving Dravidians in that part of the subcontinent, may use pipal (leaves) to protect against evil forces.[61]

In keeping with the above is the likelihood that a name in the *Rig-veda* refers to a non-Aryan cult of tree worshippers (who were disparaged by the Aryans, though there is no reason to believe that tree worship itself was "un-Aryan").[62] The pipal and banyan trees, on their part, did not grow along the Inner Asian route of Aryan migration, and the Aryans cannot have been familiar with them until they arrived in India.[63]

Role in Hindu Ritual and Religion

The centrality of the pipal tree in Hindu religious thinking is revealed in three sayings. One, "I am going to the pipal tree," has the meaning "I am going to say my prayers."[64] The second, "She has watered the pipal tree," means "She has done something pious."[65] The third saying, "She has done (worshipped) tulsi and pipal," means "She has carried out much good work."[66]

Supernatural Beings to Whom Sacred Fig-Trees Are Tied

In Vedic times, the pipal (aśvattha) reigned over all other trees,[67] and the gods were said to assemble beneath a celestial pipal tree.[68] Later, the pipal also came to be the residence of, symbolic of, and sacred to, the Trimūrti, the triad of great gods mentioned previously.[69]

In later Hindu tradition, Vishnu was said to have been born beneath a pipal tree.[70] He also took the form of that tree, which was representative of and sacred to him and his incarnations.[71] Appropriately, Lakshmī, wife of Vishnu and goddess of good luck and abundance, has been associated with the pipal tree in some places and is thought to live in it every week on Sunday, a favorable day for its worship.[72] Krishna, one of Vishnu's leading incarnations, is also said to pervade the pipal, and, in addition, the tree is deified and worshipped as Vasudeva, father of Krishna.[73] In Kerala, a pipal leaf on which an image of Krishna has been modelled is kept in many Nair households. In 1964, moreover, people there were startled to hear that an image of Krishna as an infant had been discovered on the leaf of a giant pipal tree at Trichur, a Cochin town with one of the most ancient temples in India. Many people went to view the image, but, it is said, only the faithful could make it out.[74]

In explanation, perhaps I should add that images on pipal-tree leaves are common in India, for people paint figures on the skeleton leaves of the pipal tree (Figure 14) to create attractive works of art.[75] During the festival of the Muharram, first month of the Islamic calendar, for example, Indian Moslems make lamps of such leaves, some of them beautifully constructed, which they hang in their houses and out of doors.[76]

The pipal tree clearly enjoys a special tie with Vishnu and his incarnations, but, as we shall see, it has notable ties with Shiva, too.[77] Pipal trees may also be inhabited by a broad range of other deities, both national and local.[78] They may be occupied by demons or by evil or benevolent spirits;[79] spirits of certain human dead;[80] and snake people (to be considered in detail later). It is not surprising that, from an introduced monotheistic perspective, Malabar Christians have called the pipal the devil's tree.[81]

14. Skeleton leaf of the pipal tree (from Condit, 1969).

15. Hindu ascetics and shrines under a banyan tree (from Ragozin, 1902).

The banyan has been seen in a quite similar light. It has been a resting place for the triad of later Hindu gods.[82] All three members of the triad have had clear ties to the banyan, but those of Shiva are especially well developed.[83] It is thus fitting that a famous banyan tree, to be considered in detail later, was dedicated to Pārvatī, a major wife of Shiva.[84] As with the pipal, the banyan has also been tied to and occupied by many other deities, major or minor, regional or local.[85] The banyan, like the pipal, has been tied to saints;[86] to spirits, good and evil;[87] and to snake people. In any case, it is because of this association with deities that ascetics and other persons seeking enlightenment may take up residence beneath pipal or banyan trees (Figure 15) and that, beneath or near them, images, altars, and other ritual objects may be set up and shrines constructed (Figure 16).[88] In the Ramayana, there is a fine description of such a sacred banyan tree. It was "like a bright cloud." It covered a vast space, and was located in the center of "a level and charming spot over which cool breezes blew resembling heaven itself . . . [a tree] where many sages sheltered . . . [a tree] frequented by groups of great sages."[89]

16. Shrines beneath a sacred fig-tree (from Crooke, 1896a).

Sacred Fig-Trees as Protective, Purifying, Healing, and Wish-granting

The "wishing tree," *kalpa-vṛiksha* (also *kalpa-druma* or *kalpa-taru*), is a tree found in ancient Indian myth, art, and sculpture, both Hindu and Buddhist.[90] In earliest times, when all was pure, it is said to have grown on earth. People then needed no land, homes, or other possessions. They could simply sit under the tree and make a request for their needs to be met. In later eons, because of human aspirations and depravity, it was found in Indra's paradise.[91] In the Sanskrit literature, trees of various species have been referred to as the kalpa-vṛiksha, among them the banyan, which is said to provide food, drink, clothing, jewelry, children, beautiful young women, and more.[92] A banyan tree has also been depicted in sculpture as the kalpa-vṛiksha. In a sculpture at the Mahābodhi temple, to be considered later, two human arms reach out from a banyan tree. In one hand is a plate of food, and, in the other, a drink. They extend toward a man who puts out his right hand to receive them.[93] Elsewhere, gold pieces may be shown falling from the tree, with containers beneath overflowing with coins (Figure 17).[94] The kalpa-vṛiksha was sup-

17. The banyan as a wishing tree (*kalpa-vṛiksha*), from a
temple of Kubera, lord of the earth's treasures (third century
B.C.). Shown among the banyan tree's aerial roots are a pot
and two bags, all overflowing with coins. Note the railing
around the tree (from Coomaraswamy, 1993).

posed to have counterparts in various sacred places on the earth.[95] In
modern times, though other trees have been called wishing trees,[96]
Chowbe has argued that only two trees measure up to the mythical kalpa-
vṛiksha. One is the famous "undying banyan tree" (*akshaya-vaṭa*) at Allahabad. The second is a tree of the same name at the city of Gaya.[97] Both

of these are pilgrimage centers to be mentioned again later. One should note here, however, that the banyan is especially well suited for the role of an "undying tree," because its habit of continually sending down aerial roots that develop into new trunks suggests longevity. There is a Hindu belief that the life of another person can be extended by planting a tree in his name, caring for it, and having it grow. Planting a banyan seems especially well suited for achieving longevity.[98]

In addition to the trees mentioned above, there are other famous banyan and pipal trees in the subcontinent, as well as local trees, to which appeals may be directed. Appeals may simply involve prayer carried out at a tree. However, they usually also entail other things, such as offerings of water and food, circumambulation, wrapping a thread around a tree's trunk (symbolic of a gift of clothes), making vows, or the practice—found widely in the Old World—of hanging rags or worn clothes on trees as votive offerings.[99] A pipal tree may also be honored by carrying out a ceremony of investiture with the sacred thread as if it were a Brahmin.[100]

Ancient or modern works indicate that appeals to or rituals involving pipal or banyan trees have been carried out to destroy enemies;[101] avert evil forces;[102] protect against disasters;[103] heal illness;[104] pardon sins;[105] and gain prosperity, wealth, and happiness.[106] Even soil near the roots of a sacred fig-tree is sometimes used for such purposes, as when certain Bombay Brahmins in the hope of gaining wealth[107] dig such soil from a pipal or banyan tree and make an image of Parthishwar, lord of the earth.[108] It is thought that animals may seek safety in pipal trees, as revealed in a Rajasthani saying: "Whenever he is in some trouble or danger, the squirrel is able to run and climb the pipal tree; he can go no further than this."[109]

It seems, however, that most human ritual involving pipal and banyan trees from Vedic times to the present has been based on the fertility associations of these trees. Notable in this regard is the belief in Bengal that the banyan tree is inhabited by and associated with Shashthī, goddess of childbirth and children. The goddess is worshipped as a banyan branch full of fruit. This may be a planted branch or a wall painting of one. It is said that the banyan is tied to Shashthī because of its many fruit.[110] The banyan has phallic associations, too, as shown in the fact that, if no temple is available, the liṅga of Shiva—a phallic symbol to be considered again later—may be placed at the foot of a banyan tree for public worship.[111] Not to be overlooked are: the tale of a woman who gained her husband by worship of a pipal tree;[112] the employment of pipal leaves in marriage ceremonies to ward off the evil eye; the worship of the pipal tree at marriage rites to assure good fortune;[113] the use of "the wedding robe of the bride" to decorate a banyan tree in Gujarat;[114] the ceremonial planting of a pipal tree in Bengal by childless individuals and persons whose infants have died after birth;[115] and the belief that devotion to the pipal tree leads to a happy marriage.[116] Also notable is the rite Aśvattha-pata-vrata, performed by Bengali women to honor the pipal tree on the last day of Vaiśākha (April-May), an auspicious month, for the purpose of enhancing family happiness and wealth.[117] Hartland has written of a tiny plate of gold, or *tāli* (a badge of marriage that is tied around a South Indian Hindu bride's neck at her wedding), that is formed like the leaf of an "Indian fig tree" (pipal?) and represents the phallus. He writes further that in the eighteenth century, when Roman Catholic missionaries tried to get their converts in India to replace the tāli with the cross, the missionaries encountered so much resistance that they had to compromise: the tāli could continue to be worn, but only if a cross had been engraved on it. Meyer has observed, however, that Hartland's association of the pipal leaf with the phallus is contrary to early Indian sources that associate the pipal leaf with the vulva, and Meyer insists that the intent of a tāli-vulva was to strengthen young women and their vulvas.[118]

More should be said about appeals to pipal and banyan trees for children. Such appeals have typically been made by barren wives who want sons.[119] It is thought that the spirits of Brahmin boys who died before they were married live in pipal trees and that such tree spirits are capable of making women fertile. Such beliefs explain two interesting practices. One is that most women wear veils when they pass such trees. Another is that infertile women may remove their clothing at night and, while naked, circumambulate a pipal tree a specified number of times.[120] Women desirous of children are also reported as circumambulating a pipal tree 108 times or some multiple of 108.[121] There is a report that, when a woman who has circumambulated a pipal tree bears a child, she might hang a cradle on the tree.[122]

Men may also be involved in such appeals. Men without offspring may honor or worship a pipal tree with water each day in the expectation of obtaining a son.[123] Even Brahmins may undertake such ritual, sometimes in an impressive manner. This is shown in an early tale of wealthy but childless Brahmin named Nyagrodha, who appealed to the god of a large nyagrodha (banyan) tree in a city, Nyagrodhika, named after the tree. The Brahmin arranged to have the ground around the tree sprinkled, purified, and decorated. He covered it with flowers, perfume, and incense, and he erected flags and standards. Then he entertained 800 Brahmins, presented them with gifts, and appealed to the god of the tree to grant him a son. The Brahmin used a carrot-and-stick approach. He promised the tree god that if his wish were granted he would honor the tree in a similar way for an entire year. If not, he warned the god, he would cut the tree down, break it into chips, burn them, and scatter the ashes or throw them into a running stream. Eventually, the tale goes, the tree god arranged the matter, though with outside supernatural assistance because he himself was a minor figure. In time, a son was born, and, appropriately, he was named Nyagrodhaja.[124] All the above is in keeping with Hindu use of various plant parts of pipal or banyan trees (bark, aerial root, fruit, milky juice or latex) as aphrodisiacs, to encourage sperm production and to make women fruitful.[125] Also common has been the worship of pipal and banyan trees by married women who seek to put off becoming widows by appealing for longevity for their husbands.[126] Chowbe notes that, when the night of the new moon (ama-vāsya) in a Hindu lunar month falls on a Sunday, upper-caste Hindu women, in an effort to assure longevity for their husbands and joy in the hereafter, worship a pipal tree by circumambulating it 108 times. At each round, moreover, they present a gold or silver coin, a sacred thread, fruit, or sweets.[127] In the month of Jyeshtha (May–June), moreover, Hindu women everywhere fast and worship at a banyan tree to protect themselves from widowhood.[128] That occasion[129] is named for Sāvitrī, a lovely, chaste, and faithful wife whose tale is recounted in the Mahabharata and in the Puranas. When her husband, Satyavān, died, Sāvitrī held his body in her arms while sitting under a banyan tree awaiting the appearance of Yama, lord of the dead. When Yama came to take Satyavān's soul, Sāvitrī followed Yama and made repeated appeals that he return her dead husband to life. Though reluctant at first, Yama, impressed by her dedication, finally granted her wish.[130]

Sacred Fig-Trees, Truthfulness, Proper Behavior, Innocence, and Guilt

In the same way that leaves of the tulsi plant serve in Hindu oath-taking, so do leaves of sacred trees such as the pipal.[131] As described in the nineteenth century, a person making a deposition under oath or a defendant being tried asks the deity of the tree to kill him if he says anything but the truth. Then, after crushing a pipal leaf, he begins his testimony.[132] At the end of the last century, it was said to be customary for a Hindu to take an oath by placing a pipal leaf on his head.[133] Somewhat different in the way it involved the pipal tree, however, was the principal oath of the Aheriya, a tribe of hunters, fowlers, and thieves of northwestern India. That oath was made on Ganges water, but was considered more binding if the oath-taker stood beneath a pipal tree or held a pipal leaf in his hand.[134] Nor, it is said, will a devout Hindu risk telling a lie or vary from strict standards of behavior while he is standing under a pipal tree.[135] Relevant in this regard is an interesting story, whether true or invented for European tourists, of some Hindu merchants objecting to the planting or seeking the removal of pipal trees in their bazaar, since they could not operate without some measure of trickery. If they were to operate in the shade of pipal trees, the merchants argued, their bargaining would be paralyzed because they would no longer be able to falsify and deceive.[136] From the perspective of the merchants' Hindu customers, it may be that pressures for the merchants to be truthful and behave in an upright manner were reassuring.

In a similar vein, one reads that in a trial by fire in the past an individual who had been accused walked barefoot over burning pipal leaves or pipal wood. If he was burned, he was guilty; if he was unhurt, he was innocent.[137] In northern India (Oudh) in the middle of the last century, a Brahmin explained why oaths taken on a pipal tree are more effective than ones administered in the courts established by the British. In the latter, the Brahmin insisted, a man feels little hesitation about lying because he does not face divine retribution or dishonor in his village or caste. Far more effective in determining truth, the Brahmin said, is the Hindu system, under which a man accused of wrongdoing is called before village or caste members. If he refuses to admit his guilt and to compensate his accuser, he is instructed to bathe, place his hand on a pipal tree, and state aloud his innocence. This is done in the belief that no one would risk taking an oath on a sacred fig-tree and then telling an untruth. Should a person do so, he would risk punishment by the gods who live in the tree. Thus, if an accused refuses to take the oath, he is judged guilty and may be told to compensate his accuser for damages incurred. If he does not do so, the accused is avoided by other people and his life is made wretched.[138] In nineteenth-century Bastar in Central India, the pipal served in quite a different way in establishing guilt. Two pipal leaves were used in a first step to determine the guilt or innocence of a woman accused of witchcraft. One leaf represented her; the other, her accusers. The position of her leaf, when it was cast onto her outstretched hands, raised suspicions of guilt or innocence, but the final verdict was determined by "the usual water ordeal."[139]

Ritual Use of Their Wood

Fire, personified as the god Agni, has been an object of veneration by Hindus since antiquity. As a result, ceremony has been involved in various aspects of the fire sacrifice, including the gathering of firewood, the building of the sacred fire altar, and the setting up and lighting of the fire. There was, moreover, not merely one form of fire sacrifice but many, each with a different purpose in public worship or household ritual. Several of these involved starting the fire by friction using fire sticks (Sanskrit: *araṇi*) made from the wood of the aśvattha (pipal) and *śamī* (*Prosopis spicigera* or *Acacia suma*) trees.[140] Macdonell and Keith, writing of Vedic India, have said that the lower of the two, apparently a block of wood used in making sacrificial fires, was made from wood of the śamī tree, and the upper (the drill), from the wood of the aśvattha (pipal) tree.[141] Hopkins has noted that, in epic mythology, the sacred fig-tree represents "the male element in the production of fire" and that the śamī is the birthplace of Agni and that Agni is the son of śamī.[142] Gupta has observed that the aśvattha was the male and the śamī the female, a highly inflammable wood regarded "as the goddess-incarnate," and that there is a clear analogy between making a sacred fire and sexual intercourse.[143] From a slightly different perspective, Dymock et al. have pointed out that wood of the pipal tree personifies masculine power, and that when rubbed against wood of the śamī tree, which represents female power, it brings on fire, which symbolizes reproduction.[144] It is interesting that, in a striking parallel, Hindu women in the Sind may rub themselves against a pipal tree in order to obtain offspring.[145] Also of interest is the Vedic practice of lighting a fire with fire sticks of aśvattha and śamī wood in an effort to obtain male offspring.[146] In such a ceremony in the *Atharva-veda*, the sexual symbolism is quite clear: "The aśvattha [pipal, which, in this case, was male] . . . has mounted the śami . . . : then a male child was produced."[147] Also of interest is the fact that Agni, who personifies fire, is noted for his amorous nature,[148] and that in the modern fire drill used in northern India, the base of the rotating part of the drill is called *sanku*, "spike" or "dart," and the cavity that contains the tinder is called *yoni*, "vulva."[149] Whatever the details of the practices and the meaning of the symbolism involved, use of the wood of the pipal tree in making sacred fires has made it central to some of Hinduism's most ancient and sacred rituals.

Indeed, S. M. Gupta[150] has suggested that the sanctity of the pipal tree may derive from its ancient use in making sacrificial fires. One could equally well make a case that pipal wood was used for such fires because it already enjoyed sanctity. In either case, pipal wood was used as a talisman.[151] Pipal and banyan wood were also used for making certain ritual vessels, such as for holding the sacred soma juice so important in Vedic ritual.[152] Pipal wood has been used in modern times for making the spoons used to pour ghee onto the sacred fire.[153]

Other Expressions of Sanctity

The sanctity of the two trees, moreover, has been reflected in a surprising range of ways, of which I would mention just a few examples. One is the use of the pipal and banyan as art motifs from antiquity onward, including their depiction on early Hindu coins.[154] Another example is that *pipal* appears in many place-names.[155] A third is that a variety of silkworm that feeds on the leaves of the pipal tree is called divine because of the tree's sacredness, and that its silk, in part because of this, is very highly regarded.[156] A fourth example, from early in the nineteenth century, involves mildew that continued to destroy wheat crops over a period of several seasons in an area of Central India. The cause of the blight was a matter of speculation, with many regarding it as punishment for human wrongdoing. Thus, among the explanations for how to end the blight, one was to eliminate cow slaughter, another, to fight the increase in adultery. Then a cowherd had a vision that if a cultivator took water from a particular stretch of a small river, then carried the water to his field in containers that did not touch the ground on the way, and finally made a circle of water around his field, his wheat would be unaffected by the blight. People came to obtain water in great numbers (400,000 people in one six-week period) and from distances of more than 100 miles. Of special interest to us, however, is that the water had to be taken from a spot beneath a large pipal tree that had fallen into the river, and, before taking water, a person obtained the blessing of Vishnu priests stationed on the shore. One explanation of the water's effectiveness was that the pipal tree, the above-water branches of which remained alive, made the water holy.[157]

Planting, Care, and Protection of Sacred Fig-Trees

Planting

Why and Where They Are Planted.—Before taking up the question of why and where sacred fig-trees are planted, we should note that the Bodhi tree is different from other Buddhist symbols and even from relics of the Buddha's body (which are widely honored), for, as Coomaraswamy has noted, the tree is virtually the Buddha personified.[158] This is demonstrated in the Jatakas, where the Buddha is made to say that, to those who wish to show their reverence to him when he is away on a trip, the Bodhi tree is the only proper substitute for himself.[159] It is also reflected in the story of Ashoka, the famous Buddhist ruler, who bestowed kingship on the Bodhi tree and dedicated it as sovereign of his land.[160] When King Tissa of Ceylon received a branch of the Bodhi tree sent by Ashoka, another story goes, he worshipped it by granting it the kingship of Ceylon, while, symbolically, he assumed the role of a doorkeeper. After Tissa planted the branch, moreover, eight young Bodhi trees sprang up, and Tissa, awed, honored them with the gift of a white parasol as a symbol of their royal status.[161] In Buddhist art, the Bodhi tree may be represented with a parasol above it. This not only indicates its status but also implies that, as a symbol, the tree represents the Buddha as well as, or better than, an anthropomorphic figure could.[162]

The pipal tree is such a central element in the imagery of Buddhism that, wherever the tree is able to survive local conditions, Buddhism's adherents have planted them near temples, monasteries, and relic chambers (*dāgobas*).[163] In sculptures in the Buddhist ruins of Sanchi and Amaravati in India, the pipal tree is shown as ornamented with garlands and encircled with worshippers.[164] In Ceylon, one of the main areas of the Indian subcontinent where Buddhism has continued to be practiced through the millennia, a pipal tree can be found near all Buddhist temples.[165] Since people gain religious merit by planting a pipal tree, moreover, Buddhists in Ceylon also plant them in many other places, such as in human settlements, along roads, in fields, and even, in memory of the deceased, where human remains are burned or have been interred.[166]

Among Hindus, the idea that a person may gain religious merit by planting sacred trees, such as the pipal and banyan, has persisted from antiquity to the present day.[167] In the Puranas, for example, it is said that a person who plants trees will receive heavenly bliss and that one who plants a pipal or a banyan tree will never go to hell.[168] A man plants a pipal tree near a tank in modern India, it is said, so that its leaves may fall into the water to serve as offerings to his ancestors.[169] Nor has the person who plants such a tree been blind to its effect on his social standing, for example, a magistrate who sought to gain the goodwill of people in his district by planting pipal trees.[170] Except in places such as the Himalayas, where temperatures are too cold, nearly every village in Hindu India has a pipal tree, commonly near a temple or in some other prominent place, particularly where Brahmins perform their ablutions.[171] In Kerala, it is said, the prominence of a temple is reckoned by the height of its pipal tree.[172] Devout Hindus may also plant pipal trees near their homes to have them convenient for worship.[173] Banyan trees are also widely planted along roads, at crossroads or village squares, or near temples and shrines.[174]

Because they can provide abundant shade—an important matter in hot climates—meetings may be held under pipal and banyan trees, thus one of the names for the latter: "tree of councils."[175] Rulers in Kerala have been chosen under a pipal tree.[176] Traditional courts of justice, too, have commonly been held under pipal trees, which is especially appropriate because the great sanctity of the tree deters lying.

There may also be plantings, not of a pipal tree by itself, but of a pipal with other sacred plants. In the tulsi chapter, we saw that a tulsi shrub is a frequent companion of the pipal tree typically grown on a raised platform in a village. A pipal tree and a banyan tree may also be planted next to each other.[177] A pipal may be planted with a neem.[178] There are also triads of sacred trees, for three is a blessed number. Pipal, banyan, and neem trees are a common triad and the object of remarkable devotion.[179] In North India, such a triad was reported at a Shiva temple in Hardwar, one of Hinduism's seven sacred cities. That triad of trees, moreover, was considered as sacred as the junction of Hinduism's triad of holy rivers at Allahabad, which is called *triveṇī* or *triveṇī sangama*.[180] One also reads of a triad of sacred trees consisting of pipal, bael, and neem;[181] of pipal, bael, and śamī;[182] and of three different fig species (pipal, banyan, and *pākar* or *Ficus venosa*).[183] In Kerala, moreover, there is a sacred triad of temple trees consisting of a pipal, a neem, and a mango (*Mangifera indica*). Though the mango and neem at first provide shade to the pipal, ultimately they are overshadowed and die.[184] Five is an auspicious number, and five sacred trees grown together also constitute a very sacred group.[185] There was an assemblage of five sacred trees (*pañcha-vaṭi*) in ancient times[186] consisting of a pipal, planted on the east side; a banyan, on the west; bael, on the north; an *āmlā* tree (emblic myrobalan, *Emblica officinalis*),[187] on the south; and an *aśoka* (*Saraca indica*), on the southeast.[188] One also reads of a modern assemblage of five also called pañcha-vaṭi—a pipal, banyan, neem, mango, and emblic myrobalan—at which devout Hindu men regard it as a sacred duty to stay.[189] Each of the trees in the two groups of five is sacred and auspicious. Collectively they possess truly remarkable abilities: to remove sin and pollution; to eliminate sorrow and bring great happiness; to assist women in finding a husband; to bring on fertility; to facilitate the birth of male offspring; and to create prosperity, great wealth, and longevity.[190] To assemble and plant more than five trees in one place for purposes of worship strikes one as quite a difficult undertaking. Though this has been reported,[191] in all likelihood it was not carried out by ordinary folk with any regularity.

Tree Marriage.—Assemblages of sacred trees such as those mentioned above have a clear advantage over an individual tree in dealing with human needs—for not only do assemblages represent greater power, but also, as we have seen, they possess a broader range of abilities to improve human life. This advantage, moreover, may be enhanced by binding them further by means of "tree marriage," a solemn ritual in which trees are formally married, whether to other trees, humans, deities, or other things.[192] It is considered highly meritorious to sponsor a tree marriage, and the ceremony may be followed by an enthusiastic public celebration that lasts for several days and entails considerable expense.[193] Tree marriage may involve two trees of the same species, as in the case of two pipal trees that were growing nearby and were considered husband and wife.[194] It may involve two fig trees of different species, as when a pipal tree is married to a banyan tree—a common union and one popular in Bengal.[195] A pipal or banyan tree, on the other hand, may be married to a tree of a different genus (the preferred partner for the pipal is the neem) or to more than one such tree, as would be true of most cases mentioned in our previous paragraph. More than proximity may be entailed. A married pair of trees (for example, a pipal and a banyan) may grow with their branches intertwined, like a married couple in loving embrace.[196]

Pipal and banyan trees may also be married to gods[197] or to humans who can gain real advantages through such unions.[198] The marriage may tie a bride and groom to a powerful natural force capable of bestowing some of its reproductive vigor on the couple.[199] A human bride and bridegroom may, as an alternative, pass on to the tree some evil force that otherwise would affect their marriage, particularly one threatening its fertility.[200] In Oudh, for example, it is thought to be quite ominous for a young man and woman to marry if his ruling stars are stronger than those of his proposed bride. Risk can be avoided, however, by having the young woman first marry a pipal tree.[201] A somewhat similar situation is dealt with in an astrological treatise that cites Hindu religious or philosophic works in explaining what a man should do when he is convinced that his daughter has been born at such an ill-fated time that she is certain to become a child widow. First, according to the treatise, he should have his astrologer determine an auspicious time for him to leave home to start setting things right. Then he should go to a deserted place and fast in homage to the pipal tree. His daughter, on her part, should take a morning bath, put on clean new clothes, go out alone and in secret to dig up a young pipal tree, carry it to a location where a bael and a śamī tree are growing, and then plant and water it. Then, every day for a specified lunar month, she should worship a Brahmin or Brahmin woman, as well as an image of the goddess Pārvatī. Finally, on a day identified by an astrologer as favorable for that purpose, her marriage to the pipal tree should be consummated employing all the ritual used in an ordinary human marriage. If these instructions have been followed and the young woman subsequently marries a human husband, the treatise concludes, she will be at no risk of becoming a widow.[202]

In some cases, the tree may be a replacement for a human spouse. For a young Hindu woman, marrying a tree may save her and her family from the scorn that, according to popular thinking, results when a daughter has attained adulthood but remains unmarried.[203] A married woman, on her part, may also gain from marrying a tree. If she does so, she can eliminate the risk of widowhood, an undesirable state. Her gain in marrying a tree is that, even if her human husband were to die, she would still be married—to the tree.[204] Not only has tree marriage served to eliminate the risk of widowhood, but it has also been employed by Hindus to facilitate the remarriage of widows, which, though legal, is commonly frowned upon.[205]

Marriages to trees or shrubs have also served to make it easier to take multiple wives. Among certain Brahmins at the turn of the century, for example, not only was a third marriage considered highly inauspicious, but it was also believed that the third wife would soon die. When a Brahmin interested in taking a third human wife first married an *arka* plant (*Calotropis gigantea*, an erect, perennial shrub), however, that plant became his third wife, and his new human wife became his fourth. The plant, it was believed, would soon die (or was deliberately cut down), but the fourth wife was not affected adversely.[206]

Care and Protection

Sacred fig-trees may be damaged by animals, wild and domestic, that feed on their foliage. There are also reports of elephants and camels feeding on pipal and banyan trees,[207] of banyan leaves being fed to elephants, and of pipal leaves being cut and fed to cattle.[208] In addition, there is a report from Oudh during the mid-nineteenth century that, though herders were not permitted to touch pipal trees in villages and cultivated fields, the foliage of banyan and pipal trees found in jungle areas might be cut as fodder for the livestock of peasants as well as for the camels and elephants of local officers.[209]

Sacred trees have, however, been protected against injury in various ways. Priests have served, or guardians have been appointed, to protect sacred fig-trees, such as at the pilgrimage sites of Bodh Gaya and Anuradhapura.[210] The common practice of planting sacred fig-trees on mounds or platforms[211] and laying stones around them also serves a protective role. It has been called a typical and nearly essential feature of Buddhist and Hindu shrines to be enclosed by a wall or railing, and this is reported for sacred fig-trees as well.[212] Early Buddhists, for example, placed stone railings around sacred fig-trees (note Figure 17). One also reads of the tree at Anuradhapura being kept in an enclosure, its branches supported by masonry pillars and its main stem supported by retaining walls. In a similar vein, Buddhist rulers circled the compound of the Bodhi tree at Bodh Gaya with stone or brick walls.[213] One famous pipal tree, the

Vidur aśvattha, is described as "built round with various shrines for protection."[214]

The area beneath sacred fig-trees may be cleaned, as by sweeping.[215] Indeed, "god's tree"—as both Valentijn and Knox call the pipal tree in Ceylon because of its sanctity to the Buddha—is more respected and better cared for in that land than any other tree.[216] As for Hindus, they are careful not to plant a pipal tree too close to a house, out of concern that its roots would grow under the hearth and get burned.[217] For Hindus, watering pipal trees is a religious duty.[218] On Sunday, when Lakshmī, goddess of good fortune and prosperity, is thought to be in the pipal tree, Hindus, after taking a bath, pour water, to which milk and sugar may be added, on to the ground under such a tree.[219] Watering has also been done at any time of need or illness[220] or on other special occasions. Watering may be carried out, for example, as a result of a vow made by the relative of a dying man,[221] or when a childless man, in an effort to obtain a son, pays homage to a pipal tree every day by giving it water.[222] One also reads that, on the death of a high-caste Hindu, a pitcher—with a small hole in its bottom that is stuffed with kuśa grass—may be filled with water and suspended from the branch of a pipal tree. Water drips steadily from the pitcher for the ten days of death rituals,[223] to the benefit of the tree. In a similar vein is the account of a son pouring 360 brass containers of water at the foot of a pipal tree to guarantee the tranquility of his dead father.[224] Ward has observed, moreover, that Hindu women seldom go out on the streets, and that some of them may plant a sacred tree in their compounds in order that they may gain merit from watering it during the hot season. He adds the observation that, to honor Brahmin wives, lower-caste (śūdra) women may carry water to Brahmin household trees.[225] Young prop roots of the banyan tree may be safeguarded from damage by encircling them with bamboo tubes.[226] Health problems may also receive attention, as in preventing further damage to a pipal tree infested with lac insects by taking one of the affected branches to the Ganges and putting it into the sacred river.[227]

Sacred fig-trees, whatever their origin, may cause serious damage to wells, houses, temples, tombs, and other structures. Despite this, Hindus become quite upset when one is injured. They are also reluctant, unwilling, or afraid to cut them down, or even to cut them away from places where they are causing damage.[228] Such fears are based on concern with the supernatural beings who live in the trees and the serious punishments they can mete out to a Hindu who injures them. Among these are impoverishment, childlessness, and the inability to have a son, which means that the injurer's family would become extinct and that he would have serious problems in the next world.[229] An awareness of the risk is revealed in the Ramayana when the demon-king Rāvaṇa protests, "I have not cut down any fig tree in the month of Vaiśākh, why then does the calamity befall me?"[230]

Buddhists have similar concerns about sacred fig-trees. If one interpretation of an early Buddhist work is correct, to hurt a pipal tree is an offense as serious as killing one's mother or father or raping a nun.[231] One early Buddhist tale tells of a caravan of treasure-seeking merchants who camped beneath a huge banyan tree. As they cut off one branch of the tree after another, out came food, drink, women, and valuables, gifts from the *nāga-rāja* (snake ruler), whose tree it was. Greedy and thirsting for still greater rewards, they decided to cut the entire tree down. Whereupon the nāga-rāja became so incensed that he had his nāga subjects attack and kill the entire group of merchants, except for their leader, who had objected to chopping the tree down.[232] The sacred Bodhi tree of the Buddhists at Anuradhapura cannot have its branches lopped off; even its leaves, which are highly valued by pilgrims, are normally obtained only when they fall to the ground.[233] Indeed, when Tennent mentioned to a Ceylonese officer in charge of the sacred tree that he would like to have a few of its leaves, the officer "undertook to bring them . . . *at night.*"[234]

Members of other ethnic groups may also be at risk, whether from humans or from supernatural forces, if they damage sacred fig-trees. This is shown by the riots against Moslems after they have cut pipal branches back.[235] Foreigners are not altogether free from danger either, as shown by the story of a British engineer, who, in order to carry out construction at a fort, had to cut down a banyan tree. His act so angered local Brahmins that they poisoned him.[236] One judges that, even if Europeans are not punished for cutting a tree, blame may fall on them. The Maghs of Bengal, for example, consider it dangerous to down trees except when Europeans are present to assume the guilt.[237] Even animals have been reported as being punished for damaging sacred fig-trees. This is shown in the tale of an elephant who accidentally ate a single leaf of a banyan tree that was highly venerated. The elephant died within three days.[238]

Fitting with the above are observations that to fell a pipal tree would be a terrible impiety, unpardonable or not readily forgiven;[239] that it is forbidden to cut down a pipal tree;[240] that it is a crime to damage or demolish either a pipal or a banyan tree;[241] that it is an impiety to injure a pipal tree in any way; and that it is strictly forbidden to use pipal wood as fuel.[242] The reluctance to fell pipal trees applies even to ones growing in forests, which may explain a medieval Bengali story of clearing a forest to establish a settlement and of cutting down nearly all the forest trees except the pipal.[243] Similar ideas apply to the *deodār,* the Himalayan cedar (*Cedrus deodara*), which in the Himalayas assumes the role of the pipal tree as the most sacred tree. In the last century, for example, one Himalayan rāja granted a contracting firm a lease to cut deodār for timber in the territory he ruled, whereupon his subjects rose in revolt, requiring him to seek protection from the British authorities. The argument of his subjects was that the rāja did indeed own the land, but the trees were owned by the gods.[244]

Cutting a tree accidentally can also bring on punishment, as among Oriyan tribes, in which an accidental cutting of a banyan tree requires sacrifice of a goat to the deities who live in the tree.[245] Even disrespect for a pipal tree may be sufficient to bring on distress.[246] In Ceylon there is a tradition of "the leprous king," who developed leprosy because, when he passed under a pipal tree, he failed to give the tree the honors to which it was entitled.[247] Indeed, tree spirits sometimes cause injury with little or no provocation. In one Bengal folktale, for example, the spirits of a banyan tree would wring the necks of all people who dared to approach the tree at night.[248]

Famous Sacred Fig-Trees of the Indian Subcontinent

Those of Gaya District in Bihar and Anuradhapura in Ceylon

In antiquity, the Gaya District of the modern province of Bihar was part of Magadha, that celebrated Indian kingdom in which Buddhism originated. The district contains many places of importance in Buddhist tradition, but, of them, the sacred complex at the village of Bodh Gaya ("Gaya of the Enlightenment"), six miles from the city of Gaya itself, is by far the most important. For Buddhists, Bodh Gaya is the holiest place on earth, for, according to tradition, it was here that the Buddha meditated under a pipal tree—the Bōdhi-druma (Sanskrit; later Bo or Bodhi), the "tree of enlightenment."[249] In the words of one ancient account, ". . . having made his resolution, [the Buddha] sat down to obtain perfect knowledge at the foot of the great holy tree."[250]

Bodh Gaya and its Bodhi tree have been a goal for pilgrims from India and the entire Buddhist world for more than two millennia, making this pilgrimage one of the world's longest-lived of all that are still carried out. The site is also more important today than any other Buddhist pilgrimage site in India, with one recent work (published in 1994) claiming that each year its famous temple is visited by millions of pilgrims and tourists from all over the world.[251] Bodh Gaya has been likened to Jerusalem for the exciting associations it elicits, not only among devotees, but also among others who appreciate its central place in a religious system that has had a major impact on some of the greatest civilizations in the history of the world.[252]

Though pilgrims may consider the Bodhi tree growing in modern Bodh Gaya to be the very one under which the Buddha sat, disinterested observers credit it with being a descendant of that holy tree—one of a long line of successors.[253] Thus, the Bodhi tree at Bodh Gaya, though it had "five huge trunks" in 1992,[254] was not large in size at all times in the past. Even so, a visit to the holy tree when Bodh Gaya was in its prime must have been awe-inspiring. The pilgrim, for one thing, came face to face with an object of unusual sanctity and meaning. It could, moreover, be approached only by passing among an imposing array of sacred structures as well as lakes, rivers, ponds, and other landscape features important in Buddhist lore. Among them, with stupas or other religious structures nearby, were a place along a river where the Buddha had bathed, a stone on which he had washed and dried his robes, a banyan tree where he had been exhorted, and a lake associated with the nāga-rāja Muchalinda,[255] who, as we shall see, sheltered the Buddha at the time of his enlightenment.

In the seventh century A.D., Chinese Buddhist pilgrim Hsüan-tsang (Xüan-zang) reported that the Bodhi tree at Bodh Gaya was only 40 or 50 feet tall, far below the several hundred feet it was reputed to have been in the Buddha's day. The tree that Hsüan-tsang observed was located in a compound that took 500 paces to walk around. The compound was encircled by a brick wall, high and strong, and it had four gates. Under the tree was the *vajrāsana* ("diamond throne"), an immortal throne thought to be at the earth's center and the place where all Buddhas had sat, or would sit in the future, in order to gain genuine enlightenment.

Also in the compound were sacred structures so numerous, Hsüan-tsang noted, that it would be difficult to describe them individually. Hsüan-tsang reported that people came to Bodh Gaya to seek cures, and that spontaneously every year, on the day of the Buddha's death, the Bodhi tree was visited by thousands and tens of thousands of worshippers—including laymen, clergy, and princes—who bathed the tree with "scented water and perfumed milk," scattered flowers, provided music, and made religious offerings.[256] Judging from Hsüan-tsang's account and from modern remains and observations,[257] in its prime Bodh Gaya and the surrounding area were crowded with structures that had been erected as memorials by devout persons from India and other lands, especially Ceylon and Burma. Among the structures, large and small, were: stupas;[258] temples, monasteries, and retreats (including caves carved out of solid rock); statuary, carvings, and other art; uncommon trees and flowers; and other trees, including pipals and banyans, that played a role in Buddhist lore. The most famous temples were at or near the Bodhi tree. One of these was the "Ashoka temple," built in the third century B.C. Another was the temple of the Mahābodhi, "The Great Enlightenment." This temple may have been built in the second century A.D. and seems to have existed in roughly its present form in the seventh century A.D. Whatever the actual dates of its construction may have been, the Mahābodhi temple, which has been restored again and again, still stands today (Figure 18).[259]

Over the millennia, though certain Buddhist structures at Bodh Gaya have been restored, most have fallen into ruins. A century ago it was said, ". . . the number of images scattered about this place, for 15 or 20 miles in all directions, is almost incredible; yet they all appear to have originally belonged to the great temple or its vicinity, which seems to have been the grand quarry" for the whole area.[260] The Bodhi tree, on its part, has been blown down in a storm. It has also been cut down more than once by persons hostile to Buddhism. In the third century B.C., for example, it was cut down by the famous Buddhist king Ashoka before he accepted the Buddha's teachings.[261] In the seventh century A.D., moreover, it was cut down by Śaśāṅka, king of Gauḍa in Bengal.[262] In such cases, tradition has it, the tree was miraculously restored to life, or, as Western observers believe, a new tree grew up from a seedling that was planted or from seed that was sown, perhaps in a crevice on the dead or dying tree.[263] Late in the last century, for example, reconstruction of the temple at the Bodhi tree required that it be transplanted to a garden nearby. Hearing of this

18. The Mahābodhi temple at Bodh Gaya as restored in 1884 (from Monier-Williams, 1889). The sacred Bodhi tree is not depicted because it had to be removed during the restoration. It has since been replanted.

19. The Bodhi tree at the Mahābodhi temple in 1891. At the tree are a Japanese Buddhist monk and Angarika Dharmapala, famous Ceylonese Buddhist and founder of the Mahābodhi Society (from Guruge, 1965).

and hoping to assure the life of the sacred tree, groups of pilgrims from Burma and Ceylon arrived at Bodh Gaya to cover the stem of the tree with gold leaf and to pour scents over its roots and fertilize them. Despite this, the tree died, and a new pipal tree was planted behind the restored temple (Figure 19).[264]

In addition, seed, seedlings, and cuttings from the sacred pipal tree at Bodh Gaya have, since antiquity, been carried to Buddhist centers throughout mainland India. Tradition has it that such transfers began already during the Buddha's lifetime. The Buddha himself had a branch of the original tree planted in the garden of the monastery at Śrāvastī (Sewet), where he preferred to live.

Such transfers were also made to foreign lands, and Monier-Williams thought it likely that most sacred trees near Buddhist temples, not only in India, but also in Ceylon and Burma, originated from seed brought from the sacred tree at Bodh Gaya.[265] The first Bodhi tree to reach China was presumably a seedling from Bodh Gaya. It was carried by sea from Magadha to China about 1,400 years ago, where it was planted in a monastery courtyard at Canton.[266] Most memorable of all foreign transfers, however, was one mentioned previously, the branch of the Bodhi tree at Bodh Gaya that was carried to Ceylon in the third century B.C., which, by one tradition, was a precious gift from Ashoka to Tissa, king of Ceylon, who, along with his lords and commoners, had become a Buddhist.[267] That branch, carried to Ceylon by Ashoka's daughter, was planted at Anuradhapura, Tissa's capital, to become the most celebrated tree on that island. Even after Ceylon's capital was moved elsewhere and the area around Anuradhapura virtually abandoned from the twelfth to the mid-nineteenth century, a pipal tree, watched over by Buddhist monks, continued to survive and to be worshipped (Figure 20). Should it have died, it would have been a catastrophe bringing dismay and fear not only in all parts of Ceylon but in foreign Buddhist lands as well.[268] For one thing, the sacred tree at Anuradhapura would have been lost for purposes of worship.[269] For another, the source of supply for pipal trees grown in temple and monastery grounds throughout Ceylon would be gone.[270]

In regard to Bodh Gaya, it is interesting that the sacred complex, including the Bodhi tree,[271] has long been a pilgrimage site not only for Buddhists but also for Hindus. Even more, there is clear evidence that, as the Buddhist complex fell into ruins in past centuries, Bodh Gaya was being taken over by Hindus. It is believed, for example, that in the fourteenth century the Bodhi tree and the nearby temple were taken over for Hindu rites. At the close of the fifteenth century, a monastery dedicated to Shiva was built near the main temple at Bodh Gaya, mainly with material taken from the ruins. Moreover, in the year 1727 or thereabouts, the Moslem emperor of Delhi gave the village as a grant to the abbot (mahant) of the Shiva monastery. Though Buddhists were still permitted to visit and worship there, the former Buddhist temple was in the possession of Śaivite ascetics.[272] It has been suggested that, with the decline of Buddhism, Brahmins likely adopted the Bodhi tree as a sacred object in order to make a profit from Buddhists who continued to worship it.[273] Early in the nineteenth century, however, there was a stairway, built by some zealous Hindu, to enable orthodox Hindus to "pass without . . . seeing the hateful image of Buddha.[274] In the nineteenth and early twentieth centuries, differences between Brahmins and Buddhists over control of the

20. Sacred Bo tree at Anuradhapura in the mid-nineteenth century (from Tennent, 1859).

sacred complex found expression in judicial actions. These were brought
by Buddhists—the Mahābodhi Society of Ceylon and India—who
wanted to regain possession of the Mahābodhi temple at Bodh Gaya.[275] A
compromise was finally reached in 1952, when authority over the temple
was transferred from the Hindu mahant to a joint Hindu-Buddhist committee.[276] Despite this, the matter has continued to be surrounded by

controversy. Buddhists are concerned with what they regard as a tilt in committee arrangements to favor the Hindus. Some of them object to what they see as the committee's corruption, to clandestine meetings with Hindu extremists, to the misappropriation of funds, and to the cutting of branches from the Bodhi tree to obtain bits of wood for sale as souvenirs. Many are also upset with the presence of Hindu priests in the temple and by what they regard as Hindu efforts to assimilate Buddhism in practice as well as in theory. In 1992, on the anniversary of Buddha's enlightment, Buddhists staged a protest in which busloads of people, over 1,000 altogether, came to the temple and harassed the Hindu priests. Hindus, on the other hand, have quite a different perspective. Some argue that the Buddha was simply an incarnation of Vishnu, that Buddhists and Hindus are thus worshipping the same god, and that Buddhism is part of Hinduism.[277]

Among modern evidences of a Hindu presence at Bodh Gaya are its Hindu temples and monasteries. In the inner chamber of the Mahābodhi temple, one finds Shiva's liṅga on the floor immediately in front of an image of the Buddha. Images of Hindu gods, among them Vishnu and Shiva, are found near the temple entrance. Hindus also worship many Buddhist images at the temple, and certain Hindu rites for the ancestors are carried out there. In addition, directors of the nearby Hindu monastery are buried at the side of the Mahābodhi temple.[278]

There is also a separate Hindu place of pilgrimage in the city of Gaya itself.[279] It is located in the sacred section of Gaya, which has been called Old Gaya or Respected Gaya to distinguish it from the city's secular section.[280] Sometimes Old Gaya has also been called Brahmā Gaya or Hindu Gaya,[281] terms that somewhat reduce the possibility of its being confused with the Buddhist complex at Bodh Gaya. Involved in development of Gaya (Hindu Gaya) as a place of pilgrimage was the conversion of Buddhist buildings and images into Hindu ones,[282] much as pagan temples in the Roman world were sometimes converted into Christian churches. At the same time, Hindu pilgrims to Gaya have continued to include a side trip to Bodh Gaya and its Bodhi tree in their itineraries.[283] Indeed, after a storm struck Bodh Gaya and blew over the Bodhi tree in 1876 and one of its seedlings was planted to replace it, an additional seedling was planted[284] some distance away for Hindu pilgrims to worship. This meant that there were two sacred Bodhi trees in Bodh Gaya, one for use by Buddhists, the other, for Hindus.[285]

Gaya (Hindu Gaya) contains many sacred centers, major and minor.

21. *a.* Footprints of Vishnu, from India (from Crooke, 1896a); *b.* footprint of the Buddha, an artistic rendering of the footprint at Sara Buri in Thailand (from Alabaster, 1871). The drawing of the Sara Buri footprint, which is rich in Buddhist and Hindu symbolism, contains three prominent elements and 108 small compartments (108 is a mystical number that represents the heavens). Their meaning is explained in detail by Alabaster (1871: 286–310), but two of the prominent elements are (1) the *chakra* (wheel) (at the center of the footprint), which here represents the wheel of the law, the instruction of the Buddha, the means of eliminating sin and suffering; and (2) the ornamental boundary, a design that derives from the lotus, a plant important in religions of Indian origin whose flower symbolizes matchless beauty and harmony.

They represent all major Hindu sects, and centers commonly serve different human needs and have their own festivals held at various times of the year.[286] It is said that every Hindu should visit Gaya at least once during his lifetime to carry out rites for his dead ancestors,[287] and indeed the most important single series of rites carried out at Gaya is that relating to honoring one's ancestors (śrāddha).[288] Prominent among śrāddha rites carried out by Hindu pilgrims are devotions carried out at the temple of Vishnu's footprint (Vishnupād or Vishnupāda). This is a single footprint in stone that in earlier times had been the Buddha's.[289] Similar footprints are honored in various places by Hindus and Buddhists (Figure 21).[290] In the last century, the Vishnupād temple was described as made of black stone (Vishnu is depicted with a dark complexion) and as having a high dome with a gold pinnacle. Today, moreover, there are two beautiful

21. *b.*

parks at the rear of the temple, appropriately called Vishnu Park and Tulsi Park.[291]

The Vishnupād temple is surrounded by crowds and is located in the midst "of a labyrinth of courts, temples, and convents." The footprint itself, left when Vishnu came to earth to destroy the holy demon Gaya, consists of an indentation in a rock. When Monier-Williams visited Gaya in 1876, he wrote of the footprint as being "in a large silver basin, under a silver canopy, inside an octagonal shrine." Space was provided nearby for carrying out the Vishnupād śrāddha, and various types of offerings, including rice balls, were placed around the footprint.[292]

The śrāddha rites carried out at Gaya are thought to be among the most effective of all śrāddhas in bringing emancipation to family ancestors. Indeed, it is said that, for carrying out śrāddhas, the temple of Vishnu's footprint at Gaya is visited more than any place in India[293] and that, once a man has carried out a śrāddha at Gaya, he never has to carry out another one.[294] A śrāddha at Gaya may be quite involved and time-consuming. Often it involves performing rites at about 100 different places in the Gaya area, among them the Phalgu-śrāddha, bathing in and worshipping at the holy waters of the Phalgu River, and the Vaṭa-śrāddha, at the undying banyan tree, the akshaya-vaṭa.[295] At a minimum, the entire sequence takes 8 days, and it can take as much as 15 days. Moreover, the payments made to the priests who officiate at the rites, Brahmins of a caste called Gayāwal, can be quite high.[296]

Some Other Famous Trees

The literature on India—ancient and modern, Indian and foreign—contains many additional references to celebrated fig-trees. The earliest Greek and Latin authors to mention giant fig-trees in India—including a banyan tree large enough to shelter an army—look back to the time of Alexander the Great.[297] More specific are early Indian and Chinese references to what many Hindus regard as India's oldest banyan tree, the akshaya-vaṭa located at or near Allahabad. Balfour[298] has suggested that a giant banyan tree mentioned in the Ramayana was the akshaya-vaṭa of Allahabad. He seems to be referring to a wish-fulfilling banyan tree and "haunt for perfected beings" called Śyāma, which the god Rama, his wife Sītā, and his half-brother visited after leaving Allahabad, and which Sītā honored and circumambulated, her hands folded in reverence.[299] In the seventh century A.D., in front of a Hindu temple in Allahabad, the Chinese Buddhist pilgrim Hsüan-tsang observed a banyan tree that was surrounded by human bones. These, he said, were bones of pilgrims who had sacrified themselves by jumping from the tree.[300] The remains of a tree in an underground temple in modern Allahabad, described as a stump bearing a few branches to which numerous pilgrims came to worship, were said to be those of the akshaya-vaṭa of Hsüan-tsang.[301] Now, it seems, there is a different, more visible, tree for pilgrims to view, but it is said to lack the standing of the akshaya-vaṭa that made Allahabad famous.[302]

Another renowned banyan tree is the Kabir-bar, said to have been named Kabir after a noted Vaishnava reformer of that name (A.D. 1440–1518; *bar* = "banyan"),[303] which apparently still grows on an island in the Narbada River (second in sanctity only to the Ganges) not far from Broach in Gujarat. This seems to be the banyan tree, a place of pilgrimage, described by Pietro della Valle early in the seventeenth century. The tree was dedicated to Pārvatī, Shiva's wife. On its trunk, a bit above the ground, was a crudely carved circle representing the face of the goddess. Bright, flesh-colored paint was applied to her face with ritual and on a regular basis. Her eyes were made of silver and gold, and she wore jewels that were gifts from persons she had cured. Around her face were bunches of fresh flowers along with leaves of betel pepper. The flowers were constantly replaced and, when removed from time to time, were passed out to worshippers, sacred souvenirs that people kissed and placed on their heads. There was a bell, apparently hanging from the tree, that was used by worshippers to get the attention of the goddess, and nearby was a small chapel visited by childless women in an effort to become fruitful. Valle mentions a yogi standing on a mound near the image of the goddess. He was a person responsible for care of the image, and alms were given to him. Also carried out at the tree were prayers, offerings to the goddess, circumambulation, and other ceremonies. All the above indicates that this was a well-established ritual center. Historical records of the Kabir-bar, moreover, go back hundreds of years before Valle visited it, and, indeed, a native tradition holds that the tree is 3,000 years old.[304] Whether or not this is so, at one time[305] it was described as having 320 large trunks, more than 3,000 smaller ones, and, even after much destruction had occurred, a circumference of 2,000 feet. When they happened to be nearby, Indian armies might camp under the tree, for it was said to be capable of providing shelter for 7,000 people.[306]

Role of Sacred Fig-Trees in the Snake Cult of India

Background on the Snake Cult

Before considering the sacred fig-tree in snake worship among Hindus, some background on the snake cult may be needed for the Western reader. In Hindu India, there is a cult of snakes in which the cobra, role model for the snakes of India, is especially revered;[307] thus, when I use the word *snake* henceforth, unless otherwise stated, it usually refers to the cobra. The cobra, aroused and ready to strike, bears a notable resemblance to an erect human phallus, and, in any case, the snake cult, in a rich variety of ways, relates to fertility concerns. It is also tied to sacred trees, as illustrated in Maity's article, "Tree Worship and Its Association with the Snake Cult in India."[308] There have been snake people (*nāga*s or *nāg*s) and their rulers, commonly multiheaded cobras,[309] in Hindu mythology since antiquity.[310] Nāgas changed readily into human form and often entered the human sphere as companions, marriage partners, and ancestors of many princely families.[311] Nāgas have sometimes been depicted as handsome men or beautiful women or, in the manner of a mermaid, as having the torso of a human and a snake tail for its lower half.[312] It is thought that nāgas sometimes live in the moist soil under the roots of trees. Indeed it has been suggested that the ties between tree worship and serpent worship may have come about because many snakes like to live in such places.[313] Nāgas, however, also live in water bodies, such as springs, fountains, tanks, ponds, wells, rivers, lakes, and the ocean, and they can bring on precipitation and floods—an awesome power in a land such as India, which today, as throughout its history, has been a land highly dependent on its numerous agricultural villages.[314] Perhaps in part because water is so vital to farmers, many Kunbis, members of a caste of cultivators, worship only the snake, and they do so with more feeling than other Hindus show.[315] On the other hand, the worship of snakes is not limited to cultivators, but occurs among Hindus of all castes and sects, among the literate and well educated as well as the illiterate.[316]

Most authorities believe that the cult of snakes in India preceded the arrival of the Aryans (1500 B.C.?), who over time, and after hostility with snake worshippers, incorporated snake cultists' ideas into the Aryan system of religious beliefs.[317] The cobra is rarely depicted on seal tablets of the Indus Valley civilization, though it does appear on one "as a 'witness' to an 'enthroned chief'"[318] in a way reminiscent of the cobras (nāgas) depicted with the Buddha or with Hindu deities in later times. On the grounds of representations on seals, potsherds, and amulets, some authorities have concluded that it is likely, or even certain, that snakes were venerated if not worshipped by people of the Indus Valley civilization (c. 2500–1700 B.C.). Others have held that snake worship was common in India, or among the Dravidians of South India, before the arrival of the Aryans.[319] The above observations fit with the fact that the *Rig-veda*, which looks back to the earliest days of Aryan settlement in India (1500–900 B.C.?), makes no mention of a snake cult. Instead, it presents the snake as a wise but wily creature linked with wolves and demons, one that kills and is to be killed. On the other hand, there is clear evidence of a snake cult in subsequent Vedic accounts.[320] Early Hindu works refer to offerings made to snakes, to snake images being worshipped, and to snake people who had an influence on human life, competed with other supernatural beings, and had leaders called nāga-rājas.[321] Some of these had greater prominence than others, especially Śesha (sometimes identified with Ananta), the serpent who, in Hindu cosmology, supports the world on his head and is sometimes called the ruler of all nāgas.[322] In popular Hindu thinking, earthquakes are believed to be caused by Śesha yawning or shaking his head when he thinks of the sins of the world.[323] In addition, Śesha (or Ananta) forms a couch on which Vishnu reposes.[324] There is also a serpent world within the earth, whose capital is built principally of precious stones.[325]

References to the snake cult are also found in accounts of Jains and Buddhists and in their writings.[326] With respect to the latter group, one should first be aware that Buddhist writers stress the point that the ancient Hindu gods were inferior and subordinate to Gautama Buddha, a view they apply to the nāgas as well.[327] In Buddhist legends, snakes represent earthly life, for they are the principal actors in the control of atmospheric and terrestrial waters. They are grouped with other deities concerned with fertility, good health, and prosperity who, though benevolent, are considered unseeing. In contrast, the Buddha represents a step beyond, a triumph of asceticism and spiritual release over blind commitment to worldly matters.[328]

Buddhist literature depicts nāgas in various ways. Some are savage demons, but most possess human qualities and sometimes even turn into humans. At first appearance, they may be stormy and mutinous, but often, under the Buddha's influence, they abandon their paths of violence to other creatures and become docile beings who embrace his ideas.[329] In any case, there is no such persistent antagonism between savior and snake as found in literature and art in the Western world.[330]

Nāgas and nāga-rājas play roles at various times during the life of the Buddha.[331] One Buddhist legend has two nāga-rājas turn up and bathe Gautama Buddha just after he is born.[332] Other legends have nāgas active at the time of the Buddha's enlightenment under the Bodhi tree. One tells of the Buddha bathing in a "river of nāgas" beforehand, after which a nāga daughter presents him with a jewelled throne to sit upon.[333] A second tells of a nāga-rāja singing a song of praise to the Buddha as he approaches the tree of enlightenment.[334] A third relates to acts that follow the Buddha's enlightenment.[335] Of special note is the legend that, after seven days under the tree of enlightenment, the Buddha went a short distance to a banyan tree, called the banyan tree of the goatherds, where he sat for seven more days and savored the bliss of his emancipation. Then he went to a third tree, tree of the nāga-rāja Muchalinda, where he sat in quiet elation for an additional seven days. Muchalinda, an immense cobra who lived in the roots of the tree, emerged and, since the weather was cold, rainy, and dark, wrapped himself seven times around the body of the Buddha. He protected the Buddha further by using his great snake hood to cover the Buddha's head (Figure 22).[336] On the seventh day, Muchalinda loosened his coils, turned himself into a young man, and, placing himself before the savior, clasped and raised his hands and worshipped the Buddha. Nor do nāgas disappear from the story of Buddha's life. Some nāgas, it is true, fight him and have to be subdued. Others, however, approach him with an open mind, question him, and leave with praise. Certain nāgas assist the Buddha in crossing rivers, shelter him from harm, serve as guardians of his shadow, and, after he has died, serve as guardians of his tooth relic and of one of his stupas.[337]

Scenes of Muchalinda protecting the Buddha are found in Buddhist monuments.[338] So are scenes involving other nāgas or nāga-rājas, who are sometimes depicted as worshipping the Buddha under a sacred tree. At the stupa of Bharhut, for example, Nāga-rāja Elāpatra, another well-known figure in Buddhist legend,[339] is shown performing devotions to

22. Two views of the nāga-rāja Muchalinda sheltering the Buddha (from Vogel, 1926).

the Buddha while kneeling with joined hands at the foot of the Bodhi tree.[340] In addition, early Indian Buddhists, or some of them, participated in nāga worship. This is shown in Hsüan-tsang's account of certain Buddhist priests who considered a nāga to be their patron who brought rain and protected against plagues and other disasters. With this in mind, they erected a nāga chapel, a home for their patron where they made ritual offerings of food.[341]

Buddhism is a minor faith in present-day India, and it is in Hinduism that one finds the most abundant and interesting evidence on the snake in ritual and religion. Though the snake cult varies in detail by locale and region, it is found among Hindus in all parts of India. South India (especially the Malabar Coast), however, is usually cited as one of the greatest centers of snake worship.[342]

Hindus have also had a dread of snakes since antiquity, for the bites of various Indian species—among them the cobra, common krait (*Bungarus coeruleus*), and vipers—can cause death, and even today a significant number of Indians die of snakebite each year.[343] Fear of the cobra is enhanced by its furtiveness, its sinuous movements, its cold fixed stare and the flicking of its forked tongue, its ferocity when attacked, its aggressiveness, and the suddenness of its attacks.[344] Cobras can be fierce enemies when frustrated, for they are swift to strike out and lethal. In addition, they are thought to put curses on people that have serious detrimental effects on their lives. As Smith and Narasimha Chary have noted,[345] their curses terrorize, and, if possible, people avoid even looking at these snakes. The cobra is especially feared by women, for they often walk barefoot in the fields in the dark of early morning and also delve into the dark corners of their residences, where snakes may be lurking.[346] There is a report of a North Indian village being abandoned by its inhabitants in the last century out of fear that snakes who unexpectedly settled there were evil demons.[347] In clear support of the perception of snakes as evil, threatening, and injurious is the observation by one head priest of a temple that the snake represents one of the secretions or leftovers that remained after Murukan conquered the demons.[348]

Despite the above, Hindus believe that snakes can be benevolent, and they see no inconsistency in viewing snakes as representing ideas as opposite as "demonism and divinity, . . . violence and benevolence, . . . [and] destruction and regeneration."[349] The cult of the South Indian god Murukan (Mūrugaṇ), for example, is tied to Subrahmaṇya (Kārttikeya), Shiva's son; to Śaivism; and to serpent worship, as illustrated by the snake icons found in most Murukan shrines and temples. The snake, moreover, is considered useful in granting fertility to women, as shown in an important rite carried out among Brahmins in Kanara after marriage. The rite involves the worship of dough images of five snakes by a bride and groom, its intent being to propitiate the snake god and guarantee offspring to the couple.[350] Drawings of cobras and cobra eyes may serve to drive off evil spirits and protect against the evil eye. At the Festival of Lamps (Dīvalī), cowherds may use a large, hooded cobra made of grass in an effort to protect their cattle. The cobra's hood is folded to form a niche in which a light is placed; the cowherds then carry the cobra image from one house to another and wave it around the household cattle. The appearance of a snake at the threshing floor, moreover, is a good omen.[351]

Belief in the benevolence of snakes may be related in part to two beliefs. One is that the nāga and cobra each have an auspicious swastika mark (Sanskrit: *svastika,* "beneficial to well-being") on its head.[352] The second is that embedded in nāga and cobra heads is a precious jewel (*jī-varatna,* "life-preserving jewel") that has protective, wish-granting, and life-giving capabilities.[353] The cosmic snake Śeṣa has 1,000 heads, each decorated with the swastika and a jewel. Because of this, he is called Maṇidvīpa (from words meaning "jewel-island").[354] Furthermore, "Swastika" is the name of a mythical nāga, and other nāgas besides Śeṣa commonly have the word *maṇi* ("a pearl, a jewel") in their names, for example, Maṇi-nāga and Maṇimant, who are repeatedly included in lists of divine snakes in the Mahabharata and the Puranas.[355]

In any case, people everywhere tend to be reluctant to kill snakes.[356] If a cobra comes to live in the thatch roof of a house, it is said, not only is it left unmolested by the family, but it is also fed milk.[357] There is even a report from the past of a king in Calicut who made it a capital offense for anyone to kill a snake in his land.[358] In modern Malabar, to observe a snake with a bruised head is thought to foretell misery, and the actual killing of a snake is regarded as a heinous sin.[359] In the last century, Taylor wrote—apparently in general terms about South India—that, if a snake is killed in a village by a Moslem or someone else, people will place a copper coin in its mouth, make offerings, and burn its body to turn away harm.[360] It is also said that twice-born castes in South India perform rites for a dead cobra that involve the same formalities as funeral rites for humans.[361] A person who angers or kills a snake may suffer serious calamities such as leprosy, ophthalmia, poisoning, childlessness, and the death of a child.[362] According to Thurston, writing of South India, leprosy was thought to result not only from killing a cobra but also from contributing to the destruction of its eggs.[363] Take the case of the Coorgs of South India. They will not kill cobras found in temples, for such cobras are considered inoffensive, but they are quick to kill cobras elsewhere, which are dangerous. Despite this, for several years after one Coorg man did shoot a cobra, he was unable to father a son, which was explained by certain Brahmins in terms of the great sin he had committed in killing a sacred animal like the cobra.[364] They told him further that he would not father a son until he performed the required expiatory rites under their direction. Even then, the Brahmins said, his violation was so serious that he would not be able to have more than one son. He did perform the rites and carried out a pilgrimage to a famous cobra shrine, and sometime later his wife did indeed give birth to a son.[365] There is a fear that nāgas can bring on deformed or stillborn infants, and it is especially important that, to protect his unborn child, the husband of a pregnant woman not kill a snake.[366] A nāga's influence over a child, moreover, does not end with its birth, and a devout couple may make pilgrimages to snake shrines to ensure that a child's health remains good or is restored.[367] When a child has survived teething and the sicknesses of infancy, moreover, its hair may be shaved off and presented, along with other offerings, at the place a vow was made to a snake deity.[368] It is thus no surprise that children may be given personal names that reflect the high regard their parents have for nāgas. Among these are Nāgeśvara, Nāgarāja, Nāgaswamy, and Nāgappa for boys, and Nāgammā, Nāgamaṇī, Nāgini, and Nāgevari for girls. Such names are found among Hindus of all castes, even Brahmins.[369]

Besides snake charmers,[370] with whom most Westerners are familiar, in Hindu India there are household snakes, whether nāga images or real snakes that are fed and honored. These are objects of daily worship, honored and cared for as household deities who bestow safety, drive away evil forces, and guarantee that the family will enjoy fertility and the birth of children (Figure 23).[371] On occasion, ancestral spirits are thought to assume the form of snakes, and people often consider snakes to represent their departed ancestors who have returned home and are benevolent and protective of the family.[372] This agrees with the observation that, in Gujarat, gardeners call snakes "'father,' 'brother,' and other familiar and endearing names." They also honor snakes and never permit them to be disturbed.[373] It is also in accord with a story told to Sleeman by the principal of a small college in Central India early in the nineteenth century. According to the principal, when his great-grandfather had died and his three wives had committed suttee—immolating themselves on his funeral pyre—two snakes, one after the other, came up and cast themselves onto the pyre, too. Those watching the affair concluded that the snakes had been wives of the great-grandfather in one of his previous incarnations. Convinced of this, their śrāddha rites from that time on were not for four souls (the great-grandfather and his three wives) but for six (the man, his three wives, and the two snakes). Even in Sleeman's day, the principal,

23. Image of a household snake (from Crooke, 1896a).

members of his family, and all other Hindus who heard the story remained convinced that the two snakes were indeed members of the family
and that it was quite proper that they be included in all śrāddha rites.[374]

Snakes are also considered chthonic creatures. Thus, in Hindu snake
lore, most of the huge serpents live not in this world but in the underworld.[375] It is thought that people can make contact with the nāga world
either in caverns or "anthills" (termite mounds), the latter being favorite
haunts of snakes and snake deities.[376] Consider, in this regard, the tale of

a deified woman who had committed suicide on her husband's funeral pyre, then turned into a snake that made its home in an anthill close to the village well. When her son approached the well, she bit him, and he, too, became a snake and lived with her in her underground home.[377] The belief that the snake is a chthonic creature is in accord with the tradition that snakes or snake deities are guardians of houses, of temples, of hidden treasure,[378] and of other sacred places.[379] Cobras do indeed often live in anthills, and people go to them on certain occasions to offer milk, eggs, fruit, and flowers.[380] Cobras are thought to be fond of milk, and when one is observed at a festival drinking the milk offered at its hole, this is considered a very auspicious sign. If the snake is not observed drinking, people may anxiously return the next morning to see if the milk is gone, for if it is, it means that the offering was accepted though not as readily.[381] Eichinger Ferro-Luzzi,[382] focussing on South India in general, writes, "On a snake's sacred days gallons of milk may be poured and the snake's abode may remind one of an egg-stall."[383] Along a public road in Telugu country in the last century, a British observer noted an anthill where an old snake lived and on which a stone image of a cobra had been set up. Stuck into the ground around the anthill were pieces of wood crudely carved into a snake form. Many worshippers were women who were de-sirous of offspring and, from time to time, came to the anthill to pray and to leave milk, eggs (raw or broken), and clarified butter for the snake to eat.[384] If the women caught sight of the cobra, it was believed, the signs were positive and they were assured that their prayers for offspring would be granted.[385] Some of the earth from an anthill may be used to enhance human fertility. With similar intent, it may serve in the ceremonial sowing of seed. It may also be employed in an attempt to control weather or for making an image of the snake god at the time of a snake festival. It may also be utilized as an antidote to snake bite or be applied to parts of the body that are ailing.[386]

One also reads, for one part of India or another, of live temple snakes; of snake festivals, especially the Nāgapañchamī ("Snake's Fifth Day") (Figure 24);[387] of snake shrines and temples; of snake groves; of refuge areas for snakes in gardens at home; of collecting alms for feeding snakes; of offerings to snakes and snake deities; and more.[388] In the Himalayan foot-hills of the Punjab, a snake temple is ordinarily located in a grove of cedar trees[389] not too distant from a village, commonly near a spring or lake.[390]

24. Scene from the snake festival (from Ragozin, 1902).

A snake temple, an object of pilgrimage near Allahabad, is described as massive, located on a raised terrace in a grove of trees overlooking the Ganges. We have seen that Allahabad is the meeting place of three sacred rivers, and its waters are thus of unusual holiness. That holiness, moreover, is enhanced at the snake temple, and one reads that persons making pilgrimages to other sacred places in India take Ganges water only at the snake temple, water they consider purer than water elsewhere in Allahabad.[391] In Malabar, respectable families set aside a corner of their gardens, where a few trees are permitted to grow wild, as a sacred place or snake shrine (nāga-kotta). On a masonry platform beneath the trees, people erect and dedicate stones that have been shaped to represent cobras or cobra hoods. Every day at dusk, a lamp is lighted in the sacred area. At special times, food—eggs, milk, and plantains (Musa paradisiaca) (all symbols of life and/or fertility)[392]—may then be offered to the snakes in an effort to gain their assistance in treating barrenness or various illnesses and diseases. Malabar also has snake groves that look like small forest preserves. Snakes that appear in or near a house may be taken to snake groves. These groves are regarded as sacred areas and are provided with laterite towers for the snakes, as well as stone images of a snake king and queen.[393] Travancore, on its part, has one 16-acre snake grove (kavu) that contains two little temples sacred to the snake king and queen, as well as thousands of snake figurines carved in stone, which represent their subjects.[394] The grove also contains the home of the temple priest,[395] and it is supported by funds derived from various sources, including its own rice fields and estates.[396]

Besides nāgas and nāga-rājas, one finds regular snake deities in India, some of whom are male, some female.[397] South India, for example, has a snake goddess, Durgamma, whose shrine is constructed above a snake stone and has a neem tree growing alongside it. In household worship, Durgamma participates in the form of a cobra's head made of silver. In Bengal, her place is taken by Mānasā, a handsome goddess (Figure 25) whose symbol is the cobra. Mānasā may be depicted as sheltered by a hood of cobras or as sitting on a water-lily and dressed with snakes or in the midst of snakes. Mānasā has the ability to protect against the bites of snakes and counter their venom, thus she is also called Bishahrī (Sanskrit: viṣahari = "remover of venom"). It is said that, if she is not given sufficient attention, a member of the family is certain to die of snakebite. Mānasā sometimes lives in a pipal tree, but, in places where there are many

25. Pottery image of Mānasā, goddess of snakes (from
S. K. Ray, 1961).

snakes, a shrine may be dedicated to her or a room set aside for worshipping her. At one festival in her honor, snake charmers are described as standing on platforms and allowing themselves to be bitten by all types of snakes, while women present milk to the goddess and beg her not to harm their children.[398]

Snakes are also identified with other Hindu deities, especially those who, like the cobra, induce fear and dread in humans. Among the great

26. Shiva and the cobra (from Crooke, 1896a).

Hindu gods, the snake is closely tied to the worship of Vishnu, but Shiva, god of destruction, is most prominent in his connection with snakes.[399] In a way that recalls the tale of Buddha and Muchalinda, Shiva is commonly depicted as sitting in meditation beneath a snake-hood canopy. In a like manner, the liṅga (phallus), emblem of Shiva,[400] may be covered with a snake hood.[401] In Hindu mythology and art, Shiva's sacred thread is a snake, and his body is commonly depicted as decorated with snakes (Figure 26), thus one of the god's reputed 1,008 names or epithets, "Nāg bhushan," means "he who wears snakes as his ornaments."[402] He may wear snakes as necklaces. He may wear them as large, dangling earrings. He may wear them as a girdle, or as bangles or anklets, or as a means of tying his hair into a knot, or in other ways.[403] Snake stones and snake motifs are common in Shiva's shrines.[404] There is also an account of a snake living in a Shiva temple at Thirukalacheri in South India and being fed and worshipped daily.[405] Snake wells—wells in which nāgas are thought to live—are often found at Shiva temples.[406] Near a place of Shiva worship, moreover, one commonly finds a pipal tree, which is considered the home of snakes, the pets of the god.[407] Monier-Williams has observed that both snakes and trees are commonly thought to be occupied by demons, that Shiva is the lord of all three (snakes, plants, and demons),[408] and that this explains the close ties between Shiva worship, snake worship, tree worship, and demon worship.[409]

Hinduism also has had a rich serpent lore[410] in which there has been a great interest in extraordinary snakes, like the famous snake in what today is Uttar Pradesh, whose tail is said to extend underground from Muttra (Mathura) to Brindaban, seven miles distant.[411] Though one might think that such a snake tale would be hard to beat, a legend in the seventh century said that the body of Nāga-rāja Elāpatra, mentioned previously, extended from Taxila, a city in what today is Pakistan, to Benares, in the middle Ganges Valley of India.[412] There are also tales of snake bards (nāga-bārota) in India, wandering people who possess books on where to find certain large snakes. When they are short of money, it is said, snake bards call to snakes, who come out of their holes and give gold coins or jewels to the bards. This is in accord with the traditional belief that snakes are guardians of secret treasures hidden underground.[413]

Sacred Fig-Trees in the Snake Cult

Turning to matters relating to fig trees, Hindus, especially women desirous of bearing children, erect votive stone slabs decorated with snake motifs (nāgakals) in honor of snake deities.[414] Such slabs may be set up in villages or local areas under various sacred trees, including pipal and banyan trees, where they are worshipped by local people (Figure 27).[415] The preferred place, however, is under a pipal and a neem tree that have been formally married and whose branches may be intertwined in a way that simulates affection.[416] Not only are women the principal worshippers of trees and snakes, but they also commonly serve as the clergy who direct the worship.[417]

Such slabs may also be set up near temples, at entrances to human settlements, or near tanks or ponds.[418] Since, as we have seen, nāgas live in ponds and other water bodies, when the carving of such a slab is completed, it may be placed in a pond or well for six months, enabling the stone to take on the life force of the water; then, to make certain that

27. Praying for offspring in front of snake stones, a liṅga, and an image of the god Gaṇeśa. The images are on a stone platform beneath a tree, preferably a sacred fig-tree (*Ficus religiosa*) (from Thurston, 1912).

the stone is given life, magical formulas (mantras) are recited and other ceremonies carried out.[419]

The symbolism of the pipal and neem trees reported in some places in India (e.g., Karnataka [Mysore], Coorg, Tamil Nadu [Madras], Rajasthan, Punjab) is that the pipal is female, and the neem, male.[420] In such areas, it is said, women even cover their faces when in sight of a neem tree, for they are not supposed to display their faces to strange men.[421] Mackenzie suggests that the fruit of the neem does somewhat resemble a liṅga (phallus) and that, when it is placed on the leaf of a pipal tree, which represents the yoni (vulva), the result is a reasonable representation of an entire liṅga-yoni.[422] To help the reader who is not an Indologist better understand the symbolism involved, it seems worthwhile, before proceeding further, to elaborate somewhat on Shiva, sex, and the liṅga and yoni.

Shiva is always sexually ready, his penis hard and erect, and his semen spilling forth at the slightest stimulus, which explains two names by which he is known, "Hiraṇya-retas," having "golden semen," and "Ghṛisheś-vara," "rubbing lord," that is, lord of the sexual act.[423] As is often the case,

Hindu mythology provides us with the best understanding of the intensity, power, and danger of Shiva's liṅga and the calming effect of the yoni:

The sages cursed Śiva's *liṅga* to fall to the earth, and it burnt everything before it like a fire. Never still, it went to the underworld and to heaven and everywhere on earth. All creatures were troubled, and the sages went in desperation to Brahmā [the creator god], who said to them, "As long as the *liṅga* is not still, there will be nothing auspicious in the universe. You must propitiate Devī [= "goddess," in this case Shiva's wife Pārvatī, who is able to control his sexual urges] so that she will take the form of the *yoni*, and then the *liṅga* will become still." They honoured Śiva, and he appeared and said, "If my *liṅga* is held by the *yoni*, then all will be well. Only Pārvatī can hold the *liṅga*, and then it will become calm." They propitiated him, and thus *liṅga*-worship was established.[424]

This helps clarify how Hindus view the liṅga and yoni and why they are basic elements in the symbolism of Śaivism today, a fact illustrated especially well by M. Stevenson. Stevenson, whose observations center on Gujarat, notes that the liṅga represents the male sexual organ and that philosophically it represents the primeval man, from whom humanity derives. The yoni, on its part, symbolizes the female organ and represents the primeval female. In Shiva temples, the liṅga is kept in an inner shrine.[425] It is placed in a yoni made of stone. It may be set in such a way that water poured on the liṅga drains through the yoni into a small drain that ends outside the inner shrine "in a cow's-mouth or some other animal's head not unlike a mediaeval gargoyle."[426] In Gujarat, Stevenson has noted that at certain great Shiva festivals, and every Monday in the god's holy month, Śrāvaṇa (July–August),[427] the liṅga is "dressed in a mask of gold or silver, a necklace, and a turban," which, at other times, are kept in his temple ready for use.[428] In addition, it is on the fifth day of the waxing half of Śrāvaṇa (which falls in the middle of the rainy season, possibly because of the snake's rain-making abilities) that snakes are honored at the Nāgapañchamī, the snake festival mentioned above.[429] Snakes have long been heralds of the rainy season and the crop fertility it brings on.[430] The rainy season is also a time of anxiety. If precipitation arrives too late or is too much or too little, there is a serious danger of famine. In addition, the waters of the rainy season may force snakes from their holes and pose a special threat to humans. Thus when the Nāgapañchamī is held, women in Gujarat and the Deccan draw a picture of a snake on paper, make a snake out of cow dung, or paint a snake image on the walls of a house, and then worship it.[431] In Nagpur[432] in the last century, crude

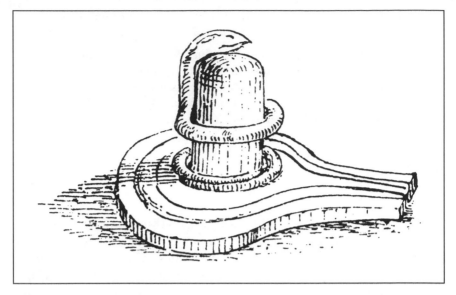

28. Cobra entwined around a liṅga and yoni in a Hindu temple (from Rivett-Carnac, 1879).

pictures of snakes were sold and passed out on this day, much like valentine cards in the West, some of them depicting snakes having sexual intercourse, others representing women and cobras in such a suggestive way as to leave no question that the snakes were phalluses.[433]

That the snake is a phallic symbol in India and is commonly found wrapped around a liṅga—as in Shiva temples and better-class Shiva shrines in Benares, where a snake or snakes may also extend down the yoni (vulva) (Figure 28)[434]—further enriches the fertility symbolism on the nāga slabs mentioned above. So does the fact that on nāga slabs one of the two usual motifs is that of snakes or snake people in sexual embrace,[435] and that a liṅga-yoni may also be engraved on their foreheads.[436] It is thus not surprising that in the state of Junagadh (Junagarh) in western India young married couples go to a famous well to worship snakes with the intent of having a happy married life.[437] Nor is it surprising to hear of the belief that children can be obtained by worshipping a cobra, that barren women often worship at their stone images, and that snakes are also worshipped at times of marriage.[438] In Maharashtra, barren women honor cobras at the Nāgapañchamī by cuddling them on their laps.[439] In one place in South India, Monier-Williams observed two or three pipal trees growing on the banks of a river (a place where nāgas live); beneath the trees were hundreds of stone images of Krishna and the liṅga of Shiva, each with a five-headed nāga shaped in such a way as to form a canopy above the image. Monier-Williams explained this by noting that, in South India if a woman is infertile and thinks this came about because, in a previous incarnation, she killed a cobra, she carries out a ceremony known as *nāga-pratishthā,* which involves erecting a snake stone beneath a tree and consecrating it by reciting texts and prayers.[440] When Monier-Williams was visiting such a place, several women were near the largest of the pipal trees, and some were circumambulating the images or sprinkling water on them.[441] It is said that in every village or local area in the Tamil, Kannada, and Telugu areas, one finds—built around a pipal tree—a platform where people worship and on which are carved images of individual snakes (cobras) or of two intertwined snakes.[442] In Tamil country, a childless woman may make a pledge that if she gives birth to an infant she will set up a stone slab beneath a pipal tree that has been married to a neem tree, a slab into which a snake image has been cut. She then worships mainly by circumambulating the tree 108 times each day for the next 45 days, after which, it is believed, she will bear children.[443] Tamil women seeking offspring favor circumambulating such married trees on Monday, an auspicious day sacred to Shiva. When Diehl observed childless women circumambulating a nāga platform in Madras, it was also a Monday.[444] In the Bangalore area, Mackenzie reported that snake stones were usually erected by Hindu women concerned with their lack of fertility, and were not under the direction of a priest. Snake stones were always located beneath pipal trees, and a stone's quality and finish were determined by a woman's devoutness and wealth. If done properly, snake stones were erected on a stone platform beneath two pipal trees growing together, a male and a female that had been formally married. Nearby on the platform there should have been a neem tree and bael tree, witnesses to the marriage. Usually on such platforms there was only one neem tree and one pipal tree, representing husband and wife. To be complete and orthodox, moreover, specific representations had to be included on the snake stones, among them a seven-headed cobra, a woman whose lower body is that of a snake, and two serpents intertwined.[445] In a similar vein, Rice, writing of Mysore (now Karnataka), has observed that stones bearing sculptured snakes are found under trees near every village; that they are commonly placed on raised platforms;

that one of the trees is always a pipal, which represents a female, and the
second, a neem, which represents a male;[446] that they have undergone a
marriage ceremony; and that trees and serpents are worshipped mainly
by women who wish to bear offspring. In addition, he has noted, a bael
tree, sacred to Shiva, is commonly planted with them.[447]

Since it embraces so many of the elements we have considered above,
it seems appropriate as an ending to this section to include a poem, "The
Festival of Serpents," by Sarojini Naidu:

> Shining ones awake, we seek your chosen temples
> In caves and sheltering sandhills and sacred banyan roots;
> O lift your dreaming heads from their trance of ageless wisdom,
> And weave your mystic measures to the melody of flutes.
> We bring you milk and maize, wild figs and golden honey,
> And kindle fragrant incense to hallow all the air,
> With fasting lips we pray, with fervent hearts we praise you,
> O bless our lowly offerings and hearken to our prayer.
> Guard our helpless lives and guide our patient labours,
> And cherish our dear vision like the jewels in your crests;
> O spread your hooded watch for the safety of our slumbers,
> And soothe the troubled longings that clamour in our breasts.
> Swift ye are as streams and soundless as the dewfall,
> Subtle as the lightning and splendid as the sun;
> Seers are ye and symbols of the ancient silence,
> Where life and death and sorrow and ecstasy are one.[448]

We leave India now to turn to a plant—mandrake—that is far better
known in the Western world than in India, and then to another—ginseng—that has gained a strong following in the Western world but has its
roots in China and East Asia. It is my hope that, having read the chapters
on tulsi and the sacred fig-trees of India, the Western reader may approach mandrake in a sympathetic frame of mind.

4 Mandrake, a Root Human in Form

With Notes on Ginseng

. . . the mandrake . . . can . . . be the herb of life or of death, a
symbol of both sensual love, the bringer of death, or of divine love,
the restorer of life.
—H. Rahner, *Greek Myths and Christian Mystery*

Whether it is gathered for good or for evil, the mandragora is
feared and respected as a miraculous plant, far stronger than any
other. It harbors extraordinary powers, which can multiply life or
strike dead. In some measure, then, the mandragora is "the herb
of life and death."
—M. Eliade, *Zalmoxis: The Vanishing God*

Identity and Geographic Occurrence of the Mandrake

The mandrake (*Mandragora officinarum* L. and *M. autumnalis* Bertol.)[1] is a
member of the nightshade family (Solanaceae), whose most economically
important plants are the potato (*Solanum tuberosum*) and tomato (*Lycopersi-
con esculentum*). More relevant to us, however, mandrake is a close relative
of belladonna, deadly nightshade (*Atropa belladonna*), which, though far
more toxic than mandrake, shares many of its pharmacological qualities.[2]
In fact, certain botanists in the past have placed *Mandragora* in the same
genus as belladonna, often calling mandrake *Atropa mandragora*.

Mandrake is a perennial herb, the best description of *M. officinarum* I
have found being that of Tristram (Figure 29): ". . . a plant of very peculiar appearance. It sends up in early spring a broad disk of leaves, lying
flat on the ground, somewhat like those of the Primrose, but more than
double their size, being a foot in length and four inches wide. In the
centre of these come out the blossoms singly, some with a stalk two or
three inches long, some with scarcely any stem. They are cup shaped, of
a rich purple colour. The fruit is the size of a large plum, quite round,
yellow and full of soft pulp.[3] It has a peculiar, but decidedly not unpleasant, smell, and a pleasant sweet taste."[4] The root is fleshy, roughly a foot
in length, and often forked.[5] Though many have failed to discern the

101

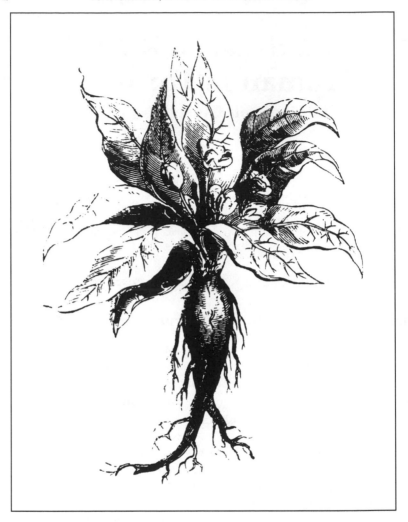

29. Mandrake plant (from Tristram, 1873).

resemblance, the root is commonly perceived as similar in form to a human body, with two legs and, in some cases, a short subsidiary root similar to the genitalia of a man.[6] Such perceptions led the mandrake to be called such names as *semihominus,* "semihuman," by the ancient Romans;[7] *anthropomorphon,* "man-shaped" or "human-shaped," by the ancient Greeks;[8] *merdom-gia,* "man-plant" or "human-plant," by the Persians;[9] and *Adam-*

kökü, "man-root" or "human-root," by the Turks.[10] Early cultivators were in a good position to discern this resemblance, for, as true in Bible lands,[11] probably the plant was common in vineyards, in wheat fields at the time of harvest, and also in abandoned fields. As we shall see, however, it is not only the root that was used, but the leaves and fruit as well, which led to names—for the fruit and the plant itself—such as "love-apple" and "devil's-apple."

Mandragora is a genus consisting of four to six species indigenous to the Mediterranean area on the west and to Iran, Central Asia, northern India, and western China on the east.[12] The species *officinarum* and *autumnalis,* on their part, have been reported as growing naturally in Spain; North Africa, especially Tunisia and Morocco; the south of France; Italy, including Sicily;[13] Illyria; Greece, from the Peloponnesus through the Greek Islands, including Crete and Cyprus; Palestine, Lebanon, and Syria; Anatolia; Mesopotamia; and Iran.[14]

Mandrake (*M. officinarum* and *M. autumnalis*) is not indigenous to northern Europe, though it has been introduced as a garden plant in some places. In the sixteenth century, for example, it was grown in gardens in both Germany and England. It was more usual in English gardens, where, in the nineteenth century, it was characterized as "not uncommon."[15] In India, there is only one indigenous species of *Mandragora* (*M. caulescens* Clarke), but it seems not to be used medicinally.[16]

Trade in Mandrake; Substitutions of Other Plants for It, and Other Fakery

Trade in mandrake roots took place both within the area where it was indigenous and with regions beyond, such as northern Europe and India. In sixteenth-century Italy, there was an active demand for mandrake roots.[17] At about the same time, Bauhin (A.D. 1541–1613) and Cherler wrote of mandrake seeds and roots exported from Crete and the Cyclades to Italy, France, and Spain to produce flowers and fruit.[18] In the sixteenth century, mandrake images were imported into England from Germany and other places, and mandrake roots, often in boxes, were sold by peddlers.[19] Early in the twentieth century, mandrake was found in many herbalists' shops in poorer areas of London. Mandrake, or plants purported to be mandrake, were also hawked by peddlers.[20] In early-nineteenth-century France, mandrake roots were displayed for sale in several seaport communities,[21] which could mean that some had been imported. Late in the nineteenth century, they were imported into Egypt.[22] They were also apparently exported from Iran or Arabia for sale in bazaars of northern India.[23]

Though such trade was widespread and often lively, mandrake roots were expensive and there was considerable fraud involving the substitution of other roots, or materials of other sorts,[24] for mandrake. This occurred even in areas where mandrakes were found naturally. In sixteenth-century Italy, for example, a man who crafted "mandrake" roots for sale confided in Mattioli that they were counterfeits, roots of other plants. Such craftsmen first cut a root into a human form. To create the hair and beard expected on a true mandrake, they planted grains of barley or millet in the false roots. Then they buried the roots until the grain had sprouted, after which they trimmed the sprouts with a sharp knife to form hair and a beard.[25]

Von Luschan[26] described two ways of shaping mandrake roots in Turkey and Syria by artists who did such work "almost as a profession." The simplest way involved shaping a fresh root by careful cutting and pressing while it remained soft, then, while it was drying, shaping it further by using pressure. The second way, far superior in its results, involved digging up a root with great care, shaping it through cutting, scraping, tying with thread, and bandaging, and then replanting the mandrake and leaving it there a sufficient time so that all bruises and other injuries were covered by further growth. When the root was finally dug up and dried, it was so natural in appearance as to make it difficult or impossible to discern where the artist shaped it (Figure 30).

In sixteenth-century Germany, Hieronymus Bock objected to dishonest dealers selling fake mandrakes to trusting people for considerable amounts of money.[27] In sixteenth- and seventeenth-century England, counterfeiting must also have been widespread, for it was condemned by various herbalists. John Gerard wrote of the "falsifying practice" of "idle drones" who carved bryony roots into human forms and sold them to gullible people as true mandrakes.[28] William Turner wrote of counterfeit images shaped by crafty thieves who mocked poor people and robbed them of their sense and their money.[29] John Parkinson wrote of fake mandrake images made "by the art and cunning of knaves and deceivers" and of the chief magistrates in London who, even though informed of the practice, tolerated it.[30] Whether people knew them to be fakes or not,

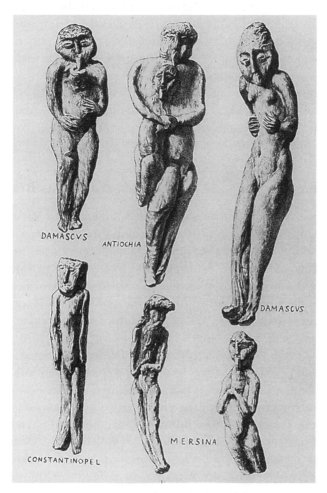

30. Carved mandrake roots from the Near East (from von Luschan, 1891).

substitutes might be called mandrake, used in the same ways as true mandrake, and surrounded by similar concerns and ritual.

The substitute most often identified is bryony of one sort or another (white bryony = *Bryonia dioica;* black bryony = *Tamus communis*), though a variety of other plants also served as mandrake substitutes.[31] It must not have been uncommon for two or more species knowingly to be used as substitutes. In modern Romania, for example, the term *mātrāgunā* ("mandragora") is applied to plants belonging to different genera. The plant most frequently called mātrāgunā in Eliade's article on the cult of the mandragora in Romania is *Atropa belladonna,* the deadly nightshade. Eliade notes, however, that white bryony (*Bryonia dioica*) takes over the role of *A. belladonna* in Romanian folk medicine.[32]

The European and Near Eastern practice of substituting other plants, such as bryony, for mandrake leads to the question of whether similar substitutions may have occurred in other parts of the Old World. This is a matter I will take up again later.

Broad Range of Ways in Which Mandrake Has Been Used

This section is intended to provide a general idea of the variety of ways in which mandrake has been used. At some times and in some places, such as Germany, mandrake served as a familiar spirit (*spiritus familiaris*). In that role it was believed to bring good fortune and prosperity to an individual and a household.[33] Germans also held that the owner of a mandrake would have no enemies.[34] Among the southern Slavs, or certain of them, bryony was also believed capable of uncovering thieves and keeping cows from being bewitched.[35]

In Saintonge, along the Bay of Biscay in France, fisherman, kelp gatherers, and others once wore necklaces or bracelets of mandrake to guard against accidents of all sorts.[36] It is also said that mountaineers in the Alps still commonly carry a mandrake charm to protect against accidents.[37] In Asia Minor, some mandrake talismans were believed effective in protecting their owners against blows, stabs, and bullets. Others were thought to make their owners invisible. Virtually every mandrake talisman, moreover, was considered capable of taking on a disease if the person who contracted that disease wore the talisman faithfully, though the mandrake could, as a result, lose its power temporarily or permanently and could even pass on the disease to a new owner.[38] In one ancient work, an even broader role for mandrake is indicated, including its use against specific health conditions and diseases, against all illnesses brought on by evil forces, and as protection against all grief, ruin, destruction, and bad events, including thievery and murder.[39]

In view of the above, it is not surprising to read of folk beliefs from various lands that Solomon's wisdom came from a bit of mandrake in his signet ring,[40] and that the power of Alexander the Great, as well as the success of Joan of Arc against the English, came from a mandrake each of them possessed.[41]

Mandrake in Matters of Love and Fertility

> Here Mandrake that procureth love . . .
> And makes the Barren fruitfull prove
> —Michael Drayton, "Muses Elizium"

The above quotation, from a poem by Michael Drayton, Shakespeare's contemporary, identifies two qualities for which mandrake has been especially noted. First is its ability to stimulate sexual passion. Second is its ability to make barren women conceive. For evidence of such beliefs I turn first to the Bible.

Among the Jews

In a Ugaritic text from Ras Shamra (fifteenth or fourteenth century B. C.) that relates to a fertility cult, one finds the word *ddym,* translated as "mandrakes," in the expression "Plant *ddym* in the earth. . ."[42] That word is nearly identical to the Hebrew noun *dudaim* (*dud'ym*), a plural form found in the Old Testament in a similar context of fertility and love. There has long been disagreement over the identity of the Hebrew *dudaim,*[43] though today nearly all scholars, biblical and otherwise, translate this word, too, as "mandrakes."[44] *Dudaim* is thought by most scriptural critics to derive from the root *dod, david,* meaning "passion," "carnal love," "beloved."[45] The sense of this is that the mandrake is the "love-plant," "fruit-of-love," or "love-apple."[46]

The word *dudaim* occurs in two places the Old Testament. In one, it appears in a song of love: "Come, my beloved, let us go forth into the field; let us lodge in the villages. Let us get up early to the vineyards; let us see if the vine flourish, whether the tender grape appear, and the pomegranates bud forth: there will I give thee my loves.[47] The mandrakes give a smell, and at our gates are all manner of pleasant fruits, new and old, which I have laid up for thee, O my beloved."[48] In the second place, a story set in Mesopotamia, the association is with fertility. Rachel, after years of marriage, bore no children by her husband, Jacob, though her sister Leah, Jacob's other wife, bore him four sons, and two servant women bore him sons as well. When Leah's son Reuben brought his mother some mandrake he found growing in the wheat fields, Rachel begged her sister, "Give me, I pray thee, of thy son's mandrakes."[49] The sisters worked out an arrangement,[50] and Rachel, for the first time, gave birth to a son.[51] The biblical account credits God with making it possible for Rachel to conceive,[52] but it has been argued that in all likelihood the earliest versions of the story acknowledged the influence of the mandrake, which later editors of Genesis dropped as a heathen notion.[53]

Whatever the reluctance of editors and biblical scholars to acknowledge the role of mandrake in love and fertility, such uses persisted in Palestine and among Jews there and elsewhere.[54] Travelling in Palestine in March of 1697, Henry Maundrell observed that it was the practice for women to lay mandrakes beneath their beds in order to facilitate conception.[55] About two centuries later, Goodrich-Freer observed Moslem and Jewish women in Palestine looking for mandrakes and hanging mandrake roots in their houses.[56] Though she could not determine the reason behind this, I suspect that things had not changed since the time of Maundrell. More revealing is the observation by Starr that there was still a demand for mandrakes among orthodox Jews in the United States at the beginning of this century. Orthodox Jews, he noted, obtained mandrakes from the Near East. They sometimes paid quite high prices for them. They wore them as talismans. They put mandrake scrapings in water to drink as medicine, and they were also convinced that mandrakes made barren women fertile. Especially touching is Starr's story about a well-to-do and influential orthodox married man in Chicago. The man wanted children to continue his line and sorrowed because he had none. Since he was also committed to establishing a Jewish homeland in Palestine, the man had been generous in directing funds to that cause. Hearing of his sorrow, some Jews in Jerusalem forwarded him a mandrake along with their best wishes.[57]

Among Other Peoples, Ancient and Modern

The use of mandrake in matters relating to love, fertility, and procreation has not been limited to the Jews or to Palestine. It has occurred throughout Europe and the Near East since antiquity.[58] Among the ancient Greeks, the philosopher Theophrastus (c. 372–287 B.C.) and the physician and pharmacologist Dioscorides (first century A.D.) wrote of the use of mandrake root in making love potions.[59] The association between mandrake and love is also displayed in use of the name "Mandragoritis" ("She of the Mandrake") for Aphrodite, goddess of love.[60] Evidence of thinking about the mandrake, sex, and reproduction in the early Greco-Roman world is also found in a text related to Hermetism, "Recital of Salāmān and Absāl."[61] According to a tale recorded in that text, an ancient king, Hermanos, complained to a sage about the fact that he had no children. The reason was that the king was not inclined toward women and could not bring himself to approach a woman. Nevertheless, the sage advised him to do so, but he refused. As a result, the sage concluded that the only way to solve the king's problem was to identify a time that astrologers regarded as propitious and to obtain a mandrake, put a bit of the king's semen in the plant, and create a child by alchemy. According to the tale, the effort succeeded with the birth of a boy, who was called Salāmān.[62]

A similar association between sperm and mandrake is found in the European folk belief that mandrake may grow beneath a gallows from the sperm of a man who was hanged for thievery or some other crime and then emitted his semen onto the ground.[63] The European folk belief, in turn, is consistent with the association of human testicles with mandrake in the Syriac language. It is also consistent with one Arabic name for mandrake: "testicles of the demon" (bayḍ al-jinn) or "apples of the demon" (tuffāḥ al-jinn).[64]

One of the most curious early associations of mandrake with sex and procreation is found in the allegory "On the Elephant" in *Physiologus* ("Naturalist"), a bestiary highly popular in medieval times. *Physiologus* was first written in Greek, apparently by a Christian or Christians in Alexandria, at some time from the second to the fourth century A.D. Then it was translated into Latin and many other languages, from Arabic and Armenian on the east to Old English and Icelandic on the west. According to one version of the allegory, which was picked up and sometimes modified in later works on natural history, the sexual intercourse of an elephant is not based on evil lust. Instead, if a male elephant decides to produce offspring, he goes with his spouse to the east, near paradise, where a tree called mandrake grows. She gives him some and charms him into consuming it. After he has eaten, they have intercourse, and she conceives at once. *Physiologus* likens the two elephants to Adam and Eve, who initially, when they still pleased God, knew nothing of sexual intercourse. When, however, Eve ate the forbidden fruit (mandrake in the case of the elephants), "she became big with evil," and she and Adam were expelled from paradise and had intercourse, which led to the birth of a child.[65]

In medieval Europe, the mandrake was highly regarded as a love talisman and aphrodisiac. The association of mandrake with fertility is made in the play "Mandragola" ("The Mandrake"), written in sixteenth-century Italy by Machiavelli.[66] "Mandragola" is about the adventurer Callimaco's efforts to seduce Lucrezia, beautiful, virtuous, but childless wife of a Florentine attorney. In the elaborate scheme followed by Callimaco, mandrake is presented to the attorney as a cure for Lucrezia's barrenness, but in fact serves as a tool in gaining amatory success for Callimaco.[67] In nineteenth-century France, mandrake was worn as a love charm;[68] and as late as 1810 mandrake manikins were purchased by persons seeking sexual stimulation or "to avoid disgrace in the domestic circle."[69] One also reads of women in eastern Europe wearing mandrake charms to guard against sterility[70] and, in an early nineteenth-century work on Greece, of young Athenians keeping bits of mandrake root in small bags they wore or carried for amatory purposes.[71]

What seems to be the most vigorous and varied modern survival of associations between "mandrake," love, and marriage is reported for Romania by Mircea Eliade.[72] Mandrake may be worn as a charm, put in water for bathing, added to food and drink, or used in other ways. It helps girls to get invitations to dances and makes certain that they perform well at them (in the hope of early marriage). It assists them in finding husbands. It helps libertines to arouse passion in men and amorous married women to get their husbands to love them. It brings good fortune in love.[73] It serves in providing fertility to married women.[74] Collecting mandrake for purposes of love and marriage involves rituals that vary considerably from place to place in Romania. It is incumbent that collectors measure up to standards such as sexual purity and cleanliness. The collection of mandrake—in which there is significant risk—commonly involves obtaining the assistance of sorceresses, "old wise women." Collection must be carried out in secret on a night when there is a full moon. It may involve prostrating oneself before the mandrake; making offerings to it, for, without payment, a mandrake will not render assistance; eating and drinking; dancing, often naked, by women and girls; embracing and fondling other participants;[75] and the recitation of magic formulas or appeals such as the following, made when girls collect mandrake to facilitate marriage:

Mandragora, Mandragora,
Marry me after a month.
If not this one, at least the next.
But marry me in any case.[76]

Among the Persian names for mandrake is one meaning "love root,"[77] which reflects the conviction that it can create love. If given to a desired person to eat without that person's knowledge, for example, mandrake is believed to encourage passion. This is in accord with the fact that Persians may wear mandrake amulets for amatory purposes or for promoting conception.[78] Though the literature on India contains scanty information on mandrake, similar beliefs are found there. They seem to have derived from Western lands or possibly from China.[79] One reads nineteenth-century accounts of mandrake roots sold as charms and worn as amulets[80] and, in a book of Ayurvedic medicine, of mandrake adding to the sexual passions of both men and women.[81] In lexicons, moreover, one of mandrake's names means "child giver," and the plant has been described as both an aid to conception and an aphrodisiac.[82]

Mandrake and the Acquisition of Wealth

Oft-mentioned qualities of mandrakes are their purported abilities to find buried treasure, to create money, and to assure the financial well-being of their owners. It was the opinion of certain Slavs that the ability of the plant to bring riches is in proportion to how far it has grown above the ground.[83] In fifteenth-century France, Joan of Arc had heard of the ability of mandrakes to create money.[84] In France and in Germany, some people held that the owner of a well-cared-for mandrake could become wealthy and, in any case, would never suffer poverty.[85] How this might come to pass is shown in the German tale about an impoverished horse dealer from Augsburg. The dealer lost a horse. Then, in his misery, he repaired to an inn where some men gave him a mandrake. When he returned home, the tale goes, he found a bag of valuable coins on his table.[86] There was also a belief that if a person were to place money next to a mandrake at night, or do that and repeat certain secret words, in the morning the amount of money would be increased or doubled.[87] Thus a household mandrake could be a source of income, and if someone seemed to be well off but with no visible source of wealth, people might suspect that a mandrake was involved. According to a fifteenth-century

English herbalist, in his youth he knew of a certain old man who was widely suspected of obtaining money in this way. On a night when the old man was gone and no one else was about, the young herbalist and three other boys tried to determine whether this was true. Their suspicions were confirmed when they broke the lock on a strong little chest the old man possessed and found therein a clean linen cloth and an image human in form and nearly a foot long, and, next to it, an unblemished penny.[88]

Caution was advised, however, not to overdo things.[89] If, say Grimm and Grimm,[90] a person expects a mandrake to serve him for a long time and not to disintegrate or die, he must not overload it. It is safe, according to Grimm and Grimm, to place a small coin (a half thaler) alongside a mandrake every night, "but no more than one ducat may be left, and then only on rare occasions—and by no means every night."

Eliade notes that in Romania, as in central Europe, people believe that if one possesses a "mandrake"[91] it will grant any wish and that mandrake can have a favorable influence in matters of business, as well as adding to wealth and abundance. The examples he provides, however, represent quite modest efforts. One involves placing mandrake under a millstone so that many customers will be attracted to a mill. Others entail putting a bit of mandrake or a few mandrake hairs in wine or spirits, or placing mandrake on or under a wine cask or barrel of spirits, to make certain that a tavern keeper has numerous and well-paying customers.[92]

Mandrake in Medicine

Mandrake as a Cure-All

To some degree, mandrake was considered a cure-all. Medieval naturalists, for example, wrote of mandrake as being a cure for all diseases "except death."[93] Di Nino[94] also wrote of mandrake as guarding against all ills. In a similar vein, an early-nineteenth-century London hawker, who sold slices of what he claimed was mandrake for a penny, assured his audience that mandrake was a cure for everything.[95] St. Hildegard of Bingen (A.D. 1098–1179), in keeping with the "doctrine of signatures" of ancient and medieval times, viewed the human form of mandrake as the key to its use in medicine: "If a man suffers from any infirmity in the head, let him eat the head of this plant: or if he suffers in the neck, let him eat of its neck: or if in his back, from its back: or if in his arm, from its arm, ... or in whatsoever member he suffers, let him eat from the similar member of its form, and he will be better."[96] In addition to such broad claims, there were specific medical uses for which it was thought particularly effective.

Mandrake as a Soporific and Narcotic

Early Greek and Latin writings contain clear indications that mandrake was highly valued for its ability to induce sleep. In those writings, one reads that the mere smell of mandrake makes a person drowsy and causes certain people to fall asleep.[97] One also reads that mandrake fruit were placed under the pillow of a patient in order to induce sleep; that mandrake and dried mandrake fruit were ingredients in sleep-inducing pills; that to bring on sleep mandrake might be eaten or taken in drinks such as wine or vinegar; and that it was also effective as an anesthetic taken before surgery.[98] In the Roman world, mandrake wine, or "death wine," was given to persons being crucified or experiencing torture or an extended or painful death.[99] Someone who consumes mandrake was said to fall into a deep sleep[100] or a coma quite similar to death.[101] Dioscorides even claimed that a person who takes mandrake falls asleep in the very position in which he was sitting when he took the drug and that he remains unaware of anything for three or four hours.[102] Pliny and Dioscorides noted that too much of a mandrake drink can kill a person, and Pliny cautioned that, when used to bring on sleep, its amount be adjusted according to a patient's "strength" (tolerance of the drug?).[103] One reads of Socrates speaking favorably of wine that lulls our sorrows "to sleep just as the mandragora does with men,"[104] and of mandrake, when it grows next to grape vines, transmitting its qualities to the wine and gentling its effect on (the sleep of) persons who drink it.[105] One also reads of an "Isle of Dreams" with a harbor city named Sleep, which is surrounded by a woodland "in which the trees are tall poppies and mandragoras";[106] of Athenians chided for being "like men who have drunk mandragora";[107] and of a man who made an error in judgment as looking like someone who had "drunk a very deep draught of mandragora."[108] An individual was described as sleeping as if he had been "drugged with mandragora."[109] In considering the position of the philosopher among ordinary men, moreover, Plato wrote of a ship's captain whose mutinous crew gained control of a ship after stupefying him with mandragora or in other ways.[110]

That such drugging with mandrake was actually carried out is suggested by the title of a Greek comedy by Alexis (c. 375–275 B.C.) which has been translated as "The Woman Drugged with Mandrake."[111] More specific evidence is found in tales of leaders who used mandrake to good effect in vanquishing their enemies. One tale, by Frontinus—a Roman soldier and author (first century A.D.)—involves Maharbal, one of Hannibal's Carthaginian officers who was sent with his soldiers to put down a rebellion by Africans. Knowing that the Africans were fond of wine, Maharbal added mandrake to a large amount of wine. Then, after a minor skirmish, he purposely withdrew, abandoning his camp and pretending to flee, though he left some luggage along with the mandrake-drugged wine. The Africans entered the camp and consumed the wine with greed and great pleasure. After a time, however, Maharbal and his force returned and either took the Africans prisoner or "slaughtered them while they lay stretched out as if dead."[112] A similar strategy was credited by Polyaenus—a Macedonian who lived in Rome (fl. second century A.D.)—to a different Carthaginian military leader. Polyaenus also related a somewhat similar tale about Caesar. Having been taken prisoner by Cilician pirates in Asia Minor, Caesar sent an emissary to borrow the ransom needed. At Caesar's command, the emissary returned not only with the ransom but also with swords and supplies needed for a great affair that included a feast and wine—but wine in which mandrake had been steeped. The pirates, who were enthusiastic about the ransom they had received, were urged to join in the feast, whereupon they ate well and drank the drugged wine in good quantities. When they fell asleep, Caesar had them killed, and he also recovered and repaid the ransom money.[113]

Awareness of its narcotic effect led some ancient Greeks and Romans to call the mandrake *circaea, circaeum,* or *circaeon.*[114] These names derive from that of the mythical sorceress Circe, who drugged the companions of Odysseus with "ill herbs" (or "malign drugs") and turned them into swine.[115] It has been suggested by some writers that the ingredient Circe used to drug Odysseus's companions may actually have been mandrake.[116] Whether or not this was intended by Homer, in the minds of the Greeks and Romans mandrake was seen as useful in drugging people.

Randolph[117] carefully weighed statements by ancient and medieval European and Near Eastern writers relating to the use of mandrake as an anesthetic prior to surgical operations.[118] He concluded that mandrake was known as an anesthetic to surgeons in those regions at least by the first century A.D. He is convinced that, to some degree, surgeons actually used mandrake in that way and that it was the main, virtually the only, anesthetic used in ancient surgery. Despite this, Randolph insisted, the use of mandrake as an anesthetic in surgery was not very commonplace either in antiquity or in the medieval period, undoubtedly because of the risks the drug posed. In any case, there are repeated references to that practice, as well as to mandrake as a soporific and narcotic, during medieval times (c. A.D. 500–1500) and into following centuries.[119] It is true that many such references derive not from personal observation but from classical sources.[120] At the same time, there is clear evidence that mandrake, along with other items, was employed in making pain-killers and anesthetics. One example of this is a "soporific sponge" in use from the thirteenth to the seventeenth century. The sponge was steeped in a mixture of mandrake, hemlock, opium, hyoscyamus, mulberry juice, lettuce, and dried ivy. When used, the sponge was moistened and given to a patient to inhale.[121]

The perception of mandrake as a soporific and narcotic became firmly entrenched in popular and scientific thinking, as shown in the writings of Drayton (A.D. 1563–1631) and Shakespeare (A.D. 1564–1616). In one case, Shakespeare's Cleopatra asks for a drink of mandrake

> That I might sleep out this great gap of time
> My Antony is away.
> (*Antony and Cleopatra* 1.5.4–5)

In another, mandrake is simply insufficient to overcome the agony of Othello's insomnia, about which the villain Iago gloats:

> Look! where he comes! Not poppy, nor mandragora,
> Nor all the drowsy syrups of the world
> Shall ever medicine thee to that sweet sleep
> Which thou owedst yesterday.
> (*Othello* 3.3.330–333)

Elsewhere Shakespeare is apparently referring to the narcotic quality of mandrake in writing:

> And duller shouldst thou be than the fat weed
> That rots itself in ease on Lethe wharf
> (*Hamlet* 1.5.32–33)

Mandrake and Madness

Ancient Greek sources contain references to mandrake bringing on madness, and one of these calls it a temporary phenomenon of short duration.[122] The onset of madness was regarded as dose-related, for in one case ancient physicians were cautioned to administer a mandrake drink in a dose less than needed to cause delirium.[123] That mandrake can indeed cause such symptoms has been confirmed by a nineteenth-century scientific study. That study found that ingestion of a tincture of mandrake can bring on dilation of the pupils of the eye, strange enlargement and confusion of vision, exaggeration of sound, sense of fullness in the brain, and a restless excitability similar to hysteria.[124]

The view that mandrake induces madness was also found in the medieval Near East,[125] as well as in Europe in later times. Shakespeare indicates that madness can be brought on either by consumption of the plant or by the frightful noise made by the mandrake when it is dug up:

> Or have we eaten on the insane root
> That takes the reason prisoner?
> (*Macbeth* 1.3.84–85)

and

> And shrieks like mandrakes' torn out of the earth,
> That living mortals, hearing them, run mad
> (*Romeo and Juliet* 4.3.47–48)

This fits with an old saying in Wales that a person who uproots a "mandrake" (black bryony) plant will die within a year while groaning or raving or while reciting prayers for having committed that offense.[126]

In the modern period, Thomson has written of an Arab belief that mandrake fruit, taken in sufficient quantity, can bring on elation and agitation to the point of insanity.[127] One reads of an Arabic name for mandrake fruit, *tuffāḥ maǧānīn,* "apples of the insane."[128] There is also a Persian belief that, if you give a person some mandrake to consume in his food without his being aware of it, he will develop a violent passion. Then if he consumes acid foods, such as lemon juice or curdled milk, he will become insane.[129] Jaworskij has noted a belief among the southern Slavs relating to mandrake and madness that seems like an elaboration on the risks, considered above, that are faced by every mandrake collector. If, according to this belief, a mandrake root is cut when being dug up, the digger is at risk of insanity.[130] In modern Romania, too, mandrake is thought capable of bringing on madness, as shown in a recitation at a ritual dance associated with mandrake collection:[131]

> Mandragora, good Mother,
> I do not take you for madness,
> I take you for love;
> I do not take you to drive me mad
> I take you to make me in love.[132]

In Moldavia, the plant itself is called mad in one folk song:

> Green herb, O mandragora,
> Beautiful bird, that is so mad
> To sing to me in the evening by moonlight.[133]

Conversely, there are also references to mandrake root serving as a cure for insanity and as a means of exorcising demons and evil spirits.[134] Indeed, the Aramaic name for mandrakes, *yabruhim*, derives from the belief that they chase away devils.[135] References to exorcising supernatural beings and curing insanity are also found in the *Herbarium of Apuleius*, an early English translation (c. A.D. 1000–1050) of a Latin work perhaps written in Africa and dating from about the fifth century A.D. According to the *Herbarium*, a drink of mandrake and warm water will cure "witlessness, that is, . . . devil sickness, *or demoniacal possession.*" Placing mandrake in the middle of a house, moreover, will drive all evils from it.[136] A similar reference is in the *Medical Formulary* of al-Kindī (c. A.D. 800–870), where the author includes mandrake in a remedy for insanity.[137] A third, found in lbn el-Beïthar, refers to the ability of mandrake to cure insanity and all ailments brought on by spirits, demons, and Satan.[138] A fourth, reported by Starr, comes from notes taken from an unidentified Armenian book on botany. According to those notes, the smoke of mandrake root drives devils and evil spirits from a room and cures insanity, especially forms in which a person is constantly speaking to himself.[139]

Other Medical Uses of Mandrake

Mandrake roots, fruit, seed, and leaves were also processed in various ways and—whether as juice, wine, oil, ointment, plaster, tablet, or in other forms—served in treating a broad range of specific ills in ancient and medieval times. Mandrake served as a pain-killer that had a soothing, cooling effect when applied externally. It was used as a plaster or poultice for reducing inflammation of various sorts. It has been applied as an eye medicine and used to treat tumors, abscesses, ulcers, and wounds. It also served in treating gout and was included in suppositories. It was apparently taken internally or externally for snake bites. Internally it was also employed against fevers and as an antispasmodic in treating nervous tic or epilepsy. It was used as an emetic, too, or as a purgative in expelling phlegm, bile, menstrua, or embryo.[140] The list of mandrake's medicinal virtues could be extended considerably, but the above is sufficient to show that it was widely used and was considered effective.

Mandrake, Underworld Forces, and Christianity

> Here Mandrake . . . In Sorceries excelling.
> —Michael Drayton, "Muses Elizium"

> The mandrake is a Janus-like plant. Its story has two faces . . . The good or the evil powers of mandrake are governed either by the gods in the heavens or by the devils in hell.
> —F. B. Kilmer, "The Mandragora"

Mention of mandrake's ability to drive out evil spirits leads to the questions regarding what the links were between (1) mandrake, sorcerers, evil spirits, demons, and the devil, on one hand, and between (2) mandrake and Christianity, on the other.

In modern Romania, mandrake can be gathered in a positive sense to facilitate love, fertility, and prosperity. Since it possesses the power of evil, however, mandrake can also be gathered for use in a negative sense— "gathered for hate," as Eliade puts it; that is, its power can be directed against and do harm to another person.[141] Mandrake's power to harm is seen as deriving from its chthonic nature and associations. This explains why, in widely scattered places and times, names for mandrake have often included "devil," "Satan," and "jinn." As Hildegard of Bingen observed, mandrake is formed from the same earth that God used to create Adam. Its resemblance to a man, however, is a deception of the devil. For this reason, she said, a mandrake must be placed in a running stream for a day and a night, before it is used, to cleanse it of its diabolic ties. After this, Hildegard wrote, it can be used to control sexual affinity between husband and wife.[142]

Also notable is the association of mandrake with witchcraft. As Lehner and Lehner[143] put it so succinctly, "In the Dark Ages [mandrake] roots were an integral part of every witch's cauldron." It was believed that witches collect mandrake, that they shape its roots into manikins, and that they sell and use mandrake for purposes of magic. This explains the use of *Zauberwurzel,* "sorcerer's root," one of mandrake's names in German.[144] It was in competition with other plants associated with witchcraft, as shown in a Sabaean fable relating to whether mandrake or another plant had greater abilities in witchcraft.[145]

Since all witches were thought to own a mandrake,[146] possession of a mandrake could place one in serious danger at various times and places. Take the case of Joan of Arc. One of the formal accusations of heresy levelled against her was that she carried a mandrake on her breast to assure wealth and success in temporal things. Joan denied the accusation completely, saying that she had never possessed a mandrake and that, though she had heard of one near her town, she had never actually observed it and had no knowledge of the uses of mandrakes.[147] During the Inquisition, too, possession of a mandrake was considered evidence of witchcraft, and many women were burned at the stake for this reason. In Hamburg in 1630, three women were executed as witches for possessing mandrakes.[148] In France in 1603, a woman was hanged as a witch near Orleans for keeping and feeding a mandrake image that looked like a female ape.[149] In 1662, the discovery of two mandrakes in the living quarters of the murdered Maréchal de Fabert was regarded by many as decisive proof that he had died because he had violated a compact with the devil.[150]

For fifteenth-century Paris, there are reports of a procedure far more humane than execution: the mandrakes were burned under orders of a Franciscan.[151] Nevertheless this, too, reflected the highly negative attitudes of some Christians toward the mandrake. Such attitudes, however, seem not to have prevailed at all times and places in Christendom. In the symbolism of early Christianity, for example, the mandrake was often portrayed in a favorable light for such things as its narcotic qualities, which were seen as spiritual medicine; its odor, which heals souls; and its ability to stimulate love and fertility.[152] To a degree, popular practices have also linked the mandrake with the cross, Christ, the Virgin Mary, and the Church. Thus, in modern Romania, the sign of the cross may be made before swallowing a mandrake drink.[153] The Virgin Mary may be quoted during a mandrake ritual. Before gathering a mandrake plant, girls may drink a toast to its good health while saying, "Glory to Jesus Christ." In addition, women may carry mandrakes to church (though hidden in their clothes) to be blessed during Lent.[154]

Ways of Collecting Mandrake

One might anticipate that, in a world considered to be inhabited by supernatural beings capable of bestowing good or evil on humans, the collection of mandrake would not have been a simple matter. Mandrake, after all, was a magical plant, a living being possessing mysterious powers of good and evil and the ability to injure and kill. Against that background, it is no surprise that, since ancient times, mandrake collection has been surrounded by uncertainty and fear and accompanied by ritual intended to protect the collector from possible harm. A person who ignored proper procedures was not merely violating a custom, but was also imprudently placing himself in great peril.

In ancient Greece, such concerns were not limited to mandrake, as was made clear by Theophrastus (c. 372–287 B.C.) in observing that druggists and herb collectors quite commonly took precautions to avoid injury by harmful plants.[155] Many precautions, moreover, were similar to those observed in mandrake collection.[156] The precautions to be taken in mandrake collection, according to Theophrastus, included using a sword to draw three circles[157] around the plant; facing toward the west when cutting it; and, when a second piece was cut from it, having someone dance around it and say "as many things as possible about the mysteries of love."[158] The dancing and speaking of love are in keeping with the aforementioned ties of mandrake with matters of love and marriage and have had an amazing persistence. In modern Romania, for example, the ritual of mandrake collection involves girls and women dancing around a plant and speaking of love and marriage. The number three also recurs in Romania, as in girls undressing and prostrating themselves three times before the mandrake plant while facing east or walking around it three times while reciting magic formulas.[159]

Pliny (first century A.D.) described a procedure for collecting mandrake that is similar to that of Theophrastus, one that, in all likelihood, derived from Theophrastus by means of intermediaries.[160] Though Pliny failed to say anything about dancing around the plant and singing of love,[161] he did mention that the digger had to face west and use a sword to draw three circles about the plant. In addition, the digger had to avoid having the wind in his face.[162]

Apparently the circles were intended to keep the mandrake from fleeing, as well as to mark one's taking possession of the plant. The circles also kept the nature and useful qualities of the plant intact and made it easier to purify the plant, to free it of natural blemishes and demonic qualities. This, in turn, might help the plant to have the desired medical or magical effect and served to protect the collector as well.[163] Because the sword was made of iron, moreover, using it to make the circles may have provided the digger with further protection from the plant, for iron has been widely used in protective magic in the Old World.[164]

Over the centuries following the time of Theophrastus and Pliny, such ideas about mandrake and its collection not only persisted but also became more elaborate. Times suitable for collecting mandrake were sometimes specified, as at midnight, or on a Friday before sunrise, or on a Tuesday in December or March when the sun is shining.[165] Recitations of magic formulas might be required, and other rules established.[166] One elaboration, which confirms the mandrake's tie with humanity, was the belief that the plant springs up under a gallows from the urine or semen of a hanged thief or other criminal (or one who has remained chaste) or of a man unjustly sentenced.[167] Moreover, it was held that, for mandrake to be effective, it must be gathered in such places, a belief used by sixteenth-century Italian mandrake sellers in explaining to potential purchasers why mandrake was so difficult to obtain.[168] Randolph has suggested that the story of the mandrake plant deriving from the body of a hanged thief represents an adaptation of a tale—as told in the *Argonautica* of Apollonius Rhodius (born c. 295 B.C.)[169]—about a plant, "the herb of Prometheus" (Medea's plant), which sprang from ethereal fluid of Prometheus that fell to the earth from an eagle that had eaten Prometheus's liver.[170] Talley has argued that the tie between mandrake and gallows originated in the Germanic area and derives from early Indo-European thinking about sacrifice, sex, and fertility.[171] In any case, the tie led to certain names for mandrake, such as the German *Galgenmännlein,* "little

gallows man," and the Icelandic *thjofarót*, "thieves' root."[172] The association of mandrake and gallows in some cases led to the view that the plant
grows in a natural state only under or near a gallows.[173] In Welsh folklore
of former times, the only place mandrake grew was next to a gallows
tree or near a crossroads, especially a crossroads where people who had
committed suicide had been buried. Gallows and crossroads were also
depicted as places where witches gathered mandrake leaves, flowers, and
roots for purposes of magic.[174] This fits with the fact that, since antiquity,
protective and exploitative magic has been practiced at crossroads, for
they have been perceived as places where supernatural beings tied to
night, death, and the underworld congregate, most notably Hecate, that
frightening chthonic goddess of ancient Greece.[175]

Another elaboration involved the mandrake shrieking, or shrieking
and groaning, when it was dug up, which fits with the fact that it was
considered a sensate being. The sound, however, was not merely disturbing but also capable of killing people.[176] The groaning or shrieking
of mandrake presented many opportunities for literary expression, as by
Shakespeare's Suffolk, who said

> A plague upon them! wherefore should I curse them?
> Would curses kill, as doth the mandrake's groan,
> I would invent as bitter searching terms,
> As curst, as harsh and horrible to hear
> (*Second Part of Henry the Sixth* 3.2.309–312)

The danger could be avoided by a mandrake collector stuffing his ears
so that he could not hear the terrible shrieks and groans and by tying a
dog (in some accounts, a black dog) to the plant to pull it up by the roots
(Figure 31). Rahner has argued that this and certain magic associated
with mandrake gathering further reveals an association with the underworld, specifically with Hecate and her dogs.[177] Though the mandrake
collector escaped injury in pulling up a mandrake with a dog, the dog,
in many versions of the story, died of the horrible noise.[178] Because mandrake was extracted in this manner, in Iran the plant came to be known
as *segken*, "dog-dug."[179]

The belief that dogs should be used in digging up mandrakes goes far
back in time, for a manuscript dating from early in the sixth century A.D.
contains a drawing of a mandrake in human form being offered to the
physician Dioscorides with the plant still tied to the body of the dog that

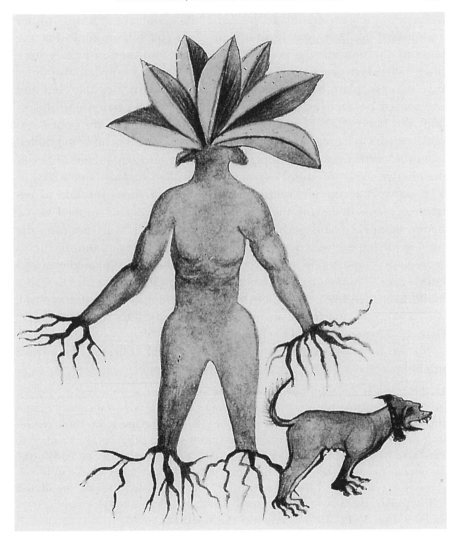

31. Mandrake, with the legendary dog used to pull it up (from Payne, 1904).

lost his life in pulling it up.[180] Similar beliefs, whether they referred to mandrake or other plants, go back several centuries earlier.[181] The Jewish historian Josephus (c. A.D. 37–100) wrote of a demon-expelling plant in Palestine, which he called baaras, being pulled from the ground by a dog that died immediately afterwards.[182] Some authorities think that the baaras plant was the mandrake, perhaps "the mandrake of Baara." Other authorities, however, remain uncertain, and still others think that the plant in question was the peony.[183] A dog was also used in pulling up a plant called *kynospastos* ("dog-dragged" or "dog-dug"). Aelian also notes that after the plant had been pulled from the earth, the dog died and was buried on the spot after mysterious rites were carried out and its body was honored.[184] The identification of this plant with the peony, it is said, appears to be reasonably sure.[185] A third case of a plant being pulled from the earth by a dog is found in a tale in an early medieval Syriac manuscript about the devil-expelling root called *kahīnā* ("splendid").[186] The above observations indicate that in ancient times the tale of extracting plants by having them pulled by dogs probably applied to the peony, mandrake, and perhaps other plants as well.[187] In any case, the story involving use of a dog, or a black dog, to pull up mandrake or its surrogates is repeated in both Europe and the Near East in medieval and later works,[188] some of which contain drawings showing a dog tied to a mandrake.[189] Indeed, the belief that it is prudent to pull up mandrake with a dog was still found in nineteenth-century Italy (the Abruzzi),[190] Greece,[191] Armenia,[192] and likely elsewhere as well.

To see how involved the entire procedure of collecting mandrake might be, consider a description in German legend:

In order to get the plant one must go out before sunrise on a Friday, stop up one's ears with cotton, wax, or pitch, take an all-black dog—he cannot have a single spot on his body—and proceed to the gallows site. One makes three crosses over the Mandrake and digs a ring all around it so that the roots are attached to the earth only by tiny fibers. One then takes a string and ties one end to the Mandrake and the other end to the dog's tail. Next, one takes a piece of bread, shows it to the dog, and then one runs off. The dog, hungry for the bread, will follow, pulling the root out. However, he will then be struck by the groaning cries and will drop dead. One then removes the Mandrake . . .[193]

Note the resemblance to the procedure followed near the end of the nineteenth century by Danubian gypsies in gathering "a kind of orchid" they knew as "boy root." The gypsies used a brand new knife to partly expose the plant's roots. Then they tied a black dog by its tail to the plant, presented a bit of donkey flesh to the dog, and, when it jumped for the flesh, it pulled the plant from the earth. The gypsies then carved the root into the shape of a liṅga, wrapped it in leather, and, in a manner reminiscent of mandrake, wore it on the arm to promote conception.[194]

A second name given by Aelian for the kynospastos plant mentioned above is *aglaophotis* ("bright shining")," because at night it was lighted like fire or a star. The baaras plant of Josephus was also said to shine at night,[195] and the mandrake, too, was thought to possess this quality, described by Thomas Moore[196] as "those hellish fires that light the mandrake's charnel leaves at night." Belief that the mandrake is luminous at night led to one of its names in Arabic, meaning "devil's candle," and to its name among the Moors of Andalusia, meaning "lamp of the elves."[197] In elaborating on the aglaophotis plant of Aelian, mentioned above, Delatte[198] has observed that plants that shine at night are associated with the moon and serve medicinally in healing illnesses, such as possession by demons (lunacy) and epilepsy, thought to be caused by the moon's influence.[199]

Care of Mandrakes

Careful attention was given to the care of mandrakes and their surrogates. When, for example, the southern Slavs removed a bryony from the ground, they bathed it in milk, dried it carefully, wrapped it in cloth, and placed it in a chest that was watched over.[200] In Germany and in France, too, a mandrake seems to have been given extraordinary care. It might be carefully washed or bathed on a regular basis, whether in water or red wine.[201] It was clothed, with some accounts specifying such costly materials as silk and velvet. It might be provided with food and drink twice daily. It might be stored in an upholstered box or casket, and more.[202] Indeed, one reads of a belief in Germany that, if mandrakes failed to get their baths, they would shriek like infants until that need was met.[203] It was also thought necessary that a mandrake be cared for properly if it is to be effective. Indeed, it was believed that, if kept with care, mandrakes would protect the family and bring on good fortune but, if neglected, would result in bad luck or destruction.[204]

Perhaps most revealing of the relationship between mandrake and man is the sixteenth-century letter written by a man from Leipzig to his brother who lived at Riga in Latvia. The brother in Riga had written of a series of calamities: damage to his house and farm, death among his livestock, souring of wine and beer in his cellars, and a threat to his very livelihood. In addition, he had serious problems in getting along with his womenfolk. The man from Leipzig consulted knowledgeable persons

32. Mandrake manikin from Leipzig (from Banks, 1932).

who told him that his brother's misfortunes came from evil persons, not from God, and that he needed a mandrake to counter them. Thus, the man from Leipzig wrote, he had purchased a mandrake at considerable expense and was sending it as a gift to his brother in Riga (Figure 32). He cautioned that the mandrake must be treated with special care. When it arrived, he said, it first had to be given three days of rest. Then it had to be bathed in warm water, and the bath water sprinkled on the doorsills or floors of the house where the brother and his women walked. Some bath water also had to be sprinkled on the livestock. This, according to the man from Leipzig, was supposed to make things turn for the better. To be certain that the problems would be taken care of, however, the mandrake had to continue to be treated well. It had to be bathed four times a year, after which it had to be wrapped in its silk dress and laid on the brother's best clothes, which were not to be worn again. The man from Leipzig also mentioned additional benefits that could be obtained from the mandrake. One was that, if a spoonful of the mandrake's bath water were drunk by a woman in labor who was unable to give birth, delivery of her child would be facilitated. Another was that a mandrake could be carried under one's right arm to assure victory in a law suit, whether one was in the right or wrong.[205]

The man from Leipzig also urged his brother not to lose the mandrake in order that it could be passed on to his grandchildren. In fact, some quite aged mandrakes were found in Germany. The German poet Rist (A.D. 1607–1667) wrote of seeing a carefully made manikin (*Erdmann*) that was over 100 years old. It was housed in a coffin, and placed on the coffin was a cloth on which was depicted a thief on the gallows, underneath which a mandrake grew.[206] By early German tradition, the youngest son inherited his father's mandrake, but, as a consequence, he assumed the obligation to place money and bread in his father's coffin. If, however, the youngest son had died before the father, the oldest son inherited the mandrake and assumed a similar obligation for his brother.[207]

Historical Notes and Conclusions

On the Ancient Near East and Europe

Some scholars have suggested that both the name "mandrake" and superstitions associated with the plant in the Western world ultimately derive from Iran, with the Greek and Latin words for the plant coming from the Persian merdom–gia, "man-plant," mentioned previously.[208] Of relevance here are the rich associations with mandrake lore of other Persian and Semitic names for mandrake,[209] reported by these and other scholars.[210] Whether or not they agree on all specifics, scholars who have examined the matter carefully also tend to look to the Near East for the origins of mandrake mythology.[211] After weighing the historical evidence, for example, Randolph[212] concluded that the major superstitions known in medieval Europe originated in the Near East or derived partly from the Near East and partly from the Greeks and Romans. He concluded further that few of the superstitions were initially tied to the mandrake but began to coalesce around it in ancient Greece and Rome. Randolph argued further that mandrake superstitions were augmented in northern Europe by elements that seem to have arrived by other routes, and that later exchanges returned the northern European accretions to the Near East.

There is a distinct possibility that, when plants of the genus *Mandragora* first arrived in northern Europe, they had been preceded by other plants that played roles similar to the one played by mandrake in the Mediterranean world. In any case, two quite different words are used for mandrake in Europe. One, related to the Greek *mandragoras,* is found in Latin and languages across southern Europe and from France to the British Isles.[213] The second, related to the German *alraun* (Old High German, *alrūna*), is found in German and Scandinavian languages. Talley,[214] in considering why the Germans failed to adopt a form of *mandragora* for the mandrake, concludes that, when mandrake first appeared among them (it was first grown in Germanic lands only in medieval times), they already had a word that could readily be extended to the mandrake. This word, *alrūna,* may go back to remote antiquity, and its linguistic roots, Talley suggests, may be *ala,* meaning "to beget, to bear," and *rūna,* meaning "secret" or "advice." It is not known exactly what the word applied to in prehistoric times, but it was associated with fertility magic. Talley has speculated that the term may have referred to a charm worn by persons who wanted children or to a root or bit of wood "on which magic symbols were inscribed." If it was an amulet, she suggests, it may have been carved into human form in keeping with beliefs about sympathetic magic. To this, I would add that, since bryony has been widely used in historical times as a substitute for mandrake in northern Europe, roots of bryony and other plants may have been shaped into human form and used in Germanic magic related to birth and fertility long before mandrake came on the scene.

There is evidence that among the early Goths there were wise women called Alirūna, or some similar-sounding name, who had skills in magic, writing, and divining the future.[215] Indeed, Grimm has argued that the term *Aurinia,* identified by Tacitus (c. A.D. 56–120) as pertaining to a woman revered by the ancient Germans,[216] actually referred to such wise women. Originally, Grimm suggests, the term *Alirūna* applied to wise women, and subsequently, similar words were applied to the plants in their custody; that is, a name originally meaning "wise woman" changed over time "from its old sense of a prophetic and diabolic spirit . . . into that of the root (mandragora, mandrake) out of which [it] is cut."[217] Grimm believed that prophecy, or divination, which was widely practiced among ancient Germanic peoples, was an important function of such women.[218] That divination with magic roots continued into later times, moreover, is shown by quotes from Grimm and Grimm: "If the owner of the Mandrake asks it questions, it will answer, and it will reveal all kinds of secret things about the future . . . ;"[219] and "He must keep an *araunl* by him, that tells him all he wants to know."[220] Returning to the association of wise women and mandrake, I would note that Eliade, writing of modern Romania, has shown the key role played by sorceresses, called *babele meş-tere* ("old wise women"), in mandrake collection and ritual.[221]

On China

Historical information on the mandrake in China, beyond the area where the plant was indigenous,[222] is scanty. It is clear, however, that long before the first record of mandrake being imported into China, a worthy competitor, ginseng, was firmly entrenched there. Ginseng, *Panax ginseng*, is a perennial herb indigenous to North China and adjacent lands, including Manchuria, Korea, and the Russian Far East. Ginseng is not in the mandrake family, Solanaceae, but in that of ivy and sarsaparilla, Araliaceae. In earliest times, its root was collected from the wild, but later, possibly by T'ang times (A.D. 618–907), it began to be cultivated in China.[223] Ginseng is highly regarded in China for its power to strengthen, stimulate, heal, and rejuvenate. It is used in treating specific illnesses, but it also serves in a general way for nurturing and restoring weak, sick, elderly, and dying people. These associations are clearly revealed in seventeenth-century Thailand (whether involving Thais or Chinese is not clear), where a soup was mentioned as containing not only ginseng but also two other items, bird's nest and chicken,[224] which are among China's most famous strengthening foods.

The similarities in form between mandrake and ginseng have struck observers (Figure 33) and have led to suspicions of a historical connection between ideas, practices, and uses relating to the two plants. Such a connection may have involved a spread from the west to China or from China

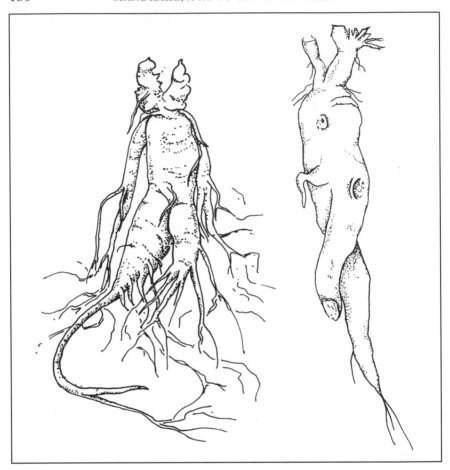

33. Ginseng (*Panax ginseng*) (left) compared with mandrake (*Mandragora officinarum*) (right) (drawn by Shelby Hall).

to the west. What are these similarities? Most striking is the fact that roots of both plants are considered human in form, and in fact *jên-shên,* one of ginseng's Chinese names, means "man-root." Both are magical roots whose effectiveness is based on their supernatural associations, as reflected in early Chinese names for ginseng meaning "divine herb" or "terrestrial essence," the latter reflecting the traditional Chinese belief that ginseng contains the life-giving power of the earth.[225] Both ginseng and mandrake are also regarded as aphrodisiacs.[226] Both are capable of making sounds.[227] Collecting them, moreover, involves great personal danger to the collector and requires that rituals be followed and other precautions be taken to assure his safety.

On the other hand, differences between ginseng and mandrake are notable.[228] Though risk is involved in collecting both roots, there have been contrasts in the precautions taken. In past accounts of ginseng collection there is no mention of three circles drawn around the plant with a sword. There is no fear that, as a plant is uprooted, the digger will die from its horrible screeching. No dog is involved in pulling it up. Instead, there are what seem to be eminently reasonable actions by the gatherer to purify himself and avoid dangerous animals and spirits.[229] I have found nothing to indicate that ginseng, like mandrake, is worn as a charm or that it serves its owner as an oracle, protector, and bestower of wealth. Nor are its supernatural powers directed, as was sometimes thought true of mandrake, toward wreaking evil on humans or killing them. Moreover, whereas mandrake's aphrodisiac qualities have been highly valued by people in the Near East and Europe, in China the aphrodisiac qualities of ginseng are of secondary importance and subordinate to its role as a general agent of restoration and fortification.[230] Unlike mandrake, ginseng is not a soporific or a narcotic. Since it lacks those qualities of mandrake, moreover, it can be used as a medicine with far less risk.[231] This also enables it to be used freely in beverages and foods, something not possible with mandrake.

Returning to the question of a possible historical connection, one should note first that ginseng was gathered from the wild in China already in ancient times.[232] There is, however, no convincing evidence that ginseng, whether the plant or its products, reached India, the Near East, or Europe in antiquity. There is evidence that ginseng was exported by Arabs from somewhere in East Asia (Korea?) by the ninth century A.D., but the destination of those shipments is unknown. Ginseng may have first reached Europe as late as the seventeenth century A.D.[233] Even in the nineteenth century, it was only occasionally, or on rare occasions, that ginseng was imported into India from China.[234] As for mandrake, Čou Mi (Chau Mih) (A.D. 1230–1320) has written of its roots being traded to China by the Arabs.[235] One cannot be certain how much earlier such trade may have existed, but there is little to support the hypothesis that Chinese views of ginseng or Near Eastern and European views of mandrake were introduced from one area to the other.

Despite the fame of ginseng, one cannot overlook the fact that the underground parts of certain other Chinese plants have also been thought to assume a human form.[236] Nor can one ignore the observation that folklore surrounding one of these, the *shang-luh* plant (*Phytolacca acinosa*), is more similar (than that of ginseng) to mandrake folklore in the Near East and Europe. Both the shang-luh and mandrake are magical plants with roots shaped like a human body. Like mandrake in the Near East and Europe, the shang-luh is said to grow in ground where a dead man has been buried, and it is both satanic itself and capable of exorcising malignant beings. Like the mandrake, the shang-luh has the ability to utter sounds, and it is said to light up.[237] In one Chinese work, a sorcerer is described as shaping a shang-luh root into a human effigy made "through [the sorcerer's] spells capable of telling the fortunes," a statement reminiscent of mandrake manikins, their role as oracles, and their ties with witches. Like the mandrake in the Near East and Europe, the fruit of the shang-luh is highly regarded by peasant women in China for its fertility-inducing qualities. Also like the mandrake, one variety of shang-luh is described as so toxic that it can make men crazy.[238]

Though the above parallels are more suggestive of a historical tie between mandrake and shang-luh than between mandrake and ginseng, it seems likely that we are dealing with a phenomenon that embraces more than a mere handful of species. We are not just dealing with mandrake and shang-luh, ginseng and shang-luh, mandrake and ginseng, or, indeed, mandrake and bryony. Instead, we are dealing with the phenomenon of "man-roots" in a more general sense, one embracing many plant species with roots that have been regarded as resembling humans. Ideas and practices do transfer, sometimes readily, from one species of man-root to another, but in the socio-religious realm, just as in the natural world, there is species competition. Sometimes a species (for example, ginseng in China) comes to play so vital a role in a human culture and society as to make it impossible for other another species (for example, mandrake) to gain a wide following.

On India

Perhaps I should add that competition among plants in the socio-religious realm may also involve species other than ones regarded as man-roots. Take the case of India, where *Mandragora officinarum* and *M. autum-*

nalis were not indigenous plants. Though mandrake was imported, sold in bazaars, recognized as resembling a human body, worn as a charm, used as an aphrodisiac, and included among India's medicinal plants at least since the time of Charaka (?A.D. 80–180?),[239] it seems not to have been well known there.[240] Though a species of *Panax* related to ginseng grows in the Himalayas of India,[241] and though ginseng from China has occasionally been brought to India from China, ginseng failed even more abjectly to became a major player in India.

Careful research needs to be carried out on the question, but I suspect that the limited appeal of mandrake and ginseng in India was based on the presence there of well-established plants that have served quite well in gaining prosperity and good health for humans, as well as in assuring their fertility and the adequacy of their sexual drives. Tulsi, for one, is believed capable of assuring wealth as well as being an aphrodisiac and inducer of fertility. Why turn to a new plant like mandrake, when tulsi is on the scene, a holy plant, a purificant that enjoys a high ritual standing in Hinduism, as well as offering rewards in the afterworld?

This matter requires more investigation, and here I would only call attention to the fact that tulsi is not alone in satisfying such vital human needs in India, that we are dealing with a competition between many species in serving such needs. Take the case of the screw pine (*Pandanus odoratissimus;* Sanskrit: *ketaki;* Hindi: *keura*) in Sikkim and India. The ketaki, like the mandrake in Europe and the Near East, is viewed in Sikkim as both a soporific and an aphrodisiac. Moreover, in a manner similar to the use of mandrake in matters relating to love, fertility, and procreation in Europe, Sikkim girls wear ketaki flowers to gain love from their lovers, and women consume a drink of milk and ketaki root to prevent miscarriages.[242] These phenomena are not restricted to Sikkim, however, for Gupta writes of the screw pine as a tree of coastal India and the Andaman Islands, one thought to be an aphrodisiac and soporific. He also points out that its seeds are believed to mend "wounds of the heart," and that girls wear its flowers in their hair to win lovers. Nair girls, however, will not do so because the plant was cursed by Shiva who, when meditating, was disturbed when Pārvatī, in disguise and wearing ketaki flowers, sought to entice him.[243]

The Decline of Mandrake

> The mandragora is the Jekyll and Hyde of drugdom. Through
> many centuries, under the fostering care of Dr. Jekyll, it cured the
> ills of mankind. When the criminal fakir, Mr. Hyde, took it in hand
> it became the tool of the mountebanks and, in turn, the outcast of
> medicine.
> —F. B. Kilmer, "The Mandragora"

Unlike the case of tulsi in Hindu India, mandrake has long occupied a
negative or, at best, an ambivalent position in Europe's major religion,
Christianity. Mandrake superstitions derived from the pre-Christian past,
and Christians were inclined to the view that mandrake was an associate
of evil spirits, demons, and Satan. Persons who possessed mandrakes
were commonly regarded as sorcerers or, at least, their dupes, and at
various times in the past they were at risk of being executed for traffick-
ing with the devil. The case seems not to have been so one-sided everywhere and at all times, but, whereas tulsi has been revered by devout
Hindus since antiquity and continues to be honored, mandrake has not
always been a favorite of devoted Christians.

Both tulsi and mandrake have played roles in traditional medicine, but
the support for tulsi is overwhelming. It is highly regarded as a remedy by
ordinary folk and among practitioners and schools of Ayurvedic medicine. Equally important, practitioners of scientific medicine in India are
sympathetic, open minded toward tulsi, whereas practitioners of scientific
medicine in Europe lacked such sympathy for mandrake. Though mandrake seems to have been honored in the pharmacopoeia of Shakespeare's day,[244] its medicinal use was already declining, and it was removed from the English pharmacopoeia in 1746 and has not been
restored.[245] One reads that in the first half of the nineteenth century,
mandrake was seldom used in modern medicine[246] and that today it is
"completely obsolete" in such medicine,[247] though it has continued to
serve as a folk remedy, especially in Mediterranean lands.[248] The decline
in use of mandrake is credited to the availability of better pain-killers. It
is also credited to the failure of adherents of scientific medicine to confirm many claims made for mandrake and to their concern with respect-
ability and their reluctance to use a plant so closely tied to superstition.[249]

One suspects that if Christianity had gained sway in India the status
of tulsi would have deteriorated just as mandrake's status did in Europe.
Had this happened, it would have been a great loss, especially for women

whose ritual activities and psychic well-being are so closely tied with the tulsi plant. As we shall see, moreover, other plants, too, play important roles in Hindu socio-religious life. Indeed, from a Hindu perspective, Christianity as it is practiced in the United States would seem strangely plantless and somehow lacking—except on Palm Sunday and Christmas.

5 A Question of Odor?

Garlic and Its Relatives as Impure Foods in the Area from Europe to China

> And, most dear actors, eat no onions nor garlic, for we are to utter
> sweet breath . . .
> —Shakespeare, *A Midsummer-Night's Dream* 4.2.42–43

> Onions and garlic are little used [in India] and people who eat
> them are ostracised.
> —T. Watters, *On Yuan Chwang's Travels in India,
> 629–645 A.D.*, quoting Hsüan-tsang

> [A man of respectable standing must perform a penance] if he has
> (knowingly) eaten garlic, or onions, or red garlic.
> —*Institutes of Vishnu* 51.3

> There are three species which [Chinese] are not allowed to eat as
> vegetarians; these are garlics, onions, and scallions, which are
> reckoned, on account of their strong taste, as being substantially
> meats.
> —J. Doolittle, *Social Life of the Chinese*

Introduction

Garlic (*Allium sativum*) and onions (*Allium cepa* and other species) are important flavorings in various of the major world cuisines.[1] Garlic also enjoys a popular reputation for having remarkable medicinal qualities, whether preventive or curative, that are useful in a broad range of human illnesses and diseases. True believers have written of "the miracle of garlic," and skeptics, of a "garlic cult" whose claims go well beyond what can be demonstrated by scientific studies. My concern in this chapter is not with the culinary role of garlic, the wonders of garlic, or the validity of claims about its medicinal effectiveness.[2] Instead, I deal with garlic and onions from a quite different perspective: that they are ritually impure and improper to eat. I consider the matter, moreover, not in general terms, but in the area of the high civilizations of the Old World extending from the Mediterranean world to China.

136

Perspectives on Bad Odor, Impurity, Disgust, and the Gods

In his classic article "Disgust and Related Aversions," Angyal[3] deemed it likely that disgust represents a primitive emotional reaction, and is not a mere reflection of human culture.[4] He argued that disgust reactions in humans involve a fear of becoming debased. In his view, the decisive element in disgust is contact with a disgusting object rather than sensory qualities such as color, sound, odor, and taste. The strength of a disgust reaction, he asserted, relates to how close the contact is with a disgusting object and the degree to which individual sensory qualities are linked to the object. Angyal emphasized that the greatest fears with respect to disgusting objects are those relating to taking them into one's mouth and ingesting them, for such objects represent oral threats to the integrity of the human body. He viewed odors as being especially distasteful because they enter the nostrils and mouth. Thus, from a disgust perspective, it is less compelling for an orthodox Jew to view the color of a pig from afar or for him to hear its distant grunting than to smell a strong pig odor or taste pork, which entails penetration of the nose or mouth and raises the possibility of ingestion.

Angyal went on to argue that disgust reactions characteristically involve what are perceived as waste products of the human or animal body. He noted that, though milk and eggs are not usually considered disgusting,[5] disgust reactions are commonly expressed for urine and feces, sweat, sputum, flesh (as for the remains of a dead animal), and similar items. Angyal's case that the primary focus of disgust is on wastes of the human and animal body is well supported in the historical and ethnographic literature. One can also find many cases to support Angyal's view that sensory qualities, such as odor, are not decisive in eliciting disgust reactions, that behind them, and the critical element in the matter, is a disgusting object of some sort. Among the Hua of highland New Guinea, the breath and body odor of a menstruating woman or a person who has recently had sexual relations is highly polluting for certain categories of individuals and can destroy their health.[6] In the Hua cases, the odors are clearly linked to impure objects, menstruating women and individuals who have recently engaged in sexual intercourse. Another situation clearly in accord with Angyal's view is that of Hindu India, a land where observant persons worry about ritual purity and pollution,[7] and where the entire range of waste products identified by Angyal, including odor, are potential pollutants. Abbé Dubois, in his observations about Hindu practices in the late eighteenth and early nineteenth centuries, accords a respectable place to odor among potential pollutants that may enter the human body.[8] A whiff of smoke, whether from a funeral pyre where a corpse is being burned or from a household fire where untouchables are cooking their food, is sufficient to pollute a Brahmin—member of one of the priestly *jātis*.[9] Dubois wrote further that in some parts of India, when untouchables see a Brahmin approaching, they will make a long detour so that effluvia coming from their impure bodies will not pollute him. When Śūdras, members of the lowest of the four *varnas* (classes), speak to a Brahmin, moreover, they maintain a respectful distance and place a hand in front of their mouths so that their breath will not reach and contaminate him. In each of the Hindu examples above, as in the Hua example, odor or breath is clearly tied to an object that is polluting, a live person who is impure or a dead body.[10]

On the other hand, in certain other cases, an individual's primary concern is not with pollution of his own body, but with not defiling and offending the gods with bad odors. This means that people try to eliminate unpleasant odors and to introduce pleasant ones. In this spirit, ancient Mesopotamians sought to soothe and delight the gods by burning things that gave off a pleasing fragrance, and took care not to offend them with bad odors.[11] Herodotus reported that each year the Babylonians offered several tons of frankincense (1,000 talents weight) for burning on one of the altars of the god Bel.[12] Jehovah instructed Moses to build in the tabernacle a wooden altar overlaid with gold for burning offerings of sweet incense.[13] Ancient Egyptian representations commonly depict a pharaoh offering incense, and, indeed, incense was thought to be the means by which prayers were transmitted to the deities.[14] Such thinking may also be implied in David's appeal, "Lord, I cry unto thee. . . Let my prayer be set forth before thee as incense. . . ,"[15] and in the observation in the Babylonian Talmud that, when the smoke of incense rises, one should say a blessing, and that the soul, not the body, derives enjoyment from fragrant odors.[16] Similar thinking is found in Hindu India today, where incense is widely used in religious rites, in part because of the wishes of worshippers that the god be pleased with the pleasant odors.[17]

Also involved in the matter of odor and the gods is the conviction that a person who approaches the high gods should be pure in mind, body, and dress, and that odor is a significant element in the purity or impurity of a suppliant or worshipper. Thus, bad body odors are to be guarded against and eliminated by all who would enter a religious sanctuary and worship its deity. In this spirit is a Sabaean inscription at Marib, a confession by two men that they had sat in the temple when they had an odor of foul plants and onions.[18] One also reads in the Babylonian Talmud that offensive breath disqualified a priest and rendered others unfit for temple service.[19]

Like the Hua and Hindus, Zoroastrians consider sweat and breath, like other emissions from the human body, as wastes capable of polluting.[20] Ancient Zoroastrian texts describe Ahura Mazda, supreme deity and god of goodness and light, as having a pleasant odor, and Ahriman, his opponent and god of evil and darkness, as having a bad odor. Ahura Mazda, Darmesteter writes, "is all perfume, [whereas] Ahriman is infection and stench."[21] According to ancient Zoroastrian texts, human souls were believed to take on the odor of their gods, and there was an elaborate rite, the Barashnūm, in which a person's body and soul could be purified, sweetened, and perfumed.[22] In the *Avesta*, Ahura Mazda is quoted as saying that after death the soul of a faithful person, an observant Zoroastrian, will, among other things, be provided with fine food. In addition, the soul will be exposed to a wind that has a sweet scent, "sweeter-scented than any other in the world," and will be greeted by a beautiful young woman, representing the deceased's conscience, who comments on his good qualities, including his sweet-scentedness. The soul of a wicked person who has died, on the other hand, will experience a foul-scented wind and will be given food that is both poisonous and of toxic stench. Another account has the wicked soul greeted by an old woman who represents the evil thoughts, evil words, evil deeds, and evil religion by which the deceased lived. Quite appropriately, the old woman is "rotten and foul-smelling" as well as dirty and hideous in appearance.[23]

Since other peoples as well have been concerned with pleasing the gods, there must have been a widespread sensitivity since antiquity to keeping smelly people out of places of worship. Sometimes such sensitivities must also have been concerned with eliminating foods and drinks of bad odor from ritual offerings. The identity of such foods and drinks deserves more careful attention, but they include items that are themselves smelly, as well as ones, like beans and other legumes, that lead humans to give off bad odors through the flatulence they cause. However many such items one may identify, clearly garlic and onions are leading actors, even superstars, among foods of bad odor.

Garlic and Onions as Foods of Bad Odor

Sokolov[24] has characterized garlic as "a plant of ill repute" that has long been avoided by English-speaking peoples because of its sharp odor. He quotes Sir John Evelyn, who, late in the seventeenth century, wrote of garlic's unacceptable pungency, which not only renders it unfit for use in salads but also, in the past, led the eating of garlic to be included among the punishments meted out for the vilest of crimes. Mennell, on his part, writes of English fear of the bad breath and gaseous emissions that consumption of garlic, leek (usually *Allium porrum*), and onions brings on—a social embarrassment that could be minimized by proper preparation.[25] This fits with Shakespeare's association of garlic-eating with unrefined people.[26] Sokolov notes Shakespeare's advice, quoted above, that actors not eat garlic (and onions) if they want "to utter sweet breath." He then goes beyond the English scene to generalize that "alliophobia," the irrational dread of garlic, has persisted in the Western world since the time of the earliest historical accounts.[27]

In fact, as we shall see, the classification of garlic and its relatives as "plants of bad odor" extends far beyond the Western world, where it occurs as early as or earlier than such views in ancient Greece.[28] Though I have found no reference to the matter in the early literature, it seems likely that the odor of garlic in combination with other odors has been considered more unpleasant than that of garlic itself. I base this on a study of 100 male and female shoppers in Finland which found that subjects judged the odor of garlic and scent, garlic and alcohol, and, most of all, garlic and sweat, more annoying than that of garlic alone.[29] However unpleasant the odor of garlic, garlicky breath, and garlic in combination with other odors may have been to the ancients, their view of garlic and its relatives as impure—which concerns us here—goes well beyond the question of bad odor. This is a matter to which we now turn.

Ties of Garlic and Onions to Underworld Forces, and Their Use in Repelling Evil

In both ancient and modern times, there has been a widespread conviction that garlic and onions are tied to underworld forces, to darkness and evil. One example of this is seen in the view of Horace, ancient Roman poet and satirist, that garlic is a toxic dish that may have been tampered with by the evil witch Canidia.[30] Another is the Moslem (or "Oriental") legend that, when Satan left the Garden of Eden following the fall of man, garlic sprang up from the place where his left foot had been, and the onion, from where his right foot had been.[31] A third is a tale found in the Bower Manuscript, a Buddhist medical treatise of the fifth century A.D., which identifies the first garlic as having originated in the blood of a demon, an enemy of the gods killed by Vishnu.[32] In a similar vein, one orthodox system of Hindu philosophy (Sāṃkhya) classifies onions and garlic with foods having the quality of *tamas* ("darkness"); that is, they are cold, uninteresting, rotten, and consist of the leavings of others.[33]

Views such as the above—that garlic and its relatives are impure and linked to the earth and underworld—mean that they are especially suitable for offering to underworld forces, whether evil spirits, demons, or underworld deities, in seeking their protection, divining their intentions,[34] repelling them,[35] or eliminating the evil they brought on, including—as we shall see later—illness and disease. In a section drawn from Persian, Egyptian, and Indian sources, a Byzantine book on the interpretation of dreams says that, if a person dreams of eating garlic, leeks, or onions, he will not only experience sorrow and grief but will also gain notoriety because of their foul odor. It goes on to say that if the vegetables are cooked, the sorrow will only be moderate; that if the person dreams that he held the vegetables but did not eat them, the suffering will be less because of the fire; and that if he dreams that he gave some garlic, leeks, and onions to a person familiar to him, that person will experience evil days in accordance with the number of the vegetables given.[36]

As for alliums in fighting evil, there is an ancient Hittite text that involves a sacrificer who removes evil from the god and himself by peeling an onion.[37] In ancient Greece, garlic was considered a powerful force protecting against the evil eye.[38] Garlic was also consumed by Greek and Roman herb collectors before they dug up white and black hellebore, medicinal plants that were thought to pose a risk of illness and death. The collection of black hellebore (*Helleborus officinalis*), which posed a greater danger, might involve swift digging, careful observation for an eagle that could cause the collector to die, as well as prayer and magical rites similar to those followed in gathering mandrake. Prominent among black hellebore's medicinal uses was the treatment of insanity, and, among other things, it was used for depression, epilepsy, paralysis, and leprosy and was also sprinkled around houses to cleanse them and protect against evil spirits.[39] In a Roman comedy by Titinius (fl. 150 B.C.), one character states that strings of garlic rebuff witches. The view that garlic is protective was widespread in ancient Italy.[40] Among the Romans, it was believed that, if it thunders when a hen is sitting, her eggs will spoil. Columella noted that people used various methods to prevent such spoilage. One included placing small branches of laurel beneath the litter of nest boxes (laurel, it was believed, is safe against lightning strikes)[41] and attaching there some heads of garlic (symbolic of sulfureous thunderbolts because of their strong odor) with iron nails (also symbolic of thunderbolts, which were perceived as iron weapons).[42]

There is abundant evidence that ancient beliefs about spirit possession, illness, disease, and garlic continued to survive over the centuries in Italy and Greece. One reads of garlic or onions worn as charms against the evil eye in Italy.[43] Garlic remains a favorite Greek preventive or remedy against the evil eye.[44] In modern times, a Greek may fasten a cluster of garlic above the house door to protect against evil,[45] and in Macedonia a merchant may hang a clove of garlic over the door of his shop.[46] The evil eye represents a danger to which infants and young children are especially at risk. Even before birth no Greek midwife would proceed without an abundant supply of garlic for use around the delivery room and for tying around the infant's neck after birth or directly after baptism.[47] In Macedonia, the Greek mother of a newborn infant may keep some garlic beneath her pillow or on her head for protective purposes.[48] The association is such that, at one Greek festival, a midwife sits on a throne as if she were Genetyllis, ancient Greek goddess of childbirth, and wears, among other things, braids of garlic and onions.[49]

According to modern Greek folk belief, infants born on Christmas day are at risk of joining evil spirits of a type (Kallikantzaroi) that live on earth during part of the year. To prevent an infant from joining these evil spirits, its mother may bind it with braids of garlic.[50] Garlic may also be sewn into a Greek child's clothes on May Day—a time of special danger in terms of magic—to protect it from evil.[51]

May Day, which marks the festival of spring, is also a time when Greek farmers seek to assure the earth's protection and good crop yields by hanging wreaths of various green plants and fruit at the doors of their houses.[52] Such wreaths always include a thistle to protect against enemies and garlic to guard against the evil eye. In some cases, they include onions as well. With similar intent, garlic (or garlic and onions) may be included in wreaths hung from a ceiling beam in Greek farmhouses on the first of September. This day is still celebrated as New Year's Day in some places in Greece, and the wreaths are called a first of the year—the initial act of the new season of cultivation.[53] In some parts of Greece, merely uttering the word for garlic is thought to protect against the evil eye, as in countering the effect of careless or unlucky words or in exclaiming, "Garlic in your eyes," to a person suspected of evil intent.[54]

Garlic's association with the exorcism of evil forces was a major factor in encouraging the ancients to use it to prevent and cure illness and disease and repel death. For example, in the writings of the Roman poet and satirist Persius (first century A.D.) one finds a reference to individuals consuming garlic to deny entry to gods (demons) "who make your body swell all over."[55] There are suggestions of such thinking in the report that the odor of garlic keeps away serpents and scorpions and that the ancients used raw garlic to cure madness.[56] It is likely no accident that Hecate, chthonic goddess of sorcery who brought on or cured illness, was offered garlic in the form of a wreath to accompany the suppers provided for her at crossroads, which, as we have seen, were associated with her, and that Hecate was believed to punish with madness anyone who dared eat her suppers.[57] Despite the rise of Christianity, Hecate and crossroads offerings did not disappear. Crossroads offerings persisted as late as the eleventh century, when there are reports of the Church attempting to put an end to them. Hecate herself, moreover, led the well-known witch ride of medieval times.[58]

In early England, garlic (along with holy water, church lichen, and lichen with "Christ's mark or cross") was among the ingredients of a drink administered to a man possessed by a devil. That masses were sung over the ingredients in preparing the drink, that the "fiend-sick man" took his drink from a church bell, that he sang a psalm as part of his treatment, and that a priest sang a benediction afterwards[59] reveal a formidable alliance of forces, among them garlic and Christianity, committed to exorcising the devil. In Germany, people believed that witches, who posed a threat to human life, did not consume garlic. Since, moreover, witches were thought to represent a greater danger during Lent than at other times of the year, it was common for Germans to protect themselves by smearing garlic on their breasts, soles, and armpits at Shrovetide.[60] To keep evil spirits from injuring her newborn infant, a seventeenth-century Danish mother might put garlic and other charms in its cradle or over the door.[61] A bridegroom in Sweden might sew garlic and other strong smelling herbs into his clothes to protect against the power of sprites and trolls.[62]

In Sir John Harington's English version (A.D. 1607) of the medieval poem *Regimen Sanitatis Salernitanum,* which derived from the medical school at Salerno, people are advised to concentrate on the virtues of garlic and to tolerate its unpleasant odor. Garlic is identified as having a secret ability to counter all poisons. Persons who eat garlic can thus drink and not worry about who prepared their drink. They can walk within houses whose air is infected. Thus, according to the poem, garlic possesses the power to protect against death.[63] Similar thinking is revealed in an early eighteenth-century account of a plague epidemic in Marseilles. During that time, thieves who plundered dead bodies protected themselves by taking a garlic decoction.[64] The use of garlic in curing specific illnesses and diseases in ancient and medieval Europe may also have been derived from its perceived ability to counter evil forces. Possible candidates are the use of garlic in the ancient Mediterranean world to repel serpents and scorpions; to cure bites and neutralize toxins; to expel intestinal parasites; to treat madness; and to cure leprosy.[65] Garlic continued to be used in treating leprosy in medieval Europe, and indeed it was so commonly used in this way that lepers were called pilgarlics, because they were expected to peel the garlic they consumed in treating the disease.[66]

Other alliums commonly played protective roles similar to that of garlic. Chives, for example, are mentioned in this regard.[67] Among early Germanic people, the leek seems to have had a protective power similar to that found in ancient Greece.[68] An interesting question in this respect is the tradition—though it is of doubtful authenticity—that, in the seventh century, Britons, led by King Cadwallader, won a battle against the Saxons because of prayers for victory offered by St. David, their patron saint, and because of the saint's requirement that during battle the Britons wear leeks in their caps. It has been suggested that St. David chose leeks as a means of identification because he was a frugal person and because leeks, which grew wild in the area where he lived, were important in his diet. It has also been suggested that he did so to frighten the enemy troops by filling the air with the horrible odor of leeks.[69] One may question, however, whether the widespread European perception of the leek as protective may also have been involved in gaining it a place in this apocryphal tale. In any case, the Welsh, descendants of the early Britons, wear leeks in their hats each year on March 1, St. David's Day. As for onions, Friend,[70] apparently referring to Bohemia, writes that, if an onion is hung up in a room, it will attract to itself illnesses that would otherwise afflict people who live there. In some places in Britain, moreover, there was a folk custom of throwing an onion after the bride, likely to protect her against evil forces.[71] In a similar vein is the old-wives' tale in England today that a cold can be prevented by wearing a bit of garlic about one's neck.[72]

Garlic is used in amulets to protect against the evil eye in Romania, as by tying it around the neck of a child or to the tail of a domestic animal. It is interesting that such garlic may be gathered on the Trinity,[73] the Sunday when the Holy Trinity is honored, which may represent a Christian strengthening of garlic's effectiveness. Of further interest are the Romanian cathartic dancers (călușari), a form of secret society dedicated to curing humans of diseases thought to be brought on by fairies (among the most common are psycho-mental disorders, epilepsy, hemiplegia, rheumatism, plague, and cholera). The sponsor of the călușari is a demigoddess known as queen of the fairies (Doamna Zînelor), who represents an altered Romanian form of Diana, ancient Roman goddess of the wild. Indeed, in Romania, Diana's very name came to mean "fairy" (zîna). Not only is Diana leader of the witches in western Europe as well, but Irodiada (= Herodiada) and Arada, two of her other Romanian names, are also well-known names among western European witches. The călușari have a flag at the top of which is tied a bag containing magical and medicinal plants, most notably garlic and mugwort, which are considered the most powerful protection against fairies. In addition, the călușari chew as much garlic as they possibly can for protective purposes, and, in an effort at curing an afflicted person, their leader spits garlic on the afflicted's face.[74]

In later Roman religion, Diana was associated with Artemis and the chthonian goddess Hecate. In this regard, I note a possible survival from ancient times in the practice, reported for nineteenth-century Cuba, of wearing around one's neck 13 cloves of garlic, suspended from a string, for 13 days in an effort to get rid of jaundice. Simply wearing the garlic, however, is not sufficient. In the middle of the night on the 13th day, the wearer must go to the junction of two streets, remove the string of garlic, cast it over his head, and then run home without looking back.[75] This procedure resembles one mentioned for ancient Greece by Theophrastus, from whose account it may be implied that a person who accidentally observed one of Hecate's suppers at a crossroads turned his back out of fear, and, in any case, returned home quickly to wash and carry out purification rites.[76] Modern parallels such as this give credence to K. F. Smith's conclusion[77] that even today "Hecate and her goblin crew are only disguised, not outworn." I would add to this that one could develop a strong case that the roots of the "cult of garlic" in contemporary America lie not only in concerns with health and disease but also in the demon theory of disease so common in antiquity.[78]

Similar beliefs and customs are reported in the other areas of primary concern to us. Among Arabs, Armenians, and Turks, garlic, or garlic, onions, and leeks, have served to repel the evil eye, witchcraft, and bad luck.[79] In Iran, there seems once to have been a "Garlic Feast" on the 14th day of the 10th month, when garlic was used to repel demons.[80] In fifteenth- and seventeenth-century Zoroastrian texts in Iran, one finds garlic, along with vinegar and rue, used to flavor a dish served to the devil, or a demon, in order to drive him away.[81] In modern Iran, garlic, like a word from the Koran, is believed to ward off the evil eye.[82] In India, garlic is highly regarded for its ability to get rid of demons, for which purpose people commonly hang it above the doors of houses.[83] When someone is eating with other persons who are not eating, two onions may be set down in front of the dishes to protect against the evil eye.[84] Apparently with similar intent, garlic may be tied around the neck of an Indian, mother or child, or a garland of onions put around the neck of a bridegroom's mother after the marriage.[85] In Konkan, when a Hindu is thought to be possessed by a certain evil spirit, an exorcist may seek to drive the spirit away by crushing some garlic into the possessed person's ears or squeezing garlic juice into his nostrils. Garlic and pepper, moreover, may be rubbed into the eyes or put up the nostrils of a person who has fainted, to get him to return to consciousness by exorcising the spirit that is troubling him.[86]

In Han times in China (206 B.C.–A.D. 220), people would hang "strong-smelling vegetables," such as garlic and onions, on red cords (red because it is effective against the evil forces of darkness) above gates and doors, at the summer solstice or other times, to keep away injurious insects and other evil forces.[87] In modern China, persons who visited a mortuary house, particularly if a death had been untimely or brought on by disease, might hide a few garlic bulbs beneath their clothes out of conviction that their strong odor would repel the forces of death.[88] A parallel to this is found in the fact that idols of Chang Ling, Taoist patriarch of exorcism, may be represented with fists of garlic or leek bulbs.[89]

Suitability of Garlic and Onions for Offering to the Gods and Use in Places of Worship

Judging from "the onion archive" (documents from the Sargonid period which date from 2260–2223 B.C.) and other sources on ancient Mesopotamia, onions, garlic, and leeks were major crops that were offered to deities as well as being consumed by important dignitaries and ordinary folk as food and for medicinal purposes.[90] Though garlic, leeks, and onions could be eaten freely at most times, they were banned at certain times of the year (for example, the first three days of the year), as well as on ritual occasions when favors were sought from the gods—possibly to avoid offending them with bad breath.[91]

Concern with keeping garlic and its relatives away from deities as well as away from other worshippers also seems to have been found in the ancient Mediterranean world. In Greece, for example, persons who ate garlic were not permitted to enter temples dedicated to Cybele, mother of the gods.[92] They seem not to have been acceptable to Nabu, an important god in Babylonia and Assyria in the first millennium B.C., for they were banned at Ezida (the "taboo of Ezida"), his shrine. Indeed, when Babylonian king Nabu-sum-iskun, despite bearing the name of the god,[93] made Nabu's temple staff consume leeks, he earned the reputation of being an irreverent ruler.[94]

Among the early Hebrews, garlic was a dietary mainstay. This is shown by their reference to themselves as garlic eaters,[95] the effects of which may have led to Roman emperor Marcus Aurelius's characterization of them as "malodorous."[96] At the same time, some Hebrews made vows against eating garlic or other alliums for a period of time.[97] Other Hebrews apparently objected to garlic's bad odor at times of worship. One reads in the Babylonian Talmud, for example, of a rabbi who, when giving a lecture, noticed an odor of garlic, whereupon he said, "Let him who has eaten garlic go out."[98] There were also early Moslem traditions that the prophet Mohammed disliked onions and garlic, or their odor, and that one should not enter a mosque after consuming them or leeks.[99]

In India, Kalhaṇa, a twelfth-century poet and historian, tells of a Hindu king who, after dedicating a new shrine, made those Brahmins who ate garlic move elsewhere.[100] There is also an early Buddhist tale of a monk who had eaten onions and sat apart at a meeting where the Buddha was preaching.[101] The monk did this so as not to annoy his fellow monks, presumably with his onion breath and body odor, but when the Buddha learned of this, he banned the eating of onions to monks so as to enable them to participate fully in meetings.

In modern India garlic and/or onions are considered impure and inappropriate for offering to Hindu gods. In North India, one cannot offer onions and garlic to Hindu gods.[102] In South India, Hindus never use garlic in foods offered to their gods, whether in temples or at home. Onions are never added to food offered in Sanskritic temples, but since feeling against onions is not as strong, they may be included in dishes offered to lesser gods, and even Brahmins may include them in dishes provided to household deities.[103] In China, on its part, Taoist divinities of the human body strongly dislike the odor of garlic and onions.[104]

Garlic and Onions Viewed as Aphrodisiacs and Stimulating and Strengthening Agents

Garlic was widely viewed as an aphrodisiac among peoples from the Mediterranean world to China. Pliny[105] says that garlic gives the body a ruddier color and, when "pounded with fresh coriander and taken in neat wine," is considered to be an aphrodisiac. The aphrodisiac qualities of garlic are also revealed in an amusing tale by Aristophanes.[106] According to the tale, some young men of Aspasia, when drunk, had gone to Megara and made off with a prostitute, and the Megarans retaliated by stealing two prostitutes from Aspasia. Aristophanes attributes these silly acts with starting the Peloponnesian War, but from our perspective what is important is that he described the Megarans as being "in agonies of excitement, as though stuffed with garlic." In ancient medicine, physicians, in seeking to excite patients suffering from what the Greeks called lethargy, had them smell garlic and onions at intervals. Physicians also attempted to stimulate a paralyzed tongue by having the patient chew garlic and onions, or to stimulate the skin of a paralyzed limb by applying a mixture that included onions.[107] An ancient Hebrew decree, attributed to Ezra, required that people consume garlic on sabbath evenings because it was an aphrodisiac and satisfied desire.[108] Rabbis in the Babylonian Talmud, commenting on the decree, said, among other things, that garlic warms the body, brightens the face, increases semen, encourages love, and that the decree applies to men who perform their marital duty every Friday night.[109] In India, onions as well as garlic are believed to stimulate the sexual appetites.[110] In China, garlic, onions, and leeks are excluded from a diet followed by Buddhists in the hope that reducing sexual desire will contribute to purity.[111]

Related to the above is the belief that strength and bravery may be enhanced by eating garlic. In ancient Greece and Rome, garlic was consumed by rural folk, soldiers, and sailors because it was thought to provide strength or strength and bravery. In Greek thinking, people fought better, were more pugnacious, if they were "garlic primed."[112] In Rome, garlic was consecrated to Mars, god of war; and, in the belief that, when eaten in large amounts, it instilled bravery in battle, legionnaires grew it in all territories they conquered.[113] In modern India, despite a widespread Hindu commitment to nonviolence and vegetarianism, it is recognized that members of the warrior castes (Kshattriyas) need martial qualities to have the greatest success in carrying out their tasks. For this reason, such groups may be permitted to consume foods such as meat, garlic, and onions (as well as alcoholic beverages), which Hindu priests and religious persons eschew. This is because—in the hot-cold classification that influences the choice of foods—meat, garlic, and onions are "very hot,"[114] and eating them strengthens, stimulates anger, and enhances the martial temperament of warriors,[115] as well as arousing them sexually and encouraging the birth of warrior sons.[116] In classical times in Greece, athletes would consume garlic to strengthen themselves before competition began.[117] In a similar vein, there is a suspicion in certain places in modern Europe that, if a runner in a race chews a piece of garlic, others will not be able to pass him.[118] One also reads that, in former times in Paris, people ate garlic and butter each day during the month of May to strengthen themselves for the remainder of the year.[119]

On the subject of animals, in ancient Greece cockfighting was popular,[120] and people believed that a cock's combativeness derived from its sexual drive. To encourage combativeness, Greeks fed garlic to fighting cocks.[121] The Greeks also rubbed garlic onto the bodies of fighting cocks[122] or smeared it onto the raised tables on which cockfights occurred so that it could revive cocks that fell or were maimed[123]—just as in modern India garlic is "administered to wounded or fainting birds."[124] In modern Bohemia, garlic is fed to cocks, ganders, and dogs to strengthen them and to make them fearless.[125] Similar beliefs have been reported in Britain. Thomas Lupton,[126] in a book published initially about A.D. 1579, cited Mizaldus (Antoine Mizaud, d. 1578) for observing that cocks that eat garlic are the ablest fighters, courageous, strong, and agile, and that, at the height of combat or battle, horses may be given garlic along with bread and wine to induce fierceness, vigor, and strength.[127]

Garlic and Onions as Flesh Food

Horace[128] wrote that to eat onions or leeks involves killing living beings, whether or not you agree with Empedocles (the Greek philosopher) that vegetables have souls. On the other hand, though Empedocles and certain others believed that plants have souls, Greeks and Romans did not ban onions and their relatives as food. Even Empedocles, Pythagoras, and the Orphics—who all believed (or, in the case of the Orphics, may have believed) in the transmigration of souls and were committed to vegetarianism in some form[129]—failed to ban them. In India, however, similar thinking did contribute to the rejection of one or another allium species. One reads, as explanations for such bans in India, that garlic originated from the body of a living creature, a demon;[130] that, when cut, onions resemble meat;[131] that their reddish color, like that of carrots, turnips, and red pulse, is similar to that of meat;[132] that, like eggplant and potatoes, onions resemble or turn into meat;[133] and that onions and garlic are shaped like a human head[134] and, by extension, that eating them is like eating flesh. These and previous explanations for garlic and onion avoidance in India are related, in that demons are thought to like blood sacrifice, meat, blood, alcohol, and strong foods and to be immoderate in their behavior and in their sexual passions.

Rejection of Garlic and Onions by Priests, Respectable Persons, and Vegetarians

I have not found a single case of an entire ethnic group rejecting garlic and onions. Nevertheless, some individuals, classes, and religious groups did develop anti-allium sentiments, usually because of associations such as those identified above. Over time, for example, the ancient Greeks came to view the use of garlic and onions as a low-class phenomenon, disgusting to persons of high social status.[135] One or another allium was also banned to priests and devotees of one cult or another in the ancient Mediterranean world. Priests of the Libyan Aphrodite, for example, refused to taste garlic.[136]

Evidence on the position of alliums in ancient Egypt, however, is quite confusing. Archeological and literary evidence from Egypt reveals that garlic, onions, and leeks were cultivated; that they were popular foods; and that onions were important in the diet of ordinary folk. Observers report that garlic and onions were included in burials; that onions and leeks were depicted as food being offered to the dead; and that the onion was used in embalming.[137] Keimer has noted that hieroglyphic inscriptions demonstrate that onions served in ritual; that they were offered to deities, especially Sokaris, lord of the dead, or chewed in front of them; and that people tied onions around their necks[138]—possibly, as with garlic elsewhere in the Mediterranean area, to protect against underworld influences. In any case, the above observations suggest that alliums were widely acceptable foods in ancient Egypt, and there is nothing in them to suggest anti-allium sentiment.

Yet certain ancient Greek or Roman writers have said, with respect to Egypt, that, when taking an oath, people swear by garlic and onions as deities;[139] that some Egyptians refuse altogether to eat onions;[140] that priests in Egypt detest onions and are careful to avoid them;[141] that it is a sin for Egyptians to eat onions and leeks;[142] or that for the people of Pelusium, east of the Nile Delta, the wild onion is a god,[143] and they do not eat onions.[144]

The conclusion seems inescapable that statements made by certain Greek or Roman writers were incorrect, and it seems likely that some Egyptians consumed alliums freely as food, whereas others refused to eat certain of them. In J. G. Griffiths's view, the differences in the Greek and Roman accounts likely derive from the contrasting views of neighboring communities in Egypt. The evidence is clear that the onion had a special ritual role in the eastern delta, and specifically in the cult of Zeus Casius.[145] The associations of that god—whether they were Egyptian, Syrian, Cretan, or otherwise—have long been a matter of scholarly controversy.[146] Some scholars, however, believe Zeus Casius to have been involved in the controversy between the Egyptian gods Horus and Seth. Indeed, it has been suggested that a statue of Zeus Casius at Pelusium, depicting a young man holding a pomegranate, was modelled on an earlier statue of Harpokrates, the young Horus, whose role was to carry out the struggle against forces of darkness. Additional ancient evidence of a tie between Harpokrates and Zeus Casius has also been found.[147] It has been noted, on the other hand, that Pelusium was in a part of Egypt regarded as the domain of Seth, and that the waning of the moon symbolized "the devouring of the 'eye' of Horus by Seth," thus tying the onion to such unclean Sethian animals as the pig.[148] Whatever the nature and origin of onion avoidance in the cult of Zeus Casius, it seems likely that such avoidance extended beyond Pelusium and the eastern Nile Delta— that, at least in classical times, onions, and possibly other alliums, were avoided in other regions by some people, whether priests or laymen. At the same time, one is forced to admit that evidence on allium avoidance in ancient Egypt is inconsistent and unclear.

For India, on the other hand, the evidence from the Sūtra period (c. 500 B.C.–A.D. 100) onward is quite clear. In early India, garlic (Sanskrit: *laśuna*), sometimes with onions (*palāndu*) or leeks, was banned to Brahmins and other respectable castes[149] who required penance for violations, as they did for tasting alcohol or unclean bodily excretions or for eating pork or beef. The *Laws of Manu* say that alliums (garlic, onions, and leeks) are unsuited for eating by twice-born men (members of the highest three castes—Brahmins, Kshattriyas, and Vaiśyas—who have undergone a second, spiritual birth following an initiation ceremony that marks a child's readiness for the honor of a Vedic education). This is because alliums emerge from unclean things, which means that, should such a person eat them, he would become an outcast.[150]

Judging from the Mahabharata, that Hindu epic poem, some of which was set down in the early centuries of the Christian era, onions and garlic were not eaten by honorable people.[151] Similar prohibitions were found in a Hindu code of law of comparable age (A.D. 100–300).[152] At the beginning of the fifth century A.D., Chinese Buddhist pilgrim Fa-hsien reported that in Gupta India, except for one group that was scorned and avoided, no one ate garlic or onions, killed animals, or consumed alcoholic beverages.[153] Seventh-century Chinese pilgrims confirmed this. I-tsing wrote that people in all parts of India refused to eat onions of any sort.[154] Hsüan-tsang, as indicated in one of the quotations at the chapter opening, noted that garlic and onions were not used very much and that persons who did eat them were ostracized. The Puranas, which were set down from the sixth to the sixteenth century A.D. and provide a legendary description of antiquity, list garlic and onions among foods unsuited for offering to one's ancestors in śrāddha rites.[155]

In early India, anti-allium feelings were also found among Jains[156] and, though apparently to a lesser degree,[157] among Buddhists, who, nevertheless, were active in fostering such views in other lands such as China.[158]

Anti-allium feelings have persisted in India into modern times. In contemporary India, the belief mentioned previously, that garlic and onions have aphrodisiac qualities, makes them inappropriate to persons, such as celibates,[159] who are concerned with avoiding sexual stimulation at all times. Also involved in garlic and onion avoidance, however, is the notion that they are exciting and, like meat, impure and to be avoided altogether by vegetarians and groups who have a strong vegetarian commitment. After a Bengali Hindu woman is widowed, for example, she avoids not only meat, fish, and eggs, but garlic and onions as well.[160] Strict Hindus in Bengal find onions unacceptable and rarely, if ever, consume them.[161] Garlic and onions may also be avoided by strict orthodox persons at times required by religious tradition, for example, during fasts.[162]

Most Brahmins are vegetarians, and many of them also avoid garlic and onions.[163] Thus, one reads a general statement that most Brahmins are not permitted to eat onions and garlic;[164] that Brahmins in a North India village avoid impure foods such as onions and garlic;[165] that in Tamil Nadu, because garlic is impure, it is not found in the normal diet of Brahmins;[166] that in a village in South India strong foods such as garlic and onions are considered inappropriate for Havik Brahmins;[167] that no strict Brahmin in Gujarat would eat garlic or onions;[168] that in Bihar, including Patna,[169] Brahmins reject both garlic and onions; and that in Benares similar attitudes are found among Brahmins.[170]

Behura[171] notes that in North India strict Hindus reject onions and leeks as well as garlic, but that this is not so in South India, where onions and leeks are permitted even to orthodox Brahmins. This fits with Eichinger Ferro-Luzzi's observation that in South India, with one exception, garlic is not consumed by Brahmins, though objections to onions are less marked.[172]

Brahmins who knowingly eat garlic and onions may be required to fast and carry out penances if they are to retain their caste status.[173] Such violations may also be of significance when a Brahmin dies. After the death of a Brahmin in Gujarat, for example, forgiveness is asked for his smaller sins (upa-pātaka), which include eating garlic and onions as well as lying, cheating, failure to give alms to deserving persons, and other acts unworthy of a person of his caste.[174]

Garlic and onion avoidance is also prominent among Vaishnavas (devotees of the god Vishnu and, as the term is often used, of his incarnations Rama and Krishna), who are noted for their strong commitment to vegetarianism.[175] In South India, Vaishnavas are stricter than other people in banning garlic and onions.[176] In North India, garlic and onions are forbidden to Vaishnavas,[177] and, for places in that region or elsewhere, there are reports of their not offering or using them in temples.[178] A Śūdra seeking to raise his ritual status in a North Indian village may become a bhagat (devotee of Vishnu) and give up not just sexual activity but also items that stimulate it, such as garlic and onions, as well as meat and alcohol.[179] Against this background, it is interesting to read that Vaishnavas have developed an acute sense of smell that enables them to tell from a person's breath whether he or she has consumed garlic, onions, or other banned objects.[180]

In modern India, anti-allium feelings are still found among Jains, who are stricter than Brahmins in the matter of food,[181] as well as among Buddhists. Buddhist lamas of the Sherdukpen of Arunachal Pradesh (formerly India's North-East Frontier Agency), for example, are not permitted to eat onions lest they become insane or develop some fatal illness.[182]

In China, garlic and onions are so widely used as flavorings that it is difficult to imagine what the country's cuisines would be like without them. At the same time, there have been millennia-long efforts to reduce or eliminate their dietary use in China. It remains unresolved whether anti-allium sentiments preceded Buddhism in China, but clearly Buddhism has been in the vanguard of the action. One example is the inclusion of an allium among the wu-hun, "five vegetables of strong odor" forbidden to Buddhist clergy, in the Brahmajāla-sūtra (which was translated in A.D. 406 by Kumarajiva, a famous Indian Buddhist scholar brought to

China by the emperor).[183] In T'ang times (A.D. 618–907), it was normal to include alliums among the wu-hun,[184] a pattern that has continued among Chinese Buddhists into modern times.[185] Of special interest is a modern Buddhist vegetarian dish, "Lohan's Delight," which is regarded as particularly appropriate for a monk (lohan) because, among other things, it includes no garlic or scallions, which are believed to stimulate passion and make it less likely that a monk attains nirvana.[186]

Bans on garlic and its relatives have not been limited to Chinese Buddhists, but have been found among Taoists and geomancers as well.[187] One also finds allium bans among minority peoples influenced by Buddhism. The Mongolian-speaking Monguors of the Kansu-Tibetan border, for example, have a sect, "those who fast," whose members consume neither garlic, nor meat, nor wine.[188]

The case of the Monguors underlines the point that allium avoidance in China is associated with fasting and vegetarianism, which led to the saying "Among the meats are three kinds of vegetables."[189] There is, for example, a Chinese vegetarian diet called *su* that is observed by Buddhists and excludes not only meat, fish, and dairy products, but garlic, onions, leeks, and alcoholic beverages as well. The Buddhist going on this diet hopes to gain purity, with animal products excluded so as not to violate the ban on killing, and alliums, to reduce the pollution that sexual stimulation can bring on.[190] In nineteenth-century China, officials participating in state religious ceremonies were expected to abstain from various acts that made them impure, among them drinking wine and eating garlic, leeks, or onions,[191] which stir the passions. Moreover when a Chinese emperor died, his entire court refrained from consuming meat and wine, as well as vegetables of strong odor.[192]

Conclusions

An initial question is how the bans on garlic and its relatives fit among the various types of food rejection and to what degree disgust may be involved. Paul Rozin and his associates have identified four psychological categories of food rejection:[193] (1) inappropriateness, the rejection of some substances, for example, paper and grass, that human cultures define as inedible; (2) distaste, in which rejection is based on the unpleasantness of a food's odor, appearance, or sensory effects in the mouth; (3) danger, in which people are concerned with the bad effects, whether in terms of health or social status, that may develop after ingestion of a food; and (4) disgust, strong rejection of potential foods that are considered polluting, foods whose very taste, smell, and/or sight are offensive, so much so that even thinking of them can bring on nausea. The rejections of garlic and onions that concern us in this chapter are not based on inappropriateness, for both are widely cultivated and highly valued as flavorings in all the societies involved. At the same time, garlic and onions may be rejected by certain groups or persons in those societies or at certain times of the year or on certain occasions. The rejection of garlic and onions does fall into the distaste category on the basis of their strong odor. The concern, however, is with the unpleasantness of the odor not only to the person who eats them but also to other persons and, even more, to the gods. In addition, the rejection of garlic and onions rests on concerns with danger, because a person's social standing can be affected by using garlic and onions, whether in ritual contexts in which they are considered improper or in the case of a person having an occupation or belonging to a social, age, or religious group for whom they are forbidden food. Finally, the rejection of garlic and onions may entail notable disgust reactions as defined by Rozin and his associates.

One can readily discern echoes of Angyal's thinking[194] in my account of garlic and onion rejection. First is the strong odors given off by onions and garlic, both in themselves and by people who have consumed them. A strong odor, in Angyal's view, may imply intimate contact with a disgusting object, which enhances the likelihood of a strong disgust reaction. To Angyal, however, a disgusting object of some sort is basic to disgust reactions, with sensory qualities, such as odor, of secondary importance. The disgusting object, moreover, Angyal sees as one linked to waste products of the human or animal body. If so, the question arises as to what there is, apart from odor, that might be considered disgusting about garlic and its relatives. In this regard, one cannot ignore the Hindu view that the color of onions or garlic resembles that of flesh and blood, and that they are shaped like human heads, making eating them, like eating meat, unacceptable to vegetarians. The association of garlic and onions with meat, however, seems to be restricted to India and religions of Indian origin, and in all likelihood this is a regional enhancement developed in a land where vegetarianism is unusually prominent. The most widespread and oft-mentioned explanation for the garlic and onion avoidance in the Old World high civilizations of antiquity was that garlic and onions, and people who eat them, give off strong, unpleasant odors, which make the vegetables unfit for offering to high gods and for use by humans prior to approaching the gods. Avoiding garlic and onions must have been a minor inconvenience to ordinary folk, who did not have contact with the high gods on an everyday basis. For some clergy and devout laymen, on the other hand, contact was frequent enough, or concern with ritual purity sufficient, to lead them to more permanent bans such as that of India's Brahmins. Concern with ritual purity in approaching the gods may have been sufficient to lead some groups to consider onions and garlic as ritually impure. In addition, however, garlic and onions are often thought to stimulate one's sexual passions, an aroused condition widely held to be ritually impure. Still another concern is that garlic and onions are tied to evil underworld forces. We seem, therefore, to be dealing with a phenomenon that cannot be explained simply in terms of a biological imperative. Instead, it is a phenomenon that reflects a blending of biological and cultural factors, and it would be wrong to relegate cultural factors to a secondary role.

6 Ritual Use and Avoidance of the Urd Bean (*Vigna mungo*) in India

With Comparative Data on Certain Related Foods, Flavorings, and Beverages

> . . . and black grain . . . is not considered fit to be eaten . . .
> —*Āpastamba Dharma-sūtra* 2.18.2

> . . . mâshas [urd beans] are expressly forbidden; for it is said
> *Ayagñiyâ vai mâshâh,* "Mashas are not fit for sacrifice."
> —F. Max Müller, in a commentary on the
> "Âpastamba's Yagña-Paribhâshâ-Sûtras"

Introduction

It has been more than a century since Sanskritist Leopold von Schroeder[1] first wrote about the striking similarities between the bans on beans of the Vedic Indians and those of the Pythagoreans of ancient Greece. Despite this, little has been done to extend von Schroeder's work, as in tracing the ban on beans beyond the Vedic period into modern India. This is my intent in this chapter, to sketch in greater detail the ritual ban and ritual use of beans in India, both ancient and modern, as well to reconsider the associations, meaning, and possible origin of the ban.

The Indian bean that concerns us here is not the bean rejected by the Pythagoreans. The Pythagorean bean was the fava bean (*Vicia faba*), a legume cultivated in the ancient Near East, Mediterranean region, and elsewhere in Europe starting in the Neolithic or in the Bronze Age (Figure 34). George Watt[2] believed it likely that the fava bean had been cultivated in the Himalayas of far northwestern India since antiquity. On the other hand, he believed that in most of India it was unknown until modern times. That the fava bean was not introduced to India by Europeans is suggested by the lack of resemblance between its Indian names and its

158

34. The fava bean (*Vicia faba,* type *major*): the plant, pods growing on the plant, and seed (from Zee and Hui, 1981).

name in Portuguese, French, or English (*fava, fève,* fava bean). Instead it has various names in India, and one of them (*bakla*) in Punjabi and Hindi is virtually the same as its name in Indo-Iranian languages to the west of India (*bakla, boklja, bogli, bagli, bakila,* etc.).[3] That the fava bean is a fairly recent introduction to most of the Indian subcontinent is supported by its absence among the legumes uncovered in ancient archeological sites. That absence is especially notable in view of the fact that certain of its wild relatives are represented in such sites,[4] along with a considerable number of domesticated legumes. Among them are legumes that seem to have originated in South or Southeast Asia (mung bean, *Vigna radiata*), or in the Near East or elsewhere in that direction (lentil, *Lens esculenta;* field pea, *Pisum arvense;* chick pea, *Cicer arietinum;* grass pea, *Lathyrus sativus;* cow pea, *Vigna unguiculata;* and hyacinth bean, *Dolichos lablab*).[5] Equally notable, the fava bean is not mentioned in the Vedic literature, and indeed there is no Sanskrit name for it.[6] Even today, the acreage devoted to fava beans in India is very small and geographically limited (to Kashmir, Punjab, Rajasthan, eastern Uttar Pradesh, Madhya Pradesh, and Karna-

35. Urd beans (*Vigna mungo*).

taka).[7] Moreover, general accounts of Indian legumes or food, and even accounts of local food and agriculture, say little, if anything, about them. Nor have I found any indication, in accounts dealing with Hindu life and religion, that fava beans play any special role in ritual or that there is a ban on them.

The bean ban of the Vedic records applied not to the fava bean but to another bean known in Sanskrit as *maśa* (*Vigna mungo* = *Phaseolus mungo*). In Hindi today, it is known as *urd* or *urid,* and in Indian English, as black gram. It is a small bean whose seed coat is commonly black in color (Figure 35).[8] It is close relative of the mung bean, *Vigna radiata* (Figure 36).[9] Like the mung bean, urd is believed to have been domesticated in India. Likely this took place in the Deccan Peninsula, and from *V. radiata* var. *sublobata,* the presumed wild ancestor of both urd and mung, which typically has black or grayish brown seeds.[10] Though urd has not spread as successfully around the world as various New World beans of the genus *Phaseolus,* it is a major pulse in India, where it is highly regarded and grown throughout the country. In the Western world, it can be purchased

36. "*Phaseolus mungo*." This illustration is from a nineteenth-century source in which the mung bean (green gram, now *Vigna radiata*) and urd bean (black gram, now *Vigna mungo*) were considered varieties of a single species, *Phaseolus mungo* (from Church, 1886).

mainly in South Asian food stores in cities that have significant populations deriving from India, Pakistan, or Bangladesh and, when prepared with curry or other spices, it is delicious.[11]

My focus here is much like that of scholars who have studied the fava bean in the Greco-Roman world, but it is on a different bean. Of special interest are the references in Indian texts, ancient and modern, to the ritual associations of maśa as they affect its use and avoidance. Before proceeding to that question, however, another matter must be considered.

Anthropologist Mary Douglas[12] has sought to understand the origin of the ancient Hebrew bans on flesh as set down in Leviticus. She has argued that one should not remove an individual ban from the context in which it is discussed; that important insights are to be gained by considering the entire range of Levitican flesh bans, which apply to such varied creatures as the hare, camel, cormorant, and fish without scales or fins; that basic to any understanding is an awareness of the strong desire of the ancient Hebrews to be holy before God; that they were convinced that to be holy they must remain apart from other peoples; that the rejection of certain flesh foods fostered their apartness; and that the model against which they judged the acceptability of animals in terms of purity and impurity was that of their herd animals, who had been blessed by God. Jean Soler[13] subsequently provided further insights into the dietary prohibitions of the Hebrews through a similar procedure, of viewing them in terms of the overall Hebrew system of beliefs as set down in the Bible. Both Douglas and Soler reached conclusions that were far more convincing than those of scholars who seek historical explanations of food habits in terms of disease or ecology.[14] Because of the success of Douglas and Soler, I will follow their lead. First I will consider certain Hindu beliefs that are essential to an understanding of their food prohibitions, including matters of social organization (caste and sectarian affiliation), concern with ritual pollution, and the color symbolism related to ritual pollution. Then I will review evidence, ancient and modern, on the use and avoidance of *Vigna mungo* in India. After that, I will turn to certain other foods and flavorings (sesame, meat, alcoholic beverages, salt, and mushrooms) that Indian texts commonly mention as those to be avoided in certain situations or by certain individuals or groups.[15] And finally, I will consider the origin of the Indian ban on eating *Vigna mungo*.

The Pollution Concept and Color Symbolism of the Hindus, Especially as They Relate to the Acceptability of Foods

Hindu Castes and Sects

Basic to any understanding of Hindu food prohibitions is the importance of the caste system, which, despite differences from one region to another, has much similarity in form throughout India. The roots of the caste system are seen in the varṇas (classes) of the *Rig-veda,* of which there were three. One was that of the Kshattriyas, warriors and rulers. A second was that of the Brahmins, priests; and a third, that of the Vaiśyas, merchants and farmers. Over time, a fourth class, the Śūdras, or artisans, was added, and then a fifth, the untouchables. As time passed, moreover, what in the *Rig-veda* had been an open system in which individuals could move from one varṇa to another evolved into the modern caste system. In this caste system there are thousands of status groups (jātis; loosely "castes") that fit into the varṇa classification but, unlike it, are endogamous functioning social units.[16]

Also important since antiquity in India have been religious sects. Hindu sects today may have adherents largely drawn from a single caste; the Satnāmis of Central India are such a sect (early in this century, virtually all adherents were *chamār*s, leather workers). Or they may attract devotees from a broad range of castes, such as the Vaishnavas (followers of Vishnu and his various incarnations such as Rama and Krishna).

Hindu Religious Views and Pollution Concerns

Closely related to the above are Hindu religious views as they pertain to one's existence in this world and in the hereafter. Three major concepts of Hinduism are *dharma,* a person's sacred duty to follow the rules of good and righteous behavior; *karma,* the law of just deserts, by which a person is ultimately repaid for good and bad thoughts and acts; and *saṃsāra,* the transmigration of souls. A Hindu considers his present life as merely one of a series of incarnations, with some, in all likelihood, still to come. A person's soul, according to the law of karma, may be reborn in a being of higher or lower ritual status, whether a human or some other living creature. A Hindu may enhance his ritual standing in his next incarnation by following three meritorious paths. Among them is "the path of service," which requires conformity to the dharma of the social groups of which he is a member.[17]

The three major attributes of dharma are truth, beauty, and purity. A thought, act, object, or human being is in accord with dharma if it is true, beautiful, but, above all, pure.[18] Purity is a state that raises a person beyond the normal human condition to a level that enables him to approach the sacred and to establish an advantageous relationship with the gods.[19] It is a condition so vital that a concerned Hindu makes serious efforts to avoid ritual pollution and, should he become polluted, to return to a state of purity. Such concerns are so pervasive that some scholars speak of a "Hindu pollution concept," without which the behavior of Hindus, whether individuals or groups, cannot be understood.

Pollution may derive from various sources. It may be a permanent or a temporary state, with temporary pollution becoming permanent if it is not removed. Pollution may also be voluntary or involuntary and external or internal.[20] Whatever its form, if at all possible it is something to be avoided or eliminated. From our perspective, it is highly significant that castes and sects establish rules of behavior intended to keep their members pure. It is also significant that among these rules are ones relating to food and eating, including the permissibility of individual foods and drinks, and that a person who eats a prohibited food or drink becomes polluted,[21] which may have dire consequences. Thus one reads in the *Laws of Manu* (composed A.D. 100–300):[22] "Through neglect of Veda study, through deviation from the rule of conduct, through remissness (in the fulfillment of duties), and through faults (committed by eating forbidden) food, Death becomes eager to shorten the lives of [Brahmins]."

It is also important that food and drink may be identified with and take on the impurity of other substances, acts, conditions, or beings. Such impurity may derive from various sources (e.g., human feces or human saliva, the latter of which is responsible for the impurity of leavings).[23] Here, however, the role of passion, killing, and death in the pollution of food and drink is of greatest concern to us. It is true that passion, in various ways, as through encouraging sexual activity and the birth of offspring, may be viewed as contributing to the survival of one's family and group. At the same time, passion must be minimized if a Hindu is to expect deliverance after death (*moksha*), for it has been associated with ritual impurity since antiquity. In Vedic India, for example, a religious student was expected to abstain from sex, apparently as a precaution against evil influences. Indeed, the term used for such a student, *brahma-chārin*, was "synonymous with 'celibate.'"[24] For similar reasons, a religious teacher was expected to abstain from sex for a day and a night prior to completing rites associated with a particularly sacred lesson.[25] Celibacy might also be required of newlyweds for the first few nights of marriage. This, Oldenberg suggests,[26] is because demons, who by their nature are lustful, could enter the woman's body at the time of sexual intercourse, making her pregnant and endangering her offspring. The period of celibacy was honored in order to mislead demons into thinking that the marriage would not be consummated, so that the demons would give up and go away. Among modern Hindus, too, sexual abstinence is essential in gaining the ritual purity needed to worship a god.[27] Killing and death, on their part, are the most serious pollutants to Hindus. This is because killing is a violation of the concept of ahimsa (nonviolence to all living creatures), one of their most cherished values (as well as of Jains and Buddhists). Death, in turn, is related to decay and to fearsome forces of the underworld. The pollution of death may affect not just the dead person's relatives but other persons as well. As described by Jindel[28] for the templed town of Nathdwara in Rajasthan, the death of a distant relative is never announced inside the temple. If this were to be done, not only would a relative hearing the news become polluted, but so would other persons and things with which he or she has contact, including the temple itself. A dead corpse, on its part, pollutes people living in a household as well as all other individuals who have contact with the corpse directly or indirectly, including those who accompany it to the place of cremation. After the cremation, friends and neighbors of the deceased can remove the pollution of death (*sutak*) by bathing and changing their clothes, after which they are permitted to enter their homes. Relatives, however, remain polluted for several days, during which time they are subject to restrictions on participating in ritual affairs. At the end of that period, certain acts are carried out to remove the pollution of death. The pollution of death also has a major impact on food use and avoidance.[29]

Scholars look back to the *Bhagavadgītā*, which may date from the first to the third century A.D., as identifying three qualities that form the basis for present-day Hindu thinking about the purity and impurity of foods. According to the *Gītā*, there are three sorts of people, each of which derives its qualities from foods they eat. First are the *sāttvika*, who are pure and wise. Second are the *rājasika,* who are ruled by passion. Third are the *tāmasika,* who are dull, lazy, and ignorant. The pure and wise value foods that are nutritious, pleasant, mild, and sweet, and that enhance good health, vigor, strength, happiness, and longevity. The passionate are inclined toward foods that are astringent, sour, saline, biting, harsh, too hot, and burning, and which bring on pain, misery, and disease. The dull, in turn, eat foods that are without taste, stale, rotten, impure, and represent the leavings of others.[30]

Present-day Hindu concerns with food, of course, go well beyond pollution. This is only one factor that may lead them to reject individual foods, whether altogether or at particular times or under particular conditions.[31] Among the most important of the Hindu's other worries are the hot (*ushṇa*) or cold (*śīta*) (heating or cooling) qualities of food and other matters relating to health, usually deriving from Ayurvedic medicine.[32] The hot-cold system, as R. S. Khare[33] has pointed out, is independent from, and does not correlate closely with the matter of primary concern to us here, the system of ritual purity and impurity. The hot-cold system focuses on and is of direct relevance to a person's body and physical being. The purity-impurity system, by contrast, is based on renunciation of one's body, but is of utmost relevance to one's spiritual condition and standing. At the same time, the two systems sometimes influence one another in ways that cannot be ignored. One example is that rājasik foods are commonly considered hot, and sāttvik foods, cold.[34] Thus, people in rural Tamil Nadu frequently speak approvingly of yogis and gurus who, because they eat "cold" vegetarian foods, can refrain from sexual intercourse and maintain spiritual as well as physical vigor.[35] Another example is that what foods are offered to the gods may be determined not just by a food's purity or impurity but also by its heating or cooling qualities.[36] Because of this, and because it is often difficult or impossible to separate the two systems in the thinking of people, from time to time I call attention to hot and cold beliefs, especially if they relate to those of purity and pollution. I do this despite the facts that there is little consistency in the ways scholars have collected data and reported on hot and cold foods; that there are striking individual and regional differences in the way Hindus classify foods in these terms; and that, at best, one can say only that most people in a group view a food as hot or cold. Indeed, Pool,[37] on the basis of research in Gujarat, has argued that the lack of consistency in the hot-cold classification of foods suggests that, in seeking understanding, one should focus not on the classification of foods but on that of diseases.

The essential element of thinking in terms of hot and cold is that a person, to be in good health, must maintain a balance so that neither overheating nor overcooling prevails. Should imbalance develop, illnesses and death may result. The goal of a concerned person, then, is to balance his or her bodily state through the use of appropriate foods. Since a person's bodily state may change from time to time, constant vigil is required. If a person's body is cold, heating foods are called for; if hot, cooling foods.

Hot and cold beliefs about food are widespread in present-day South Asia. Moreover, humoral thinking, which is basic to the concept of hot and cold foods, has been known there since antiquity.[38] Scholars have traditionally tended to credit Greece with the initial development of a humoral theory of disease.[39] It has been pointed out, however, that early exchanges in medical thinking occurred between Greece and India (prior to and following the invasion of India by Alexander the Great).[40] It has also been argued that humoral theories may have been developed in India and China as early as or earlier than in Greece.[41]

Despite the relevance of hot-cold and other factors in the making of Hindu food decisions, it is the matter of pollution that is our primary focus. Indeed in one study of food avoidances during the puerperium and lactation carried out in Tamil Nadu, nearly three-fourths of all women made decisions about when they could start using certain foods again on the basis of the concept of pollution.[42]

Hindu Color Symbolism

Turning from pollution to the color symbolism of Hindus, we note that the dichotomy between white and black is reflected in Aryans' perception of themselves as light-skinned and their perception of the Dravidians, who preceded them, as dark-skinned. In this regard there is a folk saying in present-day North India that the Aryans were light people with light animals (common cattle), and the Dravidians, dark people with dark animals (water buffalo). One suspects that the Aryans spread such ideas to Dravidian peoples. In any case, one reads that among the Tamils, a Dravidian people of South India, women prefer their children to be of fair complexion. One also reads that, to assure their offspring's fairness, pregnant women refuse to eat fruits with dark skins. If they are from wealthy families, moreover, they consume drinks that contain saffron, which is thought to lighten the skin color of the fetus.[43] White is an auspicious color, symbolic of purity, and it was, and is, the color associated with the Brahmin, or priestly, varṇa.[44]

For our purposes, however, it is not white, or yellow or green, but black and red that are of greatest concern. This is because, in a symbolism recalling that of the ancient Hebrews,[45] in India red symbolizes passion, lust, vigor, strength, and fertility, on one hand,[46] and blood, killing, and death, on the other. Red is disliked by evil spirits, and in North India blood may be considered effective in protecting against and driving out demons, as well as in healing or in curing disease.[47] Among the Kol, a tribal group of Central India, red is believed to repel demons, and in part this is why red flags are found above nearly all shrines.[48] Quite appropriately, red is symbolic of the Kshattriya, or warrior, varṇa.

Black (or dark blue, with which it is linked) symbolizes the earth's surface and underworld, and is associated with demons (asuras), the dead, and pollution.[49] It is also the color that represents the Śūdras, lowest and most impure of the four varṇas, below which are only the untouchables.[50] One reads in early texts that when making certain vows a religious student should not eat dark food. Nor should he wear dark clothes, eat flesh, or have sexual intercourse.[51] Gonda,[52] writing of early Vishnuism, notes that black or dark blue is a color, or the color, of underworld forces, of spirits of the earth, vegetation, and fertility, and magic related to them. He also notes that souls of the ancestors are commonly closely linked with such spirits. He observes further that vegetation demons, as well as humans representing them, are frequently thought to have black faces. Among Buddhists, too, frightening gods are most commonly depicted as black or dark blue, sometimes as red, but never white or green.[53]

In modern India, black is an ominous color. It is a prediction of sickness and even death to dream of black things other than a black cow. It is a bad sign to encounter a black animal when a person sets out in the morning to accomplish something. Should he or she meet a person carrying something black, moreover, it would be wise for him or her to go back home and venture out anew without the burden of blackness. If a girl is wearing black clothes when she approaches puberty, it is a bad sign. In the Sind, if a man gives a black animal to obtain a bride, the marriage, it is believed, will not be happy. At a Hindu marriage, a bridegroom should not wear black clothing, and if a black animal enters the place where a wedding is being celebrated, it will end in tragedy. For auspicious rites, moreover, a Hindu would not use a black container.[54]

Black may also serve, however, to turn away evil.[55] This is shown in the preference for black animals in offerings to chthonian powers.[56] Black was also prominent in an attempt to expel the disease godling Marī ("Death")[57] after she had introduced cholera to the community of Kotah in Rajasthan early in the last century. After a rite and sacrifice were carried out and a decree of banishment issued, a vehicle was prepared for Marī. It was adorned with funeral symbols and painted black, and it was pulled by a team of black oxen. Bags of grain, also black, were placed in the vehicle as food for Marī. The vehicle was then driven across a river amid shouts from the people and admonitions from the priests that Marī was not to set foot in Kotah again.[58] People may suspend a black pot, or a white tile or white pot with black marks on it, in a cultivated field to protect the crop. In Gujarat, to protect the door of a new house and persons who enter it against the evil eye, people may place on the door an iron hook, a black thread, and a black oily smear from a representation of Hanumān.[59] The iron in this case is not just something on which to hang things but, as a black metal, is in its own right a protection against evil.[60]

Black is also used by Hindus on their persons to protect against evil. They may, for example, wear black charms. Many people in South India put lampblack on their eyelids both to protect themselves against the evil eye from others and to keep themselves from casting evil glances.[61] Indians may smear lampblack beneath the eyes of a child or on those of a bride and groom at their wedding because black is disliked by evil spirits. When a pregnant woman is about to deliver her infant, she may mark herself with black to keep away the demon who brings on prolonged labor.[62] In South India, it is obligatory that men who undertake a pilgrimage to the noted Aiyappan temple in Kerala wear black clothes. This is apparently done to protect them while in an unsafe jungle they must pass through.[63]

As Brenda Beck[64] has observed in her study of South Indian color symbolism, the two colors black and red may be used together, and when they are, the context—for example, witchcraft and struggles with demons—is one of unruly behavior, heating and strongly polluting. From our perspective, it is significant not only that killing and death are highly polluting in Hinduism (they are, as well, in Jainism and Buddhism), but also that foods may be banned because they are of colors that symbolize blood, killing, or death.

The Urd Bean

The remains of *Vigna mungo* have been found at sites in Maharashtra in levels dating from the second millennium B.C.[65] This shows that it was an ancient cultigen in the Indian subcontinent. Moreover, there is linguistic evidence that *maśa* was an early Dravidian word that found its way into the Sanskrit language.[66] Maśa is not mentioned in the *Rig-veda*, earliest of the Vedic records, though it may have been included under the general term *dhānya* ("grains").[67] Maśa is, however, included in the *Atharva-veda* and subsequent Vedic texts.[68] Its seed came to serve as a unit of weight, whose name, *mas*, derived from the Sanskrit *maśa*.[69] In later times, the term *maśa* was also used for a coin.[70]

In nutritional terms, one can make a strong case in favor of urd, for it is an excellent high-protein food whose value is enhanced by marked anticholesterolic qualities. Ancient Indian texts suggest that maśa, like the fava bean in the Greco-Roman world, played a significant dietary role, because it was among the most common pulses in records of the Vedic period (1500–800 B.C.?) and was also popular in early Buddhist and Jain works.[71] One reads of maśa gruel, maśa porridge, and maśa cakes as everyday food in ancient India. Though, as today, it had the reputation of being difficult to digest,[72] maśa seems to have labored under no other stigma in the secular life of people. In this regard, the role of maśa in ancient India was different from the role of the fava bean among the Pythagoreans, for the latter were expected to avoid fava beans altogether.

In India, according to Crooke,[73] the "bean" and "pea" do not seem to possess any special sanctity. Their place, he observes, is taken by *Vigna mungo*, which is used in rites of many kinds. In ancient India, this bean fell into the category of black foods because of its typically black seed coat.[74] This is still the case in modern India. In Gujarat early in this century, for example, Hindus included urd ("black pulse") among the black things that must be offered to a Brahmin to counter the evil influence of Śani (Saturn), which is regarded as a black and evil planet.[75] Since Saturday is associated with Śani and is thus a sinister day—inauspicious for such things as taking an oath, starting out on a trip, plowing, wearing new clothes, or shaving—it is then that offerings are generally made to

Śani.[76] Thus, the offering of urd in Gujarat was made on Saturday, which was described as a bad and black day when the best thing any person could do is eat urd. Among the other usual offerings made to Śani, it should be noted, are sesame and salt,[77] and for similar reasons, to be discussed in more detail below. Furthermore, the metal associated with Śani is iron, which, as has been mentioned, is a black and evil metal. The lamp used in propitiating Śani, for example, is always made of iron, and Brahmins may make gifts to Śani of iron nails and iron plates.[78] Śani's image, moreover, is the only image of a Hindu god made with iron, but it is not permitted in the shrine of family gods.[79]

It is appropriate that black urd seed has also been associated with Rāhu,[80] a fictitious planet and sky demon who brings on eclipses. Hindus believe that Rāhu's shadow is polluting, and before winnowing and measuring grain they take into account Rāhu's position in the sky.[81] During an eclipse, moreover, they make loud noises to drive Rāhu away. In addition, Hindus take special actions to guard against pollution from an eclipse and, if need be, to remove that pollution (e.g., by bathing in a sacred stream, washing clothes, and throwing out clay vessels and food that were in a house during the eclipse).[82] Pregnant women are in special danger from eclipses, because eclipses may bring on deformities in the children they bear. To avoid this, they take various precautions, such as avoiding work and exposure during an eclipse and adhering closely to certain religious bans.[83]

Of special interest has been the use of maśa in rites of the dead (śrāddha).[84] This association is reported in ancient texts,[85] and it persists in modern India. Crooke,[86] for one, has noted the association of urd with death, blackness, and offerings to ancestral spirits. Among the Kol tribe of Central India, black urd is commonly scattered about the place where a human body has been cremated, an act carried out as protection against evil spirits (bhūta).[87] In modern North India, whole urd seed is prominent among the foods prepared during the time when people are polluted by death.[88] In light of the above, it is understandable that, at a Brahmin rite for the dead in modern Gujarat, Yama, lord of the dead, was offered "black pulse" (urd) on a black cloth.[89]

Crooke also describes a ritual in Uttar Pradesh, held when a new village or hamlet is being created, in which urd is used to capture and confine a village ghost so that it cannot injure the village or its crops and herds.[90] In a similar vein, one notes that a Hindu exorcist may cast urd seed on the body of a possessed person in an effort to drive out an evil spirit.[91]

The ancient association of maśa beans with darkness and death also means that they were considered unacceptable for certain ritual uses. Though maśa beans, because of their impurity, served to remove impurity from a man's head,[92] they were inappropriate for offering to higher deities.[93] Vedic texts reveal that offerings of maśa were not made;[94] that the use of maśa for sacrificial purposes was censured;[95] that substitutes might be made of various beans but not maśa, which was specifically banned as not suitable for sacrifice;[96] that for offerings made on a daily basis, maśa was banned "even if nothing else is available;"[97] and that prior to the start of a fast on the new-moon day, maśa, along with such unacceptable items as meat, salt, and honey,[98] was not to be consumed.[99]

For modern South India, Eichinger Ferro-Luzzi[100] has provided certain information that does not fit with the ancient picture sketched above and some that is clearly in accord with it. She notes, on one hand, that urd, in a sprouted, raw form or in one dish or another, is among South Indian temple offerings; that, like sesame, it is among the strengthening, energy-producing foods;[101] and that in Tamil Nadu, as a result, Hanumān, the essence of strength, is offered a spicy cake (vaṭai) made of urd, which provides more energy than any other pulse.[102] On the other hand, a Brahmin lady pointed out to Eichinger Ferro-Luzzi[103] that the use of urd in offerings to Hanumān is determined more by the pulse's color than by its energy-enhancing qualities. She also pointed out that the pulse represents the demon-lord Rāvaṇa, whom, as punishment for his offenses, Hanumān caused to be reborn in the form of urd seed. Since demons are associated with darkness and impurity, the offering of urd vaṭai to Hanumān cannot be seen as an indication that urd enjoyed full acceptability in this regard. There is, moreover, a clear South Indian ambivalence about offering urd to the gods, because its blackness, the color of death, may be disturbing and terrifying. Thus in Tamil Nadu, urd vaṭai may be offered to deities of all sorts. On the other hand, certain Kanarese Brahmins, though they will offer urd vaṭai in rituals for the dead, refuse to offer it to deities. In a similar vein, other informants replace urd with chick peas in making vaṭai for the gods. Still other informants say that, if chick peas are not available, they might use urd in a vaṭai offering. However, this could be done only if the cake were made different in appearance from a funeral cake by leaving out the central hole typical of such cakes.[104]

In Vedic India, there was also an association of urd beans with passion. For example, early Ayurvedic writers such as Charaka (?A.D. 80–180?) and Suśruta (c. A.D. 350) identified urd, among other things, as heating, aphrodisiac, and sperm producing.[105] Equally important, urd beans were tied to love, fecundity, and the bearing of male offspring. Thus, Stutley and Stutley[106] have noted that beans were used in Indian love-charms. Certain accounts tell of a pregnant woman being given two maśa beans to consume in order to assure a male child.[107] One of these, in the *Āśvalāyana Gṛhya-sūtra*,[108] tells of a woman being given curd in which two beans and one barley grain had been added for each handful of curd. "To his question why dost thou drink? . . . she should thrice reply 'Generation of a male child! Generation of a male child!'" The barley grain in the curd was symbolic of a penis, and the two beans, it is said, of testicles—the latter a symbolism mentioned for *Vicia faba* among the Pythagoreans.[109] In what are remarkable survivals, in South India a modern Ayurvedic doctor asserted that fried urd powder mixed with milk increases a man's semen production.[110] In North India, moreover, certain of R. S. Khare's informants linked urd with masculinity and male offspring. Khare[111] has emphasized, however, that once urd has been split it changes from inauspicious to auspicious. His studies show further that its inauspicious form serves in death ceremonies, and its auspicious form, in marital food transactions. Writing of South India, however, Eichinger Ferro-Luzzi[112] notes that, since the splitting of pulses prior to cooking implies contact with water, split pulse is ordinarily avoided in temple offerings, as in a cake made of rice and urd.

As for the hot-cold classification of urd, I would note first that Rizvi,[113] writing of Bangladesh, reports that both the color of a food and its physiological effect on humans are useful in understanding the basis of its classification in terms of the hot-cold system.[114] Eichinger Ferro-Luzzi,[115] from the perspective of Tamil Nadu, puts the matter in terms of four sensory traits involved in the hot-cold system. Color is one of them, with white being cold; red, hot; and black, neutral.[116] Energy production is another, with energy-rich foods such as honey, oil, and flesh food tending to be hot. Gustatory sensations—for example, dryness or burning, such as that provided by spices—are a third trait. Visible water content, her

fourth trait, may lead to a food with high moisture content being classified as cold. Problems may arise, however, when a food possesses some
qualities that contribute hotness, and others, coldness, such as a juicy red
tomato. This, it seems, may be the case with urd. The blackness of its
seed contributes a neutral or cold quality, while its energy-producing trait
contributes a hot quality. The scanty information I have uncovered on
urd as hot or cold does not permit a generalization. It could be, however,
that the different weight people give to its blackness and its ability to
produce energy[117] may have led urd to be regarded mainly as hot in Gujarat, Punjab, and the Delhi area,[118] but mainly as cold in Coimbatore
District, Tamil Nadu.[119] In any case, it is not the hotness or coldness of
urd that is of primary importance to us here. Instead, we are concerned
with its association with impurity, death, and the underworld.

Sesame

As for sesame (*Sesamum indicum* or *Sesame orientale;* Sanskrit: *tila*), various
places have been suggested as its primary center of domestication,
though Africa and India have long been the strongest candidates.[120] Certain recent studies[121] support India as the place of domestication. Whatever may have been the case, sesame seems to have been cultivated there
at least since the time of the Indus Valley civilization.[122] It is also mentioned in Vedic records from the *Atharva-veda* onward, often together
with beans (maśa).[123] The ancient literature reveals that sesame was prepared in various ways, such as in gruel and porridge. It also suggests that
sesame oil (*tailam*) was the most highly regarded vegetable oil.[124] Sesame
seed and oil also served in ritual, with the seed serving especially in ceremonies in honor of the dead ancestors.[125] Because of this, sesame seeds
have been called such names as *homa-dhānya* ("sacrificial grain") and *pitṛi-
tarpaṇa* ("oblation offered to deceased ancestors").[126] One reads in the
Laws of Manu:[127] "I will now fully declare what kind of sacrificial food,
given to the manes . . . will serve. . . . The ancestors of men are satisfied
for one month with sesamum grams . . . [and] masha [maśa] beans . . .
which have been given according to the prescribed rule." In the *Āpastamba
Dharma-sūtra* (?500 B.C.–A.D. 200),[128] in turn, sesame, beans (maśa), and
roots are among the items to be offered at śrāddha rites, and meat, too,
was provided to the ancestral spirits. The *Āśvalāyana Gṛihya-sūtra* indicates
that, in funeral rites honoring the dead, sesame seed should be put into

three sacrificial vessels, which contain kuśa grass and holy water, with this prayer: "O Tila, sacred to Soma, created by the gods during the Gosava (the cow-sacrifice, not now permitted), used by the ancients in sacrifice, gladden the dead, these worlds, and us."[129] Sesame seed and oil were also made use of in ritual directed to underworld spirits and deities, such as Yama, lord of the dead, who, indeed, has been credited with creating sesame. Its associations with death and impurity are probably why, in the *Laws of Manu,* a person is advised not to eat food containing sesame seeds after the sun has set, just as he is advised not go anywhere unpurified after eating a meal.[130] At the same time, sesame seed and oil were used in appeasing and averting evil and in removing sins. They served in gaining fame, success, and a long life. They were also employed in love magic and in connection with the birth of children.[131] The use of sesame oil in propitiating rats and mice, to reduce the damage they did, is attributed by Gonda[132] to the chthonian nature of these animals. Gonda[133] also notes that sesame and sesame seed were tied to Lakshmī, goddess of good fortune and prosperity and wife of Vishnu. He notes further that the goddess Gaurī ("Yellow" or "Fair"), one of Shiva's wives who was associated with the harvest, was honored with offerings of sesame seed. Gonda reports further[134] that at one of Vishnu's festivals, with a symbolism reminiscent of ancient Greece, people anointed themselves with sesame oil to bring good luck and avoid evil.[135] I wonder whether, as is true in South India today,[136] the sesame used on auspicious occasions was a white variety of sesame or sesame from which the seed coat had been removed to make it white.

In any case, the association of black sesame with Śani in some places[137] is especially appropriate. Śani is an inauspicious deity who is referred to as dark and evil eyed and is ordinarily depicted as dressed in black (or dark blue) and riding atop a vulture, his vāhana ("bearer" or "vehicle").[138] Eichinger Ferro-Luzzi,[139] writing of South India, notes that the black crow represents Śani (Figure 37).[140] Śani is believed to have a bad effect on the lives of people. To counter this, such things as a black animal, black gram (urd), black sesame, black cloth, and iron (black metal) may be offered to this god.[141] Margaret Stevenson,[142] writing of Gujarat, observes that if a person suspects an evil influence from Śani, he may counter it on Saturday, the day on which Hanumān (the monkey lord) vanquished the oppression of Śani. Among the things an aggrieved person should do on Saturday is to make an offering to Hanumān that in-

37. The god Śani (Saturn) riding on a black crow (from Thomas, 1961).

cludes black gram. As an alternative, an astrologer may require him to make an offering to a Brahmin, including three of the blacks mentioned above (urd, cloth, iron) or a dark blue stone called Śani. Thus, in the Gujarat case, black sesame and black urd are both involved in offerings intended to free people from the evil influence of a dark planet and deity. In North India, too, offerings to avert the misfortune brought on by Śani are black. Among the offerings are sesame, black salt, charcoal, and water buffalo. Such offerings, however, are considered bad signs, and only the lowest group of Brahmin priests will accept them.[143]

In antiquity, the ritual use of sesame might involve the seed of wild plants. In the *Taittirīya Saṃhitā*,[144] an offering of wild sesame groats is made to appease Rudra. Rudra was a Vedic god who had two sides, one merciless, harmful, and disease-causing, the other, kindly and healing.[145] In the passage in question, Rudra is identified as the fire and is associated with Agni, god of fire, whose element is the earth.

Unhulled sesame seed may vary in color from white or yellowish-white to black, with a range of intermediate colors.[146] In ancient India, however, sesame seed, like urd, was included among black foods.[147] In a rite to stimulate the growth of a Vedic man's hair, which was likely black, the "medicine-man" who applied the mixture to the sufferer's head was required to be dressed in black. He was also expected to have consumed black food such as beans and sesame.[148] This likely derives from the fact that varieties of cultivated sesame with black seed were far more common in India than varieties of sesame with white seed.[149] One wonders whether there was also deliberate selection for black seed because of its reputation for yielding the best-quality oil for medicinal purposes. This reputation is found in modern India.[150] It was also known in antiquity, for one finds in the medical treatise of Suśruta (c. A.D. 350) the statement that the black variety of sesame is best in terms of its efficacy, followed by the white variety, whereas the remaining varieties are inferior.[151] This is similar to a statement in the *Bhāvaprakāśa*, a medical work (A.D. 1600) based largely on Vedic texts, which, when comparing wild, white, red (or brown), and black sesame, notes that people consider black sesame "best" or "best suited for medicinal uses." That work also observes that black-seeded sesame yields the largest amount of oil.[152]

In modern India, which is by far the largest producer of sesame in the world, one finds a pattern remarkably similar to that of antiquity. One reads, for example, that sesame seeds (and flowers) may be used when death is near. Black sesame may be used in attempt to stave off death, to remove the contagion of death from a gravely ill person.[153] Margaret Stevenson[154] writes of the Hindu belief that if a man were to die in a raised bed he would return as an evil spirit. Thus, when he is near death, his mattress is placed on the ground nearby. This is not ordinary ground, but ground that has been sanctified by plastering it with dung from a cow, sprinkling it with Ganges water, and then scattering on it darbha grass, barley, and sesame seed—all commonly used in rites for the ancestors. In addition, sesame commonly serves in śrāddha rites. One example involves purifying the śrāddha site by scattering sesame seed and barley on the ground, a practice known already in antiquity.[155] Sesame seed is used, along with other ingredients such as rice and honey, in funerary balls or cakes (piṇḍa), which are offered to dead ancestors. It may also be used in making cakes in the form of cows (tiladhenu), which may be given to relatives and friends who attend a funeral or may be presented to a Brahmin.[156] It is also significant that sesame seeds are used in six acts carried out at certain Hindu festivals for purposes of atonement: "tilavapi, 'throwing out the seeds'; . . . tilaprada, 'offering the seeds to the dead'; . . . tilahomi, 'making a burnt offering of the seeds'; . . . tilodvarti, 'bathing in water containing the seeds'; tilasuayi, 'anointing the body with the pounded seeds'; . . . [and] tilabhuj, 'eating the seeds.'"[157] Crooke writes that when a satī (a widow or wife who sacrifices herself) approaches her funeral pyre she holds in her hand some black sesame seed. She also has in her hand some kuśa,[158] a grass that serves in funerary rites and in offerings to assure the immortality of ancestral spirits.[159] It is thus fitting that the word tilanjalī, which derives from tila for "sesame" (and had the original meaning of "a handful of water mixed with sesame, an offering to deceased ancestors or ancestral spirits"), now has the meaning of "to bid a final good-bye . . . to give up, to abandon."[160] There is also a Hindi word, tilasmā, which means "magic, magical spell, talisman."[161]

Also of relevance are the observations that South Indians do not use black sesame seed for auspicious ceremonies (weddings are auspicious, funerals inauspicious);[162] that in Tamil Nadu a sterile woman is urged to consume sesame oil, which is "hot," to stimulate sexual activity and fertility;[163] and that, because sesame seed stimulates passion, people in Tamil Nadu may have to avoid it for the time being.[164] Also notable in Tamil Nadu is the fact that sesame seed, which has particular influences in bestowing life and fertility, plays a role in rituals, including ones associated with ancestral spirits.[165] One reads further that in Gujarat an ancestral spirit may be welcomed with the casting of sesame seeds toward it, and that sesame flowers are acceptable as offerings for ancestral spirits but never for the gods.[166] Eichinger Ferro-Luzzi[167] suggests that it is because seeds symbolize life that sesame seed is a fitting offering to the ancestors, who hope for a continued existence.

Among the Nayars of Malabar, it is believed that the ghost of a dead person clings to the mourners, and that it can be driven away by rubbing the mourners with oil to which sesame seeds have been added.[168] Furthermore, in Marathi myths, sesame and urd are among the five grains offered to or associated with the god Shiva.[169] I wonder whether this is because Shiva is associated with the unknown, with ruin and death as well as with sex and rebirth. If so, the color symbolism would be in keeping with that of the hungry black dog, Shiva's frequent companion who feeds on living humans.[170]

Of particular interest are M. Stevenson's observations based on field experiences in Gujarat. She notes, in a section entitled "The Desire for a Son," that, when no child has been born in a family or when a family has had bad luck and persistent illness, family members, especially women, may carry out an elaborate ceremony in an effort to propitiate the angry ancestor thought responsible for the family misfortunes. The ceremony is related to the dead, and thus it is held away from home, such as at a temple, sacred fig-tree, or riverbank. It is also held on the blackest, most sinister day of the month. Part of the ceremony involves offering to 13 Brahmins 13 pots filled with black seed, such as black oil-seed (e.g., sesame) or black pulse (urd), though the entire affair is so black and inauspicious that it may be difficult to find Brahmins willing to accept the gift. Also of note is the role of sesame on the day the winter solstice (*makara saṁkrānti*) is celebrated (sometime between the 12th and 14th of January). This is an auspicious, joyous time when a festival is held marking the end of a period of many months (July–January, the night of the gods) during which the gods are asleep and demons are abroad to wreak evil on humans. The day is a time of purification, when men are required by their scriptures to take a morning bath in cold water and to clean their mouths, not with their ordinary tooth-stick, but by chewing sesame seed. In addition, it is the luckiest day of the year for making a pledge of marriage, as well as the most important day of the year for giving alms—among which sesame seed and sugar play a significant role. Gifts of sugar or sugar cane are made on that day. Gifts of sesame seed, a black earthenware pot containing green gram, and clothes are also made, if possible to the best of Brahmins but otherwise to the first beggar one encounters. In addition, people make balls of sesame and treacle in which they secrete a coin, and give them to beggars.[171] Though the broader meaning of the day is not mentioned, there is a report that on January 14, in an effort to foster good luck, recently married brides in Poona (Pune) wear necklaces made with sesame seed encrusted with sugar.[172]

Meat

The history of ahimsa, vegetarianism, and meat eating[173] in India has been described by others.[174] Here I would note only that, in early Vedic India, eating meat on sacrificial and other occasions was the prevailing pattern, even among Brahmins. Starting about 500 B.C., however, the practice of killing and eating animals came into conflict with the concept of ahimsa, which was popularized by Jains and Buddhists.[175] The concept of ahimsa was gradually accepted by Brahmins over the next millennium, and they came to be major advocates of the concept. This is made very clear in the *Institutes of Vishnu*,[176] which was composed from 100 B.C. to A.D. 500: "Meat cannot be obtained without injuring an animal, and the murder of animals excludes the murderer from heaven, therefore must be avoided. . . He who gives his consent to the killing of an animal, he who cuts it up, he who kills it, the purchaser and the seller, he who prepares it, he who serves it up, and he who eats it, all these are denominated slaughterers of an animal. . . He who transgresses not the law and eats not flesh . . . is beloved by men and remains free from disease. . ."

Nevertheless, the conflict over the needs for animal sacrifice and those of ahimsa continued for many centuries, with the fifth chapter of the *Laws of Manu*[177] presenting a broad range of views in the matter. On one hand, members of respectable castes were permitted to eat meat at times of sacrifice to deities and in śrāddha rites.[178] On the other hand, killing was identified as a polluting act, like sexual intercourse and consumption of alcoholic beverages; and the rejection of meat was encouraged:

"The consumption of meat (is befitting) for sacrifices," that is declared to be a rule made by the gods . . . He who eats meat, when he honours the gods and manes, commits no sin, whether he has bought it, or himself has killed (the animal), or has received it as a present from others.

There is no sin in eating meat, in (drinking) spirituous liquor, and in carnal intercourse, for that is the natural way of created beings, but abstention brings great rewards.[179]

He who injures [harmless] beings from a wish to (give) himself pleasure, never finds happiness, neither living nor dead. . . Meat can never be obtained without injury to living creatures, and injury to sentient beings is detrimental to (the attainment of) heavenly bliss; let him therefore shun (the use of) meat . . .

[In a similar vein,] to persist [in using meat except for sacrifice] is . . . a proceeding worthy of Râkshasas [a non-Aryan people who in Hindu myths are sometimes represented as demons]; [and] A twice-born man who knows the law, must not eat meat except in conformity with the law; for if he has eaten it unlawfully, he will, unable to save himself, be eaten after death by his (victims).

[If a Brahmin] has a strong desire (for meat) he may make an animal of clarified butter or one of flour (and eat that); but let him never seek to destroy an animal without a lawful reason.

The result of the controversy over meat eating is that India has become the greatest center of vegetarianism in the world, although two-thirds of all Hindus today are thought to be nonvegetarians in one sense or another.[180] Meat is eaten in India by most tribal people. It is also eaten by Moslems and many Hindus, and especially, but by no means exclusively, by members of low castes.[181] If such castes seek to raise their ritual status, however, they commonly give up the eating of meat and drinking of alcoholic beverages.[182] In addition, even members of nonvegetarian castes may ban meat at certain times in an effort to gain purity. They may do this prior to worshipping a god, on certain days of religious import, during the time of pollution following a death, at the time of a female initiation rite, or, for a mother, for seven days after the birth of her child, an event that is also polluting.[183]

Meat in general tends to be "hot" in the hot-cold classification of foods,[184] and it may be avoided for this reason. Thus, in Tamil Nadu, not only is meat defiled by death, but also, like alcoholic beverages and stimulants, it is thought to raise one's passions.[185] Many people of higher caste in Tamil Nadu believe that, because of their meat eating, persons of lower caste have more frequent sexual intercourse and produce numerous children.[186] One elderly Brahmin woman in Tanjore went beyond this. She argued that, because women of lower caste consume meat and other foods that are classified as hot, they are more readily aroused sexually and commonly become pregnant from extramarital sex. This, in turn, may lead to abortions, which are ordinarily regarded as sinful and are resented by supernatural forces. By contrast, she contended, women of higher castes, who do not eat meat, have no such problems.[187]

Most higher deities in India are inclined toward vegetarian food.[188]

This has not prevented many Hindus from making offerings of meat, or meat and alcohol, to certain lesser deities, among them village gods and mother goddesses. In addition, Hindus may make such offerings to demons, for they are already inflamed, unruly, and violent.[189] Indeed, Eichinger Ferro-Luzzi[190] tells the story of a demon who, as punishment for his hubris, was turned into a non-meat-eating bat and who ascribed his newly acquired weakness to the lack of meat in his diet.

Vaishnavas are noted for their commitment to ahimsa and vegetarianism in all parts of India. Indeed they are described by Jindel[191] as having a sort "of hatred for meat and eggs." Indeed, it is said that in North India vegetarianism is best viewed as a trait of Vaishnavas rather than of Hindus in general or even of Brahmins. It is so closely associated with them in that region that vegetarian food is considered "Vaishnava food," and vegetarian restaurants are known as Vaishnava restaurants.[192] At the templed town of Nathdwara in Rajasthan, where there is a strong Vaishnava presence, there are no slaughterhouses, and all killing of animals is banned, even for the goddess Kālī, to whom animal sacrifice is acceptable (Kālī is closely related to and often identified with Durgā). Even Moslems in Nathdwara will not eat meat, and they make a point of telling others that they are vegetarians.[193] In North India, the various incarnations of Vishnu are offered only vegetarian food. This is also true of Shiva, except in forms of Bhairava (a deity worshipped especially by untouchables). On the other hand, certain lesser deities may receive meat offerings, as do mother goddesses in the Śākta cults of the northeast. Śāktas (devotees of mother goddesses) also eat nonvegetarian food, though the many Śāktas who also worship Krishna (a vegetarian), eat only vegetarian food on the day of his birth. Moreover, when a Śākta gives up that commitment in favor of Vaishnavism or when a woman becomes a widow, the consumption of meat and fish is no longer permitted.[194]

In India today, Brahmins are mostly vegetarians, but it is difficult to generalize because meat may be acceptable to them on such occasions at śrāddha rites.[195] In addition, there are local and regional differences in Brahmin behavior regarding acceptable and unacceptable food and drink. Thus one finds Brahmin groups in Bengal,[196] Kashmir, and elsewhere who do consume fish and/or meat.[197] One also reads that early in this century in most large towns in Gujarat there were "hotels" with private access in the rear, where Brahmins could go undiscovered to obtain "red curry," as flesh dishes were designated. Should such Brahmins be detected, they would, of course, have been despised by orthodox Hindus.[198]

Because passion, strength, and martial skills are desirable qualities in warriors, however, they are permitted to consume meat and drink liquor.[199] Thus, in the same way that North Indians call vegetarian restaurants Vaishnava restaurants, in South India Tamils refer to nonvegetarian restaurants as military hotels because of the "warrior food" they offer.[200] Among the Rājputs, that caste of warriors and rulers of western, northern, and Central India, meat eating and wine drinking are believed to be essential if these warriors are to be altogether effective. Meat and wine, it is contended, stimulate the production of semen, which, in turn, contributes to courage and power and prepares Rājputs for battle. Meat and wine also stimulate passion, which, in turn, increases the birth rate, including the numbers of male offspring who, in time, become warriors.[201] One Rājput, referring to a poem, is quoted as saying: "Rajputs are very lusty, Sahib. It is because of their food and their drink. It makes them so that they have to have their lust, poor fellows."[202] One recent study[203] of vegetarians and meat eaters in India, all in apparent good health, failed to support such folk beliefs. The study did confirm that apparently healthy vegetarians in India have significantly lower vitamin B-12 levels (in this case in their seminal plasma) than apparently healthy meat eaters. Despite this, it found that, in the group of 50 men with normal sperm count and morphology, diet (vegetarian or nonvegetarian) had no significant effect on sperm count, sperm motility, or percentage of abnormal sperm.

Vegetarians, too, may eat meat, even though this is polluting, at the time of Holi,[204] that colorful Hindu festival. Mahadevan,[205] writing of the Telugu-speaking people of the Telengana region of Andhra Pradesh, says that, while it is regarded as impious to eat food of animal origin at certain other festivals, eating meat is permitted at Holi and Dassarā (a festive time of athletics and hunting, well liked by Kshattriyas). Holi is a noisy, boisterous time when the normal structure of social life is upset. Countenanced to some extent is lax behavior such as passion; sexual obscenity; noise and vulgar language and singing by children; aggressive behavior by women; certain acts of brutality by men; and the casting of colored powder and colored liquid at other people, including ones of higher status. In former times, mud, garbage, and even excrement might be employed.[206] Holi is a favorite festival of the Śūdras.[207] In a sense, everyone who participates in the festival becomes a Śūdra by indulging in polluting behavior of the sort stereotypically associated with them by members of upper castes.[208] From our perspective, however, any laxity in behavior relating to meat eating at the time of Holi is a temporary aberration. It represents a departure from the norm, a pollution that can be removed afterwards by rites of purification.

Hindus, in keeping with James George Frazer's "law of similarity,"[209] may extend their rejection of meat and blood to other foods. Thus, they may ban certain plants as food or temple offerings because their coats, flesh, or juice are similar to blood and meat in color. Members of the Baniya caste of the Punjab, for example, extend their meat prohibition to carrots, turnips, onions, and red lentils.[210] For similar reasons, beet roots and tomatoes are not served at Brahmin meals in Gujarat.[211] In a like manner, more orthodox Havik Brahmins in the hills of South India's west coast refuse to eat not only carrots, beet roots, and tomatoes, but pumpkins and radishes as well.[212] Ghāsi Dās, the reformer who established the Satnāmi ("True-Name") sect in Central India, required his followers to abstain from alcoholic beverages, meat, and, because they resemble blood in color, certain red vegetables such as tomatoes, chillies, and lentils.[213] The Pandits (Brahmins) of southern Kashmir seem to go a bit further. They explain their avoidance of red-colored vegetables (including tomatoes, carrots, and beet roots) by saying that such vegetables spring from "the blood of slain demons."[214]

It is interesting that red peppers (*Capsicum* spp.), New World domesticates, should come to be rejected in South India by some Hindus, especially Brahmins and other strict vegetarians, while forms of true pepper (*Piper* spp.), native domesticates, are respectable seasonings.[215] In South India, moreover, people distinguish between red chillies, whose color is linked to "heat, passion, and violence" (rājasik), and green chillies, which may or may not be spicier. Thus, red chillies, with one exception, seem never to be used in temple offerings in South India. On the other hand, green chillies, while not offered in Vaishnava temples, are often used in Shiva temples.[216] Not only color but also other characteristics of plants (e.g., form, texture) that suggest blood or flesh may lead them to be banned. One reads that, when rituals for vegetarian deities are carried out, certain Brahmins in South India refuse to eat vegetables that resemble meat in their stringiness (e.g., amaranth).[217] One also reads that jackfruit is seen in a similar light.[218] According to the Satnāmis, their ban on eggplant is based on the belief that it turns into meat. Members of certain Indian castes say the same thing about onions and potatoes.[219] Even the name of a plant may lead it to be prohibited. Thus, in certain temples at Mount Govardhan, a Krishna pilgrimage site near Mathura in Uttar Pradesh, Vaishnavas refuse to offer certain plant foods because their names suggest blood.[220]

Also related to the avoidance of flesh is the belief among some castes in North India that potatoes turn into meat.[221] Such thinking has led to potatoes and other roots being banned to Vaishnavas and to their being unsuited for offering to deities.[222] This recalls the Jain ban on vegetables that grow in a bulbous form—among them roots, mushrooms, and onions—which are believed to contain a multitude of living organisms.[223] It also relates to the Vedic belief that underworld forces may be embodied in roots, that roots are the property of these forces, and that offerings of roots may be made to ancestral spirits but pose dangers to humans.[224] Modern observers,[225] too, indicate that bans apply to all vegetables whose roots or stems grow in the form of a human head. This recalls the negative reaction of vegetarians in South India to the smashing of wax gourds (*Benincasa hispida*) and muskmelons (*Cucumis melo*) in symbolic blood offerings to village goddesses.[226] A further extension of this is the Jain view that "all breaking of fruits, nuts and vegetables" violates the concept of ahimsa.[227]

Alcoholic Beverages

Though alcoholic beverages were widely consumed in ancient India, there are repeated objections in Vedic texts to their use and bad effects.[228] Such objections have continued to the present day. Despite this, in modern India alcoholic beverages continue to be consumed freely by many tribal peoples, and even certain Hindus and Moslems use them, whether openly or secretly, regularly or on special occasions.[229] At the same time, alcoholic beverages are impure and unacceptable to Moslems and Jains. They are also unacceptable for Hindus of higher castes, especially Brahmins, as well as for other Hindus committed to avoiding pollution, especially Vaishnavas. Writing of Nathdwara in Rajasthan, Jindel[230] observes that Vaishnavas have an unyielding aversion to liquor, which, in their view, pollutes a drinker internally and makes him unfit for temple service. It is also notable that alcoholic beverages, or at least strong liquors, are generally classified as hot in the hot-cold scheme of things.[231] Thus their unacceptability for Hindus may rest on their ability to stimulate sex and immoderate behavior. This is because the loss of command over one's actions undermines a Hindu's chances of gaining spiritual release after death.[232] In addition, alcoholic beverages, at least in some cases, seem to be inherently impure and polluting, for which Hindus offer various explanations. One of these is that alcoholic beverages (particularly toddies) are handled by low-caste persons.[233] Other explanations are that, in brewing, insects are killed, which raises ahimsa objections similar to those against the eating of meat,[234] and that alcoholic beverages fall into the category of decaying matter, as shown by the common saying about liquor in Chhattisgarh in Central India: "It's a rotten thing."[235]

Salt

Among the world's peoples, salt enjoys a rich and varied symbolic role in everyday life and in ritual, as at times of sacrifice, divination, exorcism, birth, and death.[236] Views of salt, moreover, are not always consistent, nor have they been so among the peoples of India.[237] From one perspective, salt has been highly prized, "the best of all things," and Hindus in Gujarat may get up at dawn on New Year's Day to buy it for purposes of assuring good fortune for the coming year.[238] Salt or saline soil was often used in ancient rituals, such as in casting salt, which was symbolic of cattle, into the sacred fire in hopes that cattle numbers would increase.[239] From another perspective, salt—despite its white color when in a pure form—and salty foods, as well as sour, bitter, and pungent foods, have long been believed to be unclean because they stimulate passion.[240] Because of such views, salt was excluded in certain rituals mentioned in the Vedic Kalpa-sūtras.[241] One reads in the Gṛihya-sūtras, for example, that no saline food should be consumed for three nights of mourning (the impurity caused by death lasts for three nights)[242] or by a couple for three days and nights after marriage.[243] After the three-day abstinence by a couple, offerings are made to eliminate all evil forces that may be in the woman.[244] One also reads that a student who is undertaking certain religious vows should not eat saline, or saline or pungent, food.[245] Among the items identified in the Puranas as unsuited for offering to one's ancestors are salt (or certain kinds of salt); carrots, globular radishes, and red vegetable extracts (presumably because their color resembles flesh); and "the pulse called

Rājamásha" (urd because of its blackness?). Indeed, one list bans even things that resemble salt.[246]

In modern India, salt is believed to turn aside evil spirits and the evil eye, and it may serve in this way on various occasions.[247] In South India, for example, salt may be carried by someone and then cast into water while he or she repeats the words "Vanish, you evil eye, whosoever you may be."[248] Members of the Kol tribe believe that salt is effective against demons, and, partly for this reason, people sprinkle it over the spot where a body has been cremated.[249] In a similar manner, on "the great spirit day in October, Hindu women make marks with salt at the cross-roads,"[250] where—in India, as in widely scattered parts of the Old World—chthonic beings congregate.[251] Salt is also commonly used in charms in India. The Rautias of Bengal drive away the evil eye "by waving salt and mustard seed around a sick person."[252] In North India, people think that demons will flee from the bad odor of salt and mustard burned in a fire made with wood of the sacred neem tree.[253] Though Crooke provides no details on the practice, I suspect that similar thinking is also behind the common North Indian practice of burying Hindu ascetics in salt.[254] To return to the Kol, these people believe that, when a death has occurred in a dwelling, salt should not be added to food during the time of mourning. Nor should it be consumed by the chief mourner for an entire year following the death.[255] This is because salt is rājasik, which may lead Hindus to reject it on a temporary basis, such as in a female initiation rite, during periods of mourning, or at other times when ritual purity is sought.[256] In Gujarat, ordinary salt may be banned at times of fast.[257] In northwestern India, it may be avoided at other sacred times.[258] In rural Tamil Nadu, a woman, to counter her childlessness, may, among other things, feed and offer presents to Brahmins, visit holy men, eat sacred ash, and exclude salt from her diet.[259] In most Kerala temples, moreover, salt is not used in foods offered to the gods,[260] a practice reminiscent of the bans on salt in offerings to the gods in ancient Greece.[261] Pure salt, however, may be offered to village goddesses and to a few healing deities in South India.[262] It is likely that negative views of salt are also behind its avoidance by unmarried girls in Gujarat prior to or in connection with the great festival of Molākāta, held at the critical time in the annual cycle of life when the monsoon arrives and crops are sown.[263] At a North Indian wedding, on the other hand, salt may be waved about the heads of the bridal couple and buried as a charm close to the door of their house.[264] There is also a Gujarati practice, followed occasionally by a mother of the bridegroom, of scattering salt as she walks to the wedding ceremony. Her intention is to reduce any rudeness in the bridegroom's personality from that time onward.[265]

The periodic bans of salt by Hindus appear to have no clear biological advantage for those who observe them. Thus their origins are best sought in human thinking about purity and pollution.[266]

Mushrooms

R. Gordon Wasson[267] has argued that soma, a plant whose juice was used by Vedic Indians in preparing an exhilarating ritual beverage, was actually fly agaric (*Amanita muscaria*), a hallucinatory mushroom. If Wasson is right, we are dealing with a mushroom that was highly regarded, consumed by Brahmins, and even deified in ancient India. On the other hand, many peoples around the world associate mushrooms with decayed matter and regard them as little different from carrion and other "rotting, decaying, or dying" substances that disgust people and make them seek to keep these substances from entering their bodies.[268] Such views have also been common in India, where Hindus are vitally concerned with pollution brought on by dead and decaying things.[269] Thus, mushrooms were among the forbidden foods of the Dharma-sūtras (composed from about 500 B.C. to A.D. 600),[270] which group mushrooms with alliums as deriving from impure substances. They liken mushrooms to such disgusting or unlawful foods as excrement of a pig,[271] flesh of humans or carnivorous animals, food touched by crows or dogs, or the leavings of Śūdras. They are improper for a twice-born man to eat, and if he does so, penance is required and he may even become an outcast. If a person wishes to remain pure when he has eaten banned food unintentionally, he should vomit it up or quickly undergo purification.[272]

Though mushrooms are widely eaten in present-day India, their association with decay remains a concern to persons aspiring to ritual purity.[273] People of one North Indian village have a somewhat different perspective on mushrooms and pollution. They call mushrooms by a word meaning that they grow in places where dogs urinate. Since Brahmins look on dogs as unclean, this contributes to the impurity of mushrooms.[274] Another suggestion is that Brahmins may reject mushrooms because of their odor or because they are cooked like meat and have a flavor like meat.[275]

Conclusions

As we shall see, many scholars have had great difficulty understanding the Pythagorean ban on fava beans, in part because socio-religious ideas in the Mediterranean world changed so much that even in classical times the ban was commonly treated with amusement and scorn. This is not true of the Vedic ban on urd beans, which, with the ideas surrounding it, has enjoyed an amazing continuity up to the present day.

Certain genetically predisposed individuals in the Mediterranean world have long had a special disease risk when they consume fava beans,[276] and some scholars have suggested that it was in recognition of this that Pythagoras banned fava beans to his followers. There is, on the other hand, no special risk of disease in eating urd beans. As a result, the possibility of explaining the origin of the urd ban in such terms can be dismissed. Indeed, if the people of India had established a prohibition against eating any cultivated legume because of its danger to health, one would expect it to be the grass pea (Hindi: *khesari; Lathyrus sativus*) (Figure 38). Consumption of the grass pea can bring on the crippling disease lathyrism, a serious public health problem since antiquity, especially in North and Central India.[277] Of even more significance, Indian people have long associated this disease, which sometimes occurs in epidemic proportions, with consumption of *Lathyrus sativus*. Despite this, I can find no evidence that the grass pea was subject to ritual bans similar to those applied to urd.

All evidence, including that found in ancient texts, strongly supports the view that the bans on urd and the other foods we have considered in this chapter are related to and almost certainly derive from ancient Indian concerns with ritual purity, pollution, and spiritual well-being. It is of interest that these bans on foods have not necessarily been urged as general observances to be followed by entire classes, such as Brahmins, or religious groups, such as Jains, Hindus, or Vaishnavas. It is true that there has been pressure for such general bans on meat, alcoholic beverages, garlic and onions, and mushrooms, but apparently this has not been true of sesame and urd. The latter two, as whole seed, have been inappro-

38. Grass pea (*Lathyrus sativus*) (from Church, 1886).

priate to use only on certain occasions. In other forms, however, they may have been auspicious and, in any case, there has been no pressure that they be banned at all times by entire groups of people.

The ban on the urd bean in India goes back to antiquity, and one wonders whether Indian views of urd and prohibitions against eating it spread from outside or whether they developed in India. Did they derive from the Aryans, some other invading people, or from the Dravidians, who seem to have domesticated urd? The Vedic records reveal that the Aryans possessed clear ideas about purity and impurity, the symbolism of black, and the unsuitability of black for use in offerings to the gods. Since this fits so well with overall Vedic beliefs about the other foods we considered, one suspects that the Aryans carried all the beliefs with them when they arrived in India in the second millennium B.C. They may not have known urd before they entered India. Almost certainly, however, they had encountered other beans which, like urd, were dark in color. These may have been associated with death, the underworld, and impurity. The Aryans may have brought such ideas from the Indo-European homeland, or they may have acquired them during their migration across Inner Asia.

In this regard, I call attention to Ladizinsky's argument[278] based on plant morphology, cytology, and archeology—that the *fava bean* was in all likelihood first domesticated in Afghanistan. Even if it was not domesticated in Afghanistan, the fava bean may have been cultivated there before the time of the Aryan migration to India. Present-day cultivated fava beans in Afghanistan typically have small, roundish seeds that are brown-black in color,[279] and likely these were the sorts of beans the Aryans found there. It is possible that when the Aryans entered India, they simply extended negative views they already had of fava beans to urd, a small black bean they found cultivated by Dravidians. In a similar manner, they may have applied such views to the whole seed of sesame, another Indian domesticate that in Vedic texts shares with urd an association with the dead and the underworld.

7 The Color Black in the Pythagorean Ban of the Fava Bean (*Vicia faba*)

> the black-skinned [fava] beans . . . bounce high / under the
> whistling blast and the sweep of the winnowing fan . . .
> —Homer, *Iliad* 13.588–90

> I tell you too, as did Pythagoras,
> Withhold your hands from beans, a hurtful food.
> —Callimachus[1]

Introduction

Pythagoras, founder of an influential philosophical and religious movement in the ancient Greek world in the sixth century B.C., instituted a ban
on fava beans, though its initial form cannot be established with certainty.
The Pythagorean ban struck some ancient writers as bizarre. It was also
the object of scorn, and its origin, the subject of abundant speculation.
Though scholars have continued to speculate about it for more than two
millennia, the matter remains one of continuing debate today. In recent
decades, however, a new hypothesis, that the Pythagorean ban at least in
part was based on fear of the disease favism, has been gaining popularity
in some circles.[2] Thus a reconsideration of the entire matter is called for.[3]

This chapter represents the initial stage in my reconsideration. It focusses on the historical and ethnographic evidence on the Pythagorean
ban on beans. In carrying it out, I will first provide background on the
fava bean in the ancient Mediterranean world. Then I will present information on Pythagoras, the Pythagoreans, their bean ban, and the explanations for that ban advanced by ancient writers. This will be followed by
a review of historical evidence of fava bean use and avoidance among
other religious movements or on ritual occasions in ancient Greece and
Rome. Then, in the hope of shedding more light on the matter, I will
draw on my previous chapter, on urd, and on other sources to identify
parallels between ancient Greeks and ancient Indians in their percep-

192

tions of urd beans or fava beans. I do this in part because, despite the considerable geographic distance between Greece and India, important cultural similarities between ancient Greeks and Aryans, both of them Indo-European peoples, have long been noted by Indologists and others. Equally significant, the bean ban of India, unlike those of the ancient Mediterranean world, is known not just in the scanty records of antiquity. It can also be found in modern accounts, for it persists today in Hinduism, a religion in full vigor whose adherents number roughly 700 million people (1994 est.), or 80 percent of India's total population. My conclusions will be based on all of the above.

The Fava Bean in Antiquity

The fava bean is grown for food widely around the world today. In the Neolithic and Bronze Age, however, it was cultivated mainly in the region of its domestication (c. 7000–6500 B.C.?), somewhere from the Mediterranean area to Afghanistan, as well as in non-Mediterranean Europe.[4] As indicated in my chapter on urd, in all likelihood the fava bean was also cultivated in the mountains of northwestern India in antiquity. Nevertheless, it seems to have been unknown in most of that subcontinent prior to modern times. In a similar vein, the fava bean appears to have arrived in China only during the Yüan dynasty (A.D. 1271–1368), perhaps over the Silk Road.[5]

In addition to the fava bean, other legumes cultivated for human food in the ancient Mediterranean area included the lentil (*Lens escullenta* or *L. culinaris*), field pea (*Pisum arvense*), chick pea (*Cicer arietinum*), and grass pea (*Lathyrus sativus*).[6] Regardless of the others' eventual presence, the fava bean was "the bean" of antiquity, for it was not until after the discovery of the Americas that beans of the genus *Phaseolus* (most notably *P. vulgaris*, the common bean; and *P. lunatus*, the lima bean) were introduced to the Mediterranean area and Near East.[7] Thus in antiquity not only did the fava bean play a major role in the diet of various peoples, but it was also well regarded as food. The Romans, for example, considered fava beans to be healthy food, highly nourishing, and good for the digestion. Pliny[8] wrote of thick bean soup as "a delicacy of the table" that, though it was said to dull the senses and cause insomnia, "had a sanctity of its own in sacrifice to the gods." Macrobius wrote of the Romans offering thick bean soup and lard or fat bacon to the goddess Carna (who

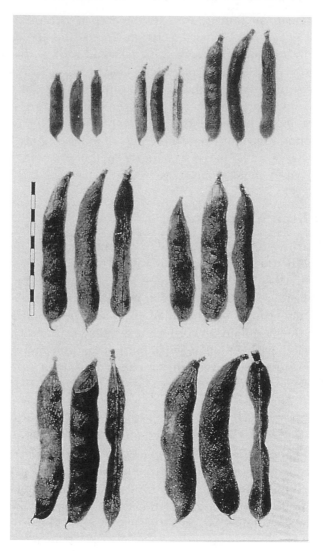

39. *Vicia faba,* type *minor,* compared with *Vicia faba,* type *major.*
a. pods of type *minor* (top row) and of type *major* (bottom row). The pods in the middle row are of type *equina,* sometimes *major equina.* Ruler length = 10 cm (from Hanelt, 1972a) *b.* Bronze Age seeds of type *minor* from Zitz in Brandenburg (left) and a modern seed of type *major* (right). Ruler length = 2 cm (from Schultze-Motel, 1972).

194

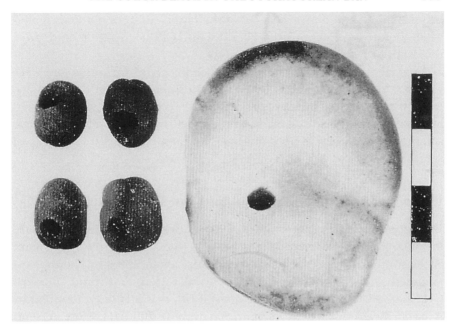

39. *b.*

cared for the vital internal organs of humans) on her holy day, the first day of June (known also as the Calends of the Beans), because these are foods that strengthen the body.[9] Ovid, on his part, wrote that the Romans consumed lard or fat bacon as well as beans mixed with spelt on that day because Carna was an early goddess who preferred the simple fare of ancient Latium. He noted further that those who ate the two foods together on her holy day were assured that nothing could injure their bowels.[10]

The fava beans of Pythagoras's day were quite different from the large, flat, light-buff-colored fava beans (type *major*) that the present-day Western reader is likely to know. For one thing, Neolithic and Bronze Age fava beans had much smaller pods and seed (type *minor*) (Figure 39), with roundish seeds common in the eastern Mediterranean area.[11] The fava beans uncovered in early levels at Jericho (Pre-Pottery Neolithic B and Middle Bronze Age), for example, are roundish and scarcely "larger than the largest peas" (*Pisum*).[12] The similarity in shape of the earliest Greek and Roman beans is indicated by the likely initial meaning of the Greek and Latin names for fava bean: "a round seed, a spherical body."[13] The elliptic, large-seeded forms (*major*) of the fava bean were not known anywhere before A.D. 500 or even later.[14] This is 1,000 years or more after the death of Pythagoras.

In ancient Greece, fava beans with seed coats of various colors were known.[15] Yet it is reasonably certain that the light-buff color of seed coats, which is recessive to black, appeared in quite recent times.[16] Thus Homer, in describing fava beans as black-skinned, may have been referring to the color that was typical in his day. This is an important fact to which I will return later.

Pythagoras, Pythagoreanism, and the Ban on Beans

Pythagoras lived from about 580 to 500 B.C. Born on the island of Samos, in Ionia, he immigrated to Magna Graecia (the area of Greek settlement at the southern tip of the Italian peninsula) about 530 B.C. There he established a philosophical-religious-political society at Croton (modern Crotone), a large and prosperous coastal city that had been founded by Achaean Greeks nearly two centuries before (c. 700 B.C.). Most present-day scholars believe that the Pythagoreans of Croton, or some of them, were members of a brotherhood characterized by communal organization and property. Whether or not this was so,[17] because of their political activities the Pythagoreans in Croton were suppressed by force about 450 B.C., and their organization was almost completely destroyed.[18] Despite this, Pythagorean societies continued to exist in Magna Graecia and elsewhere in the Greek world until nearly 350 B.C., when they became extinct. Even after that date, Pythagorean thought and legend persisted, and ultimately, about 100 B.C., there arose a Neo-Pythagorean movement which focussed mainly on mystical aspects of the Pythagorean way of life and which, starting in the second or third century A.D., was merged into Neoplatonism.

Pythagoras himself left no written works, or, if he did, none have survived.[19] Thus, persons studying Pythagoras are forced to rely on the writings of others. The earliest of these date back to about 400 B.C., a century after Pythagoras died.

Because interest in Pythagorean thinking persisted, because the movement was reborn, and because the man and his movement intrigued the ancients, sources span many centuries, to A.D. 400 and even later. Information from earliest times is scanty. There were also much invention and embellishment—to say nothing of plagiarism and outright forgery—over the centuries. Certain later writers even went so far as to identify the ingredients of the cakes supposedly consumed by Pythagoras.[20]

Understanding is also made difficult because some early writers had perspectives, philosophical or religious convictions, or agendas that made them uncritical supporters or strong critics of Pythagoras and his followers. Equally important was Pythagorean secrecy and the fact that sometimes Pythagoras spoke in mystical and symbolic terms. Also a problem is his having been regarded as a god already in his lifetime, with his true persona further obscured after his death by legends that came to surround him.

Some modern scholars follow the Neoplatonists Porphyry (A.D. 232–306) and Iamblichus (c. A.D. 250–330)[21] in saying that the early Pythagoreans were divided into two rival groups. One group was the *mathematici*, rationalists concerned with truth, mathematics, and scientific proof. The second group was the *acusmatici*, ritualists content merely with observing the *acusmata*, or *symbola*, the sayings of Pythagoras and the precepts taught by him, passed on initially by word of mouth.[22] Many of the Pythagorean acusmata have struck ancient and modern readers as strange,[23] and, indeed, Frazer[24] has pointed out that they represent superstitions of great antiquity and widespread geographic occurrence. This has led some modern scholars to consider Pythagoras not just a scientist but also a Greek shaman.[25] In any case, the Pythagorean bean ban is part of the acusmata, on which I focus, especially those relating to food and food behavior in antiquity.

The acusmata do not deal with commonsense knowledge. Instead, they represent rules of magic and ritual, some of them shared with Greek mystery cults such as that of Demeter and Persephone (Kore) at Eleusis.[26] The main concerns in the acusmata are with maintaining an individual's purity before the gods and with avoiding the dangers posed by magic and underworld forces.[27] The most conspicuous topic in the acusmata is sacrificial ritual,[28] which, as we shall see, relates to Pythagoras's ban on beans. The bean ban ultimately rests on his belief in the transmigration of souls;[29] the kinship of all living things[30] or at least those that may contain human souls;[31] and the wrongness of sacrificing animals of the latter sort.[32] In the dietary realm, such thinking led directly to Pythagorean bans on eating flesh.

Pythagorean views about the acceptability of flesh food are based on

the Greek tradition of a golden age, a state when humans lived in harmony with nature and enjoyed a just relationship with other living creatures.[33] One might expect persons who sought to emulate that ideal state
to become strict vegetarians, but ancient writers present a rich variety of
views on the patterns of flesh consumption by Pythagoras and his followers. Some say, without further qualification, that all flesh food was prohibited. Others insist that only certain organs or species were banned. Still
others—who seem to represent a minority view presented in a polemical
manner—say that Pythagoras did not institute bans on flesh at all.[34] Aristotle, among the earliest (fourth century B.C.) and most reliable observers,
said that Pythagoras did not ban flesh entirely but only that of certain
organs, such as the womb and heart, and that of a few animals.[35] Among
the views expressed by other early writers were the following: Pythagoras
abhorred killing as well as persons who killed. Thus, he not only rejected
the flesh of animals but also avoided butchers and hunters. He advised
his followers not to permit animals to be sacrificed to the gods and not to
worship at altars that had been stained with blood. He believed that, to
remain pure, one should avoid contact with births and deaths and refuse
the flesh of all animals that have died naturally, along with two fishes
(mullet and gurnard), eggs, and egg-bearing animals. One should also
observe the bans followed by persons who carry out mystic rites in
temples. Pythagoras limited his own diet to bread and honey, raw or
cooked greens, wine (only after dark), and, on rare occasions, fish. Pythagoras urged the most contemplative philosophers to give up animal
sacrifice, flesh eating, and wine drinking. Pythagoreans, on their part,
offered dried figs, cheese, and olive-cakes in sacrifice, but they avoided
animal foods during their entire lives. When in their own interest they
did offer an animal to the gods, they would merely taste it, permitting
them the illusion that they were innocent in the matter.[36]

It is clear from the above that Pythagoreans were not simple vegetarians whose views derived entirely from a high regard for all living beings.
The rejection of heart, brain, and egg, for example, is based on the view
that they are the origin of reproduction and life.[37] At the same time, all
Pythagoreans did not have the same behavior with respect to flesh food.[38]
According to Detienne, the most inflexible Pythagoreans made no flesh
offerings, ate no flesh food, and entirely avoided all intercourse with the
hunter and the cook-butcher-sacrificer (mageiros). The way of such Pythagoreans was one of austerity and rigidity in not only refusing to eat meat

but also in rejecting any association with killing and its practitioners. Their decision, Detienne insists, also entailed a rejection of the way the gods were approached in ancient Greek city-states—an approach that involved animal sacrifice and meat eating. This made such Pythagoreans deviants who set themselves apart from the politico-religious activities of Greek cities.

Other Pythagoreans, Detienne notes, were more subtle in their views of sacrifice and food. One example is their refusal to eat certain animal organs (heart, womb, brain) regarded as being "vital" and "seats of life." Another is their rejection of the flesh of certain animals. This was especially true of the plow ox, an innocent worker and companion of man. Yet they would eat animals they considered injurious or reprehensible (e.g., the pig, destructive because of its rooting and trampling). The way of these Pythagoreans, according to Detienne, was one of compromise with prevailing Greek ways, one that provided an opportunity to participate in, and perhaps to improve and rescue, civic life.[39]

Turning to the "famous, or notorious, taboo on beans,"[40] we find nearly universal agreement that it was observed by Pythagoras and the Pythagoreans.[41] It is also agreed that the ban was closely tied to their prohibitions relating to flesh. How did ancient writers explain this? Aristotle gave several reasons why Pythagoras may have recommended the ban on beans. One is that they resemble the universe in form. A second is that they are similar to "the gates of Hades" in that they alone are "unjointed." A third is that they are like genital organs. A fourth is that they are injurious. A fifth is they are associated with oligarchy through their use in elections cast by lot.[42] Since beans served in selecting persons for public office,[43] the Pythagoreans apparently viewed them as contributing to tyranny.[44] To ban beans for this reason, however, seems like an afterthought, perhaps a rationalization for an existing ban in terms of Pythagoras's hostility to the established political order.

The first of the reasons given by Aristotle, that beans resemble the universe, undoubtedly means that they were regarded as living matter.[45] All of the first three reasons, moreover, relate to life, reproduction, and death—critical events in the human life cycle that are surrounded by powerful, basic emotions. Various ancient writers make these associations more explicit in suggesting the following for the origin of the bean bans of the Pythagoreans: (1) that beans are flatulent and contain "the breath of life" and were produced at the creation of all things, when the earth was formed;[46] (2) that, in fact, they contain "the seed of man," are like testicles in their internal structure, and that, if chewed and exposed to sunshine, they even smell like semen;[47] (3) that birds who live around human habitations become sterile if they consume bean pods for any length of time, and that bean pods placed around the roots of young trees cause their shoots to wither;[48] (4) that one can obtain blood from beans in various ways, as by cooking them and exposing them to moonlight for several nights;[49] (5) that beans harbor souls of the dead, are suitable for the dead to eat, and are offered at rites in honor of the family dead;[50] (6) that beans (seed or flowers) can be transformed into female sexual organs, human heads, and even human beings;[51] (7) that one should avoid eating beans as much as one avoids eating human flesh;[52] and, indeed, (8) that eating beans is like eating the heads of one's father or parents.[53] Horace[54] pokes fun at such thinking by referring to beans as "the relations of Pythagoras." Writing in general terms, but apparently elaborating on one of Aristotle's observations about Pythagoras, Porphyry notes that beans are nearly alone among plants in their hollow, unjointed stems by which spirits may return from the underworld.[55]

Detienne[56] has presented an interesting analysis of the bean in the Pythagorean food system that draws on various of the above factors. In his view, the basic reason behind Pythagorean disgust for the fava bean is the last one in my list above, based on botany: the bean's ability, because of its lack of stem nodes, to play a special role in exchanges between this world and Hades, between the living and the dead. Detienne illustrates this with an apt quote from one of the sacred speeches of the Pythagoreans: "[Beans] serve as support and ladder for the souls [of humans] when, full of vigor, they return to the light of day from the dwellings of Hades."[57] In Detienne's view, the Pythagoreans derived all other reasons from the basic one. Among those reasons is the association of the bean with decay. This is buttressed by a myth that the bean, along with man, was the first to emerge from the original slime that characterized the universe.[58] Detienne provides another apt quotation: "At the time of the confusion that reigned at the beginning and origin of everything, when many things were mixed with the earth in germination and putrefaction, when little by little birth came to be and whole-formed animals were distinguished from plants which at that time germinated in the same decomposition, man was formed and the bean grew."[59] Despite its association with death and decay, Detienne observes, the bean also partakes of the living. This is illustrated by tales of the transformation or resemblance of beans, after exposure or burial, to blood, testicles, female sexual organs, or human heads. Thus, for Pythagoreans the bean represented an impure thing symbolic of death, as well as a terrible blend of blood and sex.[60] The bean was considered the "twin of man." Thus, eating beans was like eating human flesh, even cannibalism of the most debased sort (eating the heads of one's father or parents). Cannibalism, along with incest with one's mother, murder, temple theft, and dung-eating, was among the most polluting and disgusting acts to the ancient Greeks. According to one Greek tradition, the abandonment of cannibalism was a critical factor in the advance of mankind from primitive barbarism.[61]

Particularly troublesome to some observers is the Pythagorean likening of eating beans to eating the heads of one's father or parents. This is clarified by Onians[62] in his discussion of the ancient Greek perception of the human head. The head was seen as life or the source of life, the receptacle of the human soul, and as being holy or deserving of high honor. Onians notes that the ancient Greeks also regarded the human head as the beginning, the source of generation. This, he contends, is why the Pythagoreans equated the head to beans, for they, too, contain the principle of life, the soul, which should not be eaten.

As for the injuriousness of beans, some early writers simply say that beans are a troublesome food.[63] Others identify the trouble, as seen by Pythagoras or the Pythagoreans, as flatulence, belching, stomach upset, disturbed sleep, bad dreams,[64] and dull senses, because all of these are unsuited to a sage, a seer, or a soul seeking truth.[65] Artemidorus Daldianus, on his part, makes a general statement that recalls the widespread views of Old World peoples about the unsuitability of entering holy places after eating smelly onions and garlic. Beans, Artemidorus says, are a symbol of discord because of the shameful flatulence they bring on, and are "excluded from all festivals and holy places."[66] Plutarch, on the other hand, questions whether persons practicing holy living avoid beans and other legumes because (1) their flatulence creates abundant feces, rather than the cleanness and lightness needed for this lifestyle, or (2) because flatulence stimulates sexual passions.[67]

Also of note are the tales that Pythagoras met his death by refusing to pass through a bean field in order to evade enemies. According to one or another of these tales, Pythagoras found himself at the edge of the bean field with a group of his followers (1) when fleeing from enemies who had set fire to their place of meeting in Croton ("the house of Milo"), or (2) during a battle in Sicily when Syracusans had turned the flank of the army of Acragas (modern Agrigento), with which the Pythagoreans fought. Then Pythagoras was either (1) killed on the spot or (2) captured and put to death. Other versions of the house-burning story have Pythagoras making good his escape or have him absent altogether. Though such tales of Pythagoras's death are thought to be fabrications,[68] if true, what might Pythagoras's reasons have been for refusing to go through the bean field? Was he, as the ancients thought, unwilling to injure or tread on beans because they represented living matter, souls of the dead? Can there have been some other reason behind his refusal? Was the idea for banning beans his, or did he adopt it from some other individual or group?

Other Evidence of the Avoidance of Beans in Ancient Greece and Rome

In the Greco-Roman world, bans on eating beans were not restricted to the Pythagoreans. In seeking understanding, therefore, one is well advised to look beyond the Pythagoreans, to consider attributing the banning of beans to members of other cult groups, because, as noted by Burkert,[69] such cult groups are generally older than Pythagoreanism.

In the Cult of Demeter

One such cult group is that of Demeter and her daughter Persephone/ Kore. If Gimbutas is correct, the Demeter cult has its roots in mother goddess cults that go back to Neolithic times in eastern and southeastern Europe.[70] Demeter is a goddess of fertility, of the earth. She is also a chthonian deity with power over death and the dead. A bean ban, moreover, was associated with her cult in more than one place in Greece.[71] In her renowned Eleusinian mysteries, initiates, at least in later times, were required to abstain from beans and certain other foods, apparently on a temporary basis. Similar bans are mentioned for the Haloa, a harvest festival in honor of Demeter, Persephone, and Dionysus (god of vines).[72] It is of special interest that among the foods banned at the Eleusinian mysteries or Haloa festival were beans; eggs; egg-laying animals, including domestic fowl, especially the cock; the flesh of animals that had died naturally; fishes or certain kinds of sea creatures, among them crabs and the red mullet (*triglē*); pomegranates; and apples.[73] Porphyry explains the ban on initiates eating domestic fowl in terms of chthonic concerns.[74] He observes that Demeter is an underworld goddess to whom a cock is consecrated, put under a taboo. He says further that it would be inappropriate for persons seeking freedom from terrestrial concerns and association with celestial deities to eat birds of any sort. He explains the remaining food bans he identifies (on beans, fishes, apples, and pomegranates) in similar terms. To touch these is as defiling as touching a corpse or a woman who has recently delivered a child.[75]

The mullet, which was among the forms of sea life avoided by the Pythagoreans, is an omnivore and was believed to have a special taste for smelly, impure food and to eat human corpses and dead fish.[76] The association of the pomegranate with the dead may strike the observer as curious, for the pomegranate serves widely in fertility rites in the Old World.[77] In the ancient Greek case, however, the symbolism of the pomegranate derived from a story of the goddess Persephone. Persephone, while a captive in Hades, had been made to eat a pomegranate seed (food of the dead), which, once tasted, drew her back there for part of every year.[78]

Freese[79] includes honey among the foods banned at the Haloa festival. In ancient Greece, honey was thought to possess many virtues, purificatory, preservative, and cathartic. At the same time, the bee, perhaps because of its nesting habit (e.g., in hollows of trees, under stones, in caves, crevices in rocks, and even in animal carcasses), had special ties to Demeter and to other deities with chthonian associations. In ancient Greece, caverns and gorges were considered entrances to Hades.[80] Thus, honey was offered especially, though not solely, to underworld forces (sometimes in caves) and to souls of the dead.[81] Porphyry observed that, among other things, honey and beans were linked as symbols of death and genesis. He also observed that the ancients offered honey to underworld deities, that the priestesses of Demeter were called bees, and that Persephone was called honey-sweet.[82] It is possible that such imagery contributed to construction of the beehive-shaped tombs of the Mycenaeans, including the impressive Treasury of Atreus or Tomb of Agamemnon at Mycenae itself.[83]

Similar imagery relating to bees was found in cults on ancient Rhodes and at Ephesus in Anatolia, where it can be traced back to the Hittites.[84]

Moreover, as pointed out in my chapter on urd, honey occupied an ambivalent position in ancient India similar to that in ancient Greece.[85]

Among the Orphics

Orpheus, the mythical singer and poet, was credited by legend with founding or introducing the Eleusinian mysteries, and indeed those mysteries did bear certain resemblances to Orphic practices.[86] Furthermore, a similarity in attitude toward beans is implied in a statement by Pausanias in the first century A.D. Pausanias wrote that one cannot credit Demeter with the discovery of beans, and that a person who has observed the Eleusinian mysteries or read Orphic texts would know what he meant.[87] Though present-day scholars differ on what exchanges there may have been between the two movements and on the direction of the exchanges,[88] the Eleusinian bean ban was temporary, whereas the Orphic ban applied throughout life.

The Orphics represented a religious movement that took its name and based its beliefs and practices on ones attributed to Orpheus.[89] Though Orphic writings show clear evidence of oriental influences,[90] Thrace is usually held to be the homeland of Orpheus. Classical writers also believed that he had lived in the heroic age, prior to Homer.[91] By the sixth or fifth century B.C., the Orphic movement had spread throughout the Greek world, from Sicily and southern Italy to Scythia, and it continued to survive into Roman times.[92]

The Orphics had ties with other religious movements, especially those of Pythagoras and Dionysus (Bacchus), god of the Orphic religion. The movements of Dionysus and Pythagoras were like the Orphics in that they represented departures from or rejection of prevailing community life.[93] Especially striking are the similarities between Orphics and early Pythagoreans in beliefs and in the commitment to a life of ritual purity entailing observance of the same food bans. The movements have been called close allies that interacted and shared much common ground. Some authorities, moreover, consider the Orphics somewhat older and the prime movers in the relationship.[94] Whatever may have been the case, in the fifth century B.C. they were "almost inextricably intertwined."[95] At the same time, there were notable differences between them, particularly in the social realm.

Some scholars have written of Orphism as if it had been an organized sect. It is true that there is evidence of Orphic communities in one or more places.[96] However, scholars have been increasingly inclined to the view that most Orphics were isolated individuals committed to the religious views and behavior attributed to Orpheus by the Orphic texts.[97] If true, the Orphics represented a point of view and a movement rather than a cult. Burkert has written that the Orphics seem to have been craftsmen, itinerant priests (Orpheotelests) dedicated to such things as removing guilt and curing illness and disease by purification and magic. He has also written that their social organization did not extend beyond the individual and his family.[98] It seems, then, that Orphics, or some of them, may have been a Greek equivalent of the Mesopotamian *āšipu*, a priest-magician—a healer and expert in magic who, as a wise individual well-versed in tradition and deriving his abilities from the gods, attempted cures using such means as incantation, ritual, and exorcism.[99]

Whatever their lack of formal organization, the Orphics represented an influential ascetic movement. It has been likened in a way to that of the Puritans, who, even though there was no church that bore the name "Puritan" openly, had a significant impact on the religious history of Britain and the United States.[100] Convinced of their moral superiority and rejecting the prevailing culture of ancient Greece, the Orphics—who, according to many scholars,[101] seem to have believed in the transmigration of souls[102]—were convinced that by following a pure, simple existence in this world they would be rewarded after death.[103] In what is taken as a reference to Orphic ways, a fragment from Euripides' *Cretans* mentions the wearing of white clothing (white symbolizing purity), avoiding the impurity of birth and death, and refusing to kill animals for food.[104] Herodotus, on his part, noted that Orphics, like Egyptians and Pythagoreans, were not permitted to be buried in woolen clothes.[105] According to Guthrie, the ban on the use of wool in burials may have derived from the view that wool was obtained by stealing from sheep. This was considered an impure act related to the ban on taking life, eating meat, and the use of other animal products.[106]

Others, however, have indicated that the Orphics' dietary habits are what called attention to them or defined their way of life.[107] The Orphics stood apart from and in opposition to most Greeks in their rejection of killing. This extended to the sacrifice of animals to the gods and to the consumption of meat, eggs, and fava beans.[108] These rejections were based on the view, mentioned above, that in the age of innocence of mankind—before people began killing animals for food—humans had lived solely on vegetarian fare.[109] The philosopher Empedocles put the matter in these words: "All creatures, both animals and birds, were tame and gentle to man, and bright was the flame of their friendship. . . . Alas that the pitiless day did not destroy me first, before I devised for my lips the cruel deed of eating flesh."[110]

The Orphic rejection of eggs rested also on the belief that eggs represent the source of all life. This, in turn, is rooted in the conception of a cosmic egg from which humans and all else in the world originated.[111] Their rejection of beans, on its part, rested on the conviction that fava beans contain souls of the human dead. Thus, to the Orphics the eating of beans, like the eating of meat, was the moral equivalent of cannibalism.[112]

Among the Romans

As for the Romans, it is said that their belief that beans contain the souls of the human dead accounted for their use of beans as memorial offerings to dead family members.[113] Black beans were used in ritual during the Parentalia, a private festival that began on February 13. The Parentalia was a time when a Roman family showed respect for its dead, especially dead parents (di parentes, in later times di manes), by visiting and decorating their tombs; offering them gifts, including food, in potsherds placed in the road, apparently nearby the grave; setting up and lighting altars; and reciting prayers and making salutations.[114] The festival ended on February 21 with a public feast, the Feralia.[115]

In addition, the Romans observed the Lemuria feast (on the nights of the May 9, 11, and 13). This was a time when gifts were made to mischievous spirits (lemures, souls of persons who had not been properly buried) before sending them away. At midnight on that occasion, the father of a family would offer black beans to the lemures. First he held the beans in his mouth. Then he cast them away, and finally, with the striking of cymbals together, he demanded that the lemures leave.[116] Joannes Lydus, on his part, noted that beans were thrown into graves, perhaps at the Feralia.[117] Partly because beans were associated with the dead and served in rites honoring the family dead, Roman priests did not eat them.[118] Jupiter's priest (flamen Dialis) by tradition would not even touch beans or mention their name.[119] This recalls the attempt in the Talmud to keep from using the word swine by calling them "something else" (something not to be referred to by name).[120]

Some Parallels in Ritual Views of the Ancient Greeks and Indians; With Notes on Other Ancient Mediterranean and Near Eastern Peoples

In my previous chapter, I reviewed the bans on eating the urd bean and those of certain other foods and beverages (sesame, mushrooms, meat, alcoholic beverages, and salt) on ritual occasions in India. As indicated in that chapter, ritual purity and impurity have been prominent concerns in India from Vedic times onward. Impurity, moreover, results from sexual intercourse, birth, disease, killing, and death. Also noted, the color black is associated with death. It is for this reason that black things, including unhulled urd beans and sesame seed, have been prominent in rites associated with the dead, ancestral spirits, and forces of the underworld. A quite similar situation prevailed in ancient Greece, where episodes that greatly interfered with the normal functioning of life were thought to bring on ritual impurity of greater or lesser severity. As in Vedic India, sexual intercourse, birth, illness, disease, killing, and death were included among those episodes. People escaped impurity by avoiding contact with impure persons or things, by refraining from sexual intercourse, or by eating or avoiding certain foods. If, despite precautions taken, a Greek became polluted, the pollution had to be removed before he or she could return to normal life and approach the gods once again. This was done in a variety of ways, among them cleansing with water, fire, or earth, and dressing in newly laundered clothes.[121]

In Views of Killing, Murder, Death, and the Dead

As in India, in Greece the shedding of blood was especially polluting. Indeed, the effects of murder could extend into future generations and were thus a matter of particular seriousness. For the ancient Greeks, the term *murderer* was an insult, for it referred to one of the most vile and impure of acts.[122] It is understandable that some Greeks thought that the basic goal of Orpheus was to get people to cease their murdering, a concept that, in Orphic thinking, embraced not only the killing of humans but the sacrifice and eating of animals.[123]

Another deterrent to killing among certain Greeks was belief in the transmigration of souls, a concept found among the Pythagoreans and in the writings of Empedocles,[124] as well as in ancient and modern India.[125] In Greece, according to Burkert, transmigration of souls remained a sort of foreign element in religion. It was more at home in India, and, he insists, the possibility of an introduction from India cannot be ruled out.[126]

Death in general was also polluting. Death in a family, for example, brought impurity to the house of the deceased and his or her family. As in India, family members were excluded from normal activities for a time, and then returned to a state of purity by washing, cleansing, and making offerings to the gods.

As in Vedic India, in ancient Greece purity was of special concern to persons such as priests, who dealt with deities on a regular basis, or to other individuals who were about to approach deities. To achieve the purity needed to approach Demeter and Persephone prior to the Eleusinian mysteries, for example, the initiates bathed as a group in the sea near Athens on a specified day.[127] In a similar vein, sexual intercourse, birth, and death were not supposed to occur within a temple compound. On Delos, sacred island of Apollo, the Athenians even went so far as to excavate and remove the contents of all old graves on two occasions.[128] One reads further that a priest was not permitted to go into a house where a woman was in childbed or where the inhabitants were in mourning. He was not allowed to go to a grave or participate in a funeral banquet either. Indeed, in the ancient city of Messene in the Peloponnesus, priests and priestesses had to give up their positions if one of their children died.[129]

In another parallel with Vedic India, the ancient Greeks believed that the dead, or souls of the dead, continued to exist. They could, on one hand, injure the living or, on the other, counsel them or be useful in other ways. As a result, the living descendants respected and took care of the dead.[130] Food, drink, and other things were provided to a dead person, and each year there was a festival of souls during which the dead appeared at the house, were made welcome, and joined in the feast, after which they were asked to depart once again. Nilsson, noting the similarity of Greek practice in this regard with that of Indians and other Indo-Europeans, expresses the view that it would indeed be surprising if they were not related.[131]

In the Symbolism of Black and White

Another parallel shared by the ancient Greeks and Vedic Indians, as well as by Romans and many other peoples, is the association of white with purity, goodness, life, hope, and the high gods, and black with impurity, evil, death, sadness, and underworld forces.[132] In ancient Greece, Demeter, who had chthonic associations, was sometimes depicted as black.[133] In addition, the color of animals sacrificed to Olympian gods was typically white, and that of animals offered to chthonian deities and the dead, black.[134] On Delos, devotees who approached Zeus Cynthius did so barefoot and dressed in white. Moreover, they did so only after having observed other restrictions such as abstaining from meat and sexual intercourse.[135] One ancient explanation of Pythagoras's ban on eating white cocks was that "white represents the nature of the good [white was the color worn in appeals to the gods], black the nature of evil,"[136] which recalls the modern Greek view that a black dog should not be permitted entry to the house on New Year's Day, whereas a white dog should be welcomed and fed.[137]

Another view attributed to Pythagoras is that a worshipper should always approach the gods dressed in white, in respectful silence, and after having been purified of all pollution. In ancient Babylonia, *bārū* and *āšipu* priests wore white.[138] Zoroaster is reputed to have worn a white robe,[139] and the magi of ancient Iran also wore white robes.[140] When the Persian king prayed to Ahura Mazda he, too, set aside his royal garments and donned a white robe. Furthermore, if an ordinary Persian man or woman did not wear a sacred white shirt made of cotton, he or she was not considered a true Zoroastrian.[141] For similar reasons, the priests of ancient Haran in northern Mesopotamia wore white clothing, and so did members of the Essene sect.[142] The high priest of the ancient Hebrews, on his part, wore white clothing on the Day of Atonement, for white was the color of purity and innocence.[143] Against this background, it is no surprise to read that Pythagoras dressed in a spotless white robe and used quilts of white wool,[144] and that his followers, too, ordinarily wore white garments, both during the day and at night.[145]

In contrast, when Pythagoreans buried their dead, they placed them on leaves of black poplar, olive, and myrtle—trees sacred to underworld deities.[146] Other Greeks used myrtle branches and wreaths in funerary rites and apparently for decorating steles of the dead.[147] They also used figs and fig branches in expiatory rites, presumably for the reason reported by Tarquitius Priscus, a Roman writer of Etruscan origin and translator of Etruscan sacred books, in his *Omens from Trees*. According to Priscus, the black fig-tree and all trees with black berries or fruit were associated with underworld deities[148] (at Eleusis in Greece there was a fig tree by which Persephone was said to have descended to the under-world).[149] Priscus also reported that branches of such trees were used to burn items considered "monstrous and of ill omen."[150]

Hippocrates wrote that sorcerers, purifiers, impostors, and fakes—persons who pretend to much piety and greater knowledge than other people (Orphics?)—forbade, among other things, the wearing of black to persons afflicted with "the sacred disease" (epilepsy) because black is the symbol of death.[151] In a similar vein is an inscription (second century A.D.) that may have come from a shrine of Dionysus outside the ancient Greek city of Smyrna in Anatolia. The inscription bears signs of Orphic and Pythagorean influence[152] and reads that initiates should not approach the altars of the god when dressed in black. This was because black symbol-ized sadness, whereas the god's mysteries should be a happy occasion.[153]

Ancient Romans regarded it as shocking for a man dressed in black to go into a temple, for black was the color of clothing worn by Roman men when mourning.[154] The association of black with death is revealed in Horace's poetic description of an undertaker's employees as "black lic-tors," the real lictors being officials, probably subordinates of Jupiter's priest, who used a broom to sweep ghosts from a house after someone had died.[155] The Romans also believed that spirits living in the under-world took on its blackness, and this is how they were commonly de-picted. Black was the color of animals sacrificed to them.[156] Such spirits came out at night, and, though forces of the underworld might not be detected in the darkness, night was the time when offerings were made to them.

The association of black with impurity, evil, and death was also found among other Indo-European peoples in the ancient Mediterranean and Near East, for example, among the Hittites of Anatolia. One Hittite reli-gious text describes a ritual, that of the old woman Tunnawi, which was intended to remove impurity brought on accidentally or by black magic. Such impurity, for example, might develop in a woman who gave birth to premature infants or in a woman or man who was unable to perform normal sexual functions. To have no children to survive you, it should be noted, was an especially unfortunate state, because the well-being of a dead person depended on the offerings made to them by their descen-dants. In any case, it is fitting that black items were prominent in the Tunnawi proceedings. Among them were black clothes and shoes worn by the sacrificer, black wool stuffed into his or her ears, black utensils and containers, black sacrificial animals (ram, ewe, dog, pig), and other black objects. Such objects served in the rite because it was intended to remove the darkness and paralysis of evil, impurity, witchcraft, and sin that possessed the individual.[157] The Hittite ritual of Pupuwanni was directed against sorcery and likely also involved purification. Among other things, it called for offerings to the gods of a black puppy, a black lamb, and a black kid.[158] It may also be significant that, after cremation, the bones of a Hittite were put in a silver vessel, for silver was the Hittite metal of purity.[159] It may be no accident that among the ancient Hittites fava beans (in soup, porridge, or stew) were typically served in ritual associated with the "Black Goddess."[160]

Conclusions

Various ancient and modern writers have hypothesized that the Pythagorean ban on beans did not originate with Pythagoras. Some hold that it was adopted from preexisting beliefs and practices in Greece, whether those found in earlier cults (such as that of Demeter) or in movements (the Orphics) or among the public.[161] Other writers, ancient and modern, have looked to foreign lands as the source of the Pythagorean ban on beans. They base their views in part on assertions that Pythagoras, in his search for knowledge, had travelled abroad, whether to Egypt, Palestine, Mesopotamia, Iran, India, or elsewhere.[162] Though many of Pythagoras's supposed travels seem to be tall tales of later writers, the case for Egypt as the source of the Pythagorean bean ban deserves more careful attention. For one thing, the earliest accounts that mention Pythagoras's travels abroad, though written a century or more after his death, give Egypt as a place to which he travelled,[163] which increases the likelihood that he actually did visit that land.[164] For another, certain ancient Greek and Roman accounts contain references to the rejection of beans as food in Egypt. Herodotus,[165] for one, reported that Egyptian priests refused to eat beans.[166] The accuracy of Herodotus's report, however, may be questioned, because he also made statements about Egypt that are known to be wrong. One is the assertion that no Egyptian would plant or eat beans, which is contrary to existing evidence.[167] Another is the claim[168] that the Greek concept of the transmigration of souls came from Egypt. This view is dismissed by modern scholars, because that concept, at least in a complete form, was not found in ancient Egyptian religion.[169] Nevertheless,

Herodotus adds detail that makes one wonder whether his initial statement about priestly avoidance of beans may, after all, have been correct. He observed that if volunteer beans did spring up, Egyptian priests, because of the bean's impurity, would not even look at them. The uncovering of fava beans in Egypt in a funerary temple and their discovery inside Egyptian coffins and tombs[170] further increase the likelihood that in ancient Egypt, as in Greece and Rome, fava beans had a special tie with death and the dead, thus motivating Egyptian priests' refusal to eat them. On the other hand, Burkert[171] insists, the claim that Egyptian priests abhorred beans has not been verified by Egyptian evidence. Thus, one can only regard as unresolved the question of whether Egypt was the source of the Pythagorean bean ban. It may be that, when Egypt is named as the source of the Pythagorean bean ban,[172] this simply reflects the tendency of ancient Greeks to give credit to foreign peoples for traits that were actually Greek. The Greeks were especially likely to grant such credit, whether deserved or not, to the Egyptians, whose civilization was of much greater antiquity than that of Greece and one the Greeks regarded with great respect.[173]

Sanskritist Leopold von Schroeder,[174] impressed by strong resemblances between Pythagorean and ancient Indian philosophy and ritual (belief in transmigration of souls, commitment to vegetarianism, and a ban on beans), initially suggested that Pythagoras may have derived his ban on beans from India. After further research in which he found similar views of beans more widely among European peoples (Romans, Germanic peoples, and other Europeans as well), von Schroeder[175] reached a different conclusion: In all likelihood the roots of the bean ban go back to the Indo-European homeland (which many scholars believe to have been in the Pontic-Caspian area), where beans were associated with souls of the departed and were offered to them in ritual. Nearly five decades later, Andrews,[176] in a study of the bean in Indo-European totemism, reached a quite similar conclusion: One must look back to the ancestral Indo-European homeland in seeking the origin of the bean bans of Greece and Italy. Noting that there was no specific name for beans among the earliest Indo-Europeans, Andrews argued that it is likely that beans were not even cultivated in their homeland in that period and that the wild fava bean, which did grow there, was of little dietary importance. He suggested further that the earliest Indo-Europeans had already come to associate beans with flatulence, the spirit of life, human flesh, souls of the dead, and death.

Since parallels to Pythagorean beliefs about fava beans are found in the bean beliefs (involving various species of beans) of widely scattered non-Indo-European peoples—in Uganda, India, Japan, New Guinea, and the New World[177]—we are likely dealing with basic human reactions to beans or legumes in general. At the same time, bean bans seem to have been most widespread and best developed among Indo-Europeans, and—like von Schroeder and Andrews—I regard it as reasonable to concentrate on them in seeking the origin of the Pythagorean ban.

Though one can only speculate about such matters, some writers, ancient and modern, consider the flatulence brought on by beans to be the basic reason behind the Pythagorean or Indo-European bans. One possibility is that bean bans arose when flatulence led people to conclude that beans contained souls of the dead.[178] Related to this is Böhm's suggestion[179] that the bad dreams flatulence may bring on, which were thought to derive from unwanted chthonian influences, were sufficient reason in themselves for people to avoid beans. Other writers[180] have focused on the bean's lack of stem nodes, which made it an ideal channel for contact between the living and the dead. Hanelt,[181] a botanist whose research on fava beans gives him a special sensitivity to the physical characteristics of the plant, presents a still different view. He suggests that it is likely that the prominent black spot commonly found on each wing of a fava bean flower[182] was responsible for the plant becoming symbolic of death. Marcovich[183] adds to this that black fava bean seed as well as flower spots played a role in making such an association. This fits with Rohde's idea[184] that chthonian concerns were responsible for the Orphic and Pythagorean ban on beans. Rohde bases this on the belief that to attain purity a Greek had to be separated completely from everything associated with the realm of the dead and gods of the underworld. It also fits with ancient statements that the fava bean flower was marked with letters of ill omen, and that this contributed to the rejection of fava beans by Roman priests.[185] In addition, it is in accord with the ancient statement that it "is through bean blossoms that souls return to earth for their reincarnation."[186]

The association of blackness with evil and the underworld in all likelihood long preceded the domestication of beans. Indeed, some of the roles the bean came to play in ritual may have involved it replacing earlier items that were black.[187] It seems reasonable that in a world fraught with danger from forces of evil, people would not have overlooked the black spots on fava bean flowers. Such blackness would have alerted them to the possible danger of evil posed by the fava bean plant. I consider it likely, however, that, though warned by such black spots, the ancients would have looked for further confirmation and that this came from a second black, the seed coats of fava beans themselves. I believe further that concern with blackness was basic to both the Greek and the Indian bean bans. It is my conviction that people came to associate beans considered black (the fava bean in ancient Greece, the urd bean in Vedic India) with death, the underworld and underworld forces, impurity, and unhappiness, and therefore rejected them as unsuitable for consumption by particular persons or groups or for use on certain ritual occasions.

An association with death meant that beans were also tied to decay. This is a condition that brings on disgust reactions in humans and has led them to reject various foods, especially ones of animal origin.[188] As we have seen, beans fell partly into the latter category because the spirits of the dead they were thought to contain were active beings, which made beans a curious mixture of the living and the dead. It may be that the flatulence of beans merely served to confirm the belief that they contain active spirits. In any case, because flatulence is related to feces—which, overall, are considered disgusting by humans[189]—this may have further reinforced the view that beans are polluting. Thus, it may be no accident that Plutarch[190] linked the eating of beans with all three: flatulence, feces, and impurity.

Since ancestral spirits have also been believed to possess powers of generation that may benefit their living relatives, in both ancient Greece and India beans were also perceived as affecting sexual desire and reproduction. Despite the fact that they might play a positive role in this regard, people could not ignore the fact that they also represented meat and, even worse, human flesh. Thus, to eat beans was little different from cannibalism, another unclean, revolting act to persons seeking to maintain ritual purity, such as Orphics, Pythagoreans, and priests, including Brahmins. In a similar vein, while it was appropriate to offer black beans to ancestral spirits and underworld forces, it was commonly inappropriate, in both Greece and India, to offer them to celestial gods and goddesses.

The richness of ancient views surrounding the bean—in terms of death and the underworld, decay, spirits of the dead, flatulence, meat eating and cannibalism, sex and regeneration, and purity and impurity—makes Pythagorean revulsion at the thought of eating beans all the more understandable. Indeed, it is hard to imagine how, in banning a food, Pythagoras could have struck more basic chords of shame and dread of evil in the minds of his followers. It is especially fitting that Detienne, in his table portraying the Pythagorean food classification, ranked beans below meat as the most debased of foods, bestial and rotten.[191]

Whatever scholarly differences there may be about details, it is highly likely that dread and concern with dishonor were closely tied to the origin of bean bans among Indo-Europeans. In India, there is no credible disease concern for modern observers to seize on in explaining the ritual bans on eating urd beans. Nor can one ignore the fact that since antiquity Indians have expressed magico-religious concerns in explaining the inappropriateness of using beans on certain ritual occasions. I will leave for my next chapter the possible role of favism in the origin of the Pythagorean ban on fava beans. On the basis of the information presented above, however, the powerful magico-religious motives reported in both Greece and Rome were quite sufficient to have brought on the bans of fava beans all by themselves, without implicating favism at all.

8 Favism and the Origin of the Pythagorean Ban on Fava Beans

> . . . my suggestion is that the origin of the [Pythagorean ban on fava beans] lies in the prevalence of favism in the Mediterranean lands . . . Pythagoras himself may have suffered from this condition.
>
> —T. H. D. Arie, "Pythagoras and Beans"

> Pythagoras and many of his followers appear to have suffered from a hereditary condition, known today as favism, which is manifested in sensitivity to broad beans (*Vicia faba* L.) . . . Such persons generally appear healthy, but any form of contact with beans or the bean plant may rapidly provoke an acute attack of illness, sometimes resulting in death . . . Yet, if my thesis is correct, the Pythagoreans must have been far more vulnerable, from the physical point of view, than any ordinary political group. Their sensitivity to beans constituted an Achilles heel, which, if revealed to their opponents, could have led to their physical destruction.
>
> —E. Lieber, "The Pythagorean Community as a Sheltered Environment for the Handicapped"

> The fact of the matter is, we suggest, that this most notorious of Pythagoras' rules . . . actually fits [into the] category, "common-sense injunction." Concentrated in South Italy, Sicily, and Sardinia, there occurs a hereditary deficiency of the enzyme glucose-6-phosphate dehydrogenase (Mediterranean type), which can result in an inability to tolerate fava beans (*Vicia faba*). Persons with this anomaly (favism) find these beans a poison, for they develop a severe hemolytic anemia within a few hours of eating the beans, which in some cases is fatal . . .
>
> —R. S. Brumbaugh and J. Schwartz, "Pythagoras and Beans"

Introduction

The ban on fava beans by Pythagoras has amused and mystified observers since antiquity. Not only were fava beans a staple food in ancient Greece and Italy, as they are today, but also Pythagorean explanations of the ban in magico-religious terms struck many as bizarre. The possibility of a new explanation arose when, in mid-nineteenth-century Portugal and Sicily,

216

medical researchers first identified the disease favism and its association with fava beans.[1] This possibility, which, as I have noted, has gained favor in recent decades, is that the Pythagorean bean ban was based, entirely or partly, on knowledge of the disease favism and the health risk the fava bean poses to certain persons. Though many people—physicians and others—regard the possibility as eminently reasonable, it has not been subject to careful scrutiny against the steady accumulation of new historical and biomedical data.[2]

In chapters 6 and 7, I described (1) a similar ban, on ritual consumption of the urd bean (*Vigna mungo*) in ancient and modern India and (2) the traditional explanations advanced for the bans on fava beans among the Pythagoreans and other religious movements in the ancient Mediterranean world. In this chapter I will concentrate on the hypothesis that Pythagoras established his bean ban because of concern with favism. First I will provide brief sketches of the disease and of the hypothesis. Then I will raise a series of questions that relate to the hypothesis and will present evidence—historical, biomedical, and otherwise—that bears on each question. Finally, I will seek to reach a conclusion about the validity of the hypothesis, on whether, in view of the evidence collected, it is a reasonable one.

Favism—The Disease and the Hypothesis

The Disease

Favism is a hemolytic disease that has been most common in Mediterranean lands. It can be brought on in genetically predisposed individuals (with deficiency in the enzyme glucose-6-phosphate dehydrogenase, or G6PD, a deficiency found in approximately 400 million people around the world) when they consume fava beans.[3] Only persons with G6PD-deficiency develop the hemolytic crises of favism.[4]

Incidences of G6PD-deficiency vary greatly both regionally and locally in Mediterranean populations.[5] One study of males from all parts of Greece,[6] for example, found incidences of G6PD-deficiency by prefecture to range from 0 to 13.5 percent. A study of G6PD-deficiency in Italy[7] found incidences among males to range by region from 0 to 25 percent. Even on a single island, there may be a striking range in incidences of G6PD-deficiency from one community to another. That range, for example, is from 3 to 36 percent among Sardinian villages (males),[8] and from 8 to 35 percent among communities on Rhodes (males).[9]

It should be noted that there are hundreds of variants of the G6PD enzyme in humans around the world; that such variants differ in their characteristic levels of G6PD activity; and that the common ones found in the Mediterranean region are Class II, with low enzyme activity, which are the usual pathological variants.[10]

In young children just a few raw fresh beans may be sufficient to bring on an attack of favism,[11] and there is one report of a single bean bringing on an attack in a five-year-old patient.[12] The symptoms of favism may develop the first time an individual consumes fava beans or the first time he or she consumes them in large amounts, as in the case of a 17-year-old Greek boy who, for the first time in his life, consumed 300 grams (over a half pound) of fava beans on each of two days.[13] At the same time, only a small minority of deficient individuals who consume fava beans actually develop favism. In a study on Rhodes, of 143 G6PD-deficient boys (10–16 years of age), only 18 (12.6 percent) developed hemolysis after consuming fava beans.[14] Another study in Greece reported an incidence of favism of 10.3 percent in 223 males with G6PD-deficiency.[15] In a study in Sardinia, of 171 men and women who were over 50 years of age and G6PD-deficient, only 26 (15 percent) had experienced hemolytic episodes at some time in their lives, though the percentage was somewhat higher (19 percent) in persons who had G6PD-deficiency but not thalassemia.[16]

Most favism cases involve young children, especially those between one and five years of age. These are the years when they start to consume fava beans. In addition, it has been noted, children ordinarily consume larger quantities of fava beans in relation to body mass than adults do, the result being a greater danger of hemolytic crises.[17] In a study carried out in two hospitals serving the Caspian littoral area of Iran in 1970, 69 percent of all favism cases involved persons between one and five years of age.[18] In an Egyptian hospital, 95 percent of all favism cases involved patients under 5 years of age.[19] After age five, the incidence of favism declines notably. In the Iranian hospitals mentioned above, of 579 cases of favism, only 5 percent of all admissions involved persons over 15 years of age, and only 3.5 percent, persons over age 25.[20]

Favism may, however, develop in G6PD-deficient nursing infants two to six days after their mothers have consumed fava beans, even though the mothers may be asymptomatic.[21] There is also a report of a patient having an attack of favism after consuming the milk of a goat that had eaten fava beans.[22] Another report tells of a pregnant woman who had consumed fava beans five days before delivering an infant that had the symptoms of favism at birth. The researchers concluded that the danger of favism extends into the intrauterine stage and may threaten the life of the fetus.[23] Favism may also develop in persons of any age, among them older children and elderly individuals, who previously consumed fava beans without ill effect.[24]

Males, moreover, are far more likely than females to be G6PD-deficient and to develop severe cases of favism (male-female ratios in studies of hospital patients have ranged roughly from 2.5:1 to 21:1; that is, for every 2.5–21 male cases of favism, there was only 1 female case).[25] Persons who have experienced an attack of favism, moreover, may have repeated attacks.[26] One reads, for example, that a person who has had favism as a child may consume fava beans without difficulty for many years, but then experience a second hemolytic attack as an adult or even when quite old.[27]

Symptoms of favism may be mild or severe, and many patients with favism are never hospitalized.[28] Different forms of the disease have been described, but its characteristic symptoms, which may develop anywhere from a few hours to several days after consuming fava beans, are fatigue and weakness, pallor, jaundice, and hemoglobinuria.[29] In severe cases, an acute hemolytic anemia develops that may lead to death, especially in young children. In the first decade of this century, Fermi, a Sardinian professor of medicine, estimated that among his clinical patients with favism up to 8 percent died.[30] In the 1930s, mortality among hospital cases of favism at the University of Cagliari in Sardinia ranged from 20 to 40 percent.[31] These must have been the most serious cases, but they also received the latest and best medical treatment. As a result of health education programs, greater public awareness, screening of neonates for G6PD-deficiency, decreasing number of favism cases,[32] and treatment of favism with blood transfusions, deaths from favism in Sardinia have now become very few indeed.[33] Of 73 children with favism who were patients in a hospital in Salonika, Greece, from 1948 to 1958, 8 (10.3 percent) died.[34] Reports from Iran, Bulgaria, Tunisia, and China in the 1960s and 1970s provide a range of mortality rates among favism patients from 0 to 4.7 percent, the latter for children under two years of age.[35] One cannot, however, compare these rates directly with those from Sardinia in the 1930s, because G6PD variants and the severity of G6PD-deficiency must have been different and because of increased public awareness and improved treatment of favism over time.

The principal toxic components in fava beans are believed to be divicine and isouramil, powerful oxidizing agents which result, respectively, from hydrolysis of the compounds vicine and convicine.[36] Though vicine and/or convicine have been reported in beet juice, in the seed of the garden pea (*Pisum sativum*),[37] and in other species of *Vicia*, the amounts, with one exception, were far higher in the seed of *Vicia faba*.[38] There is, however, considerable variation in the amount of vicine and convicine in *Vicia faba* seeds, both among individual seeds and according to the state of maturity, the cultivar, and environmental conditions. Despite this, seeds of all cultivars that have been tested contain significant amounts of the compounds, and efforts to select a cultivar free of them have not succeeded.[39]

Vicine and convicine are found mainly in the seed, primarily in the cotyledons rather than in the seed coat. They are far more abundant in young seeds, for as seeds mature their vicine and convicine contents decline. A study of one fava bean variety found that the vicine content in cotyledons declined from 2.5 to 0.3 percent during seed development and that convicine underwent a similar decline. Ultimately, however, levels of vicine and convicine cease declining, and they remain significant at maturity.[40] Dried fava beans thus contain significant amounts of vicine and convicine, and these seem to be as high in frozen beans as in fresh ones.[41] The toxic factors in fava beans are at least partly soluble in water, but, since vicine and convicine are heat stable in solution, soaking and ordinary cooking reduce levels in the beans to some degree, while making the water somewhat toxic.[42]

Most cases of favism develop from eating fresh beans, raw or cooked, shortly after they are harvested (68 percent of all cases in one investigation, 97 percent in another),[43] but cases may develop at any season from consuming frozen or dry beans.[44] Posing a special danger is the practice of giving infants tender young fava bean seeds to eat, because, as we have seen, young seeds have far higher levels of toxicity than mature seeds.[45] The only certain way for a sensitive person to prevent symptoms is to exclude fava beans of all sorts from his or her diet.

Recent research has demonstrated, nevertheless, that rather simple procedures can eliminate most or all of the toxic compounds.[46] One procedure involves the use of microorganisms or microbial enzymes.[47] Another involves mixing fava bean paste with almond powder and lemon juice and letting the mixture incubate. In the latter procedure, the amount of hydrolysis of vicine and convicine depends on temperature, pH, amount of almond powder added to the fava bean paste, and duration of incubation.[48]

The Hypothesis

The arguments presented in favor of the favism hypothesis will be taken up in detail later, but most common among them is the simple fact that in the Mediterranean world—where favism in modern times has been more common than anywhere else in the world—Pythagoras banned fava beans to his followers. Also put forth as evidence are ancient tales that Pythagoras and/or his followers, when seeking to escape from enemies, risked their lives by refusing to cross a bean field. Some advocates of the favism hypothesis argue that in all likelihood this refusal was based on the fear that Pythagoras and his followers might experience attacks of favism through inhaling fava bean pollen, smelling noxious exhalations of flowering fava beans, or other contact with the beans. Some have argued that Pythagoras himself suffered from favism. One writer even suggests that the Pythagoreans were a favist society, a group of persons sensitive to fava beans, and she suggests that this is supported by the physical examination used for selecting members. She suggests further that the Pythagoreans undertook seasonal migrations into the mountains to avoid flowering fava beans under cultivation in lowland fields.

The favism hypothesis has attracted unusual, but mostly uncritical, attention in recent decades. In part, the attention derives from the discovery that G6PD-deficiency, like the sickle-cell and thalassemia traits, is effective in resisting malaria.[49] One result is that, in the minds of some observers, fava bean consumption, G6PD-deficiency, favism, and malaria have become entwined with the Pythagorean ban of beans as an unusual and interesting case of biocultural evolution.

Some Questions about the Favism Hypothesis

I turn now to a series of questions that bear on the validity of the favism hypothesis. First to be considered is whether favism was recognized as a disease in antiquity, whether it was mentioned in accounts of Pythagoras and the Pythagoreans or in ancient medical or nonmedical writings. Second, I will comment on the curious coincidence that Pythagoras banned fava beans in what today is the region where most cases of favism occur, and will consider what other explanations there might be for this. Then I will weigh a critical item in the arguments of those who favor the favism hypothesis: the tales found in certain ancient accounts that Pythagoras and his followers not only refused to eat beans but also were willing to risk death rather than cross a bean field. In regard to the bean field tales, I will consider the questions of (1) whether or not they can be regarded as trustworthy historical documents, (2) whether they contain evidence suggesting that the refusal to cross the bean field was based on fear of inhaling fava bean pollen or toxic exhalations that might bring on an attack of favism, and (3) whether indeed there is unequivocal evidence from the present-day that inhalation, especially inhalation of pollen—the most commonly cited of present-day inhalation hypotheses—can trigger attacks of favism. Then I will turn to other biomedical evidence that might cast light on the claim[50] that Pythagoras and/or his followers may have suffered from favism. With respect to Pythagoras as an individual, I will consider present-day evidence relating to the incidence of favism in his place of birth. My thinking here is that, if the disease is common there today, it may also have been common in antiquity. This, in turn, would increase the likelihood that Pythagoras suffered from the disease. With respect to Pythagoras's followers, I will weigh evidence on whether favism is common today and may have been common in antiquity, in Magna Graecia and Sicily—the centers of Pythagoras's operations—and whether he may have instituted the ban on fava beans because favism represented a threat to his adherents. Then I will examine evidence on the interesting additional hypothesis that the Pythagorean movement itself was a society of persons suffering from favism. Finally, I will consider the history of malaria in the Mediterranean region as it bears on incidences of favism and on the favism hypothesis.

Was Favism Recognized in the Time of Pythagoras?

Our initial question is whether favism as a disease and its association with the consumption of fava beans were recognized in ancient Greece. Some medical writers have made affirmative statements to that effect, sometimes presented as speculation,[51] sometimes as fact.[52] An example of a speculative statement is that of Waldron,[53] who writes that what seems like an outlandish ban against eating fava beans by Pythagoras may in fact have had solid empirical grounds. Waldron goes on to say that it may have derived from Pythagoras's recognition of the symptoms brought on in some people who had consumed fava beans. This, he argues, may have led him to make a ban on fava beans part of the observances required of cult members. An example of a statement of great certainty is that of Luzzatto and Mehta,[54] who write that favism and its ties with eating fava beans were noted in ancient times and that Pythagoras alerted his followers to the dangers of fava bean consumption. Whether such statements are presented as speculations or as matters of certainty, they are usually based on the assumption that the existence of the Pythagorean bean ban in itself demonstrates knowledge of the fava bean–favism association.

On the other hand, scholars who have sought an awareness of favism in ancient Greek medical and nonmedical sources have failed to find it.[55] This is quite surprising. Ancient Greek physicians clearly understood that excessive consumption of the seed of bitter vetch (*Vicia ervilia*) can be toxic. They also noted the paralysis of lathyrism, now known to be brought on by consumption of the grass pea (*Lathyrus sativus*).[56] Yet there is no description of favism in ancient medical accounts. On the contrary, most physicians, like most other ancient Greeks, appear to have viewed fava beans as safe foods that posed no danger to the health of humans.

The Hippocratic Collection, though attributed to the semilegendary Hippocrates, father of Greek medicine (c. 460–377 B.C.), is believed to represent a library collection written by various individuals, physicians and others. In the Hippocratic writings, all pulses are considered flatulent and capable of bringing on "biliary accidents," but fava beans themselves are viewed favorably as nourishing and binding, and thus useful in treating dysentery and abdominal upset.[57] If favism was indeed known in ancient Greece, one might expect members of the Hippocratic school to have observed it. For one thing, the authors of the Hippocratic works lived in different centuries. They represented different schools of medicine and presumably were familiar with many parts of Greece. Hippocrates, who may or may not have written works in the collection, is reputed to have travelled throughout Greece, and he, too, would have been in an excellent position to have encountered the disease.

Equally significant, Hippocrates was born on Cos (Kos) in the Dodecanese Islands, and, though the Hippocratic Collection ended up in Alexandria, various scholars associate it with the medical school on Cos, where Hippocrates taught. A famous center of the healing god Asclepius also existed on Cos in the time of the Hippocratic writers. Indeed, it was second only to the god's cult center at Epidaurus, and sick people might come from great distances to be treated. This means that Hippocrates and other doctors at the medical school were in an unusually good position to observe cases of favism had the disease been common in ancient Greece. Of equal importance is the fact that in modern Greece, Rhodes, largest of the Dodecanese Islands, is noted for its high incidences of favism and G6PD-deficiency (in one study, 22–26 percent of all Greek males tested, and in some villages, 33–35 percent) and, in former times, for being very malarious in certain places.[58] Allison et al., writing in 1963, noted that two pediatricians on Rhodes reported seeing over 100 cases of favism since 1947, despite the fact that a local ordinance banning cultivation of fava beans had been in effect the entire time. Cos is so close to Rhodes (60 miles or so) that today the islands are linked by ferry and, in summer, by hydrofoil. If favism had been present on Rhodes in antiquity, it would have been at the very doorstep of the medical school in Cos. Yet, though the Hippocratic physicians were fully aware of malaria,[59] they failed to record the presence of favism.

How can their silence in the matter of favism be explained? If favism had been a serious problem in their day, is it possible that all the Hippocratic writers—observant professionals in the vanguard of Western medical knowledge—would have overlooked it? If favism was common from the time of Pythagoras onward, it is equally surprising that clear descriptions of the disease appear only in the mid-nineteenth century A.D.— more than two millennia after the time of Hippocrates and Pythagoras.[60] Also difficult to accept is the view of some modern writers that the historian Herodotus and the philosophers Pythagoras and Empedocles recognized favism when it was unknown to physicians of their day.[61] Grmek has argued that Greek physicians' failure to link the symptoms of favism with the consumption of fava beans can be explained in terms of epistemological obstacles.[62] Even more important in my mind is the likelihood that the disease was very rare in the days of the Hippocratic school. This fits with Lieber's statement[63] that most observers regard favism as a fairly recent disease, and with a statement by Sansone, Piga, and Segni[64] that it is dubious whether favism was "known in past ages." This is a question to which I will return later.

The Occurrence of an Ancient Ban on Fava Beans in the Principal Area of Favism Today: How Remarkable a Coincidence?

Many observers are struck by the fact that Pythagoras and his followers observed a ban on fava beans in the very region where in the modern world most cases of favism occur. For some, this is simply too great a coincidence, one that strongly suggests or even proves that Pythagoras banned fava beans because of fear of favism. To persons who have studied the way beans are perceived and used in ritual across the Old World, the coincidence may be far less convincing. This is a matter I will consider in greater detail in my next chapter, but here I feel compelled to restate points made in my previous two bean chapters. First is the point that in Hindu India there is a ritual ban of a bean (the urd bean) that bears remarkable similarity to the Pythagorean ban in its magico-religious associations. Second, in the ancient Mediterranean region, similar bans were found among the Orphics of Greece, as well as among priests, or certain of them, in Egypt and Rome. The context of the bans in India, Greece, and Rome was always ritualistic or cultic, with beans identified with death and the dead, and eating them, with ritual impurity. As noted in chapters 6 and 7, beliefs that beans are associated with death and the dead, which imply danger and are only a step away from a ban, have been found not only in ancient Greece, Rome, and India, but even more widely. Some scholars have suggested that such ideas of beans likely go back to the Indo-European homeland.[65] My point is that, though some may think it too remarkable a coincidence that an ancient bean ban occurred in an area where in modern times favism is widespread, it is hardly remarkable when considered against the widespread occurrence of the noted perceptions among Indo-European peoples. It is even less so when considered against the echoes of those perceptions found among non-Indo-European peoples in distant parts of the world.[66]

Tales of the Bean Field

Tales about the refusal of Pythagoras and his followers to cross a bean field are regularly cited as evidence that they suffered from favism. Indeed, such tales constitute an element so critical in the arguments of advocates of the favism hypothesis that they deserve careful scrutiny.

Are the Tales of the Bean Field Accurate Historical Accounts?—The tales of the bean field usually cited by modern writers come from the writings of

Iamblichus and Diogenes Laertius, which date from the third or fourth centuries A.D., 700 or 800 years after Pythagoras's death (c. 500 B.C.). It is true that in most cases they credit earlier writers (Neanthes, Hippobotus, Hermippus) for the tales. None, however, is attributed to the earliest writers (fourth century B.C.) who provide accounts of Pythagoras's death, such as Aristototle, Aristoxenus, and Dicaearchus.[67] In fact, none seems to date prior to about 300 B.C., two full centuries after the death of Pythagoras.

Questions may also be raised about the motives of certain writers associated with the bean field tales. Hermippus, the only source that Diogenes Laertius provides for a bean field tale, was an Athenian writer of the Old Comedy, noted for his attacks on famous persons and given to writing insulting poems. One authority notes that the fragments of Hermippus, though they cannot all be fabrications, do contain the strangest material in the entire Pythagorean tradition.[68] Another authority characterizes Hermippus's work as "a malicious satire on Pythagoras."[69] If that is true, Hermippus's writings should be viewed with great caution, just like those of other ancient Greek literati who exaggerated and twisted the beliefs of Pythagoras and subjected them to ridicule.

As for Iamblichus, Burkert,[70] an authority on Pythagoras and ancient Greece, writes of him as being "chaotic and dogmatic," of writing hastily, of using his sources without discrimination, of being unreliable, and of deliberately altering at least one account. Burkert adds that the reader can never be certain what sorts of changes Iamblichus made. Philip,[71] another authority on Pythagoras, writes of Iamblichus's failure to cite or reconcile conflicts between his sources and of his choosing facts to suit his purpose, which, from the vantage of the fourth century A.D., was to present an ideal perspective of Pythagoras. Philip adds that, where facts were lacking, Iamblichus simply invented them. Since Iamblichus provides the only account of the bean field being in flower, I wonder whether this was one of his inventions.

In a chapter written a dozen years ago, certain advocates of the favism hypothesis[72] referred to one of the bean field tales as "circumstantial detail [that] strongly supports the suggestion . . . that Pythagoras suffered from favism." I question, however, whether it is sound practice to accept tales that, at best, date from two centuries after the fact and that in some cases derive from sources of quite dubious reliability. To give credence to such tales also goes against the expert opinion of Philip,[73] who dismisses them as fictions that seem to have been invented by Neanthes. In view of the above, it seems foolhardy to accept the bean field tales as historical fact. It is far more reasonable to deal with them gingerly and critically as part of the legend that came to surround Pythagoras over the centuries.

Do the Tales Support the View That Pythagoras and His Followers Feared Illness Brought on by Pollen Inhalation?—Tales of the bean field are so prominent in the thinking of advocates of the favism hypothesis that, for the sake of argument, I will assume they are accurate historical documents. Given that assumption, we are faced initially with the critical question of whether the accounts themselves support the hypothesis that fear of an attack of favism through inhaling pollen was behind the refusal of Pythagoras and/or his followers to cross a bean field.

As told by Iamblichus (c. A.D. 250–330), who cites Neanthes of Cyzicus and Hippobotus (third century B.C.?) as his sources, unarmed followers of Pythagoras fled from an ambush by heavily armed forces sent by the tyrant Dionysius. They were making good their escape until they came to "a field planted and fully blooming with beans." Unwilling to violate the Pythagorean prohibition against touching beans, they stopped and fought their pursuers as best they could until all the Pythagoreans were dead. As Iamblichus presents it, the Pythagoreans willingly accepted death to uphold the principles of their movement.[74] It should be emphasized that in this case, as in two early verses thought most likely to resemble the original formulation of the Pythagorean ban, the focus is on the touching of fava beans, on keeping them "far from one's hands."[75]

Iamblichus[76] follows the above tale with one of a Pythagorean husband and wife, Myllias and Timycha, who had not been able to keep up with the main group but were captured and brought before the tyrant. The couple were asked why the other Pythagoreans had been willing to die rather than step on beans. They refused to provide the answer, for that was a cult secret, even when the wife, who was pregnant, had been separated from her husband and readied for torture. Indeed, the wife cut off her tongue so that she could not be forced to disclose the secret.

Our second and third bean field tales, from Diogenes Laertius (third century A.D.), also involve Pythagoras as well as his followers. In the first of these, for which Diogenes provides no source, Pythagoras and certain adherents were in the house of Milo, Croton's most famous athlete, when it was set on fire by enemies. According to different texts, either Pythagoras was captured when he came out, or he fled until he came to a bean field, where he stopped, saying that he would rather be captured than pass through the field and would rather be killed than indulge in idle talk about his doctrines (presumably the reasons behind his refusal to cross the field). His pursuers, according to Diogenes' account, cut his throat and killed most of his followers.[77]

Our final bean field tale, for which Diogenes credits Hermippus (c. 200 B.C.), is set not in mainland Italy but in Sicily. As mentioned in my previous chapter, this is where Pythagoras and a group of his followers fought on the side of the army of Acragas in a battle against the forces of Syracuse. The Syracusans succeeded in turning the flank of their opponents, and Pythagoras was killed when avoiding passage through a bean field, while his followers were later burned at the stake for other offenses.[78]

In none of the three tales is there any suggestion of smelling beans or inhaling pollen, and only in the tale by Iamblichus were the beans in flower. None of the three accounts suggests that fear of illness or disease was a factor in the refusal to go through the bean field. Instead, the tales that do provide information about the refusal clearly state that it was based on fear of violating a cult doctrine not to touch beans, walk on them, or cross a bean field (which could have involved touching or walking on them).

Does Modern Evidence Support the View That Favism Can Be Brought on by Inhaling Fava Bean Pollen?—Even if we assume that the bean field tales are historically accurate and that Pythagoras and his followers were fearful of inhaling pollen, we would face still another question: Is there validity in the claim that, when fava beans are in blossom, inhalation of pollen by a sensitive person is sufficient to bring on an attack of favism? What is the evidence for this claim?

First, Walker and Bowman, carrying out *in vitro* studies, found that extracts of fresh fava bean seeds quickly brought on a selective drop in glutathione (GSH) levels in erythrocytes of sensitive (G6PD-deficient) persons compared with nonsensitive ones, and they had similar results with extracts of fava bean pollen or pistils.[79] Because of this, and because a sharp drop in GSH always occurs in patients during the acute stage of favism,[80] the strong likelihood is that fava bean pollen contains vicine and convicine and is toxic to G6PD-deficient persons. The possibility that inhaling pollen may bring on favism is strengthened by the implication of pollen of certain other plants (e.g., garden pea, *Pisum sativum;* garden verbena, *Verbena hybrida;* and Mediterranean stinkbush, *Anagyris foetida*) in causing, on rare occasions, another hemolytic syndrome closely resembling favism.[81] I have not, however, been able to locate tests of fava bean pollen that indicate whether, in fact, it does contain vicine and convicine.

Also of note are repeated statements in the medical literature on Italy, including Sardinia and Sicily, about favism brought on by inhalation of pollen,[82] and some writers in the past have suggested that the condition is quite common. Fermi and Martinetti,[83] for example, reviewed 1,211 cases of favism in Italy, of which 459 were thought to have derived from pollen inhalation. In Sardinia, attacks of favism from pollen inhalation are said to occur mainly in April and May, when most fava bean plants are in flower, whereas attacks from ingestion of beans occur primarily between May and August, when fresh beans are available.[84] Some Sardinians report experiencing symptoms of favism, usually milder ones, every spring when the fava fields are in flower. Others say that certain children experience attacks when they are within 100 yards of a field of flowering fava beans.[85]

Other researchers,[86] however, report a far lower percentage of pollen-induced favism: in only 15 of 500 favism patients (3 percent) in various hospitals in Sicily. Moreover, since research by Kattamis et al.[87] in Greece failed to support the pollen inhalation hypothesis, researchers seem to have proceeded with greater skepticism and care than had characterized previous studies. Perhaps because of this, Meloni et al.[88] found no cases due to inhaling pollen among 923 children (2–12 years of age) treated for favism in a north Sardinian clinic from 1965 to 1979. Instead, these researchers concluded that favism was brought on entirely by consumption of the beans themselves (fresh beans, 97 percent of cases; dried beans, 3 percent).

Research in other countries, moreover, has failed to confirm the Italian reports that favism can be brought on by pollen inhalation.[89] In the Near East, for example, few, if any, cases of favism are recorded for the period the fava bean is in flower.[90] In the provinces of Guilan and Mazanderan in northern Iran, there have been claims of favism developing from passing through a field of fava beans or from contact with fava bean pollen or flowers, but none of the reported cases developed in January or February, when fava plants are in bloom.[91] Instead, most cases occurred between mid-May and mid-June, the time when fava beans mature and are harvested.[92] Another study in the same Iranian provinces reported that only 4 of 579 persons with favism claimed that it came from pollen inhalation, and the researchers concluded that even those 4 cases were dubious.[93] Moreover, in Shiraz, in another part of Iran where a few cases of favism were reported in December and January, they may have been brought on by pollen inhalation, or they may have been cases of hemolytic anemia deriving from infection or drugs.[94]

Reports from Greece are quite similar to those from Iran. Hemolysis in patients is not brought on by mere inhalation of fava bean pollen. February and March, when fava bean plants bloom in Greece, are times when favism is of very rare occurrence. If indeed favism can be brought on by pollen inhalation, it is reasonable to expect a rise in the incidence of the disease, however slight, in those months. Not only is there no rise, but also the favism of patients admitted to hospitals during those two months seems to derive entirely from eating dry beans.[95] Seasonal peaks in cases of favism occur in Greece in April and May, but these relate to the ripening, not the flowering, of fava beans, the exact times of the peaks differing from place to place, as in Sardinia, according to latitude and altitude.[96]

Though it seems likely that fava bean pollen does contain vicine and convicine, the evidence that pollen inhalation can actually bring on favism is inconsistent, and much of it is anecdotal or based on folk belief. Because of this, it seems prudent to follow Mager et al.[97] in their conclusion that there is a lack of definite, incontestable evidence that inhalation of fava bean pollen can bring on favism. I would note further than none of three excellent reviews of G6PD-deficiency or the etiology of favism authored or coauthored by Italian researchers in the past decade[98] mention inhalation as a means of bringing on attacks of favism. Instead, they say only that the disease can be brought on in sensitive individuals by the ingestion of beans and, in infants, by means of mother's milk. Indeed, one of those researchers writes that, though there were many claims in the past that smelling fava beans or inhaling their pollen brought on attacks of favism, he knows of no reliable recent evidence to that effect.[99]

Other Evidence Bearing on the Likelihood That Pythagoras and His Followers Suffered from Favism

In regard to the question of whether Pythagoras and his followers themselves suffered from favism, biomedical researchers have demonstrated that favism is not found in persons with normal levels of G6PD, but only in persons deficient in G6PD. The argument might be made that, since Pythagoras was a Greek and since G6PD-deficiency and favism are common in modern Greece, he, too, may have been afflicted. As we have seen, however, incidences of G6PD-deficiency vary greatly from one place to another in modern Greece. Because of this, it makes sense to focus on the place where Pythagoras was born.

Evidence of Favism in the Place of Pythagoras's Birth

Most ancient writers said that Pythagoras was a native of Samos, an island in the Aegean Sea off the coast of Anatolia.[100] Indeed, he was referred to as Pythagoras of Samos or the Samian sage, and his name and representation are found on ancient coins of the island. Though certain ancient writers did suggest other places of origin, the consensus in modern times, too, is that Pythagoras was born, or probably was born, on Samos. Indeed, Samos now has a port, Pythagorio (Pythaghorio, Pithagorion; formerly Tigani), named after him.

Fortunately, there has been an excellent study by Stamatoyannopoulos et al.,[101] involving 5,156 "native Greek" airmen (adult males whose mothers and maternal ancestors were native [ethnic?] Greeks and whose mothers originated in areas of Greece other than metropolitan Athens and Salonica or in foreign Greek communities). This study found striking regional differences in the incidences of G6PD-deficiency. For the entire group of "native Greek" airmen, the incidence of G6PD-deficiency was 5.6 percent. Airmen from a few prefectures in Thessaly or Macedonia had incidences as high as 11–13 percent. In contrast, airmen from a dozen prefectures in Greece had no G6PD-deficiency at all. From our perspective, it is noteworthy that Samos was among the latter group of prefectures. Of 42 persons tested on Samos and 50 on Chios, its neighbor to the north, not one was G6PD-deficient. It is true that through history Samos has been conquered repeatedly and has received its share of immigration, including Greeks from Anatolia following the First World War. It is also true that there are reports, though all are probably inaccurate, of Samos being depopulated on five occasions in the past.[102] Tied to these are accounts of outside settlers, including non-Greeks, brought in on more than one occasion. It is clear that we cannot take modern data on G6PD-deficiency to represent the pattern that prevailed among the Greeks of Samos in Pythagoras's day. Insofar as present-day Samians do bear genes of the ancient Samians, however, the data on G6PD-deficiency provide no support for the argument that Pythagoras likely suffered from G6PD-deficiency and favism.

There is, of course, the possibility that Pythagoras's forefathers came to Samos from elsewhere. His mother was said by some ancient writers to be of Samian descent, but his male ancestors were sometimes associated with Phlius, a town in the northeastern Peloponnesus north of Argos and south of Sicyon (the latter is 10 miles northwest of Corinth).[103] Diogenes Laertius said that Pythagoras's great-great-grandfather, Cleonymus, had been exiled from Phlius.[104] Pausanias, in turn, said that Pythagoras's great-grandfather, Hippasus, had fled from Phlius to Samos for political reasons.[105] These genealogies may simply have been made up by Pythagoreans in Phlius, but, if true, they indicate that Pythagoras had a non-Samian genetic component, though a modest one. In any case, males from the modern prefectures of Corinthia and Argolis were found by Stamatoyannopoulos et al.[106] to have only moderate incidences of G6PD-deficiency (5.5 percent and 2.8 percent, respectively), far below those of the highest-incidence prefectures in Greece.

An Estimate of the Likely Incidence of Favism among Pythagoras's Followers

The argument could be made that, even if Pythagoras was not afflicted with favism, he may have instituted the ban on fava beans in the interests of his followers in Magna Graecia. By tradition, he came from Samos to Croton, and it was there that he established the Pythagorean brotherhood and there, presumably, that the bean ban was instituted. I would feel more comfortable with the position that Pythagoras established his ban in the interests of followers in Magna Graecia if they had derived from parts of Greece where incidences of G6PD-deficiency and favism are high today, or if G6PD-deficiency and favism were common in Italy today, especially in the south. The cities of Magna Graecia were likely of mixed Greek and non-Greek genetic background,[107] and this, together with the fact that its Greek settlers did not come from a single part of Greece, provides few clues. On the other hand, there is evidence on incidences of G6PD-deficiency in Italy today that may provide insights into the question.

Except for Sardinia, incidences of G6PD-deficiency in males decrease markedly in the Mediterranean area west of Greece.[108] One random sample of over 6,000 schoolboys tested in 52 villages in Sardinia, for example, found that boys from 23 of the 52 villages had incidences of G6PD-deficiency between 20 and 35 percent.[109] Other studies have confirmed that, despite striking local differences, Sardinia has by far the highest average incidence of G6PD-deficiency (about 12–15 percent of all males)[110] of any part of Italy, and, until recent decades, it had far higher incidences of favism as well (in 1905, 5.2 cases per 1,000 inhabitants).[111] I know of nothing in the tales about Pythagoras, however, to suggest that he travelled to Sardinia. Instead, his travels in the region of Italy seem to have been limited to Magna Graecia (southern Italy) and Sicily. Thus, if modern patterns of favism prevailed in antiquity and Pythagoras did observe the symptoms of favism in the Italian region, it is highly likely that he did so not in Sardinia but in mainland Italy and Sicily. This leads to the question of what modern patterns of G6PD-deficiency and favism may be in mainland Italy, especially the south, as well as in Sicily.

Compared with Sardinia, far lower incidences of G6PD-deficiency have been reported among Italian males in mainland northern and central Italy (mean for all males included in one survey of studies: 1.3 percent; range among studies: 0–4.8 percent).[112] In one test of 883 males from these two regions, for example, only 3 (0.34 percent) had G6PD-deficiency (Piedmont, Lombardy, Liguria, 0.32 percent; Emilia, Veneto, 0 percent; Toscana, Lazio, Marche, Umbria, 0.89 percent).[113] In a second study[114] only 4 of 426 males (0.94 percent) from Ferrara and Veneto were found to have G6PD-deficiency. A third study,[115] of 1,557 unselected male and female subjects from Umbria, found none who had G6PD-deficiency, which led researchers to the conclusion that the trait is extremely rare in central Italy. In another study,[116] the district of L'Aquila, northeast of Rome, was deliberately chosen because its people are descendants of early Italic tribes; because the region is isolated, set apart by high mountains; because in the past two millennia it did not experience significant immigration; and because its people have certain genetic markers that set them apart from other Italians. G6PD-deficiency was found in only 3 of 215 infant and adult males tested (1.4 percent).

People living in regions of ancient Greek settlement in southern Italy (Campania, Calabria, Basilicata, Puglia) also have low incidences of G6PD-deficiency.[117] One study at Salerno in Campania, for example, found 1.2 percent of a group of 286 unrelated males to have G6PD-deficiency.[118] Another study,[119] of schoolchildren in Campania—including some from such places of ancient Greek settlement as Ischia (Greek

Pithecusa) and Naples (Neapolis)—found that only 8 of 1,371 boys (0.58 percent) had G6PD-deficiency. A subsequent study found G6PD-deficiency in 1.3 percent (6 of 459) of randomly selected male college students born in Naples.[120] Among the studies Livingstone considered, one involved 117 men, most from southern Italy (including some from Calabria, the region where Crotone is located). None of the men had G6PD-deficiency, and only 1 of 114 women (0.87 percent) did.[121] A study by Rickards et al. of 707 unrelated male donors from Calabria found that 4.4 percent of donors from Catanzaro, 2.7 percent of those from Reggio Calabria, and 1.3 percent of those from Cosenza had G6PD-deficiency.[122] Also relevant to the question of G6PD and the ancient Greeks of southern Italy is an impressive study by Tagarelli and his colleagues[123] involving 35,660 healthy boys and girls (ages 11–13), which was carried out over a period of six years in widely scattered communities in Cosenza, the Calabrian province adjoining Crotone's province, Catanzaro, to the north. Only 209 (1.24 percent) of 16,787 male children tested in non-Albanian[124] communities in Cosenza Province, including ones located in highlands, river valleys, and coastal areas, were found to have G6PD-deficiency.[125] Because Greek settlement was primarily in coastal areas and because Greek genetic impact was concentrated there, it is notable that, of 3,855 male children from communities along the Ionian coast of Cosenza, only 74 (1.92 percent) had G6PD-deficiency.[126] This is notable because along the Ionian Sea shores of present-day Cosenza was ancient Sybaris (settled c. 720 B.C.), which, like Croton (settled c. 703 B.C.), was established by Achaean Greeks. Once Sybaris was one of the most populous, powerful, and prosperous cities of the Greek world (it was razed by armies from Croton in 510 B.C. and again in 457 B.C.). Across the highlands of Cosenza to the west and on the Tyrrhenian Sea coast were other Greek settlements: Laus (later Lavinium), a colony of Sybaris; and Tempsa (Temesa), noted for its trade in copper. Of 3,453 male children from non-Albanian communities along the Tyrrhenian coast, only 32 (0.93 percent) had G6PD-deficiency.[127] It has also been noted that in Matera, the province bordering Cosenza to the east, the frequency of G6PD-deficiency seems to be higher along the Ionian Sea and to decrease with distance from the coast.[128] Along the Ionian shores of Matera are the ruins of the ancient city of Metapontum, which was established by settlers from Sybaris and Croton about 700 B.C. and which was the place, according to Aristotle and Aristoxenus,[129] where Pythagoras died.[130] I conclude from the above that Italian males in southern Italy have incidences of G6PD-deficiency (average for all persons included in the studies cited above: 1.2 percent; range, 0.58–4.4 percent) comparable to those of northern and central Italy; that areas of ancient Greek settlement along the Ionian Sea—Pythagoras's center of activities—seem to have incidences of G6PD-deficiency higher than inland areas where Greek genetic influence is less and altitude is higher; but that, even along the Ionian Sea, present-day incidences of G6PD-deficiency among males may be only 2 to 4 or 5 percent, far lower than those in Sardinia (12–15 percent), in Achaea in Greece (8.6 percent), or in the Peloponnesus as a whole (5.9 percent).[131]

Also of interest in Cosenza Province is the fact that, in non-Albanian communities in the province's four principal geographic zones (Ionian coast, Tyrrhenian coast, Esaro and Crati river valleys, highlands), it is only along the Ionian coast that the Mediterranean phenotype of G6PD is more common than non-Mediterranean G6PD-deficiency phenotypes as a group. Furthermore, on the Tyrrhenian coast of Cosenza nearly all individuals in non-Albanian communities who carry the Mediterranean phenotype live in areas near the ancient Greek settlements of Laus and Tempsa. The non-Mediterranean G6PD-deficiency phenotypes, on their part, have a relatively even distribution, giving the impression that some or all of them are autochthonous. These G6PD phenotype distributions also agree with the view that the ancient Greeks introduced the Mediterranean phenotype (by far the most common phenotype of G6PD-deficiency in Greece)[132] first to the Ionian coast and that it then spread westward to Greek settlements on the Tyrrhenian coast. A similar hypothesis, advanced by Brancati and Tagarelli for thalassemia, is supported by a marked correspondence in Calabria between areas of ancient Greek settlement and areas where incidences of thalassemia are highest.[133]

Equally important is the fact that in southern Italy not all G6PD-deficiency phenotypes involve severe deficiency. Indeed, Rickards et al.[134] identified 11 common G6PD-deficiency variants, and, of these, 10 were associated with mild enzyme deficiency, with G6PD activity from 15 to 50 percent of normal. The percentages of all cases of G6PD-deficiency represented by mild variants differ from place to place in southern Italy. In Bari, there were no cases involving mild variants. In Matera, mild variants accounted for 30 percent of all cases; and in Naples and in southern Italy in general, 68 percent.[135] More relevant to the question of Pythagoras is the finding by Tagarelli, Bastone, et al.[136] that, in Cosenza Province, mild to moderate forms of G6PD-deficiency (enzyme activity between 5 and 60 percent of normal) accounted for more than half (53.6 percent) of all cases. What this means—since favism is less likely to develop where mild or moderate forms of G6PD-deficiency are involved—is that crude figures of incidences of G6PD-deficiency, at least in southern Italy, may lead to exaggerated expectations of favism. That would not, however, be so in places like Sardinia, where 92 percent of all cases of G6PD-deficiency are characterized by severe deficiency (G6PD activity only 0–5 percent of normal).[137]

Favism does, of course, occur today in areas of ancient Greek settlement and elsewhere in mainland Italy,[138] as well as in persons of mainland origin who have moved elsewhere.[139] At the same time, favism is not a serious public health problem in mainland Italy today, and only occasional cases are reported there.[140]

In our search to estimate what the incidences of G6PD-deficiency and favism may have been in the ancient haunts of Pythagoras in the Italian region, Sicily may provide further useful clues. It is true that favism poses a significant public health problem in modern Sicily.[141] At the same time, incidences of G6PD-deficiency are quite low in comparison with Sardinia. In one study, of 3,347 boys from all parts of Sicily, only 56 (1.67 percent) were found to be G6PD-deficient.[142] In another study, of 300 males mainly from Catania Province, only 4 (1.33 percent) were G6PD-deficient.[143] In a third study, healthy males (from 2 to 12 years of age) deriving from eastern Sicily—most coming from the two ancient Greek centers of Catania and Syracuse (principal Greek city in ancient Sicily) or their provinces—were studied and only 3 of 420, or 0.7 percent, were G6PD-deficient. The latter study also involved 677 male infants from central and western Sicily (city and province of Palermo, provinces of Trapani, Agrigento, and Caltanisseta), of whom 10 were G6PD-deficient, or 1.48 percent.[144] Finding significantly higher percentages of G6PD-deficiency was a study by Rickards et al.[145] in which 2.5 percent of 3,167 unrelated male Sicilian donors from various parts of the island were found to be G6PD-deficient, though in some places percentages were notably higher (Ragusa, 6.3 percent; Syracuse, 4.5 percent; Catania, 3.4 percent). Males from Agrigento, the Sicilian place most closely associated in lore with Pythagoras and his followers, had a frequency of G6PD-deficiency of 2.1 percent. As in southern Italy, the bulk of G6PD variants in Sicily are mild ones (with 15–50 percent of normal G6PD activity), and mild deficiency appears to be far more common than severe deficiency nearly everywhere (in Agrigento, mild deficiency characterized 100 percent of deficiency cases; in Catania, 82 percent; Syracuse, 76 percent; Ragusa and Messina, 75 percent; Palermo, 67 percent; and Caltanissetta, 25 percent).[146]

Carrying the matter a step further, we have seen that only a small minority of G6PD-deficient persons in the Mediterranean area are sensitive to fava beans, and by far the greatest number of them are young children. It is thus no surprise to read that almost all deaths from favism occur in children;[147] that generally favism is a pediatric disease;[148] and that even on Rhodes, where favism is a serious problem, it is very rare among adults, and even in busy general hospitals only isolated adult cases are found.[149]

If we were to assume that present-day incidences of G6PD-deficiency and favism are similar to those of antiquity, we would have some idea of what those incidences may have been among males in the southern Italy–Sicily area at the time of Pythagoras. Let us suppose, therefore, that at the time of Pythagoras incidences of G6PD-deficiency among Greek males in Magna Graecia and Sicily averaged 2–4 percent (as we shall see, in all probability those percentages are significantly higher today because of genetic selection related to malaria over more than two millennia). Of all G6PD-deficient Greek males, however, only a small percentage (10–13 percent) actually develop favism, even though they may continue to eat fava beans.[150] If one uses the figure of 15 percent, that would amount to about 0.3–0.6 percent of all males who experience favism. The overwhelming number of G6PD-deficient individuals, however, have favism as young children, and only a very small percentage (say, 5 percent), as adults.[151] Thus, one would expect that only about 0.015–0.03 percent males—that is, roughly 1 in 3,000 to 1 in 6,500—would normally experience the symptoms of favism at some time or another during adulthood. Thus the cases of favism among the ancient Pythagoreans, if they were similar to those of general Greek society in Magna Graecia and Sicily, were probably very few indeed, for the total number of Pythagoreans must have amounted to thousands, not millions, of people.[152] The number of severely afflicted persons may have been even lower, because women were included among members of the Pythagorean society,[153] and, as we have seen, compared with men they are far less likely to develop severe cases of the disease.

Also germane is the ability of many persons who have had an attack of favism to eat fava beans afterwards without ill effect.[154] Kattamis et al.,[155] after questioning large numbers of favism patients in Greece, found (1) that most patients who had attacks following the first time they consumed fava beans were later able to eat them without ill effect; and (2) that, among patients who had attacks only after consuming fava beans on several occasions, just a few had second or third attacks. This fits with the observation by Schilirò et al.,[156] in a study in Sicily, that, subsequent to an attack of favism, patients commonly eat fava beans with little or no difficulty. It also fits with earlier reports from Sardinia that, among 84 men who had developed overt favism but continued to eat fava beans, only about half experienced a second hemolytic attack.[157]

In light of the above, it would have made little sense for Pythagoras, or any other leader, to ban fava beans, a dietary staple, to all adult members of his group because of fear of favism. The handful of seriously afflicted adults could have stopped eating fava beans on their own, if they had been so inclined, without a formal ban of any sort.

Modern evidence suggests that self-regulation works reasonably well; that there may be restrictions on the consumption of fava beans by children; that persons who have experienced severe attacks of favism usually abstain from fava beans for a while, with varying degrees of stringency; that they do not, however, develop a revulsion for fava beans; that they usually go back to eating them on a regular basis; and that even repeated attacks and bans on cultivation of fava beans may not end consumption.[158]

Had Pythagoras been aware of the risks of favism, moreover, it would have been wiser for him to single out in his ban the young children of his followers, not adult members.[159] If disease had been his concern, failure to focus on children of members in this regard would have been especially odd in light of his favorable view of marriage and his encouragement of sex and procreation. He held that marriage is a sacred and desirable state, and that members should bear children so that after they died there would still be humans to worship the gods. Children were also considered a means of assuring the survival of the Pythagorean brotherhood.[160]

In addition, Pythagoras abhorred killing and had a great respect for life, or at least forms of life that contain souls.[161] Thus, if indeed he had known of the fava bean–favism association, it is hard to imagine that he would not have made the good news public so that it could have benefitted all people. It is also unlikely that a discovery so important in terms of public health could have remained a secret. Yet not only is there no mention of the fava bean–favism association, but also the eating of fava beans by the public continued unabated, and the Pythagorean bean ban, far from being emulated, was the butt of jokes.

Was the Pythagorean Brotherhood a Special Case, a Society of Persons Afflicted with Favism?

The possibility still remains that the Pythagorean brotherhood was not a normal cross-section of society, but rather, as Lieber[162] has suggested, a community of persons afflicted with favism. In addition to the bean field tales, Lieber presents two principal bits of supporting evidence, both from Iamblichus. One is Iamblichus's observation that it was customary for Pythagoreans to change their place of residence at different seasons of the year.[163] Lieber views these seasonal movements as transhumance, migrations between highland and lowland. Transhumant migrations have long been common in Mediterranean lands, both among herdsmen seeking pasture for their animals and among others seeking relief from the heat and illnesses of summer. Lieber suggests that the Pythagorean seasonal migrations may have been attempts to avoid the danger posed by fava beans in flower by going into the mountains where no agriculture was practiced. One objection to this suggestion is that Iamblichus said nothing to indicate that the seasonal migrations were transhumant in nature. An even more serious objection is the fact that the migration cited by Lieber was described by Iamblichus as a "migration from Tarentum to Metapontum." This migration did take the Pythagoreans through a "a craggy part of Tarentum," but basically it was a migration from one lowland city to another. Tarentum was a port on the Gulf of Tarentum. Metapontum, about 24 miles away, was at the mouth of a river that emptied into the gulf. That the intent of the Pythagorean migration was to escape into the mountains seems out of the question.

Also relevant—if pollen was, in fact, a matter of concern—is Luisada's observation[164] that fava bean pollen is liberated only in small amounts, has a high specific gravity, is sticky, and, though it may be inhaled in or near cultivated fields, is not disseminated widely. Thus if the Pythagoreans had wished to avoid inhaling fava bean pollen, remaining in Tarentum, a city that in all likelihood was largely free of such danger, would have made more sense than risking proximity to cultivated bean fields on their way to Metapontum.

Lieber[165] finds her second bit of evidence in statements by Iamblichus about candidates being carefully examined and observed before a final decision was made on granting them membership in the Pythagorean brotherhood.[166] Lieber sees this, in part, as an effort to identify individuals in particular danger of favism, who, in a society of favists, have special needs regarding strictness of diet and place of residence. Iamblichus, however, says nothing to suggest that favism may have been involved. Instead, he writes that students who wished to study with Pythagoras were first examined, tested, and questioned by Pythagoras about their relationships with their parents and relatives. Then Pythagoras observed them for inappropriate laughter and excessive talking or silence. He also considered their acquaintances and the candidates' dealings with them, as well as their leisure-time activities, desires, and things that made them happy or sad. He viewed their physiques and bodily movements, including the way they walked, because such visible things were thought to reveal the unseen character of the soul. Candidates were then supervised for three years to determine whether they were inclined toward stability and had a genuine affection for learning, and whether they disliked fame and could ignore the regard in which they were held by others. After the three years ended, candidates entered a five-year period of silence, during which they might listen to discourses by Pythagoras but not see him. This period was also intended to reveal more about candidates' character, including their morality, self-control, and suitability for the life and observances of the brotherhood. A candidate also underwent instruction in science, as well as in performing rituals and purification of the soul. Then, if the candidate demonstrated a quick mind "and alertness of . . . soul," he or she was admitted. If, on the other hand, the candidate was found ungainly and had difficulty understanding, dismissal followed.

The above procedure, described by Iamblichus several hundred years after the time of Pythagoras, strikes me as highly improbable. Indeed, it is so lengthy as to make one wonder how many candidates could possibly have become members in the mere three decades from the time Pythagoras arrived in Magna Graecia until he died. In all likelihood, we are dealing with a tall tale by Iamblichus, one that reveals a lively imagination. For Lieber to insert favism and a society of the afflicted into Iamblichus's tale is an even greater feat of imagination, and, to me, one that simply stretches credulity too far.

Malaria as a Clue to Understanding the History of Favism, and Its Bearing on the Favism Hypothesis

My final evidence on the bean ban of Pythagoras relates to the malaria hypothesis that has been championed by many scholars as an explanation for the high incidences of G6PD-deficiency in some human populations around the world.[167] According to the malaria hypothesis, G6PD-deficiency, like sickle-cell anemia and thalassemia, is a blood defect whose evolutionary role changed, at some time in the past, from representing a selective disadvantage to becoming, in balance, a selective advantage. The selective disadvantage of G6PD-deficiency is that it places infants at risk of neonatal jaundice and all individuals, but especially young children, at risk of favism. The selective advantage of G6PD-deficiency is that it provides certain carriers of the gene (heterozygote females)[168] with greater ability to escape death from falciparum malaria.[169] This, in turn, derives from the composition of their blood, from an interruption in the multiplication of malaria parasites in the presence of both G6PD-normal and G6PD-deficient erythrocytes, and from a significant reduction in parasite load.[170] The last is important because parasite load is intimately tied to mortality from malaria.[171]

Other factors, including biochemical and pharmacological ones,[172] may also be directly involved. One notes, for example, that, though females heterozygous for G6PD-deficiency can develop favism, the trait is less likely to be fully expressed, symptoms are usually milder, and severe hemolytic crises are rare.[173] Thus, such females might reasonably be expected, on average, to consume larger amounts of fava beans than persons more likely to develop severe symptoms of favism (hemizygous-deficient males, homozygous-deficient females).[174] If so, this might provide them with an enhanced selective advantage. This fits with the suggestion by Huheey and Martin[175] that the fava bean itself is directly involved in the selective process. It also fits with studies that demonstrate that toxic elements in fava beans can indeed inhibit the growth of, or kill, malaria parasites and eliminate infected erythrocytes more quickly, particularly G6PD-deficient erythrocytes.[176]

Human malaria parasites are thought to have evolved in Old World primates in tropical Africa or Southeast Asia.[177] Of the four malaria parasite species that normally infect humans, three are found in the Mediterranean area (*Plasmodium vivax, P. malariae,* and *P. falciparum*).[178] The former two parasites bring on forms of malaria in humans (*P. vivax,* benign tertian malaria; and *P. malariae,* quartan malaria) that are far less life-threatening than malaria brought on by *P. falciparum* (semitertian, or malignant tertian, malaria). *P. falciparum,* because of its virulence and specificity to humans,[179] is thought to be the most recent mutant of the four malaria parasites that normally infect mankind. It is generally found in tropical and subtropical areas, and it may be that humans were first infected by falciparum malaria in Africa, where it is endemic. In any case, falciparum malaria is the form of the disease that concerns us here. As Haldane has observed, it fully meets the criteria established for an evolutionary agent that can select for specific resistance genes (such as those for G6PD-deficiency). Falciparum malaria is, and has been over a long time span, a major killer of humans, and it can do so before humans begin to bear offspring.[180]

As Livingstone[181] has pointed out, population densities among Paleolithic hunters and gatherers were too low to have maintained malaria rates of transmission and endemicity at high levels. Conditions changed, however, when, after the domestication of plants and animals, higher densities of human population developed. After reviewing evidence on differences in gene frequencies for the sickle-cell trait, thalassemia, and G6PD-deficiency, Livingstone[182] concluded that in all probability malaria has been a major factor in genetic selection among humans for no more than 5,000 years, and more probably, for populations with which he is concerned (among them the Greeks), for 2,000 years or so.[183] Malaria of some sort does seem to have been known in the eastern Mediterranean area long before the latter date, but falciparum malaria—far and away the most serious contender for the role of primary malarial agent of selection, and perhaps the only likely one[184]—is thought to have been a late-comer, at least in Greece and Italy.

In support of a late arrival for falciparum malaria in Europe is the work of Bruce-Chwatt and Zulueta,[185] who carefully weighed conditions there from Pleistocene times onward: glacial advance and retreat; climate and climatic change; *Anopheles* mosquitoes of the region and their ability to transmit malaria parasites; temperature requirements of mosquito vectors and those needed for malaria parasites to mature; adaptation of malaria parasites to transmission by the vectors present; human population numbers and density, settlement, trade, and vegetation change as they affected the breeding of mosquitoes and/or transmission of the disease; and the spread of new species of *Anopheles* to the region. The authors conclude that in all likelihood malaria first came to Europe via the Nile Valley.[186] They contend that, though malaria may have spread widely across Europe during interglacial phases, in all likelihood most of Europe was free of malaria during a large part of the Pleistocene period. They also conclude that during the Neolithic and Bronze Age prevalences of malaria were low, and the disease, mild in form and a minor problem. Finally, they conclude that *Plasmodium malariae* and *P. vivax* remained the only malaria parasites on the Continent until relatively recent historical times.

Prior to the appearance of falciparum malaria, G6PD-deficient persons are presumed to have been at a selective disadvantage compared with normal persons. This resulted in incidences of G6PD-deficiency in the general population that in all likelihood were quite low,[187] because persons with the trait experienced higher mortality than persons without it. Some G6PD-deficient infants died of neonatal jaundice, and other G6PD-deficient individuals, especially infants and young children, died of favism. Assuming an absence of falciparum malaria, selection against G6PD-deficiency likely prevailed in the eastern Mediterranean area since remote antiquity. In the hunting and gathering stage, people collected wild forms of *Vicia* ancestral to the fava bean, which likely contained vicine and convicine in significant amounts. Later, with domestication of *Vicia faba* (7000–6500 B.C.?), selection against G6PD-deficiency probably increased because cultivated fava beans were available more widely and in much greater quantities.[188]

With the arrival of falciparum malaria, certain persons with genes for G6PD-deficiency are thought to have gained a selective advantage in terms of malaria that outweighed its selective disadvantage in terms of neonatal jaundice and favism. As a result, high incidences of G6PD-deficiency tended to develop in places where the malaria problem was particularly severe. The possibility that such changes could develop in a relatively short historical period is suggested by Szeinberg and Sheba. Their research found no G6PD-deficiency among males of the Samaritan community, which seems to have existed in Palestine since at least the eighth century B.C. They also found quite low incidences of G6PD-deficiency among male Libyan Jews (0.9 percent), who, judging from comparisons of gene frequencies of various sorts, must have left the common gene pool about 800–700 B.C. Similar low incidences of G6PD-deficiency were found among male Jews from Northwest Africa (Tunisia, Algeria, Morocco, 0.8 percent), and among male Ashkenazi (0.4 percent) and Sephardic (0.7–2.2 percent) Jews of European origin. In contrast with the above, male Kurdish and Iraqi Jews have very high incidences of G6PD-deficiency (58 percent and 25 percent, respectively).[189] The time of the historical separation of the ancestors of the Kurdish and Iraqi (Babylonian) Jews from the common gene pool, moreover, dates to about 586 B.C.[190]

A critical question remaining is, When did falciparum malaria appear in Greece and Italy? We have seen above that the Hippocratic writers knew malaria. They classified fevers as continuous and intermittent; included among the intermittent fevers tertian and quartan; and described a semitertian fever that was severe and especially likely to kill the patient.[191] Observers have generally thought that the latter was likely falciparum malaria.[192] If so, falciparum malaria was known in Greece in the fifth or fourth century B.C. On the other hand, Bruce-Chwatt and Zulueta,[193] while admitting that the Hippocratic works contain nearly certain evidence for the presence of *P. vivax* and *P. malariae* in Greece, consider the evidence for the presence of *P. falciparum* as far from convincing.

Two important historical sources on the antiquity of malaria in Greece[194] and Italy[195] point to evidence of intensive agriculture, dense settlement, and flourishing trade in areas that in later times were cursed by severe malaria and small and lethargic human populations. As to the antiquity of malaria in Greece, there is a controversial statement by Homer (ninth or eighth century B.C.) that some scholars view as referring to malaria. There are, however, questions of whether a critical word, not used again prior to the fifth century, means "heat" or "fever." Jones considers the matter to be uncertain but notes that, even if Homer was in fact referring to malaria, his statement may have applied only to the west coast of Anatolia most familiar to him.[196] Also pertinent are the writings of Hesiod (c. 800 B.C.), who lived in Boeotia, a region of central Greece that early in this century was among the unhealthiest in the entire country, barely habitable because of its severe malaria. Yet, though Hesiod does write of diseases on a few occasions, there is no clear mention of malaria. Jones also points to the fact that the ancient Boeotian city of

Orchomenus, on Lake Copais, was noted for its great wealth, an unlikely condition had malaria been a serious problem.[197] His further review of ancient Greek literature, both medical and nonmedical, led Jones to the conclusion that it is quite possible, though by no means certain, that malaria was known in mainland Greece as early as 550–500 B.C. He also views it likely that by 500 B.C. it was common in Magna Graecia and on the shores of Anatolia, and that, in any case, much of the Greek world was highly malarious by 400 B.C.[198] Bruce-Chwatt and Zulueta,[199] while accepting the view that some sections of Greece were highly malarial by that date, insist that, if falciparum malaria was known then in Greece, it must have been rare, and they suggest that *P. falciparum* probably spread across Greece at the start of the first millennium A.D.

What other historical evidence is there bearing on the importance of malaria in the Greek and Roman worlds? Celli notes that, like the Latin towns in Latium, the Greek cities of Magna Graecia were successful in the centuries following their founding but underwent a striking decline starting in the fourth century B.C., in all likelihood because of malaria.[200] Similar views, that there was a striking increase in the severity of malaria in ancient Italy, are held by other authorities as well, though they may differ about the exact dates when malaria developed into a far more serious health problem. P. F. Russell[201] suggests that malaria was common in Italy following roughly 200 B.C., that it was a major factor during the time of the Roman Republic, and that it became even more of a problem during the period of the Roman Empire. Bruce-Chwatt and Zulueta[202] write of an increase in malaria prevalences and severity in Italy starting in Hellenistic times. They suggest that the disease posed a major problem in late Roman and Byzantine times. Possibly this came about because of the introduction of *P. falciparum* (which seems to have been present in Italy by the second century A.D.). It was furthered by this parasite's adaptation to transmission by species of *Anopheles* mosquitoes long known in the Mediterranean area and by the arrival of new species of *Anopheles* that were more effective in transmitting *P. falciparum*.

In a review of archeological evidence for Sardinia, Brown[203] was struck by its more than 7,000 stone towers (*nuraghe*), which date from the Bronze Age. He was also impressed by the fact that they are found in greatest concentrations in the very areas where, in later times, malaria was severe. This, he argues, suggests that malaria was either absent or of minor consequence to the nuraghic peoples. Brown notes that most historians agree that malaria was not endemic in prehistoric Sardinia, and he suspects that there was little malaria on the island prior to the fifth century B.C., even though, during the Roman period (starting 238 B.C.), Sardinia was notorious for its insalubriousness brought on by malaria.

Brown attributes the worsening of the malaria problem in Sardinia to changes brought on by the Punic (Carthaginian) conquest of the fifth century B.C. Certain other scholars are inclined to give the Punics an even broader role in spreading malaria in the region. Laderman,[204] in a review of the early history and ecology of malaria, notes that the Punics voyaged far down the Atlantic coast of Africa into areas where the malaria parasites are presumed to have evolved. She suggests further that they may have played a key role in spreading the disease throughout the Mediterranean area and Near East.[205] She credits them with introducing malaria to Sardinia in the seventh century B.C., somewhat earlier than Brown suggested, and to Magna Graecia in the mid-sixth century B.C. She agrees that the earliest certain evidence of malaria in Greece itself dates from the fifth century B.C., and suggests that it may have been introduced to Greece by various routes from the sixth to the fourth century B.C., one possible source being the athletes and other people who came to the Olympic Games from Magna Graecia. Moreover, the longer the time after malaria became endemic in a region, Laderman insists, the higher that frequencies of G6PD were likely to be.[206]

If indeed malaria became a serious problem in Greece and Magna Graecia in the period following 550–400 B.C., selection for higher incidences of G6PD-deficiency probably began only in the time of Pythagoras or after his death in 500 B.C.[207] If this is true, when Pythagoras instituted the bean ban, incidences of G6PD-deficiency were significantly lower in southern Italy and Sicily than they came to be in later times, and favism was a quite minor problem compared with that of modern times. As we have seen, moreover, incidences of G6PD-deficiency remain low in southern Italy, even though malaria was common there in the past.[208] Such low prevailing levels of G6PD-deficiency make it still more doubtful that Pythagoras would have instituted his ban on fava beans out of concern with favism.

Such a ban would have been even less likely for Croton, for in striking contrast to the remainder of Magna Graecia, Croton remained very healthy even in the time of Strabo (c. 64 B.C.–A.D. 23).[209] This is shown in the proverb "more healthful than Croton." The city's healthiness is also reflected in the tradition that, before leaving Greece, Myscellus, founder of Croton, was asked by the oracle at Delphi whether he preferred wealth or health and, when he said health, Croton was chosen as the place for him to found. The city's salubriousness was further reflected in the repeated successes of its athletes in Olympic competition. This led to the saying "the last of the Crotoniates was the first among all other Greeks." Croton's healthy condition in Pythagoras's day is suggested by the fact that Milo, the noted athlete mentioned previously, was a companion of Pythagoras.[210]

Summary and Conclusions

There is no convincing historical evidence that favism was recognized as a disease in the time of Pythagoras. There is no evidence that people knew that consumption of fava beans could bring on hemolytic crises. Indeed, the first clear historical evidence of favism and its association with the consumption of fava beans dates from the mid-nineteenth century A.D. This, it should be emphasized, is nearly 2.5 millennia after Pythagoras died.

Nor is there anything substantial in the accounts of Pythagoras to suggest that his ban on fava beans was based on concern with their danger to human health. The principal evidence of this sort, tales of the refusal of Pythagoras and his followers to pass through a bean field, cannot be accepted uncritically, for, at the earliest, they date from 200 years after Pythagoras's death. There are also serious questions about the reliability of some of the writers in whose works such tales are found or to whom they are attributed. Thus, the tales are best viewed, not as accurate historical documents, but as part of the legend that came to surround Pythagoras over the centuries.

Even if the tales are accurate historically, there is nothing in them to suggest that the refusal of Pythagoras or the Pythagoreans was based on fear of symptoms brought on by inhalation of pollen, as certain advocates of the favism hypothesis contend. Instead, their refusal was based on an unwillingness to violate a cult doctrine not to touch beans or walk on them. Modern evidence, moreover, is equivocal on the question of whether the hemolytic crises of favism can be brought on by inhalation of fava bean pollen. Some evidence supports the possibility. Other evidence raises questions about it. Especially telling is the skepticism that prevails among recent authorities.

Also relevant, the contention that Pythagoras himself may have suffered from favism is not supported by a modern study on the incidence of G6PD-deficiency on Samos, where Pythagoras was likely born. In that study, all persons tested were G6PD-normal and thus able to eat fava beans without risk of favism. The argument that Pythagoras may have established the fava bean ban to protect his followers is not supported by studies of G6PD-deficiency in present-day southern Italy and Sicily. Despite the occurrence of favism in those regions, the disease primarily affects young children, not adults. If my estimates for Magna Graecia and Sicily are correct, only about 1 in 3,000–6,500 males is likely to experience the symptoms of favism at some time in adulthood. Such low incidences, which in the time of Pythagoras were likely far lower, would hardly have justified banning fava beans for all adult members of the brotherhood. On the contrary, to institute such a ban would have been a serious matter that may have placed members at considerable nutritional risk, because fava beans were not only a dietary staple but also a major source of protein, perhaps the most important source of protein for those Pythagoreans who were strict vegetarians.

Evidence presented for the argument that the Pythagoreans were a society of favists who migrated seasonally to avoid flowering fields of fava beans is not in accord with evidence found in the documents cited. Nor does it fit with evidence that fava bean pollen has a high specific gravity and stickness that limit its dissemination and leave towns and cities largely free of the pollen. Consideration of the malaria hypothesis, moreover, suggests that genetic selection favoring G6PD-deficiency and an increase in the incidence of favism in Greece and Italy may not have developed until the time of Pythagoras or even later.

If we look beyond the Pythagorean movement, it is difficult to believe that other Greeks would not have become aware of favism had it been a serious problem. Yet apparently they did not. Why did the members of the Hippocratic school of medicine fail to recognize the problem? The answer may be that favism was quite rare in that period. Had favism been a serious problem in the Greco-Roman world, it would be surprising that the ancients, inventive as they were with foods and their preparation, would have failed to develop techniques to eliminate the toxicity of fava beans or to record efforts in that direction. We might reasonably expect them to have practiced techniques such as those mentioned above: use of microorganisms, their enzymes, or almond powder and lemon juice. It should be noted that the almond (*Prunus amygdalus*) is believed to have been domesticated by the third millennium B.C. or before in the region from the eastern Mediterranean to Central Asia.[211] Moreover, the first citrus fruit (the citron, *Citrus medica*) arrived from Southeast Asia by the middle of the first millennium B.C. or earlier.[212]

In light of the fact that virtually none of the evidence is in agreement with the favism hypothesis, it is surprising that it has gained such a firm standing among present-day biomedical writers. This may derive from a predisposition to favor explanations of the food bans of ancient peoples in terms of disease and genetics. One of the most controversial examples of this is the ancient Hebrew ban on pork, which, some have argued, derives from a fear of contracting trichinosis—a hypothesis I have examined and found wanting.[213] Indeed, it is difficult to escape the conclusion that the favism hypothesis, like the trichinosis hypothesis, is a form of medical materialism, in this case reflecting an all-too-ready tendency of present-day people to explain the origin of a food ban in terms of concern with health and disease, even though historical evidence is scanty or lacking altogether.

In the matter of the Pythagorean bean ban, I find the explanations given by ancient writers, summarized in the preceding chapter, to be far more believable. My conclusion in that chapter was that magico-religious concerns, however out of keeping they may be with the mind-set of secularists today, are quite reasonable and sufficient in themselves to account for the Pythagorean ban. Now, having weighed the evidence on the favism hypothesis, I cannot agree with the scholars who say that this is a case of "the influence of disease on behaviour"[214] or that "there is a direct biocultural evolutionary connection between the traditional aversion to fava bean consumption and its effects on genetically susceptible individuals."[215] Nor can I agree with Grmek, who, though acknowledging an absence of proof, tends toward the view that "the prohibition against eating broad beans [was] dictated or at least prompted by the actual observation of hemolytic incidents. . ."[216] On the contrary, I submit that the interesting story of favism, glucose-6-phosphate dehydrogenase, and malaria is a separate matter from the Pythagorean ban, and should be treated as such.

9 Pythagoras Lives
Parallels and Survivals of His Views of Beans in Modern and PreModern Times

> For the comparative ethnologist, the views propounded by the Pythagoreans on the subject of beans (broad beans, *faba*) . . . represent a particular example of probably earlier ideas and practices, whose geographical distribution seems considerably greater than an enquiry limited to the ancient world would suggest . . . the ethnologist cannot but pay attention to the recurrence of the selfsame beliefs and rites not only in the ancient world and outside the school of Pythagoras, but also, in a more general way, in the Old World and, as I intend to show here, in the New.
>
> —C. Lévi-Strauss, "Pythagoras in America"

Introduction

My chapter on the urd bean demonstrated that among Hindus there has been no severing of the thread linking their views of the ritual purity and impurity of urd beans with the views of the ancient Aryans. On the contrary, modern Hindu views of the suitability for ritual purposes of the urd bean—as well as meat, alcohol, sesame, garlic, mushrooms, salt, and honey—are remarkably consistent with those recorded in Vedic accounts thousands of years ago. Moreover, present-day Hindu thinking about the ritual uses of urd beans is an integral part of a vital, ongoing religion. Such thinking, unlike that surrounding the Pythagorean ban of the fava bean, is not a mere curiosity from remote antiquity. In the face of convincing evidence, it is difficult to escape the conclusion, reached in the urd chapter, that this bean's association with death, the dead, and underworld forces was the reason it came to be considered unacceptable for use on certain ritual occasions.

Even if they accept this conclusion, many secular Westerners find it difficult or impossible to associate such thinking with the origin of the Pythagorean ban on fava beans. Their reluctance may be related to our dealing, in the case of Pythagoras and the fava bean, not with the behavior of non-Western peoples, but with our own cultural heritage. Even more, Pythagoras is part of our Western *scientific* tradition. Thus, to many of us, it may appear far more reasonable that Pythagoras would have banned fava beans because of the danger of favism, than that he would have banned them because of magico-religious thinking involving death, the dead, evil spirits, and other underworld forces. Yet, as we have seen, there is strong evidence in ancient sources that Pythagoras did indeed ban fava beans because of such magico-religious concerns. This is not as strange as it may first appear to modern observers unfamiliar with the ancient sources, for Pythagoras was a many-sided person who, among other things, had a strong commitment to magic. This is clearly shown in the ancient statement by Hippolytus: "[Pythagoras] applied himself to magic [as well as to devising] a philosophy on the origin of Nature, based upon certain numbers and measures. . ."[1]

This chapter is intended to cast further light on the survival in the premodern and modern world of views of beans and other legumes similar to those of Pythagoras. My goal is threefold. First, it is to demonstrate the occurrence of such views among widely scattered peoples. Second, it is to show that even in Europe, where the scholarly controversy about Pythagoras and beans has continued unabated over the centuries,[2] ideas similar to his have persisted in folk behavior and folklore. Third, it is to suggest that, when considered against prevailing views of life, death, and the underworld, such views are eminently reasonable.

Association of Beans with Death, the Dead, and Underworld Forces

> [The bean] was under a ban with the Pythagorean system . . . as others have reported, because the souls of the dead are contained in a bean, and at all events it is for that reason that beans are employed in memorial services to dead relatives.
>
> —Pliny, *Natural History*

The association of beans and other legumes with death and the dead has survived into modern times in Europe. A prime example of this is their use as funeral foods in various places.[3] In the past in certain parts of Berry as well as in neighboring Marche in central France, for example, people always included a dish of beans or dried peas among the items served at a funeral dinner.[4] In the Marches of central Italy, a family coming back from the burial ground joined in eating a large plate of kidney beans.[5] Beans were also a major element among funeral dishes in Sardinia.[6] In parts of Friuli in northeastern Italy, it was customary for people to eat bean soup on the day the dead are commemorated. Elsewhere a special bread or cake that includes rye and vetch (likely *Vicia sativa,* a relative of fava beans) has been served to persons who come to pray for the dead person.[7] After a funeral in the Rimini region of northern Italy, the mourners returned to the home of the deceased for a funerary dinner which consisted of chick-pea soup. The serving provided for the deceased was later consumed by a member of the family.[8] As for eastern Europe, I have uncovered a fragmentary report of beans having had ties with the dead among Slavic people, too. I refer to an account of the former Polish-Russian province of Pintschov, where beans and honey were considered foods of the dead, and at memorial dinners, food consisted of beans and peas boiled in honey-water.[9]

Beans and other legumes have also been used in Europe on All Souls' Day. This is a time set aside by the Roman Catholic church (November 2 or 3) for an annual memorial feast for all departed souls. In establishing All Souls' Day, the Church seems to have taken over a pre-Christian festival, which, among Celtic peoples, was held in early November, a time of year—the end of fall and beginning of winter—when souls of the dead returned to their homes and were fed, partly in fear that, if disgruntled, they might harm the living.[10] The association with death is revealed by the fact that in churches on this day the ceremonial color is black.

On All Souls' Day in western Europe today, people fix a meal of cooked beans, peas, or lentils, which they call soul food and give to the poor, along with meat and other edibles.[11] On All Souls' Day in the Italian Tyrol, it is bean soup that some well-to-do people give to the poor.[12] On this day in rural areas of Russia, symbolism has been reported involving wheat and honey placed on graves and then offered to passersby while saying, with solemnity, "May God forgive your sins."[13] This is in keeping with the observation made previously that honey, like beans, has associations with death and the underworld.[14]

Among the other foods associated with the dead in Europe are specially prepared "soul bread" or "soul cake." These foods have been made on All Souls' Day for distribution to visitors, the poor, and children.[15] In some places such bread or cake may simply be called souls. In Britain in the past, the custom of "souling" involved adults, children, and the poor going from house to house, singing, and receiving gifts of cakes, sweets, fruit, or money. Today the custom is still followed by children in certain rural areas of Shropshire and Cheshire.[16] In parts of Austria as well, poor persons may go from one house to the next to offer a prayer or sing a hymn in honor of the holy souls, for which they are given small loaves of soul bread.[17] There is a report that, among certain Germans of Bohemia, soul cakes have been, appropriately, black in color,[18] but I have found nothing to indicate whether flour of legumes was ever an ingredient in soul bread or soul cake, in the way Ezekiel was ordered by God to include fava bean and lentil flour in a bread to symbolize the impending destruction of Jerusalem.[19] In Sicily and in Perugia, however, the symbolism of death is unmistakable. Cakes or candies prepared on All Souls' Day bore such images as skulls, bones, skeletons, and souls in purgatory, and when they were eaten it was called eating the dead.[20] In northern Spain and in Madrid, moreover, people prepare a special All Souls' Day pastry called bones of the holy.[21] On All Souls' Day in parts of central Europe, boys are given soul cakes shaped like hares; and girls, cakes shaped like hens. This represents a curious joining of food for the dead with symbols of fertility.[22]

Cakes have also been prepared for funerals and memorial ceremonies of other sorts in Europe. In Bavaria, the rising of the dough in preparing such "corpse-cakes" was thought to absorb the good qualities of the dead person, which were passed on to the relatives who ate them.[23] In Albania, funeral "cakes," dishes of boiled wheat and other ingredients, are carried in the procession to the grave, where they are consumed by mourners after the deceased has been buried. In parts of the Balkans such cakes may bear an image of the person who has died. At Calymnos in Greece, this dish, called *kólyva,* may be carefully guarded in the house of the dead person the night before the funeral. Such dishes are carried to the church, then to the place of burial, where they are set down and passed out to mourners.[24]

Kólyva is described by Stavroulakis[25] as a dish made of boiled wheat mixed with raisins, pomegranate seeds, and honey. He notes that in antiquity this dish was used in placating chthonian deities such as Poseidon, Persephone, and Pluto. This fits with the special links honey and the pomegranate had with underworld deities, as noted previously. In addition, other ingredients—such as nuts, sesame, currants, dates, figs, sugar, cinnamon, and other flavorings or spices—may be mixed in or sprinkled on the kólyva.

Another occasion when kólyva is used in modern Greece is when souls of the deceased return to the world of the living. This occurs regularly on three All Souls' Days. On these days, one may see long processions of women and girls, dressed in black, carrying kólyva to cemeteries. It is then offered to the dead, such as by sprinkling it over their graves.[26] After offerings are made, candles may be lighted and incense burned at the family tomb.[27] Greek housewives may prepare an additional large tray of kólyva for relatives who have died childless, met their deaths abroad or in war, or have died long ago, for kólyva is considered protective against their ill will.[28] Housewives may also offer kólyva to their neighbors to gain forgiveness for the sins of dead relatives.[29]

Kólyva is also used by Turks as well as by Greek Jews, to whom it is known by the Turkish word *assuré*.[30] As is the case among Greek Christians, among Turks and Greek Jews the dish symbolizes death, or apparent death, along with hope and rebirth. Thus it is fitting that assuré is an essential dish at the festival Tu B'Shevat or Las Froutas, which is found in most Greek-Jewish communities and celebrates the onset of spring.[31]

Another food offered to the dead in Greece is a flat bread spread with honey, known as soul cake. This derives from a similar use of honey and honey cake in antiquity. In ancient times, it is likely that such honey cakes, after being offered to the dead, were cast into a cleft in the earth at a temple.[32] In modern times, this is paralleled by offerings of honey or honey cake to the Fates thought to live in the caves where such offerings are made.[33]

I have found few cases of beans or other legumes being associated with death and the dead in modern Greece. Hartland[34] has written that legumes are not mentioned as ingredients of kólyva. Even though there are exceptions—as shown by the inclusion of small white beans and chick peas in one Greek Jewish assuré dish (the symbolism, if any, is not explained)[35]—it seems that neither beans nor other legumes are essential ingredients of kólyva.[36]

White beans are, however, mentioned in connection with a Greek Christmas custom. Christmas in Greece is a religious festival. It is a time of singing, good wishes for health, happiness, and prosperity. It is a time of charity to the poor, and one when food and eating are prominent. Christmas is also a solemn occasion when the dead are honored by offerings and visits to the graveyard. It is said that, however many dishes may be prepared for the Christmas table, two dishes, kólyva broth and white beans, should not be missing. It is also said that people are expected to consume three spoonfuls of each.[37] Though the symbolism is not explained in my source, I suspect that the kólyva and beans are specified because they are foods of the dead; the number three, on its part, was probably chosen because of some special meaning it has or once had in this context;[38] and the whiteness of the beans, in turn, may express the hope for rebirth, resurrection.

The association of beans with death and the dead in Europe has been paralleled by their ties with evil spirits and other underworld forces and with divination or efforts at influencing or protecting against such evil forces.[39] According to British folk belief, beans are associated with witches, and a person who encounters a witch can be protected against her evil spells by spitting a bean at her.[40] Such thinking may account for the ancient conviction that bean fields are inhabited by ghosts and spirits. In nineteenth-century Leicestershire, there was a saying, "If you wish for awful dreams or desire to go crazy, sleep in a bean-field all night."[41] There is also a British folk belief that, if a pregnant woman eats beans, her infant may be affected mentally.[42] In a similar vein, bean blossoms are looked on with suspicion in coal-mining districts in the north and midlands of England because more mine accidents are thought to take place when beans are in flower than at other times.[43] Also of relevance is the report that, at the start of the eighteenth century on the Isle of Harries in Scotland, Molluka beans (Molucca beans),[44] especially white ones, were worn around the necks of children to protect them against the evil eye and witchcraft.[45] People believed that if any harm was directed at a child, a Molluka bean would turn black in color.[46]

According to one German folk belief, beans and peas are cult foods of demons, so people should not eat them on nights favorable for magical divination.[47] By Sicilian folk belief, beans (le fave) possess magical qualities for relieving the pains of labor, and thus in many places a woman approaching childbirth may eat nine beans, almost always black in color, one after another. When a child is born in Modica, moreover, beans may be used in a protective sense to keep the newborn from being hurt by injurious forces. The oldest woman at hand forms a cone of nine black beans on a table and recites a spell intended to neutralize certain evil spirits (le padrone di casa). This renders them incapable of harming the child.[48]

In accounts of Morocco, too, black beans are sometimes singled out as protective against illness and evil. There is one report of seven black beans being included in an amulet to protect goats or sheep from smallpox.[49] A Moroccan scribe may also seek to make himself invisible (like an evil spirit?) through an elaborate procedure involving seven black beans. Five beans may also be used in Moroccan amulets, for the number five serves in various ways to protect against the evil eye. Thus, a common amulet consists of a bean pod containing five beans or of five beans sewn into a cover of cloth or leather.[50]

Of special interest in Europe is St. John's Eve (Midsummer Eve; June 23). This is part of a Christian festival in honor of St. John the Baptist. There is no question that a festival on this date long preceded Christianity and that it was based on anxieties people felt at the time of the summer solstice. Even today, those anxieties find expression in the folk belief that this is a time when witches and demons appear on earth, which means it is a time when divination and exorcism of evil forces are prominent.[51] People in the Azores say that on St. John's Eve one can see the devil by going alone into a garden at midnight, and that St. John himself appears on that night to drive out demons and evil spirits. As in other parts of Europe, bonfires are lighted on St. John's Eve ("St. John's fires") in the Azores, sometimes on the tops of hills or peaks of mountains, to celebrate the coming light and warmth of summer and to bring good fortune and eliminate any disease, danger, and evil influence that might affect people.[52] Of interest in this regard is the medieval European practice of throwing cats into the St. John's fire, for cats, especially if black in color, were regarded as associates of witches and sorcerers.[53] Also germane has been the gathering of magical plants on St. John's Eve or St. John's Day (in some places, before dawn), which, when certain precautions are taken, are believed capable of repelling evil spirits; protecting against the spells of sorcerers; curing fever, illness, and disease; and divining the future. Perhaps most notable in this regard is St.-John's-wort (*Hypericum perforatum* or other species of its genus), an herb or shrub whose yellow flowers are likely to be in bloom for the holiday and which, along with greenery, has served as protection against evil during this holiday period. This has been done by suspending the flowers or sprigs at the entrance to a house; wearing them on one's person; or fashioning them, along with other magical plants, into garlands that serve in various ways. In some places, they have even been thrown into the St. John's fires.[54] Indeed, the demand for St.-John's-wort was so brisk at this time that the plant was thought capable of movement to avoid persons who seek its blossoms.[55] In Denmark in the past, plants of St.-John's-wort collected on

St. John's Day were placed between the beams under the roof of a house. If one of the plants grew upward, it signified a long life. If it grew down, it foretold sickness and death.[56]

Against the above background, it is no surprise that beans—especially fava beans, which have been associated with underworld forces since ancient times in Europe—may also play a role on St. John's Eve.[57] On St. John's Eve in Tuscany, for example, the St. John's fire was lighted in a field of beans in order that they ripen more quickly. At that time in Sicily, beans were eaten with a certain pomp, with people thanking St. John for obtaining from God the promise of a bountiful harvest.[58] In the Azores on St. John's Eve, a person may take three fava beans—one with its coat on, one half way peeled, and the third altogether peeled. The three beans represent, respectively, wealth, competence, and poverty. The beans may then be hidden and subsequently sought out. The fate of the finder, it is believed, is determined by which of the three fava beans he or she has found.[59]

A time of year in northern Europe that has been associated more directly and closely with legumes is Twelfth Night, evening of the twelfth day after Christmas, when the Feast of the Epiphany has been celebrated (traditionally on January 6). It has been said that on Twelfth Night, Germans, whose superstitions about beans extended to other legumes, were not supposed to eat legumes or meat,[60] presumably because that was the time, according to folk belief, that ancestral spirits return to earth.[61] For one place or another in modern Germany, there were also superstitions that a person who eats peas on Twelfth Night becomes infected with vermin or contracts leprosy, or that if he eats beans, peas, or lentils at that time he becomes ill or develops an itch.[62] In addition, Germans along with other northern Europeans[63] once selected a "King of the Bean" on Twelfth Night or on the evening before. According to some writers, this custom had its origin in the Saturnalia of the Romans, though others consider this claim unproved. Modern practice has involved selection of a bean king (usually one king per family) and sometimes also a bean queen. The selection of the bean king was by lot, as by baking a cake (English: "Twelfth-cake")[64] which contained a single bean or a single black bean, and his having chosen the piece of cake in which the bean was found. Of particular interest to us is the report that the first act of a bean king, after he had been enthroned and congratulated, involved his being lifted three times to the ceiling of the house, where he drew white crosses of chalk on the beams and rafters to protect against evil spirits, devils, and witchcraft for the coming year. Also prominent in some places have been concerns about weather and crop fertility and yield, and the cake itself served in divining good or bad things that might affect people in the ensuing year. As on St. John's Eve, bonfires and torches were lighted on Twelfth Night, for this was a dangerous time when evil forces that might damage the crops in the coming year had to be driven away.[65]

In Britain, the association of beans and other legumes with death and the underworld has been shown in other ways as well. The semilegendary sixth-century Welsh bard Taliesin, for example, described a mythical battle in which an array of plants participated. The elm "stood firm in the center of the battle . . . ; heaven and earth trembled before the advance of the oak tree . . . ; the heroic holly and the hawthorn defended themselves with their spikes . . . "; the bean, significantly, took part "bearing in its shade an army of phantoms."[66] Peas, as well as beans, have been associated with death and honoring the dead in Britain, where such practices were fostered by early Catholicism.[67] One early association of this sort relates to Passion Sunday, celebrated on the fifth Sunday of Lent, a week before Palm Sunday. Passion Sunday initiates the period of mourning for Christ's suffering, death, and burial, as shown in Catholic churches on Passion Sunday Eve, when statues, pictures, and crucifixes are covered with purple cloth.[68] In medieval England, it was universal practice on Passion Sunday to soak, fry, give away, and eat gray or brown peas, a custom that has continued into modern times in northern England and Scotland, where such peas are called carlings. In many villages in northern England, inns would provide patrons with free carlings, a practice that has persisted in pubs in some places up to the present.[69] Of particular interest is evidence that the use of peas on this day in Britain derives ultimately from the Roman practice of giving beans to the spirits of the dead, such as at the Parentalia and Feralia. It remains uncertain, however, why peas came to be substituted for beans.[70]

Such thinking seems also to have been involved in folk cures for warts as practiced in the past in Britain. According to English folk belief, warts could be cured in various ways involving animal or plant secretions, as well as death and decay. In view of their historical ties with death and decay, the use of fava beans in treating warts in England is of special interest. The soft inside of a fava bean pod was rubbed against a wart, and the shell was then thrown away or buried. It was believed that, as the shell withered, the wart would slowly disappear, and in some places a person would repeat a charm that expressed this hope: "As this Bean-shell rots away, So my warts shall soon decay."[71]

Turning to Iran, one finds echoes of the European practices and beliefs in ancient texts of the Zoroastrians. Among these is the dichotomy between forces of the sky and underworld, light and darkness, goodness and evil, as well as ancestral spirits who may return to the land of the living to benefit or harm their descendants. Beans and other legumes seem to have played little or no role in placating ancestral spirits. Instead, their place was taken by other foods. Of special note is the sacred cake, or *drōn*, made of wheat flour and water, which might be converted into another sacred cake, called *frasast,* through a person's making incisions while repeating certain words. The drōn was a small, circular pancake that was prepared with great care and concern with perfection and was then consecrated. Sacred cakes were used to propitiate angels and guardian spirits of deceased persons to gain help in fighting off demons intending to do injury in the world of the living. Such dedications were commonly made at funerals and memorial rites for the dead. Some sacred cakes were saved for use in seasonal festivals and other ceremonies, where they might be tasted or eaten by priests and other participants.[72]

In certain Zoroastrian memorial celebrations for a deceased, 33 beans, 33 eggs, and fruit were set down in front of a sacred cake. The cake was then consecrated in the presence of fire,[73] which is sacred to Zoroastrians. Modern Zoroastrians continue to use drōn and eggs (which are symbolic of immortality) in funeral and memorial rites. As reported by Mary Boyce for a contemporary Zoroastrian community, a single egg is blessed for a departing soul (and then given to a household dog, a sacred animal, to eat).[74] On the next day, however, 33 eggs—said to be for ancestors up to 33 generations ago—are offered so that the ancestors may aid their descendant in his hour of trial.[75]

In China, too, beans and other legumes have played quite minor roles as food of the dead. Instead, those roles, at least in the south, have been dominated by offerings of rice and pork, which are made in the hope that the family will obtain fertility from its deceased members.[76] Legumes are not, however, altogether absent from foods for the dead, as indicated on Taiwan among Hoklo people of Fukien origin. When a Hoklo person to be buried is young and unmarried, a salted bean, a cooked egg, and a stone must be put in the coffin. They symbolize, respectively, sprouting, rebirth, and transformation.[77] Similar cases have been reported for China proper, where various items—among them iron nails and red yeast (both protective against evil spirits),[78] as well as hempseed, peas, rice, wheat, and millet—might be scattered in a coffin or over the bottom of a grave to assure survival of the family by providing abundant food and numerous sons. The peas are intended to guarantee progeny, and, as they are added, the headman might say: "I scatter peas, in order that your descendants shall be blessed with a large posterity."[79]

In Japanese folklore, too, beans are noted for both their fertility-enhancing and their evil-expelling qualities. A dish of steamed rice and red beans (*sekihan*) is important at all auspicious times, but particularly at the Japanese New Year (by the Japanese calendar, New Year marks the start of spring).[80] Beans may also be used in modern Japan in New Year ceremonies to drive demons responsible for disease and bad luck from a house. This is done in a ceremony (called *tsuina* or *oni-yarahi* = "devil expelling") held in the evening of the last day of the old year. On that occasion, the head of a household or a servant scatters roasted beans about the house or throws them against its walls, floors, or floor mats while crying, loudly, "Out, demons," and, softly, "In, wealth." Later these beans may be eaten by those present, each person eating one bean more than the number of years in his or her age.[81] Lévi-Strauss,[82] noting that roasted soybeans are not normal fare in Japan, speculates that the beans in this ceremony (which, like other legumes, are "on the side of nature and death") may be intended for residents of the afterworld (called world of the rotten in ancient Japanese myths).

Also in Japan, bean pods and holly leaves may be included in the New Year decoration at the gate or front door of a house, holly leaves because, as in Europe, their prickles are thought to be unpleasant to demons.[83] Apparently such bean pods, like holly, are intended to discourage demons from reentering the house during the coming year.

It is said that the tsuina, the Japanese demon-expelling ceremony, which was carried out on an impressive scale in the royal court in the past, is already alluded to in an account dating from the seventh century A.D. and was likely introduced from China. In a manner reminiscent of Chinese practice, the ceremony in the Japanese royal court involved bands of masked youths, armed with halberds,[84] who drove devils away from the palace. Also similar to Chinese practice were the courtiers, armed with peach-wood staves or peach-wood bows[85] and reed arrows, who drove away a man dressed as the demon of pestilence. In addition, another man specially chosen for the purpose (called year man) spread roasted beans in all main rooms of the palace. Women of the palace then collected the beans, and each woman wrapped beans in paper in a number that equalled the years of her age plus one, and then threw them outside over her shoulder. Occasionally tsuina beans were collected by people who had reached an unlucky age, and who might include with the wrapped beans a copper coin that had been rubbed against his or her body to take on any bad luck that was there. Then the person placed the wrapped beans and coin in a bamboo tube, carried it to a crossroads, and threw it away, an act known as throwing away bad luck.[86]

In classical China, certain demon-exorcising ceremonies might involve an exorcist, shamans, a band of youthful participants, halberds, peach-wood bows and reed arrows, torches, and seeds and red pellets, with which to scatter demons and drive them away. In Bodde's description of such a classical Chinese rite,[87] the seeds are identified as those of "the five grains."[88] One finds different lists of the five grains in the literature, but Welch[89] identifies them as rice, millet, wheat, barley, and beans. This suggests that beans may have played a minor role in exorcism in China, but I have found little among de Groot's[90] assemblage of the rich variety of Chinese techniques for protecting against and exorcising evil spirits to suggest that beans or any other legume played a prominent role.[91]

In Tibet and Sikkim, too, there is an elaborate ceremony of sacrifice and exorcism that includes a practice resembling the casting of beans in the tsuina of Japan. This Tibetan ceremony is called turning away the face of the destroying devil. It is carried out within two days after a corpse has been removed and is intended to drive the death demon from the household and neighborhood. Weapons are dedicated beforehand, among them small stones, with black and white colors favored. As described by Waddell,[92] the ceremony outside the house is accompanied by such things as calling on the tutelary deity for help, beating drums and cymbals, sounding trumpets,[93] brandishing weapons, offering gifts, and shouting such things as "Be gone!" To make certain that the death demon is not hiding inside the house, a lama, carrying a bell and scepter, goes inside and makes threatening gestures with his scepter, mutters spells, and, while reciting charms, casts in all directions hot, toasted pebbles (some of the stones mentioned above?) before announcing that the demon has indeed been expelled. Regarding other Tibetan exorcism ceremonies, Waddell[94] mentioned, among other things, a cemetery as the place where demons live, and the making of noise, firing of guns, brandishing of weapons, stabbing of demons, and throwing of magic seeds and pebbles at them. In judging the fate of a Tibetan in the afterworld, black pebbles were said to represent sins, and white ones, good deeds; black and white seeds or pebbles also served in divination.[95] Also in Tibet, peas, along with items such as black radishes, onions, and garlic, may be included among unpleasant-tasting vegetables offered to wrathful deities. A collection bearing the same name is also used in a rite intended to triumph over a demon responsible for bringing on sickness and bad luck.[96]

Beans as Symbolic of Sex and as Containing the Spirit of Life

> [Pythagoras advised] abstinence from beans . . . because they are like the form of the universe . . . or . . . like the genitals . . .
> —Diogenes Laertius, *Lives of Eminent Philosophers,* quoting Aristotle

A basic element in Pythagorean thinking about the fava bean was its association with the spirit and origin of life, in which guise it was identified with human genitalia, male and female. This fits with the meaning of the word for beans to the ancient Greeks: "eggs, vessels of seed, of generation, associated with life."[97] A striking parallel to such thinking is found in an early Japanese myth about Uga-no-mikoto, who is the food *kami* (kami = something divine, awesome, and mysterious). After this kami had been killed, her body parts provided products that humans could eat or use in their efforts to survive. It is interesting that, though useful things came from various parts of her body (e.g., from her stomach, rice; from above her eyebrows, the silk worm; from the top of her head, the ox and horse), the soybean and mung bean came from her genitalia.[98] The association of beans with generation is also reported for certain mountain people of Papua New Guinea (Kamano, Usurufa, Fore, Jate). Among them, the female creation being Jugumishanta, believed to have emerged from the earth to make human beings, is referred to by some as a bean pod who bears many seeds and is even called by the name of a certain type of bean.[99] Similar fertility views are held by other New Guinea peoples (Tangu, Orokaiva) with respect to the areca nut (or betel nut) and coconut as they are linked to the fertility of both humans and their crops.[100] For the Tangu, the areca nut represents human generation, testicles, and young women capable of bearing children. The coconut (*Cocos nucifera*), on its part, represents testicles and human breasts that contain milk.[101]

Similar imagery is reported for sixteenth- and seventeenth-century France: the resemblance of peeled green beans to testicles, which gives them aphrodisiac qualities, and a like resemblance to female genitalia.[102] In one place or another in Morocco, the association of beans with sex and sexual power is displayed, as by a man seeking to enhance his sexual potency by eating beans, chick peas, peanuts, or almonds, all of which are thought to be effective because they resemble testicles. In Fez, it is said, a man who drinks the liquid in which chick peas have been soaked may even be capable of "deflower[ing] seventy-two virgin cows" in a single night. In a similar vein, if a man, on three succeeding mornings before breakfast, eats shelled almonds pounded with cinnamon and mixed with honey, he is believed to gain a lasting increase in his sexual capabilities.[103] A Moroccan scribe in Andjra, offended by the scanty payment offered by a prospective bridegroom whose sexual prowess the scribe made an effort to enhance, may seek revenge by carrying out various acts, including inscribing a charm on an egg and a bean, burying them, together with hair from the bride, beneath the entry to her home before she goes to live with her husband. This act, it is believed, will lead the bride to dislike her husband and keep him from having sexual intercourse with her.[104]

Thinking related to the above has also been found in modern Europe. At Caltanissetta in Sicily, in a parallel with Moroccan custom, the ritual food at weddings was a mixture of toasted almonds and honey. At one wedding, for example, the mother of the bride put a spoonful of the mixture in the mouth of each individual present, starting with the bride and groom.[105] At Modica in nineteenth-century Sicily, a young woman in love might plant two beans in the same pot on the first day of October. One of the beans represented her; the other, the man she hoped to marry. It was believed that, if both beans sprouted before the Festival of St. Raphaël (then celebrated on October 24), their marriage would be arranged.[106] In other places in Sicily and mainland Italy, young women who desired a husband used beans to divine what sort of man they would marry. He might be one who was wealthy and competent, or aged and infirm, or one with little or no money.[107]

In some places in the Rhineland, two black beans are baked into different New Year's doughnuts, with the expectation that an unmarried young woman and a suitable bachelor will get together.[108] There is also a

German belief that, if the bridegroom's mother throws dried peas or rice on the bride, the number of grains adhering to her dress will indicate how many children she and the groom can expect.[109] Also notable in this regard have been practices followed in Halloween divination reported for Scotland, Ireland, and England. In Scotland, two nuts (or peas if no nuts are available)—one representing a specific young man, the other, a specific young woman—are placed next to each other in a fire. If they remain undisturbed when burning, the couple will be married, the length and happiness of their marriage being determined by the brightness of the flame and the length of time the nuts burn. If, on the other hand, the nuts do not remain still when burning, but jump away from each other, no marriage will take place, the fault resting with the individual whose nut has jumped away.[110] In Northumberland in the past, scalded peas were eaten from a large bowl, and it was thought that the person who got the last pea would be the first to be married.[111] A second method was to hide a bean among the peas, with the person whose serving included the bean considered the fortunate one.[112] A far more involved process of divination with peas (*fal-e nohod*) is reported for Iran, and it is believed capable of answering not only questions of marriage, but also ones pertaining to birth, wealth, and travel.[113]

One wonders whether similar thinking may have led to the custom of casting beans or peas against houses. Thonger[114] writes of "knocking night" in Germany, one of the final three Thursdays before Christmas, when people may go from one house to another, knocking on doors, casting beans or small stones against the windows, and collecting small gifts. Others write of the German New Year's custom of casting peas against the windows of a neighbor's house.[115] This recalls the inclusion of peas among the seeds (the others being wheat, rice, and maize) used at the time of the Russian New Year, when boys and young men go from door to door, singing and casting seed to symbolize their wishes of joy and prosperity in the coming year.[116]

In Japan in the past, adzuki beans (*Phaseolus angularis*) served in "divination by gruel" associated with still another kami, the kami of pestilence: a gruel of beans and rice used in determining which crops it would be best to sow. Another form of divination in Japan involved the use of white and black beans to predict both the weather and good fortune for the forthcoming year.[117]

One may conclude from the above that beans, though not alone in this regard, have been a common symbol of generation and human sexual organs, and that such imagery may extend into the realms of magic and divination, especially in matters of fertility, love, and marriage.[118]

Avoidance of Beans by Priests and Devout Persons or on Holy Occasions

> It is not customary for the [priest of Jupiter] to touch, or even name . . . beans.
> —Aulus Gellius, *Attic Nights*

The associations of beans with death and impurity in ancient Italy and Egypt seem to have led certain priests to avoid eating them. In India, such associations have led urd beans to be rejected for use on certain ritual occasions. I have found few parallels of this sort in the Old World today, but the matter requires further investigation. One such parallel is for the Memi, a Naga people of eastern India.[119] Beans are prohibited to Memi mohvus (priests) and other persons of high social standing. Another is for the Sema Naga of eastern India, among whom harvest officials (*amthao*) are not permitted to eat certain kinds of flesh, bee grubs, or honey, or to smell beans during the time of harvest[120]—all items with excellent credentials elsewhere in terms of death, the underworld, and ritual impurity.

It is possible that views such as those above were adopted from Hindus. Yet in China proper, despite the fact that a religion of Indian origin, Buddhism, had a great impact on life starting in the early centuries of the Christian era, I have encountered few cases of avoidance of beans as food among clergy or devout persons. One exception may be the inclusion of beans on a list of the five grains to be avoided by Taoists,[121] because they may interfere with bodily harmony. In Taoist thinking, the five grains are believed to nourish the "three worms," malignant creatures within a person's body that may bring on sickness, frailty, and reduced life expectancy.

Conclusion

> Humanistic scholarship . . . has offered explanations [for the Pythagorean bean ban] that range from the mildly ridiculous to the extremely ridiculous.
> —R. S. Brumbaugh and J. Schwartz, "Pythagoras and Beans"

The above quotation reflects how intemperate some persons of scientific bent—in this case advocates of the favism hypothesis—can be in evaluating hypotheses for the Pythagorean bean ban advanced by classicists and other humanists. Though humanists may be annoyed by such criticism, their hypotheses are soundly based on the ancient literature. Their conclusions, moreover, more accurately reflect the thinking of Pythagoras, which was magico-religious as well as scientific, than the conclusions of those who espouse the favism hypothesis do.

Brumbaugh and Schwartz may not themselves believe in an underworld inhabited by demons and ancestral spirits. They may not accept the view that supernatural beings can bring on sickness and disease or affect human well-being in other ways. It is unfortunate, however, that they go so far as to scoff at the very idea that magico-religious concerns may have brought on the Pythagorean bean ban. The error of Brumbaugh and Schwartz is based on their failure to give Pythagoras his due in commitment to magic and religion as well as to science.

The data I have uncovered and presented above (which could be multiplied many times) demonstrate that in modern and premodern times, widely scattered peoples around the Old World—Indo-Europeans and others—have shared certain of Pythagoras's perceptions of beans. Such perceptions, moreover, are not rarities, but fairly common features in myth, folklore, and folk tradition. I would argue further that, if one accepts the framework of premodern people's thinking about the supernatural, their views of beans, like those of Pythagoras, are quite reasonable.

To say that humanistic explanations of the Pythagorean bean ban range from "mildly ridiculous" to "extremely ridiculous" reflects an unfortunate ethnocentrism shaped by perceptions of the supernatural world that, in historical terms, are aberrant, far from the norm that has prevailed in the past. I suspect that the ethnocentrism in question was made so extreme because the individuals in question grew up in the United States, in what Carter[122] has aptly called "the culture of disbelief." In any case, one must guard against such ethnocentrism, for it poses a special barrier to understanding and interpreting human thinking in past historical periods when supernatural forces were commonly seen as vital elements in human success and failure, life and death.

10 Further Notes, Elaborations, and Conclusions

Introduction

In this chapter, I will first consider certain characteristics of plants that appear to have influenced their use in magic and ritual. Some are characteristics mentioned more than once in this book, and I will place them here in a broader geographic and historical perspective. Then I will consider different aspects of the relationships that have developed between people and their ritual plants. One of these is the nature of those relationships. A second is the role that certain human groups have played in the spread of sacred trees in the Old World. A third is how the concerns of ancient peoples in establishing ties with ritual plants relate to the concerns of contemporary people of secular orientation.

Some Characteristics of Plants That Relate to Their Roles in Magic and Ritual

General

Not only did early humans observe plants closely, but also they were vitally concerned with how plants related to the supernatural forces believed to influence human life and well-being. It seems clear that they obtained valuable clues in determining the relationships of plants to supernatural forces[1] from the characteristics of plants—size, color, odor,

267

and such. This is the matter of initial concern in this chapter, the identification of plant characteristics that have been most important in linking them to gods, goddesses, and other supernatural beings.

Before proceeding, I would point out that, whatever characteristics present-day people regard as vital in the ritual role of a plant, one cannot be certain whether this was always so. A characteristic that contributed to a plant's ritual role in antiquity may have been overshadowed or even lost, while, over time, other characteristics may have been recognized and come to the fore.

Take, for example, the case of the peach (*Prunus persica*) in China. The peach has enjoyed a striking imagery and ritual role in China since antiquity. Indeed, more mysticism has been associated with the peach tree than with any other plant. In seeking to explain this, it is difficult to ignore the fact that the peach flowers at a critical time of year. In North China, this occurs in February, when the Chinese New Year is celebrated, with beautiful flowering peach branches, symbolic of springtime, brought home for decoration. This is the favorite time for weddings, and, as a result, the peach also symbolizes marriage, and its blossoms symbolize a bride or the face of a beautiful woman.

In a similar way, the peach has endured as a symbol of longevity and immortality in China. There was a mythical peach tree thought to grant immortality to all who consumed its fruit, and in Chinese art the god of longevity is depicted as carrying a peach or coming out of one. The peach of immortality may be depicted on the cookies and pastries that serve as gifts at birthday celebrations. When people make gifts of art in which peaches are prominent, moreover, they are expressing the wish that the recipient enjoy many years of life. Chinese Taoists, whose practices center on achieving a long life and immortality, have consumed peaches in seeking those goals. Taoists, for example, included peaches in the elixirs of life that, according to Chinese folk belief, gained immortality for certain of their priests in antiquity.

Though one might be tempted to credit the imagery and ritual role of the peach to its spring flowering and ties with marriage, longevity, and immortality, one cannot ignore the fact that peaches have also been thought to protect against and to drive away evil forces. Peach soup was drunk on New Year's Day to protect against toxic vapors and demons. Peach extracts were employed to drive out evil spirits. To guard a house against evil, people might tie a peach spray over their gates or use peach tree branches to sprinkle water on the earth around a house. The Chinese have been so convinced that evil spirits are afraid of peach wood that, to assure their safety and that of their children, they wore amulets made of peach wood or peach pits. In Han times (206 B.C.–A.D. 220), people erected peach-wood seals at the gates and doors of their houses with similar intent. In addition, the Han Chinese set up peach-wood images of two guardian deities at the doors to their houses at the time of New Year. In later times the two deities were depicted on flat boards made of peach wood, or they were painted or printed on paper. Peach-wood wands were considered especially potent weapons for repelling and exorcising evil spirits, and one reads of processions preceded by wizards who carried such wands to strike out at evil spirits and drive them away.[2] Peach-wood branches were used to strike feverous patients so as to drive out the spirit of fever. At times when epidemics occurred, moreover, a person might soak a peach twig in warm water and then use it for washing his or her body.[3]

In seeking to understand the peach's protective power in China, the question has been asked whether, in greatest antiquity, its wood, flowers, or fruit were critical. De Groot[4] has suggested that the ability of the peach tree to repel evil forces may have derived from its blossoming and fruiting at a time of the year when then yang principle is moving toward its high point, and that, as a result, the peach came to serve as a symbol of the sun. Bodde,[5] on the other hand, has noted that there is no evidence that peach blossoms were symbols of rejuvenation or marriage until well after Han times. He notes further that tales associating peach fruit with immortality also seem to be post-Han. Indeed, according to Bodde, all pre-Han accounts ascribe the protective power of the peach to its wood, though for reasons that are unclear. If he is correct, much of the peach lore and magic of modern China represent accretions that have occurred over time, additions made to an evolving imagery. In any case, they have been important in the thinking of Chinese in premodern and modern times, and they constitute vital elements in understanding the role of the peach in Chinese culture.[6]

Thorniness and Odor

The origin of the two peach-wood guardian deities of Han China remains unclear, but it has been argued that initially their figurines represented plants in human form. According to Bodde,[7] the names of the guardian deities, Shen Shu and Yü Lü,[8] derive in part from those of turmeric (*yü-chin; Curcuma longa*) and, perhaps, sow thistle (*shu; Sonchus oleraceus*). Turmeric, he argues, would have served to placate evil spirits with its pleasant aroma (or, as we shall see, turmeric may have served to drive them off), but if they persisted in seeking entry to a house, the sow thistle—thorny, bitter, and unpleasant—would have repelled them. There are, of course, many parallels to Chinese thinking about the usefulness of thorny plants in repelling evil forces.[9]

The relationship between thorniness and an ability to repel evil forces is also reflected in the meanings of the Chinese word *keng*. *Keng* originally meant "thorny" or "spiny," and specifically it referred to a thorny species of elm. From this principal meaning came that of "torment" or "distress," in the same way that a Westerner may speak of a troublesome person as "a thorn in his side." Especially important from our perspective, and apparently deriving from the principal meaning of *thorny*, is another meaning of *keng*: "to ward off 'misfortune through exorcistic rituals.'"[10]

In the example of turmeric cited above, Bodde argued that its pleasant odor was used by the ancient Chinese to satisfy evil spirits as a first step in keeping them from injuring the residents of a house. A parallel to this is the widespread use of incense to honor and placate deities.[11] In the healing centers of the god Asclepius in the ancient Greco-Roman world, for example, the burning of incense was among the purifying and healing procedures that were followed. On the other hand, humans have also used plants of unpleasant odor as repellents. In Morocco, for example, spirits may be kept away or driven off by the smells—most of them strong ones—of various plants or plant parts, with fumigation, as by burning coriander seed, commonly employed to achieve those ends.[12] In chapter 5, I noted that garlic sometimes has served to ward off evil spirits or drive them away. In addition, I noted that people have been concerned that garlic's odor might offend benevolent deities and that this may lead to the exclusion of garlic from offerings to a god, to the rejection of garlic by priests, and to the exclusion of garlic eaters from places of worship. Though their role in pleasing and repelling supernatural beings deserves more careful attention, it is clear that odors, pleasant and unpleasant, have been a serious concern in matters of ritual and religion.

Size

In weighing why the pipal and banyan trees enjoy such an exalted ritual status in India, one cannot ignore their great size. It is notable that in the

40. Baobab tree (*Adansonia digitata*) in the Sudan.

Himalayas, under climatic conditions ill-suited to the pipal and banyan, the deodār, another tall tree, has been sacred since antiquity. The importance of size is also shown in the fact that, where there are no pipal or banyan trees, Indian villagers usually honor the largest and oldest tree nearby, whatever its species.[13] One can, moreover, find examples of sacred giants in other parts of the world. Among these is one that found its way to India from the west. This is the baobab (*Adansonia digitata*), a giant tree of tropical Africa (Figure 40).[14] The baobab is found from Senegal and the Sudan, on the north, to Angola, the Kalahari, and the Transvaal, on the south. Though longer-lived than such European trees as the oak and yew, the baobab is not remarkably tall. Its trunk is not more than 25–30 feet high, and the tree's overall height is seldom more than 70 feet. The trunk, however, can develop an enormous girth in relation to the tree's height. One baobab tree observed near the mouth of the Senegal River in the mid-fifteenth century, for example, had a circumference of 112 feet.[15] The tree's impressive girth has led people in South Africa—in a manner reminiscent of the redwood country of northern California—to hollow out tree trunks[16] to serve as storerooms, temporary residences, and even as a roadside bar. Elsewhere, baobab trunks may be hollowed out to serve as places for burying human bodies or, in one case, for the keeping of prisoners.[17]

Like *Ficus indica* and *F. religiosa* in India, the baobab is commonly planted in villages, and in Yoruba country in Nigeria, villages may even be named after some remarkable tree nearby.[18] The sites of baobab trees that are found growing beyond areas where they are clearly part of the natural vegetation may be suspected of being those of former human settlements.[19] Whether such trees are indicators of former settlement or perhaps are relict plants in regions that have experienced desiccation, baobabs are striking landscape features in the open, semiarid grasslands of the Sudan belt. They may be found there as single trees or as baobab groves. Older baobab trees in the Sudan represent potential sources of water for local people and overland travellers because of that which may be found in hollows at the top of their trunks. Such hollows represent natural crevices that humans have enlarged to provide a capacity that may measure in the hundreds of gallons. Some rainwater drains into the hollows naturally. Men also raise buckets of water, by means of long ropes, from trenches dug at the base of the trees to collect water when it rains. Early in this century, it was estimated that in western Kordofan Province there were 30,000 baobabs that held water amounting to a total of 7.5 million gallons. It was also noted that during the Mahdist rebellion in the nineteenth century a retreating Mahdist army destroyed baobab trees to prevent pursuing enemy forces from using their water.[20] Indeed, baobab trees were sufficiently important in Kordofan during the colonial period that individual trees were sometimes identified on large-scale British maps to help the traveller locate them.

Africans generally regard the mature baobab with wonder and respect. It is said that, by tradition a mature baobab, like the sacred fig-trees of India, should not be cut down for firewood or for building houses, in part because it is believed to be under the protection of tree spirits. Indeed, people may avoid coming close to the tree at night out of fear of the spirits thought to congregate beneath its branches. There are also reports of baobab trees being objects of sacrifice and worship. In the Sudan and West Africa, for example, the baobab is revered as a "fertility tree," likely because of the extraordinary girth of its trunk and the widespread belief that it can make barren women fertile. Such thinking has not been restricted to those two regions. In a cave in the Limpopo Valley of southeast Africa, rock drawings depict women as having "life-sized 'seedpods' of the baobab instead of breasts."[21] In addition, there is one report that the tree is thought to herald the arrival of visitors and epidemics and that it can protect a village against smallpox.[22]

Arab merchants are said to have introduced the baobab to the Indian subcontinent at some unknown early date, and some good-sized baobabs are now found there. In the last century, one baobab, with a circumference of 47 feet, was the largest tree one observer had measured in western India,[23] but, in the Deccan, another (called the nameless great tree) was described as having a circumference of 53 feet and a height of about 87 feet.[24] The foliage of the latter tree measured 78 feet across, which explains why baobabs are used as meeting places. At the same time, it has been described as "grimmest of sacred trees," because in former times at Bijapur, southeast of Bombay, it served as an execution tree from which criminals were hanged.[25] Certain names for the plant in Indian languages mean "Gorakh's tamarind," Gorakh being a famous Hindu ascetic who probably taught his followers under the tree.[26] Thus, the baobab may be on its way to sanctity in Hindu India. If so, it will gain sanctity on the same grounds as the pipal and banyan—the ample shade it provides and its massive size.

Age

In my chapter on the sacred fig-trees of India, I noted that famous ones are thought to be quite old, with their ages often measured in thousands of years. Antiquity has always been a matter of wonder to people, and contacts with antiquity can be reassuring. Thus, great trees, as survivors of the distant past, can be viewed as satisfying the human need for comfort and good cheer, as enabling a stronger link between contemporary worshippers and their gods than would be the case if they relied just on sacred works, myths, and traditions. The faithful, after all, believe the Bodhi tree at Bodh Gaya to be the very tree under which the Buddha meditated and received enlightenment in the fifth century B.C. That tree's offspring, the sacred tree at Anuradhapura in Ceylon, is thought to go back to the third century B.C. The still-sprouting remains of a tree at Allahabad are regarded as those of the never-dying banyan tree mentioned in the Ramayana, and local tradition has it that the Kabir-bar, that famous banyan tree of Gujarat, is 3,000 years old.

Ancient trees were important in ancient Greece as well. In the second century A.D., Pausanias, after weighing Greek traditions, concluded that the oldest living, healthy tree in Greece was the willow (*Salix?*)[27] that grew in the sanctuary of Hera at Samos, one of Greece's oldest sanctuaries. Next in age, according to Pausanias, came the sacred oak (*Quercus*) of Zeus at Dodona in Epirus, in northwest Greece.[28] Third and fourth were the olive (*Olea*) on the Acropolis in Athens and the olive at Delos, the island on which there was a cult center of Apollo. Pausanias suggests, as a runner-up, the plane tree of Menelaus (presumably *Platanus orientalis*)[29] near Caphyae in Arcadia. This tree had reputedly been planted by Menelaus when he was assembling an army to attack Troy.[30] Note that some of these ancient trees were associated with specific deities and their ritual centers (Samos, Dodona, Delos). Another was associated with a religious complex in a capital city (the Acropolis).[31] Still another, the plane tree of Menelaus, was tied to a great man of the past.[32] On other lists of the oldest living trees of the Greco-Roman world, individual trees may differ. On his list of the oldest living trees of Greece, for example, Theophrastus (c. 372–287 B.C.) had two of Pausanias's trees. These included the olive on the Acropolis and the plane tree near Caphyae. Theophrastus, however, also included a palm tree at Delos,[33] a wild olive at Olympia, and oaks at the tomb of Ilos at Ilium.[34] All these trees are located in situations quite similar to those of Pausanias's trees. So are the oldest living trees of the Greco-Roman world identified by the Roman naturalist Pliny (A.D. 23–79).[35] So, too, are the reputedly oldest living fig-trees of the Indian subcontinent. The olive tree on the Acropolis, for example, recalls the pipal tree at Anuradhapura, Ceylon's ancient capital; and the plane tree of Menelaus recalls the Kabir-bar of Gujarat, a banyan tree reputed to have been named for a noted Vaishnava reformer.

Over the millennia, individual sacred fig-trees in India, such as the one at Bodh Gaya, have died in one way or another, but devout people often persist in believing that a present-day tree represents the very one that lived in antiquity. A similar problem existed with the sacred oak of Dodona, reputed to be the most ancient oracle in Greece.[36] By the second century A.D., there had been an oak of Zeus at Dodona for roughly a millennium, and likely Dodona had such an oak long before that.[37] Almost all ancient authorities on Dodona, moreover, referred to its sacred oak in the singular, as if it were one tree. Parke, however, has raised the question of how long an oak tree can live. He concludes that it would be very unusual for an oak to live more than 500 years, and that 700 or 800 years might be its maximum life span. This assumes, of course, that a tree remains in good health and does not suffer some life-threatening injury. How, then, was the matter of continuity handled? Parke has speculated that, when their sacred oak showed evidence of decay, the priests of Dodona planted one of its acorns to perpetuate it,[38] which would mean that—as with sacred pipal and banyan trees in India—worshippers over a long historical period were dealing with a succession of sacred trees, not with an undying one. Also deserving more attention is another parallel, to be considered shortly, provided by the sacred oak at Dodona.

Movement

Fergusson tells a tale of nineteenth-century India that reveals how a plant's movements can gain it sanctity.[39] One day while managing a factory in Jessore in Bengal, Fergusson noticed large crowds passing nearby and thought they were simply going to a fair. However, when, on succeeding days, the crowds increased in size and seemed to be more religious in nature, he asked about the matter, and was informed that they were going to a tree, about six miles away, in which a deity had appeared. The following morning he rode to that spot and found an old, decaying tree, on which garlands and offerings were hanging. There was also much ritual activity going on, and around the tree were houses occupied by the Brahmins who looked after things. When Fergusson asked how the deity made his presence known, he was told that the tree raised its head in welcome when the sun came out in the morning and bowed its head when the sun went down in the evening. A return visit, at noon, confirmed the miracle. The tree did indeed raise its head. Further investigation provided an explanation acceptable to "the man of science"—that the branches of the tree had at first grown over the main pathway through the village, but had dropped so low that people could not pass beneath them. So they pulled the tree to one side and fastened its branches parallel to the road. In doing this, its roots had been twisted like the strands of a rope. When the morning sun struck them, the roots dried and contracted and had a tendency to untwist, which raised the head of the tree. With the dew of evening, they relaxed and became twisted again, and the head of the tree bowed.

Quaking and Rustling of Leaves

One type of oracle at Dodona, at least in later times, was obtained from the sacred oak by priests or priestesses. They determined Zeus's message from the rustling of its leaves, which seems to have been considered the voice of the god.[40] One finds many references to this phenomenon. One reads, for example, of the "panting oak" of Zeus at Dodona and of its leaves "that are famed to rustle" at his bidding.[41] The Dodona oak's oracular ability was recognized already in great antiquity, for Homer, who may have lived in the ninth or eight century B.C., wrote in the *Iliad* of Achilles addressing Zeus as "lord of Dodona" and of the god's prophetic priests there.[42] In the *Odyssey*, Homer was even more specific in writing of Odysseus going to Dodona to hear the will of Zeus at his "high-crested oak."[43] That oracular oak was so identified with the god that, when the ship *Argo* was constructed for Jason, a timber from that oak was fitted into the ship's prow, apparently so that Zeus might be present to make his will known in directing the vessel and assuring its safety. As further assurance, however, Jason consulted the oracle at Dodona and obtained Zeus's approval before assembling the Greek nobles and sailing off.[44]

Along with the oracles of Delphi and Zeus Ammon at Siwa Oasis in North Africa, moreover, Dodona ranked among the three most famous oracles in the Mediterranean world.[45] How did it come to be established? Herodotus (fifth century B.C.) reported an Egyptian tale that the oracles at Dodona and Siwa (then Ammonium) had both been established by priestesses from the center of Zeus (Ammon-Ra) at Thebes in Egypt. Herodotus was told a myth by the priestesses at Dodona that expressed a similar origin. According to that myth, two black doves left Thebes. One flew to Siwa; the other, to Dodona. The Dodona dove landed in an oak tree and, speaking in a human voice, announced that an oracle of Zeus was to be established there. The Siwa dove, on its part, instructed the Libyans to establish an oracle of Zeus Ammon. Herodotus was of the opinion that, instead of doves, two Theban priestesses had been carried away as slaves, and that, after arriving in Siwa and Dodona, they had set up oracles of the sort they knew in Thebes. This, in Herodotus's view, explains why the oracular practices at Dodona and Thebes were so similar,[46] though he provided no detail about what those similarities might be. Various myths of a common origin were repeated in later times. However, Parke's careful weighing of Herodotus's statements[47] raises serious questions about the motives of Herodotus's informants and whether he himself had been too ready to accept an Egyptian origin for the oracle of Dodona because he was committed to the view that Greek religion had derived from Egypt. Parke's review of the early histories of the cults at

Dodona and Siwa, moreover, strongly suggests that the two cults had quite independent origins.[48]

Of interest here, however, is the possibility that, at least in later times, oracular oaks were found at the cult center at Siwa. This possibility is suggested by Lucan and Silius Italicus in the first century A.D. Lucan was impressed with a grove of trees (not identified as to species) at the oracular center of Zeus Ammon, "the only green trees that exist in all Libya."[49] Silius Italicus went into the matter in detail. The grove at Zeus Ammon's shrine, he wrote, consisted of tall oaks that were sacred and were worshipped "with steaming altars." The god revealed the future "in his prophetic grove"; and when the god entered the priest, the trees beat against one another, a deep humming sound passed through the grove, and then a loud voice spoke out and delivered the prophecy.[50] It was because of this and other evidence that A. B. Cook concluded that, like the oak of Zeus at Dodona, the oak or oaks of Siwa were oracular.[51] Parke, on his part, dismisses Silius's account as "a mixture of literary reminiscence and his own imagination."[52]

The laurel (*Laurus nobilis*) and its association with Apollo is well known. Moreover, it has been suggested that at Delphi his sacred laurel may once have been oracular, too. This is based on a statement, by the author of the Homeric hymn "To Apollo,"[53] that Apollo prophesies "from his laurel tree below the dells of Parnassus."[54] Though the meaning of this statement may not be altogether clear, it suggests that Apollo spoke from his sacred laurel at Delphi just as Zeus spoke from his sacred oak at Dodona, probably through priests, who interpreted his speech in the rustling of leaves.[55] If that was the case, however, that type of prophecy at Delphi ended before the time of Greece's historical periods, and indeed there were no oracular trees in classical Greece apart from the oak at Dodona.[56] Nevertheless, in later times the laurel did play a minor role in oracular ritual at Delphi. It was often used to decorate Apollo's shrine. A prophetess may have chewed laurel leaves to call Apollo to her, though some consider this doubtful.[57] She burned laurel wood or leaves along with barley flour on an altar. She also seems to have carried out some sort of fumigation before proceeding with the prophecy.[58] When she sat on the tripod from which she delivered Apollo's message, moreover, she wore a crown of laurel, and she seems to have held in her hand a laurel shoot, which she shook from time to time.[59]

Returning to India, we see that the literature contains numerous references to the quivering or quaking of leaves of the pipal tree. It also contains references to the sound they make. That sound, like the sound of leaves at ancient Dodona, represents a means by which supernatural beings and humans communicate. An Indian holy man who sat beneath a pipal tree possessed oracular abilities;[60] and it has been suggested that the Buddha may have chosen a pipal tree under which to receive enlightenment because he was anticipating communication with the supernatural world. Buddhists in nineteenth-century Ceylon said that the quivering of pipal leaves dates from the time the Buddha sat beneath the Bodhi tree.[61] In any case, while the quivering and rustling of leaves are important, they represent just one aspect of behavior with respect to "talking trees" and "tree oracles," the varied and widespread role of trees in the Old World in communicating with gods.[62]

The quaking of leaves may, however, also find its way into religious thinking along avenues different from the ones cited above. The leaves of aspens in western Europe (European aspen = *Populus tremula*) are said to quake because of offenses they committed against Christ. German tradition has it that the aspen, among all trees, failed to acknowledge Jesus in the flight to Egypt; that, as a result, Jesus cursed the aspen; and, that when he spoke the aspen began to quake. In Syria, people say that the cross was made of aspen and that, ever after Christ was crucified, its leaves have quivered in remembrance of that event. In Brittany, too, aspen leaves are said to quiver because its wood was used for the cross or because, when Christ was suffering on the cross, all the world's plants and trees bowed their heads except the aspen, which asked why it should weep and tremble when it had committed no offense. Tradition has it that before the aspen had completed that statement, it began to quiver, and that this will persist until the day of judgment.[63]

Seed

I have noted the belief that the banyan tree is inhabited by and associated with Shashṭhī, goddess of childbirth and children, an association said to derive from that tree's many fruit. There are many parallels to this. One example is the ancient trait, still widespread in the Old World today, of casting cereals, other seeds, or fruits at the bride, the bridegroom, or both of them.[64] Fruit and seeds may also serve in seeking to make a barren woman fertile. One of the most interesting examples of this is reported for Isfahan in Iran, where a barren woman may be taken to a certain mosque, where she breaks one nut for each step she takes when mounting its tower. When she leaves the mosque, she carries the nutmeats, together with some raisins, in her veil. Then, as she walks home, she offers a few nuts and raisins to certain men she encounters who make a favorable impression on her. The belief is that this procedure should end her sterility. A European who refused an offer of nuts and raisins from a woman who approached him on an Isfahan street (because he thought she was a prostitute) thus sent her the unintended signal that her barrenness had not ended.[65]

In ancient Mediterranean lands, the pine cone may have come to be associated with Dionysus, god of vegetation and fruitfulness, because, as the seed pod of an evergreen tree, it was symbolic of developing life.[66] In addition, three trees with many-seeded fruit were among the earliest domesticated fruit trees in the Mediterranean and Near East.[67] These were the pomegranate, true fig, and sycamore fig (*Ficus sycomorus*).[68]

The pomegranate (*Punica granatum*) is well suited for a role as a symbol of fecundity. Not only does its fruit have abundant seed, but it possesses the color red as well. This resemblance to blood, the "life fluid" of humans, thus ties the fruit more firmly to the human sphere. People's association of the pomegranate with human fertility, life, abundance, and prosperity is amply demonstrated in the literature and art of ancient Near Eastern and Mediterranean lands (Figure 41).[69] Solomon likened his bride's temples to a piece of pomegranate and the bride herself to an "orchard of pomegranates, with pleasant fruits."[70] Apparently with a symbolism of life, fertility, and prosperity, hundreds of pomegranates were depicted on the pillars of Solomon's temple, as well as on Aaron's priestly robe.[71] Numerous representations of pomegranates are also found in the art of ancient Babylonia, Assyria, Egypt, and Iran.[72] One Assyrian love-charm involved a suitor reciting a charm over a pomegranate and then presenting it to his intended.[73] At Assyrian and Babylonian wedding feasts, moreover, pomegranates were served as symbols of love and fecundity.[74] In the ritual of Syria and Phoenicia, the pomegranate was so conspicuous that *rimmon,* the name used for its fruit, was also in the name for the sun god, Hadad-Rimmon.[25] Attis, a god with roots in western Asia, was reputed to have been born miraculously of a virgin who conceived him when she placed on her breast a pomegranate[76] that had grown from the severed genitals of a man-monster.[77] In ancient Greece and Rome, the pomegranate tree and its fruit were cult objects symbolizing fruitful-

41. Stylized holy pomegranate-tree on an Assyrian cylinder seal (ninth century B.C.; from Muthmann, 1982), in what appears to be a fertility ritual. The tree seems to be wearing a headdress or crown, and hovering above it is a flying disk representing Assur, the sun god. Each of the royal figures who face the pomegranate tree holds in one hand a beam coming from the sun, while he raises his other hand, perhaps to honor the tree. The branches of the tree, tipped with fruit with large blossoms, also seem to be reaching out horizontally in greeting. The winged, eagle-headed figures each carry a pomegranate blossom (for use in pollination?) and a square-handled container of some sort (in hopes of an abundant harvest?).

ness and generation, as well as death and destruction.[78] Various Greek deities are depicted with pomegranates or described as having ties with them.[79] One of them is Hera,[80] for whom, as the goddess presiding over marriage, it was thus quite appropriate as a symbol.[81] Nevertheless, pomegranates were linked especially to Dionysus, from whose blood, according to ancient Greek myth, the pomegranate tree sprouted.[82] Pomegranates also served in rites of marriage, and one interpretation of Homer's having Pluto give pomegranate seed to Persephone to eat—which bound her in marriage to him—was that this was an ancient marriage

42. Christ and two pomegranates, central design in the floor mosaic of an early villa in England (fourth century A.D.) (from Muthmann, 1982). Behind Christ's head is the sacred Chi-Rho monogram, representing the first two letters of the Greek word for *Christ*. This was said to have been a heavenly sign observed by the emperor Constantine prior to a great military victory, and it became his symbol, used on his standard and on the shields of his soldiers. It also appeared on early Christian coins, lamps, vessels, and tombs. The floor mosaic in England thus appears to symbolize victory (Chi-Rho) and eternal life (pomegranate) through Christ.

rite.[83] With the coming of Christianity, moreover, the pomegranate came to symbolize the hope of an everlasting life (Figure 42)[84]

Turning to later times and to the Near East, the Prophet Mohammed said that every pomegranate contains a growing seed from paradise. In Morocco, it is thought to possess *baraka,* or "holiness,"[85] and Moslems there and elsewhere believe the pomegranate to have magical and medicinal virtues. There is a tale in *The Thousand and One Nights* of a renowned sultan who had everything he wished except a child, for which he prayed to God unceasingly. One night a man who seemed holy, like a prophet, appeared in the sultan's dream and instructed him on how he could make his wish come true by praying, obtaining a pomegranate from his head gardener, and consuming as many of its seeds as seemed desirable. When the sultan awoke, he ate 50 pomegranate seeds, one for each of his wives. Then he had sexual intercourse with each of them in turn. In time, the tale goes, 49 of his 50 wives became pregnant.[86] In modern Iran, on the morning of his wedding, a bridegroom may meet the bride coming to their new home, whereupon he breaks open a pomegranate.[87] A Turkish bride may cast a ripe pomegranate to the ground, with the number of seeds that fall out indicating the number of children she will bear.[88] Similar thinking is probably involved when an Arab bride smashes a pomegranate on the front post or threshold of the bridegroom's tent or house, and then throws the seeds inside.[89] In a comparable situation among the Maronites of Syria, the actions are reminiscent of casting the bridal bouquet in the Western world. The Maronite bride is taken to her new home. She is pelted with raisins and cereal grains. On entering it, she throws a pomegranate into the middle of the bridal party, and it is enthusiastically snatched and portioned out by the bridegroom's friends.[90] Among the Mandaeans of Iraq and Iran, the pomegranate is one of the five most sacred foods, and pomegranate twigs, symbolic of life and fertility, may be carried by boys accompanying the bride in a wedding rite.[91]

At the Panja or Parwanaiia, a joyous and holy spring feast of the Mandaeans, moreover, pomegranates are among the fruits, nuts, cereals, and vegetables displayed on ritual tables as symbols of fertility, life, and rebirth.[92] Among certain modern Moroccan groups, pomegranates serve in rites intended to assure crop fertility and protect crops against the evil eye. When the plowing of a field is about to commence, pomegranates, figs, raisins, and bread may be taken to the field. A pomegranate may be squeezed on one horn of the plow oxen or crushed on the plowshare in the hope that the cereal grains will be as many and as plump as the pomegranate seeds. If people have no pomegranates, they may touch the plow point with dried figs or tear a fig into small pieces above the plow point, because the fig, too, has many seeds.[93]

In popular thinking in modern Greece, the pomegranate still represents "immeasurable number" and abundance; a bright red pomegranate blossom, moreover, is symbolic of intense love.[94] In hopes for abundance, on New Year's Day on Chios a member of the household sprinkles a mixture of pomegranate seeds, currants, and beans over the house and its inhabitants.[95] The ancient Greek practice of casting a pomegranate with great force onto the threshold or floor of a house, still carried out today on New Year's Day, also expresses the hope for good fortune and prosperity during the coming year.[96] On September 1, the start of the ancient new year, the people of Carpathos cast one pomegranate onto the floor in such a way as to scatter its seeds throughout the house.[97] On the island of Amorgos, the person selected to be first to enter the house on New Year's Day takes two steps inside while saying, "Come in, good luck!" Then he takes two steps back, saying, "Out, bad luck!" After doing this three times, he enters the house and throws a pomegranate down with great force, so that it will split open. The inhabitants of Lemnos, on their part, put pomegranates on the table on New Year's Day to symbolize abundance. In former times on the eve of the Greek festival of spring (May 1), moreover, cultivators of Pergamum suspended on their household doors wreaths that contained clusters from various seed- or fruit-bearing plants. These might include a pomegranate branch with a fruit or a fig branch with figs.[98] Similar symbolism was found in Greek weddings in the nineteenth century. When a bride in Crete first entered her new husband's house, she was handed a pomegranate that she broke open and then cast the seed onto the floor.[99] In Aegina, pomegranate seeds and peas were cast at a bride immediately after the wedding to assure her fertility.[100]

In India, the pomegranate has been a symbol of Gaṇeśa, that elephant-headed deity who, to devotees in certain of his early sects, was held to be creator of all the gods. Perhaps for this reason, Gaṇeśa was depicted as holding a pomegranate in one hand while embracing his śakti, or female energy. In China, there are no records of the pomegranate prior to the third and fourth centuries A.D. When the tree was introduced, moreover, it was accompanied by symbolism prominent in the Near East and Mediterranean area. The fruit, with its many seeds, came to symbolize fertility, numerous sons and grandsons, and perpetuation of the family.[101] Pomegranate fruit became highly regarded wedding gifts. They also played a role at wedding dinners.[102] Their fertility symbolism is well illustrated in a Hong Kong procession carrying furniture to the future home of a couple soon to be married. The most highly valued item, a modern toilet, was at the head of the procession, but, since no article might be empty, the toilet was filled to overflowing with pomegranates and eggs—two outstanding symbols of fertility.[103] After marriage, Chinese women desirous of children sometimes offer pomegranates to the goddess of mercy, whose temple porcelain bears representations of pomegranate fruit.[104] This imagery extends to the pomegranate flower as well.[105] In this regard, one reads of a Hong Kong funeral procession in which carts carrying the wives of the deceased's grandchildren bore a special emblem, a red pomegranate flower. Since the pomegranate symbolizes "continuity of the clan,"[106] in all likelihood the flower motif was intended to announce, and perhaps assure, the family's continued survival.

There is abundant evidence that the numerous seeds of the fig *Ficus carica* have also been recognized by many peoples, ancient and modern. Hoffner, though he says nothing of the fig's symbolism among the ancient Hittites, has noted that they were impressed by two qualities of its fruit: its sweetness and the fact that it contains "a thousand seeds."[107] A medieval Greek and Arabic text on the interpretation of dreams says that, if a person dreams he is collecting ripe figs from a tree, a very wealthy man will provide him with money. He will receive the money, as well as other riches, in an amount in keeping with the number of seeds in the fruit.[108] In modern Morocco, dried figs are a popular type of alms given to the dead, because figs have many seeds, each of which has merit, according to Moroccan belief.[109] In sub-Saharan Africa, many groups use *Ficus capensis* and likely another fig species as fertility charms to benefit both humans and their crops, an idea, it is said, that probably came from their numerous clustered fruits. In addition, the Fulani and Zulu feed the fruit and leaves of these fig trees, or an infusion of them, to domestic animals to increase their milk production and/or their numbers. In East Africa, moreover, *F. capensis* is often found at shrines and places where sacrifices are carried out.[110]

The association of figs with prosperity and peace is revealed in biblical expressions like "And Judah and Israel dwelt safely, every man under his vine and under his fig tree . . ."[111] Baskets of figs were widely represented with mythical significance in the ancient world,[112] commonly in a context of love, marriage, fertility, and abundance. In the Greek world, the fig is represented in a manner that suggests sanctity already in the Minoan and Mycenaean eras.[113] In later times, the fig was dedicated to Hermes, no doubt in his erotic form,[114] but it was associated especially with the god Dionysus, who was thought to have discovered the fig and given it to humans.[115] In Attica, figs were among the indispensable offerings to him in the form of Dionysus rusticus.[116] The ancient Spartans worshipped a form of Dionysus called Dionysus of the Fig.[117] One ancient source also refers to the god as "the fig-wood Dionysus,"[118] perhaps because the phallus in the procession of Dionysus was made of fig wood[119] or because certain images of Dionysus were made of fig wood or had fig-wood masks or faces.[120] In one description of a Dionysus procession, two celebrants, following each other, carried a jug of wine and the branch of a grape vine. Then came a celebrant pulling a male goat. That celebrant, in turn, was followed by a person carrying a basket of dried figs, and by another person carrying a phallus.[121] Because the fig, like the grape and phallus, was a symbol of Dionysus, and because the fig, as a fruit, represented the female genitalia, figs seem to have been included in the procession as an appropriate companion for the phallus.[122] Similar fertility links were displayed when an ancient Greek bride first entered the bridegroom's house and was showered with such things as figs and dates, nuts, and coins.[123]

Exudations

Prominent among the exudations of trees and other plants is the milky juice, or latex, that appears in certain species when they are wounded. Indian trees of that sort have been called milk trees, and, in the Indian literature, species of figs have been conspicuous among milk trees since antiquity.[124] Hutton thinks it likely that such milky juice led fig trees to be tied to fertility cults in India, as well as in Italy, Africa, and New Guinea.[125]

In the Brahmanas, juice from the descending roots of the banyan tree and from the fruit of banyan, pipal, udumbara, and *plakṣa*[126] trees served the Kshattriya (warrior, knightly, royal) castes as a substitute for the holy soma (which was allotted to Brahmins). The drinking of this juice (designated "milk") provided the Kshattriyas with the tree's valuable qualities, among them royal power, vigor, and independence.[127] Sanskrit writers noted that the fruit of another fig species, *F. hispida,* enhances the secretion of milk and protects a fetus in the womb.[128] The udumbara (*F. glomerata*) is called milk tree or golden juiced by Sanskrit writers, and, in popular thinking in modern India, an extract of its juice is thought to enhance the production of mother's milk and prevent abortion.[129] In the Deccan in modern times, boys may cast stones into a milk bush (*Euphorbia tirucalli*), then gather the stones and wave them around the udder of a cow or goat or the breasts of a woman to increase her milk supply.[130] Milk and milk-exuding trees, such as the jackfruit tree (*Artocarpus integrifolia*),[131] play a role in marriage rites of the Coorgs. The Coorgs may also propitiate their ancestors at a platform built at home around the trunk of a milk-exuding tree.[132] Some tribal groups of modern Orissa regard the banyan tree as mother, and one of their tales is of two orphan children being left beneath a banyan and kept from starvation by consuming its milky juice.[133] Fig-tree juice, or latex, is also prominent in a myth of the Kuttia Kond tribal people of Orissa. When people were first on earth, the myth goes, they had no proper food, so the earth mother and creator Nirantali told the banyan tree, "Feed the people with your milk." After the banyan denied having any milk in its body, Nirantali struck it with an axe and said, "Let milk come." Milk flowed from the incision, and people let it fall into their mouths, and survived in this way until cereals came to the world.[134] The close ties of Indian "milk trees" with fertility concerns are further shown by the use of the milky juice of the pipal tree as an aphrodisiac in India. In addition, one reads of a requirement that the central pole of the threshing floor come from a tree with milky juice.[135]

In ancient Rome, various writers commented on the milky juice of the fig tree and of young figs,[136] and, according to Macrobius,[137] "'milk' is the term properly used for the juice of figs." The association between figs and milk was enhanced by use of fig-tree "milk" as rennet, to curdle milk in making cheese.[138] Also noteworthy, the fig tree was sacred to the goddess Rumina, whose name comes from *ruma*, an old Latin word for "breast." Rumina was the goddess of suckling animals and the rearing of young children, and the fig tree was sacred to her.[139] It was appropriate, according to Varro, that a fig tree was planted near Rumina's shrine at the foot of the Palatine Hill in Rome. It was also fitting, he said, that milk offerings were made to her rather than offerings of wine and suckling animals.[140] Varro wondered, indeed, whether a fig had been planted at her shrine because its "milk" served in making cheese.[141] Some scholars have argued further that the "milk tree" of Rumina became the fig tree on the Palatine (*Ficus ruminalis*), at which, according to legend, Romulus and Remus were nursed by a wolf.[142]

Juice of a wild fig-tree was also offered to the goddess Juno Caprotina ("Goat Juno") at the festival of Nonae Caprotinae in Rome (July 7).[143] In this festival, Juno seems to have represented the female principle.[144] Frazer has noted, moreover, that a goat was sacrificed to her under a wild fig-tree (which the Romans called *caprificus*, "goat fig-tree"), because both the goat and the wild fig-tree represented the male principle in fertilization. He also noted that the festival may have been carried out at the time of fig caprification.[145] A striking parallel is found among the modern

Kikuyu and Kamba of Kenya, who, in rites with strong sexual implications carried out at sacred fig-trees (a species akin to *Ficus capensis*), smear the tree's milky juice on a barren woman's entire body, or on her loins and navel, in an effort to make her fertile.[146]

The above suggests that, because the latex of fig trees resembles milk, humans have involved them in ritual associated with childbirth, nursing infants, and human fertility. It also recalls the suggestion that the milky juice of the pipal and other species of *Ficus* may have contributed to their being tied to fertility cults in India and other parts of the Old World.[147] Many plants have milky latex, and fig trees are not the only plants with that quality to play a role in the folklore of milk and fertility. One version of a folktale of the Kaffirs of South Africa tells of a poor family that obtained milk from a tree by squeezing it—an event that may have occurred before people used the milk of animals.[148] Among the Ndembu of Zambia, the tree *Diplorrhyncus condylocarpon*, which has a white latex that appears whenever its bark is scratched, plays a prominent role in fertility ritual. Women say that, because of its white latex, the tree represents both milk and the breasts that provide it. The "milk tree," as investigator Victor Turner calls it, serves in a girl's puberty rites. Those rites are carried out "when a girl's breasts begin to ripen," and entail wrapping her in a blanket and laying her at the foot of a milk-tree sapling. The camp where Ndembu boys are circumcised is dominated by a thorn tree called *chikoli* (*Strychnos spinosa*), which, among other things, symbolizes an erect penis, sexual virility, manliness, power, bravery, perseverance, hunting skill, and a long life in good health. The actual circumcision, however, takes place under a milk tree, and an uncircumcised boy, like a girl who has not gone through puberty rites, is called one who lacks whiteness.[149]

Another tree of note for its exudations is the ash, which provides a sugary substance from its bark and leaves that, even as late as the start of this century, seems to have been fed to newborn infants in Germany and the Scottish highlands.[150] In addition, ash exudations have been marketed as "manna," a general term for sweet edible substances that may be exuded by plants or excreted by insects.[151] In one work on the plants of Europe, four species of ash are identified, and two are singled out as manna-producing. One of the two is *Fraxinus ornus*, which grows in many parts of Greece as well as in other Mediterranean lands.[152] Prior to the end of the eighteenth century, it came under cultivation, to become the principal source of medicinal manna in Europe.[153] The second manna-producing ash is *Fraxinus excelsior,* the tallest leaf tree in northern Europe and the only ash species that grows there. It yields less manna than *F. ornus* does.

In Germanic mythology, there is a cosmic ash, Yggdrasil, a tall and sacred tree for which *Fraxinus exelsior* must have been the model.[154] The ash was the principal and most sacred seat of the gods, who held council under it daily.[155] The first man was formed from an ash tree, and indeed he was named Ask ("Ash"). In a Norse myth, a goat consumes stems of the cosmic ash and then provides honey-wine from its udders for those feasting in Valhalla. After the twilight of the gods, moreover, mankind will be renewed by a man and woman who, safe within the cosmic ash, are nourished by dew.

Echoes of these beliefs were found in ancient Greece, where, in mythology, Zeus is nursed on bee honey in the Diktean Cave on Crete. In addition, Hesychius, in his lexicon, linked the term *mankind* with *seed of ash.* On the basis of the above observations, as well as parallels with soma in ancient Iran and India,[156] Dumont concludes that the cosmic tree of early Indo-Europeans was a mead tree that dropped heavenly honey on the earth. As for the ash, Dumont judges it highly likely that its production of fermentable manna led early Indo-Europeans to single the tree out as the nurse of both gods and humans and to give its manna a major role in their myth and ritual.[157] In support of this view, he also cites a modern parallel—involving ritual use of a honeylike exudation of the linden tree—among the Cheremis, a Finno-Ugric group living along the Volga River, whose mythology bears striking similarities to Norse mythology, including a cosmic tree.[158]

Shape

One of James George Frazer's laws of sympathetic magic is "the law of similarity,"[159] which states that things that resemble each other do, in fact, share basic qualities. In China, this is expressed in the belief that the pointed, dagger-shaped leaves of sweet flag are weapons of which spirits are quite fearful.[160] In a similar vein in India is Brahmins' and Jains' refusal to eat vegetables, among them mushrooms, garlic, and onions, which they perceive as being shaped like a human head.[161] Among the plants we have considered in detail, mandrake and ginseng are the most striking examples of how the human shape of a plant has contributed to its use in magic, and indeed the magical beliefs surrounding these two man-roots have persisted since antiquity.

43. Buddha's-hand citron (*Citrus medica* var. *sarcodactylis*)
(from Bailey, 1935).

Another example of the inclination of humans to see reflections of themselves in plants is the Oriental perception of the fruit of a particular variety of citron as a human hand. I am referring to the fingered citron (*Citrus medica* var. *sarcodactylis*), a highly valued variety called Buddha's hand (*fo-shou-kan*) in China. In this variety, which has a strong, pleasant odor and is used for perfuming clothes and rooms, the carpels of the fruit naturally separate and grow so as to bear a certain resemblance to fingers (Figure 43).[162] This resemblance may have been of special significance, because for Buddhists, as for Hindus and Moslems, the imprint of a five-fingered hand, commonly colored red or yellow (as with turmeric), has been considered a protection against evil, especially the evil eye, as well as being an auspicious decoration and a mark of honor.[163]

Though China has made important contributions to the world's store of citrus fruit,[164] the fingered citron appears to have been introduced to China from abroad at some time between the fourth and tenth centuries A.D.[165] Swingle, a leading citrus researcher, has suggested that fingered citron originated in India and that Buddhist monks brought it to China.[166] Indeed, there is a tradition that the Buddha, on picking a citron and finding it bitter and of no use, stretched out his hand to make the tree disappear. Then, relenting, he informed the tree that it could live if it altered its fruit so as to be pleasing to humans, whereupon the tree reshaped its fruit to that of Buddha's outstretched hand.[167] At the same time, while India is held by many scholars to be the place where citron was first domesticated, there is no named variety of citron in India.[168] Furthermore, early representations of the citron in India, though they are few, depict fruit of a normal citron form that in no way resembles the fingered citron.[169] Certain scholars have suggested that the citron may have been domesticated to the west of India, and, though this is a minority view, it is possible that the fingered-citron variety was developed there. Indeed, there are claims that the fingered citron is depicted in ancient Egyptian and Assyrian ruins, though Tolkowsky, a leading authority on the history of citrus fruit, has judged the claims for fingered citron in ancient Egypt to be quite unconvincing, and is noncommittal about the Assyrian plant, which he calls pineapple-shaped and a rarity being carried to a king or his officials.[170] Despite this, one cannot dismiss out of hand the possibility that the fingered citron was developed to the west of India, and that Arab sea traders, who had early contacts with China, introduced it there. At the same time, there is no convincing evidence of the fingered citron either in early India or in lands to the west, which suggests that Southeast Asia deserves careful investigation as the possible source of Buddha's-hand citron. South China had extensive early sea trade with Southeast Asia that involved a broad range of commodities, among them various fruits,[171] which provided a ready means for introducing the fingered citron to China. In China, moreover, the fingered citron is cultivated in parts of the country adjacent to Southeast Asia. This includes South China and Central China from the Yangtze Valley southward. Finally, Buddhism has been prominent in Southeast Asia, and the fingered citron also seems to have played a ritual role in that region, for example, as an altar offering in Indochina.[172]

Though its origin remains a mystery, in traditional China fingered citron was the most common citron variety.[173] It has long enjoyed an important role as a symbol of happiness, wealth, and longevity. The tree is an ornamental and a popular pot-plant, and both the tree and its fruit are highly prized gifts, especially at the time of New Year. This is because they enjoy an envious reputation for bestowing good fortune on a household. Buddha's-hand citron has also been a common offering in temples or at shrines of household gods, both at New Year and other times.[174] In addition, the fruit has been a common art motif, as on jade or ivory carvings, or, with stems, leaves, and flowers, on lacquered wood panels.[175] The plant's role is well illustrated on a plate described and depicted by Yetts,[176] which is rich in fruit symbolism: the pomegranate for numerous offspring; the Buddha's-hand citron for happiness and wealth; and the peach for longevity.

Color

As for color, I have noted the suggestion that tulsi achieved sanctity in Hinduism because its purplish to black hue led people to link it with Krishna, whose name means "dark" or "black" and who is depicted with a blue, blue-black, or dark skin. A similar association is suggested for *Eugenia jambolana* Lam.,[177] an Indian tree whose fruit (Hindi: *jamun*) is dark in color (purple) like Krishna. Because of this, the tree is "very dear to him," and is "therefore, worshipped, and Brahmins . . . fed under it."[178] A black color may, however, lead to quite different associations, for black is also an unlucky color.[179] The black color of urd seed in India, for example, led it to be associated with the earth and underworld, as well as with underworld forces, death, and pollution. This made urd suitable for use in rites relating to the dead and underworld forces, but unacceptable in certain other rites requiring great purity, such as in offerings to the high gods. I noted further (1) that sesame seeds, which in antiquity were often linked to urd and included among black foods, may, have come to be viewed in a similar light, especially if they were black; and (2) that fava beans in the ancient Mediterranean world, which in Homer's day appear typically to have been black in color, also came to be tied to impurity, death, and the underworld and, as a result, were forbidden on some ritual occasions and to certain priests as well as to groups such as the Pythagoreans and Orphics.

There are many cases in which plants are avoided as food or used or avoided in ritual because of their color. For many Hindus, meat is an unacceptable food. Thus, members of the Baniya caste in the Punjab pro-hibit carrots, turnips, onions, and red pulse as food because they are red in color and thus resemble flesh.[180] In the nineteenth century in the low-lands of Scotland, green was considered the color that fairies had selected for themselves. Because of this, it was believed, they would be offended by and would demolish a human who wore green at a wedding. Thus, green, an inauspicious color, should never be worn at a wedding. Nor, on a wedding day, should anything green be used in other contexts; for example, kale and other green vegetables should not be served at a wed-ding dinner.[181]

A striking case of the opposite sort is that of turmeric, which gained a prominent role in the ritual of India because yellow is a sacred color, and its rhizome provides a yellow dyestuff. Though turmeric has other uses as well, especially as a flavoring, its name in various languages, among them Sanskrit, is synonymous with "yellow," and it is likely that its yellow color led humans to domesticate the plant.

In India, turmeric is the source of an important ceremonial color. Its role is critical at times of Hindu marriage, for yellow has erotic connota-tions, which is true also in the eastern Mediterranean area, where saffron was the ancient yellow dyestuff. A few days before a Hindu couple are to be wed, they are sprinkled with a mixture of turmeric and oil. The bride then puts on a robe dyed with turmeric, which she continues to wear until the wedding. The wedding invitations are colored with turmeric, and turmeric is splattered on the wall and worshipped by the newlyweds. The intent of all this is to purify the couple, to protect them from evil forces, to encourage communion between them, to facilitate the birth of offspring, and to foster well-being and happiness.[182]

In India, a turmeric root may serve as a charm to repel the evil eye.[183] It plays a special role at times of birth and death. It is, for example, a Hindu practice in Bombay to cut off the umbilical cord and bury it along with turmeric. There is also a Telegu-speaking Hindu practice of smearing the mother with turmeric on the seventh day following her child's birth, and burying the afterbirth in a pot about which turmeric-dyed string has been wound. A corpse may be rubbed with turmeric prior to cremation. In former times, when a Hindu woman was taken to her husband's funeral pyre to commit suicide (suttee), she wore a cloth dyed with turmeric. In a similar vein, when Rājputs, members of that warrior caste, went into a battle where they were badly outnumbered and likely to die, they wore yellow robes.[184]

The ritual role of turmeric in Southeast Asia and the Pacific region differs from that found in India, perhaps most notably in its use in ceremonies to assure crop fertility. Whatever the ritual role turmeric plays in Southeast Asia and the Pacific area its color, as in India, is of paramount concern.[185]

Place and Method of Growth

Even among peoples who are not given to tree worship, individual trees growing in places of great sanctity or possessing unusual qualities may themselves gain sanctity. Generally India's Sikhs do not worship trees. Despite this, they regard a certain jujube tree (*Zizyphus jujuba*), one that grows in the compound of their Golden Temple at Amritsar, as sacred and capable of removing sorrow. Sikhs also hold sacred an unusual *āmlā* (emblic myrobalan) tree near Bareilly in Uttar Pradesh. Though most of this tree's branches produce bitter-sour fruit, one of them bears sweet fruit—a condition, according to Sikh tradition, that came about because one of their gurus had once rested under the tree. The branch that shaded him, Sikhs say, bore sweet fruit ever after.[186]

Other locations may bring plants to the attention of humans on a regular basis. Mandrake seems to have been a volunteer in abandoned and cultivated fields, and tulsi, in waste places everywhere. This suggests that ancient cultivators regularly encountered these plants, that their existence and qualities were constantly being called to the attention of humans, and that they were in an ideal position to be singled out for ritual use by humans. Whether or not a wild plant grew close at hand, ancient humans must have been quite sensitive about where particular species grew and about their growth habits, and sometimes they used this knowledge to establish a plant's role in magic and ritual and its suitability for dietary use. In the chapter on urd, we have seen that some peoples have believed that mushrooms spring from impure substances. Ancient Hindu writings, for example, compared mushrooms to pig dung and the leavings of persons of low caste. Modern Hindus, too, may tie mushrooms to decay or to places where dogs urinate. The fear is that, since mushrooms grow in polluted places, the person who eats them partakes of that pollution. Therefore, persons concerned with maintaining ritual purity should avoid them. This is in accord with the observation that in India flowers growing in cemeteries are not suitable for use in weddings or rites in which prosperity is sought.[187]

Even plant species that are not restricted to a particular location may, in popular thinking, be assigned one that seems appropriate. Early tales in Europe, for example, often depict mandrake as growing in places apparently chosen to emphasize its ties with humanity, on one hand, and with death and underworld forces, on the other. Thus mandrake was commonly said to spring up under a gallows, where it grew in the urine or semen of a man who had been executed there. Such associations, it has been suggested, evolved from early Indo-European thinking about sacrifice, sex, and fertility. In Welsh folklore, mandrake always grows near a gallows tree or a crossroads, particularly a crossroads where persons who killed themselves are interred. Gallows and crossroads are also places where witches were reputed to gather mandrake for their infernal purposes. Crossroads, since ancient times and among many peoples, have been places where underworld forces gather and where people have carried out magical rites for protective and other purposes. Thus, like gallows, they are highly appropriate places to expect mandrake, a plant with underworld ties, to grow.

Place and method of growth may combine in influencing a plant's imagery and ritual role, as suggested by Rahner in considering the willow tree in ancient Greece.[188] The willow, he noted, enjoyed a dual symbolism of life and death: "of fresh and bubbling life, and also of the womb of death to which all things must return." Thus, on one hand it was sacred to mother goddesses such as Hera, and on the other it symbolized infertility.

In part, the willow's infertility symbolism seems to derive from its premature loss of seed. The recognition of this quality is shown by Homer's calling the willow tree "fruit-destroying." Theophrastus and Pliny took that expression to mean that, though the willow reproduces readily from shoots, most willow species lose their seed before it approaches ripeness.[189] In what seems to be an extension of this idea, Aelian wrote that if a man crushes "the fruit of a willow tree . . . and drinks it, his semen loses its procreative strength."[190] Pliny, on his part, noted a drug of willow seed that makes a woman barren.[191]

Rahner, while accepting the idea that its seeding pattern played a role in the willow's imagery of infertility, implies that this also related to the place the tree usually grows. The willow, he observes, is a water-loving tree which in Greece grows in moist, low-lying places near streams or springs—places, in ancient Greek thinking, that provide ready access to the underworld. As a result, the Greeks regarded the willow as a chthonic tree frequented by nymphs who came from the underworld. Rahner notes further that in Greece all "unfruitful trees" were tied to the land of the dead. This, he argues, implies that the willow's "unfruitfulness" derived partly from its ties with the underworld and death. In any case, the Greeks believed that the willow could not only contribute to infertility but also suppress "amorous appetites." This led it to become a symbol of sexual continence as well.

Another example of how a plant's growth habits may influence its ritual role is that of the strangler figs. I have noted that the ability of a pipal tree to strangle a host tree on which it grew led Vedic Indians to appeal to the pipal tree for help: "As thou climbest up the trees, O Aśvattha, and renderest them subordinate, thus do thou split in two the head of my enemy, and overcome him!"[192] Thus a strangler tree is asked for assistance to do more of the same, but in the human sphere and in the interests of a human appellant. Abbott, moreover, writes in the present tense of such appeals to the pipal tree to destroy one's enemies, as if these appeals are still made among modern Hindus.[193]

The sacred fig-tree's strangling abilities have also served to enhance an effectiveness in ritual that it already possessed. In our chapter on the sacred fig-tree, we saw that in Vedic India certain sacrificial fires were prepared with a fire drill made from wood of the sacred fig (aśvattha) and śamī trees. In such fires, fig wood served as the male element, the drill; and śamī wood, the female element, the base. The preferred wood for fire sticks, however, was that of a sacred fig-tree that had grown on a śamī tree. The fig's growth involved its tendrils grasping the śamī, which, in Vedic thinking, was visualized as a man embracing a woman, which made such wood especially well suited for the sexual intercourse that Vedic fire-making symbolized.[194] Apparently, moreover, such growth was deliberately arranged, for Gonda[195] writes of the root of a sacred fig-tree, whose wood was intended for use in fire-making, being "inserted" into a śamī tree for growing.

Symptoms Experienced by Humans Who Consume Plants

Certain ancient writers have suggested that the Pythagorean ban on fava beans was based on the stomach gas and intestinal upset, troubled sleep, disagreeable dreams, and abundant excrement that are brought on when one eats them. These, it has been noted, are signs of a disturbed state, a heaviness inappropriate to persons visiting sacred places, attending festivals, or seeking truth—occasions when purity and lightness are needed.

Some ancient observers viewed such flatulence in a different manner. For them, flatulence was a sign that fava beans contained life, the souls of deceased humans. Because of this, it was detestable and defiling to consume fava beans, which involved eating decayed matter and even one's own relatives. It was because of such thinking, some have argued, that bans on the fava bean, such as that of Pythagoras, were established. By either of the two views, the symptoms experienced by people when eating fava beans were critical in determining their acceptability on everyday and ritual occasions.

One could make a similar case that the exhilarating and intoxicating effect of soma—whose juice, along with other ingredients, was used by Vedic Indians in making a fermented drink used at sacrifices—led it to become a "divine herb," both sacred and a deity in its own right. Mandrake, which can induce drowsiness, sleep, and death, may represent another example of this sort, but one that led to an association with sorcery and the underworld. Taste may also affect the ritual role of a plant, as is the case with the tamarind tree (*Tamarindus indica*) in India, which is not used in auspicious rites because its fruit is so sour. People believe that, if they should use the tamarind tree in a rite, the rite would also become sour and thus pointless and without meaning.[196]

Relationships between People and Their Ritual Plants

The Nature of Those Relationships

One observation to emerge from this study is that ritual plants have enjoyed unusually rich and varied associations with other aspects of human life and culture. One plant—for example, garlic or urd—may be polluting to certain people or on certain occasions. Another—for example, the tulsi plant or the pipal tree—may be purifying. A plant may be tied to prosperity, good health, fertility, marriage, and life, on one hand, or to poverty, illness, sterility, widowhood, and death, on the other. A plant—tulsi, for example—may be worshipped to attract a mate or make a marriage fruitful. Beliefs and practices relating to ritual plants may find expression in sacred literature as well as in myth and folktale. They may relate to society as a whole or to specific groups, as with the fava bean, which was widely used in diet in the Mediterranean world, but not by Pythagoreans and Orphics. They may be subject to considerable regional variation. They may enjoy an amazing persistence, as shown by the pipal tree, whose sanctity seems to go back to the time of the Indus Valley civilization, if not before—a time span of at least three or four millennia. Or, like all beliefs and practices, those related to ritual plants may be subject to change, as shown in the striking decline in the standing of mandrake, brought on in Europe by the rise of Christianity and scientific medicine. A new religion may, on the other hand, take over earlier ritual uses of plants. This is shown in India, where Buddhists took over Hindu views about the sanctity of fig trees, though they identified individual sacred trees with the Buddha rather than with Hindu deities. Even if a new religion does not adopt earlier views and practices involving ritual plants, moreover, they may continue to be expressed in folk belief and practice.

Also notable is the desire of humans to be in the presence of a sacred plant and to protect it against injury, as with a Hindu housewife who maintains and watches over a tulsi plant at home. It seems to be preferred that sacred plants be located reasonably close to home. It is possible that this is the reason why in the Himalayas, where the pipal tree does not do well, the deodār is the sacred tree on which ritual is centered. Sometimes, however, a lengthy journey may be necessary to reach a sacred tree. People from various parts of the ancient Greek world travelled to the sacred oak of Zeus at Dodona for oracular purposes. Buddhists from Ceylon, Burma, and China have gone on pilgrimage to Bodh Gaya to worship at the tree where the Buddha received enlightenment. In India, however, merely being near a sacred plant may not suffice. To gain further merit for a human or for the good of the plant, people practice circumambulation, as by walking around a tulsi plant or pipal tree 108 times, an auspicious number.

The ritual power of a plant may be enhanced by employing more than one species of plant that share a trait or that have traits that complement each other. The value of a plant in ritual may also be increased by a species with which it grows, as we saw above in the case of the aśvattha tree that has grown upon a śamī. An equally interesting case is that of mistletoe that grows on an oak. Among the Celts of ancient Gaul, as among Celts elsewhere, the oak was a sacred tree. Mistletoe is not often found growing on oaks,[197] but when it did in Gaul, both the mistletoe and the oak on which it grew were regarded as the most sacred of all things, and the mistletoe was collected by druids in a great ceremony that involved animal sacrifice and feasting. Pliny noted that in Gaul mistletoe was given to barren animals in a drink to make them fertile. It was also used to treat all illnesses and served as an antidote to poison. In another place, Pliny, apparently referring to Italy, reported that women carry mistletoe to help them conceive. Frazer, who has noted parallels between Celtic and early Latin religious practices, observed further that mistletoe above all was considered effective in protecting against witchcraft.[198]

In Celtic Britain, too, mistletoe had healing and amatory roles,[199] and it is significant that the usual names for mistletoe in modern Celtic languages (Welsh, *olhiach;* Irish, *uileiceach;* Breton, *ollyiach*) mean "all-healing."[200] The special value of mistletoe associated with the oak is suggested by the discovery, in a Bronze Age tumulus, of an oak coffin that not only was covered with oak branches, but also, inside with the human remains, contained a large amount of what has been identified as mistletoe.[201]

In ancient Greece, too, mistletoe growing on an oak was of special significance. In one of his tragedies, Ion called mistletoe "the sweat of the oak," perhaps implying that it was the concentrated essence of the oak tree. We have seen that the framing of the ship *Argo* included some wood from the Dodona oracular oak. One ancient writer also wrote that the *Argo* was built with wood from the "lion tree," which, he said, was like a mistletoe-bearing oak, impervious to destruction by water or fire, just like mistletoe itself.[202]

Taking the matter a bit further is an observation by Drayton that mandrake grown "in the shade of the mystic mistletoe" is the supreme "love-compelling agent."[203] It is also striking that mistletoe, especially when it had grown on an oak, was considered effective in some of the same ways mandrake was.[204]

Ritual power may also be enhanced by deliberately planting more than one sacred species together, as, for example, the triad of sacred trees (pipal, banyan, and neem) found at a Shiva temple in Hardwar, one of Hinduism's most sacred cities. Ritual plants may be associated with sacred objects of other sorts. One example of this is the association of tulsi with the śālagrāma stone in the ceremony celebrating the plant's marriage to Vishnu. Another is the worship of the "undying banyan tree" along with Vishnu's footprint and the holy waters of the Phalgu River at the Hindu pilgrimage center at Gaya. The ritual power of a sacred plant may be increased by marrying it to a sacred plant of its own or another species, for example, by Hindus who carry out a formal wedding ceremony for a pipal and a neem tree. A human, too, may be married to a plant to achieve useful ends, as when a married woman marries a tree to do away with the risk of widowhood, an undesirable state. That risk is eliminated because, if her human husband were to die, she would still be married to the tree.

Ritual plants may be tied to nature cults. The link between sacred fig-trees and the snake cult in India is an example of this. Ritual plants have also developed relationships with a broad range of supernatural beings, such as deities, evil spirits, and ancestral spirits. In ancient Greece, for example, the laurel was Apollo's tree at Delhi; and the willow, Hera's tree at Samos. Such relationships were not usually exclusive, however, for trees and other ritual plants have usually related to more than one deity. In India, the tulsi plant has strong ties with Vishnu, but Shiva is not left out. The banyan tree, on its part, has strong ties with Shiva, but Vishnu is not left out, nor are a range of other deities. Urd and sesame, in a similar manner, have ties with death, ancestral spirits, evil spirits, devils, and chthonic deities such as Yama, lord of the dead, and Śani (Saturn), a dark and evil planet.

Ritual plants may also relate to broader religious concepts relating to life, or to the world, the underworld, or the hereafter. The pipal tree in India, for example, is the local representative of the cosmic tree, a tree that represents the universe and is the source of all life. Oak trees in early Prussia and at Dodona in Greece were forms of oracular trees. The concept of the transmigration of souls, moreover, is represented in widespread belief in the Old World that trees are inhabited by ancestral spirits, and is demonstrated as well in the Pythagorean conviction that fava beans contain souls of the ancestors. Deities and other supernatural beings may also enter plants, as when Vishnu turned Vṛindā into a tulsi plant.

Finally, ritual perceptions of plants may find expression in medicine, whether traditional or scientific medicine. In Ayurvedic medicine, for example, tulsi serves as a purificant in preventing and curing illness and disease; and various parts of pipal or banyan trees serve in stimulating sex, encouraging the production of sperm in men, and eliminating barrenness in women.

Human Agents in the Diffusion of Sacred Trees

In my chapter on the sacred fig-trees of India, I noted that Buddhists have played a prominent role in the diffusion of the pipal tree. Their interest, moreover, has been in pipal trees with pedigrees, most notably the holy tree at Bodh Gaya in Bihar. Even while the Buddha was alive, he directed that a branch of the holy tree be brought to the monastery where he preferred to live. He is also reported to have said, "He who worships it will receive the same reward as if [he had] worshipped me in person."[205] This provided an outstanding precedent for a transfer of sanctity through carrying and planting seed, seedlings, and cuttings of the Bodh Gaya fig-tree elsewhere. The most notable of those transfers involved a branch carried and planted at Anuradhapura, then the capital of Ceylon, in the third century B.C. The Anuradhapura fig-tree, in turn, became the primary source for pipal trees planted throughout that island. The full story of Buddhist transfers of pipal trees is yet to be told. Clearly, however, it goes far beyond Bodh Gaya and Anuradhapura and into distant parts of the Buddhist world. In addition, it was done on a scale that may be unique among transfers made from individual trees of great sanctity.

We have also seen that Hindu traders sometimes plant pipal and banyan trees near their places of business in shops and bazaars. They have also served as agents of diffusion for these trees. The activities of such traders have not been limited to local communities, districts, provinces, regions, or even to India, for Indian merchants have migrated across the Old World to places as distant as Gibraltar and Hong Kong. Their enterprise and skills, moreover, have led them to become essential factors in the trade of many lands around the Indian Ocean and beyond. From our perspective, it is notable that *Baniya* is a term used for Hindu castes of traders, shopkeepers, and money lenders. It refers especially to the trading castes of western India,[206] who are in an excellent geographic position to establish trade in ports of Arabia and Africa. It is also notable that such traders, Baniya, are credited with introducing the banyan tree to places along the Persian Gulf and to Arabia and Africa when they set up business there. In fact, the European names "l'arbre des banians" and "banyan tree" derive from this fact or from a famous tree on the Persian Gulf under which Indian traders had set up a shrine.[207]

The full story of the Baniya role in the diffusion of Indian sacred fig-trees remains to be told. An unanswered question is how far back in time that diffusion may have occurred. Near the end of the fifteenth century, Vasco da Gama, on his famous voyage of exploration, found Hindu residents and Hindu Indian merchants and their ships in Arab ports in East

Africa.[208] Moreover, the merchant-author of *The Periplus of the Erythraean Sea* indicates that already in the first or second century A.D. there was a well-established sea trade—in which Indian Ocean monsoon circulation was critical—between India, on one hand, and Arabia, Egypt, and East Africa, on the other. Though most of that trade seems to have been in Arab hands, the *Periplus* says that on one island in southwestern Arabia (Kanē) the inhabitants were "a mixed people, consisting of Arabs and Indians, and a few Greeks who have come there to trade."[209] Furthermore, trade between the Indus Valley and the Near East, whether overland or by way of the Indian Ocean, goes back to the time of the Indus Valley civilization (c. 2500–1700 B.C.) and beyond. At the same time, it cannot be proven whether or not any of this was direct trade or whether Indus Valley traders or trading colonies had been established, for example, in Mesopotamia.[210]

Another story about agents in the diffusion of a ritually important tree also deserves mention. This is the case of the citron, "a goodly tree" of the Hebrews (*etrog; Citrus medica* var. ethrog), which came to play an essential role at the Feast of Tabernacles or Feast of Booths (Sukkot). This is a happy fall festival of thanksgiving. At that time, modern Hebrews come to the synagogue either with a citron fruit in their hands or with citron fruit attached to myrtle, willow, and palm branches.[211] They also eat citron preserves during that period.[212] The citron was the first citrus tree to be cultivated in the eastern Mediterranean area,[213] but it is not clear when or why it came to serve in the Feast of Tabernacles.[214] Isaac has concluded that the citron assumed that role at least by the first century A.D., and likely long before.[215] According to Midrashic commentators, the citron fruit represents the human heart, and its use in the Feast of Tabernacles was intended to atone for sins of the heart.[216] The citron was thought to enhance a man's sexual potency and to help a pregnant woman give birth to a son; and in Roman times the Hebrews used citrons to adorn their bridal chambers.[217] In any case, a supply of citron fruit was needed for Hebrew ritual purposes. This led citron cultivation to spread from one Hebrew community to another across the Mediterranean world, thus making the Hebrews a major force in the plant's diffusion.[218] The case of the Hebrews and citron not only presents a clear example of the importance of ritual needs in plant diffusion, but also provides an excellent parallel to that of Buddhists and sacred fig-trees.

Concerns of Ancient Peoples in Their Dealings with Ritual Plants Compared with Concerns of Secular People Today

True believers among present-day material determinists might pore over the stories of the plants considered in this book to seek an explanation of their ritual roles in medical, economic, environmental, or techno-environmental terms. Bans on the fava bean did occur in the Mediterranean world, where favism is prevalent today, though, as we have seen, existing evidence does not support the idea that the Pythagorean ban on fava beans derived from awareness of and concern with favism. Persons who suggest otherwise are on as shaky ground as those who have argued that the ancient Hebrew ban on pork derived from concern with trichinosis or environmental deterioration.[219] An imaginative determinist might argue that tulsi's sanctity derived from recognition of its abilities to repel mosquitoes, that it makes very good sense to have a mosquito-repellent plant growing at home. He or she might also argue that citron became the goodly tree of the Hebrews because it was a good source of vitamin C. Tulsi does indeed have mosquito-repelling abilities, and citron is a source of vitamin C. Yet these are quite minor aspects of the human needs served by these and other ritual plants considered in this book. As Andrew P. Vayda has observed[220] in criticizing the approach of techno-environmental determinist Marvin Harris, Harris is wrong because he thinks that there are "general formulas, laws, or prescription[s]" that can explain changes in human life over time. Harris is also wrong, writes Vayda, because of his monism, the idea that one key, a techno-environmental one, will open all doors. In regard to the matter that has concerned us in this book, I would go further. I would argue that in order to gain an understanding of the role of plants in ritual through history, Harris's and other forms of material determinism open very few doors, whereas many can be opened by careful weighing of the physical characteristics of plants along with the basic needs of humans.

Of overwhelming importance in those ritual relationships was a desire for good health and prosperity; a fear of violence, evil, impurity, death, and decay; and concern with one's prospects after death. Also powerful were hopes for fertility and continued ability to have children, without which a family's generational survival would be jeopardized and care of the elderly threatened. Often, moreover, the paths to follow were established by the scriptures, as indicated in the Hindu Upanishads, which were set down in their present form between 400 and 200 B.C.: "What is set forth in the Vedas, that is Truth. / By what the Vedas tell, wise men live their life."[221]

In our present-day political scene some of the ancient vital concerns persist. Social Security, Medicaid, Medicare, and other means of caring for the aged and infirm are all vital issues. These may be viewed as runaway expenditures that are bankrupting the nation or as humane programs that are vitally needed and fully justified. Taxation and income redistribution are of similar concern. From one perspective, people focus on taxation and income redistribution as they destroy the incentive to work and the ability of wage-earners to prosper. From another perspective, they focus on what are called the greedy rich, and on why their money should be taken and given to the deserving poor. Minimum-wage laws may be condemned because they destroy jobs or praised because they provide many low-income workers with a living wage. NAFTA and other free-trade agreements may be seen as unfairly taking jobs from American workers or as improving efficiency and benefitting the nation as a whole. Abortion may be approached from the perspective of civil rights, the right of a woman to make her own decisions with respect to aborting or giving birth to a fetus; or it may be approached in terms of a fetus's right to live.

Though certain of the ancients' concerns may have been quite similar to those of contemporary people, one big difference is that, for them, the family was more basic in the struggle for survival. Thus in matters of assuring their health, fertility, and well-being, individuals were more likely to take action at a family level.[222] Young people, moreover, were far more understanding and appreciative of the views their forefathers, and had a greater recognition that they were part of cultural traditions that might have deep historical roots. That is still the case in India and many other non-Western lands. By contrast, the predominant focus of modern American youth has been on self and age group. Their focus is also on the present rather than on their roots in Western civilization. Equally important, however, the people of antiquity, or at least many more of them, lacked the secular view that prevails in the Western world today. Today there is an unusual focus on the material and the sensate, on houses, motor vehicles, clothes, loud and crude music, sex, violence, and drugs. Since secularism has prevailed for decades, it is especially difficult for Americans of any age to appreciate the thinking of their forefathers, in whose world supernatural forces—gods, devils, and spirits good and evil—were important to human well-being. One classification of queries addressed in historical consultations with the oracle at Delphi in ancient Greece revealed that 43 percent of the queries (24 of 55) related to worship of the gods and a desire to please and honor them, or to religious problems such as how to maintain the sanctity of shrines and whether to open sacred lands to farming. Of the remaining queries that were of great concern to individuals and families (rather than primarily to communities and states), virtually all fell into the categories of family welfare; contemplated enterprise or career; crimes committed by the person who made the query; wish to learn one's origin, the identity of one's parents; need to change residence, captivity, exile, loss of country; lack of children and desire for progeny; plague, famine, drought, catastrophe; and death.[223] Since similar concerns were basic not only to the ancient Greeks but also to other ancient peoples of the Old World, the ritual relationships they developed with plants were perfectly reasonable. Avoiding the use of garlic and onions before entering a temple, keeping and caring for a mandrake at home, worshipping a tulsi plant in the morning, nurturing and circumambulating a pipal tree—all of these make great sense given the prevailing framework of thinking. Indeed, I am convinced that, contrary to what many cultural materialists believe, basic human concerns were the prime movers in determining the ritual roles that plant species came to play, and that techno-environmental, medical, and nutritional factors were quite secondary in the matter.

Notes
Bibliography
Index

NOTES

Chapter 1. Introduction

1. I have included material in many chapters on ancient and traditional uses of plants in curing sickness and disease, but particularly if they relate to magic and ritual. Though it is now somewhat out of date, Sheldon Saul Hendler's *The doctors' vitamin and mineral encyclopedia* (New York: Simon and Schuster, 1990) contains useful information and brief bibliographies on the nutritional and medical merits of certain plants mentioned in this book (garlic and onions, mushrooms, mistletoe, ginseng, St.-John's-wort). The state of scientific thinking about such matters is constantly changing, however, and the interested reader is well advised to consult recent studies, which may readily be identified in *Medline*.

Chapter 2. Tulsi, Holy Basil of the Hindus; With Notes on Sweet Basil in the Mediterranean World

1. Sanskrit: *tulasī;* Hindi: *tulsī*. Among the other Sanskrit names for the plant are *parnāsa* and *surasā* (Ainslie, 1826, 2: 426; G. Watt, 1889–96, 5: 443; Dutt, 1922: 220; Godbole et al., 1966: 146; Roxburgh, 1971: 463). The word *tulasī* is not found in ancient Ayurvedic texts or in the Vedic Brahmanas or Samhitas. Instead, one finds in them the word *surasā* or *surasa*, which interpreters have taken to be *tulasī*, a word which seems to have derived from *surasā*. It is said that the latter name for the plant prevailed in antiquity; that the word *tulasī* first appeared in the medieval period (ninth and tenth centuries A.D.); and that the

307

word *tulasī* gained prominence between the twelfth and fourteenth centuries A.D. and became the plant's principal name. The possible sequence was *surasā* > *surasī* > *sulasī* > *chulasī* > *tulasī* (P. V. Sharma, 1973).

2. Pande, 1965: 36.

3. Indianists have retained a lively interest in India's sacred plants, as shown in recent decades by the publication of books such as *Le culte de l'arbre dans l'Inde ancienne*, by Odette Viennot (1954); *Tree symbol worship in India*, by Sankar Sen Gupta (ed.) (1965); *Plant myths and traditions in India*, by Shakti M. Gupta (1971); *Tree worship in ancient India*, by Binod Chandra Sinha (1979); *Sacred trees across cultures and nations*, by Sankar Sen Gupta (1980); and *Sacred plants of India*, by Brahma Prakash Pandey (1989).

4. There is confusion about the terms *darbha* and *kuśa grass*. Many writers, ancient and modern, have considered the two terms to be identical and interchangeable; and modern writers of this persuasion have commonly identified the grass in question as *Poa cynosuroides* or *Eragrostis cynosuroides* (Monier-Williams, 1887: 338; G. Watt, 1889–96, 3: 254; Crooke, 1926: 295; B. Walker, 1968, 1: 405; Gonda, 1985: 29, 52, 97). Other writers, however, have distinguished clearly between the two and, in modern times, have even placed them in separate genera (Gonda, 1985: 29, 52). In any case, darbha is not the only sacred grass of Hinduism, but it is said that it is the holiest. It serves at all religious rites, including funeral ceremonies, and is cast on the ground before all sacrifices, for it purifies everything with which it comes into contact; it consecrates the soil and creates the holiest of all places to sit; and, when it is wrapped around one's fingers, it serves as an amulet and makes the fingers suitable for use in the most hallowed rites (Monier-Williams, 1887: 310, 338; G. Watt, 1889–96, 3: 253–54; Dubois, 1906: 651–52; Crooke, 1926: 295; B. Walker, 1968, 1: 405–6; Stutley and Stutley, 1977: 157–58). For a scholarly review of the ritual uses of darbha and other grasses in Vedic religion, see Gonda, 1985.

5. Sanskrit: *aśvattha;* Hindi: *pipal.*

6. Sanskrit: *nyadgrodha* or *vaṭa;* Hindi: *bor, bar, ber, bargat.*

7. Hindi: *neem;* Sanskrit: *nimba.* In India, the neem, or margosa, tree is linked to the lesser deities of disease. It is believed to be the residence of Śītalā, goddess of smallpox, and her six sisters. Therefore, a platform for the goddess may be set up beneath a neem tree (for a photo of a shrine of Śītalā and village godlings, see Crooke, 1896a, 1: opp. 126; according to M. Stevenson [1915: 266–67], Jain women, too, almost always worship at shrines of Śītalā when smallpox strikes). Well-to-do Hindus may pay Brahmins to worship the tree daily during the hot season, when the coming of the goddess of smallpox is greatly feared. Moreover, when the weather is hot, or at noon, children are usually not permitted to approach a neem tree in a lonely place, out of concern that the goddess will descend on their heads. When smallpox does occur in a village, town, or city, moreover,

women worship the neem tree and the goddess, and for protection or propitiation people may place neem leaves on the door of a house or neem garlands on the bed of the afflicted individual. Neem serves a broad range of other medicinal uses as well, and is employed in staving off death, gaining wealth, obtaining offspring, and assisting at the birth of a child.

Neem also enjoys a belief in its general ability to purify, protect, and cure illness, which is based on myths that the tree derives from nectar of the gods or that a few drops of such nectar fell onto the tree. People may eat neem leaves on New Year's Day to protect against disease during the coming year. For purposes of protection and purification, they may burn neem leaves in their houses or place garlands of neem leaves across streets or across the doorways of their houses. Neem leaves may also be placed in the mouth as a symbol of sorrow by people returning from a funeral. Neem leaves or branches also serve to purify funeral mourners and sever them from all connection with the dead and the impurity of death, as well as to protect against and exorcise evil spirits. To protect a mother and her newborn child from evil forces, a twig with neem leaves may be placed above the door of her house. With similar intent, people may also place outside a door an earthen brazier in which a small fire is burning, at which persons pause before entering the house to enable the fire to dispel any evil they may have (Crooke, 1896a, 1: 125–32; 2: 104–6; 1926: 410; Chowbe, 1899: 228; M. Stevenson, 1920: 157, 288, 362; Colthurst, 1924: 75–76; Aiyar, 1931–32: 427; B. Walker, 1968, 1: 399; Abbott, 1974: 31, 263, 314, 317, 320, 321, 322–23, 325, 326, 329, 388; Sen Gupta, 1980: 54; Stutley, 1985: 103; Pandey, 1989: 3–4; Jeffery et al., 1990: 9).

8. Monier-Williams, 1883: 330–39; Crooke, 1896a, 2: 29–30, 94–115; 1926: 404–10; Chowbe, 1899; Dubois, 1906: 649–53; Geden, 1908–26a: 232–33; 1983: 176; Basak, 1953: 106–9; Sen Gupta, 1965b, esp. chapters by Chandervaker, Desai, Mahapatra, Maity, Pande, and Upadhyaya; B. Walker, 1968, 1: 357–58, 405–6; 2: 214–19; Gonda, 1969: 11–14; 1970: 111–13; Ward, 1970, 3: 203–5; S. M. Gupta, 1971: 50–58; Sen Gupta, 1980: 26, 36–54.

Hindi: *bael* or *bel;* Sanskrit: *bilva*. In English, the bael tree is sometimes called the wood-apple tree. For the differences between the two trees, bael and wood-apple or elephant-apple (*Limonia acidissima*), see G. Watt, 1889–96, 1: 117; and Hayes, 1966: 414–15. For more on the bael—cultivation and economic uses of the tree and its fruit, see G. Watt, 1889–96, 1: 117–24; Naik, 1949: 455; Prakash, 1961: passim; Hayes, 1966: 414–15; Achaya, 1994: passim; S. K. Roy, 1985: passim. The role of the bael tree in ritual and religion will be touched on when, later in this chapter, the ties between Shiva and tulsi are considered.

9. Risley, 1891, 1: 393.

10. In South India, a Hindu may wear around the neck a small plate of gold or copper containing a representation of the god Hanumān for protection against

the evil eye (Woodburne, 1981: 62). For more on the use of copper in Hindu ritual, see Abbott, 1974: 210–12.

11. E.g., the village of Tulsī mentioned by Babb, 1975: 80.

12. There is, for example, the girl's name "Tulasī" and the man's name "Tulasīdāsa"—"slave, servant, or devotee of Tulsī"—made famous by the great Hindu poet Tulsīdās (B. Walker, 1968, 2: 525; Smith and Narasimha Chary, 1991: 248).

13. Pickering, 1879: 687.

14. Crooke, 1896a, 2: 110.

15. In west tropical Africa, for example, two basil species (*O. viride* Willd., the fever plant or mosquito plant; and *O. canum* Sims [= *O. americanum* L.]), hoary or American basil) are commonly cultivated in household gardens for use as medicinals (Dalziel, 1937: 462–63).

16. Parlby, 1850, 1: 43, 217; G. Watt, 1889–96, 5: 440–45; Dymock et al., 1890–93, 3: 83–88; Crevost and Lemarié, 1917: 155–56; Ridley, 1922–25, 2: 643; Furtado, 1926–29: 416–17; Bois, 1927–37, 3: 179–80; Bailey, 1935, 2: 2319; Uphof, 1959: 251; Burkill, 1966, 2: 1597–1603; Balfour, 1976, 7: 5–6; Perry, 1980: 189–90; Sundararaj and Balasubramanyam, 1986: 166; Vartak and Upadhye, 1989.

17. Darrah, 1974: 63, 67.

18. Darrah, 1972: 8; 1974: 63.

19. Vavilov, 1949–50: 32.

20. Vartak and Upadhye, 1989: 5, 9.

21. Hooker, 1872–97, 4: 608; G. Watt, 1889–96, 5: 441; Laufer, 1919: 587–88; Parry, 1945: 166; Roxburgh, 1971: 464; Darrah, 1972: 3; Pruthi, 1976: 29; Y. S. Lewis, 1984: 171; Farrell, 1990: 38.

22. Darrah, 1972: 4.

23. Laufer, 1919: 586.

24. Parlby, 1850, 1: 217; Sheriff, 1869: 184–85; Dymock et al., 1890–93, 3: 83; G. Watt, 1889–96, 5: 441.

25. *sabzā* (Lord, 1908–26: 472).

26. Sheriff, 1869: 184–85; G. Watt, 1889–96, 5: 441; Dymock et al., 1890–93, 3: 83; Mukhopadhyay, 1965: 162; Pruthi, 1976: 29; Sundararaj and Balasubramanyam, 1986: 166–67.

27. Zeven and Zhukovsky, 1975: 49; Mathon, 1981: 77; Zeven and de Wet, 1982: 56.

28. Hooker, 1872–97, 4: 607–9; Balfour, 1885, 3: 944; 1976, 7: 5–6; G. Watt, 1889–96, 5: 440–45; Dymock et al., 1890–93, 3: 83–88; Dutt, 1922: 221; Gamble and Fischer, 1956–58, 2: 777–78; Mukhopadhyay, 1965: 162; Godbole et al., 1966: 145–46; Roxburgh, 1971: 463–65; Pruthi, 1976: 29; Sundararaj and Bala-

subramanyam, 1986: 166; Satyavati et al., 1987: 354–55; Vartak and Upadhye, 1989.

29. Parlby, 1850, 1: 43, 217.

30. G. Watt, 1889–96, 5: 443; Dymock et al., 1890–93, 3: 88; Dutt, 1922: 220–21; P. V. Sharma, 1973: 232.

31. In premodern and modern times, many terms have been used, and not always consistently, for *Ocimum* species, including *O. sanctum*. The result is that readers are often confused about the identity of the plant being considered. Some confusion stems from the use of *tulsi* or *tulasi* in a general sense without indicating the species, whether *O. sanctum* or otherwise, that is being discussed. Further confusion is brought on by certain Indian writers who use those words for a plant in the Western world without specifying that it is *O. basilicum* they are talking about.

32. E.g., More, 1989: 15.

33. G. Watt, 1889–96, 5: 443; Darrah, 1974: 65–66; *The useful plants of India*, 1986: 405; Palange, 1989: 23. For descriptions of a green-leafed form of *O. sanctum* widely cultivated in the United States and a purple-leafed form from India but largely unknown in the United States, see Darrah, 1974: 65–66.

34. Darrah, 1974: 65–66.

35. Das, 1965: 26; Gonda, 1970: 111.

36. Upadhyaya, 1965: 13.

37. Rai, 1992: 31.

38. R. S. Khare, 1976a: 102.

39. Zimmer, 1955, 1: 164–65.

40. *tri-mūrti* = "three-forms." Although some of the principal Vedic gods were joined in triads (Macdonell, 1897: 19, 54, 69, 93–94; B. Walker, 1968, 1: 395), the joining of Vishnu, Brahma, and Shiva in a triad is a later development, and, indeed, mention of it is absent in the epics except in one late passage (Hopkins, 1969: 223–24, 231).

41. For this these and other tales of how the Krishna-tulsi relationship came about, see Crooke, 1896a, 2: 110–11; Kincaid, 1908: 3–8; Underhill, 1921: 129–30; Enthoven, 1924: 121; Thomas, 1961: 133–34; Kabiraj, 1965: 154; B. Walker, 1968, 2: 584–85; Gonda, 1970: 111; Ward, 1970, 3: 204; S. M. Gupta, 1971: 75–78; Babb, 1975: 107–8; Chandola, 1976: 108–9; and Sen Gupta, 1980: 43. In art, the goddess Tulasī is depicted as having four arms and dark skin. She is dressed in white, wears a crown and numerous ornaments, and sits on a lotus throne (Stutley, 1985: 146).

42. Monier-Williams, 1883: 333; Frazer, 1935, 2: 26; Mahapatra, 1965: 129; Sen Gupta, 1965a: xxv; R. S. Khare, 1967: 6; Babb, 1975: 107.

43. B. Walker, 1968, 1: 396; Abbott, 1974: 5.

44. For excellent accounts of the Ganges, or the Ganges and other rivers, in

Hindu sacred geography, see Eck, 1982; and Kinsley, 1986: 187–96. For such an account of the river goddesses Gaṅgā and Yamunā (Jumna), see Viennot, 1964. For Hindu views of the power of water, see Abbott, 1974: 161–71. For Hindu views of the origin of all life in the waters, expressions of Hindu water cosmology in early literature, and a discussion of nymphs and goddesses of springs and rivers, including Gaṅgā, as they have appeared in art, see Coomaraswamy, 1993: 105–12, 169–75.

45. One version of the story of reincarnation has the hair of Vṛindā become the tulsi plant, and her body, the Gandaki River. This and other place-names mentioned in the text are included on the map at the end of the text.

46. Sālagrāma stones are ammonites, rounded stones that contain imprints of fossil shells. They range in size from small pebbles to large rocks that have been eroded and washed into the lowland from limestone rock in the Himalayas. They are especially numerous in the bed of the Gandaki River (Dubois, 1906: 648; B. Walker, 1968, 2: 584; Sleeman, 1973: 121–22).

47. The stone itself is an object of worship, since it represents the deity. To gain merit, devotees may wear a śālagrāma stone. Even if broken, a stone may remain useful in driving away evil (Abbott, 1974: 13, 245, 470).

48. "Hari" ("tawny") is one of the names by which Vishnu is called.

49. Dymock et al., 1890–93, 3: 87; Crooke, 1896a, 2: 110; Pande, 1965: 38; Upadhyaya, 1965: 12; Chandola, 1976: 109; Sen Gupta, 1980: 43.

50. R. S. Khare, 1967: 6.

51. Stutley, 1985: 146.

52. Monier-Williams, 1883: 333; Dymock et al., 1890–93, 3: 87; Crooke, 1896a, 2: 111; Geden, 1908–26a: 232; 1983: 176; M. Stevenson, 1920: 141; Enthoven, 1924: 121; Frazer, 1935, 2: 26; Thomas, 1960: 30, 35; Sen Gupta, 1965a: xix, xxv; S. M. Gupta, 1971: 78; V. Mani, 1975: 797, 798; Stutley and Stutley, 1977: 306; Smith and Narasimha Chary, 1991: 246–47.

53. V. Mani, 1975: 798.

54. Enthoven, 1924: 121; Pandey, 1989: 35; Smith and Narasimha Chary, 1991: 246–47.

55. G. Watt, 1889–96, 5: 444; Pandey, 1989: 35.

56. Smith and Narasimha Chary, 1991: 247.

57. Basak, 1953: 108; Bhattacharyya, 1953: 174; Chandola, 1976: 109; R. S. Khare, 1976a: 102; Rai, 1992: 11.

58. R. S. Khare, 1976a: 102.

59. Watt, citing Lisboa, describes a ceremonial offering in which the worshipper took two tulsi leaves, dipped them into water, and threw one onto the brass dish of food and the other onto the god (G. Watt, 1889–96, 5: 444–45).

60. Upadhyaya, 1965: 12; Toomey, 1986: 72.

61. Parlby, 1850, 1: 42–43; Balfour, 1885, 3: 944; 1976, 7: 6; Palange, 1989: 22–23, 25; Sivarajan and Balachandran, 1994: 485.

62. Palange, 1989: 25.

63. Also in use is a term that incorporates the god Rama's name—*Ram* or *Rama tulsī*, which is usually applied to *O. gratissimum.*

64. Parlby, 1850, 1: 43; Drury, 1873: 317; Balfour, 1885, 3: 944; G. Watt, 1889–96, 5: 443; Dymock et al., 1890–93, 3: 85; Desai, 1965: 54; Roxburgh, 1971: 463–65; Chandola, 1976: 108; Bedi, 1978: 283; *The useful plants of India,* 1986: 405; Palange, 1989: 22–23; Rai, 1992: 20, 23–24.

65. Pickering, 1879: 687, citing W. Jones.

66. In certain Indian languages the term *kala* or *kālī* ("black") *tulasī* is also used for *O. sanctum* or its dark cultivar (Ainslie, 1826, 2: 426; G. Watt, 1889–96, 5: 443; S. M. Gupta, 1971: 77; Roxburgh, 1971: 463; Balfour, 1976, 7: 6; *The useful plants of India,* 1986: 405; Satyavati et al., 1987: 355).

67. The number seven is prominent in Hindu religion and ritual and often serves in efforts to fight evil and evil spirits. There are not only seven sacred cities, seven sacred rivers, seven sacred islands, and seven sacred sages, but also a container of water being waved seven times around the head of a bridegroom to repel evil, water drawn from seven wells serving as a cure for infertility, a seven-day course of medical treatment, and more (Abbott, 1974: 301–3).

68. Hinduism's "seven sacred cities" are not always the same. According to Walker, those most often mentioned (they are located on the map), are Ayodhya, Rama's birthplace; Mathura, Krishna's birthplace; Gaya, sacred city of Vishnu; Benares, sacred city of Shiva; Dwarka, Krishna's capital; Hardwar, where the Ganges River enters the lowland; and Allahabad (Prayāga), meeting place of three sacred rivers—the Ganges, Jumna, and the mythical Saraswati (B. Walker, 1968, 2: 510). The Saraswati is actually lost in the sand about 400 miles northwest of Allahabad, but Hindus believe that the Saraswati joins the other two rivers underground. Indeed, there is an underground temple in Allahabad, where water trickling from the stone walls is identified as being from the Saraswati.

69. Desai, 1965: 54.

70. Among related words, *kanthibadala,* or "necklet exchange," is a marriage ceremony, found among Vaishnavas in Bengal and certain other sects, in which necklets, commonly of beads, are exchanged between bride and groom; and *kanthika* is a spoken mantra, a psalm of praise (B. Walker, 1968, 2: 26, 42).

71. Crooke, 1908–26b: 443; K. N. Sharma, 1961: 49; Gonda, 1970: 111; Babb, 1975: 80; Sen Gupta, 1980: 42; Rai, 1992: 31.

72. Abbott, 1974: 13.

73. Parlby, 1850, 1: 217; Balfour, 1885, 3: 944; 1976, 7: 6; G. Watt, 1889–96, 1: 432; 5: 444; Dymock et al., 1890–93, 3: 87; Dutt, 1922: 221; Diehl, 1956: 80,

220; Gamble and Fischer, 1956–58, 2: 778; Desai, 1965: 54; Upadhyaya, 1965: 13; Burkill, 1966, 2: 1602; Gonda, 1969: 14; 1970: 111, 120; Rai, 1992: 31; Francis, 1984: 195, 204; Smith and Narasimha Chary, 1991: 247.

Rosaries are used by Christians, Moslems, and Buddhists, and, though used by Hindus today, they are post-Vedic in India (Gonda, 1980: 154). Various kinds of rosaries are found in India, and beads may be made of various substances of plant origin and otherwise (G. Watt, 1889–96, 1: 426–33; Francis, 1984: 195 and passim; Stutley, 1985: 5, 87). Among Hindus, a rosary (mālā) serves for counting the number of prayers or mantras recited by a devotee. A rosary may be held by hand, wrapped around the wrist or elbow, or worn as a necklace (B. Walker, 1968: 2: 294). For more on the use of rosaries in India, see *North Indian Notes and Queries,* Vol. 2 (1892–93): 215, and Vol. 3 (1893–94): 22, 27–28, 37–38, 57–58, 73–74; Crooke, 1906: 407–10; and B. Walker, 1968, 2: 294. For the use of rosaries by Jains, see M. Stevenson, 1915: 243, 254, 258.

74. Wilson, 1958: 20–21 n 9; Gonda, 1970: 120.

75. "Rudra" is one of Shiva's names. *Rudrāksha* means "Rudra's eye." The latter term relates either to the third eye of the god from which the seeds are said to fall as tears or to the urethral tube by which Shiva is said to discharge the seed (B. Walker, 1968, 2: 217).

76. In the Punjab, however, the word *rudrāksha* appears to be used for seeds of the "jujube tree" (Crooke, 1906: 408), though Crooke does not indicate whether, among the species of *Zizyphus* cultivated in India, he is referring to *Zizyphus vulgaris,* the common jujube; or to *Zizyphus jujuba,* the Indian jujube; or to both.

77. On the other hand, among certain sects in India, worshippers take special care to hide their beads when they engage in prayer so that they avoid being injured by means of magic or the evil eye (Crooke, 1906: 409).

For more on Hindu beliefs about the evil eye and their efforts to avert it, see B. Walker, 1968, 1: 351; and Abbott, 1974: 116–48.

78. G. Watt, 1889–96, 1: 431; 3: 205; Crooke, 1906: 408; 1908–26b: 443; B. Walker, 1968, 2: 217; S. M. Gupta, 1971: 38–40; Francis, 1984: 195, 200.

One reads also of Śāktas, worshippers of female deities, having rosaries of dead men's teeth and similar relics; of fakirs (mendicants or itinerant wonder-workers) possessing rosaries made of snake bones to indicate their possession of a charm to cure snake bites; and of snake charmers who, for protection, may suspend such rosaries from the pipes they play in front of snakes (Crooke, 1906: 408).

79. Dymock et al., 1890–93, 3: 87; M. Stevenson, 1920: 199; S. M. Gupta, 1971: 78, 81; Mahindru, 1982: 72.

80. Tripathi, 1936: 170, 173; Das, 1965: 27, 28.

81. Fawcett, 1901: 314–15.

82. Zimmer, 1955, 1: 165; Abbott, 1974: 337.

83. Beads made from the bark and wood of the bael tree are worn by *Śūdras* to indicate that they are Hindus, not Moslems (G. Watt, 1889–96, 1: 430).

84. In Hindu thinking, persons and things with innate power, among them sacrificial food, should not touch the ground, for this nullifies their power and negates the effectiveness of religious rites (Abbott, 1974: 153–59).

85. Until recent times, child marriage was quite common among Hindus. In early times it seems not to have been unusual for girls to marry at ages of four, five, and six. Child marriage continued into the modern period, but in 1929 it was made illegal for a girl to marry if she is less than 14 years of age (B. Walker, 1968, 1: 230–32; 2: 39).

86. Monier-Williams, 1883: 336–37; G. Watt, 1889–96, 1: 123; Crooke, 1896a, 2: 112; 1908–26a: 482; and 1926: 414; Macdonell and Keith, 1912, 2: 68; M. Stevenson, 1920: 232, 305, 392; Enthoven, 1924: 84; Basak, 1953: 108; B. Walker, 1968, 2: 217; Gonda, 1969: 197 n; 1970: 111–12; S. M. Gupta, 1971: 21–24; Stutley and Stutley, 1977: 48; B. C. Sinha, 1979: 33, 34–35; Sen Gupta, 1980: 46–48. The wood may, however, be used for making amulets and serve in certain Hindu rites, as in funeral pyres for wealthy persons. When a venerated old person dies, moreover, a bael tree may be planted on his grave and worshipped regularly in the hope that the dead will assist the living. When a bael tree grows spontaneously on a grave, it is thought to be the dead person who has returned (Abbott, 1974: 334–35).

87. Nair, 1965: 95.

88. Das, 1965: 28.

89. Dymock et al., 1890–93, 3: 87; Nair, 1965: 93; S. M. Gupta, 1971: 78, 81.

90. Nair, 1965: 93.

91. M. Stevenson, 1920: 230. A phallic symbol to be discussed in the next chapter.

92. Abbott, 1974: 244 n.

93. Babb, 1975: 107.

94. Beck, 1987: 407.

95. Bhattacharyya, 1953: 199; B. Walker, 1968, 2: 217.

96. Crooke, 1908–26a: 482. At seeming odds with this, Śrī (Lakshmī), wife of Vishnu and goddess of abundance, is involved in the mythology surrounding the bael tree, which sprang from her milk and is thus called Śrīphala ("fruit of Śrī"). Thus, the bael tree is sacred to her, and its leaves are depicted as bringing pleasure to Vishnu, too (G. Watt, 1889–96, 1: 123; Crooke, 1896a, 2: 112; Gonda, 1969: 197–98; S. M. Gupta, 1971: 21–22, 24; Sen Gupta, 1980: 46).

97. Dymock et al., 1890–93, 3: 88; Geden, 1908–26a: 232; 1983: 176; Dutt, 1922: 221; Yule, 1913–16, 1: 116 and n; Das, 1965: 25; Nayak, 1965: 123; B.

Walker, 1968, 2: 584; Ward, 1970, 3: 203; Darrah, 1972: 4; Pandey, 1989: 34–35; Vartak and Upadhye, 1989: 12; Rai, 1992: 39; Sivarajan and Balachandran, 1994: 485.

Late in the last century, Dymock et al. (1890–93, 3: 88) observed that, in Calcutta, tulsi was found even in compounds of Europeans—close to the doors of virtually all huts occupied by their native servants.

98. Monier-Williams, 1883: 333; Frazer, 1935, 2: 26; Thomas, 1961: 133; R. S. Khare, 1967: 6–7 n; Chandola, 1976: 107; Rai, 1992: 11, 19.

99. Dubois, 1906: 650; Whitehead, 1908–26: 239; Underhill, 1921: 129.

100. Beck, 1987: 407.

101. Balfour, 1885, 3: 944; 1976, 7: 6; Underhill, 1921: 131; Thomas, 1960: 30, 35. Even when a tulsi plant is not growing at a house where Vishnu is the principal deity, its pedestal may be present (Beck, 1987: 407).

102. Nair, 1965: 93, 94.

103. Smith and Narasimha Chary, 1991: 246.

104. Rai, 1992: 13.

105. Monier-Williams, 1883: 334; 1887: 334.

106. Pickering, 1879: 687 n; Dymock et al., 1890–93, 3: 88; Fryer, 1909–15, 2: 120 n; Gamble and Fischer, 1956–58, 2: 778; Yule and Burnell, 1903: 931; Roxburgh, 1971: 463; Darrah, 1972: 4; Mehra et al., 1975: 44; Vartak and Upadhye, 1989: 12; Rai, 1992: 19.

107. Smith and Narasimha Chary, 1991: 247.

108. Das, 1965: 25; Gonda, 1970: 111.

109. Parlby, 1850, 1: 43; Dubois, 1906: 650; Yule, 1913–16, 1: 116 n; Yule and Burnell, 1903: 931; Day, 1969: 13; Rai, 1992: 18, 19.

110. Darrah, 1972: 4; Balfour, 1976, 7: 6.

111. Abbott, 1974: 336.

112. Abbott, 1974: 281–82.

113. Pandey, 1989: 34–35. Dubois (1906: 650) described such a pillar as square, three or four feet high, with a "hollow at the top, with its four sides facing the four points of the compass."

114. Parlby, 1850, 1: 43; Pickering, 1879: 687 n; Monier-Williams, 1883: 333; Dubois, 1906: 650; Fryer, 1909–15, 2: 120 and n; Yule, 1913–16, 1: 116 n; Thurston, 1912: 291 n; Geden, 1908–26a: 232; 1908–26b: 143; 1983: 176; Underhill, 1921: 129; Frazer, 1935, 2: 26; O'Malley, 1935: 106; Gamble and Fischer, 1956–58, 2: 778; Nair, 1965: 93; B. Walker, 1968, 2: 584–85; Yule and Burnell, 1903: 931; Day, 1969: 13; Ward, 1970, 3: 203, 204; Rai, 1992: 12.

115. Smith and Narasimha Chary, 1991: 244–45.

116. Das, 1965: 25.

117. Rai, 1992: 10.

118. Parlby, 1850, 1: 43.

119. Babb, 1975: 108.

120. Geden, 1908–26b: 143; Rai, 1992: 10.

121. "Vṛindāvana" (Sanskrit) is the name of an area important in Krishna lore, and now the town there, Brindaban (in present-day Uttar Pradesh near Muttra, or Mathura), is an important Vaishnava pilgrimage center.

122. Dymock et al., 1890–93, 3: 88 and n; Dubois, 1906: 650; Thurston, 1912: 291 n; Underhill, 1921: 129; Tripathi, 1936: 173; Nair, 1965: 93; B. Walker, 1968, 2: 584–85; Abbott, 1974: xi; Sen Gupta, 1980: 44.

123. Rai, 1992: 10.

124. Dymock et al., 1890–93, 3: 86–87; Rai, 1992: 18.

125. Dubois, 1906: 650.

126. S. M. Gupta, 1971: 78–79; Chandola, 1976: 107.

127. Fryer, 1909–15, 2: 120; Basham, 1954: 319; Nair, 1965: 93; Nayak, 1965: 123; B. Walker, 1968, 2: 585; Beck, 1987: 407; Pandey, 1989: 35.

128. Monier-Williams, 1883: 333–34; Geden, 1908–26a: 232; 1908–26b: 143; 1983: 176; Enthoven, 1924: 121; Frazer, 1935, 2: 26; Das, 1965: 26–27; R. S. Khare, 1967: 6–7 n; Sen Gupta, 1980: 44; Smith and Narasimha Chary, 1991: 245.

129. R. S. Khare, 1976a: 102.

130. Smith and Narasimha Chary, 1991: 247.

131. For more on cow dung as a purificant, see Simoons, 1974: 26–30.

132. Parlby, 1850, 1: 43; Dymock et al., 1890–93, 3: 88; Dubois, 1906: 649, 650; Thurston, 1912: 291 n; Yule, 1913–16, 1: 116 n, quoting Vincenzo Maria; Dutt, 1922: 221; Enthoven, 1924: 291, 294–97; Das, 1965: 26; Upadhyaya, 1965: 12; Ward, 1970, 3: 203–4; B. Walker, 1968, 2: 585; Chandola, 1976: 107; Smith and Narasimha Chary, 1991: 245–46; Rai, 1992: 11, 14, 39.

133. Parlby, 1850, 1: 43; Dymock et al., 1890–93, 3: 88; Underhill, 1921: 129; Das, 1965: 25–26; Upadhyaya, 1965: 12; Babb, 1975: 165; Balfour, 1976, 7: 6; Chandola, 1976: 107; Rai, 1992: 11, 14; Sivarajan and Balachandran, 1994: 485.

134. M. Stevenson, 1920: 291–95; Underhill, 1921: 32.

135. Das, 1965: 27.

136. Parlby, 1850, 1: 42; Dymock et al., 1890–93, 3: 87; Ward, 1970, 3: 203–4.

137. S. M. Gupta, 1971: 78–79; Rai, 1992: 11.

138. Das, 1965: 26; Upadhyaya, 1965: 12; Darrah, 1972: 4; Chandola, 1976: 109; Sen Gupta, 1980: 42; Smith and Narasimha Chary, 1991: 247.

It is Hindu custom to maintain the union of Krishna and Tulasi by keeping a tulsi leaf on the śālagrāma stone (a common household god), or one on it and one beneath it (Parlby, 1850, 1: 42; Monier-Williams, 1883: 335; Ward, 1970, 3: 204).

139. Dubois, 1906: 650.

140. Underhill, 1921: 130.

141. Das, 1965: 26; Upadhyaya, 1965: 12; Chandola, 1976: 109.

142. Crooke, 1896a, 2: 111.

143. Abbott, 1974: 336–37.

144. Smith and Narasimha Chary, 1991: 247.

145. Sleeman, 1973: 122.

146. Crooke, 1906: 455; Underhill, 1921: 129–31; Frazer, 1935, 2: 26–27; B. Walker, 1968, 2: 585; Sen Gupta, 1980: 42.

147. S. M. Gupta, 1971: 80.

148. Abbott, 1974: 26.

149. Basak, 1953: 108.

150. Underhill, 1921: 129.

151. Dymock et al., 1890–93, 3: 87; Enthoven, 1924: 121; Sen Gupta, 1965a: xix, xxv; Darrah, 1972: 4.

152. Sen Gupta, 1980: 42.

153. Abbott, 1974: 115.

154. Abbott, 1974: 213, 217, 219. The magical role of iron in India or elsewhere in the Old World is considered in more detail in our urd and mandrake chapters.

155. Underhill, 1921: 129; Enthoven, 1924: 121; B. Walker, 1968, 2: 584–85. In Orissa, the explanation of the ban on night picking of tulsi leaves is different: it deters individuals who might carelessly rip leaves off (Das, 1965: 28).

156. Das, 1965: 28.

157. Dymock et al., 1890–93, 3: 87.

158. Upadhyaya, 1965: 12.

159. Parlby, 1850, 1: 43.

160. Ward, 1970, 3: 204.

161. A right-hand circumambulation is clockwise and auspicious. A left-hand circumambulation is counterclockwise and inauspicious, tied to evil, illness, and death, and utilized in devil worship (B. Walker, 1968, 2: 598).

162. The liṅga will be considered in detail in the chapter on the sacred fig-trees of India.

163. Circumambulation is also practiced by Buddhists. This may involve circumambulating a sacred tree, or it may involve circumambulating stupas or other sacred structures which usually have paths for circumambulation. For Buddhists, like Hindus, right-hand circumambulation is auspicious. There is an interesting Buddhist tradition that a migrating flock of wild geese or swans, on becoming aware of the Buddha's presence below, made a solemn clockwise "circumambulation" in the air (Zimmer, 1955, 1: 77, 211, 233, 234, 237, 240, 246 n, 248, 326 and passim; B. Walker, 1968, 2: 213, 437).

164. O'Malley, 1935: 101.

165. pers. comm., Deryck O. Lodrick.

166. For the sanctity of fire in Hinduism, see B. Walker, 1968, 1: 358–59. For the role of fire in Indian ritual and belief, see Abbott, 1974: 172–205.

167. Circumambulation of a corpse is part of the funeral rites. According to B. Walker (1968, 2: 598), it is done with the corpse to the left of people walking around it. This is the inauspicious direction. M. Stevenson (1920: 145, 152), however, writes of circumambulation of a Brahmin corpse with the corpse on the right hand, the auspicious direction, when the corpse is in the house and the primary focus is on its divinity. In contrast, circumambulation of the corpse when it is on its funeral pyre, or circumambulation of the pyre as the fire dies, is done with the object on the left hand, the inauspicious direction. It is of interest that, though Buddhist Tibetans practice circumambulation with the image on their right, followers of Bon, the indigenous religion that preceded Buddhism in Tibet, circumambulate an image in the opposite direction (Crooke, 1906: 453).

168. M. Stevenson, 1920: 35, 85, 86–87, 176; Enthoven, 1924: 294–97; O'Malley, 1935: 101; B. Walker, 1968, 2: 213, 598; Abbott, 1974: 97, 199; Eck, 1982: 166.

169. Simoons and Lodrick, 1981: 128–29.

170. M. Stevenson, 1920: 248, 290–91, 300; Enthoven, 1924: 54, 290, 291, 294–97; B. Walker, 1968, 1: 358; 2: 585; Ward, 1970, 3: 204; Abbott, 1974: 288, 317, 322, 333, 335. For more on circumambulation in Hinduism, see B. Walker, 1968, 2: 213, 598–99.

Enthoven (1924: 295) observed that, when a sacred tree is circumambulated, water is poured at its foot once each circuit.

171. Monier-Williams, 1883: 333.

172. Balfour, 1885, 3: 944; Darrah, 1972: 4.

173. M. Stevenson, 1920: 248; Thomas, 1960: 30, 35; Ward, 1970, 3: 204.

174. Geden, 1908–26a: 232; 1983: 176; Underhill, 1921: 129.

175. Parlby, 1850, 1: 43.

176. Nair, 1965: 93.

177. Enthoven, 1924: 54, 291, 295, 296. For the quite negative Hindu and Moslem Indian perceptions of, and restrictions placed on, married women without children, see Abbott, 1974: 109–10.

178. Monier-Williams, 1883: 334.

179. Dymock et al., 1890–93, 3: 87; Das, 1965: 25; Gonda, 1970: 111.

180. Das, 1965: 26; Chandola, 1976: 110, 112; Sen Gupta, 1980: 44, 45.

181. R. S. Khare, 1967: 6; Gonda, 1970: 111; Sen Gupta, 1980: 42.

182. Chandola, 1976: 110. In India, boys are greatly preferred over girls. For an interesting discussion of this preference, see Jeffery et al., 1990: 20–23.

183. Cain, 1875: 197; Thurston, 1906: 306; 1912: 53.

184. Bhatnagar, 1965: 91, citing R. C. Temple.

185. Wakil, 1895–96: 76. In a similar vein, it is said that in Nepal every Newār

girl, while still a child, is married to a bael fruit, which is cast into a sacred river after the rites. A Newār woman may later obtain a human husband, but she cannot become a widow, for the bael fruit of her initial marriage is thought to remain in existence (Crooke, 1926: 418).

186. Gold, 1988: 248.

187. Crooke, 1896a, 2: 116. Marriage between a tulsi plant and a sacred fig tree (pipal) is also reported (Desai, 1965: 55; Pandey, 1989: 21).

188. Crooke, 1896a, 2: 116; Bhatnagar, 1965: 91.

189. Das, 1965: 27.

190. Das, 1965: 25–26, 27; Ward, 1970, 3: 203.

191. Parlby, 1850, 1: 44, citing Ward.

192. S. M. Gupta, 1971: 81; Chandola, 1976: 108. Researchers have reported that short-term dietary use of an extract of tulsi leaves also significantly reduced the sexual behavior of adult male rats (Kantak and Gogate, 1992).

193. Reghunandanan et al., 1995: 83, 84–86.

194. Sen Gupta, 1980: 45; Reghunandanan et al., 1995: 83, 85. In 1980, research was being conducted in India by family planning bodies on the effectiveness of tulsi against "sex hunger" (Sen Gupta, 1980: 46).

195. B. C. Sinha, 1979: 28.

196. *Nelumbium speciosum*. For more on the lotus in Hindu and Buddhist art, lore, and symbolism, see Zimmer, 1955, 1: 158–230; B. Walker, 1968, 2: 216; S. M. Gupta, 1971: 65–70; and Coomaraswamy, 1993: 155–60.

197. Das, 1965: 26.

198. V. Mani, 1975: 798.

199. Woodburne, 1981: 63; Smith and Narasimha Chary, 1991: 246.

200. Abbott, 1974: 164.

201. Smith and Narasimha Chary, 1991: 246.

202. G. Watt, 1889–96, 5: 444.

203. Dymock et al., 1890–93, 3: 88; Crooke, 1896a, 2: 110; Upadhyaya, 1965: 12; Gonda, 1970: 111; Abbott, 1974: 317–18, 336; Babb, 1975: 107; Chandola, 1976: 108; Sen Gupta, 1980: 43.

204. Sen Gupta, 1980: 61.

205. Bhattacharyya, 1953: 184.

206. Penzer, 1924–28, 2: 82; Abbott, 1974: 268–69.

207. Crooke, 1896a, 1: 21–22; S. M. Gupta, 1971: 82; Chandola, 1976: 108; Sen Gupta, 1980: 43.

208. Abbott, 1974: 269, 336.

209. Also of interest in this regard is the observation that a person who has gained merit by a vow can, while mantras are recited, transfer his or her merit to another person by pouring water over tulsi leaves onto the hands of that other person (Abbott, 1974: 15, 168).

210. Nair, 1965: 93.

211. Eichinger Ferro-Luzzi, 1990: 42, citing Bhanumati.

212. Das, 1965: 25.

213. Abbott, 1974: 336; Smith and Narasimha Chary, 1991: 246.

214. Abbott, 1974: 160.

215. Rai, 1992: 31.

216. Rai, 1992: 11.

217. R. S. Khare, 1976a: 103. Tulsi, like other things to be offered to a deity, can itself become polluted by contact with the earth (Enthoven, 1924: 84).

218. Rai, 1992: 31.

219. Crooke, 1896a, 1: 49.

220. M. Stevenson, 1920: 141; Smith and Narasimha Chary, 1991: 247.

221. V. Mani, 1975: 798.

222. Abbott, 1974: 173.

223. Dubois, 1906: 650; S. M. Gupta, 1971: 79; Darrah, 1972: 4.

224. Nair, 1965: 94.

225. Abbott, 1974: 336.

226. Pande, 1965: 38; Stutley and Stutley, 1977: 306; Stutley, 1985: 146; Rai, 1992: 13, 15.

227. Pande, 1965: 38.

228. Fawcett, 1901: 245. Gold is auspicious, purifying, protective, and imperishable. For gold as a means of purification in the Vedas, see especially Gonda, 1991: 30–31. For more on the meaning and role of gold in Vedic ritual, see Gonda, 1980: 140–41; and Gonda, 1991. For gold in modern Indian ritual and belief, see Abbott, 1974: 206–10.

229. M. Stevenson, 1920: 141.

230. Desai, 1965: 54.

231. Darrah, 1972: 4.

232. Dymock et al., 1890–93, 3: 87.

233. Abbott, 1974: 336.

234. Dymock et al., 1890–93, 3: 87.

235. Darrah, 1972: 4.

236. Bhatnagar, 1965: 91; Upadhyaya, 1965: 13; Abbott, 1974: 336; Sen Gupta, 1980: 43.

237. Dubois, 1906: 649–50.

238. Sen Gupta, 1980: 44.

239. Parlby, 1850, 1: 43; Ward, 1970, 3: 204.

240. Yule and Burnell (1903: 931) write that tulsi is commonly planted in a pot on a masonry pedestal near Hindu temples or houses. They also write that, on occasion, "the ashes of deceased relatives are preserved in these domestic shrines." I have been unable to find a confirmation of this statement.

241. Ward, 1970, 1: 277.

242. S. Roy, 1983: 58–59. After gold, the Kōlīs regard silver as the purest form of metal. For silver as protective and purifying in modern India, see Abbott, 1974: 210. In the Vedas, silver, which is tied to the moon and involved in lunar symbolism, is also sometimes linked with gold as auspicious and purifying, for which see Gonda, 1991: 63–68.

243. M. Stevenson, 1920: 143, 147.

244. G. Watt, 1889–96, 1: 432; Crooke, 1906: 408; Mehra et al., 1975: 43–44. One also reads of Jain rosaries of 108 beads (M. Stevenson, 1915: 243, 254). In addition, the necklace of the principal Buddhist priest of Nepal was said to have 108 beads, and so were the rosaries of Tibetan Buddhists (Crooke, 1906: 408, 409). Crooke (1906: 408) writes that the rosaries of Shiva devotees contain 32 beads, like the rosary depicted in the text (Figure 4), or double that number. B. Walker (1968, 2: 294), on the other hand, writes that rosaries of Śaivites may contain 12, 18, 28, 32, 64, 84, 108, or more rudrāksha seeds.

245. Chaubé, 1893–94: 28.

246. Monier-Williams, 1883: 334; Chowbe, 1899: 228; Crooke, 1906: 408; Thurston, 1912: 133, 184; M. Stevenson, 1920: 151, 152, 232–33, 248; O'Malley, 1935: 101; Upadhyaya, 1965: 4; B. Walker, 1968, 2: 137. For more on auspicious and inauspicious numbers in India, see B. Walker, 1968, 2: 136–37; and Abbott, 1974: 284–309. A source I have been unable to obtain is R. C. Das's *Numbers in Hindu magic and religion* (1913).

247. Stutley and Stutley, 1977: 306.

248. V. Mani, 1975: 798.

249. M. Stevenson, 1920: 160–61, 172, 177–78.

250. Smith and Narasimha Chary, 1991: 247.

251. With a similar intent, orthodox Hindus may pour water onto other sacred plants and at places where cows gather (Enthoven, 1924: 142).

252. R. S. Khare, 1967: 5–7.

253. Thurston, 1912: 291.

254. Enthoven, 1924: 39.

255. For more on oath-taking in India, see Abbott, 1974: 434–38.

256. Hutton, 1963: 105–6; Balfour, 1976, 3: 960; Crooke, 1906: 348–49; Stutley and Stutley, 1977: 48. In a similar vein, it is said that no Hindu would dare to tell a lie when he has a bit of gold in his mouth (Monier-Williams, 1887: 336 n).

257. Abbott, 1974: 336, 337, 435.

258. Desai, 1965: 55.

259. Parlby, 1850, 1: 44. For the role of the goddess Gaṅgā and the Ganges River in Hinduism, see B. Walker, 1968, 1: 378–80, and Kinsley, 1986: 187–96.

260. Upadhyaya, 1965: 13.

261. Balfour, 1885, 3: 944.

262. Hutton, 1963: 105.

263. Balfour, 1885, 3: 944; 1976, 3: 960; G. Watt, 1889–96, 5: 445. In a similar manner, early in the colonial period the British had people take oaths on Ganges water or by holding a cow's tail, though such oaths were later abandoned (Crooke, 1906: 348).

264. J. W. Bennett, 1843: 55.

265. Upadhyaya, 1965: 13.

266. Prakash, 1961: 282; Achaya, 1994: 213.

267. E.g., Mahindru, 1982: 71.

268. For example, Agarwal, 1986: 260; and Vartak and Upadhye, 1989: 12.

269. G. Watt, 1889–96, 5: 442. Further mention of the use of *Ocimum* of one sort or another in making tea or other beverages is found in Parlby, 1850, 1: 217; Vartak and Upadhye, 1989: 7; and Rai, 1992: 17, 34.

270. G. Watt, 1889–96, 5: 444; Balfour, 1976, 7: 6.

271. E.g., Sundararaj and Balasubramanyam, 1986: 166–67.

272. Dymock et al., 1890–93, 3: 87.

273. Rai, 1992: 17.

274. Smith and Narasimha Chary, 1991: 248.

275. For which, see Simoons, 1991: 410–14.

276. For its effectiveness in this regard, see Hasan and Deo, 1994.

277. *Charaka Saṃhitā* 27, trans. in P. Sharma, 1981: 208; Ainslie, 1826, 2: 426; Drury, 1873: 317; G. Watt, 1889–96, 5: 444; Dymock et al., 1890–93, 3: 88; Dubois, 1906: 650–51; Dutt, 1922: 221; Chopra et al., 1958: 517; Ward, 1970, 3: 203; Chandola, 1976: 107–8; Stutley and Stutley, 1977: 306; B. C. Sinha, 1979: 28; Sen Gupta, 1980: 45; Stutley, 1985: 146; Agarwal, 1986: 260; Satyavati et al., 1987: 355–56; Palange, 1989: 21; Paranjpe and Paranjpe, 1989; Sivarajan and Balachandran, 1994: 485; Reghunandanan et al., 1995: 83.

For animal studies by scientific researchers of the usefulness of tulsi leaves or tulsi-leaf extract or oil as antiinflammatory, anticarcinogenic, antiulcerogenic, or cholesterol-lowering agents, see Aruna and Sivaramakrishan, 1992; Mandal et al., 1993; Prashar et al. 1994; Sarkar et al., 1994; and S. Singh et al., 1996. For a human study of the potential of a tulsi-leaf extract for treating non-insulin-dependent diabetes mellitus, see Agrawal et al., 1996.

278. Sen Gupta, 1980: 44.

279. S. Sinha, 1966: 65, 68, 73, 78, 87.

280. Sen Gupta, 1980: 44.

281. Risley, 1891, 1: 255–56.

282. W. G. Griffiths, 1946: 56, 188.

283. Hutton, 1963: 116.

284. K. Singh, 1965: 87.

285. Crawfurd, 1820, 1: 438.

286. Bartlett, 1926: 35.

287. Burkill, 1966, 2: 1601.

288. Burkill, 1966, 2: 1601.

289. Furtado, 1926–29: 416.

290. Burkill, 1966, 2: 1602.

291. Ridley, 1922–25, 2: 643; Furtado, 1926–29: 416–17.

292. Laufer, 1919: 590; Bartlett, 1926: 35; Furtado, 1926–29: 417; Burkill, 1966, 2: 1598, 1601, 1602.

293. R. J. Wilkinson, 1924: 49; Overbeck, 1926.

294. Heyne, 1950, 1: 1338; Perry, 1980: 189. In the first century A.D., both Dioscorides and Pliny mentioned sweet basil in a similar context. Dioscorides (*De materia medica* 2.171) simply said that basil "calls out milk." According to certain versions of Pliny's *Natural history*, basil applied to the breasts was believed to drain milk or promote its flow, though the common version is that basil "checks the flow of milk" (Pliny, *Natural history* 20.122–23). Also see notes by translator W. H. S. Jones, Vol. 6: 72 n, 73 n. For a similar statement by Galen, see H. Phillips, 1827, 1: 62.

295. Laufer, 1919: 590; Burkill, 1966, 2: 1598.

296. Darrah, 1974: 65.

297. Seeds of Change, P. O. Box 15700, Santa Fe, N. M. 87506–5700.

298. Laufer, 1919: 586–87.

299. Darrah, 1972: 4.

300. Pliny, *Natural history* 20.123.

301. D'Andrea, 1982: 32.

302. Massé, 1954: 216, 296. The color of leaves and form of fruit of certain species of the genus *Elaeagnus* bear a striking resemblance to those of the olive tree (G. Watt, 1889–96, 3: 204).

303. Skinner, 1911: 59.

304. Gubernatis, 1978, 2: 35.

305. Gubernatis, 1978, 2: 35.

306. Megas, 1963: 49.

307. Faithfull, 1985: 249.

308. Faithfull, 1985: 249.

309. Sermini, 1911, 2: 100–109.

310. Boccaccio, 1972: 366–70. This is a theme later taken up Keats in his poem "Isabella; or, The Pot of Basil" (Keats, 1899: 110–19). For a discussion of Boccaccio's symbolism in the story of Lisabetta, see Faithfull, 1985.

311. Gubernatis, 1978, 2: 35.

312. Gubernatis, 1978, 2: 35.

313. Thiselton-Dyer, 1898: 101; Skinner, 1911: 60.

314. Darrah, 1972: 5; Gubernatis, 1978, 2: 35.

315. D'Andrea, 1982: 32.

316. Gubernatis, 1978, 2: 35–36; Darrah, 1972: 6. One can also discern elements of hope in the symbolism of basil among Greek Christians. On Christmas Eve on the island of Kios in the Sea of Marmara, village girls gather at a friend's house, open the shutters, and put a sprig of dried basil in a basin of water, and, nearby, an icon of the Virgin Mary. Then they proceed with their celebration of Christ's birth (Megas, 1963: 32).

317. Drower, 1956: 87 n.

318. Darrah, 1972: 6.

319. Moore, 1895: 469.

320. Friend, 1981: 570.

321. Moore, 1895: 469 n; Skinner, 1911: 59. Basil has been cultivated in Egypt at least since Ptolemaic times (Keimer, 1967: 23).

322. Lawson, 1964: 13.

323. Hyde, 1923: 170–71; Megas, 1963: 37.

324. Forty is a magic, valuable number for the Greeks (Hardie, 1981: 120–21). This is shown especially well on the Day of the Forty Saints (March 9), an auspicious day. At Metrae in Thrace, this day is regarded as the best time for planting sweet basil, for only if it is planted then "will it grow green and thick—with forty shoots." The number 40 is also prominent in the celebration that honors the memory of 40 Christians killed in Greece in the fourth century for preaching Christianity. One reads, for that celebration, of preparing 40 sheets of pastry or 40 pancakes, of a dish made with 40 different sorts of wild herbs, of 40 glasses of wine drunk by men, and of a cloth embroidered or woven with 40 sorts of thread (Megas, 1963: 85–86).

325. Megas, 1963: 98.

326. Bent, 1966: 327–28.

327. Megas, 1963: 154. The symbolism of the pomegranate will be considered in chapter 10.

328. The work in question is attributed to Abu Ma'shar (Albumasar) (d. A.D. 886). Gubernatis, 1978, 2: 37.

329. Oberhelman, 1991: 189.

330. According to the legend, a certain Sassanid king was holding a public audience. During that audience, people heard a call of distress coming from a hole in the floor of the audience chamber. Then, discovering a snake in an underground struggle with a horrible beast, people freed the snake. At the next year's public audience, the same snake emerged from the same hole carrying a small branch in its mouth. People took the branch and sowed the seed found on it, which grew into a basil plant that proved effective against a cold with which the king was afflicted (Massé, 1954: 210).

331. Coats, 1971: 291; Darrah, 1972: 6.

332. Phillips reported the view that when basil was introduced into cold areas like the British Isles it was no longer capable of creating snakes but that, if basil was chewed and placed in the sun, worms and maggots were produced (H. Phillips, 1827, 1: 61).

333. Dioscorides, *De materia medica* 2.171; Pliny, *Natural history* 20.119–20; Maimonides, *On poisons and their anecdotes* 1.2.1; Culpepper, 1778: 32–33; H. Phillips, 1827, 1: 60–64; Coles, 1938: 76; Coats, 1971: 292–93; Darrah, 1972: 6.

334. G. Watt, 1889–96, 5: 442, 444; Satyavati et al., 1987: 354–55.

Chapter 3. Sacred Fig-Trees of India

1. Two etymologies have been suggested for *aśvattha*. One, based on the tale that the fire god Agni, in the form of a horse, took refuge in the tree, is that it derives ultimately from **aśva-stha*, "the standing place of a horse." The second is that *aśvattha* derives from **a-svastha*, or *non in se constans*. According to the second etymology **a-svastha*, in the sense of "not settled," "unstable," and "changeable," refers to its tremulous leaves, or, in the sense of "not self-dependent," to the fact that it commonly begins life as an epiphyte (Lassen, 1858–74, 1: 304 n 1; Kuhn, 1886: 174; Emeneau, 1949: 369–70).

In the Vedic records the word *pippala* means "berry" in a mystical sense, whether referring to a berry in general or, possibly, a berry of the sacred fig-tree. It is interesting that a certain Vedic teacher was called *pippalāda*, "eater of berries"; that in later literature the term *pippala* denoted the sacred fig-tree itself (Macdonell and Keith, 1912, 1: 531–32); and that it was indeed a tree under which the devout achieved spiritual understanding, as when the Buddha received his enlightenment.

2. Less commonly, in the English literature, it is spelled *peepal, peepul, pippal,* or *pippul*.

3. Rather than use the term *sacred fig-tree* or *sacred fig-tree of India* for *F. religiosa*, I will use the term *pipal* throughout to distinguish it clearly from the banyan, the other sacred fig-tree on which we focus.

4. *Vāyu Purāṇa* 2.49.34, 36, trans. in Tagare, 1987–88, 2: 958; *Vishṇu Purāṇa* 1.22, trans. in Wilson, 1961: 125; G. Watt, 1889–96, 3: 360; Dubois, 1906: 652; Pandey, 1989: 21.

5. *Bhagavadgītā* 10.24–26, trans. in Telang, 1882: 89.

6. Ainslie, 1826, 2: 10; Monier-Williams, 1887: 337; Ragozin, 1902: 29; Macdonell and Keith, 1912, 1: 462; Bhatnagar, 1965: 89.

One reads, for example, that the banyan is one of the most sacred of Hindu trees, that it is meritorious to plant a banyan tree, that people are reluctant to cut one down, that they worship at and make offerings to banyan trees, that banyan leaves are used in ritual as platters and for pouring libations, that pious holy men wear a cloth of banyan fiber, that Brahmins prefer to eat from plates made of banyan leaves, and that other Hindus eat off such plates, too (Drury, 1873: 213; G. Watt, 1889–96, 3: 346; Philpot, 1897: 35; Chowbe, 1899: 227; Roxburgh, 1971: 640; Balfour, 1976, 3: 1101). These disposable plates are used because they reduce the possibility of the eater being ritually polluted (Achaya, 1994: 63).

Besides the pipal and banyan, a fig species commonly used in ritual, and often called sacred, in India, ancient and modern, is the *gūlar* or *umbar* (Sansk.: *udumbara; Ficus glomerata*) (Crooke, 1881; G. Watt, 1889–96, 3: 353, 360; Crooke, 1896a, 2: 97, 99; 1926: 407, 408; Macdonell and Keith, 1912, 1: 87; M. Stevenson, 1920: 33–34, 330; Chandervaker, 1965: 44; B. Walker, 1968, 1: 358; Gonda, 1969: 11–12; Hopkins, 1969: 6–7; S. M. Gupta, 1971: 55–56; B. C. Sinha, 1979: 32, 84; Gonda, 1980: 109–110; Sen Gupta, 1980: 26; Stutley, 1985: 147; Pandey, 1989: 20–21).

7. *Vishṇu Purāṇa* 2.4, trans. in Wilson, 1961: 163, 166.

8. *Mahābhārata* 3.186.65–90, trans. in van Buitenen, 1973–78, 2: 569, 588–89.

This tale is alluded to more than once in the early literature, as in the *Vāyu Purāṇa*, which tells of an "infant boy . . . who sleeps on the top of the Vaṭa tree in that vast sheet of cosmic waters" (*Vāyu Purāṇa* 2.49.96–99, trans. in Tagare, 1987–88, 2: 964). There are, however, different versions of the flood myth in the early Hindu literature, for which see B. Walker, 1968, 2: 544–45; and Coomaraswamy, 1993: 19 n 5, 147–49, 201 n 17.

9. Hooker, 1872–97, 5: 513; Trimen, 1893–1900, 4: 90; G. Watt, 1889–96, 3: 358; Cooke, 1903, 3: 149; Brandis, 1921: 601; Gamble and Fischer, 1956–58, 3: 953; and Kirtikar et al., 1975, 3: 2318.

10. Hooker, 1872–97, 5: 499; Trimen, 1893–1900, 4: 86; G. Watt, 1889–96, 3: 344; Cooke, 1903, 3: 145; Brandis, 1921: 600; Roxburgh, 1971: 639; Gamble and Fischer, 1956–58, 3: 952; Chopra et al., 1958: 508; Kirtikar et al., 1975, 3: 2312; Nadkarni, 1976, 1: 543.

11. Brandis, 1921: 600, 601, 602; Condit, 1969: 101; Roxburgh, 1971: 642. The banyan is subject to damage from severe frosts. It has done well when planted in Hawaii and southern Florida, but in California it grows well for a few years, is hurt by severe frost, and rarely becomes large. When the pipal has been introduced to the United States, it, too, has proved hardy enough only for Hawaii and certain areas of Florida and southern California (Condit, 1969: 100, 178).

12. The true fig is now cultivated in various parts of India. Though it is one of the earliest cultivated fruit trees of the eastern Mediterranean (Zohary and Spiegel-Roy, 1975: 324), it appears to have been a late arrival in India. The fig is not among the fruits whose remains were found in early Indian archeological sites considered by Vishnu-Mittre (1968: 97; 1977: 584–85). It is not mentioned

in the early medical literature of India (Achaya, 1994: 205). Literary evidence in India, moreover, suggests that the true fig was not known there prior to the fourteenth century A.D. (Gode, 1941–42: 126, 130–35; 1943).

13. In nineteenth-century Ceylon, banyan fruit were the favorite food of wild swine. Indeed, wild swine were so fond of banyan fruit that, when its red figs were ripe, they could not be deterred from coming to a tree at night, even in the face of considerable danger. European hunters who stationed themselves under such trees, for example, were able to kill swine until they tired of the slaughter, for though the ground under the tree would be littered with the bodies of dead swine, the survivors would return to the same tree several times during a night (J. W. Bennett, 1843: 230).

14. Lassen, 1858–74, 1: 301, 302, 305; G. Watt, 1889–96, 3: 345, 359; *Phallic tree worship,* 1971: 14; Balfour, 1976, 3: 1101; Roxburgh, 1971: 640, 642; *The useful plants of India,* 1986: 221, 223. In the Hindu epics, there are references to people eating the fruit of pipal and banyan trees. At the same time, it is said in the Mahābhārata that if a man is desirous of his own good and wishes to be prosperous and enjoy glory, he should never eat the fruits of the pipal, banyan, and udumbara trees (*Mahābhārata* 13.104, trans. in *Anuśanaparva,* 1893: 510; Prakash, 1961: 114, 115, 128).

Eating the fruits of the pipal tree, along with those of the banyan, udumbara, and two other fig trees, is banned to Jains because to eat such fruit is thought to involve taking life, the many small organisms found in the fruit (Prakash, 1961: 220; R. Williams, 1963: 53, 110, 112, 113). The Jain respect for life of all sorts is, of course, remarkable, and perhaps its most touching expression is in the bird hospitals and animal shelters and homes Jains have founded in many parts of India. A fascinating study of animal homes—in which Jains play a major role—is Deryck O. Lodrick's *Sacred cows, sacred places: Origins and survivals of animal homes in India* (1981).

The situation is different among at least some tribal groups in India, for one reads of banyan and pipal fruit being eaten and pipal leaves consumed as potherbs (G. Watt, 1889–96, 3: 359; Elwin, 1939: 50, 51; I. Singh, 1944: 20; Fuchs, 1960: 65). This suggests that tribal peoples in general make greater dietary use of pipal and banyan trees than Hindus do.

Pipal and banyan wood and other plant parts do have nonritual uses, including medicinal ones, for which see Ainslie, 1826, 2: 11; Parlby, 1850, 1: 218; Drury, 1873: 213, 217; G. Watt, 1889–96, 3: 345–46, 358–59; Dymock et al., 1890–93, 3: 339–41; Dutt, 1922: 236; Chopra et al., 1958: 508, 673, 674; Burkill, 1966, 1: 1021, 1030; Balfour, 1976, 3: 1101; Kirtikar et al., 1975, 3: 2312–13, 2318; Nadkarni, 1976, 1: 543–44, 552–53; B. C. Sinha, 1979: 26–27; Sen Gupta, 1980: 38–39; *The useful plants of India,* 1986: 221, 223. The wood of the pipal tree, however, is "very light, coarsely fibrous, perishable, . . . takes an inferior polish," and is of little use (Drury, 1873: 213; G. Watt, 1889–96, 3: 359). Banyan wood, though durable under water and useful for making well curbs and certain other things, is open-grained, soft, and, it, too, is of little value or use (Lassen, 1858–74, 1: 301; Drury, 1873: 213; G. Watt, 1889–96, 3: 346).

15. The banyan is the best known species of *Ficus* for this growth habit, which, however, is found in many *Ficus* species.

16. If severed from the main trunk, the secondary ones are able to survive on their own (Gamble and Fischer, 1956–58, 3: 952).

17. Lassen, 1858–74, 1: 301–2; Hooker, 1872–97, 5: 499; Drury, 1873: 213; Cooke, 1903, 3: 145; G. Watt, 1889–96, 3: 344; Trimen, 1893–1900, 4: 86; Emeneau, 1949: 346; Ragozin, 1902: 24–29; Roxburgh, 1971: 639; Balfour, 1976, 3: 1100–1101.

Surprisingly, however, *The Guinness book of world records, 1997* lists the giant banyan in the Botanical Garden, Calcutta, which covers three acres and has a circumference of 1,350 feet, as the tree of "greatest spread" in the world (Young, 1996: 43). David (1996), who calls the Calcutta banyan "the previous Guinness world-record holder," grants that honor to the Thimmamma Marimanu, a banyan in Andhra Pradesh that covers 5.2 acres.

18. Fryer, 1909–15, 1: 265 n 3. For a poet and novelist who claimed "banyan-identity" because he had lived and had roots in many lands, see Depestre, 1996.

19. Caul, 1806: 345.

20. pers. comm., W. P. Armstrong.

21. Drury, 1873: 213.

22. Fryer, 1909–15, 1: 265.

23. Lassen, 1858–74, 1: 301; Yule and Burnell, 1903: 66, quoting Heber; *Phallic tree worship*, 1971: 13.

24. The largest pipal trees observed by Roxburgh in India, for example, had trunks about 20 feet in circumference (Roxburgh, 1971: 642).

25. A tribal myth of certain Saora of Orissa has the pipal not only the world's first tree but also one created to provide shade. "Before the creation of the world, Kittung and his sister used to live in a gourd. When the new world was made and the gourd broke open, brother and sister came out and made their home on Kurabeli Hill. There were no trees on the earth at that time, and the two had to sleep in the open under the sky. . . When the hot weather came, the girl said 'How can I live in this heat when there is no shade?' Kittung cut off his . . . hand, and put it on a stone. It soon grew into a tree, and gave shade beneath which Kittung's sister sheltered. This was the *onjerneban* [the pipal tree] . . ." (Elwin, 1955: 207).

26. McLean and Ivimey-Cook, 1956: 1747.

27. Eliade, 1958: 273–74; James, 1966: 147–55.

28. Alabaster, 1871: xxxi–xxxii.

29. Birds' service as agents of dispersal is demonstrated in an interesting tribal

myth of certain Kuttia Kond of Orissa: "At first there were no trees or shrubs, and the earth looked ugly and naked without any ornament. Rani-aru [a legendary creator of things] went to the place where she had been born and found a pipal fig. She put it behind her house. Two months later a shoot came up; she tended it carefully and in twenty years it was mature. When it was about to bear fruit, the tree said to Rani-aru, 'I have all this fruit on my body; what am I to do with it?' She said, 'Birds will eat your fruit and from their bellies seeds will drop and trees will spring up everywhere.' The tree said, 'Call them quickly, for I am weighed down by this burden.' Rani-aru called the birds and they sat on the tree and ate and then flew to the surrounding hills and new trees grew from their droppings" (Elwin, 1954: 131).

30. Tennent, 1859, 1: 95–97; Drury, 1873: 213; Hooker, 1872–97, 5: 513; G. Watt, 1889–96, 3: 344, 358; Ragozin, 1902: 29–30; Cooke, 1903, 3: 149; Brandis, 1921: 601; Burkill, 1966, 1: 1030; Gamble and Fischer, 1956–58, 3: 953; Condit, 1969: 99; Roxburgh, 1971: 640; Balfour, 1976, 3: 1100–1101. For a description of the strangling process used by fig trees, see Tennent, 1859, 1: 95–96; and, with the eye of a botanist, E. J. H. Corner, pp. 664–65 of Vol. 1 of his *Wayside trees of Malaya* (Singapore: Government Printing Office, 1952). For illustrations of strangler figs at an early stage of growth or as they develop, see Emeneau, 1949: 348 and opp. p. 345.

31. Emeneau, 1949: 350.

32. *Atharva-veda* 3.6, trans. in Bloomfield, 1897: 91–92; Macdonell and Keith, 1912, 1: 43. For more on strangler figs in Sanskrit literature, see Emeneau, 1949: 350–64.

33. Yule and Burnell, 1903: 692; Yule, 1968: 265 n.

34. Caul, 1806: 345.

35. Crooke, 1906: 497.

36. S. M. Gupta, 1971: 51.

37. Monier-Williams, 1889: 517.

38. Parlby, 1850, 1: 218.

39. Dubois, 1906: 652; J. J. Meyer, 1937, 2: 133.

40. *Atharva-veda* 4.37.4–5, trans. in Bloomfield, 1897: 33; Macdonell, 1897: 134. In another Vedic account, apsarās and their male counterparts, gandharvas (celestial minstrels), live in pipal and banyan trees. As portrayed in the Vedas and epics, not all apsarās and gandharvas were mere performers, for, among other things, they commonly tied to sexuality, seduction, and love. One celebrated gandharva was Viśvāvasu (a title also used for the god Vishnu), who played the lute with such sensitivity that each listener thought the minstrel was playing solely for him. Viśvāvasu was also thought to have sexual intercourse with every bride prior to her husband's consummation of the union. In the *Atharva-veda*, apsarās and gandharvas living in trees were asked to be benevolent to a passing wedding procession. In one of the Brahmanas, moreover, apsarās and gandharvas regu-

lated human fertility, and people who wanted children offered prayers to them (B. Walker, 1968, 1: 371–72; Hopkins, 1969: 153, 154, 156, 160–64). For more on apsarās and gandharvas in Vedic and epic mythology, see Macdonell, 1897: 134–37; B. Walker, 1968, 1: 371: 372; 2: 143–44; and Hopkins, 1969: 152–58, 159–64, and passim.

41. Yule and Burnell, 1903: 691; J. J. Meyer, 1937, 2: 133; Nair, 1965: 99–100.

42. Coomaraswamy, 1993: 42 n 8.

43. Elwin, 1954: 432–33; Monier-Williams, 1889: 517–18. The role of the leaves of sacred trees in communication with the gods in India deserves more investigation. The rustling of leaves falls into the Sanskrit category of sound called *āhata*, "struck," that sound "produced by the physical action of one thing upon another." It also falls into the subcategory of āhata called *dhvani*, "sounds of animate nature, such as the call of animals, the song of birds . . . clapping, breaking wind and snoring" of humans, but not their voiced sounds (B. Walker, 1968, 2: 426–27). I wonder whether the sound of a sacred tree's rustling leaves—such as that of the pipal—would fall into the further subcategory of dhvani called *divyadhvani* (*divya* = "celestial"), or "celestial sound." Jains believe that a celestial sound emanated from Mahāvīra's body and from the bodies of other holy teachers of antiquity (*jina*s: human teachers who attained infinite knowledge and preached salvation). The sound occurred as a jina sat perfectly still in an all-knowing state after he had attained jinahood. Jains believe further that such celestial sound was translated by a jina's chief disciples, that they passed his teachings on to others, and that these were set down to form the Jain scriptures (Jaini, 1979: 2–4, 35, 42–43). Mahāvīra's renunciation is reputed to have taken place under an *aśoka* tree (*Saraca indica*) (M. Stevenson, 1915: 31; S. M. Gupta, 1971: 97; Jaini, 1979: 12), but what role, if any, did sounds of the tree have in communication with the supernatural world?

44. Monier-Williams 1887: 330; 1889: 514–15; Campbell, 1894–1901, 27: 109–10, 111; Hartland, 1894–96, 2: 175–231; Philpot, 1897; Crooke, 1926: 400–412; Frazer, 1935, 2: 7–96; Bode, 1955; James, 1966; *Phallic tree worship*, 1971: 15; Sen Gupta, 1980: 21–27.

45. Hutton, 1933: 397; 1963: 223, 231. It is impossible, however, to tell whether practices of tribal peoples in the Indian subcontinent preceded or were adopted from Hinduism or Buddhism. We have seen that the pipal tree was not native to Ceylon. Yet the Vedda, the island's most primitive people, are said to sit around pipal trees when they worship. They also set up stone platforms beneath them and set lamps on the platforms (Yule and Burnell, 1903: 108) in a way strikingly like Buddhist practice on Ceylon. Similar questions may be raised about the parallels between Hindu practices and those of tribal groups in mainland India, which can be striking indeed. See, for example, Crooke, 1926: 400ff. (general); W. G. Griffiths, 1946: 200 (Kol); and Elwin, 1955: 81, 124, 207 (Saora).

46. Fairservis, 1992: 90.

47. Fairservis, 1983, 1992.

48. Coomaraswamy, 1993: 11, 63, 64, 70, 71.

49. Coomaraswamy, 1993: 11, 62, 64. For the meaning and etymology of the word *yaksha* and the yakshas' role in the Vedas and Upanishads, see Coomaraswamy, 1993: 9–24. Yaksha worship might also involve shrines and practices typical of modern Hindu worship, including "the use of images in temples, the practice of prostration, circumambulation, the offering of flowers . . ., incense, food, and cloths, the use of bells, lighting of lamps, the singing of hymns, [and] the presentation of a drama dealing with the . . . deity." The only difference was that food offerings were different, for yakshas ate meat and drank liquor (Coomaraswamy, 1993: 74, 80, 125 n 24).

50. Fairservis, 1992: 23, 47, 90, 139, 161, 187. Chidambaram, a place of pilgrimage with a famous Shiva temple, has, according to Crooke (1908–26e), the Sanskrit name Chitāmbara, meaning "atmosphere of wisdom."

51. Fairservis, 1992: 138, 148, 196, 220.

52. Pipal leaves, while apparently no longer used to form a canopy, are still used in wedding booths in modern Gujarat. As described by Margaret Stevenson (1920: 28–29, 61–62, 65, 101, 103, 143), the booth set up at the home of a Brahmin bride rests on four posts. Two additional sticks of wood are put in the ground near one of the posts. One stick is of green bamboo, symbolizing auspiciousness and the hope that the family will be green and prosperous. The second is a piece of wood a foot long called the ruby pillar. On the top of the latter, two sticks are tied crosswise to represent the four faces of the god Brahma. Set on these are several items, among them pipal leaves (presumably for fertility), turmeric (of a sacred color, auspicious, purifying, protective, and with erotic connotations), and a fruit of the *madana* (apparently the shrub or small tree *Randia dumetorum*). *Madana*, also one of the names for Kāma, god of love, means "rutting," "'drunk' (with love)," and a ravenous, tormented desire for the other (B. Walker, 1968, 1: 514–15, 609). In keeping with this, Stevenson says that during the wedding the priest bores the hard madana fruit and ties it to the wrist of the bride and bridegroom with the intention of keeping the couple from excesses of passion during the days following the wedding. G. Watt (1889–96, 4: 214; 6, pt. 1: 391), though he does not explain the meaning of the practice, has noted that *R. dumetorum* is sacred to Shiva, and that at weddings of the Vaiśya caste the fruit, together with that of the shrub *Helicteres isora*, is tied on the wrists of the bride and bridegroom.

For a description of Gujarati Brahmin wedding practices, which are rich in symbolism, see M. Stevenson, 1920: 58–95.

53. B. Walker, 1968, 1: 483–84.

54. Marshall, 1931, 1: 64; Fairservis, 1992: 207, 220.

55. Marshall, 1931, 1: 63–65; Mackay and Mackay, 1948: 58; James, 1966: 23; Stutley and Stutley, 1977: 27, citing Bosch; Fairservis, 1992: 191, 197, 203.

56. Mackay, 1943: 89, 93, and plate 31, 2 and 3; plate 32, 1a; and plate 36, 9 and 37.

57. For a good account of the construction, uses, and history of the platform beneath the sacred Bodhi tree at Bodh Gaya in Bihar, see R. Mitra, 1972: 92–95.

58. Mackay and Mackay, 1948: 59, 61.

59. It is risky to project associations from prehistory into historical periods, but in later times, the tiger or lion has been the vāhana of Durgā, a warrior goddess and wife of Shiva who is often identified with Pārvatī, another wife (B. Walker, 1968, 1: 509, 2: 540). A male god of the Indus Valley civilization, moreover, has widely been regarded as a proto-Shiva, though that identification has been questioned.

60. Hopkins and Hiltebeitel, 1987: 221.

61. For the sanctity of trees, including the pipal, to the ancient Indus Valley people, and for similarities of their practices to those of modern Hindus: Marshall, 1931, 1: 63–66; Heras, 1938: 32–33; Vats, 1940, 1: 333; Mackay and Mackay, 1948: 58–61; Karmarkar, 1950: 189–90; James, 1966: 23–24; B. Walker, 1968, 1: 483–84; Stutley and Stutley, 1977: 27; Hopkins and Hiltebeitel, 1987: 221; and Fairservis, 1992: 14–23, 117. For the pipal as a repeller of evil forces among the Brahui: Bray, 1913: 16.

62. Coomaraswamy, 1993: 20 n 11.

63. Coomaraswamy, 1993: 63.

64. Yule and Burnell, 1903: 692, citing John Trotter.

65. Desai, 1965: 55.

66. Desai, 1965: 55.

67. *Aitareya Brāhmaṇa* 7.32, trans. in Haug, 1922: 334–36.

68. *Atharva-veda* 5.4.3, trans. in Bloomfield, 1897: 4, 415; Macdonell and Keith, 1912, 1: 44.

69. Monier-Williams, 1887: 335 n; G. Watt, 1889–96, 3: 360; Crooke, 1896a, 2: 98; J. J. Meyer, 1937, 2: 132–33; Upadhyaya, 1965: 3; James, 1966: 24; S. M. Gupta, 1971: 51, 52; Sen Gupta, 1980: 16.

70. Dubois, 1906: 652; B. Walker, 1968, 1: 358; Balfour, 1976, 3: 1101; Pandey, 1989: 22.

71. Rheede, 1673–1703, 1: 48; Dubois, 1906: 652; J. J. Meyer, 1937, 2: 133; Basak, 1953: 107; Thomas, 1960: 30; Chandervaker, 1965: 44; Mahapatra, 1965: 126; Pande, 1965: 37, 44; Hopkins, 1969: 7, 208; Gonda, 1969: 12; 1970: 113; Ward, 1970, 3: 203; S. M. Gupta, 1971: 51–52; Stutley and Stutley, 1977: 27; B. C. Sinha, 1979: 33; Sen Gupta, 1980: 36, 37, 39, 40, 59.

72. Crooke, 1896a, 2: 100; 1926: 408; Mahapatra, 1965: 127; Upadhyaya, 1965: 4; James, 1966: 25; Sen Gupta, 1980: 16, 59.

73. Monier-Williams, 1887: 335; Crooke, 1896a, 2: 98; 1896b: 10; 1908–26a: 482; 1926: 407; Chowbe, 1899: 227; James, 1966: 25; Sen Gupta, 1980: 16, 38.

74. Nair, 1965: 99. This incident is remarkably similar to one being reported

in my home state, Washington, as I am writing this (April 1997). Initial television reports indicated that in the Yakima Valley, a rich agricultural area with a sizable Hispanic population, images of what was reputed to be the Virgin Mary were found on the backs of highway signs. The images had soft, glowing colors resembling ones used in paintings of Our Lady of Guadalupe, patron saint of Mexico. Thousands of people arrived to view two of the signs, and there is talk that, in the interests of public safety, they may be moved elsewhere, away from traffic. Representatives of the state Department of Transportation suggested that the visions seem to be mere discoloration deriving from a chemical coating intended to prevent oxidation. Similar visions, however, were reported on highway signs some distance away, in the city of Moses Lake, which also has a large Hispanic population. Danger to the hundreds of viewers of one Moses Lake sign led the Department of Transportation to remove it, for which the department received many complaints. Meanwhile one visitor in the Yakima Valley said, "This is a miracle from God," whereas the Catholic Diocese of Yakima said that "it was too soon to decide whether [the] vision of the Virgin Mary . . . on highway signs in the Yakima Valley . . . has religious significance." Regardless, the Washington State Patrol prepared for possible crowds of out-of-towners in the Yakima Valley over the next weekend. Though visitor numbers were down, in nearby parking lots vehicles were seen with licenses not only from Washington but also from Oregon, Idaho, California, and British Columbia (Nicholas K. Geranios, "Another road sign attracts crowd seeing Mary," *Spokesman-Review* [Spokane, Washington], 114th Year, No. 305 [April 9, 1997]: B3; "Faithful may flock to road signs. Law officers prepare for crowds coming to see images of Virgin," *Spokesman-Review*, 114th Year, No. 307 [April 11, 1997]: B4; "Crowding eases at Mary sightings near Sunnyside," *Spokesman-Review*, 114th Year, No. 311 [April 15, 1997]: B6).

75. For instructions on their preparation, see Parlby, 1850, 2: 502.

76. Parlby, 1850, 1: 218.

77. J. J. Meyer, 1937, 2: 133; Desai, 1965: 55; Maity, 1965: 47; Gonda, 1970: 112; S. M. Gupta, 1971: 52.

78. Chowbe, 1899: 227; Thomas, 1961: 135; Upadhyaya, 1965: 4; Sen Gupta, 1980: 36, 37, 39, 59.

79. Thurston, 1906: 307–8; S. C. Mitra, 1939–40: 446; Nayak, 1965: 121, 122; S. M. Gupta, 1971: 55; Sen Gupta, 1980: 86.

80. Chowbe, 1899: 227–28; R. V. Russell, 1908–26: 315; Crooke, 1926: 408; S. M. Gupta, 1971: 51.

81. Rheede, 1673–1703, 1: 48. In a similar vein, monotheists in Palestine have considered fig trees to be the abodes of devils capable of destroying people, especially a father of children who sleeps beneath such a tree (Baldensperger, 1893: 204).

There is, on the other hand, an interesting account of a Moslem holy man in Bengal who persuaded his co-religionists to make offerings to pipal and banyan trees (S. C. Mitra, 1939–40: 449), though that was not mainstream Islamic behavior. Jains, like Hindus and Buddhists, regard the pipal as a sacred tree (Dymock et al., 1890–93, 3: 339; James, 1966: 24). Sikhs view the pipal tree as the creator and consider its leaves sacred (Sen Gupta, 1980: 38).

82. Sen Gupta, 1980: 37.

83. For notes on the ties of the banyan to Brahma, Vishnu, and/or Shiva, see Chowbe, 1899: 227; Enthoven, 1924: 120; Thomas, 1961: 135; Wilson, 1961: 166; Chandervaker, 1965: 44; Nair, 1965: 99; Pande, 1965: 44; B. Walker, 1968, 1: 357; Gonda, 1969: 11–12; 1970: 113; Hopkins, 1969: 7, 208; Ward, 1970, 3: 203; S. M. Gupta, 1971: 56, 58; Stutley and Stutley, 1977: 211; Sen Gupta, 1980: 41; Stutley, 1985: 103.

84. Valle, 1892, 1: 35. Pārvatī is one of Shiva's most important wives, though local goddesses, as well as major goddesses such as Durgā and Kālī, are also commonly presented as Shiva's wives and even as manifestations of Pārvatī or of Satī, Shiva's first wife. For an excellent description of the relationships that may develop among Hindu goddesses because of the Hindu tendency to view all goddesses as aspects of a single great goddess, see Kinsley, 1986: 132–33.

85. Crooke, 1906: 46; Mahapatra, 1965: 127–28; S. M. Gupta, 1971: 58; Sen Gupta, 1980: 39, 40, 41; Coomaraswamy, 1993: 124 n 10.

86. S. C. Mitra, 1939–40: 447; Sen Gupta, 1980: 41. One famous banyan tree, an object of pilgrimage in Andhra Pradesh today, is believed to have sprung from the banyan poles that supported the funeral pyre where a pious wife, Thimmamma, committed suttee (self-immolation) after her husband had died (fourteenth century A.D.) (David, 1996).

87. Moore, 1895, 2: 438 n 3; Crooke, 1906: 46; Enthoven, 1924: 120–21; S. C. Mitra, 1939–40: 446, 447; Banerjea, 1953: 76–77; Nair, 1965: 99; Nayak, 1965: 122; Pande, 1965: 37; Rousselet, 1975: 41.

88. Noehden, 1827: 131, 132; Valle, 1892, 1: 39; Moore, 1895, 2: 438 n 3; Yule and Burnell, 1903: 65, 66; Fryer, 1909–15, 2: 78; Enthoven, 1924: 121; Reeves, 1971: 230; *Phallic tree worship*, 1971: 13; Balfour, 1976, 3: 1100; B. C. Sinha, 1979: 35; David, 1996.

89. *Rāmāyaṇa* 3.33, trans. in Shastri, 1957–62, 2: 75.

90. Monier-Williams, 1889: 520; Crooke, 1906: 47; Chowbe, 1899: 224–25; Agrawala, 1943; Karmarkar, 1950: 193; Zimmer, 1955, 1: 132; 2: plates 242, 243, 479c; B. Walker, 1968, 2: 218; S. M. Gupta, 1971: 57.

91. Chowbe, 1899: 224–25; B. Walker, 1968, 2: 218.

92. Agrawala, 1943: 4; Upadhyaya, 1965: 3; S. M. Gupta, 1971: 57. For a Jain tale of gifts bestowed by the kalpa-vṛiksha, see M. Stevenson, 1915: 273.

93. Crooke, 1906: 47.

94. Crooke, 1906: 47; Stutley, 1985: 108; Coomaraswamy, 1993: 62, 64, 240–41.

95. Monier-Williams, 1889: 520.

96. Rice, 1897, 1: 455.

97. Chowbe, 1899: 225.

98. Abbott, 1974: 325, 333.

99. G. Watt, 1889–96, 3: 360; Crooke, 1896a, 1: 161–64; 1906: 498; M. Stevenson, 1920: 290, 318–19; Enthoven, 1924: 54, 84, 120, 142, 290, 291, 294–97; S. C. Mitra, 1939–40: 447, 448–49; James, 1966: 24, 25; S. M. Gupta, 1971: 52, 53, 55, and passim; Abbott, 1974: 326; Sen Gupta, 1980: 36–41; Pandey, 1989: 20, 21–22.

100. Monier-Williams, 1887: 335; Crooke, 1896a, 2: 98; S. M. Gupta, 1971: 53.

101. *Atharva-veda* 3.6, trans. in Bloomfield, 1897: 91–92, 334.

102. Crooke, 1896b: 10; Leach, 1949–50, 2: 872.

103. Gonda, 1970: 113.

104. *Atharva-veda* 8.7.19–20, trans. in Bloomfield, 1897: 43; S. C. Mitra, 1939–40: 449; Basak, 1953: 107.

105. Dubois, 1906: 243, 653; S. M. Gupta, 1971: 52.

106. B. C. Sinha, 1979: 33; Sen Gupta, 1980: 37.

107. Or, in the case of the pipal tree, the hope of gaining wealth and male offspring.

108. Enthoven, 1924: 84.

109. Gold, 1988: 134–35.

110. Mahapatra, 1965: 127–28; Sen Gupta, 1980: 41, 72.

111. Chowbe, 1899: 227; J. J. Meyer, 1937, 3: 335.

112. Crooke, 1896a, 2: 99.

113. Crooke, 1896a, 2: 99; 1926: 407–8; Thurston, 1912: 118; M. Stevenson, 1920: 61; Upadhyaya, 1965: 4.

114. James, 1966: 25.

115. Sen Gupta, 1980: 72.

116. Crooke, 1896a, 2: 99.

117. Mahapatra, 1965: 127. For the association of women and trees in early Hindu and Buddhist literature and art, see Vogel, 1929; and Coomaraswamy, 1993: 83–89.

118. Hartland, 1908–26: 826, citing Dulaure and Sonnerat; J. J. Meyer, 1937, 1: 231–32. Walker writes that South Indian use of the tāli is a survival from an ancient *devadāsī* rite, in which a girl was consecrated to the god of a Hindu temple (*deva-dāsī* = "god's slave") where she served as a temple prostitute (B. Walker, 1968, 2: 42, 246–47). For further notes on use of the tāli by Hindu women, see Dubois, 1906: 224, 226, 353, 492; Thurston, 1912: 46, 47, 48, 51, 143, 153, 158, 195; Diehl, 1956: 97, 189, 204–5, 236. For use of the tāli in the festival marriage

of a local goddess in South India and in a sham marriage between a heifer and a bullock, see Thurston, 1912: 165–66, 297.

119. Valle, 1892, 1: 39; Crooke, 1896a, 2: 99; 1926: 408; Chowbe, 1899: 227; Enthoven, 1924: 290, 291; Leach, 1949–50, 2: 872; Mahapatra, 1965: 127–28; Pande, 1965: 37; Upadhyaya, 1965: 4; James, 1966: 24; Gonda, 1970: 113; B. C. Sinha, 1979: 31; Sen Gupta, 1980: 37, 38, 39, 41.

120. R. V. Russell, 1908–26: 315; Crooke, 1926: 408; Leach, 1949–50, 2: 872. In later times that practice changed, with such a woman winding a cotton thread about the trunk of the pipal tree 108 times (Crooke, 1926: 408).

121. Abbott, 1974: 333.

122. Abbott, 1974: 322.

123. Chowbe, 1899: 227.

124. von Schiefner, 1926: 186–90. This tale is from the *Bka'-'gyur*, a Tibetan Buddhist collection of sacred works, most of them translated from Sanskrit, that was assembled in the thirteenth century A.D. The Brahmin was called Nyagrodha because he, too, had been born after his father had appealed to the nyagrodha tree for a son.

125. G. Watt, 1889–96, 3: 345, 359; Kirtikar et al., 1975, 3: 2313, 2318; Nadkarni, 1976: 544, 552; Stutley and Stutley, 1977: 27; Sen Gupta, 1980: 41. Among certain tribal groups, such as the Santal, there are reports of young aerial roots of banyan trees being wrapped around the neck as a charm to promote conception (Pandey, 1989: 20). A surprising exception is the use of pipal leaves in an abortistice among one Indian group (Lal and Lata, 1980: 274).

126. Dymock et al., 1890–93, 3: 339; Enthoven, 1924: 295–96; Crooke, 1926: 407; Mahapatra, 1965: 127; Upadhyaya, 1965: 4; Pandey, 1989: 20.

127. Chowbe, 1899: 228. Crooke (1896a, 2: 99) tells this in a slightly different way and with different timing, worship occurring when the night of the new moon falls on a Monday.

128. For other days when pipal and banyan trees are worshipped by circumambulation, see Enthoven, 1924: 295, 296.

129. Vaṭa-Sāvitrī-vrata ("banyan-Sāvitrī-vow"). The exact time of the fast in Jyeshṭha varies from one region to another. In some cases, moreover, women fast for three days, but, if they cannot do this, they observe the fast for one day (Crooke, 1896a, 2: 99; M. Stevenson, 1920: 300; Enthoven, 1924: 120; B. Walker, 1968, 1; 358; Sen Gupta, 1980: 40). In Bengal, worship of the banyan tree is not limited to Sāvitrī's day in Jyeshṭha, but occurs on every Saturday in that month (Mahapatra, 1965: 127; Sen Gupta, 1980: 41).

130. *Mahābhārata* 3.280–81.70, trans. in van Buitenen, 1973–78, 2: 766–73. For thirteenth- and seventeenth-century accounts of the ceremony, which derive ultimately from the Puranas, see A. H. Allen, 1900: 59–66. The ceremony was an elaborate affair in which a banyan tree was essential.

131. Crooke, 1906: 348; Abbott, 1974: 337, 435.

132. Parlby, 1850, 1: 219; Sleeman, 1973: 385.

133. Chowbe, 1899: 228.

134. Crooke, 1896b, 1: 47.

135. Monier-Williams, 1887: 336; Crooke, 1906: 497; Nair, 1965: 99; Geden, 1983: 176.

136. Monier-Williams, 1887: 336; Crooke, 1896a, 2: 100; 1906: 497; Sleeman, 1973: 385 n 1.

137. Yule and Burnell, 1903: 692, citing Halhed; Balfour, 1976, 3: 960.

138. Reeves, 1971: 228–29.

139. Crooke, 1896a, 2: 273.

140. Dymock et al., 1890–93, 3: 338–39; Crooke, 1896a, 2: 99–100, 107, 192–96; Ragozin, 1902: 159–60; Macdonell and Keith, 1912, 2: 511–12; Frazer, 1935, 2: 248–50; B. Walker, 1968, 1: 358–59; Hopkins, 1969: 97–107; S. M. Gupta, 1971: 20, 53, 54; Gonda, 1980: 163–75; Stutley, 1985: 122. For a discussion of the identification of śamī with *Prosopis spicigera* or *Acacia suma*, see Frazer, 1935, 2: 250 n.

141. Macdonell and Keith, 1912, 1: 43; 2: 355, 511–12. One also reads, however, of other possibilities, as of both fire sticks made of aśvattha wood (*Śatapatha Brāhmaṇa* 11.5.1.16–17, trans. in Eggeling, 1882–1900, 44: 74) or, the preferred choice, from the wood of an aśvattha tree that has grown on a śamī tree (Kuhn, 1886: 40, 66, 175; Eggeling, 1882–1900, 12: 275; Gonda, 1980: 164). The hole in a fire drill cannot be shaped with iron, which is impure and inauspicious, and, though this is not strictly observed today, at one time fire sticks were formed by use of the holy darbha grass (Abbott, 1974: 214).

142. Hopkins, 1969: 6, 100.

143. S. M. Gupta, 1971: 20, 54. See, in this regard, the *Rig-veda* 3.29, trans. in R. T. H. Griffith, 1963, 1: 343–44.

144. Dymock et al., 1890–93, 3: 338. See also Frazer, 1935, 2: 248–50.

For a description of a modern fire drill, see Crooke, 1896a, 2: 194–95. Crooke, writing of northern India, notes that the lower bed of the fire drill is usually made from the hard wood of *Acacia catechu* (*khair* or *khadira*), and that the part of the drill that rotates to provide friction is a softer wood, usually pipal. It is of interest that the resinous extract (catechu) of *A. catechu* is taken by Hindu widows to curb their sexual urges (G. Watt, 1889–96, 1: 43).

In their fire drill, Hindus regard the epiphyte—the fig tree—as male, and the host as female. On the other hand, in their fire drill the ancient Greeks at the time of Theophrastus appear to have considered the epiphyte—ivy, for one—as female, and the host—laurel—as male, for the base was commonly made of ivy or another vine, and the drill, of laurel (Theophrastus, *Enquiry into plants* 5.9.6–7). Despite this, the word for ivy in ancient Greek is a masculine word, and for laurel, feminine (Frazer, 1935, 2: 251–52).

145. Abbott, 1974: 323.

146. Frazer, 1935, 2: 250; Gonda, 1980: 217.

147. *Atharva-veda* 6.11, trans. in Bloomfield, 1897: 97, 460.

148. Hopkins, 1969: 103–5.

149. Crooke, 1896a, 2: 195. In Vedic India, cereal grains and śamī leaves might be scattered over the joined hands of a bridal couple (Gonda, 1980: 113). Among modern Hindus, moreover, śamī trees play a role in Hindu ceremonies involving marriage and childbirth. Examples of this are: the bridegroom who carries a śamī twig to his wedding to ensure the success of his marriage; the expectant mother who worships a śamī tree to protect and warm her unborn child; and the mother who, after her child is born, sleeps on the ground with several śamī thorns (Dymock et al., 1890–93, 3: 338; Crooke, 1896a, 2: 101–2; 1926: 408; M. Stevenson, 1920: 86, 115–16; B. Walker, 1968, 2: 216).

150. S. M. Gupta, 1971: 53.

151. Bloomfield, 1897: 334.

152. *Rig-veda* 1.135.8, and 10.97.5, trans. in Griffith, 1963, 1: 188 and n 8, and 2: 533 and n 5; *Taittirīya Saṃhitā* 7.4.12, trans. in Keith, 1914, 2 (19): 611; *Śatapatha Brāhmaṇa* 12.7.2.14; 13.2.7.3, trans. in Eggeling, 1882–1900, 44: 220, 317 and n 1; Dymock et al., 1890–93, 3: 338–39; B. Walker, 1968, 1: 358. Many suggestions have been made regarding the identity of the original soma plant of India and the etymologically similar *haoma* plant of Iran, though the matter remains a mystery. R. Gordon Wasson (1968) has made a case for fly agaric, the psychedelic mushroom *Amanita muscaria*. David S. Flattery has made a case for wild rue, *Peganum harmala* (Flattery and Schwartz, 1989: 1–102). Other plants have been implicated in the matter as well, whether as the original soma or as additives to or substitutes for it. Among those plants are: garden rue, *Ruta graveolens;* species of *Ephedra* that contain an alkaloid which, when consumed, acts like adrenalin; *Asclepias acida* (= *Sarcostemma brevistigma*), a trailing shrub with a milky sap that is called mild and acidic; Indian hemp plant (marijuana, *Cannabis sativa*); sugar cane (*Saccharum officinarum*); hop (*Humulus lupulus*); mandrake; ginseng; pomegranate (*Punica granatum*); an Afghan grape; and more. Much has been written on the subject, and information on soma and plants thought to be soma may be found in many places, among them G. Watt, 1889–96, 3: 246–51; 6, pt. 2: 477–78; Macdonell and Keith, 1912, 2: 474–79; Ray, 1939; B. Walker, 1968, 2: 418–21; Wasson, 1968; S. M. Gupta, 1971: 27–31; Flattery and Schwartz, 1989; and Achaya, 1994: 38, 57–58, 108. A sizable bibliography on matters relating to soma appears in Flattery and Schwartz, 1989: 153–72.

153. Dymock et al., 1890–93, 3: 339; G. Watt, 1889–96, 3: 360; Crooke, 1896a, 2: 99–100; Pandey, 1989: 22.

154. Cunningham, 1962: 108. In Burma, the tongues of bells in Buddhist temples are commonly shaped like pipal leaves (Burkill, 1966, 1: 1030). At a mon-

astery in Thailand, the holiest building, or *bort*, was bounded by eight stones carved to look somewhat like pipal leaves. These, by unchanging custom, identified it as the most sacred area of the temple (Alabaster, 1871: 272).

155. Desai, 1965: 55.

156. Ragozin, 1902: 42. Though Ragozin did not identify that silkworm further, I wonder whether he was referring to the pipal- and banyan-feeding species called *deo-muga* (*Theophila religiosa*) (G. Watt, 1889–96, 6, pt. 3: 4–5).

157. Sleeman, 1973: 204–6.

158. Coomaraswamy, 1993: 11–12, 76–77.

159. *Jātaka* 479, trans. in Cowell, 1969, 4: 142–43.

160. *Mahāvaṃsa* 18.35–36, trans. in Geiger, 1960: 125.

161. *Mahāvaṃsa* 19.29–32, 59, trans. in Geiger, 1960: 130–31, 133.

162. Coomaraswamy, 1993: 11–12, 64, 76–77. The use of a parasol above a pipal tree was adopted by Buddhists from an earlier tree cult (Coomaraswamy, 1993: 64).

163. Monier-Williams, 1889: 517.

164. Bode, 1955: 48.

165. Tennent, 1859, 2: 616; Trimen, 1893–1900, 4: 90.

166. Knox, 1911: 29; Arasaratnam, 1978: 179; Hardy, 1989: 239; Pandey, 1989: 21. The *Śatapatha Brāhmaṇa*, that Vedic priestly guide to ritual and prayer, says, on the other hand, that a grave should not be located near banyan or pipal trees because of possible harmful influences from their magic (*Śatapatha Brāhmaṇa* 13.8.1.16, trans. in Eggeling, 1882–1900, 44: 427).

167. G. Watt, 1889–96, 3: 346, 360; Chowbe, 1899: 227; Ward, 1970, 3: 205; Rousselet, 1975: 41.

168. B. C. Sinha, 1979: 33.

169. Abbott, 1974: 335.

170. Monier-Williams, 1887: 336.

171. Drury, 1873: 213; Pickering, 1879: 239; Yule and Burnell, 1903: 691; Dubois, 1906: 652; Whitehead, 1908–26: 238; Leach, 1949–50, 2: 872; Desai, 1965: 55; Nair, 1965: 98; Day, 1969: 12; Gonda, 1970: 112.

The role of fig trees among India's tribal people deserves careful investigation. Here, however, I would call attention to the role of fig trees among the Lhota Naga. The Lhota are a tribal people of the Naga Hills in Assam who, in earlier times, were headhunters. Heads of enemies killed in war were kept at a head-tree, usually a magnificent fig tree that grew on a mound in the center of the village. The head-tree was the most conspicuous object in a Lhota village. It was also sacred. Agricultural rites were carried out at the tree, and in a way the tree determined the success of a Lhota village. When the Lhota established a new village, moreover, a site was chosen where a tree suitable for use as a head-tree was already growing. Care was taken not to injure a head-tree, but when one did die, a new tree was planted at the same site (Mills, 1922: 28–29, 108, 129).

172. Nair, 1965: 98–99.

173. Drury, 1873: 213; Ward, 1970, 3: 203.

174. Cooke, 1903, 3: 145; S. C. Mitra, 1939–40: 446; Gamble and Fischer, 1956–58, 3: 953; S. M. Gupta, 1971: 58; *Phallic tree worship*, 1971: 13.

175. Moore, 1895, 2: 438 n 3.

176. Nair, 1965: 99.

177. Ragozin, 1902: 29; S. C. Mitra, 1939–40: 446.

178. Mackenzie, 1875: 5; Rice, 1897, 1: 455; Crooke, 1906: 498; Dubois, 1906: 653; Thurston, 1912: 133; Nair, 1965: 100; Nayak, 1965: 121–22; B. C. Sinha, 1979: 84.

179. Chowbe, 1899: 228–29.

180. Chaubé, 1895–96b; Srinivas, 1952: 215. The term *triveṇī* means "three-stranded" or "three-braided." The spot where the three rivers (Ganges, Jumna, and the mythical Saraswati) join at Allahabad is one where the sanctity of the Ganges is said to "exceed all bounds," and, in Hindu thinking, this makes Allahabad one of the holiest places on all the earth (B. Walker, 1968, 2: 303; Hopkins, 1969: 6). Allahabad itself is sometimes called Triveṇī because of its geographic position at the place where the three rivers meet (B. Walker, 1968, 1: 29). At Hardwar, this term is also used by temple priests for the triad of sacred trees growing there (Chaubé, 1895–96b).

181. Rice, 1897, 1: 455.

182. Chaubé, 1895–96a.

183. Crooke, 1926: 404.

184. Nair, 1965: 100. In our chapter on tulsi, the neem and bael trees were identified and their sanctity was considered. For notes on the sanctity of the other trees mentioned in this section—mango, myrobalan, and aśoka—see Monier-Williams, 1889: 516–17; G. Watt, 1889–96, 5: 156; 6, pt. 1: 221; 6, pt. 2: 476; Crooke, 1896a, 2: 102, 109–10; 1906: 497–98; Chowbe, 1899: 225–26, 229; Colthurst, 1924: 36–38; S. M. Gupta, 1971: 40–41, 61–62, 95–97; Stutley and Stutley, 1977: 22; and Sen Gupta, 1980: 71–72.

185. In Hinduism, the number five transforms a great deal of diversity into a meaningful measure. It is also a highly auspicious number, as, for example, in the *pañcha-gavya*, "five products of the sacred cow," and *pañcha-vṛiksha*, "the five trees" of Indra's paradise (B. Walker, 1968, 2: 137, 218; Abbott, 1974: 295–301; Stutley and Stutley, 1977: 218; Stutley, 1985: 107).

186. In modern times, the revered reformer Ramakrishna (A.D. 1836–86) sought enlightenment under the shade of pañcha-vaṭi, a group of five sacred trees at Dakshineswar, not far from Calcutta (Ghosal, 1965: 110).

187. *Emblica officinalis* = *Phyllanthus emblica* (G. Watt, 1889–96, 6, pt. 1: 217).

188. Colthurst, 1924: 38; B. C. Sinha, 1979: 33; Sen Gupta, 1980: 38.

189. Chowbe, 1899: 229.

190. G. Watt, 1889–96, 3: 346, 359–60; 6, pt. 1: 221; Crooke, 1896a, 2: 99, 102, 104–6; S. M. Gupta, 1971: 41, 61–62, 95; B. C. Sinha, 1979: 33–34.

191. For example, the *Vāyu Purāṇa* (2.15.28–29, trans. in Tagare, 1987–88, 2: 599) mentions a mountain where six different species of trees grow in one place, and observes that people who carry out ablutions and holy rites there attain heaven. The *Skanda Purāṇa*, on its part, recommends an arrangement of trees that includes a myrobalan, 4 banyans, 5 baels, and 25 aśokas (B. C. Sinha, 1979: 33).

192. For more on marriages involving trees or other plants in India, see Monier-Williams, 1887: 334–35; Crooke, 1896a, 2: 115–21; 1926: 415–18; Abbott, 1974: 287, 293, 335–37, 363, and passim; and Sen Gupta, 1980: 74–77. Tree marriage, though quite important in India, is not the only form of "mock marriage" carried out there. Mock marriages involving humans may wed a person to a god, a plant, an animal, or some inanimate object, such as a sword (Monier-Williams, 1887: 327; Chaubé, 1895–96a; Crooke, 1896a, 1: 236; 2: 118, 119, 121, 185; 1926: 418; Frazer, 1918, 1: 525).

193. Mackenzie, 1875: 5; Dubois, 1906: 653; Sen Gupta, 1980: 38, 72, 77.

Early in the last century, Sleeman reported that in Jubbulpore in Central India each mango tree in a planted grove had to be married to a tree of some other sort (often a tamarind) before the man who planted it, or his wife, could harvest and eat the fruit. In a case he cited, moreover, an old couple had to sell all their silver and gold ornaments as well as borrow as much as possible to pay for the entire grove to be married with the proper pomp and ceremony (Sleeman, 1973: 31–32).

Apparently there are cases in which no formal marriage ceremony is carried out. Perhaps this was so in one case where a banyan tree was embracing (strangling) a palmyra palm, which was regarded by Hindus as "a holy marriage instituted by providence" (Roxburgh, 1971: 640).

194. Mackenzie, 1875: 5.

195. G. Watt, 1889–96, 3: 346; Ragozin, 1902: 29; Mahapatra, 1965: 126; S. M. Gupta, 1971: 52–53.

196. Ragozin, 1902: 29; Dubois, 1906: 653; S. M. Gupta, 1971: 53, 56.

197. For the description of a ceremony in Rajasthan in which a household pipal tree was married to a local deity, see Gold, 1988: 248–51. The ceremony was a meritorious one involving hopes of continued prosperity and ties to fertility and pilgrimage.

198. At one time, Frazer thought that totemism might be a factor in tree marriage in India. Later, however, he judged the evidence insufficient and deemed a

tie between tree marriage and totemism unlikely (Frazer, 1935, 2: 57 n 4; 1968, 1: 32–33; 4: 210).

199. Crooke, 1896a, 2: 121; 1908–26c: 4; 1926: 417; Frazer, 1935, 2: 57; 1968, 4: 210.

200. Crooke, 1896a, 2: 120–21; 1908–26c: 4; 1926: 416–17; Frazer, 1935, 2: 57 n 4; Sen Gupta, 1980: 74.

201. Crooke, 1896a, 2: 116.

202. Chaubé, 1895–96a.

203. Crooke, 1896a, 2: 120; Sen Gupta, 1980: 74–75. In South India early in this century, parents with adult, unmarried offspring might purchase two wooden figurines—representing their son or daughter and a spouse—and have them married in a formal ceremony in the hope that this would facilitate their offspring's marriage to a human spouse (Thurston, 1912: 159).

204. Crooke, 1896a, 2: 120. A Hindu prostitute, apparently for similar reasons, may marry a plant, but if it dies she becomes a widow (Sen Gupta, 1980: 77).

205. Sen Gupta, 1980: 75–76. Similar customs about widow remarriage are found among Indian tribal groups, who may facilitate such unions by first having one or both members of the prospective union marry trees (Sen Gupta, 1980: 75, 76).

206. G. Watt, 1889–96, 2: 48; Crooke, 1896a, 2: 115–16, 117; Thurston, 1912: 51. The role of *Calotropis gigantea* in the ritual of marriage and birth deserves more scholarly attention. In addition to its use in Hindu mock marriage, among the Kunbis of the Konkan, the coastal area around Bombay, this plant serves in ritual to facilitate birth when a woman in labor is experiencing difficulty in delivering her child (Crooke, 1896a, 2: 120–21).

207. Sleeman, 1973: 566–67.

208. G. Watt, 1889–96, 3: 345, 359.

209. Reeves, 1971: 97, 200, 218.

210. Tennent, 1859, 2: 617; Hardy, 1880: 175 n.

211. This practice may go back to great antiquity, for Mackay and Mackay (1948: 59–60) described an Indus Valley clay amulet on which a large tree of unknown species is depicted. Around the base of the tree is a high platform, much like the raised platforms so common around sacred trees in modern India.

212. Coomaraswamy, 1993: 68. In this context, Coomaraswamy notes a Buddhist legend of a rich but childless man who observes near a road a lofty forest tree with wide-spreading branches. Desirous of offspring and convinced that the tree must be occupied by a potent tree spirit, he made his request to the tree only after he had the ground cleared beneath it, a wall built around it and sand scattered within the compound, and the tree decorated with flags and banners (Coomaraswamy, 1993: 68, quoting Burlingame).

213. Tennent, 1859, 2: 616, 618–19; Watters, 1904–5, 2: 114–15; Fergusson, 1910, 1: 229; Cunningham, 1966: 15–16; Beal, 1968, 2: 115.

214. Rice, 1897, 1: 455.

215. Knox, 1911: 29; Arasaratnam, 1978: 178.

216. Knox, 1911: 29; Arasaratnam, 1978: 178.

217. M. Stevenson, 1920: 290 n.

218. Sen Gupta, 1980: 38.

219. Crooke, 1896a, 2: 100. Crooke notes elsewhere (1908–26a: 482) that watering after a morning bath is done especially in the month of Vaiśākha (April-May).

220. Crooke, 1908–26a: 482; Basak, 1953: 107.

221. M. Stevenson, 1920: 142–43.

222. Chowbe, 1899: 227.

223. Chowbe, 1899: 227.

224. Crooke, 1896a, 2: 100.

225. Ward, 1970, 3: 203.

226. McLean and Ivimey-Cook, 1956: 1747.

227. Crooke, 1896a, 2: 100.

228. Parlby, 1850, 1: 219; Drury, 1873: 217; Pickering, 1879: 239; Monier-Williams 1887: 336; G. Watt, 1889–96, 3: 346, 360; Valle, 1892, 1: 39; Cooke, 1903, 3: 149; M. Stevenson, 1920: 290; Upadhyaya, 1965: 3–4; Reeves, 1971: 123–24; Sleeman, 1973: 442–43.

229. Bakhsh, 1892–93; Chowbe, 1899: 227; Leach, 1949–50, 1: 114; 2: 872; Upadhyaya, 1965: 3–4.

230. B. C. Sinha, 1979: 32.

231. Davids, 1890–94, 36: 78 n 1.

232. *Jātaka* 493, trans. in Cowell, 1969, 4: 222–23.

233. Tennent, 1859, 2: 615–16.

234. Tennent, 1859, 2: 616.

235. M. Stevenson, 1920: 290 n.

236. G. Watt, 1889–96, 3: 346; Yule and Burnell, 1903: 66.

237. Crooke, 1926: 401.

238. Valle, 1892, 1: 39.

239. Chowbe, 1899: 227; Dubois, 1906: 652; Condit, 1969: 99.

240. Leach, 1949–50, 2: 872.

241. Ragozin, 1902: 30.

242. Upadhyaya, 1965: 3.

243. Mahapatra, 1965: 126.

244. Oldham, 1901: 466. Crying for further attention by culture historians is the question of religious beliefs in South and Southeast Asia as they have slowed, reduced, or even prevented environmental degradation. In India, such beliefs

may lead to reluctance to cut down particular species of trees wherever they are found, as detailed by Abbott (1974: 331–32). They may, on the other hand, lead to the preservation of an entire habitat, as in the sacred groves studied by Gadgil and Vartak (cited by Gold and Gujar, 1989). Gold and Gujar present an interesting account of their own, with several stories that illustrate how, in Rajasthan, concern with the sensibilities of deities has protected trees from being cut down in the domains of those deities. These domains are homes of the gods, and humans who enter them are guests who must behave with proper respect toward their supernatural hosts. It is a punishable act for a human to cut down a deity's trees, injure the small animals to whom the deity has granted sanctuary, or use in unacceptable ways the streams and other water bodies in the deity's domain. The result is a powerful influence for environmental preservation in such places, which also exists in other parts of India. Gold and Gujar call the phenomenon divine conservation, and they regard it as far more effective than conservation efforts by the government's forestry agents, who lack moral authority.

There are various aspects to this phenomenon, as shown in an account from Bengal during the colonial period that, when a clearing was to be made, no Hindu woodcutter would strike a blow with his ax until the European supervisor had done so first, thereby directing the anger of the spirit or deity to himself. In Thailand, the cutting down of trees is considered evil, and people are reluctant to cut down trees of any sort out of fear of angering the tree gods. There is one report that, before felling trees, a Thai offers them cakes and rice (Sen Gupta, 1980: 11). Indeed, tree-felling was considered so vile in the last century that one European road builder in the Bangkok area was provided with a gang of the basest criminals to cut down trees, and, even then, the removal of any particularly holy tree was banned by the government (Alabaster, 1871: 221).

245. S. M. Gupta, 1971: 57.

246. Mahapatra, 1965: 126.

247. J. W. Bennett, 1843: 333–34; Hardy, 1989: 239. Before the discovery that leprosy was caused by a bacillus, *Mycobacterium leprae,* people around the world were quite imaginative in identifying causes, natural and supernatural, of the disease. They were also imaginative in prescribing ways of warding off and treating the disease. Among Hindus, leprosy was commonly believed to be brought on by sin, for example, by telling a lie in a certain sacred grove of trees. To treat leprosy, therefore, purificatory rites, such as bathing in sacred waters or eating algae growing in them, might be carried out (Crooke, 1896a, 1: 58–59, 125, 221; 2: 91). In Ayurvedic medicine in India, moreover, the leaves of banyan trees and bark of banyan and pipal trees have been used in treating leprosy (Kirtikar et al., 1975, 3: 2313; Nadkarni, 1976, 1: 553). Similarly, in China, people might seek protection from leprosy by putting a small branch of the banyan tree over their doors (de Groot, 1964, 1: 45).

248. Philpot, 1897: 64.

249. It has been suggested that the sacred fig-tree at Bodh Gaya may have already been sacred prior to the Buddha's day, that his followers came to associate his name with a tree that was already renowned (Davids, 1903: 231; Grierson, 1908–26: 183 n, citing Bloch). This view does not conflict with the Hindu view that the sacred fig-tree at Bodh Gaya was planted by Brahma (Hardy, 1880: 173 n).

Other Buddhas also received enlightenment under sacred trees, but each had his own species of tree. The Bodhi trees of the three Buddhas who immediately preceded Gautama Buddha, for example, were the banyan (for Kāśyapa Buddha); the gūlar, *Ficus glomerata* (for Kanaka Muni); and the *sirisha*, *Acacia sirissa* or *Albizzia lebbek* (for Krakuchhanda) (Monier-Williams, 1889: 515–16; Philpot, 1897: 40–42; Davids, 1903: 229–30; Cunningham, 1962: 45–46, 107, 108; S. M. Gupta, 1971: 56, 58; Sen Gupta, 1980: 90). In a similar vein, the tree of enlightenment of the Jain founder or reformer Mahāvīra, a contemporary of the Buddha, was the aśoka (*Saraca indica*). Legend has it that in Mahāvīra's later life an aśoka tree grew wherever he preached (M. Stevenson, 1915: 31; Thomas, 1961: 190–91; S. M. Gupta, 1971: 97).

250. *Buddha-Carita of Aśvaghosha* 12.116, trans. in Cowell, 1894: 136.

251. Keyes, 1987: 348; Ahir, 1994: xi.

252. Monier-Williams, 1889: 396.

253. Monier-Williams, 1887: 338; 1889: 392–93; Grierson, 1908–26: 184; Hardy, 1989: 236–37.

254. McDonald, 1992: 28.

255. H. A. Giles, 1923: 53–56; Beal, 1968, 1: 126–29.

256. Watters, 1904–5, 2: 114–17; Beal, 1968, 2: 114, 115–36.

257. See, for example, R. M. Martin, 1838, 1: 69–77; Monier-Williams, 1889: 390–401; Grierson, 1908–26; Vidyarthi, 1961; *Buddhist shrines in India*, 1968: 15–21; R. Mitra, 1972: esp. 59–180; B. Barua, 1975; D. K. Barua, 1981; Thakur et al., 1981; Ahir, 1994.

258. Originally stupas may have been burial mounds. By the time of Ashoka, however, stupas had become shrines that held relics or ashes or merely served as memorials (Zimmer, 1955, 1: 5–6).

259. For more on the Ashoka and Mahābodhi temples, see Monier-Williams, 1889: 390–99; Watters, 1904–5, 2: 116–18; Grierson, 1908–26: 183–85; Beal, 1968, 2: 118–19; and *Buddhist shrines in India*, 1968: 15–20; D. K. Barua, 1981; Ahir, 1994.

260. Hardy, 1880: 173 n. In a similar way, Jain temples in India were used by Moslems as quarries to build their mosques. In addition, however, Jain temples were made over into mosques (M. Stevenson, 1915: 283).

261. At the beginning of the fifth century A.D., Fa-hsien, a Chinese pilgrim to India, reported another tale about King Ashoka and the destruction of the Buddha's sacred fig-tree at Bodh Gaya. After Ashoka had been converted to Buddhism, the tale goes, he regularly went to the Bodhi tree, in part to ask forgiveness for his transgressions. He was absent from home so much that his queen, after discovering the reason, had some men cut the tree down. When Ashoka saw what had been done, he was paralyzed with sorrow, fell to the ground, and was finally revived by his courtiers, who cast water in his face. Then, however, Ashoka had the stump of the sacred tree banked up with bricks and its roots wet with 100 pitchers of cow's milk, after which he threw himself to the ground and swore never to rise again if the tree did not live. Immediately, according to the tale, the tree began to grow, and when Fa-hsien visited, it was nearly 100 feet tall (H. A. Giles, 1923: 58–59). For another version of this story, by seventh-century Chinese Buddhist pilgrim Hsüan-tsang, see Beal, 1968, 2: 117–18.

262. Crooke, 1906: 48; Grierson, 1908–26: 184; Beal, 1968, 2: 117, 118. For a history of the life and death of Bodhi trees at Bodh Gaya, see R. Mitra, 1972: 95–99.

Śaśāṅka's intent is made clear by his order, given to one of his officers, to replace a statue of the Buddha with one of Shiva (Beal, 1968, 2: 121).

263. Monier-Williams, 1889: 392–93; Crooke, 1906: 48; Grierson, 1908–26: 184; Rousselet, 1975: 586.

264. Monier-Williams, 1889: 393–94.

265. Monier-Williams, 1889: 393.

266. Stuart, 1911: 488.

267. The story of the transfer of the branch is told in detail in the *Mahāvaṃsa*, that early chronicle (fifth or sixth century A.D.) of Ceylon (*Mahāvaṃsa* 18–19, trans. in Geiger, 1960: 122–35).

268. There is a report of such a catastrophe actually taking place near the beginning of this century. A violent storm, one of the worst ever experienced in Ceylon, threw the sacred Bodhi tree to the ground. This event is described as "an irreparable calamity" (Daniels and Stevans, 1971, 2: 855). In 1948, moreover, there was a news report that the Bodhi tree at Anuradhapura was withering and that its prospects were bad, that word of the problem was spreading through the Buddhist world, and that pilgrims, in an effort to help the tree, were pouring gallons of milk around its trunk ("The sacred Bo," 1948).

269. For a chronology of events relating the sacred fig-tree at Anuradhapura, from the third century B.C. to the eighteenth century A.D., see Tennent, 1859, 2: 632–36.

270. Tennent, 1859, 1: 97–98; 2: 613–36; Legge, 1886: 103–4; Monier-Williams, 1887: 338; Trimen, 1893–1900, 4: 90; Crooke, 1906: 48; Davids, 1903:

302; Barns, 1908–26: 450; Davids, 1908–26a; 1908–26b: 747–48; Fergusson, 1910, 1: 228–29, 243; H. A. Giles, 1923: 68; Ludowyk, 1958: 90–91; *Phallic tree worship*, 1971: 55–56; B. C. Sinha, 1979: 85; Hardy, 1989: 236.

271. *Vāyu Purāṇa* 2.49.33–34, trans. in Tagare, 1987–88, 2: 957–58.

272. Grierson, 1908–26: 185.

273. Vidyarthi, 1961: 24.

274. R. M. Martin, 1838, 1: 75.

275. Vidyarthi, 1961: 25. For more on this society, its founding by Anagarika Dharmapala, a noted Ceylonese Buddhist, and its actions see Guruge, 1965, especially 688–89 and 731–50.

276. Vidyarthi, 1961: 25.

277. McDonald, 1992. The problem is exacerbated by the fact that many Indian Buddhists were formerly Hindu untouchables. As followers of B. K. Ambedkar—postindependence leader of the untouchables, who urged that they become Buddhists to escape their lowly status in the Hindu caste system—untouchable converts to Buddhism expected that they would finally be free of the caste system and of Brahmin priests. To see Brahmins in the Mahābodhi temple is more than many new Buddhists can bear. For more recent information on the struggle of Buddhists and Hindus over Bodh Gaya, see Ahir, 1994.

278. Hardy, 1880: 173 n; Monier-Williams, 1889: 398–99; Grierson, 1908–26: 183, 184, 185; Vidyarthi, 1961: 3, 24; R. Mitra, 1972: 4; McDonald, 1992: 28.

279. For an excellent account of Gaya, its sacred centers, performances, and specialists, see Vidyarthi, 1961. See also R. M. Martin, 1838, 1: 47–65.

280. Vidyarthi, 1961: 1–2.

281. Grierson, 1908–26: 182; Vidyarthi, 1961: 3; R. Mitra, 1972: 9.

282. Grierson, 1908–26: 183. It may be, however, that, as Grierson (1908–26: 182–83) has suggested, in earliest times the community of Gaya was a Hindu pilgrimage site where people came to worship at a sacred fig-tree (banyan) to gain offspring; that in the fifth century B.C. it became Buddhist; and that later, between the fifth and seventh centuries A.D., it once again became Hindu.

283. Grierson, 1908–26: 184; Vidyarthi, 1961: 3, 24–25; Rousselet, 1975: 586.

284. The additional seedling was planted, not by Buddhists or Hindus, but by J. D. Beglar, who, at that time, was in charge of renovating the temple of the Mahābodhi (Grierson, 1908–26: 184).

285. Grierson, 1908–26: 184.

286. Vidyarthi, 1961: 5–17.

287. Monier-Williams, 1887: 311; Grierson, 1908–26: 182; Stutley and Stutley, 1977: 96.

288. Vidyarthi, 1961: 33–49. The view that a pilgrimage to Gaya benefits one's ancestors goes back to an unknown ancient date. The Mahabharata, that epic which may have been set down from 200 B.C. to A.D. 500, says that a man should

covet many sons so that at least one may go to Gaya to perform the śrāddha for his ancestors, that a pilgrimage and stay in Gaya for a specified period of time is capable of purifying a man's "lineage to seven generations," and that a pilgrim may gain many sons as well (*Mahābhārata* 3.82.84–85; 3.85.6–9, trans. in van Buitenen, 1973–78, 2: 390, 399; *Mahābhārata* 13.88, trans. in *Anuśanaparva*, 1893: 430–31). In the Ramayana (which may have achieved its final form by roughly A.D. 250), King Gaya, when honoring his ancestors at Gaya, chanted a verse to the effect that a man should have many sons in order that at least one of them may go to Gaya to save him from hell (*Rāmāyaṇa* 2.99.11–14, trans. in Goldman and Pollock, 1984–86, 2: 298; which is the same as *Rāmāyaṇa* 2.107.11–14, trans. in Shastri, 1957–62, 1: 412). Similar sentiments are found in the Puranas, including the *Vāyu Purāṇa* (c. A.D. 500), which extols the merits of pilgrimage to Gaya and offerings there for purposes of purification, removing sin, obtaining sons, and salvation in the afterworld both for the pilgrim's ancestors and for himself (*Vāyu Purāṇa* 2.15.97–98; 2.43.8–44, trans. in Tagare, 1987–88, 2: 606, 911–15; *Vishṇu Purāṇa* 3.16, trans. in Wilson, 1961: 266). References to the Gaya śrāddha are also found in the *Institutes of Vishnu* (100 B.C.–A.D. 400) (*Institutes of Vishnu*, 85. 4, 22, 40, trans. in Jolly, 1880: 256, 257, 259). For an early legendary account of the holy demon Gaya, as well as the establishment of the pilgrimage center, the greatness of the city, and the performance of the pilgrimage (including the śrāddha rites), see the *Vāyu Purāṇa* 2.43–50, trans. in Tagare, 1987–88, 2: 910–72.

289. Grierson, 1908–26: 183; Vidyarthi, 1961: 13; B. Walker, 1968, 1: 384; R. Mitra, 1972: 17–18, 20; B. Barua, 1975: 62; Rousselet, 1975: 585–86. *Vishṇupād* means "Vishnu's foot" (Vidyarthi, 1961: 217) or "Vishnu's footstep," and comes from the Sanskrit *pāda*, "foot" of a bird or other animal (Macdonell and Keith, 1912, 1: 516).

When Francis Buchanan visited the temple at the beginning of the nineteenth century, he did not view Vishnu's footprint, but was told that it was an imprint in a rock like that made in clay by a human foot. It was, however, much larger than human size (R. M. Martin, 1838, 1: 65). Barua (1975: 62, 63) also writes of it as a single footprint, in contrast with the *footprints* of the Buddha found at Bodh Gaya. In writing of the rites performed by pilgrims at Gaya (Hindu Gaya), the *Vāyu Purāṇa* has observed that Vishnu's footprint "is divine and destructive of sins by its very sight. . . By touching and worshipping it, sins are dispelled" (*Vāyu Purāṇa* 2.49.55, trans. in Tagare, 1987–88, 2: 960).

290. Among the other footprints of Vishnu or his incarnations that are honored in India are one footprint of Vishnu at Bodh Gaya and another at a bathing ghat adjacent to the temple of Gangadwara at Hardwar in Uttar Pradesh. Sacred footprints of other Hindu deities and saints are also honored in India (even at early Gaya, for which see *Vāyu Purāṇa* 2.49.55–71, trans. in Tagare, 1987–88, 2: 960–62). Indeed, Monier-Williams (1889: 508) noted that in travelling in India

he repeatedly came to shrines that appeared to be empty but actually contained two footprints on a small raised stone altar. In addition, footprints of Jain saints have been the objects of pilgrimage (Monier-Williams, 1889: 509–10; Jaini, 1979: 193), as well as ones of the Prophet Mohammed. One of the latter was on a stone kept at a mosque in Lucknow. It had reputedly been brought from Arabia by a pilgrim, but disappeared during the Indian Mutiny (Crooke, 1896a, 2: 200).

Mitra (1972: 18) has written that nowhere else in India is the worship of footprints by Hindus as prominent as at Gaya, which, in his view, derives from the Buddhist origin of footprint worship there. Whatever the age and sequence of Hindu and Buddhist footprints at Gaya and Bodh Gaya, footprints of the Buddha have been objects of worship for Buddhists since antiquity. This is shown by their being included, along with other sacred objects (e.g., Bodhi trees, wheels), in sculptures on the Buddhist stupa of Bharhut (Cunningham, 1962: 106). In addition, footprints of the Buddha occur elsewhere in the Buddhist world, in Burma, Thailand, Tibet, Mongolia, and China. Most famous are those at Adam's Peak in Ceylon and Sara Buri in Thailand, which have long been the goals of pilgrimage (Monier-Williams, 1889: 506–14; Keyes, 1987: 349). It is questionable whether the Buddha ever went to Ceylon. Nevertheless, at the start of the fifth century A.D., Fa-hsien, a Chinese Buddhist pilgrim, mentioned a sacred complex—including a large pagoda and a monastery with 5,000 monks—near one "footprint of the Buddha" in that land. There was also a second footprint on a peak (now Adam's Peak), which Buddhists, then and to the present day, have regarded as the Buddha's. The latter is the most famous footprint in the Buddhist world, and facsimiles of it are found in Buddhist establishments elsewhere in Ceylon. That footprint, moreover, has long been an object of pilgrimage not only of Buddhists but of Hindus and Moslems as well. Hindus consider the footprint to be Shiva's, and Moslems regard it as Adam's, thus the place-name in English, "Adam's Peak." Christians, who also come to worship, regard the footprint as St. Thomas's (Legge, 1886: 102 and n; Monier-Williams, 1889: 511; Yule, 1913–16, 2: 359; H. A. Giles, 1923: 67; Leach, 1949–50, 1: 9; Ludowyk, 1958: 12–23; Gibb and Beckingham, 1958–94, 4: 854; Arasaratnam, 1978: 48–49; Keyes, 1987: 349). In the fourteenth century, Ibn Baṭṭūta described two tracks followed by pilgrims to the summit of Adam's Peak. One was Eve's track, which was the easy one. The other was Adam's track, steep and difficult. For more on Ibn Baṭṭūta's pilgrimage, see Gibb and Beckingham, 1958–94, 4: 853–55. Despite Islamic and Christian overlays, some have regarded the footprints on Adam's Peak as symbolizing India's cultural impact on Ceylon, with Ludwyk calling his book on the Buddhist art and monuments of early Ceylon *The footprint of the Buddha.*

Buddha's footprint at Sara Buri was discovered and authenticated at the beginning of the seventeenth century A.D. The discovery may have been made by a Thai who had seen the footprint on Adam's Peak, but, in any case, it is a far more recent discovery than Buddha's footprint on Ceylon. For a discussion of the Sara Buri footprint (over which is a shrine was erected) and other notable footprints, Buddhist and otherwise, see Alabaster, 1871: 243–62; and Monier-Williams, 1889: 506–14. For a representation of Buddha's footprint at Angkor Wat in Cambodia, see Zimmer, 1955, 2: plate 556.

291. Vidyarthi, 1961: 28.

292. Monier-Williams, 1887: 309.

293. Monier-Williams, 1887: 308; Rousselet, 1975: 585–86. As we have seen, Gaya is commonly mentioned among the seven most sacred Hindu cities. On the other hand, two surveys of Hindu pilgrims elsewhere as to which places of pilgrimage they regard as the most-sacred in India raise questions about its rank. One survey found that pilgrims did not rank Gaya in the top three, and the other, that they did not rank it in the first ten (Bhardwaj, 1973: 100–103, 113). Despite this, it has been estimated that Gaya was visited by 31,000 pilgrims in 1805; 300,000 in 1906; and, in each of the several years preceding 1961, from 50,000 to 80,000 (Vidyarthi, 1961: 91, 97).

294. M. Stevenson, 1920: 124–25. An extension of the view that śrāddha rites carried out at Gaya are highly effective is an elaborate ancestral offering of 108 rice balls, which is carried out in villages elsewhere and is named "the Fort of Gaya" because it, too, is regarded as very potent (M. Stevenson, 1920: 124).

Monier-Williams has written that śrāddha rites are carried out in auspicious places, such as cow houses. Most favorable for śrāddhas, however, are the shores of sacred streams or pools and locations hallowed by Vishnu's footsteps. In this regard, he notes, the banks of certain holy tanks at Benares represent an ideal spot, though their merit for certain śrāddhas may be exceeded by that of the temple of Vishnu's footstep at Hindu Gaya (Monier-Williams, 1887: 308). In addition to Hindu Gaya and Benares, however, Allahabad (in Uttar Pradesh), Kurukshetra (in the Punjab), and Sidhpur (in Gujarat) are identified as among the sacred places where especially meritorious śrāddhas may be carried out (B. Walker, 1968, 2: 428). According to M. Stevenson (1920: 124–25), the best śrāddha rites for female ancestors are those carried out at Sidhpur. There are also times of special merit for carrying out śrāddhas, and there are foods and drinks that may be preferred, for which see B. Walker, 1968, 2: 427–28.

295. Walker writes of "the immortal banyan tree" near the Vishṇupād at Hindu Gaya and the offerings that are made to it (B. Walker, 1968, 1: 384), and Vidyarthi, of the "undying banyan tree; name of a sacred centre in Gaya represented by the banyan tree" (Vidyarthi, 1961: 205).

The Vaṭa-śrāddha at Hindu Gaya, which is mentioned in the Mahabharata (*Mahābhārata* 3.82.70–74, trans. in van Buitenen, 1973–78, 2: 390; *Mahābhārata* 13.88, trans. in *Anuśanaparva*, 1893: 430–31), recalls the pilgrimage to a huge fig-tree, known as the vegetable giant, that grows in the ruins of "Padjajarian"

(Pajajaran, once capital of a Hindu-Buddhist state) in Java. Pilgrims in Java are convinced that souls of the ancestors live in the branches of the tree (Skinner, 1911: 113).

296. Monier-Williams, 1887: 309–12; Grierson, 1908–26: 183. For details on the performance of śrāddhas at Hindu Gaya in modern times, see the pages in Monier-Williams cited above; and Vidyarthi, 1961: 33–49. For a detailed account of the Gayāwals and their way of life, see Vidyarthi, 1961: 50–110.

297. See, for example, Theophrastus, *Enquiry into plants* 4.4.4. For a history of Greek and Roman knowledge of the banyan tree, see Noehden, 1827.

298. Balfour, 1976, 3: 1100.

299. *Rāmāyaṇa* 2.49, trans. in Goldman and Pollock, 1984–86, 2: 189–90, 417; this is the same as *Rāmāyaṇa* 2.55, trans. in Shastri, 1957–62, 1: 298–301.

300. Neither of the translations of Hsüan-tsang's account I have consulted describes the suicides in this way. Some writers, however, have said that the Allahabad banyan tree once extended over the Ganges, and that people committed suicide by throwing themselves from the tree into the river in the belief that this would gain them salvation (Monier-Williams, 1883: 337; Crooke, 1926: 407; Upadhyaya, 1965: 5–6). If so, this "jump of salvation" would have been rich in symbolism, involving one of Hinduism's most sacred trees and its most sacred river.

301. Monier-Williams, 1887: 337; Crooke, 1896a, 2: 98; 1906: 47–48; 1926: 407; Murray-Aynsley, 1900: 112; Watters, 1904–5, 2: 362–63; Beal, 1968, 1: 232–33; Condit, 1969: 177; Balfour, 1976, 3: 1100; Sen Gupta, 1980: 39.

Tradition has it that this tree goes back 5,000 years and is the oldest and most sacred banyan tree in India (Sen Gupta, 1980: 39). As for its possible ties with the akshaya-vaṭa of the Ramayana, Balfour has noted that the latter was on the opposite side of the river from the modern remnant (Balfour, 1976, 3: 1100). If so, the modern remnant may nevertheless represent a descendant or successor of some sort in the same general region. The matter, however, is quite uncertain, and, indeed, Europeans believe that trickery is involved in presenting the underground stump as a living tree that bears leaves seasonally (Murray-Aynsley, 1900: 112).

For a possible parallel in ancient Greece, in which oracles may have been delivered from a tree stump, see A. B. Cook, 1904–7, 15: 414–15.

302. Gold, 1988: 216 and n.

303. As an alternative, Balfour raises the possibility that it comes from the Arabic *kabir,.* "great" (Balfour, 1976, 3: 1100).

304. Some observers have even suggested that this may be one of the giant banyan trees described by Nearchus, who accompanied Alexander the Great, as being capable of sheltering an army of 10,000 men (Arrian, *Indica* 8.11.7–9; G. Watt, 1889–96, 3: 344; Crooke, 1906: 49; *Phallic tree worship,* 1971: 14; Balfour, 1976, 3: 1100).

305. Floods had caused significant damage to the tree by the late eighteenth century by eroding the shores of the island on which the Kabir-bar grows and carrying off part of the tree as well. Moreover, a violent hurricane in A.D. 1783 half destroyed the tree. Enough survived for it to be described as "one of the noblest groves in the world" almost a half-century later. By 1876, when Monier-Williams visited, the tree was gradually decaying or, at least, had lost its forest aspect, though it was still an object of seasonal pilgrimage. A few decades later, Crooke wrote, "floods, storms, and old age have almost completed its ruin" but noted its "scanty remains" continued to survive. Apparently it recovered quite well, for Desai, writing in 1965 of tree worship in Gujarat, described it, using the present tense, as a large tree and an object of worship and pilgrimage (Monier-Williams 1887: 337 and n; Ragozin, 1902: 27–28; Crooke, 1906: 49; Balfour, 1976, 3: 1101; Desai, 1965: 55).

306. Monier-Williams, 1887: 337; Valle, 1892, 1: 35–39; Ragozin, 1902: 27–29; Crooke, 1906: 49; *Phallic tree worship*, 1971: 13–14; Balfour, 1976, 3: 1100–1101.

For references to still other notable fig-trees in the Indian subcontinent, see Drury, 1873: 213; Sinclair, 1875: 66; Trimen, 1893–1900, 4: 86; G. Watt, 1889–96, 3: 334; Rice, 1897, 1: 455; Cooke, 1903, 3: 145; Crooke, 1906: 49–50; Enthoven, 1924: 120–21; Yule and Burnell, 1903: 65–66, 692; Condit, 1969: 99, 177; Rousselet, 1975: 41; Balfour, 1976, 3: 1100, 1101; and Young, 1996: 43. For an interesting account of a banyan tree called Thimmamma Marimanu ("Thimmamma's big tree"), which grows in a village in Andhra Pradesh, see David, 1996.

307. Rice, 1897, 1: 454; Oldham, 1901: 462; Vogel, 1926: 270; Mundkur, 1983: 84–85; Eichinger Ferro-Luzzi, 1987, 1987: 84.

308. Maity, 1965. For more on the cult of snakes in India, and, in some cases, its ties with tree worship, see especially Mackenzie, 1875; Rivett-Carnac, 1879; Monier-Williams, 1883: 319–26; *Ophiolatreia, or serpent worship*, 1889: 94–98 and passim; Crooke, 1896a, 2: 121–45; 1906: 439–44; Thurston, 1912: 121–36; Oldham, 1901, 1905; Vogel, 1926; Aiyar, 1931–32; A. P. Iyer, 1938–39; Karmarkar, 1950: 157–71; Srinivas, 1952: 166–69; Howey, 1955: esp. 42–70, 367–75; Maity, 1965; B. Walker, 1968, 2: 387–90; Fergusson, 1971; Stutley and Stutley, 1977: 198–99; and Smith and Narasimha Chary, 1991: 235–41.

309. In Hindu myths, the term *nāga* may refer to an elephant, to an ordinary snake, or to supernatural beings "half human, half serpentine in form, not necessarily evil, but often beautiful, wise, and good, and, although armed with a deadly venom, possessing also the elixir of life and immortality, and able to bestow it upon others" (Monier-Williams, 1883: 321–22; *Ophiolatreia, or serpent worship*, 1889: 97–98; Vogel, 1926: 281; Stutley and Stutley, 1977: 198). It is of interest that among Hindus both the snake (as we shall see) and the elephant (B. Walker, 1968, 1: 326; Kinsley, 1986: 22) have long been thought capable of bringing on rain and fertility.

The word *Naga,* as applied to tribal peoples, such as the Angami Naga, Lhota Naga, and Sema Naga, who live in northeastern India, seems not to derive from similar-sounding Sanskrit words that relate to snakes (for example, *nāga,* "snake people"). Though many suggestions have been made for the origin of the tribal name, most likely it represents a European modification of an Assamese word meaning "naked" (Sanskrit: *nāgna*) (Hutton, 1969: 5 n).

310. One early work even gives the nāgas their own caste system (Karmarkar, 1950: 168, citing the *Bhaviṣya Purāṇa*).

311. Zimmer, 1955, 1: 354.

312. Zimmer, 1946: 72–73; Brodrick, 1972: 137; Mundkur, 1976: fig. 1; Stutley and Stutley, 1977: 198.

313. Monier-Williams, 1887: 331.

314. For more on the role of snakes in controlling water, see Crooke, 1908–26d: 415. For an interesting account of a noted nāga well in Benares, which was both a place of snake worship and an object of pilgrimage, see Rivett-Carnac, 1879: 21–24.

315. Rivett-Carnac, 1879: 24. In South India, people think that snakes build their nests near springs of underground water, that they favor finely pulverized soil, and that they contribute to soil fertility and the good health of cattle. This, according to Aiyar, is likely the reason that many priests in South Indian snake temples have a background as farmers (Aiyar, 1931–32: 428). At the same time, Eichinger Ferro-Luzzi (1987: 90) has suggested that the role of snakes in controlling water, rain, and the fertility of crops appears to be less in South India than in North India.

In ancient Epirus, there was a grove of trees sacred to Apollo where tame snakes, fed by a virgin priestess, were used to predict whether or not a year will be prosperous and free of sickness (Aelian, *On the characteristics of animals* 11.2).

316. Smith and Narasimha Chary, 1991: 241.

317. Monier-Williams, 1883: 320–21; Aiyar, 1931–32: 424; Karmarkar, 1950: 159–68; Hutton, 1963: 225, 228–29; B. Walker, 1968, 2: 388; Stutley and Stutley, 1977: 198.

318. Fairservis, 1992: 190, 197, 199, 206.

319. Aiyar, 1931–32: 424; Mackay, 1937–38, 1: 360; Mackay and Mackay, 1948: 65; Karmarkar, 1950: 157–68, 190; Maity, 1965: 47; B. Walker, 1968, 2: 388; Mundkur, 1983: 99.

320. *Rig-veda,* 6.52.15; 7.38.7; 7.94.12; 7.104.9–10; 10.63.4, trans. in Griffith, 1963, 1: 623; 2: 43, 90, 99, 471; Monier-Williams, 1883: 320–21; Crooke, 1908–26d: 414–15; Stutley and Stutley, 1977: 198.

321. In Hindi today, the term *nāg* means "snake" or, more specifically, "cobra" (also "elephant"), and *"nāgrāj,"* a mythological "serpent king" (Vogel, 1926: 281; Chaturvedi and Tiwari, 1970: 307).

322. E.g., *Vishṇu Purāṇa* 1.22 and 2.5, trans. in Wilson, 1961: 125, 169–70. In 1836, Sleeman, in describing the old city of Delhi, noted a metal pillar (apparently erected in the fourth or fifth century A.D.) whose base, according to Hindu belief, rested on the head of Śesha (Sleeman, 1973: 497–99). In building a new house in modern Gujarat, an astrologer identifies the spot in the foundation that is directly above Śesha's head. Then a mason drives a peg into the ground at that spot to make certain that the snake does not shake its head and damage the house. In erecting a wedding booth in Gujarat, moreover, great care is taken in inserting a ceremonial pillar into the ground, lest it puncture Śesha (M. Stevenson, 1920: 62, 354). Śesha is not only accepted as real, but is still worshipped in modern India, for example, in Rajasthan (Tod, 1971, 3: 1648) and the Himalayas (Oldham, 1901). In addition, Śesha is a personal name given to boys, and Śeshammā, to girls (Smith and Narasimha Chary, 1991: 241).

323. Crooke, 1896a, 2: 288; M. Stevenson, 1920: 354; Abbott, 1974: 149.

324. Zimmer, 1955, 1: 12–14, 44, 165–68; 2: plates 111 and 286; B. Walker, 1968, 2: 388–89; Fergusson, 1971: 70.

325. Monier-Williams, 1883: 320–23; Vogel, 1926: esp. 47–92, 166–219; Basham, 1954: 316–17, 319; B. Walker, 1968, 2: 387–90; Hopkins, 1969: 23–29; Stutley and Stutley, 1977: 198–99.

326. Monier-Williams, 1883: 321; Karmarkar, 1950: 161, 168, 171; Basham, 1954: 297; Brodrick, 1972: 138; Eichinger Ferro-Luzzi, 1987: 89–90.

327. Vogel, 1926: 93; Zimmer, 1946: 66, 69.

328. Zimmer, 1946: 66, 69.

329. Vogel, 1926: 93.

330. Zimmer, 1946: 66; 1955, 1: 354. Fergusson thought that there was an initial suppression of serpent worship under Buddhism (Fergusson, 1971: 62 and n). Whether or not that was the case, serpent worship persisted, and indeed it became a major element in Buddhist mythology.

331. For which, see Vogel, 1926: 93–131.

332. Vogel, 1926: 95–97.

333. Vogel, 1926: 97–98. The role of the nāgas in this incident is not consistent. This is indicated by the fact that, after the Buddha had eaten and thrown his golden food bowl into the water, the nāga-rāja attempted to make off with it (Vogel, 1926: 97).

334. *Buddha-Carita of Aśvaghosha* 12.112–16, trans. in Cowell, 1894: 135–36; Vogel, 1926: 98–102.

335. *Mahāvagga* 1.2–3, trans. in Davids and Oldenberg, 1881–85, 13: 79–81; Vogel, 1926: 102; Zimmer, 1946: 67–68.

336. There is a similar myth about the Jain saint Pārśvanātha (Sanskrit: "Lord Serpent"; eighth century B.C.?), who preceded Buddha by some centuries. When he was seeking enlightenment, Pārśvanātha was sheltered from a heavy rain by a

snake that spread its hood over the saint like an umbrella (M. Stevenson, 1915: 48–49; Zimmer, 1955, 1: 58–59, plate B2b/c; 2: plate 247).

337. Vogel, 1926: 97–131.

338. Vogel, 1926: 103–5; Karmarkar, 1950: 171; Zimmer, 1955, 1: 63–67, 243; 2: plates 557, 559, 561. In modern Burma, a gold image of the Buddha sheltered by the hood of a snake is a favorite gift found in pagodas (Crooke, 1908–26d: 415). Similar scenes, of a nāga sheltering a god or savior, are also common in Hindu and Jain art (Crooke, 1908–26d: 415; Vogel, 1926: 104; Karmarkar, 1950: 170–71; Zimmer, 1955, 1: 65–66).

339. For the legend of Elāpatra and the Buddha, see Vogel, 1926: 105–7. In the seventh century A.D., the Chinese Buddhist traveller Hsüang-tsang visited a tank dedicated to the Elāpatra in northwestern India. Its waters were pure and sweet, and it contained lotus flowers of different colors. Alongside the tank, moreover, were shamans to whom people came to request the atmospheric conditions they desired, whether rain or clear weather (Beal, 1968, 1: 137). This is in keeping with the ability of nāgas to control weather, mentioned earlier.

340. Cunningham, 1962: 106.

341. Beal, 1968: xli–xlii.

342. For example, Thomas (1960: 35) regards South India and Bengal as the great centers of snake worship in India; Stutley and Stutley (1977: 198) recognize South India, Bengal, and Assam as places where snake shrines are especially common. Vogel (1926: 268, 270, 273) singles out South India as a region where snake worship prevails, including the Malabar Coast; he also notes that southern and western India, especially the western part of Gujarat, are places where live snakes are worshipped in an undisguised way. Crooke (1906: 442; 1908–26d: 413) writes of snake worship as more general in South India than any other part of the country and identifies both Malabar, in the south, and Kashmir, in the northwest, as major strongholds of snake worship. Whitehead (1908–26: 239) says that snake worship is particularly widespread along the Malabar Coast, and Eichinger Ferro-Luzzi (1977c: 547) writes of the modern South Indian state of Kerala, along the Malabar Coast, as the most celebrated Indian state in terms of snake worship.

343. Mundkur, 1983: 5, 43–44, 61–62. Between 1940 and 1949, known human deaths from snakebite in India averaged more than 13,000 per year (Mundkur, 1983: 43). Human deaths from snakes have been far more numerous than deaths brought on by other animals; in the year 1919, over 20,000 people were killed by snakes in India, and only 2,637 by all other animals together. Snake-caused mortality, moreover, must have been much higher in past centuries when far more jungle remained (Vogel, 1926: 7).

In India, the mongoose (*Herpestes* spp.), regarded as an inverterate enemy of the cobra, has also been thought by many to be immune to cobra venom. It is not likely, however, that snakes form an important element in mongoose diet, nor is it true that the mongoose is immune to cobra venom (Crooke, 1906: 440–41; Lodrick, 1982: 195–96). Some have suggested, as an alternative, that the animal uses the "mongoose plant" (*Ophiorrhiza mungos*) as an antidote to the bites of cobras and other poisonous snakes. There are reports of people using that plant for the same purpose and of its root serving as a charm to protect against snake bites (G. Watt, 1889–96, 5: 488–89). For other Indian remedies against snake bites, see Crooke, 1906: 441–42. For an interesting account of the mongoose in Indian history and culture, including folklore, literature, and iconography, see Lodrick, 1982.

344. Crooke, 1896a, 2: 123; 1908–26d: 412; Brodrick, 1972: 136. For a revealing account of the fear Indians have for the cobra, see Eichinger Ferro-Luzzi, 1987: 87.

A person may use various charms, among them an ornament shaped like a hooded serpent, as protection against snake bite, and someone who has been bitten by a snake may go to a snake shrine bearing gifts of food and making a vow that if he lives he will give the food to Brahmins (Crooke, 1908–26d: 417; M. Stevenson, 1920: 314–15).

345. Smith and Narasimha Chary, 1991: 237.

346. Crooke, 1896a, 2: 123; 1908–26d: 412.

347. Monier-Williams, 1883: 325.

348. B. Walker, 1968, 1: 532–33; Clothey, 1978: 187–88.

349. Monier-Williams, 1883: 320.

350. Abbott, 1974: 248.

351. Abbott, 1974: 142–44, 204, 396.

352. Vogel, 1926: 27–28, 83, 91, 171. The swastika is an ancient Indian symbol employed already by people of the Indus Valley civilization (Volčok, 1976: 83; Fairservis, 1992: 190, 197, 218). Both right-hand and left-hand swastikas are known in India. A right-hand, or male, swastika is one in which the end of the right horizontal bar bends downwards and the ends of the other three bars are all in the same rotary direction so that the swastika moves clockwise. In modern India, it represents the spring sun and, like right-hand circumambulation, is auspicious, whereas the left-hand, or female, swastika represents the fall sun and is inauspicious (B. Walker, 1968, 2: 469–70). The auspicious swastika has served in a broad range of ways in Hindu symbolism and ritual. It appears on ancient Hindu coins, on textiles, and on Hindu books of accounts. A swastika of turmeric or saffron (which are auspicious and protective) may be drawn on the feet of a bride and groom and their parents. A swastika may be drawn in saffron powder over the carving of a lotus flower (the national flower of India and a widely used symbol) on the foundation stone of a house. A swastika may also be drawn at the threshold or door of a house, as during the Festival of Lamps. It may be drawn on the head of a young boy at the time of his ceremonial haircut. It may also be

drawn on a sacred tree, or on a pipal leaf used in a postwedding ritual. In another ritual, a swastika made of green pulse (mung beans) is made near the head of a god. A swastika may also serve as a seat for the sun deity; it may, in western India, be found on the wooden ladles that serve in worshipping the fire god; and it may be worshipped as representing a goddess (Crooke, 1896a, 1: 11–12, 160; 2: 101; 1906: 452–53; 1926: 408; M. Stevenson, 1920: 18, 22, 36, 109, 110, 316, 335, 355, 358, and 415; Enthoven, 1924: 41; Karmarkar, 1950: 169–70; B. Walker, 1968, 2: 469–70; Abbott, 1974: 283).

The present-day Western perception of the swastika has been strongly influenced by the use of its right-hand form as a symbol for Nazi Germany. For many Westerners, that swastika has come to represent unthinkable evil, unwarranted violence, killing, executions, and the Holocaust. This is in sharp contrast with its perception by the Jains, the Indian sect most closely associated with nonviolence. That swastika, symbolic of well-being, has appeared in nearly all Jain iconography from antiquity to the present day. In ancient times, certain Jain saints used it as their symbol. It has appeared regularly in Jain temples and books. It also serves in ritual, as when a Jain worshipper arranges a rice offering in the form of a swastika (M. Stevenson, 1915: 53, 56, 97, 251; Jaini, 1979: 108, 192, 200).

353. Crooke, 1896a, 2: 143–44; 1908–26d: 416; Vogel, 1926: 25–26, 77, 148–49, 171, 194, 198, 271; B. Walker, 1968, 1: 385; 2: 388; Eichinger Ferro-Luzzi, 1987: 92).

354. Crooke, 1896a, 2: 125; B. Walker, 1968, 1: 385; 2: 388–89.

355. Vogel, 1926: 218.

356. Crooke, 1908–26d: 416–17; Whitehead, 1908–26: 239; M. Taylor, 1971: 237.

357. Whitehead, 1908–26: 239.

358. *Ophiolatreia, or serpent worship,* 1889: 95, citing Samuel Purchas.

359. Thurston, 1912: 123.

360. M. Taylor, 1971: 237. When a Hindu burns a snake in this manner, it is said, not only is he freed of that sin, but also, if he carries out the act on a Saturday, the burned copper can serve in a ring that is powerful in repelling spirits (Abbott, 1974: 211).

361. Crooke, 1908–26d: 418.

362. Monier-Williams, 1883: 324; Crooke, 1908–26d: 413; Vogel, 1926: 274. Persons afflicted with these ills may repair to serpent shrines to conciliate the serpent gods (Monier-Williams, 1883: 324), who can also cure them. In Kerala, a South Indian state noted for snake worship, there are two major snake shrines. One is at Manarsala, where the snake grants appeals for children. The other is at Pambumakkat (Pampumekat), where the snake cures skin problems. Perhaps, it has been suggested, the snake came to be regarded as effective in treating leprosy and skin problems because it sheds its skin and emerges fresh and well (Eichinger Ferro-Luzzi, 1977c: 547; 1987: 90–91).

The snake's shedding of its skin is noted already in the Vedic and epic literature. Skin that had been shed, moreover, was used for its magical power, for the act of shedding suggests purification, renewal of life, and immortality (Crooke, 1896a, 2: 123–24; 1908–26d: 412; Vogel, 1926: 7, 13–14). In this regard, one recalls a Malayali folktale in which Shiva discovered that his son Subrahmaṇya had become a snake. When Shiva touched the snake's head, Subrahmaṇya came out of his skin and the earth once again became light and harmony was restored, Subrahmaṇya's emergence representing rebirth, "the coming of a 'new creation'" (Clothey, 1978: 187–88). The purity of snake skin is reflected in the fact that some modern Brahmins always keep a snake skin in one of their sacred books (M. Taylor, 1971: 237).

363. Thurston, 1912: 124.

364. There may be ways of avoiding such guilt. In mid-nineteenth-century Ceylon, Bennett observed that it was not unusual for persons who crossed rivers or travelled on them to find floating bags that were made of matting and contained one or more cobras. Such bags were tied at their mouths, but they did contain food such as boiled rice and an egg or two. This led Bennett to conclude that, despite the sanctity of cobras, devout Buddhists were not deterred from sending them on an aquatic voyage from which they could not escape (J. W. Bennett, 1843: 115).

365. Srinivas, 1952: 169.

366. Abbott, 1974: 109; Smith and Narasimha Chary, 1991: 238.

367. Eichinger Ferro-Luzzi, 1987: 92.

368. M. Taylor, 1971: 236.

369. M. Taylor, 1971: 237; Smith and Narasimha Chary, 1991: 241.

370. For more on snake charmers in India, see Dubois, 1906: 74–75; Thurston, 1912: 92–96, 129; and Aiyar, 1931–32: 429. For snake charmers in India and other lands, see Howey, 1955: 207–17.

371. Brodrick, 1972: 136; Smith and Narasimha Chary, 1991: 241.

372. Crooke, 1896a, 2: 133; 1908–26d: 416; Fryer, 1909–15, 2: 78 n; Karmarkar, 1950: 168; B. Walker, 1968, 2: 388. For Jain women's propitiation of snakes as their ancestors, see M. Stevenson, 1915: 266.

373. *Ophiolatreia, or serpent worship*, 1889: 95, citing Forbes.

374. Sleeman, 1973: 29.

375. Karmarkar, 1950: 168, 169; Thomas, 1960: 35.

376. Vogel, 1926: 28–29, 30; Brodrick, 1972: 137; Eichinger Ferro-Luzzi, 1987: 93.

377. Eichinger Ferro-Luzzi, 1987: 89.

378. Snake charmers are reputed to have the ability to identify snakes that are guardians of treasure, to follow them to their holes, and to request that they point out the treasure's location (Crooke, 1896a, 2: 135).

379. Crooke, 1896a, 2: 144–45; 1906: 443–44; 1908–26d: 416; Thurston,

1912: 121–36; Karmarkar, 1950: 168, 169; B. Walker, 1968, 2: 388; Stutley and Stutley, 1977: 198; Eichinger Ferro-Luzzi, 1987: 92.

In A.D. 1313, the rock fortress of Chitor in Rajasthan was stormed by Moslems, and the Rājputs who had fled to the fortress, together with their wives and children, died by fire in an underground chamber that has ever after been sacred. Tradition has that chamber now guarded by an enormous snake whose toxic breath puts out the lights of all who seek to enter "the place of sacrifice" (Tod, 1971, 1: 311).

380. Crooke, 1908–26d: 413, 418; Thurston, 1912: 134. For an excellent account of the anthill in Hindu myth and ritual, including its ties with snakes and deities, see Eichinger Ferro-Luzzi, 1987: 93–98. The widespread Indian belief that cobras *always* live in anthills is not true (Eichinger Ferro-Luzzi, 1987: 93).

381. M. Taylor, 1971: 236.

382. Eichinger Ferro-Luzzi, 1977c: 548.

383. As for eggs and milk, Eichinger Ferro-Luzzi has observed that they are the principal offerings to snakes in India, and she considers it likely that this is because they are linked with life and fertility. She notes, however, that, while the practice of offering milk to snakes is found throughout India, the offering of eggs to snakes appears to be restricted to certain sections of South India. Even there, she observes, eggs are offered to snakes only when people do so at anthills without a priest being present, or where the snake is tied to a village goddess and is served by a *pūjāri*, a socially inferior Brahmin who supervises the daily offerings made to her. Where snake worship has been Sanskritized, however, snakes are, as a rule, vegetarians who are not given eggs to eat (Eichinger Ferro-Luzzi, 1977c: 547–48; 1987: 87–88).

384. There is a legend in Rajasthan about the origin of the names of the village of Pipār and its lake, Sāmpu. According to the legend, a Brahmin named Pipa regularly carried an offering of milk to a snake deity who lived in a hole on the shores of a local lake. The snake deity rewarded the Brahmin by giving him two pieces of gold. When the Brahmin had to leave town on one occasion, he arranged to have his son make the usual offering. The son, however, saw this as an opportunity to seize the snake's entire treasure. With this intent, he armed himself with a stick, and, when the snake came out to eat, the boy gave it a powerful blow. However, the snake, though injured, was able to take refuge in its hole. When the son told his mother the tale, she was so fearful of retribution by the snake that she made plans to send the son away to join his father. In the morning when she went to wake her son, however, she was shocked to find in his bed a giant coiled snake rather than the boy. When Pipa, the Brahmin father, returned home, he was grief-stricken, but, despite this, he propitiated the snake with liberal offerings of milk. The snake was so pleased that he showed Pipa his treasure and directed him to erect a monument that would record the event for future

generations. Thus, the legend goes, "Pipār," the name of the town, comes from "Pipa," the Brahmin's name, and "Sāmpu," the lake, comes from *sampa*, "serpent" (Tod, 1971, 2: 852).

385. Mackenzie, 1875: 6; and Thurston, 1912: 132, citing Cornish.

386. Thurston, 1912: 134; Abbott, 1974: 160, 349–50; Eichinger Ferro-Luzzi, 1987: 96–97.

387. The festival's name derives from the fact that it is held on the fifth day of the waxing half of the month of Śrāvaṇa (July–August). It is called Nāgapañchamī in North India and Nāgara-pañchamī in South India (Crooke, 1908–26d: 418; Thurston, 1912: 123, 124, 135). Taylor (M. Taylor, 1971: 237) has observed that the Nāgapañchamī is held during or after the season in which snakes have shed their skins and are believed to have become pure (see note 362 above). For more on the Nāgapañchamī festival, see Rivett-Carnac, 1879: 26–27; Crooke, 1896a, 2: 137–40; 1908–26d: 418–19; Dubois, 1906: 571; M. Stevenson, 1920: 314–16, 407; Vogel, 1926: 275–80; B. Walker, 1968, 1: 355; M. Taylor, 1971: 236, 237; Stutley and Stutley, 1977: 198; and Mundkur, 1983: 84. For other times of snake worship, see M. Taylor, 1971: 236–37; and Smith and Narasimha Chary, 1991: 238–39.

388. Mackenzie, 1875: 5–6; Crooke, 1906: 442–44; 1908–26d: 418; Dubois, 1906: 571, 641–42; Thurston, 1912: 121–36; B. Walker, 1968, 2; 388; M. Taylor, 1971: 236–37.

389. The cedar in question is *Cedrus deodara,* mentioned earlier, which is the principal source of timber in northwestern India. In Sanskrit, this tree is known as *deva-dāru,* "godly dāru" or "godly wood," but it is best known by its contracted Hindi name, "deodār." As its name intimates, the deodār is sacred, and today it is the tree of the gods, the most revered tree in the western Himalayas, found at elevations of between 4,000 and 10,000 feet. The pipal does not do well or cannot survive at such elevations, and the deodār takes its place there. Like the pipal tree, the deodār tree can reach impressive size and height, with one tree described as reaching a height of 250 feet (G. Watt, 1889–96, 2: 235; Crooke, 1906: 498). Deodār wood served in making sacrificial posts in Vedic times (it must have come from the Himalayas, since the deodār does not grow in the lowland plains). In the modern Himalayas, the deodār is planted near temples, like the pipal in lowland India. Deodār trees are believed to be inhabited by spirits and deities, and they are worshipped to repel sickness, death, and other evils. Deodār branches may, for example, be burned at sacrificial rites to keep evil spirits away, and deodār smoke is inhaled by inspired prophets (who speak for a deity) for the same purpose. The tree is also linked to Shiva, who is said to have meditated beneath a deodār, and to nāga-rājas, and most Himalayan temples dedicated to nāga-rājas are constructed of massive deodār logs and are sheltered in deodār groves (G. Watt, 1889–96, 2: 237; Murray-Aynsley, 1900: 113; Oldham, 1901:

465–66; Macdonell and Keith, 1912, 1: 353; 2: 11; Crooke, 1926: 414; Ghosal, 1965: 110; B. Walker, 1968, 2: 216; S. M. Gupta, 1971: 9).

390. For details on the construction, appearance, and operation of such snake temples in the Himalayas, see Crooke, 1896a, 2: 125–31; Oldham, 1901; and Vogel, 1926: 247–50.

391. Vogel, 1926: 267.

392. Plantain and banana trees (*Musa paradisiaca* and *M. sapientum*) are sacred, auspicious, and symbolic of fertility. Thus women may worship the plantain tree to become fertile. In addition, plantain and banana leaves, fruit, and even entire plants may serve in Hindu marriage ceremonies (Crooke, 1896a, 2: 108; S. M. Gupta, 1971: 63–65; Sen Gupta, 1980: 66).

393. Crooke, 1906: 442–43; Thurston, 1912: 121–23; Srinivas, 1952: 167.

394. There is an interesting tale explaining the origin of this noted snake grove. A family was so poor as to be unable to provide a dowry for their daughter when she married. As an alternative, they made her a gift of a stone serpent, of which they had many, since they held snakes in great honor. The daughter worshipped and took good care of the stone serpent, and in short order she became pregnant and gave birth both to an infant boy and a baby snake. When it matured, the snake had numerous progeny, which were taken to a single place, and this explains the origin of the present-day snake grove (Thurston, 1912: 126). This tale has a far happier ending than the case, reported in newspaper stories in October 1996, of three girls in India whose parents were also unable to provide a dowry, a problem the girls solved by committing suicide.

395. In Cochin, there is a caste of Brahmins who are the snake priests and the only ones permitted to cut or use the trees in a snake grove (Crooke, 1906: 443).

396. Thurston, 1912: 125. For details on how snake worship was carried out in this famous grove of trees, see A. P. Iyer, 1938–39.

397. Crooke, 1896a, 2: 131–33.

398. Crooke, 1906: 443; 1908–26d: 413; Vogel, 1926: 278; Thomas, 1960: 35; Maity, 1965: 48–50; B. Walker, 1968, 2: 389; Stutley and Stutley, 1977: 198; Mundkur, 1983: 44, 45, 174.

399. For more on Shiva's ties with snakes, see Rivett-Carnac, 1879; Howey, 1955: 61–70; and Eichinger Ferro-Luzzi, 1987: 84, 87–88. For notes on the snake and nāgas in Vaishnavism, see *Ophiolatreia, or serpent worship*, 1889: 95–98; Crooke, 1908–26d: 415; Whitehead, 1908–26: 239; Vogel, 1926: passim; Karmarkar, 1950: 170–71; Howey, 1955: 42–54; B. Walker, 1968, 1: 355; Gonda, 1969: 96, 101–2, and 150–53; and Eichinger Ferro-Luzzi, 1987: 84, 88.

400. A linga is ordinarily made of stone, metal, wood, or earth, though temporary ones may be made of other substances. Especially valued are stone lingas called *bāṇa-liṅga* or *vāna-liṅga* ("arrow-liṅga"), which are obtained from the bed of the sacred Narbada River. Bāṇa-liṅgas are pebbles or small elliptical stones,

apparently of white quartz, that are permeated by the spirit of Shiva and require no consecration. The bāṇa-liṅga is the Śaivite equivalent of the śālagrāma stone of the Vaishnavas, mentioned in my tulsi chapter (B. Walker, 1968, 1: 594; 2: 73; Sleeman, 1973: 122 n). For more on the liṅga in Hinduism, see Zimmer, 1955, 1: 22–25; B. Walker, 1968, 1: 594–97; Stutley and Stutley, 1977: 162–63; and T. A. G. Rao, 1985, 2, pt. 1: 73–102.

401. Monier-Williams, 1883: 321; Karmarkar, 1950: 170; Howey, 1955: 64; Desai, 1965: 55. Various objects that somewhat resemble a phallus have been found in sites of the Indus Valley civilization, and various authorities have concluded that some of them certainly, or almost certainly, are formalized representations of a phallus (liṅga), and that phallic worship played a major role in the religion of the Indus Valley people (Marshall, 1931, 1: 58–61, 63; Mackay and Mackay, 1948: 61–62; Basham, 1954: 24, 298; Zimmer, 1955, 1: 22, 25). Some have believed that phallic objects were tied to the worship of an Indus deity, commonly referred to as a proto-Shiva, who is depicted on Indus seals, and that this fertility deity may have evolved into Shiva. It has been deemed likely, too, that snakes were honored, if not worshipped, among the Indus Valley people (Mackay and Mackay, 1948: 65; Zimmer, 1955, 1: 26). On pottery uncovered for one period at the Indus site of Chanhu-daro, representations of serpents are always associated with one of the cone-shaped objects (Mackay, 1943: 91), which might tempt one to raise the further question of whether the snake, too, may have been tied to phallic worship and to the "proto-Shiva" of the Indus Valley civilization. The entire argument, however, rests on a dubious conclusion: that the Indus Valley cones actually represent phalluses, a view that some have questioned (see, for example, Dales, 1984; Srinivasan, 1984: 83–87). Equally serious are the arguments that the Indus Valley deity cannot be linked to Shiva (for which, see Sullivan, 1964; Srinivasan, 1975–76, 1984; Hiltebeitel, 1978; Ghurye, 1979: 157; and Hopkins and Hiltebeitel, 1987: 221–22).

402. Rivett-Carnac, 1879: 24.

403. Karmarkar, 1950: 170; Howey, 1955: 64; Thomas, 1960: 35; B. Walker, 1968, 2: 387, 407–8; O'Flaherty, 1981: 243–44 and plates 8, 10, and 12. The Ramayana of Tulsīdās shows the context of terror into which snakes fit: "Siva's attendants began to dress their lord, arranging his serpent, crest and crown of matted locks; with snakes for his earrings and bracelets of snakes for his wrists; his body smeared with ashes and a lion's skin about his loins; the moon on his brow, the lovely Ganga on the crown of his head, his eyes three in number and a serpent for his Brahminical cord; his throat black with poison; a wreath of dead men's skulls about his breast. In such ghastly attire, was arrayed, the great god Siva. With trident in hand he advanced riding on a bull, while the drums beat and instruments of music were played . . ." (Growse, 1966: 47).

Many saintly human beings as well as other Hindu deities, among them

Vishnu, may also be ornamented with snakes or depicted as sitting under a snake canopy, for snakes are symbolic of immortality. Shiva, however, appears to be more richly bedecked with snakes, and invariably they are his attendants (Rivett-Carnac, 1879: 17; *Ophiolatreia, or serpent worship*, 1889: 95–98; Moor, 1968: 23; Fergusson, 1971: 69–71).

404. For this, see particularly Rivett-Carnac, 1879.

405. Aiyar, 1931–32: 426.

406. Rivett-Carnac, 1879: 23.

407. Desai, 1965: 55; Gonda, 1970: 112.

408. One name used for Shiva is "Bhūteśvara," "lord of demons" (B. Walker, 1968, 2: 408).

409. Monier-Williams, 1887: 331.

410. Crooke, 1896a, 2: 141–42; Vogel, 1926: 247–80; Aiyar, 1931–32: 425–26; Howey, 1955: 367–75; Thomas, 1960: 35.

411. Crooke, 1896a, 2: 131.

412. Beal, 1968, 1: 137 n 44.

413. Crooke, 1896a, 2: 134–36; Aiyar, 1931–32: 428; M. Stevenson, 1920: 315.

414. For additional representations of such votive stones, see Vogel, 1926: plates 29–30; Zimmer, 1946: plate 8; 1955, 1: plate B2a; Mundkur, 1976: 431; 1983: 175; and Smith and Narasimha Chary, 1991: 236. For a detailed description of a typical snake stone, see Smith and Narasimha Chary, 1991: 239–40.

415. Whitehead, 1908–26: 239; Srinivas, 1952: 168; Diehl, 1956: 160.

416. Rice, 1897, 1: 455; Thurston, 1912: 133; Vogel, 1926: 270; Aiyar, 1931–32: 426; J. J. Meyer, 1937, 3: 195; Zimmer, 1946: 72; Diehl, 1956: 160.

Even in areas of high precipitation, such slabs can remain in good condition for centuries, as shown on a photograph of snake stones under a tree in Mysore State (now Karnataka), which date from the seventeenth and eighteenth centuries A.D. (Zimmer, 1946: plate 8). Indeed, they sometimes far outlast trees under which they were erected. Thus, when Diehl found that most snake stones at Vellore in Tamil Nadu were located under neem trees, he concluded that they were survivors of tree marriages in which the pipal trees had died (Diehl, 1956: 254).

417. Whitehead, 1908–26: 239.

418. Vogel, 1926: 270; Zimmer, 1946: 72; 1955, 1: 49.

419. Thurston, 1912: 133; Vogel, 1926: 270; Zimmer, 1946: 72; 1955, 1: 49.

420. Mackenzie, 1875: 5; Rice, 1897, 1: 455; Crooke, 1908–26d: 417; Whitehead, 1908–26: 239; Diehl, 1956: 254; S. M. Gupta, 1971: 52; B. C. Sinha, 1979: 84. In marriages between pipal and neem trees elsewhere, however, people commonly regard the pipal as male, and the neem, female (S. M. Gupta, 1971: 52; B. C. Sinha, 1979: 84; Hopkins and Hiltebeitel, 1987: 221).

The gender of the pipal tree, however, has varied from time to time and place to place. In marriages with the banyan, it has been the female, and the banyan, the male (G. Watt, 1889–96, 3: 359; S. M. Gupta, 1971: 52–53; Pandey, 1989: 20, 21). On the other hand, *pippala,* as used for the sacred fig-tree in later Sanskrit literature, was masculine (Macdonell and Keith, 1912, 1: 531 n 3). The pipal tree (aśvattha) has also been described as a king among trees, a Brahmin, and a representative or embodiment of such male gods as Brahma, Shiva, and Vishnu (Chowbe, 1899: 227; Pande, 1965: 44; Gonda, 1970: 112–13; S. M. Gupta, 1971: 51–52).

421. S. M. Gupta, 1971: 52; B. C. Sinha, 1979: 84.

422. Mackenzie, 1875: 5.

423. B. Walker, 1968, 2: 407, 409.

424. O'Flaherty, 1981: 257, quoting the *Padma Purāṇa.*

425. Though a liṅga is found in every Shiva temple, two liṅgas are considered particularly sacred. One is in Benares—that great center of Shiva worship—at a temple where Shiva is honored as Viśveśvara, "lord of all" (Geden, 1908–26b: 143; B. Walker, 1968, 1: 118–19).

426. The fertility symbolism in the cult of Shiva is enhanced by the practice of placing the model of an egg, that universal symbol of life and fertility, on the roof of a Shiva temple. In the dedication of a Śaivite temple in western India, first the liṅga is lowered, by means of a sling made of silk, through a hole in the roof. Then, after the liṅga is installed in the temple and the hole is filled in, a brass, gilt, or stone egg is placed on the temple dome, after which the temple flag is raised (M. Stevenson, 1920: 408–9).

427. All Mondays of the year are sacred to Shiva, but those of Śrāvaṇa are especially so (M. Stevenson, 1920: 305).

428. M. Stevenson, 1920: 305, 313, 314, 375.

429. Crooke, 1908–26d: 418; Vogel, 1926: 275; B. Walker, 1968, 1: 355; Smith and Narasimha Chary, 1991: 239.

430. Zimmer, 1955, 1: 353; Brodrick, 1972: 136, 137–38; Smith and Narasimha Chary, 1991: 237.

431. Crooke, 1908–26d: 418; M. Stevenson, 1920: 314.

432. The term *nāga* occurs in many place-names in India. In some cases, it derives from an ancient people called Nāga. Their land extended from Iran and Afghanistan into northwestern India, and their culture seems to have involved worship of the sun and serpents. The name of the city of Nagpur, however, may derive from the common occurrence of cobras in the area or from a snake temple that is located there (Rivett-Carnac, 1879: 24; Crooke, 1908–26d: 414; B. Walker, 1968, 2: 106–8).

433. Rivett-Carnac, 1879: 26. For a survey of the sexual symbolism of the serpent around the world, see Mundkur, 1983: 172–208.

434. Rivett-Carnac, 1879: 17–18; Monier-Williams, 1883: 321; M. Stevenson, 1920: 234 n, 375, 382; Fergusson, 1971: 70; O'Flaherty, 1981: 244; Mundkur, 1983: 174.

435. Mundkur, 1976: 431. Aiyar (1931–32: 426), writing of South India, seems to have been referring to this motiff in a more delicate way when he wrote of "stone images representing crossed serpents." The motif of entwined serpents in loving embrace is an ancient and widespread one, found, for example, in early Mesopotamia and apparently known in India before the Aryans arrived on the scene (Zimmer, 1946: 72–73).

436. Diehl, 1956: 159–60. Also of interest is the fact that in Mirzapur, a city in Uttar Pradesh, a liṅga, as is widely the case with nāgas, may be used to bring on rain (Crooke, 1896a, 1: 73, 76).

437. M. Stevenson, 1920: 315.

438. Thurston, 1912: 121–36 passim; Karmarkar, 1950: 168.

439. Eichinger Ferro-Luzzi, 1987: 91, citing Kapre.

440. That South Indians explain barrenness in terms of a woman having killed a snake in a previous incarnation is confirmed by others (South India in general: Monier-Williams, 1883: 324; Tamils: Diehl, 1956: 160). Punishment of a snake killer can also occur in this life rather than in a subsequent incarnation (Monier-Williams, 1883: 324). One example of this, cited in our text, is that of the Coorg man who killed a snake and was unable to father a son. Also relevant, Aiyar (1931–32: 426) has noted that in South India sterility in women is attributed to *sarpa śāpa*, the curse of the serpent, "either in this life or in the previous one."

441. Monier-Williams, 1883: 324–25.

442. Srinivas, 1952: 167–68. The motif of intertwined snakes is an ancient one, found, for example, on a Sumerian goblet dating from about 2600 B.C. (Zimmer, 1946: 73 and plate 11).

443. Thurston, 1912: 133; Vogel, 1926: 270.

444. M. Stevenson, 1920: 305; Diehl, 1956: 159, 160, 254.

445. Mackenzie, 1875: 5.

446. This association of neem and pipal trees is explained in one folktale as follows: Seven beautiful daughters of an evil spirit were on their way to a river to bathe. The god Krishna observed them, fell in love, and asked their hands in marriage. Though they turned down his request, he did not go away, upon which, to be free of him, the sisters turned themselves into a pipal tree. Thereupon, Krishna responded by turning himself into a neem tree which held them, in their form as a pipal tree, in a passionate embrace. This, according to the tale, is the origin of the tradition of worshipping the two trees together (Nayak, 1965: 121–22).

447. Rice, 1897, 1: 455–56.

448. Naidu, 1912: 66.

Chapter 4. Mandrake, a Root Human in Form; With Notes on Ginseng

1. Linnaeus thought that the mandrakes of the Mediterranean region belonged to a single species, which he identified at first as *Mandragora officinarum*. Certain modern botanists have continued to hold to the one-species view, but most believe that the mandrakes of the Mediterranean belong to more than one species. Some present-day botanists write of two species: (1) *M. officinarum* L. (= *M. vernalis* Bertol.) and (2) *M. autumnalis* Bertol., though Linnaeus regarded the latter not as a species but as a variant of *M. officinarum* (Hawkes, 1972: 356–57; Jackson and Berry, 1979).

Both variants are found in the same countries in the Mediterranean region, though *M. officinarum* L. is more cold-resistant and can grow farther north than *M. autumnalis*. *M. officinarum* produces leaves and flowers in early spring, thus its classification as *M. vernalis* by some botanists. *M. autumnalis*, by contrast, flowers in autumn. The roots of the two variants are similar in form, but both roots and fruit of *M. officinarum* are larger than those of *M. autumnalis* (Jackson and Berry, 1979: 508–9, citing Tercinet).

In ancient works on biology, medicine, and agriculture, as well as in poetry and fiction, there are references to male and female forms of mandrake (e.g., Pliny, *Natural history* 25.147; and Dioscorides, *De materia medica* 4.76). In the medieval and postmedieval literature, one finds descriptions and drawings of "male" and "female" mandrakes (known in English folklore as mandrakes and womandrakes). Drawings depict them as differing in such things as length of leaves, size of fruit, and robustness of root. Sometimes, moreover, the root is depicted as having the body of a man or a woman (W. Turner, 1568: pt. 2, fols. 45–46; Bock, 1577: 315a; T. Wright, 1845: 179; Frazer, 1918, 2: 378; Lehner and Lehner, 1960: 90–91; Boullet, 1960: 24–25, 27; Woodward, 1969: 194–96).

The idea that plants of many sorts had male and female forms was based on a limited understanding of sexual reproduction in plants in ancient times. Indeed, when the ancients wrote of male and female plants they usually referred to plants that belonged to different species (Bonser, 1963: 326–27; and Singer, 1975: 86–88). This is in keeping with the modern botanist Tercinet's identification of *M. autumnalis* Bertol. as "female mandrake" and *M. officinarum* L. as "male mandrake" (Jackson and Berry, 1979: 508, 509).

2. Mandrake contains some of the same alkaloids as belladonna, but the latter, along with certain other plants, constitutes a readier source of those alkaloids (Grover, 1965: 100; N. Taylor, 1965: 147).

3. For color photographs of mandrake in flower and mandrake with unripe fruit, see Baumann, 1993: 98.

4. Tristram, 1873: 466–67.

5. Tristram, 1873: 467; Moldenke and Moldenke, 1952: 137; Graves and Patai, 1966: 219.

6. Graves and Patai, 1966: 219.

7. Columella, *On agriculture* 10.19–20.

8. Dioscorides, *De materia medica* 4.76; Isidore of Seville, *Etymologiae* 17.9.30, trans. in Sharpe, 1964: 33 n 241.

9. Herbelot, 1777–79, 1: 275; Veth, 1894: 200; Richardson, 1984: 79; Besnehard, 1993: 127.

10. von Luschan, 1891: 728; Veth, 1894: 201. As we shall see, human feelings were often attributed to the mandrake, as revealed in a poem by Langhorne late in the eighteenth century: "Mark how that rooted mandrake wears / His human feet, his human hands" ("Some notes about mandrakes," 1891: 60).

11. Ibn el-Beïthar, *Traité des simples* 1177 (or 1877–83, 2: 247); W. Smith, 1896: 515; Post, 1932–33, 2: 262; Moldenke and Moldenke, 1952: 138; Fleisher and Fleisher, 1994: 248.

12. Hooker, 1872–97, 4: 241–42; G. Watt, 1889–96, 5: 144; Greuter and Rechinger, 1967: 104; Lu An-ming, 1986: 81–82; Symon, 1991: 147.

The so-called North American mandrake, the herb *Podophyllum peltatum* L., is a New World species and member of a different genus. For more on *P. peltatum,* its medicinal use and toxicity, see Mack, 1992.

13. In the last century, Don (1831–38, 4: 455) and Pickering (1879: 247) wrote that mandrake grew in, or was a native of, Switzerland, but Beyer wrote that the most northerly point where mandrake has certainly been found is along the southern edge of the Venetian Alps (Beyer, 1891: 738; Frazer, 1918, 2: 379).

14. Ibn el-Beïthar, *Traité des simples* 1177 (or 1877–83, 2: 247); Mattioli, 1554: 478; Sibthorp, 1806–13, 1: 153; Ainslie, 1826, 1: 208; Don, 1831–38, 4: 455; Pickering, 1879: 247; Milne Edwards, 1864: 56; Tristram, 1873: 466, 468; Dymock et al., 1890–93, 2: 583; "Some notes about mandrakes," 1891: 60; "Mandrake," 1893–96; W. Smith, 1896: 515; Thomson, 1911, 2: 379–80; J. R. Harris, 1917b: 377; Steier, 1928: cols. 1028–29; Post, 1932–33, 2: 262; Moldenke and Moldenke, 1952: 138; Maundrell, 1963: 82; Greuter and Rechinger, 1967: 103–4; Woodward, 1969: 196; Beveridge, 1971, 1: 11; Parkinson, 1976: 378; Feinbrun-Dothan, 1978: 167; Jackson and Berry, 1979: 508, citing Tercinet. According to Pickering, mandrake is also known to grow in Siberia (Pickering, 1879: 247).

15. W. Turner, 1568: pt. 2, fol. 46; Woodward, 1969: 196; Rhind, 1840: 552.

16. Hooker, 1872–97, 4: 242; Dymock et al., 1890–93, 2: 581. *M. caulescens* is found in Sikkim at elevations of 12,000–13,000 feet above sea level.

17. Frazer, 1918, 2: 379, citing Mattioli.

18. Bauhin and Cherler, 1650–51, 3: 617, citing Lobelius.

19. W. Turner, 1568: pt. 2, fol. 46; Cotes, 1904: 67, 69; Friend, 1981: 293–94.

20. Lovett, 1913: 121.

21. Friend, 1981: 294.

22. Pickering, 1879: 247. For mandrake as a magical and medicinal plant in

ancient Egypt, see Brugsch, 1891; Starck, 1917: 76–77; Steier, 1928: cols. 1031–32; Dawson, 1929: 113; Keimer, 1967: 20–23; and C. J. S. Thompson, 1968: 43–45.

23. Balfour, 1885, 2: 844; Dymock et al., 1890–93, 2: 583; G. Watt, 1889–96, 5: 144). I have not been able to confirm Agarwal's statement (1986: 228) that *Mandragora autumnalis* is grown in Indian gardens.

24. Beyer (1891: 740–41) reported that one *alraun* (mandrake) in a museum in Berlin was made, not from a root, but from the knot of a tree, and that many others were not made from plant materials at all. One alraun that came from Switzerland, for example, was crafted from a dried frog but had a head made from the root of a plant, *Alpinia officinarum*.

25. Beyer, 1891: 739–40; Starr, 1901: 262; Frazer, 1918, 2: 379.

26. von Luschan, 1891: 728.

27. Bock, 1577: 315 a; Grimm and Grimm, 1981, 1: 344–45. To get an idea of the variety in form of mandrake manikins, see von Luschan, 1891: 727 (Turkey and Syria); Banks, 1932: before p. 429 (Leipzig); and Boullet, 1960: 23, 33 (France?).

28. Woodward, 1969: 195–96. For additional references to counterfeit mandrakes by English writers, see Browne, *Pseudodoxia epidemica* 2.6.1; Lupton, 1612: 44–45; and Dymock et al., 1890–93, 2: 583.

29. W. Turner, 1568: pt. 2, fol. 46.

30. Parkinson, 1976: 377.

31. Browne, *Pseudodoxia epidemica* 2.6.1; Dymock et al., 1890–93, 2: 583; Beyer, 1891: 739, 740–41; "Some notes about mandrakes," 1891: 60; Jaworskij, 1896: 353 and passim; Starr, 1901: 261, 262, 264; Cotes, 1904: 67; Hazlitt, 1905, 2: 386; Trevelyan, 1909: 92; Coles, 1938: 72; Langdon-Brown, 1941: 36–37; Moldenke and Moldenke, 1952: 138; Woodward, 1969: 195–96; Friend, 1981: 293; Grimm and Grimm, 1981, 1: 344.

32. Eliade, 1972: 204 n, 219 n, 220.

33. Beyer, 1891: 741–42; Starck, 1917: 57–64; Frazer, 1918, 2: 383. In Germany, familiar spirits of one sort or another, among them mandrakes, were often kept in a sealed glass bottle (C. J. S. Thompson, 1968: 138; Grimm and Grimm, 1981, 1: 94). Illustrations of mandrake manikins enclosed in glass may be found in Boullet, 1960: 33.

34. Grimm and Grimm, 1981, 1: 94.

35. Jaworskij, 1896: 354.

36. Frazer, 1918, 2: 387 and Sébillot, 1968, 3: 484, citing Noguès.

37. Biswas and Chopra, 1982: 3, citing T. J. Williams. Use of mandrake or its substitutes as charms which reputedly provides assistance to people without requiring them to ingest mandrake has been reported across a broad geographic belt from Europe to India. References to the practice include the following: En-

gland: "The folk-lore of Drayton," 1884–85, 2: 148; Moldenke and Moldenke, 1952: 138–39; Germany: Moldenke and Moldenke, 1952: 138; France: Thiselton-Dyer, 1898: 101; Sébillot, 1968, 3: 484; the Alps: Biswas and Chopra, 1982: 3, citing T. J. Williams; Greece: J. R. Harris, 1917b: 374, citing Sibthorp; Romania: Eliade, 1972: 213, 214, 216; eastern Europe: Biswas and Chopra, 1982: 3, citing T. J. Williams; Asia Minor: von Luschan, 1891: 728; Iran: Ascherson, 1891a: 737 n 3, citing Haussknecht; Ploss, 1899, 1: 605; and India: G. Watt, 1889–96, 5: 144, citing Dymock.

38. von Luschan, 1891: 728.

39. Hermes, cited by Ibn el-Beïthar in Sontheimer, 1840–42, 2: 14, 16; and in Ibn el-Beïthar, *Traité des simples* 1177 (or 1877–83, 2: 246–47); Hertz, 1905: 276.

Hermetic texts, written in Greek or Latin and likely dating from the first through the third centuries A.D., are revelations attributed to the Egyptian god Thoth (Greek: Hermes Trismegistos), and deal with philosophical and religious topics and astrology, magic, and alchemy.

40. Belief in a link between mandrake, on one hand, and the abilities of Solomon and Alexander, on the other, go back at least to the early centuries of the Christian era, when Hermes (cited by Ibn el-Beïthar) mentioned such beliefs.

41. Hermes, cited by Ibn el-Beïthar in Sontheimer, 1840–42, 2: 14, 16, and by Ibn el-Beïthar, *Traité des simples* 1177 (or 1877–83, 2: 246); Beyer, 1891: 742; Starr, 1901: 265.

42. Graves and Patai, 1966: 220.

43. Browne, *Pseudodoxia epidemica* 7.7; Calmet, 1845–46, 3: 316–17; W. Smith, 1896: 515; Brim, 1936: 355–56; Moldenke and Moldenke, 1952: 138, 283; Löw, 1967, 3: 364–66; Ramban, 1971: 369–70.

44. Post, 1932–33, 2: 261; Moldenke and Moldenke, 1952: 137; Feinbrun-Dothan, 1978: 167; Fleisher and Fleisher, 1994: 245. Other writers have identified dudaim as citrons, mushrooms, or flowers, whether field flowers in general or specific ones, such as jasmine, violets, and lilies (Browne, *Pseudodoxia epidemica* 7.7; Calmet, 1845–46, 3: 316–17; Brim, 1936: 355–56; Moldenke and Moldenke, 1952: 138, 283; Cruden, 1953: 302; Ramban, 1971: 369; Parkinson, 1976: 378–79).

For more on the derivation, or possible derivations, of *dudaim,* see Frazer, 1918, 2: 372 n; R. C. Thompson, 1926: 101–2; 1949: 218; Brown et al., 1953: 187, 188; Löw, 1967, 3: 364; and Fleisher and Fleisher, 1994: 246. In all possibilities suggested in the above sources, the concept of love or sex is prominent.

45. J. R. Harris, 1917b: 378–79; Moldenke and Moldenke, 1952: 283; Fleisher and Fleisher, 1994: 245–46.

46. Tristram, 1873: 466; J. R. Harris, 1917b: 358.

47. In the Talmud, wine is portrayed as an aphrodisiac. One cup makes a

woman attractive. Two cups are debasing. Three lead her to solicit in public; four and she "solicits even an ass in the street and cares not" (Kethuboth 65a, trans. in Daiches and Slotki, 1936, 1: 393).

48. Song of Solomon 7.11–13.

49. Some experts have stated that neither the flowers nor the fruit of the mandrake plant have a pronounced smell, whether pleasant or unpleasant (Moldenke and Moldenke, 1952: 138). Others say that, while it is well known that the smell of the mandrake plant is not strong, it is unpleasant or offensive, at least to Europeans (Browne, *Pseudodoxia epidemica* 7.7; W. Smith, 1896: 515; Tristram, 1873: 468). Still others, however, have described the smell of the fruit in more favorable terms such as "agreeable," "sweet," or "sweet and fresh like an apple" (Dioscorides, *De materia medica* 4.76; Tristram, 1873: 467; Cotes, 1904: 66–67; Joret, 1976, 1: 498). In the most careful examination of the question that I have found, Fleisher and Fleisher (1994: 247–50) admit that the smell of mandrake is elusive, but they insist it can be detected when the fruit is fully ripe, and that, in a newly harvested grain field, its smell may permeate the air. The smell is not, they observe, like that of roses, jasmine, or other aromatic flowers, but rather it is suggestive of subtle danger, as well as being exciting and addictive. Fleisher and Fleisher also mention Hebrew sources that credit the smell of mandrake with stimulating human sexual feelings and heightening the appetite for making love; thus, they suggest, the smell of mandrake may have aroused Rachel and given her a new perspective on life.

50. It is a matter of dispute, among those who think that Rachel did eat the mandrake, as to whether she consumed the fruit or grated root (Graves and Patai, 1966: 220 n 8).

51. Genesis 30.14–24.

52. "And God remembered Rachel, and hearkened to her, and opened her womb" (Genesis 30.22).

53. W. H. Bennett, 1904: 293 n; Frazer, 1918, 2: 373–74; Gunkel, 1964: 124–26. Various eminent Jewish scriptural commentators, as well, have denied that either Rachel or Leah used mandrake to facilitate pregnancy (Ramban, 1971: 369–70; Fleisher and Fleisher, 1994: 249).

54. "Some notes about mandrakes," 1891: 60.

55. Maundrell, 1963: 82.

56. Goodrich-Freer, 1907: 67.

57. Starr, 1901: 267.

58. E.g., Albertus Magnus, *Book of secrets* 1.5; Grimm, 1883–88, 4: 1674; Leyel, 1926: 108–9; Woodward, 1969: 196.

59. Theophrastus, *Enquiry into plants* 9.9.1; Dioscorides, *De materia medica* 4.76.

60. Randolph, 1905: 502; J. R. Harris, 1917b: 359; and Frazer, 1918, 2: 375.

This comes from the lexicon of Hesychius of Alexandria (fl. fifth century A.D.). Hesychius wrote the most complete lexicon known for the ancient Greek language, one that drew on other lexicons going back to the first century B.C.

61. This text was translated into Arabic from a Greek original, now lost, by Ḥunayn ibn Isḥāq, a noted translator (d. A.D. 873).

62. Corbin, 1960: 211–12.

63. Grimm and Grimm, 1981, 1: 344. Such beliefs, found among Germanic peoples and other groups in northern Europe, are unknown in Romania (Eliade, 1972: 224).

64. Ibn el-Beïthar, *Traité des simples* 422 (or 1877–83, 1: 314); R. C. Thompson, 1926: 101; 1949: 217, 218; Post, 1932–33, 2: 261; Levey, 1966: 330; Fleisher and Fleisher, 1994: 245.

65. *Physiologus* 20, trans. in Curley, 1979: 29–32; T. Wright, 1845: 177–78; *An early English version of Hortus Sanitatis,* 1954: 41. For more on this allegory, its origins and symbolism, and a version that differs somewhat in detail from that presented here, see Rahner, 1963: 255–57.

66. For more on the mandrake in novels, poems, and folktales, see Vernaleken, 1859: 253–61; La Fontaine, 1883–97, 5: 22–59; Hertz, 1905: 259–60; Schlosser, 1912; Starck, 1917: 48–57; Schmidt, 1958: 95–121; and Hävernick, 1966.

67. Machiavelli, 1957; Sices and Atkinson, 1985: 15–16. The question has been raised (Gubernatis, 1978, 2: 214) whether Machiavelli knew of "The Woman Drugged with Mandrake," an early Greek comedy by Alexis to be mentioned again later.

68. Thiselton-Dyer, 1898: 101.

69. Friend, 1981: 294.

70. Biswas and Chopra, 1982: 3, citing T. J. Williams.

71. J. R. Harris, 1917b: 374, citing Sibthorp.

72. Eliade, 1972.

73. Unfortunately, mandrakes may also be used in Romania in a negative way, to see that girls are not invited to dances or that girls or women are disliked or unattractive to men.

74. Interestingly, it also induces cows to give more milk.

75. Eliade (1972: 224) notes that, when gathering mandrake leaves, girls lie on top of each other, imitating the sexual act.

76. Eliade, 1972: 206.

77. One also reads of a Persian word, *mihr-gyah,* "herb of love"; and, somewhat surprisingly, of another, *istarang* or *astereng,* which means "mandragora, mandrake. Barren, unfruitful" (Massé, 1954: 215; Löw, 1967, 3: 366; Richardson, 1984: 79).

78. Ploss, 1899, 1: 605; Massé, 1954: 215, 295–96.

79. Dymock et al., 1890–93, 3: 581.

80. Dymock et al., 1890–93, 3: 583; G. Watt, 1889–96, 5: 144, citing Dymock.

81. Nadkarni, 1976, 1: 764.

82. Dymock et al., 1890–93, 2: 581.

83. Jaworskij, 1896: 353, 355.

84. Quicherat, 1841–49, 1: 214; Frazer, 1918, 2: 384.

85. Chéruel, 1899, 2: 726–27; Frazer, 1918, 2: 386–87; Du Cange, 1954, 5: 214; Sébillot, 1968, 3: 487; Grimm and Grimm, 1981, 1: 94.

86. Friend, 1981: 533.

87. Chéruel, 1899, 2: 726; Beyer, 1891: 742; Grimm and Grimm, 1981, 1: 94; Friend, 1981: 294.

88. T. Wright, 1845: 182.

89. Beyer, 1891: 742.

90. Grimm and Grimm, 1981, 1: 94.

91. As noted previously, in Romania the term *mātrāgunā* ("mandragora") is used for plants from quite different genera.

92. Eliade, 1972: 204, 216, 220–21, 224.

93. T. Wright, 1845: 181.

94. di Nino, 1879–91, 1: 86.

95. Lovett, 1913: 121.

96. Hildegard, *Physica* 1.56 [2.102], in Migne, 1882: cols. 1151–52; see also Bonser, 1963: 250–51.

97. This is confirmed in a nineteenth-century study in which a French physician and a second person repeatedly, but at short intervals, smelled the juice pressed from a mandrake plant without the root (it was reported to have a nauseating smell resembling that of reptile's flesh). Their symptoms included running nose, hoarseness, slight cough with expectoration, laborious breathing, shivering, "heaviness and confusion of the head," and weariness of body. The unpleasant symptoms were gone after a night in bed but were followed by a light perspiration. All symptoms had disappeared in from three to eight days, depending on diet and treatment (T. F. Allen, 1964: 150–51, citing Dufresne).

98. Aristotle, *On sleep and waking* 3.456b.28–32; Theophrastus, *Enquiry into plants* 9.1; Dioscorides, *De materia medica* 4.76; Pliny, *Natural history* 25.150; Celsus, *Of medicine* 3.18.12 and 5.25.2, 3B; Macrobius, *Saturnalia* 7.6.7; Basil, *Homilies* 5.4; Randolph, 1905: 509–30.

99. N. Taylor, 1965: 138; C. J. S. Thompson, 1968: 225–26. How mandrake wine was prepared—usually, it seems, from the root—is discussed by Pliny (*Natural history* 25.147–50) and Dioscorides (*De materia medica* 4.76).

100. Philo Judaeus, *On the contemplative life* 45.

101. Apuleius, *Metamorphoses* 10.11.

102. Dioscorides, *De materia medica* 4.76.

103. Pliny, *Natural history* 25.150; Dioscorides, *De materia medica* 4.76. Evidence that some persons can tolerate mandrake is found in Tristram's statement (1873: 467) that, despite its reputation as a soporific, he ate mandrake frequently without feeling at all sleepy. From the perspective of mandrake as a poison, however, the medieval Jewish physician Maimonides (A.D. 1135–1204) observed that some people can suck the root of *Mandragora autumnalis* without ill effect but that its skin and seeds are bad for everyone (Maimonides, *On poisons and their antidotes* 2.4.9).

104. Xenophon, *Banquet* 2.24.

105. Plutarch, *How the young man should study poetry* 1; Randolph, 1905: 510.

106. Lucian, *A true story* 2.33.

107. Demosthenes, *Fourth philippic* 6.

108. Julian, *Epistles* 42.

109. Lucian, *Timon* 2.

110. Plato, *Republic* 6.488.

111. Randolph, 1905: 501; Edmonds, 1957–61, 2: 441. Unfortunately only fragments of the comedy survive, and it is impossible to determine whether the woman was drugged for purposes of seduction or for some other purpose. Even more serious are questions about whether the plant involved was mandrake, for in his translation of Athenaeus's *Deipnosophists* (e.g., Vol. 2, p. 75)—where fragments of Alexis's comedy are presented—Gulick gives the title as "The woman who drank belladonna."

112. Frontinus, *Stratagems* 2.5.12.

113. Polyaenus, *Stratagems of war* 5.10.1; 8.23.1.

114. Dioscorides, *De materia medica* 4.76; Pliny, *Natural history* 25.147.

115. Homer, *Odyssey* 10.210–43.

116. T. Wright, 1845: 179; Murr, 1890: 202; Randolph, 1905: 501–2 n, citing Dierbach; Lehner and Lehner, 1960: 90; Rahner, 1963: 223, 228–29.

In a similar manner, some have sought to identify the plant moly—which was given by Hermes to Odysseus to protect him from bewitchment by Circe—with mandrake. Though many translators simply identify the plant as moly, and go no further in identifying it, Mandelbaum's recent translation of the *Odyssey* (1990) reads, "When that was said, he gave his herb to me; he plucked it from the ground and showed what sort of plant it was. Its root was black; its flower was white as milk. It's *moly* for the gods; for mortal men, the mandrake—very hard to pluck; but nothing holds against the gods." For problems in identifying moly as mandrake, see Lang, 1885: 147–48, 150–55. For some of the ways in which moly has been classified botanically, see Rahner, 1963: 184–90, who favors the view that it was not a real plant, but a mythological one. For moly and mandrake in pagan and Christian symbolism, see Rahner, 1963: 179–277.

117. Randolph, 1905: 513–30.

118. Randolph cites numerous ancient and medieval writers—from Pliny and Dioscorides to Isidore of Seville and Avicenna—as mentioning the use of mandrake in surgery in ancient and medieval times. For an additional reference, for the postmedieval period, see Grindon, 1883: 291, citing Lyte.

119. Isidore of Seville, *Etymologiae* 17.9.30, trans. in Sharpe, 1964: 33 n 241; *Herbarium of Apuleius* 132.2; Ibn el-Beïthar, *Traité des simples* 2300 (or 1877–83, 3: 419–20); W. Turner, 1568, pt. 2: fol. 46; Porta, 1658: 217–18; Hone, 1845: col. 1564; T. Wright, 1845: 181; Grindon, 1883: 291; "The folk-lore of Drayton," 1884–85, 2: 361; "Mandrake," 1893–96; Hazlitt, 1905, 2: 386; Randolph, 1905: 512, 515–22; Budge, 1913, 2: 713; Leyel, 1926: 144–45; Coles, 1938: 72; T. F. Allen, 1964: 151; Grover, 1965: 100; Levey, 1966: 330; de Vigo, 1968: fol. 193; C. J. S. Thompson, 1968: 119–20, 187–97, 204, 207, 209, 210, 213, 217, 226–28; Woodward, 1969: 196; Rubin, 1974: 137 and 198, citing Bartolomeus Anglicus; Arano, 1976: color plate XX and black and white plate 187; Parkinson, 1976: 378–79.

120. Randolph, 1905: 512, 515–22, 524.

121. Leyel, 1926: 144.

122. See, for example, Aretaeus, *On the causes and symptoms of chronic diseases* 1.6; and Columella, *On agriculture* 10.19.

123. Hippocrates, *Places in man* 39.

124. T. F. Allen, 1964: 150–51, citing B. W. Richardson.

125. E.g., Ibn el-Beïthar, *Traité des simples* 2300 (or 1877–83, 3: 420).

126. Trevelyan, 1909: 92.

127. Thomson, 1911, 2: 380.

128. Goodrich-Freer, 1907: 68.

129. Massé, 1954: 296.

130. Jaworskij, 1896: 353.

131. Eliade, 1972: 204.

132. Eliade, 1972: 210.

133. Eliade, 1972: 215.

134. The *baaras* root, which, in the minds of some scholars, may have been a mandrake, was also thought to have the ability to drive demons out of patients quickly (Josephus, *Jewish war* 7.6.3).

135. Graves and Patai, 1966: 220.

136. *Herbarium of Apuleius* 132.5, 7.

137. Levey, 1966: 279, 330.

138. Ibn el-Beïthar, *Traité des simples* 1177 (or 1877–83, 2: 246–47).

139. Starr, 1901: 265.

140. Theophrastus, *Enquiry into plants* 9.9.1; Hippocrates, *Diseases II* 43; Hippocrates, *Places in man* 39; Hippocrates, *Fistulas* 9; Hippocrates, *Diseases of women* 1.74, 80 and 2.199; Dioscorides, *De materia medica* 4.76; Pliny, *Natural history*

25.147–150; Maimonides, *On poisons and their antidotes* 1.3.1, 13; *Herbarium of Apuleius* 132.2–4, 6; Ibn el-Beïthar, *Traité des simples* 1177, 2300 (or 1877–83, 2: 246–47; 3: 419–20); Randolph, 1905: 507–8; Kilmer, 1932: 80; Levey, 1966: 279, 330.

141. Eliade, 1972: 204, 206–7, 209, 211, 213, 219, 224, 225.

142. Hildegard, *Physica* 1.56. See also Frazer, 1918, 2: 378; and Rahner, 1963: 254, 261.

143. Lehner and Lehner, 1960: 90.

144. Bacon, *Natural history*, Century 7.616; "Some notes about mandrakes," 1891: 61; Thiselton-Dyer, 1898: 101; Trevelyan, 1909: 92, 93; Frazer, 1918, 2: 383; Coles, 1938: 72; Lehner and Lehner, 1960: 90; Friend, 1981: 293.

145. Maimonides, *Guide for the perplexed* 29.

146. Haupt, 1862–63, 1: par. 66.

147. Quicherat, 1841–49, 1: 213–14; Frazer, 1918, 2: 383–84.

148. Skinner, 1911: 169.

149. Friend, 1981: 532.

150. "Some notes about mandrakes," 1891: 60.

151. Frazer, 1918, 2: 386.

152. J. R. Harris, 1917a: 139–40; Rahner, 1963: 247–77.

153. One wonders whether this may be done to protect against the mandrake, as seems to be the case in Wales, where, by folk tradition, a digger makes the sign of the cross three times before digging around a mandrake (bryony) (Trevelyan, 1909: 93).

154. Eliade, 1972: 208–9, 212, 214, 216.

155. Theophrastus, *Enquiry into plants* 9.8.5–8.

156. Randolph, 1905: 489–99.

157. Three is a magic number, and the making of three circles with a sword is specified for other plants as well, for example, gladwyn (Theophrastus, *Enquiry into plants* 9.7) and Pisidian iris.

158. Theophrastus, *Enquiry into plants* 9.8.8.

159. Eliade, 1972.

160. Randolph, 1905: 490.

161. As Randolph has observed (Randolph, 1905: 490), Pliny may have left out such material because, as he had stated not long before (Pliny, *Natural history* 25.25), he had no confidence in aphrodisiacs "or any other unholy magic," and, since he had already denounced such practices, he intended to say nothing further about them except, as needed, in warning and condemnation.

162. Pliny, *Natural history* 25.148.

163. Colley March, 1901: 341; Delatte, 1938: 78–79; Bonser, 1963: 322, 331. For more on the practice and meaning of making magic circles around plants

(with iron, gold, silver, ivory, or other things) before collecting them, see Delatte, 1938: 68–79.

164. There is a widespread conviction in the Old World that iron and steel are associated with underworld forces. To work iron, a blacksmith needs the assistance of such forces. Thus in modern Ethiopia, blacksmiths are feared as sorcerers and associates of evil spirits, and are thought to use magic in order to shape iron (Simoons, 1960: 180–81). In nineteenth-century Ethiopia, there was a belief that, if a Christian emblem or bit of scripture were present when a blacksmith was seeking to work iron, it would neutralize the power of the god of metalworking to transform the metal (W. C. Harris, 1844, 2: 295). Iron's association with underworld forces was likely behind Jehovah's insistence that, in building him an altar, the Hebrews employ no cut stone, lest, by using tools, the altar become polluted (Exodus 20.25). It may also have been behind the fact that no iron tools were used in constructing Solomon's temple in Jerusalem (1 Kings 6.7). Such thinking may also have been responsible for the general practice of excluding iron from sanctuaries in ancient Greece and for the requirements that the chief magistrate of the city of Plataea never touch iron and that, with one exception, he wear white clothing (Plutarch, *Aristides* 21; Frazer, 1935, 3: 226–27). It may also account for the reluctance of the ancient Romans to use iron in association with religion or religious personages, as illustrated by the tradition of cutting the hair of priests with bronze, rather than iron, implements (Frazer, pp. 48–50, 94–95, in Vol. 4 of his trans. of Ovid, *Fasti;* Frazer, 1935, 3: 226).

Iron and steel are also believed to protect humans against evil forces, as in modern Italy, where iron in any form, but especially a horseshoe, is considered effective against a person who gives the evil eye to others (Pitre, 1981: 134–35). There are also widespread folktales in Europe in which iron repels fairies and elves and renders them impotent. It is as if they are creatures of the Paleolithic and that iron, a new metal, is abhorrent and damaging to them (Tylor, 1958: 140). The view that fairies dislike iron is reported in the Scottish Highlands (Frazer, 1935, 3: 229). Certain Germanic peoples, on their part, sought to prevent elves from substituting another child for a newborn infant by placing in its cradle a key, steel, and needles, or a piece of the father's clothing (Grimm, 1883–88, 2: 468–69). A seventeenth-century Danish mother included steel in one form or another among the amulets placed over a door or in the crib of her newborn infant to protect it from the evil eye (Brand, 1893–95, 2: 73). The practice of mounting iron horseshoes over stable doors in contemporary England represents a survival of such beliefs (Tylor, 1958: 140).

In the Near East, evil spirits are in such dread of iron that its very name is considered protection against them (Tylor, 1958: 140). In modern Morocco, it is widely believed that not only do such spirits fear iron, but that they fear steel, especially steel weapons, even more. Thus, swords, daggers, and needles are commonly used at weddings for protection against earth spirits. People may wear a steel ring, or carry a horse nail to protect themselves, or use objects made of steel to protect the grain being threshed (Westermarck, 1920: 53–54; 1973: 8, 9). For more on such views of iron in medieval England, see Bonser, 1963: 229, and Rubin, 1974: 78–79, 117; and around the world, Frazer, 1935, 3: 225–36.

165. Neither Theophrastus nor Pliny specified a time suited for gathering mandrake, though they did note propitious times for gathering other plants. Both, for example, reported the opinion that a peony should be uprooted at night lest a woodpecker, sacred to Mars, observe the act and defend the peony by attacking the eyes of the person uprooting the plant (Theophrastus, *Enquiry into plants* 9.6; Pliny, *Natural history* 25.29).

166. Jaworskij, 1896: 353–54; Beyer, 1891: 744; Starr, 1901: 265; Grimm and Grimm, 1981, 1: 93–94.

167. Don, 1831–38, 4: 455; Grimm, 1883–88, 3: 1202; Beyer, 1891: 744; Randolph, 1905: 495–96; Trevelyan, 1909: 93; J. R. Harris, 1917b: 357, 372; Jacob, 1965: 58–59; Grimm and Grimm, 1981, 1: 93, 344 n. For representations of gallows or other execution scenes in connection with mandrake, see Boullet, 1960: 12–13.

168. Starr, 1901: 261–62.

169. Apollonius Rhodius, *Argonautica* 3.843–68.

170. Randolph, 1905: 495–96; see also R. J. Clark, 1968.

171. At the eastern edge of the distribution of Indo-European languages in Eurasia, Crooke (1896a, 1: 226) reports that a hangman in Bombay was noticed as being unusually careful with the rope that was used in hanging a criminal, especially the section of rope that circled the neck. This, the hangman said, was because he could sell every bit of such a rope to people who thought that it turned away ghosts and evil spirits and likewise precluded death from hanging. Crooke also notes that infertile women in India may seek to end that condition by bathing beneath a person who has been hanged or by obtaining a piece of the gallows wood for the same purpose.

172. Talley, 1974: 162–68.

173. At the end of the sixteenth century, Gerard noted the "ridiculous tale," apparently current in England, that mandrake is seldom, if ever, found growing naturally except under a gallows (Woodward, 1969: 195).

174. Trevelyan, 1909: 92, 93.

175. For an excellent review of the meaning of ancient Greek and Roman superstitions and rituals linked with crossroads, especially those associated with Hecate, see Johnston, 1991. The burying of dead persons and the making of offerings and carrying out of rites at crossroads in connection with demons and underworld deities have also been reported in many other lands (J. M. Campbell,

1894–1901, 27: 105–6; Westermarck, 1906–8, 2: 256 n 2; Gonda, 1980: 238–39, 259).

176. As late as the 1930s in England, Money-Kyrle was told by an old lady that her husband, who had refused to listen to warnings, had dug up a mandrake and died a little while later (Money-Kyrle, 1934).

177. Rahner, 1963: 235–39.

178. T. Wright, 1845: 178–79; Tristram, 1873: 467; Grimm, 1883–88, 3: 1202, 1203–4; Dymock et al., 1890–93, 2: 582, 583; Beyer, 1891: 744; Starr, 1901: 265; Trevelyan, 1909: 93; J. R. Harris, 1917b: 356, 366; Frazer, 1918, 2: 381, 387–91; Boullet, 1960: 19–20; Bonser, 1963: 330–31; Woodward, 1969: 195; Grimm and Grimm, 1981, 1: 93–94.

There is a later Jewish version of the tale of Jacob and the mandrakes that has a donkey, by accident, pull a mandrake free of the earth and then die, a version that Frazer suspects may have been known to and suppressed by the writer of Genesis or his editor (Ginzberg, 1909–38, 5: 298–99 n 189; Frazer, 1918, 2: 393).

179. Dymock et al., 1890–93, 2: 583; Veth, 1894: 200; Starr, 1901: 261; Löw, 1967, 3: 366, citing Wetzstein. This tale had found its way to China by medieval times when Čou Mi reported the practice among Moslems far to the west, and indeed the name he used for mandrake, *ya-pu-lu,* is quite close to the Arabic *yabrūh* and Persian *jabrūh* (Minakata, 1896: 344; Laufer, 1917: 1–4; 1919: 447 n, 585).

180. Bonser, 1963: 330; Singer, 1975: 61–62.

181. Though several similarities have been noted between beliefs surrounding the mandrake and those associated with Medea's plant, the "the herb of Prometheus," in the *Argonautica* of Apollonius Rhodius, Apollonius said nothing about a dog pulling up the plant (R. J. Clark, 1968).

182. Josephus, *Jewish war* 7.6.3.

183. Randolph, 1905: 491 and n, citing Langkavel; Ginzberg, 1909–38, 5: 297–98 n 189; J. R. Harris, 1917b: 365; Frazer, 1918, 2: 390–93; Moldenke and Moldenke, 1952: 137, 138; Bonser, 1963: 331–32; Rahner, 1963: 239–42; Hartland, 1971: 46; Friend, 1981: 291.

Early in this century, Skinner (1911: 215) wrote that it was still the practice of parents in Sussex "to put strings of beads carved from peony roots about the necks of their children," in part to keep away illness and evil spirits.

184. Aelian, *On the characteristics of animals* 14.27.

185. Dioscorides, *De materia medica* 3.157; Randolph, 1905: 491 n, citing Langkavel; Frazer, 1918, 2: 389; W. H. S. Jones, Vol. 7, p. 113 n in the trans. of Pliny's *Natural history* by H. Rackham and others. For a contrary view, see Rahner, 1963: 242–46.

186. Budge, 1913, 2: 708–10. Bonser has said that clearly the *kahīnā* was the mandrake (Bonser, 1963: 331–33), though Budge does not make such a claim.

187. For more on the ancient use of dogs in pulling up plants and the reasons for the practice, see Delatte, 1936: 110–14. Though tales of a dog pulling up mandrake came to be widespread in both Europe and the Near East, they are not found in modern Romania, where "mandrakes" are still collected (Eliade, 1972: 224).

188. *Herbarium of Apuleius* 132.1; Don, 1831–38, 4: 455; T. Wright, 1845: 179–80; Payne, 1904: 73; Hazlitt, 1905, 2: 385; Trevelyan, 1909: 93; J. R. Harris, 1917b: 366; Woodward, 1969: 195; Grimm and Grimm, 1981, 1: 93–94.

189. For medieval and premodern representations of a dog pulling up mandrake or tied to it, see T. Wright, 1845: 179; Payne, 1904: figs. 3, 5–6; J. R. Harris, 1917b: following p. 358; Schmidt, 1958: following p. 68; Boullet, 1960: 10, 15–17, 20–21; and Singer, 1975: 71. The role of the dog in mandrake collecting is described well in the Anglo-Norman bestiary of Philip de Thaun (twelfth century):

> The man who is to gather it must dig round about it,
> Must take great care that he does not touch it;
> Then let him take a dog bound, let it be tied to it,
> Which has been close shut up, and fasted three days,
> And let it be shewn bread, and called from afar;
> The dog will draw it to him, the root will break,
> And will send forth a cry, the dog will fall down dead
> At the cry which he will hear; such virtue this plant has,
> That no one can hear it, but he must always die.
> And if the man heard it, he would immediately die:
> Therefore he must stop his ears, and take care
> That he hear not the cry, lest he die,
> As the dog will do which shall hear the cry.
>   (Philip de Thaun, trans. in T. Wright, 1845: 180)

190. di Nino, 1879–91, 1: 86–87; Gubernatis, 1978, 2: 215 n.

191. Ascherson, 1891a: 732 n, quoting von Heldreich.

192. J. R. Harris, 1917b: 366.

193. Grimm and Grimm, 1981, 1: 93–94.

194. Hartland, 1894–96, 1: 154–55, citing von Wlislocki.

195. Josephus, *Jewish war* 7.6.3.

196. Moore, 1895: 452.

197. Idrisi, cited by Ibn el-Beïthar, *Traité des simples* 1177 (or 1877–83, 2: 247–48); Idrisi, cited by Ibn el-Beïthar in Sontheimer, 1840–42, 2: 16–17; Herbelot, 1777–79, 1: 275; Frazer, 1918, 2: 390; Richardson, 1984: 79.

198. Delatte, 1936: 111–12.

199. For more on luminous plants, including mandrake, see Bonser, 1963: 327–28.

200. Jaworskij, 1896: 354.

201. In collecting mandrake in Romania, the plant may be offered wine or sprinkled with wine. In a similar vein, a newly gathered mandrake may be washed in wine (Eliade, 1972: 206, 216, 221, 224).

202. Grimm, 1883–88, 3: 1203; 4: 1674; Chéruel, 1899, 2: 726; Du Cange, 1954, 5: 214; Sébillot, 1968, 3: 487; Grimm and Grimm, 1981, 1: 94, 344.

203. Beyer, 1891: 740.

204. Starr, 1901: 262, 264.

205. Elton, 1882: 220 n 1; Beyer, 1891: 741–42; and Banks, 1932; all citing J. G. Keysler.

206. Friend, 1981: 533.

207. Elton, 1882: 219–20, 221; Grimm, 1883–88, 3: 1203; Beyer, 1891: 742; Grimm and Grimm, 1981, 1: 94.

208. Ascherson, 1891b; Veth, 1894; Löw, 1967, 3: 366.

209. The Semites are believed to have been intermediaries, the first to receive these ideas from Iran.

210. Herbelot, 1777–79, 1: 275; Ascherson, 1891b; Veth, 1894; C. J. S. Thompson, 1968: 20–21; Richardson, 1984: 79.

211. Starr, 1901: 261; Randolph, 1905: 498; Starck, 1917: 38, 65, 72–79.

212. Randolph, 1905: 489–500.

213. For the possible origins of this word, see Besnehard; 1993: 127–28. France has had an unusual range of spellings in names for mandrake. In the twelfth and thirteenth centuries, the French names given for mandrake are *mandragore*, still in use today, and *mandegloire* (Littré, 1863–72, 3: 416–17; Robert, 1953–64, 4: 410; Bloch and Wartburg, 1960: 382). In the fourteenth century, an earlier name was modified, in popular usage, to *main-de-gloire*, "hand of glory" (Talley, 1974: 160, citing Hoffman-Krayer and Bächtold-Stäubli). Among the other spellings used regionally and/or in the past are *mandagoire, mandeglore, mandraglore, madagloire,* and *mandragloire*.

214. Talley, 1974.

215. Talley, 1974: 157; Grimm, 1883–88, 1: 404; 3: 1201; Grimm and Grimm, 1981, 2: 15, 245–46.

216. Tacitus, *A treatise on the situation, manners, and inhabitants of Germany* 8.

217. Grimm, 1883–88, 1: 95, 404–5; 3: 1202. For a note on linguistic problems with deriving *alraun* or *alrūna*, "mandrake," from *Alirūna*, see Donald Ward's commentary in Grimm and Grimm, 1981, 2: 246.

218. In Welsh folk tradition, witches sell bits of mandrake to persons who want to learn secrets (Trevelyan, 1909: 93).

219. Grimm and Grimm, 1981, 1: 94.

220. Grimm, 1883–88, 3: 1204, citing H. Jörgel.

221. Eliade, 1972.

222. However, two other species of its genus, *Mandragora caulescens* and *Mandragora chinghaiensis*, are found in western or southwestern China (Lu An-ming, 1986: 81–82).

223. M.-W. Hong, 1978: 35; Hou, 1978: 44.

224. Tachard, 1981: 271.

225. Willoughby-Meade, 1929: 272; S. Y. Hu, 1976: 11.

226. For references to the use of ginseng as an aphrodisiac or in treating impotence in East Asia and other lands, see Collyer, 1903: 29; S. Y. Hu, 1976: 23; Keys, 1976: 86; Siegel, 1979: 1614, 1615; Perry, 1980: 43; and Carlson, 1986: 245, 246.

227. Ginseng's ability to communicate is demonstrated in a Chinese tale that, during the Sui dynasty (A.D. 581–618), householders living in the ginseng area of northwest China heard a man calling out during the night somewhere behind their residence. They could find no man who made the calls, but, finally, nearly a mile away, they discovered a remarkable ginseng plant. On digging, it turned out to have a man-shaped root five feet long, and, for that reason, was called spirit of the ground (Willoughby-Meade, 1929: 272; F. P. Smith, 1969: 301–2).

228. For a discussion of similarities and differences, see Laufer, 1917: 18–21.

229. Early in this century it was said that, when ginseng gatherers in Manchuria discovered ginseng in a mountain forest, the plant was dug up carefully, and with an eye out for panthers and tigers, who were also believed to seek ginseng and were likely to attack a person who had some. More than anything else, however, gatherers were afraid of the tiny red-eyed demon who was said to protect ginseng and might destroy a gatherer's eyesight or drink his blood (Ossendowski, 1924: 118–20). For a month before seeking ginseng, some gatherers would abstain from sexual intercourse, strong alcohol, and meat in an effort to assure their purity and the success of their venture. In addition, prior to departing, a gatherer would bathe in cold water and make offerings to the deities. When he found a ginseng plant, moreover, he feared that it might disappear because of his unworthiness. For this reason, while keeping the plant in sight, he prostrated himself before it while saying aloud, "Don't flee. I am a pure man, my soul is free from having been soiled, my heart is open and free of any bad intentions" (Symons, 1981: 7).

230. Anderson and Anderson, 1977: 369; Anderson, 1988: 192–93.

231. One exception is ginseng abuse syndrome, for which see Siegel, 1979.

232. Bretschneider, 1882–95, 3: 18–25; Baranov, 1966: 403; S.-K. Hong, 1982: 429; Duke, 1989: 27.

233. M.-W. Hong, 1978: 19.

234. Ainslie, 1826, 1: 154–55; Dymock et al., 1890–93, 2: 163.

235. Minakata, 1896: 344; Laufer, 1917: 1–7, 21; 1919: 447.

236. Minakata, 1896: 343; Laufer, 1917: 21.

237. The shang-luh is reputed to light up when *ignis fatuus* ("foolish fire") clusters about it as it is ready to gain the ability to speak (Minakata, 1896: 343). Ignis fatuus is a phosphorescent light observed hovering above the ground, mainly over marshes, and is popularly called jack-a-lantern or will-o'-the wisp.

238. Minakata, 1894–95, 1896.

239. In the materia medica of India, narcotic, sedative, and anesthetic uses of mandrake are prominent, with the plant viewed as similar to belladonna in its action, but weaker (Chopra et al., 1969: 64; Nadkarni, 1976, 1: 764; *The useful plants of India,* 1986: 353).

240. Ainslie, 1826, 1: 206–8; G. Watt, 1889–96, 5: 143–44; Khory and Katrak, 1981: 478–79.

241. I refer here to *Panax pseudo-ginseng,* which is indigenous, among other places, to the Himalayas of Nepal, Sikkim, Bhutan, and northeastern India (Hooker, 1872–97, 2: 721; Hara, 1970, 1971: 90–91).

242. Biswas and Chopra, 1982: 3.

243. S. M. Gupta, 1971: 83–84.

244. "The folk-lore of Drayton," 1884–85, 2: 361.

245. Kilmer, 1932: 81; Langdon-Brown, 1941: 36.

246. "Mandragore," 1816–19: 175; Rhind, 1840: 552.

247. N. Taylor, 1965: 147.

248. Kilmer, 1932: 81. For modern uses of "mandrake" in folk-medicine in Romania, see Eliade, 1972: 217–18, 219, 220.

249. C. J. S. Thompson, 1968: 237–45; Grover, 1965: 100.

Chapter 5. A Question of Odor? Garlic and Its Relatives as Impure Foods in the Area from Europe to China

1. Though some may be tempted to classify raw garlic and onions, like bitter substances (for example, coffee) and perhaps ones that are very acid (sour) or irritating, as "innately unpalatable substances," continued dietary exposure leads many people to like them (Rozin and Vollmecke, 1986: 436, 445–46). Indeed, sometimes such substances become essential flavorings in a cuisine. For the way in which the initial perception of the chili pepper (*Capsicum* spp.) as an irritant may change to that of a favored flavoring, see Rozin and Schiller, 1980; Rozin, 1982: 236–40; Rozin et al., 1982; Lawless et al., 1985; Rozin, 1990.

2. For which, see Watanabe, 1974; Dausch and Nixon, 1990; Biedermann, 1995; and Resch and Ernst, 1995. Of special interest in recent decades are studies that suggest that garlic and/or other alliums have an antitumor effect (Niukian et al., 1987; Knasmüller et al., 1989; Nishino et al., 1989; You et al., 1989; Zhang et

al., 1989; Dorant et al., 1996) as well as promise in fighting cardiovascular disease (Lau et al., 1983; Ernst, 1987; Kendler, 1987; Ali and Thomson, 1995; Orekhov et al., 1995).

3. Angyal, 1941.

4. For recent perspectives on disgust and food, see Rozin and Fallon, 1987; and Rozin et al., 1993.

5. Angyal (1941: 396) recognized that a degree of disgust may develop when it is pointed out that milk and eggs derive from the body of an animal, but he failed to mention the fact that animal milk and dairy products have been considered disgusting in many human cultures around the world (Simoons, 1954, 1970) and that for some groups, especially in Africa, chicken eggs (sometimes also chicken flesh) are objects of disgust (Simoons, 1994: 144–67).

6. Meigs, 1978: 305.

7. For an excellent account of the Hindu pollution concept, including the links between human emissions and ritual pollution, see H. N. C. Stevenson, 1954.

8. Dubois, 1906: 188.

9. A Hindu of good caste, or food being cooked for him, may become polluted merely by the shadow of or a glance from an impure person (Ketkar, 1909: 6; Thurston, 1912: 109; H. N. C. Stevenson, 1954: 51; Hutton, 1963: 72).

Odor has been a matter of concern in India since antiquity. In ancient times, it was believed that good or evil could be passed on through smelling substances or, when they were burned in a fire, by inhaling their smoke. Smoke could be polluting, as in the case mentioned in my text sentence, but generally it was purifying, as in fumigating a newborn infant with the smoke of mustard seed and small grains to protect it from the demons of epilepsy (Gonda, 1980: 82, 139–40, 259, 281, 409).

In modern Gujarat, a father may remove evil influences from his infant son by ceremonially smelling its head. A father may also smell his son's head when the latter returns home for the first time after he has married or if the son returns after becoming famous in some way or after a victory in war (M. Stevenson, 1920: 132–33 n).

10. A related belief, found in Irish myths, is that the breath of elves is capable of bringing on illness and death in humans and animals (Grimm, 1883–88, 2: 460–61).

11. van der Toorn, 1985: 34.

12. Herodotus, *History* 1.183.

13. Exodus 30.1–9.

14. Farbridge, 1970: 267.

15. Psalms 141.1–2.

16. Berakoth 43a, b, trans. in Simon, 1984.

17. Crooke, 1896a, 2: 21.

18. van der Toorn, 1985: 34.

19. Kethuboth 75a, trans. in Daiches and Slotki, 1936, 4: 470.

20. Choksy, 1986: 180–81.

21. Darmesteter and Mills, 1880–87, 4: 214 n 3.

22. Darmesteter and Mills, 1880–87, 4: xciv and n 7, 214 n 3. The Barashnūm rite (described or discussed in the *Vendidad* 9.1–57, trans. in Darmesteter and Mills, 1880–87, 4: 119–33; *Pahlavi Vendidad* 9.1–145, trans. in E. W. West, 1880–97, 18: 431–54; and the *Sad-Dar* 36.1–10, trans. in E. W. West, 1880–97, 24: 296–98) served in the purification of living persons who had been badly defiled. Originally it was performed to remove defilement brought on by contact with the dead. Later, it also came to be performed to remove pollution brought on by other causes, without contact with a corpse (Darmesteter and Mills, 1880–87, 4: xciv and n 7, 119; E. W. West, 1880–97, 18: 431).

23. *Avesta, Yasht* 22.1–36, trans. in Darmesteter and Mills, 1880–87, 23: 314–21 and 319–20 n.

24. Sokolov, 1975.

25. Mennell, 1985: 301.

26. *Measure for measure* 3.2; *Coriolanus* 4.6; *First part of Henry the Fourth* 3.1.

27. Sokolov, 1975: 70.

28. Ancient Greeks' consideration of garlicky breath as unpleasant is shown by the liberal use of garlic by women during the Skira festival so that they might be as repulsive to their men as possible (Burkert, 1983: 145, 170, 193).

29. Rosin et al., 1992.

30. Horace, *Epodes* 3.8.

31. Grieve, 1931, 1: 342; Moldenke and Moldenke, 1952: 32.

32. Bower Manuscript, 1.10–12, trans. in Hoernle, 1893–1912: 11 and n. For references to other early Indian accounts dealing with the origin and nature of garlic, see Hoernle, 1893–1912: 11 n 6.

33. B. Walker, 1968, 2: 264, 344.

34. The onion, for example, serves in fortune-telling in Bohemia (Friend, 1981: 277). For notes on divination with onions or garlic in Britain, see Brand, 1893–95, 3: 356–57; Hazlitt, 1905, 2: 464–65; and Whitlock, 1979: 81.

35. According to Crooke (1896a, 2: 21), writing of modern northern India, bad odors not only drive off evil spirits but also may be used to tell whether evil remains in a person or has come out. Thus, one can determine whether an ill child remains under an evil influence by means of the odor given off after passing around its head and burning a mixture of bran, ground chili peppers, mustard, and sometimes the child's eyelashes. If the odor is very bad, it indicates that the evil influence is no longer in the child. A similar procedure, involving the burning of chili peppers, nail and hair clippings, and other things to determine whether

an evil spirit has been expelled from the body of a child, is reported in southern India (Thurston, 1912: 115–16).

The view that evil spirits are sensitive to the odor of garlic and onions is not limited to Hindus in India. For example, the Sema Naga, a tribal group of the Naga Hills, believe that the *teghāmi,* spirits of the earth who are closely tied to humans and are usually malevolent, are repelled by strong or unpleasant odors such as those of garlic, ginger, and lemon grass (Hutton, 1968: 199 and n). In a similar vein, the Lhota Naga may keep a small onion or a cowrie shell on their persons for protection against evil spirits. Ginger is regarded as especially effective in this way (Mills, 1922: 27, 34, 132, 169).

36. Oberhelman, 1991: 190.

37. Hoffner, 1974: 108–9; Burkert, 1985: 76.

38. Ussher, 1960: 154–55; Rusten et al., 1993: 111 n. Bulbous roots of the squill, or "sea onion" (*skilla*), are mentioned repeatedly in ancient Greek accounts as agents of purification that were hung outside doors to ward off evil spirits, toxicity, or infection. The squill is usually identified as *Urginea maritima* or species of the liliaceous genus *Scilla.* The squill in question, however, may have been a different plant, *Ornithogalum pyrenaicum* (Hehn, 1888: 158; Parker, 1983: 231–32; Burkert, 1985: 76). In modern Morocco, certain Arabs use squill, because of its odor, to repel vermin (Westermarck, 1926, 2: 243).

39. Dioscorides, *De materia medica* 4.150–51; Theophrastus, *Enquiry into plants* 9.8.6, 8; Pliny, *Natural history* 25.49–61.

40. Wünsch, 1908–26: 463.

41. Pliny (*Natural history* 2.146; 15.134–35) noted that laurel is the only plant that grows in the ground, or the only one planted by man, that is never struck by lightning.

42. Columella, *On agriculture* 8.5.13; Gubernatis, 1872, 2: 281. Pliny (*Natural history* 10.153–54) noted the practice of protecting eggs against damage from thunder by putting a nail, or some earth from a plowshare, beneath the straw on which the eggs rest. The use of a nail for this purpose is still found in modern Sicily, where the nail is thought to attract and absorb all sorts of noise that might be harmful to the chickens (Gubernatis, 1872, 2: 281).

43. Pitre, 1981: 137.

44. Moor, 1834: 326; Clodd, 1898: 214; Lawson, 1964: 13–14; Hardie, 1981: 111–12.

45. Lawson, 1964: 140.

46. Hardie, 1981: 111.

47. Lawson, 1964: 13. In modern Estonia, there is a superstition that garlic placed unobserved in a child's clothes at its baptism protects it from sorcery. A superstition reported for modern Austria is that, when a child is born, its mother "should take three bites of an onion, be lifted and set down three times on the

stool, draw her thumbs in, and blow three times into each fist" (Grimm, 1883–88, 4: 1807, 1845).

48. Hardie, 1981: 110.

49. Megas, 1963: 54.

50. Megas, 1963: 33–34.

51. Megas, 1963; 120–21.

52. In a similar vein, people in Bologna purchased garlic at the midsummer festival as a charm against poverty during the ensuing year, and considered garlic as symbolic of plenty (Thiselton-Dyer, 1898: 227).

53. Megas, 1963: 116–17, 153–55.

54. Moor, 1834: 326; Clodd, 1898: 214; Murray-Aynsley, 1900: 144; Lawson, 1964: 14; Hardie, 1981: 111–12.

55. Persius, *Satires* 5.186–88.

56. Pliny, *Natural history* 20.50, 52.

57. K. F. Smith, 1908–26: 565–66, 567; Ussher, 1960: 154–55.

58. K. F. Smith, 1908–26: 567.

59. Cockayne, 1864–66, 2: 137, 139.

60. Grimm, 1883–88, 3: 1078.

61. Brand, 1893–95, 2: 73.

62. Chambers, 1967, 1: 720.

63. Harington, 1970: 86.

64. Sokolov, 1975: 70.

65. Pliny, *Natural history* 20.50–57.

66. Leyel, 1926: 40.

67. Friend, 1981: 277.

68. Hehn, 1888: 160.

69. G. Watt, 1889–96, 1: 171; Skinner, 1911: 150; Friend, 1981: 398–99.

70. Friend, 1981: 277.

71. Friend, 1981: 357.

72. Harfouche, 1981: 106 note f, citing M. Gelfand.

73. Murgoci, 1981: 127.

74. Eliade, 1973: 115–16, 118–19, 120; 1976: 78–82.

75. Gubernatis, 1978, 2: 7–8, quoting Piron.

76. Theophrastus, *Characters* 16.14; Ussher, 1960: 154–55.

77. K. F. Smith, 1908–26: 567.

78. For interesting chapters on "disease, bewitchment, and purifiers" and "divine vengeance and disease" in ancient Greece, see Parker, 1983.

79. Friend, 1981: 270, 543; Harfouche, 1981: 103, 104.

80. Flattery and Schwartz, 1989: 90 n 27.

81. Shea and Troyer, 1843, 1: 348; Flattery and Schwartz, 1989: 89 and n.

82. Adams, 1901: 230.

83. Crooke, 1896a, 2: 35.

84. Abbott, 1974: 129.

85. Mahadevan, 1961: 393; Abbott, 1974: 343.

86. Campbell, 1894–1901, 24: 225.

87. Bodde, 1975: 290, 291, 302–3, 306, 311, 392.

88. de Groot, 1964, 1: 32; 6: 1080. In Tibet, too, garlic and onions are thought to protect against evil and may be among the unpleasant-tasting vegetables offered to wrathful deities or used in a rite to triumph over a demon responsible for bringing on sickness and bad luck (de Nebesky-Wojkowitz, 1956: 346, 514–15, 522). Japan, as well, is included among lands where garlic is used in a similar protective manner (Friend, 1981: 270).

89. de Groot, 1964, 6: 1078.

90. Jastrow, 1898: 661; R. C. Thompson, 1949: 52–55; Gelb, 1965: 60, 62; Saggs, 1965: 61; Brothwell and Brothwell, 1969: 108–9; Ellison, 1983: 147; Limet, 1987: 137.

91. R. C. Thompson, 1903–4, 2: xlvii–xlviii; 1949: 53, 54; van der Toorn, 1985: 33–34.

92. Athenaeus, *Deipnosophists* 10.422d; Hehn, 1888: 155; Grieve, 1931, 1: 342.

93. This was true of many personal names, for example, the biblical Nebuchadrezzar or Nebuchadnezzar (= Nabu-kudurri-usur, "O Nabu, protect my boundary stone"), the Babylonian king who destroyed Jerusalem in 586 B.C.

94. van der Toorn, 1985: 34. In Egypt, onions were not offered to Zeus Casius of Pelusium, east of the Nile Delta (Sextus Empiricus, *Outlines of Pyrronhism* 3.224), but in this case, as we shall see, it may have been because the wild onion was sacred to the deity.

95. Babylonian Talmud, Nedarim 31a, trans. in Freedman, 1936: 89.

96. Ammianus Marcellinus, *Chronicle of events* 22.5.5; Feliks, 1971–72b: col. 329.

97. Jerusalem Talmud, Nedarim 6.8, 6.9, trans. in Neusner, 1985: 118, 128; Babylonian Talmud, Nedarim 63b, trans. in Freedman, 1936: 202.

98. Babylonian Talmud, Sanhedrin 11a, trans. in Schachter and Freedman, 1987 (unpaginated).

99. Shea and Troyer, 1901: 358; Wensinck, 1960: 85, 135, 155, 180.

100. *Rājataraṅginī* 1.341–43, trans. in Stein, 1900, 1: 51.

101. *Kullavagga* 5.34.1, trans. in Davids and Oldenberg, 1881–85, 20: 153–54.

102. K. N. Sharma, 1961: 47. For a classification of the deities in a Hindu village and a discussion of their characteristics and roles, see Harper, 1959.

103. Eichinger Ferro-Luzzi, 1977b: 370; 1981: 248.

104. Maspero, 1981: 269.

105. Pliny, *Natural history* 20.56–57.

106. In Athenaeus, *Deipnosophists* 13.569f–570a.

107. Celsus, *Of medicine* 3.20.1–2; 3.27.1D; 4.4.

108. Jerusalem Talmud, Megillah 4.1.75a, trans. in Neusner, 1987: 149.

109. Babylonian Talmud, Baba Kamma 82a, trans. in Kirzner, 1935: 466, 467.

110. G. Watt, 1889–96, 1: 169; B. Walker, 1968, 2: 215; Hasan, 1971: 59, 62, 66; Katona-Apte, 1975: 320; Madan, 1975: 87; Katona-Apte and Apte, 1977: 10–11.

111. Gould-Martin, 1978: 40.

112. Aristophanes, *Knights* 494, 946; Rogers, in his trans. of *Knights,* 71 n, 133 n; Aristophanes, *Acharnians* 161–66; Rogers, in his trans. of *Acharnians,* 30 n.

113. Leach, 1949–50, 1: 441; Lehner and Lehner, 1962: 103.

114. Garlic always seems to be considered "hot" or "very hot" in the hot-cold classification of foods in India. The onion, too, is reported to be hot in most accounts of India (G. Watt, 1889–96, 1: 169; Minturn and Hitchcock, 1966: 74; B. Walker, 1968, 1: 461; Hasan, 1971: 62, 66; R. S. Khare, 1976a; Kakar, 1977: 187; Gopaldas et al., 1983: 7; Pool, 1987: 390), though I have found a few cases in which onions were regarded as cold (Beck, 1969: 567; Babb, 1975: 131). In the Chhattisgarh area, Madhya Pradesh, moreover, onions are considered so cold that people may carry them when the weather is hot to prevent sunstroke (Babb, 1975: 131).

115. Hasan, 1971: 62.

116. For more on dietary concessions made for warrior groups in Hindu India, see Simoons, 1994: 9–10, 330 n.

117. Norman, 1972: 235.

118. Grieve, 1931, 1: 342–43. In Hungary, a jockey may attach a garlic clove to the bit of his horse in the hope that other horses will fall back when they get a whiff of the garlic (Grieve, 1931, 1: 343).

119. Norman, 1972: 235.

120. For notes and references relating to cockfighting in the ancient Mediterranean world, see Goodenough, 1953–68, 8: 62; D. W. Thompson, 1966: 34–36; Taran, 1975: 110; and Lonsdale, 1979: 155; for cockfighting in Great Britain, see Brand, 1893–95, 2: 57–63; in India, Kipling, 1892: 38–40, Thurston, 1906: 569–70, and Rosner, 1955; and in China, Cutter, 1989.

121. Gulick, in his trans. of Athenaeus, *Deipnosophists,* Vol. 6: 79 n; Stadler, 1924: col. 991.

122. D. W. Thompson, 1966: 35.

123. Lonsdale, 1979: 155.

124. D. W. Thompson, 1966: 35.

125. Skinner, 1911: 205; Moldenke and Moldenke, 1952: 32.

126. Lupton, 1612: book 8, no. 79.

127. Similar observations were made by botanist William Coles (Cole) in *Art of simpling,* published initially in A.D. 1656 (Coles, 1938: 112–13). Coles noted

further that, in a garden troubled with moles, if one places garlic, leeks, or onions in their passages, the moles will leap out of the ground. Though this suggests a view that moles, too, may be made lively by alliums, this does not seem to have been Coles's meaning. I say this because his story about moles apparently derives from *The marvels of the world* (par. 57), a medieval source ascribed to Albertus Magnus, and because, in an English edition of that work, one reads: "If thou wilt take a Mole. Put in his hole an Onion, or a Leek or Garlic and she will come soon forth without strength." The account adds that serpents and dogs also avoid garlic or refuse to eat food dipped into garlic. In the sixteenth century, Thomas Hill (in *The profitable arte of gardening*), acknowledging Albertus, suggests further that somehow garlic, onions, and leeks are similarly repulsive to the moles (in the translation of Albertus Magnus [1973: 100 n 57]).

128. Horace, *Epistles* 1.12.21–22; Wilkins, 1937: 168.

129. Keith, 1909: 575–76, 583–84, 601; Rohde, 1925: 342, 345–47, 375, 398 n 50, 406 n 96; Guthrie, 1952: 196–98, 217–18; 1962–81, 2: 249–51; Dodds, 1963: 143–44, 149, 154; Burkert, 1972: 120–26, 133.

130. Bower Manuscript, 1.12, trans. in Hoernle, 1893–1912: 11.

131. Prakash, 1961: 221.

132. "Panjab—red food forbidden—Hindus," 1886. Harper (1964: 155), in discussing foods inappropriate for use by Havik Brahmins in a South Indian village, puts onions and garlic in a separate category from foods that are like meat in color (tomatoes, carrots, radishes, and pumpkins). Others (e.g., Toomey, 1986: 67) explain the rejection of such reddish vegetables by saying that, in their color or name, they suggest blood. Madan (1975: 87) carries the matter further in writing that Brahmins (Pandits) living in villages in southern Kashmir reject as food all vegetables of red color, including tomatoes, carrots, and beets, because they spring "from the blood of slain demons," apparently referring to the story, cited above, of the demon slain by Vishnu. The Pandit rejection of onions and garlic, however, he attributes to other causes.

133. Crooke, 1885: 41; Prakash, 1961: 221.

134. Dubois, 1906: 189; B. Walker, 1968, 2: 264; Hasan, 1971: 59. This resemblance has been noted by other peoples, as well, and may be reflected in their use of words. There is evidence, for example, that the ancient people of Locri, a Greek city in southern Italy, used the word *kephalē*, "head," also in the sense of "onion-head" (Hehn, 1888: 156). A play with the Latin words *caepa* ("onion") and *caput* ("head"), found in Ovid's *Fasti* (3.339–40), implies recognition of a dual similarity, in shape as well as in sound. Hebrew recognition of alliums' resemblance to the human head, in turn, is reflected in the Mishnah by the use of *kaflutin*, "with a head," for the leek bulb (Feliks, 1971–72c).

135. Hehn, 1888: 157–58.

136. Sextus Empiricus, *Outlines of Pyrrhonism* 3.224.

137. J. G. Wilkinson, 1883, 1: 180, 181; 2: 402–3, 515; 3: 350–51, 417–19; Murr, 1890: 178; Budge, 1909: 74, 119, 160, 180, 214, 239; Brothwell and Brothwell, 1969: 108; J. G. Griffiths, 1970: 280–81; Feliks, 1971–72c; Täckholm and Drar, 1973, 3: 93–113; Darby et al., 1977, 2: 656–63, 673–75.

138. Keimer, 1933.

139. Pliny, *Natural history* 19.101.

140. Diodorus Siculus, *Library of history* 1.89.4.

141. Plutarch, *Isis and Osiris* 8.

142. Juvenal, *Satires* 15.9.

143. Lucian, *Zeus rants* 43.

144. Aulus Gellius, *Attic nights* 20.8.7, quoting Plutarch.

145. J. G. Griffiths, 1970: 280.

146. A. B. Cook, 1964–65, 2, pt. 2: 985–87.

147. A. B. Cook, 1964–65, 2, pt. 2: 986.

148. J. G. Griffiths, 1970: 280–81; Täckholm and Drar, 1973, 3: 100–101; Darby et al., 1977, 2: 662.

One explanation Plutarch gave for the Egyptian avoidance of onions—in general and by the people of Pelusium—is that, contrary to all other vegetables, the onion dries up during the waxing of the moon but grows and buds during the waning of the moon (Plutarch, *Isis and Osiris* 8; Aulus Gellius, *Attic nights* 20.8.7, quoting Plutarch).

149. *Āpastamba Dharma-sūtra* 1.5.17.26, trans. in Bühler, 1879–82, 2: 63; *Vāsishtha Dharma-sūtra* 14.33, trans. in Bühler, 1879–82, 14: 73; *Gautama Dharma-sūtra* 17.32, trans. in Bühler, 1879–82, 2: 266; *Laws of Manu* 5.5, 19, trans. in Bühler, 1886: 170, 172; *Institutes of Vishnu* 51.3, trans. in Jolly, 1880: 162; *Yājñavalkya Dharma-sūtra* 1.171, 176, trans. in Vidyârṇava, 1918.

150. *Laws of Manu* 5.5, 19, trans. in Bühler, 1886: 170, 172.

151. *Mahābhārata, Karṇa-parva* 44.17 and *Mahābhārata, Anuśāsana-parva* 91.38, 39, trans. in P. C. Roy, 1919–30, 5: 111; 10: 156.

152. *Yajñavalkya Smriti* 1.171, 176, trans. in Vidyârṇava, 1918.

153. Legge, 1886: 43; H. A. Giles, 1923: 21. More than a millennium later, Father Montserrate observed in Gwalior that Moslems, when they consumed an intoxicating poppy-pod drink, avoided eating, among other things, "meat, garlic, onions or anything of that kind" (Hoyland and Banerjee, 1922: 25). Apparently these Moslems were concerned with possible ill effects, but I wonder whether a survival of ancient Indian beliefs about these foods may also have been involved.

154. Takakusu, 1896: 44–45, 137–38.

155. *Vāyu Purāṇa* 2.16.11b–14, trans. in Tagare, 1987–88, 2: 611; *Vishṇu Purāṇa* 3.16, trans. in Wilson, 1961: 266.

156. *Acaranga-sūtra* 2.1.8.13, trans. in Jacobi, 1884: 110.

157. I say this in part because of a tale in the Jatakas (c. 450 B.C.), an early Buddhist collection of tales, legends, riddles, and puzzles, which reveals widespread use of garlic by Buddhists, with the Buddha objecting only to the greed exhibited by nuns in collecting it (*Jātaka* 1.136, trans. in Cowell, 1969, 1: 292–93). A story in the *Vinaya Piṭaka,* early regulations with respect to Buddhist monastic life, does have the Buddha ban the eating of onions. At the same time, the rule seems to have been a pragmatic one, and nothing in the account suggests that onions or other alliums were viewed as unclean. Indeed, the Buddha is quoted as permitting monks to eat onions for medicinal purposes (*Kullavagga* 5.34.1, 2, trans. in Davids and Oldenberg, 1881–85, 20: 153–54). This agrees with the use of garlic in various formulas in an Indian Buddhist medical treatise, the Bower Manuscript (Bower Manuscript 1.1–43, trans. in Hoernle, 1893–1912: 10–15).

158. Simoons, 1991: 157–58.

159. B. Walker, 1968, 2: 215.

160. Chakravarty, 1959: 42; Chakravarti, 1974: 405.

161. G. Watt, 1889–96, 1: 171.

162. Katona-Apte, 1975: 320–21, 324, 325; Katona-Apte and Apte, 1977: 10–11.

163. B. Walker, 1968, 2: 215; Hasan, 1971: 58–59; Madan, 1975: 87.

164. Chakravarti, 1974: 403.

165. Hasan, 1971: 66.

166. Eichinger Ferro-Luzzi, 1975: 479.

167. Harper, 1964: 155.

168. M. Stevenson, 1920: 241.

169. R. M. Martin, 1838, 1: 121.

170. pers. comm., D. O. Lodrick.

171. Behura, 1962: 132.

172. Eichinger Ferro-Luzzi, 1977b: 370.

173. Basak, 1953: 112.

174. M. Stevenson, 1920: 165–66.

175. As Gonda has noted, the term *Vaishnava* used in its strictest sense refers to adherents of Vishnu, though commonly it embraces worshippers of Rama and Krishna as well. European writers and British administrators, moreover, have tended to use the term quite broadly, with H. A. Rose using it to embrace "any 'orthodox' Hindu who does not eat flesh, onions, or garlics and does not drink spirits." In a similar vein, in Sindh and certain other places, the term *Vaishnav* is synonymous with "a vegetarian" (Gonda, 1970: 171 n 2).

176. Eichinger Ferro-Luzzi, 1978a: 101.

177. K. N. Sharma, 1961: 47; Hasan, 1971: 59–60.

178. Jindel, 1976: 183; Toomey, 1986: 67.

179. Hasan, 1971: 59–60.

180. Jindel, 1976: 183.

181. Dubois, 1906: 698.

182. Paul, 1958: 156.

183. de Groot, 1896: 42; Laufer, 1919: 303.

184. Schafer, 1977: 132.

185. Welch, 1967: 112.

186. Y. Martin, 1984: 218.

187. Stuart, 1911: 28; Welch, 1958: 132; Maspero, 1981: 269.

188. Schram, 1954: 117.

189. Doolittle, 1865, 2: 183; Stuart, 1911: 28.

190. Gould-Martin, 1978: 40.

191. "The state religion of China," 1831–35: 51–52.

192. S. E. Thompson, 1988: 74.

193. Fallon and Rozin, 1983; Rozin, 1984: 594–96; 1988a: 140–41; 1988b: 170–73; Rozin and Vollmecke, 1986: 438–41.

194. Angyal, 1941.

Chapter 6. Ritual Use and Avoidance of the Urd Bean (*Vigna mungo*) in India; With Comparative Data on Certain Related Foods, Flavorings, and Beverages

1. von Schroeder, 1884: 31–39.

2. G. Watt, 1889–96, 6, pt. 4: 234–35.

3. Hanelt, 1972b: 217.

4. I refer to the weeds *Vicia sativa* (common vetch) and *V. tetrasperma*, uncovered at Navdatoli-Maheshwar (mid-second millennium B.C.) (Vishnu-Mittre, 1968: 97; 1974: 25). Common vetch, or a variety of it, is found wild in parts of modern India, too, but, in contrast with the situation in Europe, it is not cultivated as a fodder crop (G. Watt, 1889–96, 6, pt. 4: 235–36; Kachroo and Arif, 1970: 316).

5. Vishnu-Mittre, 1968: 96–97; 1974: 23–25; 1977: 574, 576, 577, 578; Allchin, 1969: 326; Kajale, 1977: 105; Costantini, 1981: 277.

6. de Candolle, 1919: 318; D. Khare et al., 1984: 7.

7. D. Khare et al., 1984: 7.

8. Though urd seed is generally black, there are forms whose seed is brown, olive-green, gray, or mottled (Kachroo and Arif, 1970: 149; Smartt, 1976: 68; Kay, 1979: 378).

9. Translators usually give maśa as a specific bean, known today as *Vigna mungo* (Oldenberg and Müller, 1886–92, 30: 352; Macdonell and Keith, 1912, 2: 156; Prakash, 1961: 264). Some, however, translate it as "maśa bean" or "maśa pulse," and still others, simply as "bean."

10. Zeven and de Wet, 1982: 76; Ignacimuthu and Babu, 1987: 418, 420.

11. Recipes for several tasty urd dishes are included in Valerie Turvey's *Bean feast* (San Francisco: 101 Publications, 1979), my favorite being "Curried urd dal."

12. Douglas, 1966: 41–57; 1972: 71–79; 1973: 60–64; 1975: 261–73, 282–89, 304–9.

13. Soler, 1979.

14. Simoons, 1994: 64–92.

15. Garlic has been considered in the previous chapter, but it is commonly linked with these foods and flavorings. In the Vedic Kalpa-sūtras (ritual texts comprising the Śrauta-, Gṛihya-, and Dharma-sūtras), for example, salt, garlic, onions, leeks, and mushrooms were all banned on certain ritual occasions or to respectable persons (Gopal, 1959: 163). Even the handling of such foods might be restricted. The lawgiver Nārada (A.D. 140–450), for example, wrote that at times of misfortune Brahmins are permitted to gain their livelihood in the manner set down for two of the three castes below them in rank, Kshattriyas and Vaiśyas, but never that of the Śūdras ("vile caste") (*Nāradīya-dharma-śāstra* 1.56–65, trans. in Jolly, 1889: 55–57). Should a Brahmin make his living as a Vaiśya, however, he is subject to certain restrictions on what he might sell, and he must never sell meat, alcoholic beverages, strong seasonings (presumably including garlic and onions), salt, sesame, or animals lacking cloven hoofs.

16. H. N. C. Stevenson, 1954: 48–49.

17. H. N. C. Stevenson, 1954: 46–47.

18. Mathur, 1964: 97.

19. Dumont and Pocock, 1959: 31; Babb, 1970: 293–94.

20. H. N. C. Stevenson, 1954: 50–52.

21. Blunt, 1931: 87–103; H. N. C. Stevenson, 1954: 52–62; Hutton, 1963: 71–78.

22. *Laws of Manu* 5.4, trans. in Bühler, 1886: 170.

23. The leavings of "good" deities, on the other hand, are pure and acceptable for consumption by devotees. For a discussion, from the perspective of North Indian Hindus, of the impurity of human leavings (*juthā*) and excreta (*gū*) as compared with the purity of leavings (*prasāda*) and excreta of supernatural beings, see R. S. Khare, 1976a: 92–110; 1976b: 91–93. For more on juthā and prasāda, see Babb, 1970: 294–99; 1975: 53–61; Eichinger Ferro-Luzzi, 1977b: 357–59; and Katona-Apte and Apte, 1977: 7–9.

24. B. Walker, 1968, 1: 85; Oldenberg, 1988: 224, 248.

25. Oldenberg, 1988: 224.

26. Oldenberg, 1988: 125–26, 134.

27. Bhattacharyya, 1953: 173; Gough, 1955: 64.

28. Jindel, 1976: 186–87.

29. R. S. Khare, 1976b: 170–82.

30. *Bhagavadgītā* 17.7–10, trans. in Radhakrishnan and Moore, 1957: 155; Basak, 1953: 110–11; Eichinger Ferro-Luzzi, 1977c: 544–45.

31. R. S. Khare, 1976a: 81–113.

32. Eichinger Ferro-Luzzi, 1975.

33. R. S. Khare, 1976a: 85.

34. R. S. Khare, 1976a: 83–84 n 2.

35. S. B. Mani, 1981: 202.

36. R. S. Khare, 1976a: 85 n 5.

37. Pool, 1987.

38. D. V. Hart, 1969: 33–34.

39. For development of the concepts of hot and cold, and dry and wet, in Greek philosophy, see Lloyd, 1964.

40. Filliozat, 1964; Venzmer, 1972: 53.

41. Logan, 1977: 90; Manderson, 1987: 329.

42. Eichinger Ferro-Luzzi, 1974: 15.

43. S. B. Mani, 1981: 214.

44. Hutton, 1963: 66; Beck, 1969: 558; Abbott, 1974: 279–80. One reads of similar traditions among the Mandaeans of Iraq and Iran. Their origin was in the north, a highland which is the home of the gods. Its people are light in color. The south, a lowland, has black people whose "appearance is ugly like demons." This is in accord with the Mandaean view, to be mentioned again later, that white is the color of purity, and black, the color of impurity and evil (Drower, 1937: 9, 39, 197, 222).

45. Farbridge, 1908–26: 150.

46. Abbott, 1974: 281–82.

47. Crooke, 1896a, 2: 20; 1908–26b: 444.

48. W. G. Griffiths, 1946: 181. In modern Greece, people may hang pieces of red cloth, or red kerchiefs or red blankets, from their windows during the Easter season, apparently because of the protective power of the color red. In former times in one community of northern Thrace, such cloth was colored red by dipping it in the red dye used to color Easter eggs. The red eggs of Easter, on their part, are blessed in church by one means or another. Such "eggs of the Resurrection" or "eggs of the Good Word" are believed capable of bringing on miracles (Megas, 1963: 95, 107–8).

49. Crooke, 1926: 294–95; Beck, 1969: 558–60.

50. Hutton, 1963: 66; Gonda, 1980: 47.

51. *Gobhila Gṛihya-sūtra* 3.1.17, 23; 3.2.13–14, 30, trans. in Oldenberg and Müller, 1886–92, 30: 70, 71, 73.

52. Gonda, 1969: 209–10.

53. Bussagli, 1987: 564.

54. Abbott, 1974: 276–77.

55. Abbott, 1974: 277–79.

56. Crooke, 1926: 292; Beck, 1969: 559.

57. Marī is a godling of pestilence who has special ties with cholera. Among her other names is Marī Māī, "Mother Death." For more on Marī and other godlings linked to cholera, see Crooke, 1896a, 1: 137–46; 1906: 107; Abbott, 1974: 249. For more on other Hindu disease godlings, see Crooke, 1896a, 1: 123–74; B. Walker, 1968, 1: 399; Kinsley, 1986: 155, 160, 198, 200, 204–5, 208–11.

58. Tod, 1971, 3: 1733–34.

59. M. Stevenson, 1920: 356. Hanumān, as we shall see, was victorious over a representative of Śani (Saturn), the black and cruel planet (M. Stevenson, 1920: 256).

60. In the Indian subcontinent, iron is an impure, inauspicious metal that is avoided in religious ceremonies but may protect people in a broad range of ways (Frazer, 1935, 3: 233–36; Abbott, 1974: 213–30). Iron nails may be offered to spirits and deities living in trees in the hope that this will ward off evil, including illness, death, and loss of livestock and crops (S. M. Gupta, 1971: 9). Iron nails may be driven into the threshold of a house for similar protective purposes (Abbott, 1974: 23). As told by W. G. Griffiths (1946: 182) for the Kol tribe of Central India, iron may be buried in the floor near the entrance of a new house. Though unseen to humans, it is sensed by demons, who, as a result, will not enter the house. Kol women, who are thought particularly subject to evil influences, should always have a bit of iron, such as a ring, bracelet, or anklet, for protection. An iron key, a bit of iron suspended from a string, and even the nails in footwear all help. With this in mind, a Kol should have a bit of iron beneath his head while he sleeps, and he may also drive iron nails into the four corners of his wooden cot. In a similar manner, a Kol bridegroom carries iron to the wedding ceremony, and there is iron in the wedding booth. A sick man, in turn, is well advised because of his weakened state to have iron nearby for protection. For more on iron in Hindu ritual and belief, see especially Abbott, 1974: 213–30.

61. Woodburne, 1981: 56.

62. Crooke, 1896a, 2: 3–4, 28, 29; 1908–26b: 444; 1926: 294; W. G. Griffiths, 1946: 181, 182 (Kol); Beck, 1969: 571 n 4; Abbott, 1974: 277–79.

63. Beck, 1969: 571 n 4.

64. Beck, 1969: 558–59.

65. Vishnu-Mittre, 1977: 578.

66. Burrow, 1948: 390.

67. Macdonell and Keith, 1912, 1: 398; Ray, 1933: 221, 225.

68. Macdonell and Keith, 1912, 1: 182; 2: 156.

69. Yule and Burnell, 1903: 530.

70. B. Walker, 1968: 2: 140.

71. Prakash, 1961: 11, 61.

72. Krishnaswamy, 1974: 9; Eichinger Ferro-Luzzi, 1977c: 548. For protein digestibility (*in vitro*) of urd, which improved significantly with soaking, cooking, autoclaving, and sprouting, see Jood et al., 1989.

73. Crooke, 1896a, 2: 27.

74. Bloomfield, 1897: 536 n 3; Gonda, 1980: 44.

75. M. Stevenson, 1920: 256–57.

76. Saturday is not only tied to Śani but is also a Hindu day of choice for carrying out acts to ward off evil and expel evil spirits. Even to speak the words "born on Saturday" is thought to be sufficient to cure the effects of the evil eye (Abbott, 1974: 274). For more on Śani and Saturday, see Abbott, 1974: 274, 437.

77. Abbott, 1974: 274.

78. Abbott, 1974: 221.

79. Abbott, 1974: 213.

80. M. S. A. Rao, 1986: 137.

81. Abbott, 1974: 383.

82. Crooke, 1896a, 1: 18–23; Thurston, 1912, 42ff.; M. Stevenson, 1920: 351–52; B. Walker, 1968, 2: 272; S. B. Mani, 1981: 213.

83. Crooke, 1896a, 1: 22; S. B. Mani, 1981: 214. Pregnant women in Iran are also believed to be in special danger during solar and lunar eclipses. The danger is that if a pregnant woman touches herself the infant will have a dark spot at the corresponding part of its body, or that if she or someone else touches her abdomen the infant will bear freckles. Because of such concern, a pregnant Persian woman may wear gloves during an eclipse to avoid touching her body (Massé, 1954: 8–9).

84. Oldenberg, 1988: 340 n 135. For more on śrāddha rites and the relationship to dead ancestors, see M. Stevenson, 1920: esp. 156–92; Stutley and Stutley, 1977: 284; B. Walker, 1968, 2: 427–29; and Oldenberg, 1988: 319–33.

85. E.g., *Āpastamba Dharma-sūtra* 2.7.16.23, trans. in Bühler, 1879–82, 2: 141; and *Laws of Manu* 3.266–67, trans. in Bühler, 1886: 124; Gonda, 1980: 120.

86. Crooke, 1926: 294.

87. W. G. Griffiths, 1946: 186.

88. R. S. Khare, 1976a: 179–80, 182–86 passim; 1976b: 173, 175, 176, 211 n 10.

89. M. Stevenson, 1920: 171.

90. Crooke, 1881.

91. Campbell, 1894–1901, 27: 239.

92. *Taittirīya Saṃhitā* 5.1.8.1, trans. in Keith, 1914, 2: 398.

93. Gonda, 1980: 120.

94. *Śatapatha Brāhmaṇa* 1.1.1.8–10, trans. in Eggeling, 1882–1900, 12: 5–6.

95. Prakash, 1961: 12.

96. Oldenberg and Müller, 1886–92, 30: 352.

97. Gonda, 1980: 178, citing the *Gobhila-Smṛti* 1.131; 3.114.

98. In Vedic texts, honey (*madhu,* a word related to the English *mead* but which, especially in earlier Vedic texts, referred to any sweet that served as food or drink) was a magical substance imbued with strengthening, healing, erotic, and fertility powers. It was also associated with underworld forces and was offered in rites for the dead. As a result, honey, like meat and salty or pungent foods, was inappropriate for use on occasions where ritual purity was of special importance (Gonda, 1969: 16; 1980: 107–8, 187, 274–75, 336, 453, 455). Thus one reads of a religious student who, during his period of study, must not eat honey (Oldenberg, 1988: 248). Similar sentiments are found in the Sanskrit writings of Amitagati (eleventh century A.D.), which say that the quality shared by honey, meat, and alcohol is an ability to arouse sexual passion (R. Williams, 1963: 52).

In modern times, honey plays a significant role in ritual. It is one of the five nectars (pañchamṛita) of the Hindus. It is the base for another ritual nectar (*madhuparka*) offered to guests, a bridegroom, a pilgrim, a king, and to saints. It may be taken to a place of worship and then to a field or threshing platform to bless the grain. It is offered to people on the first day of the new year, and it is used for washing images (Abbott, 1974: 313).

Jains have taken a somewhat different view in banning honey because bees are killed in collecting it, which leads to the saying "He who eats honey takes on himself the sin of burning seven villages." In addition, Jains object to honey because it comes "from the vomit or spittle of insects" (R. Williams, 1963: 55).

In terms of present-day thinking about hot-cold foods, one might expect honey, an energy-producing and exciting food, to be "hot," much like raw sugar or jaggery seems to be (Wiser, 1955: 359; Hasan, 1971: 62; Eichinger Ferro-Luzzi, 1975: 477; S. B. Mani, 1981: 200; Pool, 1987: 390). Hotness, however, does not necessarily apply to all types of sugar or sweets (see, for example, Wiser, 1955: 359; Beck, 1969: 568; Eichinger Ferro-Luzzi, 1977c: 539; Kakar, 1977: 194; and Pool, 1987: 390). The evidence I have uncovered on honey, though scanty, indicates that in general it is hot (very hot, a general statement: B. Walker, 1968, 1: 461; very hot in Punjab: Kakar, 1977: 195; hot in Bengal: Jelliffe, 1957: 135; Lindenbaum, 1977: 144; and in Tamil Nadu: Eichinger Ferro-Luzzi, 1975: 475, 477), but cold in its Coimbatore District (Beck, 1969: 569).

99. Gopal, 1959: 166; *Śāṅkhāyana Śrauta-sūtra* 4.1.1–3, trans. in Caland, 1953: 77.

100. Eichinger Ferro-Luzzi, 1977a: 510, 512; 1978a: 103–8 passim.

101. Eichinger Ferro-Luzzi, 1973a: 170; 1977c: 548.

102. Eichinger Ferro-Luzzi, 1977c: 548.

103. Eichinger Ferro-Luzzi, 1977c: 549.

104. Eichinger Ferro-Luzzi, 1977a: 510; 1977c: 548–49.

105. *Charaka Saṃhitā* 27.24, trans. in P. Sharma, 1981: 196; *Suśruta Saṃhitā* 46.15, trans. in Bhishagratna, 1963, 1: 475.

106. Stutley and Stutley, 1977: 184.

107. Bloomfield, 1897: 534; Gonda, 1980: 120, 321.

108. *Āśvalāyana Gṛihya-sūtra* 1.13.2–3, trans. in Oldenberg and Müller, 1886–92, 29: 179–80.

109. Oldenberg and Müller, 1886–92, 29: 179 n 2; see also Gonda, 1980: 215, and Stutley and Stutley, 1977: 184.

110. Eichinger Ferro-Luzzi, 1977c: 548–49.

111. R. S. Khare, 1976a: 180 n, 182–98 passim; 1976b: 198, 211 n 10.

112. Eichinger Ferro-Luzzi, 1977b: 360–61.

113. Rizvi, 1986: 230.

114. See also Lindenbaum, 1977: 145. For more on hot-cold thinking around the world, see the articles included in "Hot-cold food and medical theories: Cross-cultural perspectives," a special issue of *Social Science and Medicine* (Vol. 25, No. 4, 1987) edited by Lenore Manderson. For problems encountered in ethnographic research on the hot-cold theory of disease, see especially Logan, 1977: 94–107; and Manderson, 1987.

115. Eichinger Ferro-Luzzi, 1975: 474.

116. Nichter (1986: 194), however, observes that in South Kanara District, Karnataka, most people associate black not with neutral, but with either hot or cold.

117. I base this on Eichinger Ferro-Luzzi's observations, for Tamil Nadu in general, that urd is thought to be more energy-producing than any other pulse, that this quality would make it hot, and that it may even be likened to meat in that regard. On the other hand, she observes, its blackness would make it neutral or cooling (Eichinger Ferro-Luzzi, 1975: 475; 1977c: 548).

118. O. Lewis, 1958: 286; Kakar, 1977: 33; Gopaldas et al., 1983: 6–7.

119. Beck, 1969: 567.

120. Vavilov, 1949–50: 28, 38; Nayar and Mehra, 1970: 26–29; Nayar, 1976: 232–33; Darby et al., 1977, 2: 497; Mathon, 1981: 51, 79; Zeven and de Wet, 1982: 78, 144–45; Bedigian and Harlan, 1986.

121. Bedigian et al., 1985: 136–37; Bedigian et al., 1986: 354, 362.

122. Vats, 1940, 1: 6; Mehra, 1967: 94; Vishnu-Mittre, 1968: 97; 1974: 25; 1977: 576; Allchin, 1969: 324; Bedigian and Harlan, 1986: 140.

123. Macdonell and Keith, 1912, 1: 182, 312; Mehra, 1967: 94–95.

124. Ray, 1934: 18; Prakash, 1961: 266; Bedigian and Harlan, 1986: 141.

125. *Laws of Manu* 3.210, 223, 234, 267, trans. in Bühler, 1886: 114, 117, 118, 124; *Śāṅkhāyana Gṛihya-sūtra* 4.1.3, trans. in Oldenberg and Müller, 1886–92, 29: 107; Ray, 1933: 227–28; Mehra, 1967: 96, 98; Gonda, 1969: 13–14; Hopkins, 1969: 12, 32, 69; S. M. Gupta, 1971: 97–98; Gonda, 1980: 120–21; Bedigian and

Harlan, 1986: 142; Oldenberg, 1988: 200. For a thorough list of early Indian sources that mention sesame, including references to the continuing use of sesame in śrāddha rites in later times, see Mehra, 1967.

126. Dutt, 1922: 218.

127. *Laws of Manu* 3.266–67, trans. in Bühler, 1886: 124.

128. *Āpastamba Dharma-sūtra* 2.7.16.23, trans. in Bühler, 1879–82, 2: 141.

129. Dymock et al., 1890–93, 3: 26.

130. *Laws of Manu* 4.75, trans. in Bühler, 1886: 141.

131. Dymock et al., 1890–93, 3: 26; Hopkins, 1969: 16–17, 69, 146; S. M. Gupta, 1971: 98; Gonda, 1980: 113, 120–21, 131–32, 182, 256, 266, 267, 272–73, 393, 403–4, 442, 443, 445, 451; Bedigian and Harlan, 1986: 142.

One reads, for example, of a myth in which a man who has no sons makes an offering of cows—or, in lieu of live cows, "cow-cakes" made of sesame—with the wish that his ill luck will change (Hopkins, 1969: 16–17).

For notes on the ritual use of sesame to symbolize "life germinating, life triumphant, and rebirth" among modern Near Eastern peoples, see Drower, 1956: 37, 230, 247.

132. Gonda, 1980: 102.

133. Gonda, 1969: 14.

134. Gonda, 1969: 13, 14 n 12.

135. For sesame in another fertility rite associated with Vishnu, see Gonda, 1969: 259–62.

One wonders whether this is related to the difference between sesame seed and sesame oil in the hot-cold classification of foods. My sources suggest that sesame seed is ordinarily considered hot or very hot in certain places (Tamil Nadu: Eichinger Ferro-Luzzi, 1973b: 264; and S. B. Mani, 1981: 200, 212; Gujarat: Pool, 1987: 390), whereas sesame oil occupies a less clear position. In some cases it has been reported as hot (Punjab: Wiser, 1955: 359; Kerala: Eichinger Ferro-Luzzi, 1975: 476; rural Tamil Nadu: S. B. Mani, 1981: 200); in others, as cold (Coimbatore District, Tamil Nadu: Beck, 1969: 567; Bangladesh: Lindenbaum, 1977: 144); and, in one, as occupying an ambivalent position in the hot-cold scheme (Tamil Nadu: Eichinger Ferro-Luzzi, 1975: 476; 1985b: 495).

136. Eichinger Ferro-Luzzi, 1977c: 551.

137. Crooke, 1896a: 2: 16; Eichinger Ferro-Luzzi, 1977c: 550–51, 555; M. S. A. Rao, 1986: 137.

138. Crooke, 1896a, 2: 16, 156; B. Walker, 1968, 2: 458–59; Ward, 1970, 3: 70–71.

139. Eichinger Ferro-Luzzi, 1977c: 551. Diehl has observed (1956: 159) that, on Śani's day in South India, his vāhana, the crow, with salutations and mantras, should be fed before a person eats.

140. Vultures and crows are tied to the underworld, evil, death, and impurity.

Their scavenging habits are a factor in this. So is their blackness, as shown in the *Atharva-veda:* "What this black bird flying forth towards (me) has dropped here— may the waters protect me from all that misfortune and evil!" and "Whatever the black bird, that has come hither stealthily, has touched of that which has stuck to the rim, or whatever the wet-handed slave girl does pollute—may ye, O waters, purify (that) mortar and pestle!" (*Atharva-veda* 7.64.1; 12.3.13, trans. in Bloomfield, 1897: 167, 186).

Modern Hindus believe crows to be evil spirits, and at funerals they may make offerings to them so that the crows will be inclined favorably to the deceased person. If crows do not accept the offering, it is quite a bad sign for that person (Dubois, 1906: 487). Among the Coorgs of South India, it is believed that, if a crow's droppings fall on someone, he or she must dip in a tank or river for 1,000 times. The Coorgs believe that, if crows perch on a roof and caw, someone within the building will die. A Coorg man who observes two crows mating, it is thought, will die soon afterwards, though he can avoid this by quickly sending his relatives a false message that he has died, which in modern times may involve sending a telegram (Srinivas, 1952: 105–6). For Hindu offerings to Yama, lord of the dead, and to crows and vultures in śrāddha rites at Gaya, see Vidyarthi, 1961: 36, 38. For statements in Vedic and later Hindu mythology about vultures as messengers of Yama; to the king of vultures as the ruler of the underworld; to demons assuming the form of vultures; to crows knowing the secret of hell because they had lived there for eons; to vultures and crows as unlucky, and as blood drinkers who enter the bodies of persons who disobey their gurus, see Macdonell, 1897: 152, 163; B. Walker, 1968, 1: 155; and Hopkins, 1969: 19, 110.

141. Abbott, 1974: 279; Eichinger Ferro-Luzzi, 1977c: 551.

142. M. Stevenson, 1920: 256.

143. Crooke, 1896a, 2: 16.

144. *Taittirīya Saṃhitā* 5.4.3.2, trans. in Keith, 1914, 2: 430.

145. B. Walker, 1968, 2: 313–14.

146. G. Watt, 1889–96, 4, pt. 2: 504–5; Bedigian and Harlan, 1986: 138.

147. Bloomfield, 1897: 536 n 3; Gonda, 1980: 44.

148. Bloomfield, 1897: 536–37; Gonda, 1980: 44.

149. G. Watt, 1889–96, 6, pt. 2: 506; 1908: 982–83, 986. It is suggested that the dominant genotype of sesame involving black seeds and purple plant color evolved in India. The wild Indian sesame (*Sesame orientale* var. *malabaricum*) that some believe to be the progenitor of domesticated sesame also belongs to the purple group of Indian sesames (Bedigian et al., 1986: 359).

150. G. Watt, 1889–96, 6, pt. 2: 506, 507; 1908: 983, 986.

151. *Suśruta Saṃhitā* 46.16, trans. in Bhishagratna, 1963, 1: 476–77.

152. Dutt, 1922: 217–18; Ray, 1933: 238. The above statements need to be weighed against modern evidence. Though this is beyond the scope of my in-

quiry, I would note that Chakraborty et al. (1984: 291, 294–95) found one white-seeded variety of sesame in West Bengal to contain more oil (42 percent) than one black-seeded variety (39 percent), though when no nitrogen fertilizer was applied, oil yields per hectare were higher in the black-seeded variety. The researchers noted further that white-seeded sesame sells for at least 30 percent more than black- or brown-seeded varieties because of its high oil content and culinary utility.

153. Abbott, 1974: 56.

154. M. Stevenson, 1920: 142.

155. *Laws of Manu* 3.234, trans. in Bühler, 1886: 118.

156. G. Watt, 1889–96, 4, pt. 2: 26; Dymock et al., 1890–93, 3: 26; Crooke, 1896a, 2: 28; 1926: 294; M. Stevenson, 1920: 159, 160–61, 172, 173, 184, 185; Underhill, 1921: 64; B. Walker, 1968, 2: 149, 428; Eichinger Ferro-Luzzi, 1973b: 264; Bedigian and Harlan, 1986: 142.

157. Dymock et al., 1890–93, 1: 26–27.

158. Crooke, 1926: 294.

159. Ghosal, 1965: 117; B. Walker, 1968, 1: 405.

160. Crooke, 1896a, 2: 28; 1926: 294; Chaturvedi and Tiwari, 1970: 249.

161. Chaturvedi and Tiwari, 1970: 249.

162. Eichinger Ferro-Luzzi, 1977a: 510.

163. S. B. Mani, 1981: 200–201.

164. Eichinger Ferro-Luzzi, 1975: 479. Though sesame seed, which is considered very hot, is thought to have a favorable effect on a woman's fertility, it is also believed to induce menstruation. For this reason, women in Tamil Nadu avoid it during pregnancy because of fear of abortion, or, if an abortion is desired, they may consume it (Eichinger Ferro-Luzzi, 1973b: 264, 266; S. B. Mani, 1981: 200, 211). It is interesting that in Tamil Nadu another common emmenagogue is also dark in color: "a paste of black cumin seeds and unrefined jaggery (usually dark brown in color)" (S. B. Mani, 1981: 200). In a similar vein, among the Bhat community of India sesame is included in a mixture believed to be a powerful sterilizer, an aid in regulating human fertility (Lal and Lata, 1980: 274).

165. Eichinger Ferro-Luzzi, 1973b: 264.

166. M. Stevenson, 1920: 161 n 183. An exception to this is the offering of sesame seeds to Yama, lord of the dead, as in rites for the ancestors at Gaya (Vidyarthi, 1961: 36).

167. Eichinger Ferro-Luzzi, 1973b: 264.

168. Crooke, 1908–26b: 442.

169. Katona-Apte and Apte, 1977: 13.

170. B. Walker, 1968, 2: 406–8.

171. M. Stevenson, 1920: 126–27, 272–74; see also B. Walker, 1968, 1: 196, 355.

172. pers. comm., Makarand S. Jawadekar, cited by Dorothea Bedigian, unpublished manuscript, 1996.

173. In general, I use *meat* in the broader sense of "flesh food," to include meat and fish in much the same way as Hindus of North India do when using meat (*māns*) in a generic sense (R. S. Khare, 1976a: 21 n 8).

174. Hopkins, 1906; W. N. Brown, 1957; Alsdorf, 1961; M. M. Singh, 1967: 70–75; Mehendale, 1970.

175. In medieval Jain thinking, to consume meat was a violation of ahimsa that also entailed the acceptance of "vultures, wolves, and tigers as one's gurus" (R. Williams, 1963: 54).

For insights into Indian views on the spiritual similarities between humans and other animals, as background to the emergence of ahimsa concerns, see Jaini, 1987.

176. *Institutes of Vishṇu* 51.71–74, trans. in Jolly, 1880: 170–71.

177. *Laws of Manu* 5.31–32, 33, 37, 45, 48, 56, trans. in Bühler, 1886: 174, 176, 177.

178. For references to Brahmins eating meat, see Ray, 1934: 24; and Gonda, 1980: 120, 450. In a similar vein, Daṇḍin, a Sanskrit poet and novelist (c. A.D. 600), wrote that the eating of meat and drinking of alcohol, though forbidden in general to Brahmins, is permitted to them if it has been an offering to the gods or when, at śrāddha rites, meat has been offered to the ancestors (D. K. Gupta, 1972: 248–49, 250). The Jain monk and scholar Hemachandra (A.D. 1088–1172) also alluded to meat eating in connection with śrāddha rites (R. Williams, 1963: 54).

179. One reads in the Gṛihya-sūtras that abstinence from sexual intercourse and meat eating was required of officiating priests at the time of a sacrifice (*Āśvalā-yana Gṛihya-sūtra* 1.23.23, trans. in Oldenberg and Müller, 1886–92, 29: 197). It was also required of an instructor before teaching secret doctrines (*Śāṅkhāyana Gṛihya-sūtra* 2.11.6; 2.12.8; and 6.1.2, trans. in Oldenberg and Müller, 1886–92, 29: 77, 81, 141).

180. Chakravarti, 1974: 403.

181. Hira Lal, 1925: 64–66; Chakravarti, 1974: 402–6.

182. Srinivas, 1961: 247.

183. Behura, 1962: 127; Gough, 1955: 63–64; Jindel, 1976: 187–88.

184. Jelliffe, 1957: 135; Harper, 1961: 294; Hasan, 1971: 62, 66; Kakar, 1977: 196; Lindenbaum, 1977: 144; Eichinger Ferro-Luzzi, 1977c: 544; Vidyarthi et al., 1979: 98; S. B. Mani, 1981: 202; Gopaldas et al., 1983: 6; Pool, 1987: 390.

185. Eichinger Ferro-Luzzi, 1975: 477.

186. S. B. Mani, 1981: 202.

187. S. B. Mani, 1981: 212. Despite the tendency for meat to be considered hot, there are striking differences in the way animal species may be classified in

hot-cold terms (B. Walker, 1968, 1: 461; Beck, 1969: 561, 567–68; Wandel et al., 1984: 98; Rizvi, 1986: 229; Pool, 1987: 390). From our perspective, it is significant that purity considerations and color symbolism are involved in at least some of these hot-cold differences, as, for example, in the case of goatflesh in South India. In Tamil Nadu, though goatflesh tends toward hotness because it is meat, it comes from an herbivore (which, unlike omnivores and carnivores, does not kill and eat other animals). This makes it "the purest of all meats" and "relatively 'cooling'" (Eichinger Ferro-Luzzi, 1975: 476). There is, however, a difference of opinion as to where the balance should lie, with some Tamil women rejecting goatflesh as too cold, and others, as too hot (Eichinger Ferro-Luzzi, 1974). In Coimbatore District, Tamil Nadu, goatflesh and goat blood, both of which are consumed, are said to be cooling when consumed by humans. The flesh and blood of sheep, on the other hand, are said to be heating, which Beck (1969: 570) relates to the different color symbolism of the two animals. Both of them, she notes, are called by similar terms, but the term for *goat* has *white* as a modifier and that for *sheep* has *red*. Purity concerns over the scavenging habit of chickens are also known to lead some people in India to avoid chickenflesh (Eichinger Ferro-Luzzi, 1973b: 260; 1974: 9), and one wonders whether this may be involved in any of the cases in which chickenflesh is reported to be heating (Mahadevan, 1961: 390; Beck, 1969: 567; S. B. Mani, 1981: 200, 212).

188. Harper, 1959: 227–28; Babb, 1975: 54; Eichinger Ferro-Luzzi, 1981: 261–62.

189. L. K. A. Iyer, 1909–12, 1: 64, 113, 131–32, 136, 152, 168, 178, 183, etc.; Thurston, 1909, 4: 312–14, 317, 375; 5: 432; 6: 230; Hira Lal, 1925: 66–67; Nanjundayya and Iyer, 1930, 3: 342–43, 470; Harper, 1959: 227; K. N. Sharma, 1961: 48, 52; Madan, 1975: 87–88, 91–93; Eichinger Ferro-Luzzi, 1977b: 362–63, 365–66; 1977c: 548; 1978a: 89, 91, 101; 1981: 243.

190. Eichinger Ferro-Luzzi, 1985b: 496.

191. Jindel, 1976: 185.

192. K. N. Sharma, 1961: 54, 55.

193. Jindel, 1976: 185.

194. K. N. Sharma, 1961: 48, 50–51.

195. Senart, 1930: 48; B. Walker, 1968, 2: 428. On the other hand, Behura (1962: 127) says that during śrāddha rites nearly all Hindus eat vegetarian food and avoid alcohol. He observes that in Orissa in the distant past venison was offered to ancestral spirits, but that today this is not done because of the scarcity of game.

196. Chakravarty (1959: 38, 42, 43, and Preface, p. 1) suggests that in ancient Bengal strict Brahmins and other puritanical Hindus were vegetarians, as they are today. He also says that there has been a falling away from that practice by Hindus in Bengal because of the region's abundant supply of fish and the influ-

ence of tantrism, non-Vedic sects widely considered base by other Hindus. Those sects, among other things, preach self-indulgence, including the consumption of flesh and drinking of alcoholic beverages (B. Walker, 1968, 2: 482–86).

197. Srinivas, 1956: 74; 1961: 247; K. N. Sharma, 1961: 45–46; R. S. Khare, 1966; Chakravarti, 1974: 403–5; Madan, 1975: 87; Eichinger Ferro-Luzzi, 1985a: 166.

198. M. Stevenson, 1920: 241.

199. Hasan, 1971: 62; Chakravarti, 1974: 403; Eichinger Ferro-Luzzi, 1981: 242; 1985b: 496.

200. Eichinger Ferro-Luzzi, 1981: 242; 1990: 42.

201. Carstairs, 1957: 87, 109–10, 118, 165, 188; Harlan, 1992: 127 and n.

202. Carstairs, 1957: 188.

203. Jathar et al., 1976.

204. Babb, 1975: 173.

205. Mahadevan, 1961: 389.

206. Crooke, 1896a, 2: 313–22; M. Stevenson, 1920: 282–87; Marriott, 1966; B. Walker, 1968, 1: 354; Babb, 1975: 168–75.

207. Marriott, 1966: 201; R. S. Khare, 1976b: 147.

208. Babb, 1975: 173, 174.

209. Frazer, 1935, 1: 52–174.

210. "Panjab—red food forbidden—Hindus," 1886.

211. M. Stevenson, 1920: 241.

212. Harper, 1961: 293; 1964: 155.

213. R. V. Russell and Hira Lal, 1916, 1: 309.

214. Madan, 1975: 87.

215. Eichinger Ferro-Luzzi, 1973a: 171; 1977b: 370. Margaret Stevenson (1920: 289) has also reported a similar distinction between the use of red pepper and black pepper in ritual in Gujarat.

216. Eichinger Ferro-Luzzi, 1977b: 370; 1981: 247–48.

217. Nichter, 1986: 193.

218. Eichinger Ferro-Luzzi, 1975: 479.

219. Crooke, 1885. R. V. Russell and Hira Lal (1916, 1: 309) write more specifically about the Satnāmis that Ghāsi Dās, founder of the sect, is said to have banned eggplant because it resembles the scrotum of a water buffalo (for Hindus, the water buffalo, unlike the cow, is an impure animal: Hoffpauir, 1982: 227). It is interesting that both the potato (Wiser, 1955: 359; Minturn and Hitchcock, 1966: 74; B. Walker, 1968, 1: 461; Beck, 1969: 567) and the eggplant (Kakar, 1977: 185; Beck, 1969: 566; Pool, 1987: 390) seem commonly, but not universally (Sri Lanka: Wandel et al., 1984: 96), to be included among "hot" foods.

220. Toomey (1986: 67, 78 n 21) includes carrots, tomatoes, *masūr* lentils, onions, garlic, potatoes, and cauliflower in an overall list of banned plants. However,

he does not indicate which are banned because their color or name recalls blood. In all likelihood, carrots, tomatoes, and masūr lentils belong to that group. Cauliflower, in turn, is improper as an offering because its name, *gobhi,* suggests the sacred cow (*go*), and cooking it recalls the abhorrent practice of cow slaughter.

221. Crooke, 1885.

222. K. N. Sharma, 1961: 47.

223. Dubois, 1906: 698; R. Williams, 1963: 113–16.

224. *Laws of Manu* 3.267, trans. in Bühler, 1886: 124; *Āpastamba Dharma-sūtra* 2.7.16.23, trans. in Bühler, 1879–82, 2: 141; Gonda, 1980: 123–24; Oldenberg, 1988: 132, 175 n 451.

225. Dubois, 1906: 189; Hasan, 1971: 59; Jindel, 1976: 183.

226. Eichinger Ferro-Luzzi, 1977c: 552.

227. Eichinger Ferro-Luzzi, 1977c: 552. Certain roots and tubers may also be rejected because they are newcomers to India or are associated with foreigners. Harper (1961: 293), for example, explains the rejection of potatoes by certain Havik Brahmins of South India in terms of their "being Englishman's food." Toomey (1986: 78 n 21), writing of Hindu pilgrimage sites in Uttar Pradesh, notes that potatoes and other foods brought in from outside India are unsuitable as offerings. Such objections are, of course, quite common in India. In South India, tomatoes, carrots, cabbage, and other "English" vegetables are not employed in temple cooking (Eichinger Ferro-Luzzi, 1981: 248). In a similar way, the rejection of lentils at a Hyderabad temple may derive partly from Moslems' fondness for them (Eichinger Ferro-Luzzi, 1977b: 369, citing G. S. Aurora); and in Maharashtra, many orthodox Hindu women reject certain vegetables on auspicious occasions because they are recent introductions deriving from the New World and not mentioned in the sacred Vedic texts (Katona-Apte and Apte, 1977: 10–11). In Tamil Nadu, Eichinger Ferro-Luzzi (1974: 13) noted a similar tendency, for there to be greater objections to the consumption of recently introduced tubers by women during the puerperium and lactation. She insists, however, that there is more than this to the objections against newly introduced tubers (manioc, white potato, sweet potato), for the sweet potato has a particularly bad image and is considered especially dangerous to women during those times. In addition, more Brahmin women (96 percent) refused sweet potatoes than women of other castes (79 percent). Eichinger Ferro-Luzzi suspects that the lowly standing of the sweet potato may relate to both its sweetness and its color. Kalhaṇa, a twelfth-century poet and historian of Kashmir, explained the rejection of garlic by some people in India by saying that the practice of eating garlic had been introduced by foreigners (Prakash, 1961: 221). Crooke (1896a, 2: 35; 1926: 291), on his part, observes that in Sanskrit garlic was designated "the foreigner's root" (*mlechha kanda*), which may mean, he suggests, that it is a late introduction to India.

228. R. Mitra, 1873; Ray, 1934: 25–34; Saletore, 1943: 118–23; Gopal, 1959: 166–68; Prakash, 1961: 24–26; M. M. Singh, 1967: 75–79.

229. Dubois, 1818, 1: 237–38; Hira Lal, 1925: 66–68; Chopra and Chopra, 1933: 665–67.

230. Jindel, 1976: 184–85.

231. Mahadevan, 1961: 390; Minturn and Hitchcock, 1966: 74; B. Walker, 1968, 1: 461; Beck, 1969: 561, 569; Hasan, 1971: 66; Vidyarthi et al., 1979: 98; S. B. Mani, 1981: 200, 202, 212; Gopaldas et al., 1983: 6; Pool, 1987: 390, 391.

232. Carstairs, 1957: 97–98; H. N. C. Stevenson, 1954: 55.

233. Mathur, 1964: 125, citing Srinivas.

234. Mathur, 1964: 125.

235. Babb, 1975: 48, 173–74.

236. Trumbull, 1899: esp. 53–70, 81–106, 133–38; Latham, 1982: 29–42, 163–66.

237. See, in this regard, Abbott's discussion of "the power of salt" (Abbott, 1974: 232–38).

238. M. Stevenson, 1920: 140, 264.

239. *Śatapatha Brāhmaṇa* 2.1.1.6; 5.2.1.16, 17; 7.1.1.7–8, 16; 7.3.1.8; 13.8.1.14, trans. in Eggeling, 1882–1900, 12: 278; 41: 33–34, 299–300, 302, 343; 44: 426–27.

240. *Bhagavadgītā* 17.9, trans. in Radhakrishnan and Moore, 1957: 155; Prakash, 1961: 41–42, 180; Katona-Apte and Apte, 1977: 10–11; Eichinger Ferro-Luzzi, 1977b: 370–71; 1978b: 413. On the other hand, salt may be placed at the root of coconut trees because it is believed to increase fertility, too. It may also be placed on the stems of fruit trees when their fruit is developing, and then watered well, to increase the yield of fruit (Abbott, 1974: 237).

241. Gopal, 1959: 163.

242. *Āśvalāyana Gṛhya-sūtra* 4.4.16, trans. in Oldenberg and Müller, 1886–92, 29: 244.

243. *Hiraṇyakeśi Gṛhya-sūtra* 1.7.23.10, trans. in Oldenberg and Müller, 1886–92, 30: 197; *Gobhila Gṛihya-sūtra* 2.3.15, trans. in Oldenberg and Müller, 1886–92, 30: 48. For a similar belief among modern Hindus, see Abbott, 1974: 238.

244. Oldenberg, 1988: 246.

245. *Āśvalāyana Gṛhya-sūtra* 1.22.19, trans. in Oldenberg and Müller, 1886–92, 29: 192; *Hiraṇyakeśi Gṛhya-sūtra* 1.2.8.2, trans. in Oldenberg and Müller, 1886–92, 30: 158; *Āpastamba Gṛhya-sūtra* 4.11.21, trans. in Oldenberg and Müller, 1886–92, 30: 274; etc.

246. *Vāyu Purāṇa* 2.16.11b–15, trans. in Tagare, 1987–88, 2: 611; *Vishnu Purāṇa* 3.16, trans. in Wilson, 1961: 266. The touch of polluted people or things, or the sight of unholy and dishonored creatures such as fowl, pig, and dogs, would also ruin a śrāddha (*Vāyu Purāṇa* 2.16.36–41, trans. in Tagare, 1987–88, 2: 614).

247. Abbott, 1974: 232–35.

248. Woodburne, 1981: 62.

249. W. G. Griffiths, 1946: 186.

250. Crooke, 1908–26b: 444.

251. For crossroads in ritual in India and other lands, see J. M. Campbell, 1894–1901, 27: 105–6; for crossroads in Indian ritual and healing and different ways of placating evil forces who live there, see M. Stevenson, 1920: 146, 414–15; Abbott, 1974: 22, 56, 69, 128–30, 139, 155, 283, 285, 296, 393; and Gonda, 1980: 238–39. For the use of earth or dust from crossroads to counter the evil eye and sickness in India, see Abbott, 1974: 124, 129, 159–60, 234. Providing a more intimate feeling for the role of crossroads in ritual, some lower castes in South India take a black hen, pass it three times around a person afflicted with the evil eye, then cut its neck and throw it away at a place where four roads join (Woodburne, 1981: 62).

252. Crooke, 1908–26b: 444.

253. Crooke, 1908–26b: 442.

254. Crooke, 1896a, 2: 23. A parallel custom, once common in parts of England, is to set a plate containing salt on a corpse. One explanation of the custom is that salt is symbolic of immortality and hated by the devil. Another is that the salt slows the passage of air into the bowels of the deceased, thus slowing distention and making it simpler to close the coffin (Hazlitt, 1905, 2: 533).

255. W. G. Griffiths, 1946: 186.

256. Gough, 1955: 63–64; Eichinger Ferro-Luzzi, 1975: 479; 1977b: 371; 1978b: 413; 1981: 247; 1985a: 163.

257. M. Stevenson, 1920: 289.

258. Frazer, 1968, 4: 223.

259. S. B. Mani, 1981: 204.

260. Eichinger Ferro-Luzzi, 1977b: 371; 1977c: 544, 553; 1978a: 95; 1981: 247; 1985a: 163. Sea salt is banned at ritual and festive times in certain provinces of North and Central India and is strictly banned for use in foods offered in śrāddha rites (Behura, 1962: 133). This, however, may derive from the fact that in North India sea salt is considered less pure than rock salt, in part because it is handled by low castes (Eichinger Ferro-Luzzi, 1977b: 371). In any case, sea salt may also be banned in India on celibate fast days, when rock salt is permitted (M. Stevenson, 1920: 289).

261. Oldenberg, 1988: 288 n 338.

262. Eichinger Ferro-Luzzi, 1977b: 371–72; 1977c: 553; 1978a: 91.

263. M. Stevenson, 1920: 51–52, 259, 301.

264. Crooke, 1896a, 2: 23.

265. M. Stevenson, 1920: 72.

266. Eichinger Ferro-Luzzi, 1978b. One other possibility for the origin of the salt bans should be mentioned: the association of salt with the earth. In certain medieval Śvetāmbara Jain texts, for example, salt is regarded as earth (*mṛd*), virtually all sorts of which were banned for eating because earth contains living organ-

isms or souls and because of fear of intestinal ills. Salt, because it is needed to sustain life, was the sole exception in not being banned (R. Williams, 1963: 110, 111). Despite this, one wonders whether the classification of salt as earth by Jains or others may in some situations have contributed to its impurity.

267. Wasson, 1968.

268. Meigs, 1978: 312–13, 316–17; Rozin and Fallon, 1987: 28.

269. H. N. C. Stevenson, 1954: 51.

270. *Āpastamba Dharma-sūtra* 1.5.17.28, trans. in Bühler, 1879–82, 2: 63; *Vāsishtha Dharma-sūtra* 14.33, trans. in Bühler, 1879–82, 14: 73; *Gautama Dharma-sūtra* 17.32, trans. in Bühler, 1879–82, 2: 266; *Laws of Manu* 5.3, 19; 6.14; 11.155–62, trans. in Bühler, 1886: 170, 172, 201, 462–63.

271. Both the pig and mushrooms, as items of impurity, might be held responsible for a person becoming ill or suffering other calamities. The death of the Buddha, for example, is held by some scholars to have been brought on by his eating pig's flesh. Wasson, however, has argued that the Buddha died from eating mushrooms, a food of which pigs are fond (Wasson, 1982).

272. *Laws of Manu* 5.3, 19; 11.155–62, trans. in Bühler, 1886: 170, 172, 462–63; *Vāsishtha Dharma-sūtra* 14.33, trans. in Bühler, 1879–82, 14: 73.

273. Srinivas, 1961: 247; Eichinger Ferro-Luzzi, 1974: 14; 1975: 479.

274. Hasan, 1971: 59.

275. Eichinger Ferro-Luzzi, 1974: 14.

276. The disease in question is favism, which can bring on acute hemolytic anemia and even death to genetically predisposed individuals with deficiency in the enzyme glucose-6-phosphate dehydrogenase (G6PD). For significant numbers of clinical cases of favism to occur, one needs both low-activity G6PD variants and widespread dietary use of fava beans. For this reason, favism is more common in the Mediterranean region than elsewhere in the world, for fava beans are widely consumed there, and many of the deficiency variants of G6PD found there are Class II, involving severe deficiency, with G6PD activity less than 10 percent of normal. Tests carried out so far in the Indian subcontinent, however, suggest that, though G6PD-deficiency is widespread and variants characterized by severe deficiency (Class II) do occur, by far the most common deficiency variants are ones with moderately deficient enzyme activity (10–60 percent of normal) (Baxi et al., 1961, 1963; Meera Khan, 1964; Azevedo et al., 1968; McCurdy and Mahmood, 1970; Mourant et al., 1976: 725–45 passim; Meera Khan and Wijnen, 1986; Panich, 1986).

It may be of historical interest that the Mediterranean variant, most common of the severe deficiency variants in Greece and Italy, has been reported in persons originating in India's northwest (in 3 of 15 individuals tested), where there was a long-continued Greek presence following the invasion of India by Alexander the Great. None of the three individuals had a medical history that suggested favism

(Azevedo et al., 1968: 374, 377), and there is also some question whether this variant was in fact Mediterranean. It has been noted that when the Indian study was carried out, in the 1960s, it was not known that what was then called the Mediterranean variant actually consisted of many distinct variants. As a result, one cannot be certain whether that Indian variant was what today would be called Mediterranean (Luzzatto and Battistuzzi, 1985: 271), though one individual with the Mediterranean variant was also identified in a later study in India (Meera Khan and Wijnen, 1986: 246). Moreover, though sensitivity to antimalaria drugs (a common trait in G6PD-deficient persons) is frequent in the Indian subcontinent, none of the studies that I have consulted suggests that favism occurs there. This may reflect the fact that the fava bean is a minor crop limited in its geographic occurrence, not that favism is altogether absent. If the disease does occur in the subcontinent, however, it is likely quite rare.

277. Shourie, 1945; Gopalan, 1950; Govil et al., 1959; Dwivedi and Prasad, 1964; S. L. N. Rao et al., 1969; Mitchell, 1971; Padmanaban, 1980.

278. Ladizinsky, 1975: 80, 82, 87.

279. Hanelt, 1972a: 111.

Chapter 7. The Color Black in the Pythagorean Ban on Eating the Fava Bean (*Vicia faba*)

1. Variations of this oft-quoted line have been ascribed to Pythagoras (Callimachus, in Aulus Gellius, *Attic nights* 4.11.1–2; Callimachus, "Fragments" 553, Trypanis), Orpheus (Didymus, in *Geoponica* 2.35.8; also Kern, 1922: 301–2), and Empedocles (Empedocles, in Aulus Gellius, *Attic nights* 4.11.9; Empedocles, "Fragments" 128, Wright). Whatever its origin, it would be difficult to find a stronger statement of bean rejection than the one attributed to Empedocles: "Wretches, utter wretches, keep your hands off beans!"

2. See, for example, Arie, 1959; Lieber, 1970, 1973; Brumbaugh and Schwartz, 1979–80; Grmek, 1980: 87–102, 112–21; G. D. Hart, 1980: 47–48; W. M. S. Russell, 1980: 374–75; Scarborough, 1981–82; W. M. S. Russell and C. Russell, 1983: 100; Bollet and Brown, 1993: 573; P. J. Brown, 1993: 723–24.

3. For reviews of the ancient literature on Pythagoras and beans, see von Schroeder, 1901; Wünsch, 1902: 31–46; Böhm, 1905: 14–17; Delatte, 1930; Marcovich, 1964; and Grmek, 1980. For excellent accounts of Pythagoras's perceptions of food, including beans, see Detienne, 1970; and of the bean in Indo-European tradition, Andrews, 1949.

4. Hopf, 1969: 356; Hanelt et al., 1972: 273; Schultze-Motel, 1972; Renfrew, 1973: 107–9; Cubero, 1974: 47; Ladizinsky, 1975; Zohary and Hopf, 1973: 892–93; D. Zohary, 1977: 39; Kislev and Bar-Yosef, 1988: 177.

5. Hanelt, 1972b: 216, 221; Bond, 1976: 180–81.

6. Renfrew, 1973: 105; Zohary and Hopf, 1973; Kislev and Bar-Yosef, 1988. Bitter vetch, *Vicia ervilia,* also seems to have been cultivated during the Neolithic and Bronze Age, but authorities (Renfrew, 1973: 116; Zohary and Hopf, 1973: 893) differ over whether it was used as human food.

7. A. M. Evans, 1976.

8. Pliny, *Natural history* 18.118.

9. Macrobius, *Saturnalia* 1.12.32–33.

10. Ovid, *Fasti* 6.169–82. For more on the use of beans or bean porridge at religious rites among the Romans, see Frazer, p. 146 in Vol. 4 of his trans. of Ovid, *Fasti;* Frazer, p. 241 in Vol. 4 of his trans. of Pausanias, *Description of Greece;* and Fowler, 1899: 130–31.

11. Andrews, 1949: 274, 284; Moldenke and Moldenke, 1952: 101 n 56a, citing W. T. Stearn; Hopf, 1969: 357; Hanelt, 1972b: 221; Schultze-Motel, 1972: 350; Zohary and Hopf, 1973: 892.

12. Hopf, 1969: 357.

13. Andrews, 1949: 284.

14. Hanelt, 1972b: 221; Schultze-Motel, 1972: 350; Zohary and Hopf, 1973: 892; Bond, 1976: 181.

15. Hanelt, 1972b: 210.

16. Bond, 1976: 181.

17. For a weighing of the historical evidence and a contrary view, see Philip, 1966: 138–46.

18. Philip, 1966: 25–26; Burkert, 1972: 115–17; 1982: 14.

19. Philip, 1966: 192–94, countering the claims of Diogenes Laertius, *Lives of eminent philosophers* 8.6–7.

20. Philip, 1966: 1.

21. Porphyry, *Life of Pythagoras* 37; Iamblichus, *On the Pythagorean life* 81–89.

22. Guthrie, 1962–81, 1: 191–93; Philip, 1966: 28–29, 145–46; Burkert, 1972: 166–218; 1982: 20–21.

23. Among the acusmata thought strange: When you go abroad, don't turn around at the border. Don't stir the fire with a knife. Don't leave the imprint of a pan on the ashes. Don't urinate on or stand on your nail- or hair-clippings (Diogenes Laertius, *Lives of eminent philosophers* 8.17); or "Don't spit upon the trimmings of your hair and finger-nails" (Iamblichus, cited in Kirk and Raven, 1957: 227 n; and Burkert, 1972: 173 n 57). The ancients sought to provide meaning for these, though some explanations were not the real ones (Iamblichus, *On the Pythagorean life* 86; Porphyry, *Life of Pythagoras* 42; Jerome, *Apology against Rufinus* 3.39). In any case, some of them would be familiar to present-day culture historians and ethnologists. One reads in an ancient Mesopotamian text (1350–1050 B.C.?), for

example, that it is a violation, an impurity, to step on nail-parings or armpit hair-shavings (Reiner, 1956: 143; Geller, 1990: 113). Concern with hair- and nail-clippings continues to be widespread in the modern world, because they may be polluting in themselves or used in witchcraft to injure a person. Among the Hua of highland New Guinea, for example, body hair is considered strongly polluting, in part because of its own nature as a bodily emission and in part because it is covered with other emissions (body oils and sweat). The Hua fear the pollution of fingernails mainly because of their use in witchcraft, such as a woman putting shavings from her fingernails in the food of her victim, who then withers away and dies. At the same time, hair- or nail-clippings of dead Hua may be worn by their children to enhance their growth and fecundity and that of their plants and animals (Meigs, 1978: 305, 306, 309). Among modern Zoroastrians in Iran, hair- and nail-clippings are considered dead matter, the property of Ahriman, god of darkness, and too impure to be permitted to touch the good earth. Special care was taken to dispose of such clippings. Should nail-clippings fall onto the ground, some Zoroastrians said, "they would be seized by demons and made to slash their owner in the hereafter" (Boyce, 1977: 107–9). Similar care is taken with hair- and nail-clippings in India, and it is only at shrines and pilgrimage places, which are protected against sorcery by their sanctity, that they are left lying around (Crooke, 1896a, 1: 280; 2: 277–78).

24. Frazer, 1890.

25. Dodds, 1963: 140–47; Philip, 1966: 158–62; Burkert, 1972: 162–65.

26. Burkert, 1972: 176–78; Parker, 1983: 358–59.

27. Parker, 1983: 294–96; Burkert, 1985: 302–3.

28. Iamblichus, *On the Pythagorean life* 85; Burkert, 1972: 174.

29. To persons who believe in transmigration, the soul of a person who dies may be reborn in some other living form, whether a human, an animal, or otherwise. In the words of another believer, the famous Greek philosopher Empedocles (c. 490–430 B.C.): "For before now I have been at some time boy and girl, bush, bird, and a mute fish in the sea" (Empedocles, "Fragments" 108, Wright).

The transmigration of souls actually having been one of Pythagoras's beliefs is attested to by fragments from Xenophanes, a contemporary of Pythagoras. Xenophanes reported that Pythagoras had once recognized the soul of a friend in the barking of a dog (Xenophanes in Diogenes Laertius, *Lives of eminent philosophers* 8.36). Diogenes Laertius (*Lives of eminent philosophers* 8.4–6), citing Heraclides of Pontus (fourth century B.C.) as his authority, said that Pythagoras could actually recall and name the persons in whom his soul had previously lived. In the fifth century B.C., Herodotus wrote that certain Greek writers, early and late, had adopted the doctrine of transmigration of souls from Egypt, though they presented it as their own (Herodotus, *History* 2.123). Unfortunately, Herodotus declined to name the Greeks he had in mind, but it is likely that Pythagoras was among them (Rawlinson, p. 197 n, Vol. 2 of his trans. of Herodotus, *History;* Kirk and Raven, 1957: 222–23). If so, the account of Herodotus would provide further early evidence that Pythagoras believed in the transmigration of souls, though Herodotus was wrong in saying that Egypt was the source of Greek views on transmigration (Kirk and Raven, 1957: 224; Werblowsky, 1987: 22). Pythagoras's belief in transmigration is further confirmed in the writings of Aristotle (384–322 B.C.) (Aristotle, *On the soul* 407b.19–26), and it became an integral part of the legend that surrounded Pythagoras. For more on Pythagoras and the transmigration of souls, see especially Philip, 1966: 151–71; and Burkert, 1972: 120–65. For the concept of transmigration in ancient Greece and India, or in Greece and other parts of the world, see von Schroeder, 1884; Keith, 1909; Frazer, 1935, 8: 300–302; and Werblowsky, 1987.

30. Dicaearchus (?), in Porphyry, *Life of Pythagoras* 19; Kirk and Raven, 1957: 223–24; Guthrie, 1962–81, 1: 186–87; R. J. White, p. 77 n 74 in his trans. of Artemidorus Daldianus, *Interpretation of dreams.*

31. Philip, 1966: 147.

32. Diogenes Laertius, *Lives of eminent philosophers* 8.13, including an attribution to Aristotle; Iamblichus, *On the Pythagorean life* 85; Guthrie, 1962–81, 1: 190; Burkert, 1972: 182.

33. Detienne, 1970: 157. This Greek tradition contrasted with a second tradition, that the earliest humans lived in a savage state (Detienne, 1970: 157).

34. Guthrie, 1962–81, 1: 190–91; Detienne, 1970: 142–48.

35. Aristotle, cited by Plutarch in Aulus Gellius, *Attic nights* 4.11.11–13; and in Diogenes Laertius, *Lives of eminent philosophers* 8.19.

36. Diogenes Laertius, *Lives of eminent philosophers* 8.13, 19, 22, 33–34; Porphyry, *Life of Pythagoras* 7, 43–45; Porphyry, *On abstinence from animal food* 2.28; Athenaeus, *Deipnosophists* 4.161a–e; Lucian, *Philosophies for sale* 6; Iamblichus, *On the Pythagorean life* 85, 107–9, 225–26; Guthrie, 1962–81, 1: 187–91; Detienne, 1970; Burkert, 1972: 180–83.

37. Burkert, 1972: 181–82; Detienne, 1979: 85–87. The Pythagorean rejection of eggs may have involved more than this, for while eggs were indeed symbolic of life and fertility in Greece and Rome, they also served as offerings to the dead (Nilsson, 1908). Though this was done in the belief that they were life-giving and in the interests of survival of the soul of the deceased, the association with death may also have implied impurity. Apparently with this in mind, Nilsson (1957: 139–40) has suggested that Pythagorean rejection of eggs may have been based on their use as offerings to the dead.

In any case, the use of eggs as funerary offerings and in burials extended beyond Greece and Rome. Among Hebrews in the Greco-Roman period, for example, "seeds," because of the life force they contained, were essential among food offerings to the dead, and among the "seeds" were eggs, along with beans and lentils (Goodenough, 1953–68, 6: 169). Even today, such thinking about and uses of eggs continue among various Near Eastern peoples, for which see Drower, 1956: 8, 25–26, 38, 223.

38. Burkert, 1972: 180–83; Detienne, 1970; 142–48; 1989: 5–6.

39. Detienne, 1970: 155–62; 1977: 40–59; 1979: 60–61; 1989: 6, 8, 12.

40. Burkert, 1972: 183.

41. One exception in earliest times was Aristoxenus, whose account is difficult to believe and may have had a polemical intent, but who, centuries later, was seconded by Aulus Gellius (Aulus Gellius, *Attic nights* 4.11; Burnet, 1930: 93–94; Guthrie, 1962–81, 1: 191; Burkert, 1972: 107, 183, 198).

42. Aristotle, cited in Diogenes Laertius, *Lives of eminent philosophers* 8.34.

43. In Athens, for example, they served in selecting judges by lot (Lucian, *Philosophies for sale* 6).

44. Iamblichus, *On the Pythagorean life* 260.

45. Guthrie, 1962–81, 1: 184.

46. Diogenes Laertius, *Lives of eminent philosophers* 8.24; Hippolytus, *Philosophumena* 1.2.13.

47. Lucian, *Philosophies for sale* 6; Porphyry, *Life of Pythagoras* 44; Hippolytus, *Philosophumena* 1.2.13; Delatte, 1930: 42–43; Guthrie, 1962–81, 1: 184.

Also relevant in the ties of beans with sex, some ancient writers link the bean to the female reproductive organs (Guthrie, 1962–81, 1: 184). Clement of Alexandria (c. A.D. 150–215), in a somewhat different tack, asserts that beans bring on sterility in women, and expresses the view that they were banned by Pythagoreans, after their families were grown, as a means of birth control (Clement of Alexandria, *Miscellanies* 3.3.24).

48. Clement of Alexandria, *Miscellanies* 3.3.24; Theophrastus, *Causes of plants* 5.15.1–2.

49. Lucian, *Philosophies for sale* 6; Delatte, 1930: 42–43; Andrews, 1949: 278–79. Joannes Lydus (*On months* 4.29) records the use of bean juice as a substitute for blood in a Roman ritual.

50. Pliny, *Natural history* 18.118–119; Lucian, *Dialogues of the dead* 6 (20).3; Plutarch, *Roman questions* 95; Cicero, *On divination* 2.119. The association of beans with the dead may have led ancient diviners to use them, together with salt, which was also linked with the dead. This, in turn, seems to have led people to call persons who kept secrets to themselves "men concerned with salt and beans" (Erasmus, *Adages* 1.1.12; Frazer, p. 241 in Vol. 4 of his trans. of Pausanias, *Description of Greece*).

51. Porphyry, *Life of Pythagoras* 44; Hippolytus, *Philosophumena* 1.2.13–14; Delatte, 1930: 42.

52. Porphyry, *Life of Pythagoras* 43.

53. Lucian, *Dream, or the cock* 4; Lucian, *Dialogues of the dead* 6 (20).3; Clement

of Alexandria, *Miscellanies* 3.3.24. For references to other statements of this sort, see Frazer, p. 240 in Vol. 4 of his trans. of Pausanias, *Description of Greece*.

54. Horace, *Satires* 2.6.63–64.

55. Porphyry, *Cave of the nymphs in the "Odyssey"* 19.

56. Detienne, 1970: 153–55; 1977: 49–59; 1979: 60–61.

57. Detienne 1977: 50.

58. For more on primeval slime, man, and beans in the thinking of Pythagoras, see Gorman, 1979: 37, 58.

59. Detienne, 1977: 50.

60. For more on the sexual connotations of beans among the ancient Greeks, see Lévi-Strauss, 1979: 37–38.

61. Detienne, 1970: 154; 1979: 58–59; Parker, 1983: 305, 326, 360.

62. Onians, 1973: 93–122.

63. E.g., Callimachus, "Fragments" 553, Trypanis.

64. Plutarch (*Table-talk* 8.10.1; see also *Geoponica* 2.35) wrote in general terms that, because beans interfere with sleep and bring on bad dreams, people were instructed to avoid them when they attempted divination by means of dreams.

65. Diogenes Laertius, *Lives of eminent philosophers* 8.24; Pliny, *Natural history* 18.118; Cicero, *On divination* 1.62; 2.119; Tertullian, *On the soul* 48.3; Burkert, 1972: 184; see also Clement of Alexandria, *Miscellanies* 3.3.24.

66. Artemidorus Daldianus, *Interpretation of dreams* 1.68.

67. Plutarch, *Roman questions* 95. For more on the reasons advanced in antiquity for the Pythagorean bean ban, see Olck, 1897: cols. 619–20.

68. There are also other, more believable accounts of his death. Stories involving a bean field, which Philip (1966: 191) calls "fiction," appear in two of four versions of Pythagoras's death presented by Diogenes Laertius's *Lives of eminent philosophers* (8.39–40) in the third century A.D. Diogenes gives no source for one of the two stories, but cites Hermippus of Smyrna (c. 200 B.C.) for the other. Though it remains a matter of speculation who the ultimate inventors may have been, one must admit that the bean-field tales fit well with the legends that surround Pythagoras and his relationship with beans. For still another bean-field tale, one involving not Pythagoras but his followers, see Iamblichus, *On the Pythagorean life* 31.190–91.

69. Burkert, 1972: 178.

70. Gimbutas, 1982: 211–15.

71. Lang, 1901, 2: 283–87.

72. Harrison, 1955: 145–50; Schmitt, 1955: 100; Deubner, 1959: 60–69; Avery, 1962: 513; Burkert, 1972: 177; Parker, 1983: 358. For an account of the unacceptability of beans to Demeter on another occasion, see Pausanias, *Description of Greece* 8.15.3–4. On Dionysus in the Eleusinian mysteries, see Bianchi, 1976: 7–9.

73. Porphyry, *On abstinence from animal food* 4.16; Harrison, 1955: 148–50; Schmitt, 1955: 100; Deubner, 1959: 61 n 5; Burkert, 1972: 177; Parker, 1983: 358.

74. For more on the role of the cock in ancient Greek ritual and religion, see Simoons, 1994: 154–56.

75. Harrison, 1955: 150.

76. Aelian, *On the characteristics of animals* 2.41; 9.65; Parker, 1983: 358–59, 362–63. Also of possible relevance, the red mullet is blood-colored and was dedicated to and eaten by Hecate, an underworld goddess who relished blood (Athenaeus, *Deipnosophists* 325a–d, 358f; Parker, 1983: 360–61, 362–63). Also mentioned in connection with the avoidance at Eleusis was the fact that initiates honored the red mullet, whether for its unusual fecundity or because it kills "sea hares" (sea slugs?), which are lethal to humans (Aelian, *On the characteristics of animals* 9.51, 65; Plutarch, *Whether land or sea animals are cleverer* 983f; Parker, 1983: 350–62).

77. The pomegranate, with its many seeds, is symbolic of both fertility and abundance (Muthmann, 1982; Simoons, 1991: 245), and in early Christianity it came to symbolize hope for an everlasting life. Such symbolism was found in ancient Greece as well, but there was another side to this, for, while the pomegranate tree and fruit as cult objects did symbolize fruitfulness and production, they also symbolized death and destruction.

78. Harrison, 1955: 149.

79. Freese, 1910–11: 981.

80. Hyde, 1923: 213.

81. Roscher, 1890: 49 n 199, 65, 108–9; Robert-Tornow, 1893: 144; A. B. Cook, 1895: 12–24; 1964–65, 2: 977, 1056, 1142; Schrader, 1908–26: 27; Hyde, 1923: 114; Guthrie, 1955: 221–22, 227–28; Lawson, 1964: 121–22, 150–51, 533–34; Burkert, 1992: 65.

A curious practice relating to bees and death, once common in Britain, was that of "telling the bees." It was carried out after the death of a person who kept bees, when a servant, relative, heir, or successor of the deceased informed his bees of their master's death (along the Welsh border of England people said that telling must be done in the middle of the night). A piece of black crepe might be put on the hive as a symbol of mourning, and funeral food might be offered to the bees. It was believed that, if the bees were not told, they would either die or leave their hives and not return. In Devonshire, it was thought that, if people failed to tell bees of their master's death, someone else in the household would die before year's end (G. L. Gomme, 1892: 12; Hazlitt, 1905, 1: 38–39; E. M. Wright, 1914: 281–82; Dorson, 1968, 1: 327, quoting Gomme). Related to the above is the superstition, once found in many parts of England, that, if bees abandon their hive (or are removed from it without taking certain precautions?), their owner will soon die (Hazlitt, 1905, 1: 38).

82. Porphyry, *Cave of the nymphs in the "Odyssey"* 15–19. For references to the

use of *bees* or related terms for clergy and/or devotees of Demeter, Artemis, and other deities, see Roscher, 1890: 65, 108; and A. B. Cook, 1964–65, 1: 443–44.

83. The "Treasury of Atreus" (c. 1300–1250 B.C.)—a tall dome of corbelled construction with no interior support—was the largest domed structure covering the greatest uninterrupted space in all the ancient world prior to completion of the Roman Pantheon more than a millennium later. For illustrations of the so-called treasury, which was almost 50 feet in diameter, see Gardner, 1980: 102–3.

84. A. B. Cook, 1895: 12–14; Barnett, 1956: 218–19.

85. Parallels also exist in the Near East. In ancient Mesopotamia, honey was among the propitiatory offerings made to the dead (Burkert, 1992: 65). In ancient Egypt, honey served in funerary offerings, and, as elsewhere in the classical world, dead bodies were sometimes preserved in honey (including that of Alexander the Great), perhaps in part because of honey's sanctity (Budge, 1925: 208, Drower, 1956: 8 n 2; Darby et al., 1977, 1: 430–31, 440). For notes on the symbolism and ritual use of honey in the Near East, see Drower, 1956: 8 and n 2.

86. Linforth, 1941: 262; Harrison, 1955: 544–45; Boyancé, 1962: 474–80; 1972: 21–31; Graf, 1974: 22–39.

87. Pausanias, *Description of Greece* 1.37.4.

88. Guthrie, 1952: 153–56; Graf, 1974: 22–39; Alderink, 1981: 100 n 8.

89. Some scholars have suggested that Orpheus was not merely a mythical figure, but may have been a historical personage whose life and character were embellished by later tales (Robbins, 1982: 11). In either case, Orpheus is credited in Greek texts with having had an impact on a broad range of religious cults and practices in addition to the Eleusinian mysteries (Linforth, 1941: 261–76).

90. Guthrie, 1952: 86–87; Reitzenstein, 1978: 90 n 2; Burkert, 1983: 119; 1985: 296; 1992: 125–27.

91. Nilsson, 1949: 215; Guthrie, 1952: 26.

92. Willoughby, 1929: 108–12; Guthrie, 1952: 10–11, 19–20, 253. In one form or another, there is clear evidence that Orphism survived in the Roman Empire even after the rise of Christianity. Guthrie notes, in this regard, that early in the fourth century the patriarch Athanasios expressed anger at an old woman who, for a price, would provide an Orphic spell. He also notes, however, that early in the sixth century Joannes Lydus wrote of Orphic mysteries that "used to be performed."

93. Willoughby, 1929: 90–91, 103; Nilsson, 1957: 12, 121–22; Pollard, 1965: 102–4; Detienne, 1975, 1979: 68–94; 1989: 5–8; M. L. West, 1983: 1–26.

94. Guthrie, 1952: 94, 218; Wili, 1955: 83–85.

95. Burkert, 1972: 39.

96. Burkert, 1982: 12; M. L. West, 1983: 3.

97. Linforth, 1941: 58–60, 288–92; Guthrie, 1952: 204–5; Pollard, 1965: 95; Detienne, 1979: 70–72; 1989: 6–7; Alderink, 1981: 8–15; M. L. West, 1983: 2–3.

98. Burkert, 1982: 3–12.

99. By contrast, the Mesopotamian *asû* (physician), sometimes in competition and sometimes in cooperation with the āšipu, focussed primarily on natural causes of illness, on the body of the ill person, on washing and rubbing, on collecting and administering medicines, on bandages, and on other hands-on treatments (Ritter, 1965).

100. Rose, 1943: 34.

101. E.g., Willoughby, 1929: 97; Reinach, 1942: 87; Guthrie, 1952: 197, 217–18; Wili, 1955: 76; Dodds, 1963: 149; Werblowsky, 1987: 22–23; Grmek, 1989: 214, 217–18.

102. It is not certain, however, that the transmigration of souls was an Orphic belief, and some scholars reject the idea (Burkert, 1972: 120–35; Alderink, 1981: 83–84).

103. Guthrie, 1952: 195–201; Pollard, 1965: 100.

104. Euripides quoted in Porphyry, *On abstinence from animal food* 4.19; Guthrie, 1952: 109–12, 199; Harrison, 1955: 478–79.

105. Herodotus, *History* 281.

106. Guthrie, 1952: 198.

107. Euripides, *Hippolytus* 952–53; Plato, *Laws* 782c; Burkert, 1985: 301.

108. Euripides, *Hippolytus* 952–53; Plato, *Laws* 782c; Plutarch, *Table-talk* 2.3.1; Aristophanes, *Frogs* 1032; Kern, 1922: 301–2; Rohde, 1925: 357–58; Linforth, 1941: 55, 59, 70, 97–98, 286–88; Guthrie, 1952: 16–17, 196–97, 217, 254; Graf, 1974: 93 n 61; Detienne, 1975: 60; 1979: 60, 61, 85–86; Alderink, 1981: 80–85; M. L. West, 1983: 14–15, 21; Burkert, 1985: 301–2; Grmek, 1989: 214.

109. Plato, *Laws* 782c; Empedocles, "Fragments" 118–25, Wright; Guthrie, 1952: 197–98; 1962–81, 2: 248–51.

110. Empedocles, "Fragments" 119–20, Wright.

111. Plutarch, *Table-talk* 2.3.1; Linforth, 1941: 286–87; Guthrie, 1952: 92–95, 254; Harrison, 1955: 625–29; Nilsson, 1957: 136, 140–42; Detienne, 1979: 85–86. For more on the concept of the cosmic egg in various parts of the world, see Hellbom, 1963.

112. Guthrie, 1952: 196; Detienne, 1979: 61–62, 86; Grmek, 1989: 217–18.

113. Plutarch, *Roman questions* 95.

114. Similar festivals of the dead were found in ancient Greece, among them the Genesia, at which the dead were honored in Archaic times (c. 800–500 B.C.). Little detail is available except for the annual Genesia festival as practiced in Athens, where it seems not to have been observed after about 400 B.C. (Rohde, 1925: 167–68; Jacoby, 1944; Bremmer, 1987).

For speculation that the honoring of the goddess Carna in June, mentioned above, resembled the Parentalia in being a rite for the dead, see Fowler, 1899: 131.

115. Ovid, *Fasti* 2.533–82; Frazer, pp. 431–52 in Vol. 2 of his trans. of Ovid,

Fasti; Frazer, p. 241 in Vol. 4 of his trans. of Pausanias, *Description of Greece;* Rose, 1941: 91; Schilling, 1987a, 1987b: 461.

116. Ovid, *Fasti* 5.419–44; Fowler, 1899: 106–10; Frazer, pp. 36–46 in Vol. 4 of his trans. of Ovid, *Fasti;* Frazer, p. 241 in Vol. 4 of his trans. of Pausanias, *Description of Greece;* Rose, 1941.

117. Joannes Lydus, *On months* 4.29; Frazer, p. 241 in Vol. 4 of his trans. of Pausanias, *Description of Greece.*

118. Pliny, *Natural history* 18.118–19.

119. Aulus Gellius, *Attic nights* 10.15.11–13; Festus, *On the meaning of words:* "fabam," p. 77, ed. Lindsay.

120. Feliks, 1971–72d.

121. Nilsson, 1949: 83–86; de Vogel, 1966: 127; Burkert, 1985: 75–84; Parker, 1983. I do not cite pages for Parker, 1983, because the entire work, which is unusually rich and scholarly, is devoted to pollution and purification in early Greek religion. 136 For excellent material on the impurity of shedding blood and ritual purification carried out for homicide in ancient Greece, see Parker, 1983: 104–43, 370–74. The symbolism of red in ancient Greece and the role of blood in ritual had parallels with those of Vedic India. In both places, blood sacrifices were made to the gods, though killing was a polluting act. Most fishes did not serve in ancient Greek sacrifieces, but the tuna, as "a fish that bleeds," was regarded as suitable for sacrifice to the gods (Durand, 1989: 127–28).

122. Parker, 1983: 360.

123. Detienne, 1975: 60.

124. Frazer, 1935, 8: 300–302; Burkert, 1972: 120–65.

125. M. Stevenson, 1920: 194–96, 198–99, 436–38; Dandekar, 1953: 125–30; Macdonell, 1968: 115, 223–25, 277–78, 383, 386–89, 422; B. Walker, 1968, 1: 340–41.

126. Burkert, 1972: 133; 1985: 298. Werblowsky (1987: 23) agrees. He calls attention to a remarkable likeness between Indian thinking about transmigration and thinking expressed on "Orphic" tablets found close to the hand of a dead person at Compagno, near Naples, which refer to the soul's escape from "the sorrowful weary wheel" (Harrison, 1955: 667–69; for more on such Orphic views, see Guthrie, 1955: 323). See Grmek (1989: 214) for further comments on possible philosophical exchanges between ancient India and Greece.

127. Burkert, 1985: 78.

128. Nilsson, 1949: 83–84.

129. Nilsson, 1949: 84.

130. Reinach, 1942: 85–86; Nilsson, 1949: 99–104.

131. Nilsson, 1949: 102.

132. See, in this regard, Grimm, 1883–88, 1: 54, 312–13; 2: 840–41; 3: 993, 1042; 4: 1814; Farbridge, 1908–26: 150; 1970: 278; Bussagli, 1987: 563; and

Dölger, 1971. Christ, for one, is seen as the lord of light who, like the sun, comes from the east to bring enlightenment to mankind, whereas Satan is the lord of darkness, an evil being who lives in the west (Rahner, 1955: 399). It is thus fitting that in one German legend a black dog, death, and mandrake are linked, and that in another legend, emissaries of the devil ride on black horses (Grimm and Grimm, 1981, 1: 93–94; 2: 163–64). That such imagery is ancient in northern Europe is shown by the fact that Velnius, pre-Christian, Lithuanian (and Baltic) god of the dead, who was much feared because of his killing tendencies, rode on a black horse and might turn up as a black pig that shrieked and scared people to death or, in a cemetery, as a black dog whose bites never healed (Gimbutas, 1974: 91).

133. Grimm, 1883–88, 1: 313 n; Lang, 1901, 2: 285.

134. Rohde, 1925: 169; Frazer, pp. 273–76 in Vol. 2 of his trans. of Ovid, *Fasti;* Guthrie, 1955: 221.

135. Burkert, 1972: 177.

136. Diogenes Laertius, *Lives of eminent philosophers* 8.34.

137. Megas, 1963: 48. Interestingly, the Eastern church is said to lack a defined sense of liturgic color, though ordinarily vestments are white or red, with gold embroidery. In the modern Roman Catholic church, on the other hand, there is an established order for the color of vestments that clergy wear. Black vestments are used in funeral rites for adults, in masses for the dead, and in a certain mass on Good Friday, the day Christ died. White vestments, on the other hand, serve on many other occasions, as in bridal masses, in all festivals of the Virgin Mary and of Christ (except those associated with his death), and in funeral rites for children (W. A. Phillips, 1910–11: 1059–60).

138. Drower, 1937: xxiii n 2, citing R. Campbell Thompson. Among the Babylonians and Assyrians, bārū priests were diviners who usually predicted the future through hepatoscopy, inspection of the liver of animals (their name comes from *bārū*, "to see" or "to inspect"). Āšipu priests, as indicated above, were priest-magicians who treated illness and disease (Smith and Whitehouse, 1910–11: 317).

139. Dhalla, 1922: 175.

140. Drower, 1937: 39. The ceremonial dress of the modern Parsis, both priests and laymen, is also white. So is that of the Yezidis, as well as that of the Mandaeans of Iraq and Iran, for white symbolizes "the dress of light in which the pure soul is clad." The Mandaeans also say that at one time they always wore white clothing, that it was a sin to wear color. They also cover their sacred books, or rolls, in white cloth, and an orthodox priest was quite upset when Drower bound such a sacred work in leather (Drower, 1937: 22–23, 30, 36, 39, 91, 166, 167).

141. Dhalla, 1922: 174–75, 259, 315–16, 365.

142. Drower, 1937: 39, 165.

143. Farbridge, 1970: 278.

144. Diogenes Laertius, *Lives of eminent philosophers* 8.19, 33.

145. de Vogel, 1966: 187, citing Iamblichus; Burkert, 1972: 190; 1985: 302.

146. Pliny, *Natural history* 35.160; Rohde, 1925: 192 n 61; A. B. Cook, 1964–65, 2: 470–72, 843, 1165.

147. Plutarch, *Aristides* 21; Burkert, 1983: 56–57. In ancient Greece, the myrtle, an evergreen shrub, also symbolized immortality, and, because it was sacred to Aphrodite, goddess of love and beauty, it symbolized love (Hehn, 1888: 170–71; Skinner, 1911: 190–91; Lehner and Lehner, 1960: 41). For the myrtle in modern Near Eastern ritual and belief—especially that relating to life, death, baptism, resurrection, marriage, and happiness—see Drower, 1937: 35–36, 70, 87–88, 105–6, 111, 121–22, 144–45, 179, 205, 206, 230, 392, and passim; 1956: 34, 36, 37, 81–83, 85, 229–30, 231, 237, 241, 245; and Farbridge, 1970: 47–48.

148. This recalls the ban on black figs, black grapes, black berries, and any fruit with black juice in modern Greece on August 29, the annual celebration of the beheading of John the Baptist. In this case, however, black fruit is banned because of an association with a revered saint: the black color of the fruit is thought to have derived from St. John's blood (Megas, 1963: 152).

149. Macrobius, *Saturnalia* 3.20.2–3; Rohde, 1925: 320 n 81, 590; Burkert, 1983: 259; 1985: 82–83.

150. Macrobius, *Saturnalia* 3.20.2–3.

151. Hippocrates, *Sacred disease* 2.1–30. The association of black with death in Greek thinking is also shown in Artemidorus Daldianus's *Interpretation of dreams* (5.35): "A man who had a rich sister who was sick dreamt that a fig tree sprouted up in front of his sister's house from which he plucked and ate a total of seven black figs. After his sister had lived another seven days, she died, leaving the dreamer as her heir. The reasons are obvious."

152. Among these were a ban on the use of eggs in the banquet in honor of Dionysus and a ban on initiates eating mint, a common flavoring in the preparation of fava beans (Nilsson, 1957: 136, 137; Detienne, 1979: 86, 115 n 104).

153. Nilsson, 1957: 134–35; and Detienne, 1979: 86, citing J. Keil.

154. Cicero, *On Vatinius* 13.31–32; Frazer, pp. 152, 192–93, 273–76, and 301 in Vol. 2, and pp. 310–11 in Vol. 3 of his trans. of Ovid, *Fasti;* Cumont, 1923: 166.

155. Horace, *Epistles* 1.7.6; Frazer, p. 282 in Vol. 2 of his trans. of Ovid, *Fasti*.

156. Seventeenth-century Persians used somewhat different reasoning. Because they considered black unlucky, a contemptible color associated with the devil, black clothing was inappropriate for persons in mourning (Chardin, 1927: 215). See also Massé, 1954: 91, 353, 354, 356.

157. Goetze and Sturtevant, 1938: 5–25, 98–102.

158. Collins, 1990: 223–24.

159. Gurney, 1977: 60–61, citing Haas and Wilhelm.

160. Hoffner, 1974: 98–99, 102. This goddess was presumably an underworld deity such as Erishkigal, Allatum, or Allani. For more references to these goddesses, see Gurney, 1977: 4, 5, 13, 18, 55. For Hittite funerary rituals in which an underworld goddess received offerings, see Gurney, 1977: 59–83.

This pattern is also reported in the modern Near East. The Mandaeans of Iraq and Iran, for example, detest black, for it is the color of evil, death, and mourning (Drower, 1937: 167, 197, 222). In modern Morocco, white is the appropriate color for holy persons and places. Black, on the other hand, is a bad omen, and actions and events at night or in the dark are hazardous (Westermarck, 1973: 6–8, 70, 127, 132).

161. Andrews, 1949: 277 n 33; Pollard, 1965: 97, 111; Burkert, 1972: 178; Parker, 1983: 358–59.

162. Kirk and Raven, 1957: 224; Philip, 1966: 189–91; Burkert, 1972: 112.

163. Philip, 1966: 189, 190; Gorman, 1979: 56–63.

164. For more on early claims that Pythagoras visited Egypt, see Grmek, 1989: 215; Lefkowitz, 1995: 67–69, 76–77, 98, 103–4.

165. Herodotus, *History* 2.37.

166. In this, Herodotus is followed by Plutarch (Plutarch, *Table-talk* 8.8.2; Plutarch, *Isis and Osiris* 5). Diodorus Siculus (*Library of history* 1.89.4), on his part, says only that some Egyptians refused to eat beans. For more on the bean in ancient Egyptian ritual, see Hopfner, 1974: 305–13 (pars. 529–31).

167. J. G. Wilkinson, 1883, 1: 180; 2: 402, 409; Darby et al., 1977, 2: 682–85.

168. Herodotus, *History* 2.123.

169. Kirk and Raven, 1957: 224; Burkert, 1972: 126, 128; Werblowsky, 1987: 22; Lefkowitz, 1995: 67–69.

170. Schweinfurth, 1884: 201; Andrews, 1949: 274, 277 n 34; Moldenke and Moldenke, 1952: 101; Darby et al., 1977, 2: 682.

171. Burkert, 1972: 128.

172. Plutarch, *Table-talk* 8.8.2.

173. Keith, 1909: 573; Burkert, 1972: 128, 157–58. For an evaluation of ancient claims for the derivation of Greek traits from Egypt, see "Ancient myths of cultural dependency" in Lefkowitz, 1995: 53–90.

174. von Schroeder, 1884: 35–39.

175. von Schroeder, 1901.

176. Andrews, 1949: 287–90.

177. Frazer, 1935, 9: 143–44; 1968, 2: 310, 492; Lévi-Strauss, 1979.

178. Diogenes Laertius, *Lives of eminent philosophers* 8.24; Delatte, 1930: 54–56; Andrews, 1949: 285–86, 289–90; Onians, 1973: 112 n 2.

179. Böhm, 1905: 15, 17; Andrews, 1949: 285.

180. E.g., Detienne, 1970: 153.

181. Hanelt, 1972b: 209.

182. For a discussion of the coloring of fava bean flowers and representations of different patterns of wing spots (usually black, black-purple, brown-black, or brown in color) on *minor, major,* and other varieties, see Sirks, 1931: 281–83; Hanelt, 1972a: 91–92.

183. Marcovich, 1964: 31 n 36.

184. Rohde, 1925: 357–58.

185. Varro, cited in Pliny, *Natural history* 18.119; Festus, *On the meaning of words:* "fabam," p. 77; *Geoponica* 2.35.

186. Burkert, 1972: 183.

187. In Tibetan divination, white and black pebbles may be used, or, in one form of drum divination, black and white sections on a drum skin. If the seed representing an ill person moves into the white section, his illness can be cured; if it moves into the black section, his case is hopeless (de Nebesky-Wojkowitz, 1956: 457–59).

188. Meigs, 1978: 312–14; Rozin and Fallon, 1987: 28; Rozin and Nemeroff, 1990: 212; Rozin et al., 1993: 579–82.

189. Angyal, 1941: 409; H. N. C. Stevenson, 1954: 51; Meigs, 1978: 305, 306–7, 308–9, 310–13; Rozin and Fallon, 1987: 29; Rozin et al., 1993: 579–81.

190. Plutarch, *Roman questions* 95.

191. Detienne, 1970: 160; 1977: 59.

Chapter 8. Favism and the Origin of the Pythagorean Ban on Fava Beans

1. Sansone, Piga, and Segni, 1958: 7–10, 221; Russo, 1967: 318; Lieber, 1973: 35–36; Mager et al., 1980: 266; Grmek, 1980: 87–88; 1989: 224–25.

2. The only review to qualify in this regard is that of Grmek (1980), originally published a decade and a half ago and reissued, with certain additions and modifications, nearly a decade ago (Grmek, 1989: 210–44).

3. G6PD-deficiency is also involved in bringing on neonatal jaundice, acute hemolytic anemia in persons who take antimalaria drugs such as primaquine, and certain other clinical conditions (Beutler, 1960; Luzzatto and Mehta, 1989: 2244–49; Piomelli, 1986; Verjee, 1993; Mehta, 1994: 873). For a list of drugs to be avoided by G6PD-deficient persons, see Verjee, 1993: 44; and Mehta, 1994: 873.

4. Szeinberg et al., 1957: 608–9, 610–11; Sansone, Piga, and Segni, 1958: 176–78, 224; Motulsky, 1960: 48; Zannos-Mariolea and Kattamis, 1961: 37–38; Kattamis et al., 1969b: 34; Mager et al., 1980: 269; Kattamis, 1986: 29–30; Luzzatto and Mehta, 1989: 2246; Mehta, 1994: 873.

5. For excellent summaries of those data, as well as references to studies of G6PD-deficiency in populations bordering on Greece and Italy, see Mourant et al., 1976; and Livingstone, 1985.

6. Stamatoyannopoulos et al., 1966: 300–302.

7. Salvidio et al., 1969: 333.

8. Siniscalco et al., 1966: 383.

9. Kattamis et al., 1969a: 289. Rhodes is also characterized by high incidences of favism. The incidence of favism from one area to another is not always proportional to the incidence of G6PD-deficiency (Kattamis et al., 1969a; Kattamis, 1986: 28–29).

10. Luzzatto and Battistuzzi, 1985: 251–77; Luzzatto and Mehta, 1989: 2237, 2241; Arese and De Flora, 1990: 4; Mehta, 1994: 871. The most common G6PD-deficiency variant in Greece, Sicily, and mainland Italy is called Mediterranean, which is characterized by G6PD activity only 0–5 percent of normal. The Mediterranean variant, despite its name, is not the most common variant in Egypt and is not reported in Algeria at all (Luzzatto and Battistuzzi, 1985: 265–70).

It has been noted that favism has not been certainly demonstrated in G6PD-deficient blacks (Motulsky, 1965: 153); that favism has not been described in Africans; and that it is thought not to be associated with the African (A-) variant of G6PD (Verjee, 1993: 45). The Republic of the Sudan is clearly an exception, for several cases of acute hemolytic anemia have been reported in Khartoum in G6PD-deficient boys (ages seven months to nine years) who had consumed fava beans, which are called Egyptian beans (Hassan, 1971). If favism has not been confirmed elsewhere in Africa, moreover, this may simply reflect the fact that fava beans are not cultivated to any degree, if at all, in tropical Africa, for, in Italy, deficient persons with the African (A-) variant—including Negroid, Caucasoid, and mixed individuals—have developed favism from consuming fava beans (Calabrò et al., 1989; Galiano et al., 1990). This is in accord with Mehta's statement (1994: 874) that it is incorrect to say that favism occurs only in persons with polymorphic variants of G6PD (especially G6PD Mediterranean), or that G6PD A- is not tied to favism.

Favism is reported in South China and Taiwan, where Class II variants of G6PD are common and fava beans are eaten (Sansone, Piga, and Segni, 1958: 29; Belsey, 1973: 4; Panich, 1986: 200–201; Arese and De Flora, 1990: 4; Kantha, 1990: 107), but clinicians in Thailand often note anecdotally that favism is absent there. This has been confirmed by one study, but it remains uncertain whether it is because G6PD mutants in Thailand are different (by far the most frequent variant is Mahidol, a Class III, moderately deficient variant also common in southern China) (Panich, 1986: 197, 200, 216); because fava beans in Thailand have limited toxicity; or because Thai methods of preparation destroy the toxic compounds (Kitayaporn et al., 1991).

11. Arese, 1982: 127.

12. Luisada, 1941: 233.

13. Riepl et al., 1993: 932, 933.

14. Kattamis et al., 1969a: 288.

15. Kattamis et al., 1969b: 38.

16. Siniscalco et al., 1961: 1180.

17. Corchia et al., 1995: 808.

18. Hedayat et al., 1971: 151.

19. Belsey, 1973: 5.

20. Hedayat et al., 1971: 151.

21. Sansone, Piga, and Segni, 1958: 46–47; Emanuel and Schoenfeld, 1961; Russo, 1967: 321; Kattamis et al., 1969b: 35–36; Plato et al., 1964: 273; Hedayat et al., 1971: 151; Kattamis, 1971; Taj-Eldin, 1971; Belsey, 1973: 7–8, 9; Schilirò et al., 1979: 185, 186–87; Mager et al., 1980: 267; Luzzatto and Mehta, 1989: 2247; Kattamis, 1986: 27; Arese and De Flora, 1990: 5.

22. Luisada, 1941: 233.

23. Corchia et al., 1995: 807–8.

24. Sansone, Piga, and Segni, 1958: 46; Arese and De Flora, 1990: 4–5; Yahya and Al-Allawi, 1993: 290.

25. Sansone, Piga, and Segni, 1958: 47–48, 222; Veras, 1961: 348; Zannos-Mariolea and Kattamis, 1961: 39, 40; Plato et al., 1964: 273, 276; Russo, 1967: 322, 339; Donoso et al., 1969: 514, 516; Kattamis et al., 1969b: 35, 36; Hedayat et al., 1971: 150; Russo et al., 1972: 856; Belsey, 1973: 5–6; Meloni et al., 1983: 84, 85; Kattamis, 1986: 26–28; Arese and De Flora, 1990: 5; Yahya and Al-Allawi, 1993: 291.

Sansone, Piga, and Segni (1958: 47–48, 222) have written that male children are much more likely to develop favism than female children. Among youths and adults, however, females have incidences of favism as high as or higher than males. Studies in Greece (Plato et al., 1964: 276; Kattamis, 1986: 27–28) and Iran (Hedayat et al., 1971: 150, 151), however, found far more males than females among adult hospital cases of favism. Sartori (1971: 463–64) reported that though incidences of favism were approximately the same between males and females (ages not given) selected at random in three Sardinian villages, all severe cases of favism occurred in males in the village where the matter was investigated. In a similar vein, Kattamis (1986: 28) suggests that male-female ratios in hospitalized patients are not the real ones, that they are skewed because female heterozygotes may experience such mild symptoms as to escape detection.

26. Kattamis et al., 1969b: 38; Hedayat et al., 1971: 153–54; Belsey, 1973: 3; Calabrò et al., 1989; Meloni et al., 1992: 31.

27. Arese and De Flora, 1990: 31.

28. Crosby, 1956: 91.

29. Belsey, 1973: 1; Arese, 1982: 127–28; Mehta, 1994: 873–74.

30. Fermi and Martinetti, 1905: 81, 86.

31. Crosby, 1956: 91.

32. The incidence of favism in Sardinia dropped from 5.20/1,000 residents in 1905 to 0.73/1,000 in 1975 and to 0.33/1,000 in 1979 (Arese and De Flora, 1990: 4). That drop seems to be continuing, for in the district of Sassari, northern Sardinia, the number of favism cases dropped from 508 in 1961–70 to 144 in 1981–90 (Meloni et al., 1992).

33. Deaths from favism in Sardinia have dropped from roughly 250 a year in 1936 to negligible numbers in recent decades (Arese and De Flora, 1990: 4).

34. Veras, 1961: 348, 350.

35. Donoso et al., 1969: 516; Hedayat et al., 1971: 153, 154; Belsey, 1973: 6–7.

36. Mager et al., 1980: 277–85; De Flora et al., 1986: 79; Arese and De Flora, 1990: 7–13.

37. Though some researchers have failed to find either vicine or convicine in garden peas (Griffiths and Ramsay, 1992: 464–65), Jamalian et al. (1977b: 210) did find a trace of vicine in them. They also identified one G6PD-deficient man who was afflicted with favism and who, though he never ate fava beans, occasionally developed jaundice from eating garden peas (Jamalian et al., 1977a: 214–15).

38. Jamalian et al., 1977b: 210–11; Mager et al., 1980: 279; Pitz et al., 1981: 7. Griffiths and Ramsay, 1992: 463, 464–65. The exception is *Vicia bithynica*, which was found to have amounts of vicine and convicine similar to those of *V. faba* (Griffiths and Ramsay, 1992: 463, 464–65).

39. Collier, 1976; Jamalian, 1978; Olsen and Andersen, 1978; Pitz and Sosulski, 1979; D'Aqino et al., 1981: 1302; Pitz et al., 1981; Gardiner et al., 1982; Arese et al., 1986: 50, 51; Arese and De Flora, 1990: 8.

40. Burbano et al., 1995: 268–69.

41. Sisini et al., 1981: 1499.

42. Collier, 1976: 158; Jamalian et al., 1976: 333; 1977a; Jamalian and Bassiri, 1978; Pitz and Sosulski, 1979; Sisini et al., 1981; Pitz et al., 1981.

According to Arese et al. (1986: 51), boiling or drying and storing fava beans did not reduce the amounts of vicine and convicine they contain. However, Collier (1976: 158) found, in boiling two lots of fresh fava beans for 30 minutes, that their vicine was reduced by 21 percent and 58 percent and that the amounts lost equalled those found in the cooking water. Jamalian et al. (1977a: 216–17), on their part, reported that water in which dry fava beans had been soaked brings on a drop in glutathione levels in the erythrocytes of favism-prone subjects.

For more on convicine and/or vicine reduction in fava beans through soaking in water and/or other methods of preparation, see Hegazy and Marquardt, 1983: 102–3; and Abd Allah et al., 1988: 207–9. For heat treatment of ground fava beans and destruction of vicine and convicine, see Arbid and Marquardt, 1985: 842–43. For fava bean dishes in the Near East and North Africa, see Donoso et al., 1969: 513–14; and Belsey, 1973: 9–10.

43. Pitz and Sosulski (1979) found fresh green beans to contain 2.5 times more total vicine and convicine than dried beans.

44. Luisada, 1941: 232; Sansone, Piga, and Segni, 1958: 50–51, 222; Russo, 1967: 321, 339; Kattamis et al., 1969b: 36; Hedayat et al., 1971: 151–52; Sartori, 1971: 462, 467; Belsey, 1973: 7; Schilirò et al., 1979: 185; Meloni et al., 1983: 84; Corchia et al., 1995: 807; Arese et al., 1986: 45; Luzzatto and Mehta, 1989: 2247; Arese and De Flora, 1990: 5; Mehta, 1994: 874.

Vicine and convicine have also been reported in certain other plant parts (e.g., seedlings, leaves, pods), but the seed, because of its dietary importance, poses the principal danger to sensitive persons. In one study, Brown and Roberts (1972: 3203, 3204) found vicine and convicine to remain constant at very low levels in young seedlings in their first two weeks of growth. They detected no vicine or convicine either in very young fava bean pods (up to 10 cm long) or in their seeds. Vicine and convicine were not found in larger pods (13–15 cm long), but they did occur in seeds of those pods. Sisini et al. (1981: 1498), however, found significant amounts of total vicine and convicine in fava bean pods (0.70 percent of dry weight) and also found total vicine and convicine in seed coats to be nearly as high (1.73 percent of dry weight) as levels in cotyledons (1.88 percent). Burbano et al. (1995: 268–71) found vicine and convicine mainly in the cotyledons (0.3–2.5 percent), but also in seed coats and pods at various stages of growth, in pods at very low levels (less than 0.1 percent). Jamalian et al. (1977b: 210, 211) found no vicine in either the flowers or the pods of fava beans, though significant amounts occurred in the seed, both seed coat (hull) (0.30–1.89 percent of dry weight) and cotyledon (dehulled seed) (0.61–2.38 percent). In still another study, Pitz and Sosulski (1979: 95, 97) found green pods to contain neither vicine nor convicine. However, they found seed to contain significant amounts of vicine and convicine, but seed coats contained only about one-tenth the amount found in whole mature seed. Studies by Collier (1976), Jamalian (1978), and Jamalian and Bassiri (1978) confirm the fact that seed coats contain vicine but in amounts far lower than in cotyledons.

Sisini et al. (1981: 1498) reported about as much total vicine and convicine in fava bean leaves (1.81 percent of dry weight) as in seed coats and cotyledons. Luisada (1941: 232, 233), on his part, demonstrated that in unusual cases fava bean leaves can bring on clinical symptoms, such as when a sensitive person drinks water from a container in which these leaves had been stored.

45. Jamalian and Bassiri, 1978; Pitz et al., 1981; Burbano et al., 1995: 268–70.

46. Hegazy and Marquardt, 1983; Arbid and Marquardt, 1985; Abd Allah et al., 1988; Donath and Kujawa, 1991; McKay, 1992.

47. Donath and Kujawa, 1991; McKay, 1992.

48. Arbid and Marquardt, 1985.

49. For a review of the ties between malaria and the sickle cell trait, thalassemia, and G6PD-deficiency, see Vogel and Motulsky, 1986: 458–72.

50. Arie, 1959: 77–80; Lieber, 1973: 34; W. M. S. Russell, 1980: 375.

51. E.g., Arie, 1959; Lieber, 1970: LV; Mager et al., 1980: 266.

52. Luisada, 1941: 229; Szeinberg et al., 1957: 603; Kattamis, 1986: 26.

53. Waldron, 1973.

54. Luzzatto and Mehta, 1989: 2238, 2246. See also Mehta, 1994: 872.

55. Veras, 1958; Grmek, 1980: 80–87, 113; 1989: 238–39.

56. Grmek, 1980: 83–87.

57. Hippocrates, *Regimen* 2.45; Hippocrates, *Epidemics* 2.6.7; Hippocrates, *Regimen in acute diseases (appendix)* 47, 64.

58. Allison et al., 1963; Stamatoyannopoulos et al., 1966; Kattamis et al., 1969a; Valaes et al., 1969; Livingstone, 1973: 170; 1985: 151–52.

59. Hippocrates, *Epidemics* 1.6–9; P. F. Russell, 1955: 7–9; Bruce-Chwatt and Zulueta, 1980: 17–19; Gilles, 1993a: 1.

60. Needing careful reexamination is the evidence pertaining to whether or not ancient physicians may have become aware of favism over the centuries following the time of the Hippocratic writers. Dioscorides (c. A.D. 40–90), a well-travelled physician and pharmacologist, noted in his famous herbal that fava beans are flatulent, difficult to digest, and bring on troublesome dreams, but also that they are nourishing and useful medicinally, as in stopping diarrhea and vomiting (Dioscorides, *De materia medica* 2.127). Significantly, however, he said not a word that suggests an awareness of favism. Yet, according to Scarborough (1981–82: 357), an authority on Roman medicine, there is certain evidence that "a form of favism" was known in "ancient medical dietetics." He cites, as an example, a passage in the writings of Galen (*Commentary on Hippocrates' "Epidemics"* 2.4.3, trans. in Galen, 1964–65, 17, pt. 1: 474–75), that noted physician (c. A.D. 129–199) whose travels carried him from Anatolia to mainland Greece, Egypt, and Rome. This took him across much of the modern Mediterranean belt of favism.

61. Veras, 1958: 6.

62. Grmek, 1989: 224, 240–42.

63. Lieber, 1970: LIV.

64. Sansone, Piga, and Segni, 1958: 221.

65. von Schroeder, 1901; Andrews, 1949.

66. Lévi-Strauss, 1979.

67. Burkert, 1972: 117; Philip, 1966: 191.

68. Burkert, 1972: 102–3.

69. Rohde, cited in Burkert, 1972: 103.

70. Burkert, 1982: 13.

71. Philip, 1966: 17–18, 22 n 14.

72. W. M. S. Russell and C. Russell, 1983: 100.

73. Philip, 1966: 191.

74. Iamblichus, *On the Pythagorean life* 189–91.

75. Grmek, 1989: 213.

76. Iamblichus, *On the Pythagorean life* 192–94.

77. Diogenes Laertius, *Lives of eminent philosophers* 8.39; Philip, 1966: 191.

78. Diogenes Laertius, *Lives of eminent philosophers* 8.40.

79. Walker and Bowman, 1960; Bowman and Walker, 1961.

80. Jamalian et al., 1977a: 213–14; Mager et al., 1980: 269, 281, 283; Luzzatto and Mehta, 1989: 2249; Arese and De Flora, 1990: 5–6.

81. Mager et al., 1980: 266, citing Larizza, Brunetti, and Grignani.

82. Crosby, 1956: 91; Sansone, Piga, and Segni, 1958: 8–15, 48–51, 222; Motulsky, 1960: 48; Sartori, 1971: 462; Russo, 1967: 321; Schilirò et al., 1979: 183, 185.

Motulsky and Campbell-Kraut once said that contrary to popular belief it is not pollen that brings on hemolysis but, rather, volatile products deriving from the fava bean plant when it is in flower. In support of this, they cite the case of people working in bins where fava beans are stored, places where the air contains no pollen, who develop hemolysis through inhalation of the volatile products (Motulsky and Campbell-Kraut, 1961: 188).

83. Fermi and Martinetti, 1905: 83.

84. Luisada, 1941: 231. Crosby (1956: 91) puts the situation in Sardinia somewhat differently, saying that most cases of favism occur in April and May, "when the beans are fresh and the pollen of the blossoms is in the air." Sartori (1971: 462–63), on his part, associates the April and May peaks of favism in Sardinia with the ripening of the fava beans.

85. Crosby, 1956: 91.

86. Schilirò et al., 1979: 183, 185.

87. Kattamis et al., 1969b.

88. Meloni et al., 1983: 83.

89. Belsey, 1973: 8; Mager et al., 1980: 266.

90. Belsey, 1973: 7.

91. Belsey, 1973: 8.

92. Donoso et al., 1969: 516.

93. Hedayat et al., 1971: 151, 155–56.

94. Belsey, 1973: 8.

95. Kattamis et al., 1969b: 39; Kattamis, 1986: 31.

96. Sartori, 1971: 462–63; Kattamis, 1986: 30–32.

97. Mager et al., 1980: 266.

98. Arese et al., 1986: 45; Luzzatto and Mehta, 1989: 2246–47; Arese and De Flora, 1990: 4–5.

99. Arese, 1982: 127–28.

100. Philip, 1966: 185–86; Burkert, 1972: 111 and n.

101. Stamatoyannopoulos et al., 1966.

102. Shipley, 1987: 105 and 105 n 15, 302.

103. Philip, 1966: 186–87; Burkert, 1972: 111 n 12, 206 n 77.

104. Diogenes Laertius, *Lives of eminent philosophers* 8.1.

105. Pausanias, *Description of Greece* 2.13.2.

106. Stamatoyannopoulos et al., 1966.

107. According to Strabo, the Iapyges, an Indo-European but non-Latin people, had once lived at Croton (in the area of Croton?) (Strabo, *Geography* 6.1.12). The Iapyges had linguistic affinities to peoples of the Balkans, and, according to one ancient tradition, they came from Illyria, across the Adriatic Sea. The general region of Croton, however, was more properly the country of non-Latin Italic peoples (Bruttii). The Greek cities of Magna Graecia, on their part, were settled by people from various parts of the Greek world. That settlement took place over a period of centuries. Croton itself was founded about 700 B.C., reputedly by Myscellus, a Greek from Rhype in Achaea (Diodorus Siculus, *Library of history* 8.17). Metapontum, like most early cities of Magna Graecia, was also established by Achaean Greeks. Tarentum, however, was a Dorian colony that was later affiliated with Sparta. Siris and Elea were established later by Ionian Greeks. Because Greek settlers came from such varied places and because of interbreeding among Greeks, Iapgyes, Bruttii, and perhaps other non-Greeks—the peoples of Magna Graecia must have had considerable genetic diversity.

108. For maps of incidences of G6PD-deficiency in the Mediterranean area, see Luzzatto and Battistuzzi, 1985: 268; and Cavalli-Sforza et al., 1994: genetic map 169. These sources also have maps of G6PD-deficiency in other parts of the world.

109. Siniscalco et al., 1966: 383.

110. Tagarelli, Bastone, et al., 1991: 141.

111. Crosby, 1956; Sansone, Piga, and Segni, 1958: 17–21, 221; Sansone, Segni, and de Cecco, 1958; Livingstone, 1967: 294–305; 1973: 180–85; 1985: 212–21; Salvidio et al., 1969; Mourant et al., 1976: 727, 737, 739, 745; P. J. Brown, 1981: 375; Meloni et al., 1983: 86–87, citing Sartori; Luzzatto and Battistuzzi, 1985: 268.

112. Livingstone, 1985: 194–212.

113. Salvidio et al., 1969: 333.

114. Gallo, 1968.

115. Brunetti et al., 1965: 212, 219.

116. Corbo et al., 1981.

117. Fifteen of 1,777 males, or 0.8 percent, mostly from these regions, included in Livingstone, 1985: 193–96.

118. Rickards et al., 1988: 571; pers. comm., Olga Rickards.

119. Renga et al., 1968.

120. Colonna-Romano et al., 1985: 228.

121. Salvidio et al., 1969: 333.

122. Rickards et al., 1988: 571; pers. comm., Olga Rickards.

123. Tagarelli and Brancati, n.d.; Tagarelli, Bastone, et al., 1991; Tagarelli et al., 1992.

124. All my text discussion of Cosenza Province deals with non-Albanian communities. I have set aside the interesting material on G6PD-deficiency in towns of the Albanian ethnic minority of Cosenza, who first settled in southern Italy in the fifteenth century. Persons from Albanian towns were found to have somewhat higher frequencies of G6PD-deficiency (15 of 510 boys tested, or 2.9 percent) than those of non-Albanian communities (Tagarelli and Brancati, n.d.: 3, 6, 15; Tagarelli et al., 1992). Also set aside were two other studies. One was set aside because it represents a likely case of random genetic drift in a somewhat isolated population. This study was done in San Giovanni in Fiore, a highland town in Cosenza Province, and reported a 4.3 percent incidence of G6PD-deficiency (27 of 629 boys tested). This is much higher than incidences in other highland communities of the province and, indeed, one of the highest found so far in mainland Italy (Tagarelli and Brancati, n.d.: 4, 17; Tagarelli, Bastone, et al., 1991: 146, 149; Tagarelli et al., 1995: 249, 254–55). The second of these two studies that I set aside (Gallo, 1968) involved males from Matera in Basilicata and found that 1 of 14 (7.1 percent) had G6PD-deficiency. The latter study was set aside because of its small sample size and because a subsequent study found that only 2.8 percent of unrelated male donors from Matera (numbers not given) had G6PD-deficiency (Rickards et al., 1988: 571, 572).

125. Tagarelli and Brancati, n.d.: 8; Tagarelli, Bastone, et al., 1991: 141, 142; Tagarelli et al., 1997a: 205–6.

126. Tagarelli and Brancati, n.d.: 8; Tagarelli, Bastone, et al., 1991: 143, 146, 149; Tagarelli et al., 1997a: 205–6.

127. Tagarelli and Brancati, n.d.: 8; Tagarelli, Bastone, et al., 1991: 144, 148, 149; Tagarelli et al., 1997a: 205–6. In former times, malaria was of high to moderate endemicity in both coastal areas of Cosenza.

128. Rickards et al., 1988: 571.

129. Burkert, 1972: 112, 117.

130. Still another study (Modiano et al., 1965) was carried out in the province of Lecce (at the tip of the boot heel) in the region of Puglia. Lecce was chosen for various reasons. It was malarial. Thalassemia and favism are not uncommon there. Certain other published gene frequencies among its peoples vaguely resembled those of Sardinia. It has archeological ruins (stone towers, megalithic monuments) that resemble ones found in Sardinia but are nearly absent elsewhere in Italy. In addition, Lecce has people in certain areas who speak non-Italian languages, particularly 10 communes of Greek-speaking people believed to have come from the Peloponnesus in Byzantine times. Despite Lecce's malaria, only 6 of 275 randomly selected males (2.2 percent) were found to be G6PD-

deficient. Furthermore, the gene frequencies of Lecce's people in general turned out to have no significant resemblances to those of Sardinians. The people of its Greek-speaking communes, on their part, seemed to differ little in this way from peoples of other areas of the province.

131. Stamatoyannopoulos et al., 1966: 298, 300.

132. Luzzatto and Battistuzzi, 1985: 268; Tagarelli et al., 1997a: 205.

133. Tagarelli and Brancati, n.d.: 9, 12; Brancati and Tagarelli, 1982: 147, 148; Tagarelli, Bastone, et al., 1991: 146–49; Tagarelli et al., 1997b: 202–3. Significant genetic differences between the Ionian and Tyrrhenian coasts of Cosenza Province have also been found in the incidence of phosphoglucomutase 1 (PGM1) (Tagarelli, Mazzei, et al., 1991).

134. Rickards et al., 1988: 571, 572.

135. Colonna-Romano et al., 1985: 231; Rickards et al., 1988: 572; Viglietto et al., 1990: 12.

136. Tagarelli, Bastone, et al., 1991.

137. Rickards et al., 1988: 572. The Mediterranean variant of G6PD is found in Sardinia, but other variants characterized by severe deficiency (Cagliari, Sassari, Seattle-like) also occur. Indeed, the latter three variants account for the bulk of G6PD-deficiency cases there (Testa et al., 1980; Fenu et al., 1982; Luzzatto and Battistuzzi, 1985: 268; Rickards et al., 1988: 572–73).

138. Fermi and Martinetti, 1905: 89–90; Luisada, 1941: 230–31; Sansone, Piga, and Segni, 1958: 17–21; Brunetti et al., 1965; Modiano et al., 1965: 19; Bottini et al., 1971; Calabrò et al., 1989; Galiano et al., 1990.

139. E.g., Ferrarans in Sardinia: Motulsky and Campbell-Kraut, 1961: 173.

140. Arese and De Flora, 1990: 4; pers. comm., P. Arese.

141. Russo, 1967; Schilirò et al., 1979.

142. Schilirò et al., 1979: 183.

143. Salvidio et al., 1969: 333.

144. Russo, 1967: 323, 339.

145. Rickards et al., 1988: 570–72. The datum presented above is not in agreement with Grmek's observation (1989: 231), insofar as it applies to southern Italy and Sicily: "By contrast [with northern Italy], the B- [Mediterranean] variant of G6PD deficiency is extremely common in Sicily, the fatherland of Empedocles, in Sardinia, and in the parts of Calabria where the Greek colonies once stood and Pythagoras held forth. There, up to one-third of the autochthonous males have the favic defect."

146. Rickards et al., 1988: 572.

147. Luisada, 1941: 236.

148. Belsey, 1973: 5.

149. Kattamis et al., 1969a: 290; 1969b: 34; 1971.

150. Kattamis et al., 1969a: 290; 1969b: 38.

151. One study in Cyprus found that only 4 percent of all patients hospitalized with favism from 1955 to 1960 were age 17 or over (Plato et al., 1964: 276).

152. To put the matter in a modern perspective, in 1961 Sicily had a male population of 2.3 million, of whom, by Russo's estimate, 1.2 percent, or 27,000 individuals, were G6PD-deficient (Russo, 1967: 324). One might expect 15 percent of those males to develop favism at some time in their lives, or roughly 4,000 individuals. Assuming a single episode of favism in a lifetime and a life span of 50 years, one would expect about 80 cases of favism among males in Sicily per year. Problems arise with estimating the actual numbers of favism cases because of such factors as public health education, which may prevent the disease, failure of afflicted persons to see a doctor, and failure of doctors to diagnose, report, and hospitalize those who do seek medical attention. In fact, the total number of hospital admissions for favism reported in Sicily in 1961 was 32. By 1965 and 1967 those numbers had increased to 44 and 58, largely because of increasing medical awareness of the disease (Russo, 1967: 320). These figures include both males and females, but Russo reported that males accounted for 94 percent of all cases of favism in Sicily (Russo, 1967: 322), which would, in 1965 and 1967, have amounted to 41 and 55 cases. Whatever the year, however, adult male cases reported (5 percent of the total male cases of favism) were likely no more than 2 or 3 out of a total male population of more than 2 million.

153. Philip, 1966: 139–40; Burkert, 1982: 17–18.

154. *Haemoglobinopathies and allied disorders,* 1966: 17. In Iraq, three patients who had been treated for favism were given fava beans to eat two to three months after complete recovery, and were followed for at least a month after the subsequent ingestion. None of the three experienced a hemolytic episode during that time (Yahya and Al-Allawi, 1993: 290, 291).

155. Kattamis et al., 1969b: 38; Kattamis, 1986: 27–28.

156. Schilirò et al., 1979: 187.

157. Arese and De Flora, 1990: 31, citing Marcolongo.

158. Crosby, 1956: 91; Allison et al., 1963: 239; Sartori, 1971: 462, 465; Belsey, 1973: 10; Hedayat et al., 1981: 111, 112; Meloni et al., 1992: 31.

159. The same argument applies to the speculation that Egyptian priests banned fava beans out of fear of hemolysis (Motulsky and Campbell-Kraut, 1961: 188). Nearly all Egyptians eat fava beans, and high incidences of G6PD-deficiency have been reported in males, an average of 26 percent for the country as a whole (Ragab et al., 1966).

160. Burkert, 1972: 171, 178 n 94, 185; 1982: 17–18.

161. Guthrie, 1962–81, 1: 187–91; Philip, 1966: 147; Detienne, 1970; Burkert, 1972: 180–83.

162. Lieber, 1973.

163. Iamblichus, *On the Pythagorean life* 189.

164. Luisada, 1941: 231, 232.

165. Lieber, 1973: 36–37.

166. Iamblichus, *On the Pythagorean life* 71–74, 193, 226–27.

167. For reviews of evidence for the malaria hypothesis in general, see Motulsky, 1960: 42–55; Cavalli-Sforza and Bodmer, 1971: 148–58; Livingstone, 1971, 1983, and 1985: 6–10; Luzzatto, 1979; and Vogel and Motulsky, 1986: 460–72. For reviews of evidence relating specifically to malaria and G6PD-deficiency, see especially Luzzatto and Battistuzzi, 1985: 295–300; Luzzatto et al., 1986; Vogel and Motulsky, 1986: 464–65; and Luzzatto and Mehta, 1989: 2252–54. Geographic evidence for a link between malaria and G6PD-deficiency is of two sorts. High amounts of G6PD-deficiency occur only in areas where serious malaria has been present for many generations (numbering from dozens to hundreds). Within populations that are otherwise genetically relatively homogeneous, moreover, the incidence of G6PD-deficiency usually corresponds to the amount of exposure to malaria (Luzzatto, 1979: 962–63; Luzzatto and Battistuzzi, 1985: 296). For studies relating to geography, malaria, and G6PD-deficiency in the Mediterranean area, see especially Choremis et al., 1962; Stamatoyannopoulos and Fessas, 1964; and Stamatoyannopoulos et al., 1966 (Greece); Plato et al., 1964 (Cyprus); and Siniscalco et al., 1966; and P. J. Brown, 1981 (Sardinia).

At the same time, the matter of G6PD-deficiency is complex. Malaria is not the only factor determining its frequencies. In addition, the evidence is not always consistent (Livingstone, 1983: 21–31, 35–36; Luzzatto and Battistuzzi, 1985: 295–300). Nevertheless, Livingstone (1983: 31) concludes that, after three decades of speculation and inquiry, the malaria hypothesis still provides the only reasonable answer to the geographic distributions of the red-cell abnormalities in question. For the malaria hypothesis and G6PD-deficiency, Luzzatto et al. (1986: 181) consider the evidence sufficiently convincing that they have objected to continued use of the term *malaria "hypothesis."* Roth and Schulman (1989: 83–85), on their part, write of it "as virtually proven by a wealth of epidemiological surveys and in vitro investigations." They suggest that it be renamed *malaria theory* or some similar term to reflect its rise from being a simple hypothesis to a scientific truth.

168. G6PD-deficiency is a gender-linked gene, and heterozygotes are found only in females. Heterozygote females are believed to enjoy a selective advantage in terms of malaria over both homozygote females and hemizygote males, whether they are G6PD-normal or -deficient (Luzzatto et al., 1986; Cavalli-Sforza et al., 1994: 152–53, 186).

169. Motulsky, 1960: 48–55; Allison et al., 1963: 237, 240; Luzzatto et al., 1969; Cavalli-Sforza and Bodmer, 1971: 156–57; Luzzatto, 1979: 969–70; Roth et al., 1983; Luzzatto et al., 1983: 167–68; 1985; Luzzatto and Bienzle, 1979; Luzzatto and Battistuzzi, 1985: 295–300; Luzzatto and Mehta, 1989: 2253–54; P. J. Brown, 1993: 723; Verjee, 1993: 41; Mehta, 1994: 872.

170. Luzzatto et al., 1983: 167–68; 1985: 205, 207–8, 212–14; 1986: 190–92.

171. Livingstone, 1971: 39; Vogel and Motulsky, 1986: 464; Verjee, 1993: 41.

172. Katz, 1987: 139–42.

173. Kattamis et al., 1969b: 39; Kattamis et al., 1971; Russo et al., 1972; Mager et al., 1980: 271–72; Arese et al., 1986: 46; Kattamis, 1986: 28; Luzzatto and Mehta, 1989: 2247; Arese and De Flora, 1990: 5.

174. Though there are references to sensitive individuals refusing to eat fava beans, I have identified only one study that casts light on the amounts of fava beans consumed by persons afflicted with favism as compared with persons who are unafflicted. That study (Hedayat et al., 1981: 110, 111) was carried out in Iran, and involved 361 hospital patients with favism, along with 42 G6PD-deficient and 168 normal schoolchildren who lived in the same area. It found, with respect to mean weekly intake of raw fava beans, that the favism patients, as compared with the other two groups, consumed such beans a bit less frequently and in somewhat smaller amounts.

175. Huheey and Martin, 1975: 1146.

176. Golenser et al., 1983; I. A. Clark et al., 1984: 485; Ginsburg et al., 1996: 7, 14–16.

177. Dunn, 1965; Laderman, 1975: 589; McNeill, 1976: 16; Bruce-Chwatt and Zulueta, 1980: 9; Livingstone, 1984: 417–19; Gilles, 1993a: 1.

178. A fourth malaria parasite normally found in humans is *Plasmodium ovale.* Since it occurs mainly in tropical Africa and sporadically in Southeast Asia, southern China, and the western Pacific area (P. F. Russell et al., 1963: 72; Garnham, 1980: 111; Wernsdorfer, 1980: 15, 17, 74, 77; Beaver et al., 1984: 174; Livingstone, 1984: 419; Bruce-Chwatt, 1985: 33–34; Gilles, 1993b: 24), it will not be mentioned further.

179. According to Wernsdorfer (1980: 22), there are no reports of nonhuman primates becoming infected with *P. falciparum* naturally. Success has been obtained, however, in certain experimental attempts to infect nonhuman primates with *P. falciparum* (Garnham, 1966: 393–95; 1980: 121, 125–27; Wernsdorfer, 1980: 21, 22).

Plasmodium reichenowi, which occurs naturally in chimpanzees in tropical Africa, closely resembles *P. falciparum,* though it seems to bring on mild or minimal symptoms in chimpanzee hosts. Experimental attempts have failed to introduce *P. reichenowi* into humans by injections with infected chimpanzee blood. The erythrocytes of the chimpanzee, on their part, have been found only "feebly susceptible" to *P. falciparum* (P. F. Russell et al., 1963: 106–7; Garnham, 1980: 119–20, 121; Wernsdorfer, 1980: 22).

180. Motulsky, 1960: 43; P. F. Russell et al., 1963: 396–97; Angel, 1966: 761, 762; 1967: 387; Laderman, 1975: 589; Livingstone, 1971: 42; 1984: 413; Luzzatto, 1979: 963, citing Haldane; Garnham, 1980: 103–15; Beaver et al., 1984: 204–5; Luzzatto et al., 1986: 182; Gilles, 1993b: 25.

Plasmodium falciparum, unlike *P. vivax* and *P. malariae,* is able to invade red blood cells of all ages, and is thus able to parasitize an extremely high percentage of a host's erythrocytes. In addition, *P. falciparum* multiplies more rapidly than other *Plasmodium* species that affect humans, and, since it is common for more than one parasite to grow in a single erythrocyte, the total number of falciparum parasites is inclined to be greater. Cells infected with *P. falciparum* also become sticky and tend to block the host's small blood vessels, which can cause severe damage to the host's body. It is because of its greater malignancy that falciparum malaria is responsible for most deaths from malaria around the world (Garnham, 1966: 360–62, 376, 377–78, 383, 395–99; Beaver et al., 1984: 194–97; Dunn, 1993: 859).

181. Livingstone, 1984: 417; 1989: 297–98.

182. Livingstone, 1964: 447–48.

183. In a later article, "Simulation of the diffusion of the β-globin variants in the Old World," Livingstone (1989) remains convinced that "malaria is a recent selective factor" among humans. He develops a case for this view by first assuming that each of the Old World hemoglobin variants S, C, and E, whose high frequencies are widely thought to derive from selection by malaria, had a single origin, and that β-thalassemia developed in many separate mutations. Then, after simulating rates of mutation, selection, and gene flow of these traits among 600 human groups from West Africa to Southeast Asia, Livingstone concludes that present-day high frequencies most likely came about in 100–150 generations of selection and diffusion. Assuming, as Livingstone does, that one generation equals 25 years, this would be a process that started from roughly 1750 B.C. to 500 B.C., perhaps in the region where falciparum malaria first made its appearance. For a further discussion of time, evolution, the sickle-cell trait, and thalassemia, see Cavalli-Sforza et al., 1994: 146, 148, 150–52.

184. Cavalli-Sforza and Bodmer, 1971: 148, 153, 156–57; Luzzatto et al., 1986: 182.

185. Bruce-Chwatt and Zulueta, 1980: 1, 9–16.

186. P. F. Russell (1955: 3) has suggested that in Egypt, as in Europe, malaria was not a major problem in pre-Greek times. On the other hand, there are hints of what appears to have been malaria in ancient Egyptian papyri (Edwin Smith Surgical Papyrus, Ebers Papyrus) dating from 1600 B.C. and 1550 B.C. (Garnham, 1966: 3; Wernsdorfer, 1980: 2). Studies of Egyptian mummies, moreover, have found blood defects such as thalassemia that would have provided resistance to malaria (Rabino Massa, 1997); even more telling, *Plasmodium falciparum* antigen has been identified in three Egyptian mummies of Predynastic age (pre-c. 3100 B.C.) (Miller et al., 1994), which suggests that falciparum malaria itself was known in Egypt in considerable antiquity.

187. Livingstone, 1964: 441; 1967: 27; 1985: 7; Laderman, 1975: 593.

188. Not to be overlooked is the possibility that the fava beans of antiquity

were significantly more toxic than those of the present day and that, in times before falciparum malaria arrived, its absence, too, may have been a factor in keeping incidences of G6PD-deficiency low. It is known that the fava beans of the ancient Mediterranean area (before c. A.D. 500 or 1000) were of type *minor.* Unfortunately, however, I have found little evidence on the comparative toxicity of *minor* and *major* types of fava beans grown in the Mediterranean region.

Nearly all medical studies fail to identify whether the fava beans are *minor* or *major* in type. This is also true of many assays of the convicine and vicine content of fava beans. So far as I can determine, moreover, there is no study, whether in the Mediterranean area or elsewhere, carried out to compare average vicine and convicine levels in *minor* and *major* seed. We are left, then, to seek out suggestive bits. In one study done in Canada, Collier (1976: 158) reported that two lots of fresh *major* seed "gave 0.50 and 0.53% vicine, wet weight, and two lots of . . . *minor* . . . gave 0.89 and 1.07% wet weight," which at best raises the question of whether this may be true in general. Gardiner et al. (1982) provide information on the vicine and convicine content of mature seeds from 78 genotypes of *V. faba* raised in Canada. Though the researchers do not identify their genotypes as *major* or *minor,* I was able to identify a handful of them as *minor* by using other sources (Pitz et al., 1981; Arbid and Marquardt, 1985: 840). The two genotypes at the top of the Gardiner et al. list, higher in total glucosides (vicine and convicine) than all other genotypes, were forms of *minor.* Closer examination revealed other *minor* genotypes in the list, both in its top and bottom half, but, without the identity of all genotypes on the list, no conclusion could be reached regarding the average vicine and convicine content of *minor* and *major.* In any case, these are modern cultivars grown in Canada, not ancient ones from Greece and Italy.

Further hints come from Vural and Sardas (1984: 176–77), who, in a study in Turkey, reported a greater drop in GSH levels in erythrocytes of G6PD-deficient persons (from 58.9 mg/100 ml red blood cells to 17.8 mg/100 ml) when exposed to extracts of the one *minor* variety (Milas) used in the study than when exposed to extracts of the one *major* variety (Sakiz) used (from 58.9 mg/100 ml to 30.6 mg/ 100 ml). The scanty evidence above, however, is insufficient to tell whether *minor* cultivars, on average, have higher total glucoside levels and are more likely to bring on hemolytic attacks in sensitive individuals. If, however, subsequent re- search proves that *minor* varieties used in the Mediterranean area are indeed more toxic, this greater toxicity may have helped keep the incidence of G6PD- deficiency low prior to the arrival of falciparum malaria.

189. Szeinberg, 1963: 70–72.

190. Szeinberg and Sheba, 1958: 165; Motulsky and Campbell-Kraut, 1961: 175; Sheba, 1971: 1336–37. Mourant et al. (1978: 29) write that the Jewish depor- tees, especially persons from the malarial swamps around former Lake Huleh, may have carried the G6PD-deficiency gene with them from Palestine, but that

their incidences of G6PD-deficiency became very high through continuing intense genetic selection, possibly because they had cultural characteristics different
from those of their non-Jewish Kurdish neighbors, who have much lower incidences of G6PD-deficiency. As an example of such cultural factors, Mourant et al.
cite the case of the Parsis of Bombay, Zoroastrians who have open water tanks in
their house compounds, which were ideal breeding places for mosquitoes, and
who today have higher incidences of G6PD-deficiency than their Hindu neighbors. For more on the Kurdish Jews and selection pressures needed to have
brought on their very high present-day incidences of G6PD-deficiency, see Motulsky and Campbell-Kraut, 1961: 175; Livingstone, 1967: 65–68; and Cavalli-Sforza
and Bodmer, 1971: 174–77.

Cavalli-Sforza and Bodmer point out that the intensity of genetic selection
brought on by malaria may vary from place to place and from one time period to
another. Because of doubts about specific factors that may have been involved
and their importance, estimates of selection pressure and of the length of time it
took to bring on present-day incidences of G6PD-deficiency in the Mediterranean
area are matters of great uncertainty. For discussions of fitness and/or the time
factor in reaching high incidences of G6PD-deficiency, see Livingstone, 1964:
448; 1971: 49–50; 1983: 22–25; Siniscalco et al., 1966: 389–91; Cavalli-Sforza and
Bodmer, 1971: 176–77; and Luzzatto et al., 1986: 182–83, 184.

191. Hippocrates, *Epidemics* 1.5–9 and *Aphorisms* 4.43, 59.

192. Jones, 1909: 63–64; Patrick, 1967: 242; Wernsdorfer, 1980: 2.

193. Bruce-Chwatt and Zulueta, 1980: 18–19, 34.

194. Jones, 1909.

195. Celli, 1933.

196. Jones, 1909: 23–25.

197. Jones, 1909: 25–26.

198. Jones, 1909: 29, 58–59, 69. For a recent review of Jones's work on the
history of malaria in the Greek world, see Grmek 1989: 279–83.

The early accounts are not always convincing. There is, for example, a questionable story that the philosopher Empedocles (c. 490–430 B.C.) freed the city of
Selinus (Selinunte) in Sicily from a pestilence that some modern writers believe
to have been malaria. The pestilence, which killed ordinary citizens and women
in childbirth, was thought to have come from the bad odor of a nearby river.
Empedocles is reputed to have stopped the pestilence by having two nearby rivers
directed to the place, thereby mixing and sweetening the waters (Diogenes Laertius, *Lives of eminent philosophers* 8.70; Jones, 1909: 32–33; Ackerknecht, 1965: 89).

199. Bruce-Chwatt and Zulueta, 1980: 19, 33–34.

200. Celli, 1933: 12, 24.

201. P. F. Russell, 1955: 9–14. In an article on the history of malaria in Calabria, Tagarelli (1997) presents a similar reconstruction and dates.

202. Bruce-Chwatt and Zulueta, 1980: 21–27, 89–90.

203. P. J. Brown, 1981: 378–80.

204. Laderman, 1975: 590–93.

205. For Phoenicians, Carthaginians, Greeks, and the spread of genes for thalassemia in the Mediterranean area about 2,500–3,000 years ago, see Cavalli-Sforza et al., 1994: 150–52, 260.

206. An introduction of malaria to Greece from Magna Graecia (or Sicily) does not fit, however, with the fact that present-day incidences of G6PD-deficiency seem far lower in areas of Greek settlement in southern Italy and Sicily than in the areas of Greece from which people of the Greek settlements came. For example, incidences of G6PD-deficiency along the Ionian coast of Cosenza Province in Calabria, home of Sybaris, which was founded by Achaeans, are less than a fourth (1.92 percent) of those reported in modern Greece for Achaea (8.6 percent in the study by Stamatoyannopoulos et al., 1966: 300). In Sicily, Syracuse was founded by Corinthians, and Catania, by persons from Naxos whose origins were in the city of Chalcis on the Greek island of Euboea. Today the 1 percent estimate of G6PD-deficiency for Syracuse and Catania is far below those of the ancestral areas in Greece (Corinthia, 5.5 percent; Euboea, 2.8 percent; Stamatoyannopoulos et al., 1966: 300). Also not in accord with the idea that malaria was introduced to Greece from Magna Graecia is the evidence, discussed in the text, on geographic patterns of G6PD-deficiency and the Mediterranean phenotype of G6PD in Cosenza Province in Calabria.

207. Not all scholars agree with such late dates for malaria becoming a serious problem in Sardinia, Magna Graecia, Sicily, and Greece, or with the time when G6PD-deficiency became common (Laderman, 1975: 589–90). E. Giles (1962: 288–89), in attempting to relate the fava bean, favism, and the Indo-European kinship system, speculates that malaria and selection for G6PD-deficiency probably go back to 2000 B.C. or earlier in the Indo-European homeland. Siniscalco et al. (1966: 382), citing Livy, suggest the likelihood that malaria was endemic in prehistoric Sardinia, though P. J. Brown (1981: 378) points out that most historians would disagree with that view. Angel (1964, 1966, 1967), on the basis of incidences of porotic hyperostosis (osteoporosis symmetrica) in human skeletons uncovered in ancient Anatolia and Greece, has claimed that malaria was endemic in the eastern Mediterranean long before 2000 B.C., and that the mutations that created *P. falciparum* and selection for the sickle-cell trait, thalassemia, and G6PD-deficiency appear to have occurred there prior to the seventh millennium B.C. Laderman (1975: 589–90) has noted, however, a statement by Angel that porotic hyperostosis can also develop from other factors (e.g., childhood malnutrition, severe dysentery) unrelated to malaria, on which grounds she questions Angel's conclusions. Bruce-Chwatt and Zulueta (1980: 15), on their part, suggested that, in terms of climate, *P. falciparum* is unlikely to have been found in Anatolia at

Chatal Hüyük, one of the places where Angel reported porotic hyperostosis in human skeletons. Of special interest in Angel's evidence, however, is an increase in porotic hyperostosis in Greece from Hellenistic to modern times (Angel, 1966: 761). I wonder whether the latter increase came about because of the arrival of falciparum malaria.

208. Salvidio et al., 1969: 337; Bruce-Chwatt and Zulueta, 1980: 98.
209. Jones, 1909: 30–31.
210. Strabo, *Geography* 6.1.12, 6.2.4.
211. Zohary and Hopf, 1988: 163–65.
212. Isaac, 1959; Andrews, 1961.
213. Simoons, 1994: 66–71.
214. W. M. S. Russell and C. Russell, 1983: 100.
215. Katz, 1987: 134.
216. Grmek, 1989: 240, 242.

Chapter 9. Pythagoras Lives: Parallels and Survivals of His Views of Beans in Modern and Premodern Times

1. Hippolytus, *Philosophumena* 1.2.
2. Erasmus (c. A.D. 1466–1536), famous Dutch classical and religious scholar, for example, was well acquainted with ancient works on the Pythagorean bean ban and even wrote on that subject ("*A fabis abstineto*") as well as on the use of salt and beans in divination in antiquity ("*Qui circa salem et fabam*") (Erasmus, *Adages* 1.1.2.169–237; 1.1.12).
3. Hartland, 1894–96, 2: 288–89, 291.
4. Laisnel de la Salle, 1875, 2: 83.
5. Pellini, 1894–95.
6. Lawson, 1964: 535–36, citing Gregorovius.
7. Hartland, 1894–96, 2: 289, citing Ostermann; Ostermann, 1940, 1: 148.
8. Guerrieri, 1893–94: 314.
9. Schrader, 1908–26: 28, citing Kotljarevskij.
10. Frazer, 1935, 6: 81–83; 10: 223–24, 225 n; Weiser, 1952: 312–13.
11. Weiser, 1952: 313. For more on the observance of All Souls' Day in modern Europe and its associations with earlier pagan practice, see Frazer, 1935, 6: 69–83; and Weiser, 1952: 308–14. For feasts of all souls among non-Christian peoples in other parts of the world, see Frazer, 1935, 6: 51–68.
12. Frazer, 1935, 6: 74, citing Schneller.
13. Chalif, 1921: 35–36.
14. For notes on the feeding of ancestral spirits on All Souls' Day in Estonia (beans are not mentioned), see Grimm, 1883–88, 3: 913 n; 4: 1844. That account also notes that, in one district of Estonia, the spirits are greeted in the bathroom, and then bathed one by one.

15. E. M. Wright, 1914: 300; Frazer, 1935, 6: 71–72, 73, 78–80; Weiser, 1952: 313.

16. Hole, 1976: 187.

17. Weiser, 1952: 313.

18. Frazer, 1935, 6: 73.

19. Ezekiel 4.9; Feliks, 1971–72a.

20. Hartland, 1894–96, 2: 288 n. This recalls the tradition, reported by Brand for seventeenth-century England, of "sin eaters," usually poor individuals who, by accepting money and/or food and drinking ale, took on the sins of the deceased in the manner of a scapegoat. Most English of that day regarded the practice as heathen, but it seems to have found its way into at least one Christian funeral ceremony of that period. This ceremony involved making a gift over the body of the dead person—a gift of bread, cheese, drink and money—to the poorest of the deceased's neighbors. Then the minister recited the Lord's Prayer. After this, the food and drink were carried to the church, where, after a similar ceremony, the poor person offered blessings to God for the happiness of his dead neighbor and friend (Brand, 1900: 447–48, 472–74).

21. Weiser, 1952: 313.

22. Weiser, 1952: 313.

23. Hartland, 1894–96, 2: 297.

24. Hartland, 1894–96, 2: 288–89; Hyde, 1923: 202–3.

25. Stavroulakis, 1986: 131.

26. For the use of kólyva in a ceremony of communion between a mourning family and a dead woman, performed by a Greek Orthodox priest in a sacred chapel in Palestine, see Drower, 1956: 42–43. On the kólyva, priests sometimes traced a cross (sacred bread was also marked by a cross in the Mithraic mysteries: Drower, 1956: 60), and at other times, Greek letters were traced meaning "Jesus Christ conquers." After the ceremony, each participant received a piece of kólyva to take along, presumably to eat at home.

27. Among modern Greeks, kólyva may also be prepared on a variety of occasions not directly associated with the human dead. One such occasion is on December 4, St. Barbara's Day, when, especially among Greeks of Anatolia, kólyva (or honey cake) may be offered to this saint, who protects children from smallpox, at a crossroads. This is reminiscent of the crossroads food offerings to Hecate, that chthonic goddess of antiquity who was also popular in Anatolia as a protector of children (Megas, 1963: 24–25, 44, 77–78). In the Ionian islands, kólyva is offered at times of sowing and harvest in propitiation and thanks. Ionian cakes, though made mainly of wheat (symbolic of resurrection), also contain peas, almonds, nuts, raisins, and pomegranate and anise seed (Hyde, 1923: 131–32). An unmarried girl may also use kólyva in an effort to see her future husband in her dreams (Megas, 1963: 77–78).

28. Kólyva may also be protective in other ways. On the island of Lesbos, for

example, villagers may thread kólyva into wreaths that they suspend from branches of their orchard trees to protect them against the evil eye (Megas, 1963: 77).

29. Hyde, 1923: 131; Megas, 1963: 24, 44, 68–69, 77, 128; Stavroulakis, 1986: 131.

30. For two recipes for assuré, as prepared by Greek Jews, see Stavroulakis, 1986: 132–33.

31. Stavroulakis, 1986: 131–32.

32. Rohde, 1925: 168.

33. Megas, 1963: 24–25; Lawson, 1964: 121, 150–51, 533–34.

Such offerings of honey cake have not been limited to Greece. One reads, for example, of Jewish and Moslem women near Constantine in Algeria seeking fertility by sacrificing a black hen at the entrance to a cave, then entering the cave with a light, offering a honey cake, and finally bathing and leaving with the assurance that their infertility has been removed (Hartland, 1894–96, 1: 168).

For an excellent account of sacred breads and their ritual use in the modern Near East, see "Bread of life," Drower, 1956: 41–60.

34. Hartland, 1894–96, 2: 289.

35. Stavroulakis, 1986: 132.

36. In at least one place in Greece, fava beans (broad beans) themselves are mentioned at a time of ritual burial, not, it seems, because of their association with death, but because they symbolize the austere diet of Lent that is to follow. In Greece, Lent is preceded by a three-week period of eating, drinking, and merrymaking called Apokreos (Carnival). At Lefkogeia in Crete, the transition between the two periods is marked by the funeral of King Carnival. Colorfully painted villagers assemble in the village square. One of them, representing the king, lies down on a board and feigns death. Then follow a funeral procession, replete with floral wreaths and the ringing of church bells, and a symbolic burial of King Carnival by a person representing Lent. The latter is a man dressed as a woman, tall, thin, and with black clothes. At Katsidoni in Crete, on the other hand, the transition is marked by a different sort of burial, one involving the sharply contrasting foods of the two periods. On the last day of Carnival, people prepare a large pan of cooked meat, cheese, macaroni, and other "Easter food," and carry it to the fields. While it is being buried, they burn incense and cry out in sorrow, "for 'Broad bean' has arrived and sent 'Macaroni' and 'Meatman' into exile" (bean soup is acceptable during Lent, but meat, eggs, fish, and dairy products are not) (Megas, 1963: 59–75).

37. Megas, 1963: 31.

38. In ancient Greece, the number three was lucky, but in modern Greece it is unlucky, a warning of death. A modern Greek peasant may ask forgiveness for having to mention the number three. Tuesday, as third day of the week, is an

inauspicious day. Furthermore, the set days when forgiveness is sought for a deceased person all occur in units of three or multiples of three from the day of death, for example, three days, three weeks, three months, and three years (Lawson, 1964: 313, 486–87). Because Megas provides no detail, one can only wonder about the origin and meaning of the number three in the case he describes (is it good luck, bad luck, the Trinity, or what?).

39. It is believed that beans can also be used to bring injury and death to others. In a folktale of Provence, one reads that if, after uttering a prayer of malediction, an individual puts a very dry marsh bean in the oil of the lamp that burns near the altar, the person at whom the curse is directed will experience distention, illness, and death, a sequence for which there is no cure (Sébillot, 1968, 4: 481).

40. Whitlock, 1979: 65.

41. Thiselton-Dyer, 1898: 107. For references to similar beliefs in France, see Sébillot, 1968, 3: 469–70.

42. Whitlock, 1979: 65.

43. Chester, 1960: 205.

44. Molluka beans are species of *Caesalpinia* (= *Guilandina*), mostly commonly *Caesalpinia bonducella,* which has gray seeds. They are carried by the Gulf Stream from the tropics, especially the West Indies, and are found floating among seaweed on stormy shores of the Hebrides. For this reason, they are also called sea nuts or strand nuts. Some have argued that knowledge of Molluka beans provided one link in the chain of evidence that led Columbus to seek the New World (J. F. Campbell, quoted in Dorson, 1968, 2: 656). There are, however, five genera of "sea beans" from the tropics that have been known to European beachcombers since the Neolithic, all of them hard, impermeable, buoyant seeds able to float for months or years (pers. comm., Jonathan D. Sauer).

45. Because Molluka beans served among superstitious folk in Scotland as amulets and are egg-shaped, the name "fairy eggs" was also applied to them.

46. Brand, 1893–95, 3: 46, citing Martin.

47. Höfler, 1899: 109.

48. Cocchiara, 1938: 91–92.

49. In China, parched beans, thought to resemble the pustules of smallpox, were used in the hope that the pox would become dry like the beans (Doolittle, 1865, 1: 156).

50. Westermarck, 1926, 1: 212, 214, 449–50.

51. For parallels between Europe and China in methods of stimulating solar energy and warding off evil at the time of the summer solstice, see Bodde, 1975: 294, 302–4, 392.

52. Dames and Seemann, 1903: 142–43; Frazer, 1935, 10: 160–219; Weiser, 1952: 328–31; Hole, 1976: 138–39.

53. Schimmel, 1987: 122.

54. Frazer, 1935, 11: 45–75.

55. Whitlock, 1979: 84.

56. Hartland, 1894–96, 2: 50. For a somewhat similar procedure, see Grimm, 1883–88, 4: 1822.

57. One also reads that, on the first Sunday of Lent in Franche-Comté, bonfires are lighted and torches are carried through streets and fields. This is done to assure a good harvest and apparently to protect against evil in the coming year. In addition, couples who have been married within the past year make gifts of boiled peas to all young people, male or female, who appear at the doors of houses and ask for them (Frazer, 1935, 10: 110–11 and n). One wonders whether gifts of peas are made in the hope of gaining fertility and satisfying and staving off underworld forces.

58. Gubernatis, 1978, 2: 136.

59. Dames and Seemann, 1903: 143. There is also a tale about the pea on St. John's Eve that is said to have given that legume a bad reputation. According to the tale, dragons of pestilence were flying in the sky on St. John's Eve, but were kept from descending to the hills by the St. John's fires. Not to be thwarted, the dragons obtained peas that they dropped into springs and wells. The peas then rotted, gave off bad odors, and caused intestinal problems for people who drank the water (Skinner, 1911: 212–13).

60. Böhm, 1905: 16.

61. Rohde, 1925: 168. In an article on the Feast of the Epiphany, Conybeare (1910–11: 697) mentions a pagan rite with Christian undertones that, according to Epiphanius (c. A.D. 315–403), was carried out on January 5 or 6 in early Alexandria. The rite was associated with the goddess Persephone ("Kore"), daughter of Demeter, the earth goddess whose devotees, as we have seen, were expected to avoid beans on certain ritual occasions. The Alexandrian rite was carried out at the temple of the goddess. After singing hymns in the temple compound until daybreak, the worshippers, carrying torches, descended into an underground shrine of the goddess. There they brought out a wooden, naked statue of her on a litter and carried it around the main shrine seven times before returning it to its underground home. Epiphanius observed that the statue had crosses on its hands, knees, and forehead, and that the rite celebrated the fact that "today at this hour *Korē*, that is, the Virgin, gave birth to the Aeon" (a being who lives forever). Though Epiphanius considered the Alexandrian rite to be heathen, it may have represented an interesting stage in the syncretization that led pre-Christian beliefs and practices to be incorporated into early Christianity (Persephone/Kore = the Virgin Mary? Aeon = Christ?).

In any case—though Epiphanius's account does not mention it—one wonders whether the ban on beans in the cult of Demeter and Persephone may also have found its way into the early Christian Epiphany. It is known that Demeter herself became St. Demetra at her ancient cult center at Eleusis in Greece. Though uncanonized and recognized nowhere else, until the beginning of nineteenth century St. Demetra was worshipped at harvesttime in the form of an ancient statue of Demeter. In 1801, however, two Englishmen, aided by Turkish authorities, managed to take the statue away despite a riot by local Greeks. The statue, in a mutilated state, is now found in the Fitzwilliam Museum in Cambridge (Hyde, 1923: 76–77; Lawson, 1964: 79–80).

62. Grimm, 1883–88, 4: 1779, 1805, 1810.

63. This custom once occurred in Germany, Austria, Holland, Belgium, and Russia, and still survives in parts of England, France, and French Canada.

64. In many parts of continental Europe, Twelfth Day is also associated with the three wise men from the east ("kings") who appeared at the time of Christ's birth. In most of Europe, therefore, popular names for the Epiphany reflect this, as in "Day of the Three Kings," "Festival of the Kings," and "Feast of the Three Holy Kings." The association has also led Twelfth-cake in German to be called *Dreikönigskuchen,* and in French, *gâteau des rois* (Frazer, 1935, 9: 329–31; Weiser, 1952: 146–48, 152–53; Russ, 1982: 36–39).

65. Brand, 1893–95, 1: 24–29; 1900: 12–19; von Schroeder, 1901: 196–99; Hazlitt, 1905, 1: 34–35; Frazer, 1935, 9: 313–29; 10: 153 n; Weiser, 1952: 152–53; Hole, 1976: 195–99; Gubernatis, 1978, 2: 134 and n 2; Russ, 1982: 36–39.

In various places in Renaissance England, "Lords of Misrule" (in Scotland, such a person was called Abbot of Misrule, Abbot of Unreason, or Abbot of Bon Accord) were elected each year, usually at Christmas. Their role was to lead holiday merrymaking in colleges, the royal palace, homes of nobles, and such. In the colleges of Oxford, such an appointee was also designated Christmas Lord or King of the Bean (Rex Fabarum and Rex Regni Fabarum), likely because he was chosen by lot in which beans were used. His term of office commonly lasted from Christmas until Twelfth Night, at which affair a Lord of Misrule might preside. After the Reformation, the institution was criticized and preached against by Puritans as un-Christian and a relic of such pagan festivals as the Roman Saturnalia and Bacchanalia. As a result of such feelings, the institution was abolished or suppressed in both England and Scotland (Brand, 1893–95, 1: 24, 497ff.; 1900: 266–73; Hazlitt, 1905, 1: 368–71; Frazer, 1935, 9: 251, 331–34; Bastien, 1987: 526).

66. Squire, 1905: 306–7.

67. Brand, 1893–95, 1: 114–18; 1900: 57–61; Hazlitt, 1905, 1: 34–36. In one English folktale, the association is especially clear: Live children who eat beans turn green and die, then eat them as food of the dead (Briggs, 1957: 280).

68. Weiser, 1952: 179–80.

69. Brand, 1893–95, 1: 113; 1900: 57; E. M. Wright, 1914: 292; Hole, 1976: 43. In early England, Passion Sunday was also called Care, Carr, or Carle Sunday,

which alluded to the period of caring, sadness, and penance it initiated. In all likelihood, peas used on this day came to be called carlings in the same way that presents at fairs in England are called fairlings (Brand, 1893–95, 1: 113; 1900: 57–58; Hole, 1976: 43). Ultimately in northern England and Scotland the day itself also has come to be known as Carling Sunday (E. M. Wright, 1914: 292).

70. Brand, 1900: 58–59; Hazlitt, 1905, 1: 35, 36.

71. Folkard, 1884: 248; Friend, 1981: 367.

72. *Vendidad* 5.25–26, trans. in Darmesteter and Mills, 1880–87, 4: 56 and n; *Sad-Dar* 13.1–9, 87.9; *Bahman Yasht* 2.36; *Dādistan-ī Dīnīk* 30.1–4, 81.15; *Dīnkard* 9.14, 1–2; *Shāyast lā-shāyast* 3.32, 9.11, 10.2, 12.8–9, 14.1–3, 17.4, trans. in E. W. West, 1880–97, 5: 205, 283 n 6, 312, 315, 342–43, 369–71, 383 and n 5; 18: 61–63, 241; 24: 46 n 3, 273–75, 352; 37: 94 n 4, 196–97; Haug, 1978: 396, 407–8.

For a comparison of Zoroastrian and Brahminical offerings of sacrificial cakes, see Haug, 1978: 259, 280, 281, 285.

73. E. W. West, 1880–97, 5: 383 n 5.

74. When a Zoroastrian household dog dies, an egg is dedicated to its soul, just as it is to a human soul (Boyce, 1977: 163).

75. Boyce, 1977: 38, 147, 148–49, 154–55, 158, 163.

76. S. E. Thompson, 1988: 73, 77–102.

77. L. G. Thompson, 1973: 163.

78. The Chinese consider red effective in such cases because it is the color of blood, the life force, as well as of fire and light (Bodde, 1975: 302–3).

79. de Groot, 1964, 1: 89–90, 209; 6: 1032. There is also a Chinese Buddhist ceremony in which a person picks up green and yellow beans one by one while reciting the name of Buddha. When the ceremony is over, the beans are boiled and offered to passersby. This is called giving away karma-accumulating beans, because its intent is that the passersby will benefit from the good karma the beans have accumulated (Tun, 1965: 36).

80. Casal, 1967: 16–17.

81. Bastian, 1869: 367; Humbert, 1870, 2: 326; Chamberlain, 1891: 154–55; Aston, 1905: 308–9; Casal, 1967: 16 n, 17–18.

82. Lévi-Strauss, 1979: 39 and n.

83. Aston, 1905: 313.

84. For the use of swords and other weapons for exorcising evil spirits in China, see de Groot, 1964, 6: 992–1005.

85. For the peach as protective, see my conclusions chapter.

86. Aston, 1905: 308–9.

87. Bodde, 1975: 84–85, 84 n 36.

88. Five has been a number of special appeal to the Chinese since antiquity, as in the five elements, five virtues, five tastes, five colors, five classics, five heroes, five demons, five sacred mountains, five vegetables, five fruits, and more.

89. Welch, 1958: 91 n.

90. de Groot, 1964, 6: 929–1185.

91. One does read of a powder of small red peas that was one of several ingredients enclosed in wax to make "spectre-killing pills." The wax balls in question were worn or eaten in order to repel certain demons who, among other things, caused madness and delirium (de Groot, 1964, 6: 1086–87). One suspects that it is the red color of the peas that made them suitable for this purpose.

92. Waddell, 1971: 494–95.

93. The trumpets in question were specially made for summoning demons. They were constructed of human thighbones, preferably from criminals or persons who had suffered violent deaths. They might be encased in brass and might have, at one end, a copper flange on which the eyes and nose of a demon are depicted, with the opening itself representing the demon's mouth (Waddell, 1971: 300).

94. Waddell, 1971: 488, 531–33.

95. Waddell, 1971: 90, 466–67.

96. de Nebesky-Wojkowitz, 1956: 346, 514–15.

97. Onians, 1973: 112.

98. Aston, 1956: 32–33; Ross, 1965: 31–33, 35, 96. In the former Egyptian Sudan, the Kariaks provide a meal of beans twice each year to the snake and wagtail, in which they believe the spirit of the grandmother or mother of food to live (Leach, 1949–50, 1: 124).

99. Berndt, 1962: 40–42.

100. Burridge, 1969: 251, 306, 390; Schwimmer, 1973: 167–74.

101. Burridge, 1969: 251, 306, 390. In this note, I take examples only from the Old World, though they occur in the New World as well, where they commonly apply to species of *Phaseolus* and other beans domesticated in the Americas. The Iroquois, for example, held that beans were given to humans by their creator and are under the protection of one of the three daughters of the Earth Mother (Frazer, 1935, 7: 177; Leach, 1949–50, 1: 123). For more on myths of American Indian groups as they relate to the role of beans and similar-appearing fruit in ties between the living and the dead, and on the sexual symbolism of beans, see Lévi-Strauss, 1979.

102. Sébillot, 1968, 4: 473.

103. Westermarck, 1926, 1: 581.

104. Westermarck, 1926, 1: 574.

105. Hartland, 1894–96, 2: 352, citing Pulci.

106. Gubernatis, 1978, 2: 136.

107. Storniello, 1893–94: 866; Gubernatis, 1978, 2: 136.

108. Russ, 1982: 39. Also in some parts of Germany, at an affair (Mailehen, or "May fee") usually held on May Day, young men bid for unmarried girls to be

their dancing partners, and in one community, Münsterreifel, if a young woman disapproves of her partner, she gives him fava bean flowers (Thonger, 1968: 23).

109. Thonger, 1968: 55.

110. Frazer, 1935, 10: 237, 242, 245.

111. E. M. Wright, 1914: 263.

112. Hole, 1976: 43.

113. Massé, 1954: 246.

114. Thonger, 1968: 108.

115. Russ, 1982: 35.

116. Chalif, 1921: 26.

117. Aston, 1905: 341–42; Casal, 1967: 31.

118. Fava beans and beans of other sorts have also been used in rites associated with assuring crop fertility, but in this regard they are no different from seed of other sorts. A critical time in winter sowing in contemporary Greece is celebrated as a feast day on November 21 (Presentation of the Virgin Mary in the Temple). On this day, it is traditional to cast a handful of wheat, fava beans, and other seed into the fountain or well of a house while saying, "As the water flows, so may riches flow." Afterward a cupful of that water is carried into the house. The entire ceremony is reminiscent of ancient Athenian first-fruit offerings, or *panspermiá*, a name used for the modern ceremony in parts of Greece. In Arachova in Boeotia, on the evening before that feast day, members of a family consume a porridge of wheat, beans, and lentils (called panspermiá) in the hope that the Virgin will grant a favorable harvest in the coming year (Hyde, 1923: 131–32, 133; Megas, 1963: 22–23). At another farm festival on September 14 (Exaltation of the Cross), moreover, a farmer at Ghalanades, a village on Naxos, puts on a towel some barley, fava beans, and other seed he plans to sow that year. He takes the towelful of seed to the church and sets it down near the entrance. Other farmers do the same, resulting in a considerable pile of seed that the priest blesses when the day's services are over. Then each farmer retrieves his towelful of seed and, at the time of sowing, mixes it with unconsecrated seed while saying, "Come, good Jesus and Mary, bring me wealth and good fortune" (Megas, 1963: 156–57).

119. Hutton, 1969: 339.

120. Hutton, 1968: 217.

121. Welch, 1958: 91 n.

122. Carter, 1993.

Chapter 10. Further Notes, Elaborations, and Conclusions

1. There is much here that needs further investigation in cross-cultural terms. One worthy investigation would be the role of plants with trifoliate leaves in the religious beliefs and practices of various peoples in the Old World. It is clear that such plants play a significant role among Hindus, who consider all plants with

trifoliate leaves to represent the triad of great gods, Brahma, Vishnu, and Shiva (S. M. Gupta, 1971: 3). One plant of this sort is the bael tree (*Aegle marmelos*), which has already been mentioned. Among the others are the *barna* or *barun* (*Crataeva religiosa*); the *mandāra* (*Erythrina indica;* Eng.: Indian coral tree); and the *palās* (*Butea monosperma* or *Butea frondosa;* Eng.: flame of the forest) (G. Watt, 1889–96, 1: 117, 123, 555; S. M. Gupta, 1971: 3, 21, 31, 47; Stutley, 1985: 88).

The symbolic importance of three is also revealed in the practice of a newly married Hindu wife selecting, for use in postwedding ritual, a pipal twig on which three leaves are growing next to one another. The three leaves symbolize the three goddesses Gaurī, Sāvitrī, and Lakshmī. On the center leaf, the wife paints a swastika or the word *Śrī* (the latter for Lakshmī, goddess of good luck and prosperity), and on the other two, an auspicious red mark. Then, after further ritual, she pays homage to the leaves by sprinkling them with turmeric and water (M. Stevenson, 1920: 110). For another interesting ritual use of three pipal leaves, one of which represents Pārvatī, the wife of Shiva, see M. Stevenson, 1920: 304.

2. For the use of peach-wood bows in exorcism, see Bodde, 1975: 84, 127, 134.

3. This discussion is based in large part on Simoons, 1991: 217–19, where full documentation may be found.

4. de Groot, 1886: 604–6; 1964, 6: 955–56.

5. Bodde, 1975: 132–34.

6. For more on the symbolic and ritual role of the peach in China, see de Groot, 1964, 6: 957–62; and Bodde, 1975: 127–34, 136–37, 289–91, 303, 304–6, and passim.

7. Bodde, 1975: 134–35.

8. *Shen* means "spirit," and *lü,* "puppet" or "figurine," and it has been argued that initially the matched names meant "Figurines (*lü*) of the Spirits (*shen*) Shu and Yü" (Bodde, 1975: 134, citing Granet).

9. One example: the Saxons of Transylvania, who, on St. George's Day, suspended branches of wild roses or other thorny shrubs over the gates of their farmyards to repel witches, who might ride in on the backs of cows (Frazer, 1935, 2: 337–38).

10. Bodde, 1975: 132.

11. It may, however, be improper for an impure person to offer incense to the gods. For an entire month after the birth of a child, modern Chinese women, fearful that their fetal blood will anger the gods, do not burn incense to them, for this would be disrespectful (Pillsbury, 1978).

12. Westermarck, 1926, 1: 308–9, 310, 375. Strong tastes may also be used to repel spirits in Morocco (Westermarck, 1926, 1: 310).

13. Ragozin, 1902: 30.

14. The baobab is also widely known as *tebeldi* from its name in the Republic of the Sudan.

15. Dymock et al., 1889–93, 1: 218; Dalziel, 1937: 112; Owen, 1970: 24–26.

16. Baobab wood is light and spongy.

17. Dalziel, 1937: 115; Owen, 1970: 26–27. The baobab and its wood, leaves, fruit, seeds, and other plant parts have many uses in Africa, for which see Dalziel, 1937: 112–15.

18. Owen, 1970: 27.

19. Davies, 1968: 480; Hugot, 1968: 487; Owen, 1970: 36.

20. Owen, 1970: 26.

21. Owen, 1970: 28; J. M. Watt, 1972: 78.

22. Owen, 1970: 27–28, 29, 35; J. M. Watt, 1972: 78.

23. Sinclair, 1875: 66.

24. Dymock et al., 1889–93, 1: 219.

25. Crooke, 1906: 498; M. Taylor, 1986: 266–71.

26. Sinclair, 1875: 66; Dymock et al., 1889–93, 1: 218, 219; G. Watt, 1889–96, 1: 105.

27. Frazer, in his translation of Pausanias, *Description of Greece* (1: 332, 401; 3: 343–44; 4: 122), calls this tree of Hera's simply a willow. So does Rahner (1963: 290), who notes that, in addition to the willow, the chaste tree, or agnus castus— which was thought to be a species of willow—was also sacred to Hera. That thought appears to derive from Pausanias (*Description of Greece* 3.14.7). Baumann (1993: 60, 64), however, identifies both the chaste tree and the tree of Hera's at Samos as *Vitex agnus-castus*.

28. Besides the oak, other trees (especially poplar, olive, and plane trees) were, at one place or time or another, also sacred to or associated with Zeus, for which see A. B. Cook, 1904–7, 15: 295–99.

29. For photographs of *Platanus orientalis*, see Baumann, 1993: 36, 49.

30. Pausanias, *Description of Greece* 7.4.4; 8.23.4–5.

31. For more on "the eternal olive on the Acropolis," see Frazer, pp. 343–44 in Vol. 2 of his trans. of Pausanias, *Description of Greece*. The olive tree in question was near the temple of the goddess Pandrosus, but there was an altar of Zeus beneath it.

32. Earlier, however, Theophrastus (*Enquiry into plants* 4.13.2), followed by Pliny (*Natural history* 16.238), wrote that the plane tree near Caphyae had been planted by Agamemnon.

33. This must have been a famous tree long before the time of Theophrastus. I base this on Homer, whose Odysseus said, "Now in Delos once I saw . . . a young shoot of a palm springing up beside the altar of Apollo. . . when I saw that, I marveled long at heart, for never yet did such a tree spring up from the earth" (Homer, *Odyssey* 6.162–67).

34. Theophrastus, *Enquiry into plants* 4.13.2.

35. Pliny, *Natural history* 16.234–40.

36. Herodotus, *History* 2.52; Seyffert, 1895: 197; Peck, 1896: 532; Rose, 1908–26: 797; Leach, 1949–50, 1: 319; Avery, 1962: 411; Fergusson, 1971: 15–16.

37. Parke, 1967: 253.

38. Parke, 1967: 31.

39. Fergusson, 1971: 74–75 n.

40. Frazer, p. 160 in Vol. 2 of his trans. of Pausanias, *Description of Greece;* Seyffert, 1895: 197; Peck, 1896: 532; Farnell, 1896–1909, 1: 38–39; Parke and Wormell, 1956, 1: 3; Parke, 1967: 13, 86.

In addition to divining by means of a talking oak, other methods of divination alleged to have been practiced at Dodona were (1) translating the sounds of water in a bubbling stream or fountain at the foot of the sacred oak; (2) drawing of lots; (3) "by prophetesses in ecstasy"; and (4) through sounds made by a bronze vessel (Farnell, 1896–1909, 1: 38 n; Frazer, 1935, 2: 172, 358; Parke, 1967: 86–91). There are also reports that doves delivered oracles at Dodona (Parke, 1967: 42–43). Dionysius of Halicarnassus (fl. c. 20 B.C.), for example, wrote that a dove once delivered oracles at Dodona while perched on a sacred oak (Dionysius of Halicarnassus, *Roman antiquities* 1.14.5). Farnell (1896–1909, 1: 38 n) notes other ancient writers who also made vague references to talking doves, but, he insists, there is no proof that doves played a role in the oracles of Dodona, and that, in any case, "they had ceased to talk in historical times."

For notes and references on oracular waters in ancient and modern Greece or elsewhere, see Hartland, 1894–96, 2: 18, 19–24; Hyde, 1923: 120–121, 122, 123, 158–59; Frazer, pp. 5–7 in Vol. 2 of his trans. of Ovid, *Fasti;* Frazer, 1935, 2: 172; 5: 247; Parke and Wormell, 1956, 1: 27–28; and Eliade, 1958: 202, 213.

41. Statius, *Thebaid* 3.475–76; 8.201–2.

42. Homer, *Iliad* 16.220–45.

43. Homer, *Odyssey* 14.327–30; 19.296–99. For prophetic oaks among the Romans and early Prussians, see Parke, 1967: 20–24. In early Prussia, tall oaks were thought to be inhabited by gods who were able to give audible responses to queries, and in fact the high priest of a holy oak was called God's mouth. Indeed, it has been argued that the association of the oak with a sky god was an ancient Indo-European trait and that Zeus and Jupiter were his historical survivors (S. A. Cook, 1910–11: 237; Frazer, 1935, 2: 43, 349–75; Parke, 1967: 22–24, 26).

44. Apollodorus, *Library* 1.9.16.

45. Rose, 1908–26: 797.

46. Herodotus, *History* 2.54–57.

47. Parke, 1967: 52–59, 194–241.

48. Parke, 1967: 1–45, 66–67, 194–241, 254–55.

49. Lucan, *Civil war* 9.511–30.

50. Silius Italica, *Punica* 3.6–13, 673–99.

51. A. B. Cook, 1904–7, 15: 295; 1964–65, 1: 363–67.

52. Parke, 1967: 248–49.

53. The Homeric hymns are not "hymns" that served in formal religious services. Rather, they are ancient Greek poems directed to deities, and are thought

to have been presented initially in an oral form by rhapsodists as preludes to recitals of heroic poetry. Though credited to Homer by the ancient Greeks, the hymns are now believed to have been written over a period of centuries following the time of Homer by various authors of unknown or uncertain identity. The Homeric hymn "To Apollo" is credited to a famous rhapsodist, Cynaethus, who wrote it late in the sixth century B.C. (Parke and Wormell, 1956, 1: 107).

54. This refers to Mt. Parnassus, which can be seen from Delphi. "To Apollo" 394–96.

55. Farnell, 1896–1909, 4: 188 n; Parke and Wormell, 1956, 1: 3.

56. Parke and Wormell, 1956, 1: 25, 26; Parke, 1967: 20–21.

57. Farnell, 1896–1909, 4: 188; Parke and Wormell, 1956, 1: 26; Fontenrose, 1978: 225. For more on oracular methods at Delphi, see Farnell, 1896–1909, 4: 186–92; Parke and Wormell, 1956, 1: 17–41; and Fontenrose, 1978: 106–228.

58. For other references to the ritual burning of laurel in the Greco-Roman world, see Frazer, p. 146 in Vol. 2 and p. 348 in Vol. 3 of his trans. of Ovid, *Fasti*.

59. Parke and Wormell, 1956, 1: 26; Fontenrose, 1978: 224. For more on the ties between Apollo and the laurel, see A. B. Cook, 1904–7, 15: 409–11.

60. Stutley and Stutley, 1977: 27.

61. J. W. Bennett, 1843: 56 n.

62. Gaster, 1908–26: 810; S. A. Cook, 1910–11: 237; Ackerman, 1935; Frese and Gray, 1987: 31ff. A biblical example: Jehovah's command to David that he listen for a sound in the tops of certain mulberry trees to signal the time the Philistines should be attacked (2 Samuel 5.24). A Persian example, a legend and a popular art motif from the fourteenth to the sixteenth century: a talking tree that speaks through animal heads growing at the end of its branches and rebukes Alexander the Great for his craving of conquest and warns him that it is senseless to invade India (Ackerman, 1935: 67).

63. J. W. Bennett, 1843: 56 n; Leach, 1949–50, 1: 83.

64. For a thorough review of this and similar practices, see Westermarck, 1922, 2: 470–84. For rice as a Hindu symbol of auspiciousness and fertility and its place in Hindu wedding ritual, myth, and tradition, see S. M. Gupta, 1971: 82–83.

65. Massé, 1954: 6.

66. Goodenough, 1953–68, 7: 99.

67. Zohary and Spiegel-Roy, 1975: 324–25.

68. The sycamore fig (sometimes called mulberry fig) is an evergreen tree that may reach heights of 30–40 feet and have a trunk circumference of 20 feet or more and a crown as much as 120 feet in diameter. In Africa and the Near East–Mediterranean area, it has played a role reminiscent of the sacred fig-trees of India. In ancient Egypt, for example, the sycamore fig-tree was sacred to Osiris. Osiris was said to live in the tree, as shown in one of the Pyramid Texts that reads,

"Hail to thee, Sycamore, which encloseth the god." In certain rites, the image of Osiris was placed on sycamore boughs. His mother, Nut, is commonly depicted in the middle of a sycamore tree, pouring a drink for the good of the dead (Frazer, 1935, 6: 88, 110). Along with the grape (*Vitis vinifera*), the sycamore fig was among the most highly valued fruit used in Egyptian altar offerings, commonly presented in baskets or trays covered with leaves to keep the fruit fresh. Sometimes, too, sycamore figs were arranged in an uncovered basket in such a way as to "resemble the hieroglyphic signifying 'wife'" (J. G. Wilkinson, 1883, 3: 419). In central and southern Ethiopia in the past, pagan Galla people sometimes planted a sycamore fig over a priest's grave and then regarded it as sacred (Simoons, 1960: 212). For notes on the sycamore fig in the ancient eastern Mediterranean area, see Brothwell and Brothwell, 1969: 145–46; Condit, 1969: 173–75; Zohary and Spiegel-Roy, 1975: 324–25; Moldenke and Moldenke, 1952: 106–8; Darby et al., 1977, 2: 744–48; and M. Zohary, 1982: 68–69.

69. Gubernatis, 1978, 2: 167; Muthmann, 1982: passim; Baumann, 1993: 50.

70. Song of Solomon 4.1, 3, 13.

71. 1 Kings 7.41–42; Exodus 28.33–34.

72. Flückiger and Hanbury, 1879: 289; Farbridge, 1970: 35, 42.

73. R. C. Thompson, 1949: 316.

74. Lehner and Lehner, 1962: 84.

75. Hehn, 1888: 180.

76. In Phrygian myth, Attis's mother places a ripe almond on her breast, the almond being considered the father of all things (Frazer, 1935, 5: 263–64).

77. Frazer, 1935, 5: 263, 269.

78. Hehn, 1888: 180–84; Skinner, 1911: 221–22.

79. Hehn, 1888: 180–82.

80. Pausanias, *Description of Greece* 2.17.4; Frazer, pp. 184–85 in Vol. 3 of his trans. of Pausanias, *Description of Greece;* Muthmann, 1982: 52–64.

81. Hera's pomegranate has sometimes been explained in these terms. It has also been seen differently, as symbolic of blood, death, and Hera's triumph over her rivals Demeter and Persephone (Frazer, pp. 184–85 in Vol. 3 of his trans. of Pausanias, *Description of Greece*).

82. Clement of Alexandria, *Protreptikos* 2.19.3; Frazer, 1935, 7: 14.

83. Frazer, pp. 300–302 in Vol. 3 of his trans. of Ovid, *Fasti.* Use of the pomegranate was restricted in the ritual of Persephone and Demeter, her mother. Women observing the Thesmophoria festival, in remembrance of Persephone's departure for the underworld, were careful to avoid eating pomegranate seeds. In the Eleusinian mysteries, initiates were required to abstain from pomegranate fruit, whose touch polluted. At a place of Demeter and Persephone worship in Arcadia, moreover, offerings of the entire range of cultivated fruits were acceptable, but not pomegranates (Pausanias, *Description of Greece* 8.37.7; Clement of

Alexandria, *Protreptikos* 2.19.3; Porphyry, *On abstinence from animal food* 4.16; Frazer, p. 380 in Vol. 4 of his trans. of Pausanias, *Description of Greece*). For more on the pomegranate in the cult of Demeter and Persephone, see Muthmann, 1982: 67–77.

84. Skinner, 1911: 221, 222; Goor and Nurock, 1968: 73; Muthmann, 1982: 112–24.

85. Westermarck, 1973: 110.

86. Burton, n.d., 3: 269–71. Though the pomegranate's fertility symbolism has influenced its role in certain ritual contexts among Zoroastrians in Iran, in another ritual context, in which the pomegranate relates to haoma, its fertility symbolism is of no consequence (for which, see Flattery and Schwartz, 1989: esp. 76–84).

87. Massé, 1954: 67.

88. Skinner, 1911: 221–22; Gubernatis, 1978, 2: 168.

89. Musil, 1907–8, 3: 191.

90. Conder, 1883: 285.

91. Drower, 1937: 61, 188.

92. Drower, 1937: 37.

93. Westermarck, 1926, 2: 212–14.

94. Hehn, 1888: 184; Megas, 1963: 40.

95. Hyde, 1923: 154.

96. Megas, 1963: 39, 46.

97. Megas, 1963: 154.

98. Megas, 1963: 39, 40, 46, 117.

99. Wachsmuth, 1864: 98.

100. Ploss, 1899, 1: 585.

101. India: Getty, 1971: 18, 20–21; China: Yetts, 1912: 27; Laufer, 1919: 279, 286–87; Burkhardt, 1953–58, 1: 30, 120; 2: 16; Eberhard, 1968: 130.

102. Laufer, 1919: 287.

103. Burkhardt, 1953–58, 1: 118.

104. Skinner, 1911: 223.

105. Lehner and Lehner, 1960: 30–31, 104.

106. Burkhardt, 1953–58, 1: 99; 2: 16.

107. Hoffner, 1974: 116.

108. Oberhelman, 1991: 216.

109. Westermarck, 1926, 2: 533 and n 6.

110. Dalziel, 1937: 277–78; J. M. Watt, 1972: 75, 79, citing F. H. Ferreira. Among the Mandaeans of Iraq and Iran, fig leaves are woven into bridal wreaths (Drower, 1956: 7).

111. 1 Kings 4.25; see also Micah 4.4; Zechariah 3.10.

112. Goodenough, 1953–68, 7: 99.

113. A. J. Evans, 1901: 103–4, 128–29.

114. Gubernatis, 1978, 2: 140.

115. Athenaeus, *Deipnosophists* 3.78c; Frazer, 1935, 7: 4.

116. Gubernatis, 1978, 2: 138.

117. Athenaeus, *Deipnosophists* 3.78c.

118. Kerényi, 1976: 274.

119. Clement of Alexandria, *Protreptikos* 2.34.4–5; Kerényi, 1976: 274; Gubernatis, 1978, 2: 138.

120. Athenaeus, *Deipnosophists* 3.78c; Lang, 1901, 2: 255; Kerényi, 1976: 274.

121. Plutarch, *On love of wealth* 527D.

122. Goodenough, 1953–68, 6: 20 n 86.

123. Westermarck, 1922, 2: 473. The fig is involved in similar ritual in the modern world, where it retains this symbolism (Gubernatis, 1978, 2: 138–39).

124. J. J. Meyer, 1929: 75–87; 1937, 3: 195. Other tree exudations in Indian tradition should not be overlooked. In the *Vāyu Purāṇa*, for example, there is a mythical holy country, Kiṃpruṣa, where there is a fig tree that exudes honey, an excellent juice that is consumed by all the country's inhabitants, who are said to be pure in mind, to experience no sorrows, to suffer no illnesses, and to have a life span of 10,000 years (*Vāyu Purāṇa* 1.46.5–7, trans. in Tagare, 1987–88, 1: 301).

125. Hutton, 1963: 231.

126. George Watt (1889–96, 3: 355), Prakash (1961: 276), and Achaya (1994: 36, 149, 276, 287) identify plakṣa as a fig of one species or another. If correct, this would mean that all four of these trees are figs. S. M. Gupta (1971: 31), however, identifies plakṣa as the tree, mentioned above, called palās in Hindi (*Butea monosperma*). a tree associated with soma. By one account, the tree derived "from the feather of a falcon imbued with . . . soma." Its wood was made into vessels used for milking the cow earth, and its leaves served in rites to assure that female calves will became good milkers (Crooke, 1896a, 2: 111–12; S. M. Gupta, 1971: 31–33). Whether the plakṣa tree was a fig or a palās, it seems to have been appropriate company for the banyan, pipal, and udumbara trees.

127. *Aitareya Brāhmaṇa* 7.29–32, trans. in Haug, 1922: 332–36.

128. G. Watt, 1889–96, 3: 354.

129. Crooke, 1896a, 2: 97.

130. Abbott, 1974: 325.

131. This tree has unusually large fruit, from 12 to 18 inches long and 6–8 inches in diameter (G. Watt, 1889–96, 1: 332).

132. Srinivas, 1952: 74, 80, 94, 159, 160.

133. S. M. Gupta, 1971: 57.

134. Elwin, 1954: xlvi, 130.

135. Abbott, 1974: 334.

136. E.g., Pliny, *Natural history* 15.80–82; 16.181; 23.117, 126; Columella, *On agriculture* 5.11.8–9.

137. Macrobius, *Saturnalia* 3.20.5.

138. Varro, *On agriculture* 2.11.4; Pliny, *Natural history* 16.181; 23.117, 126. The use of fig-tree exudation to coagulate milk is also reported in modern Majorca (Uphof, 1959: 157).

139. Plutarch, *Romulus* 4.1; Seeley, 1881: 32.

140. Plutarch (*Romulus* 4.1) agrees in observing that no wine is offered to Rumina, but he also writes that "libations of milk are poured over her victims."

141. Varro, *On agriculture* 2.11.4–5.

142. Seeley, 1881: 32–33; Hadzsits, 1936: 307, 309. Subsequently the ruminal fig-tree, in turn, was magically moved to the Forum (Scullard, 1981: 77).

143. Macrobius, *Saturnalia* 1.11.40; Scullard, 1981: 161–62.

144. Fowler, 1899: 178.

145. Fowler, 1899: 178 n 8; Frazer, pp. 343–48, 351–53 in Vol. 2 of his trans. of Ovid, *Fasti.*

146. Beech, 1913: 4–5; Frazer, pp. 348–52 in Vol. 2 of his trans. of Ovid, *Fasti;* Frazer, 1935, 2: 316–17.

147. Crooke, 1926: 407; Hutton, 1933: 397.

148. Theal, 1886: 29–47; L. Gomme, 1908–26: 633.

149. V. Turner, 1967: 20–25, 31, 52–58, 189–91, 214.

150. Dumont, 1992: 332.

151. For an excellent account of the sources of manna in Europe and other parts of the world, see Donkin, 1980.

152. For a map of the distribution of *F. ornus* in Europe, see Donkin, 1980: 89.

153. For the production of manna from *F. ornus* in Mediterranean Europe, see Donkin, 1980: 87–97.

154. For a discussion of the ash and oak as cosmic trees in various parts of Europe, see A. B. Cook, 1904–7, 15: 291–95.

155. Fergusson, 1971: 24, quoting the Prose Edda.

156. Three species of ash, among them *Fraxinus excelsior,* are identified by Watt as growing in the Himalayas of India. Watt notes, however, that manna from *F. excelsior* seems not to be used in India at all (G. Watt, 1889–96, 3: 440–44). Donkin (1980: 87) notes that in the Himalayan foothills two species of *Fraxinus,* including *F. excelsior,* yield manna, but that their manna seems not to be gathered to a significant degree, nor is it employed in the local materia medica.

157. Dumont, 1992. For some Christian actions against the worship of sacred trees, fountains, or stones, see Fergusson, 1971: 26–27.

158. Dumont, 1992.

159. Frazer, 1935, 1: 52–174.

160. Cormack, 1935: 165, 166; F. P. Smith, 1969: 13, 53.

161. Dubois, 1906: 189, 698; K. A. Hasan, 1971: 58–59.

162. When chayote (*Sechium edule*), whose fruit bears a certain resemblance to the Buddha's-hand citron, was introduced in China from Mexico in post-

Columbian times, it was called Buddha's-hand gourd (Herklots, 1972: 339; E. N. Anderson, 1988: 132, 187).

163. Crooke, 1896a, 2: 39–40; M. Stevenson, 1920: 99; Vogel, 1920; K. Mitra, 1925; B. Walker, 1968, 1: 422; Abbott, 1974: 131–32; Woodburne, 1981: 63, 64; Coomaraswamy, 1993: 66, 71 n 15, 75.

Representations of a hand with five fingers extended also occur on tombs and buildings in ancient India, Babylon, Phoenicia, Egypt, and Carthage. Hand-shaped amulets, on their part, were employed by Etruscans, Romans, Greeks, Egyptians, and Phoenicians. In modern times, representations of the hand serve to protect against the evil eye in northern Africa, southern Europe, the Near East, and India. It seems that this was true in antiquity as well (Westermarck, 1926, 1: 469–71; Róheim, 1981: 219).

There is also a widespread gesture against the evil eye in the Mediterranean area and the Near East. It is made with five outstretched fingers, and in some places the gesture is accompanied by expressions such as "five in your eye" and "five on you" (Westermarck, 1926, 1: 470–71). Thus, one reads of a healer among Sunni Moslems in Lebanon seeking to protect an infant against the evil eye by waving it three times over the fumes of a mixture of incense, salt, garlic, and something taken from the suspected person while saying, "five in his, or her eye" (Harfouche, 1981: 103). A similar gesture and expression seem to have been known in ancient Rome (Westermarck, 1926, 1: 471).

164. Simoons, 1991: 194.

165. Tolkowsky, 1938: 8; Schafer, 1954: 67; Burkill, 1966, 1: 579; Li, 1979: 128.

166. Burkill, 1966, 1: 579.

167. Lehner and Lehner, 1960: 30.

168. Ghosh, 1985: 168.

169. Tolkowsky, 1938: 24, plates IV and V.

170. Tolkowsky, 1938: 41–42, 44.

171. Wheatley, 1961.

172. Crevost and Lemarié, 1917: 202–3.

173. F. P. Smith, 1969: 114.

174. F. N. Meyer, 1911: 45; Tolkowsky, 1938: 8–9; C. A. S. Williams, 1941: 51; Swingle and Reece, 1967: 372; H. A. Giles, 1978: 26; F. N. Anderson, 1988: 136.

175. F. N. Meyer, 1911: 45; McClure, 1933: 138; Tolkowsky, 1938: 9, plates II and III; Sowerby, 1940: 140; C. A. S. Williams, 1941: 51; Burkhardt, 1953–58, 1: 112.

176. Yetts, 1912: 27, fig. 20.

177. *Eugenia jambalana* Lam. is the equivalent of *E. cumini* L. and *Syzygium jambolanum* DC.

178. G. Watt, 1889–96, 3: 286, quoting Lisboa.

179. If, for example, one uncovers a bit of charcoal when excavating the site of a new house, it is an inauspicious sign and it is advisable to select a new site (Crooke, 1896a, 2: 50).

180. "Panjab—red food forbidden—Hindus," 1886.

181. Henderson, 1866: 21.

182. The fertility associations of both turmeric and tulsi are revealed in the observation that among certain Brahmins a priest is ultimately given the wristlet worn by a bridal couple, after which he may remove the turmeric that is ordinarily tied into the wristlet and then cast the wristlet into the household tulsi plant (Abbott, 1974: 85).

183. Woodburne, 1981: 62.

184. Dymock, 1891; Kirtikar, 1912; Crooke, 1896a, 2: 28–29; Sopher, 1964: 96–108.

185. Sopher, 1964: 108–10, 116–23.

186. S. M. Gupta, 1971: 13.

187. S. M. Gupta, 1971: 6.

188. Rahner, 1963: 286–327.

189. Theophrastus, *Enquiry into plants* 3.1.3; Pliny, *Natural history* 16.110.

190. Aelian, *On the characteristics of animals* 4.23.

191. Pliny, *Natural history* 16.110.

192. *Atharva-veda* 3.6.6, trans. in Bloomfield, 1897: 92. See also *Atharva-veda* 8.8.3.

193. Abbott, 1974: 333.

194. Kuhn, 1886: 40, 66, 175; Eggeling, 1882–1900, 12: 275, 293 n; Frazer, 1935, 2: 249–50; Gonda, 1980: 164.

195. Gonda, 1980: 164.

196. S. M. Gupta, 1971: 7.

197. The term *mistletoe* is used for numerous semiparasitic species of the families Loranthaceae and Viscaceae, but the traditional mistletoe of European literature and Christmas is *Viscum album*. *V. album* most commonly grows on apple, willow, poplar, hawthorn, and linden trees.

198. Pliny, *Natural history* 16.249–51; 24.12; Frazer, 1935, 2: 358, 362; 11: 76–94; Kendrick, 1966: 123–25.

199. Spence, 1945: 125–26.

200. Grimm, 1883–88, 3: 1206.

201. Kendrick, 1966: 124–25.

202. A. B. Cook, 1904–7, 15: 424–26.

203. "The folk-lore of Drayton," 1884–85, 2: 361.

204. The association among mistletoe, oak, and mandrake in eighteenth-century France is shown in a peasant superstition. By this superstition, a mandrake could be found at the foot of the oaks on which mistletoe grew, and such

mandrake was said to grow as deep in the earth as the mistletoe grew high on the tree (Chéruel, 1899, 2: 726, and Starck, 1917: 50, citing Sainte-Palaye).

205. Hardy, 1989: 236.

206. Hutton, 1963: 277.

207. Ragozin, 1902: 26–27 n; Yule and Burnell, 1903: 65, quoting Tavernier.

208. Da Gama mistook the Hindu Indians for Christian Indians. Ravenstein, 1898: 24 and n, 32, 35, 36 and n, 39, 40 and n, 44–45 and n, 46.

209. Huntingford, 1980: 28, 35, 37, 41–42, 47–48, 50, 52. McCrindle (1973: 92–93), in his translation of the *Periplus,* gives a somewhat different impression of Kanē's inhabitants: they consisted "of an intermixture of foreigners, Arabs, Indians, and even Greeks, who resort hither for the purposes of commerce." The implication is that the Indian inhabitants as well as the Greeks had come to Kanē as merchants, not in some other guise.

210. Lamberg-Karlovsky, 1972; Possehl, 1979: 113–14, 153–54.

211. de Candolle, 1919: 181; H. C. Powell, 1930: 57; Webber, 1943: 2–4.

212. Skinner, 1911: 88.

213. H. C. Powell, 1930: 21–22; Webber, 1943: 2–6; Andrews, 1961; Hayes, 1966: 198.

214. Isaac, 1959: 180–83; Andrews, 1961: 36–37.

215. Isaac, 1959: 181–83.

216. Abrahams, 1908–26: 144; Isaac, 1959: 183; Goor and Nurock, 1968: 155.

217. Tolkowsky, 1938: 19; Goor and Nurock, 1968: 166–67.

218. Isaac, 1959: 183–85.

219. For an evaluation of the hypothesis of environmental deterioration, see Simoons, 1994: 71–85.

220. Vayda, 1987: 507–8.

221. *Maitri Upanishad* 7.20, quoted by Coomaraswamy, 1993: 179.

222. Demonstrating how far we have moved from that perspective is a recent political advertisement on television in which an elected official from the state of Idaho was attacked for supporting the view that adult offspring, not the government, should bear the responsibility of caring for their aged parents.

223. Fontenrose, 1978: 39–44.

BIBLIOGRAPHY

Abbott, J. 1974. *The keys of power: A study of Indian ritual and belief.* Secaucus, N.J.: University Books.

Abd Allah, M. A., Y. H. Foda, Ferial M. Abu Salem, and Zahra S. Abd Allah. 1988. "Treatments for reducing total vicine in Egyptian fava bean (Giza 2 variety)." *Plant Foods for Human Nutrition* 38: 201–10.

Abrahams, I. 1908–26. "Symbolism (Jewish)." Pp. 143–45 in Vol. 12 of *Encyclopaedia of religion and ethics.* 13 vols. Ed. James Hastings. Edinburgh: T. and T. Clark.

Achaya, K. T. 1994. *Indian food: A historical companion.* Delhi, Bombay, Calcutta, Madras: Oxford University Press.

Ackerknecht, Erwin H. 1965. *History and geography of the most important diseases.* New York and London: Hafner.

Ackerman, Phyllis. 1935. "The talking tree." *Bulletin of the American Institute for Persian Art and Archaeology* 4, 2 (December): 66–72.

Adams, Isaac. 1901. *Darkness and daybreak: Personal experiences, manners, customs, habits, religious and social life in Persia.* [Grand Rapids, Mich.: By the author].

Aelian. 1958–59. *On the characteristics of animals.* 3 vols. Trans. A. F. Scholfield. Loeb Classical Library. London: William Heinemann; Cambridge, Mass.: Harvard University Press.

Agarwal, V. S. 1986. *Economic plants of India.* Calcutta: Kailash.

Agrawal, P., V. Rai, and R. B. Singh. 1996. "Randomized placebo-controlled, single blind trial of holy basil leaves in patients with noninsulin-dependent

460

diabetes mellitus." *International Journal of Clinical Pharmacology and Therapeutics* 34: 406–9.

Agrawala, V. S. 1943. "Kalpavṛkṣa: The wish fulfilling tree." *Journal of the Indian Society* (Calcutta) 11: 1–8.

Ahir, D.C. 1994. *Buddha Gaya through the ages*. Bibliotheca Indo-Buddhica Series, 134. Delhi: Sri Satguru Publications.

Ainslie, Whitelaw. 1826. *Materia indica*. 2 vols. London: Longman, Rees, Orme, Brown, and Green.

Aiyar, R. Kalyanasundaram. 1931–32. "South Indian serpent lore." *Quarterly Journal of the Mythic Society* 22: 424–30.

Alabaster, Henry. 1871. *The wheel and the law: Buddhism illustrated from Siamese sources*. London: Trübner.

Albertus Magnus. 1973. *The book of secrets*. Pp. 1–73 in Michael R. Best and Frank H. Brightman (eds.), *The book of secrets of Albertus Magnus of the virtues of herbs, stones and certain beasts. Also a book of the marvels of the world*. Oxford: Clarendon Press.

Alderink, Larry J. 1981. *Creation and salvation in ancient Orphism*. American Classical Studies, 8. Chico, Calif.: Scholars Press.

Ali, M., and M. Thomson. 1995. "Consumption of a garlic clove a day could be beneficial in preventing thrombosis." *Prostaglandins, Leukotrienes, and Essential Fatty Acids* 53: 211–12.

Allchin, F. R. 1969. "Early cultivated plants in India and Pakistan." Pp. 323–29 in Peter J. Ucko and G. W. Dimbleby (eds.), *The domestication and exploitation of plants and animals*. Chicago: Aldine.

Allen, Albert Henry. 1900. "The Vaṭa-sāvitrī-vrata, according to Hemādri and the Vratārka." *Journal of the American Oriental Society* 21, 2d half: 53–66.

Allen, Timothy F. (ed.). 1964. *The encyclopedia of pure materia medica*. Vol. 6. Ridgewood, N.J.: Gregg Press.

Allison, A. C., B. A. Askonas, N. A. Barnicot, B. S. Blumberg, and C. Krimbas. 1963. "Deficiency of erythrocyte glucose-6-phosphate dehydrogenase in Greek populations." *Annals of Human Genetics* 26: 237–42.

Alsdorf, Ludwig. 1961. "Beiträge zur Geschichte von Vegetarismus und Rinderverehrung in Indien." *Akademie der Wissenschaften und der Literatur, Mainz; Abhandlungen der Geistes- und Sozialwissenschaftlichen Klasse* 1961: 559–625.

Ammianus Marcellinus. 1948–52. *The chronicle of events*. Trans. as *Ammianus Marcellinus* by John C. Rolfe. 3 vols. Loeb Classical Library. London: William Heinemann; Cambridge, Mass.: Harvard University Press.

Anderson, Eugene N. 1988. *The food of China*. New Haven and London: Yale University Press.

Anderson, Eugene N., and Marya L. Anderson. 1977. "Modern China: South."

Pp. 319–82 in K. C. Chang (ed.), *Food in Chinese culture*. New Haven: Yale University Press.

Andrews, Alfred C. 1949. "The bean and Indo-European totemism." *American Anthropologist*, n. s. 51: 274–92.

Andrews, Alfred C. 1961. "Acclimatization of citrus fruits in the Mediterranean region." *Agricultural History* 35: 35–46.

Angel, J. Lawrence. 1964. "Osteoporosis: Thalassemia?" *American Journal of Physical Anthropology* 22: 369–71.

Angel, J. Lawrence. 1966. "Porotic hyperostosis, anemias, malarias, and marshes in the prehistoric eastern Mediterranean." *Science* 153: 760–63.

Angel, J. Lawrence. 1967. "Porotic hyperostosis or osteoporosis symmetrica." Pp. 378–89 in Don Brothwell and A. T. Sandison (eds.), *Diseases in antiquity*. Springfield, Ill.: Charles C. Thomas.

Angyal, A. 1941. "Disgust and related aversions." *Journal of Abnormal and Social Psychology* 36: 393–412.

Anuśanaparva. 1893. Pt. 2 of *The Mahabharata of Krishna-Dwaipayana Vyasa*. Calcutta: Bhārata Press.

Apollodorus. 1921. *The library*. 2 vols. Trans. James George Frazer. Loeb Classical Library. Cambridge, Mass.: Harvard University Press; London: William Heinemann.

Apollonius Rhodius. 1930. *The Argonautica*. Trans. R. C. Seaton. Loeb Classical Library. London: William Heinemann; New York: G. P. Putnam's Sons.

Apuleius. 1989. *Metamorphoses*. 2 vols. Trans. J. Arthur Hanson. Loeb Classical Library. Cambridge, Mass., and London: Harvard University Press.

Arano, Luisa Cogliati. 1976. *The medieval health handbook: Tacuinum sanitatis*. Trans. Oscar Ratti and Adele Westbrook. New York: George Braziller.

Arasaratnam, Sinnappah (trans. and ed.). 1978. *François Valentijn's description of Ceylon*. Hakluyt Society Publications, 2d ser. 149. London: Hakluyt Society.

Arbid, Mahmoud S. S., and Ronald R. Marquardt. 1985. "Hydrolysis of toxic constituents (vicine and convicine) in fababean (*Vicia faba* L.) food preparations following treatment with β-glucosidase." *Journal of the Science of Food and Agriculture* 36: 839–46.

Arese, Paolo. 1982. "Favism—a natural model for the study of hemolytic mechanisms." *Reviews in Pure and Applied Pharmacological Sciences* 3: 123–83.

Arese, Paolo, and Antonio De Flora. 1990. "Pathophysiology of hemolysis in glucose-6-phosphate dehydrogenase deficiency." *Seminars in Hematology* 27: 1–40.

Arese, Paolo, L. Mannuzzu, F. Turrini, S. Galiano, and G. F. Gaetani. 1986. "Etiological aspects of favism." Pp. 45–75 in Akira Yoshida and Ernest Beutler (eds.), *Glucose-6-phosphate dehydrogenase*. London: Academic Press.

Aretaeus. 1972. *On the causes and symptoms of chronic diseases*. Trans. Francis Adams, pp 291–373 in his *The extant works of Aretaeus the Cappadocian*. Boston: Milford House.

Arie, T. H. D. 1959. "Pythagoras and beans." *Oxford Medical School Gazette* 11: 75–81.

Aristophanes. 1902. *The Frogs*. Trans. as *"The Frogs" of Aristophanes* by Benjamin Bickley Rogers. London: George Bell and Sons.

Aristophanes. 1930a. *The Acharnians*. Trans. Benjamin Bickley Rogers. London: George Bell and Sons.

Aristophanes. 1930b. *The knights*. Trans. as *"The Knights" of Aristophanes* by Benjamin Bickley Rogers. London: George Bell and Sons.

Aristophanes. 1980. *The Acharnians*. Trans. as *Acharnians* by Alan H. Sommerstein. Vol. 1 of *The comedies of Aristophanes*. Warminster, Wilts, England: Aris and Phillips.

Aristotle. 1984a. *On sleep and waking*. Trans. as *On sleep* by J. I. Beare. Pp. 721–35 in Vol. 1 of *The complete works of Aristotle*. 2 vols. Ed. Jonathan Barnes. Rev. Oxford trans. Bollingen Series, 71, 1 and 2. Princeton: Princeton University Press.

Aristotle. 1984b. *On the soul*. Trans. J. A. Smith. Pp. 641–92 in Vol. 1 of *The complete works of Aristotle*. 2 vols. Ed. Jonathan Barnes. Rev. Oxford trans. Bollingen Series 71, 1 and 2. Princeton: Princeton University Press.

Armstrong, Wayne P. 1986. "Fig encounters of the kind." *Zoonoz* (Zoological Society of San Diego) 59, 7 (July): 17–18.

Arrian. 1929–33. *Indica*. Pp. 307–435 in Vol. 2 of *Arrian*. 2 vols. Trans. E. Iliff Robson. Loeb Classical Library. Cambridge, Mass.: Harvard University Press; London: William Heinemann.

Artemidorus Daldianus. 1975. *The interpretation of dreams, oneirocritica*. Trans. Robert J. White. Park Ridge, N.J.: Noyes Press.

Aruna, K., and V. M. Sivaramakrishnan. 1992. "Anticarcinogenic effects of some Indian plant products." *Food and Chemical Toxicology* 30: 953–56.

Ascherson, Paul. 1891a. [Comments on "Sechse Mandragora Wurzeln," by F. von Luschan]. *Zeitschrift für Ethologie* 23: 729–38.

Ascherson, Paul. 1891b. "Nachträgliche Mittheilungen über Mandragoras." *Zeitschrift für Ethologie* 23: 890–92.

Aston, W. G. 1905. *Shinto (The way of the gods)*. New York and Bombay: Longmans, Green.

Aston, W. G. (trans.). 1956. *Nihongi: Chronicles of Japan from the earliest times to A. D. 697*. London: George Allen and Unwin; New York: Paragon Book Reprint Corporation.

Athenaeus. 1927–41. *The deipnosophists*. 7 vols. Trans. Charles Burton Gulick. Loeb Classical Library. London: William Heinemann; Cambridge, Mass.: Harvard University Press.

Aulus Gellius. 1954–61. *Attic nights.* Trans. as *The "Attic Nights" of Aulus Gellius* by John C. Rolfe. 3 vols. Loeb Classical Library. London: William Heinemann; Cambridge, Mass.: Harvard University Press.

Avery, Catherine B. (ed.). 1962. *The new century classical handbook.* New York: Appleton-Century-Crofts.

Azevedo, Eliane, H. Neil Kirkman, Anne C. Morrow, and Arno G. Motulsky. 1968. "Variants of red cell glucose-6-phosphate dehydrogenase among Asiatic Indians." *Annals of Human Genetics* 31: 373–79.

Babb, Lawrence A. 1970. "The food of the gods in Chhattisgarh: Some structural features of Hindu ritual." *Southwestern Journal of Anthropology* 26: 287–304.

Babb, Lawrence A. 1975. *The divine hierarchy: Popular Hinduism in Central India.* New York and London: Columbia University Press.

Bacon, Francis. 1869–72. *Natural history.* Pp. 151–483 in Vol. 4 and pp. 7–169 in Vol. 5 of *The works of Francis Bacon.* 15 vols. Ed. James Spedding, Robert Leslie Ellis, Douglas Denon Heath, and William Rawley. New York: Hurd and Houghton; Cambridge: Riverside Press.

Bailey, L. H. 1935. *The standard cyclopedia of horticulture.* 3 vols. New York: Macmillan.

Bakhsh, Ram. 1892–93. "Mango and pipal trees." *North Indian Notes and Queries* 2: 161.

Baldensperger, Philip J. 1893. "Peasant folklore of Palestine." *Quarterly Statement, Palestine Exploration Fund* 1883: 203–19.

Balfour, Edward. 1885. *The cyclopaedia of India and of eastern and southern Asia, commercial, industrial, and scientific.* 3d ed. 3 vols. London: Bernard Quaritch.

Balfour, Edward. 1976. *Encyclopaedia asiatica.* 9 vols. New Delhi: Cosmo Publications.

Banerjea, Jitendra Nath. 1953. "The Hindu concept of god." Pp. 48–82 in Kenneth W. Morgan (ed.), *The religion of the Hindus.* New York: Ronald Press.

Banks, M. M. 1932. "Letter to the editor." *Folk-Lore* (London) 43: 429–30.

Baranov, A. 1966. "Recent advances in our knowledge of the morphology, cultivation, and uses of ginseng (*Panax ginseng* C. A. Meyer)." *Economic Botany* 20: 403–6.

Barnett, R. D. 1956. "Ancient oriental influences on Archaic Greece." Pp. 212–38 in Saul S. Weinberg (ed.), *The Aegean and the Near East.* Studies presented to Hetty Goldman on the occasion of her seventy-fifth birthday. Locust Valley, N.Y.: J. J. Augustin.

Barns, Thomas. 1908–26. "Trees and plants." Pp. 448–57 in Vol. 12 of *Encyclopaedia of religion and ethics.* 13 vols. Ed. James Hastings. Edinburgh: T. and T. Clark.

Bartlett, Harley Harris. 1926. "Sumatran plants collected in Asahan and Karoland, with notes on the vernacular names." *Papers of the Michigan Academy of Science, Arts and Letters* 6: 1–66.

Barua, Benimadhab. 1975. *Gayā and Buddha-Gayā*. 2 vols. Varanasi: Bhartiya Publishing House.

Barua, Dipak K. 1981. *Buddha Gaya temple: Its history.* Buddha Gaya: Buddha Gaya Temple Management Committee.

Basak, Radhagovinda. 1953. "The Hindu concept of the natural world." Pp. 83–116 in Kenneth W. Morgan (ed.), *The religion of the Hindus.* New York: Ronald Press.

Basham, Arthur L. 1954. *The wonder that was India.* London: Sidgwick and Jackson.

Basil, Saint. 1963. *Homilies.* Trans. as *Exegetic homilies* by Agnes Clare Way. Fathers of the Church, A New Translation, 46. Washington, D.C.: Catholic University of America Press.

Bastian, A. 1869. *Die Völker des östlichen Asien.* Jena: Hermann Costenoble.

Bastien, Joseph W. 1987. "Humor and satire." Pp. 526–29 in Vol. 6 of *The encyclopedia of religion.* 16 vols. Ed. Mircea Eliade. New York: Macmillan; London: Collier Macmillan.

Bauhin, Johann, and Johann Heinrich Cherler. 1650–51. *Historia plantarum universalis.* 3 vols. Ed. Dominique Chabre and Franz Ludwig von Graffenreid. Ebroduni.

Baumann, Hellmut. 1993. *The Greek plant world in myth, art and literature.* Trans. and augmented by William T. Stearn and Eldwyth Ruth Stearn. Portland, Oreg.: Timber Press.

Baxi, A. J., V. Balakrishnan, and L. D. Sanghvi. 1961. "Deficiency of glucose-6-phosphate dehydrogenase—observations on a sample from Bombay." *Current Science* 30: 16–17.

Baxi, A. J., V. Balakrishnan, J. V. Undevia, and L. D. Sanghvi. 1963. "Glucose-6-phosphate dehydrogenase deficiency in the Parsee community, Bombay." *Indian Journal of Medical Sciences* 17: 493–500.

Beal, Samuel (trans.). 1968. *Buddhist records of the Western world.* 2 vols. in 1. Popular ed. New York: Paragon Book Reprint Corp.

Beaver, Paul Chester, Rodney Clifton Jung, and Eddie Wayne Cupp. 1984. *Clinical parasitology.* 9th ed. Philadelphia: Lea and Febiger.

Beck, Brenda E. F. 1969. "Colour and heat in South Indian ritual." *Man,* n. s. 4: 553–72.

Beck, Brenda E. F. 1987. "Domestic observances: Hindu practices." Pp. 407–10 in Vol. 4 of *The encyclopedia of religion.* 16 vols. Ed. Mircea Eliade. New York: Macmillan; London: Collier Macmillan.

Bedi, S. J. 1978. "Ethnobotany of the Ratan Mahal Hills, Gujarat, India." *Economic Botany* 32: 278–84.

Bedigian, Dorothea, and Jack R. Harlan. 1983. "Nuba agriculture and ethnobotany, with particular reference to sesame and sorghum." *Economic Botany* 37: 384–95.

Bedigian, Dorothea, and Jack R. Harlan. 1986. "Evidence of cultivation of sesame in the ancient world." *Economic Botany* 40: 137–54.

Bedigian, Dorothea, C. A. Smyth, and Jack R. Harlan. 1986. "Patterns of morphological variation in *Sesamum indicum*." *Economic Botany* 40: 353–65.

Bedigian, Dorothea, David S. Seigler, and Jack R. Harlan. 1985. "Sesamin, sesamolin and the origin of sesame." *Biochemical Systematics and Ecology* 13: 133–39.

Beech, W. H. 1913. "The sacred fig-tree of the A-Kikuyu of East Africa." *Man* 13: 4–6.

Behura, N. K. 1962. "Meals and food habits in rural India." *Bulletin of the Anthropological Survey of India* 11: 111–37.

Belsey, Mark A. 1973. "The epidemiology of favism." *Bulletin of the World Health Organization* 48: 1–13.

Bennett, J. W. 1843. *Ceylon and its capabilities*. London: William H. Allen and Company.

Bennett, W. H. (ed.). [1904]. *The century Bible: Genesis*. Edinburgh: T. C. and E. C. Jack.

Bent, James Theodore. 1966. *Aegean Islands: The Cyclades, or life among the insular Greeks*. New and enl. ed. Chicago: Argonaut.

Berndt, Ronald Murray. 1962. *Excess and restraint: Social control among a New Guinea mountain people*. Chicago: University of Chicago Press.

Besnehard, Pierre. 1993. "Nommer la mandragore." Pp. 127–33 in Marie-Claire Amouretti and Georges Comet (eds.), *Des hommes et des plantes: Plantes méditerranéennes, vocabulaire et usage anciens*. Cahiers d'histoire des techniques, 2. Aix-en-Provence: Publications de l'Université de Provence.

Beutler, Ernest. 1960. "Drug-induced hemolytic anemia (primaquine sensitivity)." Pp. 1031–67 in John B. Stanbury, James B. Wyngaarden, and Donald S. Fredrickson (eds.), *The metabolic basis of inherited disease*. New York: McGraw-Hill.

Beveridge, Annette Susannah (trans.). 1971. *The Bābur-nāma in English (memoirs of Bābur)*. 2 vols. Trans. from the original Turki text of Zahiru'd-dīn Muhammad Bābur Pādshāh Ghāzī. New York: AMS Press.

Beyer, R. 1891. [Comments on "Sechse Mandragora Wurzeln," by F. von Luschan]. *Zeitschrift für Ethologie* 23: 738–46.

Bhardwaj, Surinder Mohan. 1973. *Hindu places of pilgrimage in India*. Berkeley, Los Angeles, London: University of California Press.

Bhatnagar, I. M. L. 1965. "Tree-symbol worship in Punjab." Pp. 89–92 in Sankar Sen Gupta (ed.), *Tree symbol worship in India*. Calcutta: Indian Publications.

Bhattacharyya, Sivaprasad. 1953. "Religious practices of the Hindus." Pp. 154–205 in Kenneth W. Morgan (ed.), *The religion of the Hindus*. New York: Ronald Press.

Bhishagratna, Kaviraj Kunjalal. 1963. *An English translation of the Sushruta Samhita based on original Sanskrit text*. 3 vols. Chowkhamba Sanskrit Series, 30. Varanasi: Chowkhamba Sanskrit Series Office.

Bianchi, Ugo. 1976. *The Greek mysteries*. Institute of Religious Iconography, State University Groningen, Iconography of Religions, 17, 3. Leiden: E. J. Brill.

Biedermann, B. 1995. ["Garlic—a 'secret miracle of God'?".] *Schweizerische Rundschau für Medizin Praxis* 84: 7–10. (Original article in German).

Biswas, K., and R. N. Chopra. 1982. *Common medicinal plants of Darjeeling and the Sikkim Himalayas*. Delhi: Soni Reprints Agency.

Bloch, Oscar, and W. von Wartburg. 1960. *Dictionnaire étymologique de la langue française*. Paris: Presses Universitaires de France.

Bloomfield, Maurice (trans.). 1897. *Hymns of the Atharva-veda*. Vol. 42 of *The sacred books of the East*. Ed. F. Max Müller. Oxford: Clarendon Press.

Blunt, E. A. H. 1931. *The caste system of northern India*. London: Oxford University Press.

Boccaccio, Giovanni. 1972. *The decameron*. Trans. G. H. McWilliam. Harmondsworth, Middlesex: Penguin Books.

Bock, Hieronymus. 1577. *Kreutterbuch*. Strassburg: Josiam Rihel.

Bodde, Derk. 1975. *Festivals in classical China: New Year and other annual observances during the Han dynasty, 206 B.C.–A.D. 220*. Princeton: Princeton University Press.

Bode, Dastur Framroze A. 1955. "The tree of life." *The Journal of the Anthropological Society of Bombay*, n. s. 9: 39–51.

Böhm, Fridericus. 1905. *De symbolis Pythagoreis*. Inaugural dissertation, Berlin.

Bois, D. 1927–37. *Les plantes alimentaires chez tous les peuples et à travers les âges*. 4 vols. Paris: Paul Lechavalier.

Bollet, Alfred Jay, and Audrey K. Brown. 1993. "Anemia." Pp. 571–77 in Kenneth F. Kiple (ed.), *The Cambridge world history of human disease*. Cambridge: Cambridge University Press.

Bond, D. A. 1976. "Field bean: *Vicia faba* (Leguminosae—Papilionatae)." Pp. 179–82 in N. W. Simmonds (ed.), *Evolution of crop plants*. London and New York: Longman.

Bonser, Wilfrid. 1963. *The medical background of Anglo-Saxon England: A study in history, psychology, and folklore*. London: Wellcome Historical Medical Library.

Bottini, Egidio, Paola Lucarelli, Rocco Agostino, Ricciotti Palmarino, Luisa Businco, and Giuseppina Antognoni. 1971. "Favism: Association with erythrocyte acid phosphatase phenotype." *Science* 171: 409–11.

Boullet, Jean. 1960. "Mandragore." *Aesculape* 43 (November): 3–37.

Bowman, J. E., and D. G. Walker. 1961. "Action of *Vicia faba* on erythrocytes: Possible relationship to favism." *Nature* 189: 555–56.

Boyancé, Pierre. 1962. "Sur les mystères d'Eleusis." *Revue des études grecques* 75: 460–82.

Boyancé, Pierre. 1972. *Le Culte des muses chez les philosophes grec*. Bibliothèque des Écoles françaises d'Athènes et de Rome, 141. Paris: Éditions E. de Boccard.

Boyce, Mary. 1977. *A Persian stronghold of Zoroastrianism*. Oxford: Clarendon Press.

Brancati, Carlo, and Antonio Tagarelli. 1982. "Thalassemia types in Calabria (southern Italy)." Pp. 147–55 in Vol. 18 of *Thalassemia: Recent Advances in Detection and Treatment*. New York: Alan R. Liss.

Brand, John. 1893–95. *Observations on the popular antiquities of Great Britain*. 3 vols. London: George Bell and Sons.

Brand, John. 1900. *Observations on popular antiquities*. New ed. London: Chatto and Windus.

Brandis, Dietrich. 1921. *Indian trees*. London: Constable.

Bray, Denys. 1913. *The life-history of a Brahui*. London: Royal Asiatic Society.

Bremmer, Jan. 1987. "Genesia." Pp. 506–7 in Vol. 5 of *The encyclopedia of religion*. 16 vols. Ed. Mircea Eliade. New York: Macmillan; London: Collier Macmillan.

Bretschneider, E. 1882–95. *Botanicon Sinicum: Notes on Chinese botany from native and Western sources*. 3 vols. London: Trübner and Co; Shanghai, Hong Kong, Yokohama, and Singapore: Kelly and Walsh.

Briggs, K. M. 1957. "The English fairies." *Folk-Lore* (London) 68: 270–87.

Brim, Charles J. 1936. *Medicine in the Bible. The Pentateuch: Torah*. New York: Froben Press.

Brodrick, A. Houghton (ed.). 1972. *Animals in archaeology*. New York: Praeger.

Brothwell, Don, and Patricia Brothwell. 1969. *Food in antiquity: A survey of the diet of early peoples*. New York and Washington, D.C.: Frederick A. Praeger.

Brown, E. G., and F. M. Roberts. 1972. "Formation of vicine and convicine by *Vicia faba*." *Phytochemistry* 11: 3203–6.

Brown, Francis, S. R. Driver, and Charles A. Briggs (eds.). 1953. *A Hebrew and English lexicon of the Old Testament*. Based on the lexicon of William Gesenius, as trans. by Edward Robinson. Oxford: Clarendon Press.

Brown, Peter J. 1981. "New considerations on the distribution of malaria, thalassemia, and glucose-6-phosphate dehydrogenase deficiency in Sardinia." *Human Biology* 53: 367–82.

Brown, Peter J. 1993. "Favism." Pp. 722–24 in Kenneth F. Kiple (ed.), *The Cambridge world history of human disease*. Cambridge: Cambridge University Press.

Brown, W. Norman. 1957. "The sanctity of the cow in Hinduism." *Madras University Journal* 28: 29–49.

Browne, Thomas. 1912. *Pseudodoxia epidemica, or enquiries into very many received tenents and commonly presumed truths*. In Vols. 1–3 of *The works of Sir Thomas Browne*. 3 vols. Ed. Charles Sayle. Edinburgh: John Grant.

Bruce-Chwatt, Leonard Jan. 1985. *Essential malariology*. 2d ed. New York: John Wiley.

Bruce-Chwatt, Leonard Jan, and Julian de Zulueta. 1980. *The rise and fall of malaria in Europe: A historico-epidemiological study*. Oxford: Oxford University Press.

Brugsch, Heinrich. 1891. "Die Alraune als altägyptische Zauberpflanze." *Zeitschrift für Ägyptische Sprache und Alterthumskunde* 29: 31–33.

Brumbaugh, Robert S., and Jessica Schwartz. 1979–80. "Pythagoras and beans: A medical explanation." *Classical World* 73: 421–22.

Brunetti, P., A. Parma, G. Nenci, E. Migliorini, and B. Brunelli. 1965. "Incidenza del difetto di G-6-PD nell'Italia centrale." *Haematologica* 50: 203–19.

Buddhist shrines in India. 1968. 2d ed. Delhi: Publications Division, Ministry of Information and Broadcasting, Government of India.

Budge, E. A. Wallis. 1909. *The liturgy of funerary offerings: The Egyptian texts with English translations.* London: Kegan Paul, Trench, Trübner.

Budge, E. A. Wallis. 1913. *The Syriac book of medicines.* 2 vols. London: Oxford University Press.

Budge, E. A. Wallis. 1925. *The mummy: A handbook of Egyptian funerary archaeology.* Cambridge: Cambridge University Press.

Bühler, George (trans.). 1879–82. *The sacred laws of the Āryas, as taught in the schools of Āpastamba, Gautama, Vāsishṭha, and Baudhāyana.* Vols. 2 and 14 of *The sacred books of the East.* Ed. F. Max Müller. Oxford: Clarendon Press.

Bühler, George (trans.). 1886. *The laws of Manu.* Vol. 25 of *The sacred books of the East.* Ed. F. Max Müller. Oxford: Clarendon Press.

Burbano, Carmen, Carmen Cuadrado, Mercedes Muzquiz, and Jose Ignacio Cubero. 1995. "Variation of favism-inducing factors (vicine, convicine and L-DOPA) during pod development in *Vicia faba* L." *Plant Foods for Human Nutrition* 47: 265–74.

Burkert, Walter. 1972. *Lore and science in ancient Pythagoreanism.* Trans. Edwin L. Minar, Jr. Cambridge, Mass.: Harvard University Press.

Burkert, Walter. 1982. "Craft versus sect: The problem of Orphics and Pythagoreans." Pp. 1–22, 183–89 in Vol. 3 of *Jewish and Christian self-definition.* Ed. Ben F. Meyer and E. P. Sanders. London: SCM Press.

Burkert, Walter. 1983. *Homo necans: The anthropology of ancient Greek sacrificial ritual and myth.* Trans. Peter Bing. Berkeley, Los Angeles, London: University of California Press.

Burkert, Walter. 1985. *Greek religion, archaic and classical.* Trans. John Raffan. Cambridge, Mass.: Harvard University Press.

Burkert, Walter. 1992. *The orientalizing revolution: Near Eastern influence on Greek culture in the early Archaic Age.* Trans. Margaret E. Pinder and Walter Burkert. Cambridge, Mass.: Harvard University Press.

Burkhardt, V. R. 1953–58. *Chinese creeds and customs.* 3 vols. Hong Kong: The South China Morning Post, Ltd.

Burkill, I. H. 1966. *A dictionary of the economic products of the Malay Peninsula.* 2 vols. Kuala Lumpur: Ministry of Agriculture and Co-operatives.

Burnet, John. 1930. *Early Greek philosophy.* 4th ed. London: Adam and Charles Black.

Burridge, Kenelm. 1969. *Tangu traditions.* Oxford: Clarendon Press.

Burrow, T. 1948. "Dravidian studies VII: Further Dravidian words in Sanskrit." *Bulletin of the School of Oriental and African Research* 12: 371–93.

Burton, Richard F. n. d. *Supplemental nights to the book of "The Thousand Nights and a Night."* 7 vols. London: Burton Club.

Bussagli, Mario. 1987. "Colors." Pp. 562–65 of Vol. 3 *The encyclopedia of religion.* 16 vols. Ed. Mircea Eliade. New York: Macmillan; London: Collier Macmillan.

Cain, John. 1875. "Native customs in the Godâvarî District." *Indian Antiquary* 4: 197–98.

Calabrò, Viola, Agostino Cascone, Patrizia Malaspina, and Giorgio Battistuzzi. 1989. "Glucose-6-phosphate dehydrogenase (G6PD) deficiency in southern Italy: A case of G6PD A(−) associated with favism." *Haematologica* 74: 71–73.

Caland, W. (trans.). 1953. *Śāṅkhāyana-Śrautasūtra.* Sarasvati-Vihara Series, 32. Nagpur: International Academy of Indian Culture.

Callimachus. 1975. "Fragments of uncertain location." Pp. 252–87 in *Callimachus: Aetia—Iambi—Lyric poems—Hecale—Minor Epic and Elegiac Poems—and Other Fragments. Musaeus: Hero and Leander.* Trans. C. A. Trypanis, T. Gelzer, and C. Whitman. Loeb Classical Library. Cambridge, Mass.: Harvard University Press; London: William Heinemann.

Calmet, Augustin. 1845–46. *Dictionnaire historique, archéologique, philologique, chronologique, géographique et littéral de la Bible.* 4 vols. 4th ed. Encyclopédie théologique, 1–4. Paris: [Migne].

Campbell, J. M. 1894–1901. "Notes on the spirit basis of belief and custom." *Indian Antiquary* 23 (1894): 333–38, 374–84; 24 (1895): 17–22, 29–32, 57–65, 121–32, 153–69, 215–31, 259–67, 292–98, 316–31, 347–56; 25 (1896): 35–48, 72–84, 125–40, 242–57; 26 (1897): 7–14, 91–104, 126–33, 245–52, 277–79, 293–304; 27 (1898): 22–26, 104–12, 137–40, 153–65, 221–23, 237–44, 270–75; 29 (1900): 45–56, 224–28, 260–61, 327–29, 382–87; 30 (1901): 97–105, 187–200, 308–10.

Carlson, Alvar W. 1986. "Ginseng: America's botanical drug connection to the Orient." *Economic Botany* 40: 233–49.

Carstairs, G. Morris. 1957. *The twice-born: A study of a community of high-caste Hindus.* London: Hogarth Press.

Carter, Stephen L. 1993. *The culture of disbelief.* New York: Basic Books.

Casal, U. A. 1967. *The five sacred festivals of ancient Japan: Their symbolism and historical development.* Tokyo and Rutland, Vt.: Charles E. Tuttle Company.

Caul, Goverdhan. 1806. "On the literature of the Hindus, from the Sanscrit." *Asiatick Researches* 1: 340–55.

Cavalli-Sforza, L. L., and W. F. Bodmer. 1971. *The genetics of human populations.* San Francisco: W. H. Freeman Company.

Cavalli-Sforza, L. Luca, Paolo Menozzi, and Alberto Piazza. 1994. *The history and geography of human genes.* Princeton: Princeton University Press.

Celli, Angelo. 1933. *The history of malaria in the Roman Campagna from ancient times.* Ed. and enl. by Anna Celli-Fraentzel. London: John Bale, Sons & Danielsson.

Celsus, Aulus. 1935–38. *Of medicine.* 3 vols. Trans. W. G. Spencer. Loeb Classical Library. London: William Heinemann; Cambridge, Mass.: Harvard University Press.

Chakraborty, P. K., S. Maiti, and B. N. Chatterjee. 1984. "Growth analysis and agronomic appraisal of sesamum." *Indian Journal of Agricultural Science* 54: 291–95.

Chakravarti, A. K. 1974. "Regional preference for food: Some aspects of food habit patterns in India." *Canadian Geographer* 18: 395–410.

Chakravarty, Taponath. 1959. *Food and drink in ancient Bengal.* Calcutta: Firma K. L. Mukhopadhyay.

Chalif, Louis H. 1921. *Russian festivals and costumes for pageant and dance.* New York: Chalif Russian School of Dancing.

Chamberlain, Basil Hall. 1891. *Things Japanese.* London: Kegan Paul, Trench, Trübner.

Chambers, R. (ed.). 1967. *The book of days.* 2 vols. Detroit: Gale Research.

Chandervaker, Pushker. 1965. "Tree-cult in Saurashtra." Pp. 41–46 in Sankar Sen Gupta (ed.), *Tree symbol worship in India.* Calcutta: Indian Publications.

Chandola, Sudha. 1976. "Tulsi plant in Indian folklore." *Folklore: India's Only English Monthly* (Calcutta) 17: 107–14.

Chardin, John. 1927. *Travels in Persia 1673–1677.* London: Argonaut Press.

Chaturvedi, Mahendra, and B. N. Tiwari. 1970. *A practical Hindi-English dictionary.* Delhi: National Publishing House.

Chaubé, Pandit Rám Gharíb. 1893–94. [Comments on rosaries]. *North Indian Notes and Queries* 3: 27–28.

Chaubé, Pándit Rám Gharíb. 1895–96a. "Marriage to a tree, or to an inanimate object." *North Indian Notes and Queries* 5: 45.

Chaubé, Pándit Rám Gharíb. 1895–96b. "Three sacred trees." *North Indian Notes and Queries* 5: 147.

Chéruel, A. 1899. *Dictionnaire historique des institutions, moeurs et coutumes de la France.* 7th ed. 2 vols. Paris: Librairie Hachette.

Chester, Paul. 1960. Letter to the editor. *Folk-Lore* (London) 71: 205–6.

Choksy, Jamsheed Kairshasp. 1986. "Purity and pollution in Zoroastrianism." *Mankind Quarterly* 27: 167–91.

Chopra, R. N., and Gurbakhsh Singh Chopra. 1933. "Some country beers of India." *Indian Medical Gazette* 68: 665–75.

Chopra, Ram Nath, I. C. Chopra, and B. S. Varna. 1969. *Supplement to Glossary of Indian medicinal plants.* New Delhi: Publications and Information Directorate.

Chopra, R. N., I. C. Chopra, K. L. Handa, and L. D. Kapur. 1958. *Chopra's indigenous drugs of India.* 2d ed. Calcutta, New Delhi: Academic Publishers.

Choremis, C., L. Zannos-Mariolea, and M. D. C. Kattamis. 1962. "Frequency of glucose-6-phosphate-dehydrogenase deficiency in certain highly malarious areas of Greece." *Lancet* 1: 17–18.

Chowbe, Pandit Ram Gharib. 1899. "On Hindu beliefs about trees." *Journal of the Anthropological Society of Bombay* 5: 224–30.

Church, A. H. 1886. *Food-grains of India*. London: Chapman and Hall.

Cicero. 1938. *On divination*. Pp. 213–539 in William Armistead Falconer (trans.), *Cicero: De senectute, De amicitia, De divinatione*. Loeb Classical Library. Cambridge, Mass.: Harvard University Press; London: William Heinemann.

Cicero. 1958. *On Vatinius:* "A cross-examination by Marcus Tullius Cicero of the witness Publius Vatinius." Pp. 240–97 in Vol 1 of *Cicero: The speeches*. Trans. R. Gardner. Loeb Classical Library. Cambridge, Mass.: Harvard University Press; London: William Heinemann.

Clark, I. A., W. B. Cowden, N. H. Hunt, L. E. Maxwell, and E. J. Mackie. 1984. "Activity of divicine in Plasmodium vinckei-infected mice has implications for treatment of favism and epidemiology of G-6-PD deficiency." *British Journal of Haematology* 57: 479–87.

Clark, Raymond J. 1968. "A note on Medea's plant and the mandrake." *Folk-Lore* (London) 79: 227–31.

Clement of Alexandria. 1949. *Protreptikos* (Exhortation). Trans. as *Le Protreptique* by Claude Mondésert. 2d ed. Paris: Éditions du Cerf.

Clement of Alexandria. 1991. *Miscellanies*. Trans. as *Clement of Alexandria: Stromateis books one to three* by John Ferguson. Fathers of the Church. A New Translation, 85. Washington, D.C.: Catholic University of America Press.

Clodd, Edward. 1898. *Tom Tit Tot: An essay on savage philosophy in folk-tale*. London: Duckworth.

Clothey, Fred W. 1978. *The many faces of Murukan: The history and meaning of a South Indian god*. The Hague, Paris, New York: Mouton.

Coats, Alice M. 1971. *Flowers and their histories*. New York, St. Louis, San Francisco: McGraw-Hill.

Cocchiara, Giuseppe. 1938. *La vita et l'arte del popolo siciliano nel Museo Pitrè*. Palermo: F. Ciuni.

Cockayne, Thomas Oswald. 1864–66. *Leechdoms, wortcunning, and starcraft of early England*. 3 vols. Chronicles and Memorials of Great Britain and Ireland during the Middle Ages, No. 35. London: Longman, Green, Longman, Roberts, and Green.

Coles, William. 1938. *The art of simpling: An introduction to the knowledge and gathering of plants*. [Milford, Conn.: Herb Lovers Book Club].

Colley March, H. 1901. "Customs relating to iron." *Folk-Lore* (London) 12: 340–41.

Collier, H. B. 1976. "The estimation of vicine in fababeans by an ultraviolet spectrophotometric method." *Journal, Canadian Institute of Food Science and Technology* 9: 155–59.

Collins, Billie Jean. 1990. "The puppy in Hittite ritual." *Journal of Cuneiform Studies* 42: 211–26.

Collyer, C. T. 1903. "The culture and preparation of ginseng in Korea." *Transactions of the Korea Branch, Royal Asiatic Society* 3: 18–30.

Colonna-Romano, S., A. Iolascon, S. Lippo, L. Pinto, S. Cutillo, and G. Battistuzzi. 1985. "Genetic heterogeneity at the glucose-6-phosphate dehydrogenase locus in southern Italy: A study on the population of Naples." *Human Genetics* 69: 228–32.

Colthurst, Ida. 1924. *Familiar flowering trees in India.* Calcutta and Simla: Thacker, Spink.

Columella. 1941–55. *On agriculture.* 3 vols. Trans. H. B. Ash, E. S. Forster, and E. H. Heffner. Loeb Classical Library. London: William Heinemann; Cambridge, Mass.: Harvard University Press.

Conder, C. R. 1883. *Heth and Moab: Explorations in Syria in 1881 and 1882.* London: R. Bentley and Son.

Condit, Ira J. 1969. *Ficus: The exotic species.* Berkeley: Division of Agricultural Sciences, University of California.

Conybeare, Frederick Cornwallis. 1910–11. "Feast of Epiphany." Pp. 695–98 in Vol. 9 of *The Encyclopaedia Britannica.* 11th ed. 29 vols. New York: Encyclopaedia Britannica.

Cook, Arthur Bernard. 1895. "The bee in Greek mythology." *Journal of Hellenic Studies* 15: 1–24.

Cook, Arthur Bernard. 1904–7. "The European sky-god." *Folk-Lore* (London) 15 (1904): 264–315, 369–426; 16 (1905): 260–332; 17 (1906): 27–71, 141–73, 308–48, 427–53; 18 (1907): 24–53.

Cook, Arthur Bernard. 1964–65. *Zeus, a study in ancient religion.* 2 vols. New York: Biblo and Tannen.

Cook, Stanley Arthur. 1910–11. "Tree-worship." Pp. 235–38 in Vol. 27 of *The Encyclopaedia Britannica.* 11th ed. 29 vols. New York: Encyclopaedia Britannica.

Cooke, Theodore. 1903. *The flora of the presidency of Bombay.* 3 vols. Calcutta: Botanical Survey of India.

Coomaraswamy, Ananda K. 1993. *Yakṣas: Essays in the water cosmology.* Ed. Paul Schroeder. New ed., rev. and enl. New Delhi: Indira Gandhi National Centre for the Arts; Oxford, New York, Delhi: Oxford University Press.

Corbin, Henry. 1960. *Avicenna and the visionary recital.* Trans. Willard R. Trask. Bollingen Series, 66. New York: Pantheon Books.

Corbo, R. M., G. F. Spennati, R. Scacchi, R. Palmarino, M. R. Della Penna, and P. Lucarelli. 1981. "A survey of serum protein and enzyme polymorphisms in the district of L'Aquila (Italy)." *Human Heredity* 31: 167–71.

Corchia, Carlo, Antonio Balata, Gian Franco Meloni, and Tullio Meloni. 1995. "Favism in a female newborn infant whose mother ingested fava beans before delivery." *Journal of Pediatrics* 127: 807–8.

Cormack, Mrs. J. G. [Annie]. 1935. *Everyday customs in China.* Edinburgh and London: Moray Press.

Corner, E. J. H. 1952. *Wayside trees of Malaya.* 2d ed. 2 vols. [Singapore: Government Printing Office].

Costantini, Lorenzo. 1981. "Palaeoethnobotany at Pirak: A contribution to the 2nd millennium B.C. agriculture of the Sibi-Kacchi Plain, Pakistan." Pp. 271–77 in Herbert Härtel (ed.), *South Asian archaeology 1979.* Papers from the Fifth International Conference of the Association of South Asian Archaeologists in Western Europe, held in the Museum für Indische Kunst der Staatlichen Museen Preussischer Kulturbesitz Berlin. Berlin: Dietrich Reimer.

Cotes, Rosemary A. 1904. *Bible flowers.* London: Methuen.

Cowell, E. B. (trans.). 1894. "The Buddha-Carita of Aśvaghosha." Pp. 1–207 in *Buddhist Mahāyāna texts,* Vol. 49 of *The sacred books of the East.* Ed. F. Max Müller. Oxford: Clarendon Press.

Cowell, E. B. (ed.). 1969. *The Jātaka, or stories of the Buddha's former births.* 6 vols. London: Luzac.

Crawfurd, John. 1820. *History of the Indian archipelago.* 3 vols. Edinburgh: Archibald Constable; London: Hurst, Robinson.

Crevost, Ch., and Ch. Lemarié. 1917. *Catalogue des produits de l'Indochine.* Tome 1: *Produits alimentaires.* Hanoi: Gouvernement Général de l'Indochine.

Crooke, William. 1881. "Exorcism of local village ghosts." *Indian Antiquary* 10: 288.

Crooke, William. 1885. "Egg-plant—potatoes—onions—unlucky." *Panjab Notes and Queries* 3, 27 (December): 41.

Crooke, William. 1896a. *The popular religion and folk-lore of northern India.* 2 vols. London: Archibald Constable.

Crooke, William. 1896b. *The tribes and castes of the North-Western Provinces and Oudh.* 4 vols. Calcutta: Office of the Superintendent of Government Printing, India.

Crooke, William. 1906. *Things Indian.* London: John Murray.

Crooke, William. 1908–26a. "Bengal." Pp. 479–501 in Vol. 2 of *Encyclopaedia of religion and ethics.* 13 vols. Ed. James Hastings. Edinburgh: T. and T. Clark.

Crooke, William. 1908–26b. "Charms and amulets (Indian)." Pp. 441–48 in Vol. 3 of *Encyclopaedia of religion and ethics.* 13 vols. Ed. James Hastings. Edinburgh: T. and T. Clark.

Crooke, William. 1908–26c. "Dravidians (North India)." Pp. 1–21 in Vol. 5 of *Encyclopaedia of religion and ethics.* 13 vols. Ed. James Hastings. Edinburgh: T. and T. Clark.

Crooke, William. 1908–26d. "Serpent-worship (Indian)." Pp. 411–19 in Vol. 11 of

Encyclopaedia of religion and ethics. 13 vols. Ed. James Hastings. Edinburgh: T. and T. Clark.

Crooke, William. 1908–26e. "Chidambaram." P. 516 in Vol. 3 of *Encyclopaedia of religion and ethics.* 13 vols. Ed. James Hastings. Edinburgh: T. and T. Clark.

Crooke, William. 1926. *Religion and folklore in northern India.* London: Oxford University Press.

Crosby, William H. 1956. "Favism in Sardinia." *Blood* 11: 91–92.

Cruden, Alexander. 1953. *Cruden's unabridged concordance to the Old and New Testaments and the Apocrypha.* Old Tappan, N.J.: Fleming H. Revell.

Cubero, José I. 1974. "On the evolution of *Vicia faba* L." *Theoretical and Applied Genetics* 45: 47–51.

Culpepper, Nich. 1778. *The English physician enlarged.* London: Lackington and Denis; Edinburgh: Patrick Anderson.

Cumont, Franz. 1923. *After life in Roman paganism.* New Haven: Yale University Press; London: Oxford University Press.

Cunningham, Alexander. 1962. *The stūpa of Bharhut.* Varanasi: Indological Book House.

Cunningham, Alexander. 1966. *The Bhilsa topes; or Buddhist monuments of Central India.* Varanasi: Indological Book House.

Curley, Michael J. (trans.). 1979. *Physiologus.* Austin and London: University of Texas Press.

Cutter, Robert Joe. 1989. "Brocade and blood: The cockfight in Chinese and English poetry." *Journal of the American Oriental Society* 109: 1–16.

Daiches, Samuel, and Israel W. Slotki (trans.). 1936. *Kethuboth.* 2 vols. Vols. 3 and 4 in pt. 3 (Seder Nashim) of *The Babylonian Talmud.* Ed. Isidore Epstein. London: Soncino Press.

Dales, George F. 1984. "Sex and stone at Mohenjo-daro." Pp. 109–16 in B. B. Lal, S. P. Gupta, and Shashi Asthana (eds.), *Frontiers of the Indus civilization.* New Delhi: Indian Archaeological Society, and Indian History and Culture Society.

Dalziel, J. M. 1937. *The useful plants of west tropical Africa.* London: Crown Agents for Oversea Governments and Administrations.

Dames, M. Longworth, and E. Seemann. 1903. "Folklore of the Azores." *Folk-Lore* (London) 14: 125–46.

Dandekar, R. N. 1953. "The role of man in Hinduism." Pp. 117–53 in Kenneth W. Morgan (ed.), *The religion of the Hindus.* New York: Ronald Press.

D'Andrea, Jeanne. 1982. *Ancient herbs in the J. Paul Getty Museum gardens.* Malibu, Calif.: The Museum.

Daniels, Cora Linn, and C. M. Stevans (eds.). 1971. *Encyclopaedia of superstitions, folklore, and the occult sciences of the world.* 3 vols. Detroit: Gale Research Company.

D'Aquino, M., G. Zaza, E. Carnovale, S. Gaetani, and M. A. Spadoni. 1981.

"Haemolytic toxic factors in fava beans (*Vicia faba*): Biological and chemical assays." *Nutrition Reports International* 24: 1297–1305.

Darby, William J., Paul Ghalioungui, and Louis Grivetti. 1977. *Food: The gift of Osiris*. 2 vols. London, New York, San Francisco: Academic Press.

Darmesteter, James, and L. H. Mills (trans.). 1880–87. *The Zend-Avesta*. 3 vols. Vols. 4, 23, and 31 of *The sacred books of the East*. Ed. F. Max Müller. Oxford: Clarendon Press.

Darrah, Helen H. 1972. "The basils in folklore and biological science." *The Herbarist* 38: 3–10.

Darrah, Helen H. 1974. "Investigation of the cultivators of the basils (*Ocimum*)." *Economic Botany* 28: 63–67.

Das, Kunjabihari. 1965. "The plant in Orissan folklore." Pp. 25–34 in Sankar Sen Gupta (ed.), *Tree symbol worship in India*. Calcutta: Indian Publications.

Dausch, J. G., and D. W. Nixon. 1990. "Garlic: A review of its relationship to malignant disease." *Preventive Medicine* 19: 346–61.

David, Stephen. 1996. "Root of a tale: The world's largest banyan tree is a part of local lore—and an object of devotion." *India Today* (September 30): 18.

Davids, Thomas W. Rhys (trans.). 1890–94. *The questions of King Milinda*. 2 vols. Vols. 35 and 36 of *The sacred books of the East*. Ed. F. Max Müller. Oxford: Clarendon Press.

Davids, Thomas W. Rhys. 1903. *Buddhist India*. New York: G. P. Putnam's Sons.

Davids, Thomas W. Rhys. 1908–26a. "Anurādhapura." Pp. 599–601 in Vol. 1 of *Encyclopaedia of religion and ethics*. 13 vols. Ed. James Hastings. Edinburgh: T. and T. Clark.

Davids, Thomas W. Rhys. 1908–26b. "Wisdom tree." Pp. 747–49 in Vol. 12 of *Encyclopaedia of religion and ethics*. 13 vols. Ed. James Hastings. Edinburgh: T. and T. Clark.

Davids, Thomas W. Rhys, and Hermann Oldenberg (trans.). 1881–85. *Vinaya texts*. 3 vols. Vols. 13, 17, and 20 of *The sacred books of the East*. Ed. F. Max Müller. Oxford: Clarendon Press.

Davies, Oliver. 1968. "The origins of agriculture in West Africa." *Current Anthropology* 9: 479–82, 494–509.

Dawson, Warren R. 1929. *Magician and leech: A study in the beginnings of medicine with special reference to ancient Egypt*. London: Methuen.

Day, Lal Behari. 1969. *Bengal peasant life. Folk-tales of Bengal. Recollections of my school-days*. Calcutta: Editions Indian.

de Candolle, Alphonse. 1919. *Origin of cultivated plants*. New York and London: D. Appleton.

De Flora, A., U. Benatti, L. Guida, and E. Zocchi. 1986. "Divicine and G6PD-deficient erythrocytes: An integrated model of cytotoxicity in favism." Pp. 77–93 in Akira Yoshida and Ernest Beutler (eds.), *Glucose-6-phosphate dehydrogenase*. London: Academic Press.

de Groot, Jan Jakob Maria. 1886. *Les Fêtes annuellement célébrées à Émoui (Amoy): Étude concernant la religion populaire des Chinois.* 2 vols. in 1. Trans. Félix Régamey. Annales du Musée Guimet, 11–12. Paris: E. Leroux.

de Groot, Jan Jakob Maria. 1896. *Le Code du Mahâyâna en Chine.* Verhandelingen der Koninklijke Akademie van Wetenschappen (Amsterdam), Afdeeling Letterkunde, n. s. 1, No. 2. Amsterdam: Johannes Müller.

de Groot, Jan Jakob Maria. 1964. *The religious system of China.* 6 vols. Taipei: Literature House. First published: Leyden: E. J. Brill, 1892–1910.

Delatte, A. 1930. "Faba Pythagorae cognata." Pp. 33–57 in *Serta Leodiensia: Mélanges de philologie classique publiés à l'occasion du centenaire de l'indépendance de la Belgique.* Bibliothèque de la Faculté de Philosophie et Lettres de l'Université de Liége, 44. Liége: H. Vaillant-Carmanne; Paris: Édouard Champion.

Delatte, A. 1936. *Herbarius: Recherches sur le cérémonial usité chez les Anciens pour la cueillette des simples et des plantes magiques.* Paris: Société d'Édition 'Les Belles Lettres.'

Delatte, A. 1938. *Herbarius: Recherches sur le cérémonial usité chez les Anciens pour la cueillette des simples et des plantes magiques.* 2d ed. Bibliothèque de la Faculté de Philosophie et Lettres de l'Université de Liége, 81. Liége: Faculté de Philosophie et Lettres; Paris: Librairie E. Droz.

Demosthenes. 1954. *Fourth philippic.* Pp. 270–313 in *Demosthenes I: Olynthiacs, Philippics, Minor public speeches, Speech against Leptines.* Trans. J. H. Vince. Loeb Classical Library. Cambridge, Mass.: Harvard University Press; London: William Heinemann.

de Nebesky-Wojkowitz, R. M. 1956. *Oracles and demons of Tibet: The cult and iconography of the Tibetan protective deities.* London: Oxford University Press; The Hague: Mouton.

Depestre, René. 1996. "The roots of the banyan tree." *Unesco Courier* 49, 10 (October): 22–23.

Desai, B. L. 1965. "Tree worship in Gujerat." Pp. 54–57 in Sankar Sen Gupta (ed.), *Tree symbol worship in India.* Calcutta: Indian Publications.

Detienne, Marcel. 1970. "La Cuisine de Pythagore." *Archives de Sociologie des Religions* 29: 141–62.

Detienne, Marcel. 1975. "Les Chemins de la déviance: Orphisme, Dionysisme et Pythagorisme." Pp. 49–79 in *Orfismo in Magna Grecia, Atti del Quattordicesimo Convegno di Studi sulla Magna Grecia, Taranto, 6–10 Ottobre 1974.* Naples: Arte Tipografica Napoli.

Detienne, Marcel. 1977. *The gardens of Adonis: Spices in Greek mythology.* Trans. Janet Lloyd. Hassocks, Sussex: Harvester Press.

Detienne, Marcel. 1979. *Dionysos slain.* Trans. Mireille Muellner and Leonard Muellner. Baltimore and London: Johns Hopkins University Press.

Detienne, Marcel. 1989. "Culinary practices and the spirit of sacrifice." Pp. 1–20 in Marcel Detienne and Jean-Pierre Vernant (eds.), *The cuisine of sacrifice among the Greeks.* Trans. Paula Wissing. Chicago and London: University of Chicago Press.

Deubner, Ludwig. 1959. *Attische Feste.* Hildesheim: Georg Olms.

de Vigo, Joannes. 1968. *The most excellent workes of chirurgerye, 1543.* The English Experience, 67. New York: Da Capo Press; Amsterdam: Theatrum Orbis Terrarum.

de Vogel, C. J. 1966. *Pythagoras and early Pythagoreanism.* Assen: Van Gorcum.

Dhalla, Maneckji Nusservanji. 1922. *Zoroastrian civilization.* New York: Oxford University Press.

Diehl, Carl Gustav. 1956. *Instrument and purpose: Studies on rites and rituals in South India.* Lund: C W K Gleerup.

di Nino, Antonio. 1879–91. *Usi Abruzzesi.* 5 vols. Florence: G. Barbèra.

Diodorus Siculus. 1933–68. *The library of history.* 12 vols. Trans. C. H. Oldfather, C. L. Sherman, C. B. Welles, R. M. Geer, and F. Walton. Loeb Classical Library. London: William Heinemann; Cambridge, Mass.: Harvard University Press.

Diogenes Laertius. 1925. *Lives of eminent philosophers.* 2 vols. Trans. R. D. Hicks. Loeb Classical Library. London: William Heinemann; New York: G. P. Putnam's Sons.

Dionysius of Halicarnassus. 1937–50. *The Roman antiquities.* Trans. as *The Roman antiquities of Dionysius of Halicarnassus* by Earnest Cary. 7 vols. Loeb Classical Library. London: William Heinemann; Cambridge, Mass.: Harvard University Press.

Dioscorides. 1959. *De materia medica.* Trans. as *The Greek herbal of Dioscorides* by Robert T. Gunther. New York: Hafner.

Dodds, Eric R. 1963. *The Greeks and the irrational.* Berkeley and Los Angeles: University of California Press.

Dölger, F. J. 1971. *Die Sonne der Gerechtigkeit und der Schwarze: Eine religionsgeschichtliche Studie zum Taufgelöbnis.* Liturgiewissenschaftliche Quellen und Forschungen, 14. Münster Westfalen: Aschendorffsche Verlagsbuchhandlung.

Don, George. 1831–38. *A general history of the dichlamydeous plants.* 4 vols. London: J. G. and F. Rivington.

Donath, R., and M. Kujawa. 1991. "Untersuchungen zum Abbau von Vicin und Convicin in Ackerbohnen Mehl durch ausgewählte Bakterienstämme." *Die Nahrung* 35: 449–53.

Donkin, R. A. 1980. *Manna: An historical geography.* Biogeographica, 17. The Hague and Boston: W. Junk.

Donoso, G., H. Hedayat, and H. Khayatian. 1969. "Favism, with special reference to Iran." *Bulletin of the World Health Organization* 40: 513–19.

Doolittle, Justus. 1865. *Social life of the Chinese.* 2 vols. New York: Harper.

Dorant, E., P. A. van den Brandt, R. A. Goldbohm, and F. Sturmans. 1996. "Consumption of onions and a reduced risk of stomach carcinoma." *Gastroenterology* 110: 12–20.

Dorson, Richard M. (ed.). 1968. *Peasant customs and savage myths: Selections from the British folklorists.* 2 vols. Chicago: University of Chicago Press.

Douglas, Mary. 1966. *Purity and danger: An analysis of concepts of pollution and taboo.* New York and Washington, D.C.: Frederick A. Praeger.

Douglas, Mary. 1972. "Deciphering a meal." *Daedalus. Journal of the American Academy of Arts and Sciences* 101: 61–81.

Douglas, Mary. 1973. *Natural symbols: Explorations in cosmology.* 2d ed. London: Barrie and Jenkins.

Douglas, Mary. 1975. *Implicit meanings: Essays in anthropology.* London and Boston: Routledge and Kegan Paul.

Drayton, Michael. 1961. *The works of Michael Drayton.* 5 vols. Ed. J. William Hebel. Oxford: Basil Blackwell.

Drower, Ethel S. 1937. *The Mandaeans of Iraq and Iran: Their cults, customs, magic, legends, and folklore.* Oxford: Clarendon Press.

Drower, Ethel S. 1956. *Water into wine: A study of ritual idiom in the Middle East.* London: John Murray.

Drury, Heber. 1873. *The useful plants of India.* 2d ed. London: William H. Allen and Company.

Dubois, Jean-Antoine. 1818. *Description of the character, manners, and customs of the people of India; and of their institutions, religious and civil.* 2 vols. Trans. from the french manuscript. Philadelphia: M. Carey and Son.

Dubois, Jean-Antoine. 1906. *Hindu manners, customs, and ceremonies.* Trans. Henry K. Beauchamp. 3d ed. Oxford: Clarendon Press.

Du Cange, Charles de Fresne. 1954. *Glossarium mediae et infimae latinitatis.* 10 vols. Graz: Akademische Druck- u. Verlagsanstalt.

Duke, James A. 1989. *Ginseng: A concise handbook.* Algonac, Mich.: Reference Publications.

Dumont, Darl J. 1992. "The ash tree in Indo-European culture." *Mankind Quarterly* 32: 323–36.

Dumont, Louis, and David Pocock. 1959. "Pure and impure." *Contributions to Indian Sociology* 3: 9–39.

Dunn, Frederick L. 1965. "On the antiquity of malaria in the Western Hemisphere." *Human Biology* 37: 385–93.

Dunn, Frederick L. 1993. "Malaria." Pp. 855–62 in Kenneth F. Kiple (ed.), *The Cambridge world history of human disease.* Cambridge: Cambridge University Press.

Durand, Jean-Louis. 1989. "Ritual as instrumentality." Pp. 119–28 in Marcel Detienne and Jean-Pierre Vernant (eds.), *The cuisine of sacrifice among the Greeks.* Trans. Paula Wissing. Chicago and London: University of Chicago Press.

Dutt, Uday Chand. 1922. *The materia medica of the Hindus.* With a glossary of Indian plants by George King. Rev. ed. Calcutta: Adi-Ayurveda Machine Press.

Dwivedi, M. P., and B. G. Prasad. 1964. "An epidemiological study of lathyrism in the district of Rewa, Madhya Pradesh." *Indian Journal of Medical Research* 52: 81–116.

Dymock, W. 1891. "On the use of turmeric in Hindoo ceremonial." *Journal of the Anthropological Society of Bombay* 2: 441–48.

Dymock, William C., J. H. Warden, and David Hooper. 1889–93. *Pharmacographia Indica: A history of the principal drugs of vegetable origin met with in British India.* 6 vols. London: Trübner; Byculla, Bombay: Education Society's Press.

Dymock, William C., J. H. Warden, and David Hooper. 1890–93. *Pharmacographia Indica: A history of the principal drugs of vegetable origin, met with in British India.* 3 vols. London: Kegan Paul, Trench, Trübner & Co.

An early English version of Hortus Sanitatis. 1954. London: Bernard Quaritch.

Eberhard, Wolfram. 1968. *The local cultures of South and East China.* Trans. from the German by Alide Eberhard. Leiden: E. J. Brill.

Eck, Diana L. 1982. "Gaṅgā. The goddess in Hindu sacred geography." Pp. 166–83 in John Stratton Hawley and Donna Marie Wulff (eds.), *The divine consort: Rādhā and the goddesses of India.* Religious Studies Series. Berkeley, Calif.: Graduate Theological Union.

Edmonds, John Maxwell. 1957–61. *The fragments of attic comedy after Meineke, Bergk, and Kock.* 3 vols. Leiden: E. J. Brill.

Eggeling, Julius (trans.). 1882–1900. *The Satapatha-Brâhmana according to the text of the Mâdhyandina school.* 5 vols. Vols. 12, 26, 41, 43, and 44 of *The sacred books of the East.* Ed. F. Max Müller. Oxford: Clarendon Press.

Eichinger Ferro-Luzzi, Gabriella. 1973a. "Food avoidances at puberty and menstruation in Tamilnad." *Ecology of Food and Nutrition* 2: 165–72.

Eichinger Ferro-Luzzi, Gabriella. 1973b. "Food avoidances of pregnant women in Tamilnad." *Ecology of Food and Nutrition* 2: 259–66.

Eichinger Ferro-Luzzi, Gabriella. 1974. "Food avoidances during the puerperium and lactation in Tamilnad." *Ecology of Food and Nutrition* 3: 7–15.

Eichinger Ferro-Luzzi, Gabriella. 1975. "Temporary female food avoidances in Tamilnad: Interpretations and parallels." *East and West,* n. s. 25: 471–85.

Eichinger Ferro-Luzzi, Gabriella. 1977a. "Ritual as language: The case of South Indian food offerings." *Current Anthropology* 18: 507–14.

Eichinger Ferro-Luzzi, Gabriella. 1977b. "The foods disliked by the gods in South India." *Annali dell'Istituto Orientale di Napoli* 37: 357–73.

Eichinger Ferro-Luzzi, Gabriella. 1977c. "The logic of South Indian food offerings." *Anthropos* 72: 529–56.

Eichinger Ferro-Luzzi, Gabriella. 1978a. "Food for the gods in South India." *Zeitschrift für Ethnologie* 103: 86–108.

Eichinger Ferro-Luzzi, Gabriella. 1978b. "More on salt taboos." *Current Anthropology* 19: 412–15. (Comments on an article by Thomas W. Neumann, with his response).

Eichinger Ferro-Luzzi, Gabriella. 1981. "The food of the gods versus human food in South India." *L'Uomo* 5: 239–65.

Eichinger Ferro-Luzzi, Gabriella. 1985a. "Divieti alimentari e sacralità del bovino in India." *L'Uomo* 9: 161–70.

Eichinger Ferro-Luzzi, Gabriella. 1985b. "The cultural uses of food in modern Tamil literature." *Annali dell'Istituto Universitario Orientale* 45: 483–502.

Eichinger Ferro-Luzzi, Gabriella. 1987. *The self-milking cow and the bleeding liṅgam: Criss-cross of motifs in Indian temple legends.* Wiesbaden: Otto Harrassowitz.

Eichinger Ferro-Luzzi, Gabriella. 1990. "Food is good to laugh: A Tamil comic view of food." *Food and Foodways* 4: 39–52.

Eliade, Mircea. 1958. *Patterns in comparative religion.* Trans. Rosemary Sheed. New York: Sheed and Ward.

Eliade, Mircea. 1972. *Zalmoxis: The vanishing god.* Trans. Willard R. Trask. Chicago and London: University of Chicago Press.

Eliade, Mircea. 1973. "Notes on the Căluşari." *The Gaster Festschrift. The Journal of the Ancient Near Eastern Society of Columbia University* 5: 115–22.

Eliade, Mircea. 1976. *Occultism, witchcraft, and cultural fashions: Essays in comparative religions.* Chicago and London: University of Chicago Press.

Ellison, Rosemary. 1983. "Some thoughts on the diet of Mesopotamia from c. 3000–600 B.C." *Iraq* 45: 146–50.

Elton, Charles. 1882. *Origins of English history.* London: Bernard Quaritch.

Elwin, Verrier. 1939. *The Baiga.* London: John Murray.

Elwin, Verrier. 1954. *Tribal myths of Orissa.* London: Oxford University Press.

Elwin, Verrier. 1955. *The religion of an Indian tribe.* London: Oxford University Press.

Emanuel, R., and A. Schoenfeld. 1961. "Favism in a nursing infant." *Journal of Pediatrics* 58: 263–66.

Emeneau, M. B. 1949. "The strangling figs in Sanskrit literature." *University of California Publications in Classical Philology* 13, 10: 345–70.

Empedocles. 1981. "Fragments." Pp. 155–298 in *Empedocles: The extant fragments.* Trans. and ed. M. R. Wright. New Haven and London: Yale University Press.

Enthoven, R. E. 1924. *The folklore of Bombay.* Oxford: Clarendon Press.

Erasmus. 1982–92. *Adages.* Trans. Margaret Mann Phillips and R. A. B. Mynors. Collected Works of Erasmus, 31–34. Toronto, Buffalo, and London: University of Toronto Press.

Ernst, E. 1987. "Cardiovascular effects of garlic (*Allium sativum*): A review." *Pharmatherapeutica* 5: 83–89.

Euripides. 1912. *Hippolytus.* Pp. 156–277 in Vol. 4 of *Euripedes.* Trans. Arthur S. Way. Loeb Classical Library. London: William Heinemann; New York: G. P. Putnam's Sons.

Evans, Alice M. 1976. "Beans: *Phaseolus* spp. (Leguminosae—Papilionatae)." Pp.

168–72 in N. W. Simmonds (ed.), *Evolution of crop plants*. London and New York: Longman.

Evans, Arthur J. 1901. "Mycenaean tree and pillar cult and its Mediterranean relations." *Journal of Hellenic Studies* 21: 99–204.

Fairservis, Walter A., Jr. 1983. "The script of the Indus Valley civilization." *Scientific American* 248, 3: 58–66.

Fairservis, Walter A., Jr. 1992. *The Harappan civilization and its writing: A model for the decipherment of the Indus script*. Leiden: E. J. Brill.

Faithfull, R. G. 1985. "Basic symbolism in Boccaccio." *Lingua e stile* 20: 247–55.

Fallon, April E., and Paul Rozin. 1983. "The psychological bases of food rejections by humans." *Ecology of Food and Nutrition* 13: 15–26.

Farbridge, Maurice H. 1908–26. "Symbolism (Semitic)." Pp. 146–51 in Vol. 12 of *Encyclopaedia of religion and ethics*. 13 vols. Ed. James Hastings. Edinburgh: T. and T. Clark.

Farbridge, Maurice H. 1970. *Studies in biblical and Semitic symbolism*. New York: Ktav Publishing House.

Farnell, Lewis Richard. 1896–1909. *The cults of the Greek states*. 5 vols. Oxford: Clarendon Press.

Farrell, Kenneth T. 1990. *Spices, condiments, and seasonings*. 2d ed. New York: Van Nostrand Reinhold.

Fawcett, F. 1901. *Anthropology: Nāyars of Malabar*. Madras Government Museum, Bulletin, Vol. 3, No. 3. Madras: Superintendent, Government Press.

Feinbrun-Dothan, Naomi. 1978. *Flora Palaestina*. Pt. 3, *Text: Ericaceae to Compositae*. Jerusalem: Israel Academy of Sciences and Humanities.

Feliks, Jehuda. 1971–72a. "Beans." Col. 355 in Vol. 4 of *Encyclopaedia Judaica*. 16 vols. Jerusalem: Keter; New York: Macmillan.

Feliks, Jehuda. 1971–72b. "Garlic." Cols. 328–29 in Vol. 7 of *Encyclopaedia Judaica*. 16 vols. Jerusalem: Keter; New York: Macmillan.

Feliks, Jehuda. 1971–72c. "Leek." Col. 1561 in Vol. 10 of *Encyclopaedia Judaica*. 16 vols. Jerusalem: Keter; New York: Macmillan.

Feliks, Jehuda. 1971–72d. "Pig." Col. 506 in Vol. 13 of *Encyclopaedia Judaica*. 16 vols. Jerusalem: Keter; New York: Macmillan.

Fenu, M. P., G. Finazzi, C. Manoussakis, V. Palomba, and G. Fiorelli. 1982. "Glucose-6-phosphate dehydrogenase deficiency: Genetic heterogeneity in Sardinia." *Annals of Human Genetics* 46: 105–14.

Fergusson, James. 1910. *History of Indian and Eastern architecture*. 2 vols. Rev. and ed. by James Burgess and R. Phené Spiers. London: John Murray.

Fergusson, James. 1971. *Tree and serpent worship: Or illustrations of mythology and art in India in the first and fourth centuries after Christ*. 1st Indian repr. Delhi: Oriental Publishers.

Fermi, Claudio, and P. Martinetti. 1905. "Studio sul favismo." *Annali d'Igiene Sperimentali* 15: 75–112.

Festus, Sextus Pompeius. 1913. *On the meaning of words.* Published as *Sexti Pompei Festi: De verborum significatu quae supersunt cum Pauli epitome.* Ed. Wallace M. Lindsay. Leipzig: B. G. Teubner.

Filliozat, J. 1964. *The classical doctrine of Indian medicine: Its origins and its Greek parallels.* Trans. Dev Raj Chanana. Delhi: Munshiram Manoharlal.

Flattery, David Stophlet, and Martin Schwartz. 1989. *Haoma and harmaline: The botanical identity of the Indo-Iranian sacred hallucinogen "soma" and its legacy in religion, language, and Middle Eastern folklore.* University of California Publications in Near Eastern Studies, 21. Berkeley, Los Angeles, London: University of California Press.

Fleisher, Alexander, and Zhenia Fleisher. 1994. "The fragrance of biblical mandrake." *Economic Botany* 48: 243–51.

Flückiger, Friedrich A., and Daniel Hanbury. 1879. *Pharmacographia: A history of the principal drugs of vegetable origin, met with in Great Britain and British India.* 2d ed. London: Macmillan and Company.

Folkard, Richard, Jr. 1884. *Plant lore, legends and lyrics.* London: Sampson Low, Marston, Searle, and Rivington.

"The folk-lore of Drayton." 1884–85. *Folk-lore Journal* 2 (1884): 111–20, 142–51, 225–35, 266–77, 357–69; 3 (1885): 79–90, 134–55.

Fontenrose, Joseph. 1978. *The Delphic oracle.* Berkeley, Los Angeles, London: University of California Press.

Fowler, W. Warde. 1899. *The Roman festivals of the period of the republic.* London and New York: Macmillan.

Francis, Peter, Jr. 1984. "Plants as human adornment in India." *Economic Botany* 38: 194–209.

Frazer, James George. 1890. "Some popular superstitions of the ancients." *Folk-Lore* (London) 1: 145–71.

Frazer, James George. 1918. *Folk-lore in the Old Testament.* 3 vols. London: Macmillan.

Frazer, James George. 1935. *The golden bough, a study in magic and religion.* 3d ed. 12 vols. New York: Macmillan.

Frazer, James George. 1968. *Totemism and exogamy.* 1st ed. 4 vols. London: Dawsons of Pall Mall.

Freedman, H. (trans.). 1936. *Nedarim.* Vol. 5 in pt. 3 (Seder Nashim) of *The Babylonian Talmud.* Ed. Isidore Epstein. London: Soncino Press.

Freese, John Henry. 1910–11. "Demeter." Pp. 980–82 in Vol. 7 of *The Encyclopaedia Britannica.* 11th ed. 29 vols. New York: Encyclopaedia Britannica.

Frese, Pamela R., and S. J. M. Gray. 1987. "Trees." Pp. 26–33 in Vol. 15 of *The encyclopedia of religion.* 16 vols. Ed. Mircea Eliade. New York: Macmillan; London: Collier Macmillan.

Friend, Hilderic. 1981. *Flower lore.* Rockport, Mass.: Para Research.

Frontinus. 1925. *The stratagems.* Trans. Charles E. Bennett. Pp. 2–327 in *Frontinus,*

The stratagems and The aqueducts of Rome. Ed. Mary B. McElwain. Loeb Classical Library. London: William Heinemann; Cambridge, Mass.: Harvard University Press.

Fryer, John. 1909–15. *A new account of East India and Persia.* 3 vols. Ed. W. Crooke. Hakluyt Society Works, 2d ser., 19, 20, and 39. London: Hakluyt Society.

Fuchs, Stephen. 1960. *The Gond and Bhumia of eastern Mandla.* London: Asia Publishing House.

Furtado, C. X. 1926–29. "Ocimum, Linn. in the Malay Peninsula." *Gardens' Bulletin Straits Settlements* 4: 416–19.

Galen. 1964–65. *Claudii Galeni opera omnia.* Ed. C. G. Kühn. 20 vols. in 22. Hildesheim: G. Olms.

Galiano, Silvana, Gian Franco Gaetani, Arrigo Barabino, Franco Cottafava, Helen Zeitlin, Margaret Town, and Lucio Luzzatto. 1990. "Favism in the African type of glucose-6-phosphate dehydrogenase deficiency (A-)." *British Medical Journal* 1: 236.

Gallo, P. 1968. "La deficienza del G6PD e le oscillazioni del tasso enzimatico eritrocitario in differenti campioni di popolazione." *Biochimica e biologia sperimentale* 7: 195–202.

Gamble, J. S., and C. E. C. Fischer. 1956–58. *Flora of the presidency of Madras. 3 vols.* Calcutta: Botanical Survey of India.

Gardiner, E. E., R. R. Marquardt, and G. Kemp. 1982. "Variation in vicine and convicine concentration of faba bean genotypes." *Canadian Journal of Plant Science* 62: 589–92.

Gardner, Helen. 1980. *Gardner's art through the ages.* 7th ed. rev. by Horst de la Croix and Richard G. Tansey. New York: Harcourt Brace Jovanovich.

Garnham, P. C. C. 1966. *Malaria parasites and other haemosporidia.* Oxford: Blackwell Scientific Publications.

Garnham, P. C. C. 1980. "Malaria in its various vertebrate hosts." Pp. 95–144 in Vol. 1 of Julius P. Kreier (ed.), *Malaria.* New York: Academic Press.

Gaster, M. 1908–26. "Divination (Jewish)." Pp. 806–14 in Vol. 4 of *Encyclopaedia of religion and ethics.* 13 vols. Ed. James Hastings. Edinburgh: T. and T. Clark.

Geden, A. S. 1908–26a. "Nature (Hindu)." Pp. 227–33 in Vol. 9 of *Encyclopaedia of religion and ethics.* 13 vols. Ed. James Hastings. Edinburgh: T. and T. and T. Clark.

Geden, A. S. 1908–26b. "Symbolism (Hindu)." Pp. 141–43 in Vol. 12 of *Encyclopaedia of religion and ethics.* 13 vols. Ed. James Hastings. Edinburgh: T. and T. Clark.

Geden, Alfred S. 1983. *Studies in Eastern religions.* Sri Garib Das Oriental Series, 9. Delhi: Sri Satguru Publications.

Geiger, Wilhelm (trans.). 1960. *The Mahāvaṃsa, or the great chronicle of Ceylon.* Colombo: Ceylon Government Information Department.

Gelb, I. J. 1965. "The Philadelphia onion archive." Pp. 57–62 in Hans G. Güterbock and Thorkild Jacobsen (eds.), *Studies in honor of Benno Landsberger on his seventy-fifth birthday, April 21, 1965.* Oriental Institute of the University of Chicago, Assyriological Studies, 16. Chicago: University of Chicago Press.

Geller, M. J. 1990. "Taboo in Mesopotamia." *Journal of Cuneiform Studies* 42: 105–17.

Geoponica. 1805–6. Trans. T. Owen. London: Printed by the translator.

Getty, Alice. 1971. *Gaṇeśa: A monograph on the elephant-faced god.* 2d ed. New Delhi: Munshiram Manoharlal.

Ghosal, Samir. 1965. "Tree in folk life." Pp. 107–19 in Sankar Sen Gupta (ed.), *Tree symbol worship in India.* Calcutta: Indian Publications.

Ghosh, S. P. 1985. "Citrus." Pp. 162–218 in T. K. Bose (ed.), *Fruits of India, tropical and subtropical.* Calcutta: Naya Prokash.

Ghurye, G. S. 1979. *Vedic India.* Bombay: Popular Prakashan.

Gibb, H. A. R., and C. F. Beckingham (trans. and eds.). 1958–94. *The travels of Ibn Baṭṭūta, A. D. 1325–1354.* 4 vols. Hakluyt Society Works, 2d ser., 110, 117, 141, 178. London: Hakluyt Society.

Giles, Eugene. 1962. "Favism, sex-linkage, and the Indo-European kinship system." *Southwestern Journal of Anthropology* 18: 286–90.

Giles, H. A. (trans.). 1923. *The travels of Fa-hsien (399–413 A.D.), or record of the Buddhistic kingdoms.* Cambridge: Cambridge University Press.

Giles, Herbert A. 1978. *A glossary of reference on subjects connected with the Far East.* 3d ed. New Delhi: Cosmo Publications.

Gilles, Herbert M. 1993a. "Historical outline." Pp. 1–11 in Herbert M. Gilles and David A. Warrell, *Bruce-Chwatt's essential malariology.* 3d ed. London: Edward Arnold.

Gilles, Herbert M. 1993b. "The malaria parasites." Pp. 12–34 in Herbert M. Gilles and David A. Warrell, *Bruce-Chwatt's essential malariology.* 3d ed. London: Edward Arnold.

Gimbutas, Marija. 1974. "The Lithuanian god Velnias." Pp. 87–92 in Gerald James Larson, C. Scott Littleton, and Jaan Puhvel (eds.), *Myth in Indo-European antiquity.* Berkeley, Los Angeles, London: University of California Press.

Gimbutas, Marija. 1982. *The goddesses and gods of Old Europe: 6500–3500 B.C.* New, updated ed. Berkeley, Los Angeles, London: University of California Press.

Ginsburg, H., H. Atamna, G. Shalmiev, J. Kanaani, and M. Krugliak. 1996. "Resistance of glucose-6-phosphate dehydrogenase deficiency to malaria: Effects of fava bean hydroxypyrimidine glucosides on *Plasmodium falciparum* growth in culture and on the phagocytosis of infected cells." *Parasitology* 113: 7–16.

Ginzberg, Louis. 1909–38. *The legends of the Jews.* 7 vols. Philadelphia: Jewish Publication Society of America.

Godbole, S. R., G. S. Pendse, and V. A. Bedekar (eds.). 1966. *Glossary of vegetable drugs in Vāgbhaṭa*. Poona: Indian Drug Research Association.

Gode, P. K. 1941–42. "Some notes on the history of the fig (*Ficus carica*) from foreign and Indian sources." *New Indian Antiquary* 4: 125–36.

Gode, P. K. 1943. "Some notes on the history of the fig—Does the word 'phalga,' used by Caraka and Suṣruta, mean 'añjīra'?" *Indian Historical Quarterly* 19: 62–65.

Goetze, Albrecht, and E. H. Sturtevant. 1938. *The Hittite ritual of Tunnawi*. American Oriental Series, 14. New Haven: American Oriental Society.

Gold, Ann Grodzins. 1988. *Fruitful journeys: The ways of Rajasthani pilgrims*. Berkeley, Los Angeles, London: University of California Press.

Gold, Ann Grodzins, and Bhoju Ram Gujar. 1989. "Of gods, trees and boundaries: Divine conservation in Rajasthan." *Asian Folklore Studies* 48: 211–29.

Goldman, Robert P., and Sheldon I. Pollock (trans.). 1984–86. *The Rāmāyaṇa of Vālmīki: An epic of ancient India*. 2 vols. Ed. Robert P. Goldman. Princeton: Princeton University Press.

Golenser, J., J. Miller, D. T. Spira, T. Navok, and M. Chevion. 1983. "Inhibitory effect of a fava bean component on the in vitro development of *Plasmodium falciparum* in normal and glucose-6-phosphate dehydrogenase deficient erythrocytes." *Blood* 61: 507–10.

Gomme, G. Laurence. 1892. "The president's address." *Folk-Lore* (London) 3: 1–25.

Gomme, L. 1908–26. "Milk (primitive religions)." Pp. 633–34 in Vol. 8 of *Encyclopaedia of religion and ethics*. 13 vols. Ed. James Hastings. Edinburgh: T. and T. Clark.

Gonda, J. 1969. *Aspects of early Viṣṇuism*. 2d ed. Delhi, Patna, Varanasi: Motilal Banarsidass.

Gonda, J. 1970. *Viṣṇuism and Śivaism: A comparison*. London: Athlone Press, University of London.

Gonda, J. 1980. *Vedic ritual: The non-solemn rites*. Handbuch der Orientalistik, Abteilung 2, Band 4, Abschnitt 1. Leiden: E. J. Brill.

Gonda, J. 1985. *The ritual functions and significance of grasses on the religion of the Veda*. Verhandelingen der Koninklijke Nederlandse Akademie van Wetenschappen (Amsterdam), Afdeling Letterkunde, Nieuwe Reeks, deel 132. Amsterdam, Oxford, New York: North-Holland Publishing Company.

Gonda, J. 1991. *The functions and significance of gold in the Veda*. Orientalia Rheno-Traiectina, 37. Leiden, New York, Copenhagen, Cologne: E. J. Brill.

Goodenough, Erwin Ramsdell. 1953–68. *Jewish symbols in the Greco-Roman period*. 13 vols. Bollingen Series, 37. New York: Pantheon Books.

Goodrich-Freer, A. (Mrs. Hans H. Spoer). 1907. "The powers of evil in Jerusalem." *Folk-Lore* (London) 18: 54–76.

Goor, Asaph, and Max Nurock. 1968. *The fruits of the Holy Land.* Jerusalem: Israel Universities Press.

Gopal, Ram. 1959. *India of Vedic Kalpasūtras.* Delhi: National Publishing House.

Gopalan, C. 1950. "The lathyrism syndrome." *Transactions of the Royal Society of Tropical Medicine and Hygiene* 44: 333–38.

Gopaldas, Tara, Anjali Gupta, and Kalpna Saxena. 1983. "The phenomenon of sanskritization in a forest-dwelling tribe of Gujarat, India. Nutrient intake and practices in the special groups." *Ecology of Food and Nutrition* 13: 1–8.

Gorman, Peter. 1979. *Pythagoras: A life.* London, Henley, and Boston: Routledge and Kegan Paul.

Gough, E. Kathleen. 1955. "Female initiation rites on the Malabar Coast." *Journal of the Royal Anthropological Institute of Great Britain and Ireland* 85: 45–80.

Gould-Martin, Katherine. 1978. "Hot cold clean poison and dirt: Chinese folk medical categories." *Social Science and Medicine* 12: 39–46.

Govil, K. K., B. M. Gupta, S. D. Kapur, N. C. Chakravarty, D. P. Bhatnagar, and K. C. Pant. 1959. "Field investigations of lathyrism in Uttar Pradesh." *Journal of the Indian Medical Association* 33: 499–506.

Graf, Fritz. 1974. *Eleusis und die orphische Dichtung Athens in vorhellenistischer Zeit.* Religionsgeschichtliche Versuche und Vorarbeiten, 33. Berlin and New York: Walter de Gruyter.

Graves, Robert, and Raphael Patai. 1966. *Hebrew myths: The book of Genesis.* New York: McGraw-Hill.

Greuter, Werner, and Karl Heinz Rechinger. 1967. *Flora der Insel Kythera.* Boissiera, 13. Geneva: [Journal de Genève].

Grierson, G. A. 1908–26. "Gayā." Pp. 181–87 in Vol. 6 of *Encyclopaedia of religion and ethics.* 13 vols. Ed. James Hastings. Edinburgh: T. and T. Clark.

Grieve, M. 1931. *A modern herbal.* 2 vols. London: Jonathan Cape.

Griffith, Ralph T. H. (trans.). 1963. *The hymns of the Rigveda.* 2 vols. Chowkhamba Sanskrit Studies, 35. Varanasi: Chowkhamba Sanskrit Series Office.

Griffiths, D. Wynne, and Gavin Ramsay. 1992. "The concentration of vicine and convicine in *Vicia faba* and some related species and their distribution within mature seeds." *Journal of the Science of Food and Agriculture* 59: 463–68.

Griffiths, J. Gwyn. 1970. *Plutarch's "De Iside et Osiride."* Cardiff: University of Wales Press.

Griffiths, Walter G. 1946. *The Kol tribe of Central India.* Calcutta: Royal Asiatic Society of Bengal.

Grimm, Jacob. 1883–88. *Teutonic mythology.* 4 vols. Trans. from the 4th ed. of *Deutsche Mythologie* by James Steven Stallybrass. London: George Bell and Sons.

Grimm, Jakob L. K., and Wilhelm K. Grimm. 1981. *Deutsche Sagen.* Trans. as *The German legends of the brothers Grimm* by Donald Ward. 2 vols. Translations in Folklore Studies. Philadelphia: Institute for the Study of Human Issues.

Grindon, Leo H. 1883. *The Shakspere flora*. Manchester: Palmer and Howe; London: Simpkin, Marshall.

Grmek, Mirko D. 1980. "La Légende et la réalité de la nocivité des fèves." *History and Philosophy of the Life Sciences* 2: 61–121.

Grmek, Mirko D. 1989. *Diseases in the ancient Greek world*. Trans. Mireille Muellner and Leonard Muellner. Baltimore and London: Johns Hopkins University Press.

Grover, Norman. 1965. "Man and plants against pain." *Economic Botany* 19: 99–112.

Growse, F. S. (trans.). 1966. *The Rámáyana of Tulsi Dás*. 8th rev. ed. Allahabad: Ram Narain Lal Beni Prasad.

Gubernatis, Angelo de. 1872. *Zoological mythology*. 2 vols. London: Trübner and Company.

Gubernatis, Angelo de. 1978. *La Mythologie des plantes*. 2 vols. New York: Arno Press.

Guerrieri, C. 1893–94. "Credenze, superstizioni e usi popolari in Rimini e suoi dintorni." *Rivista delle Tradizioni popolari italiane* 1: 314–15.

Gunkel, Hermann. 1964. *The legends of Genesis: The biblical saga and history*. Trans. W. H. Carruth. New York: Schocken Books.

Gupta, Dharmendra Kumar. 1972. *Society and culture in the time of Daṇḍin*. Delhi: Meharchand Lachhmandas.

Gupta, Shakti M. 1971. *Plant myths and traditions in India*. Leiden: E. J. Brill.

Gurney, O. R. 1977. *Some aspects of Hittite religion*. The Schweich Lectures of the British Academy, 1976. Oxford: Oxford University Press.

Guruge, Ananda (ed.). 1965. *Return to righteousness: A collection of speeches, essays and letters of the Anagarika Dharmapala*. [Colombo]: The Anagarika Dharmapala Birth Centenary Committee, Ministry of Education and Cultural Affairs, Ceylon.

Guthrie, William K. C. 1952. *Orpheus and Greek religion*. 2d ed. London: Methuen.

Guthrie, William K. C. 1955. *The Greeks and their gods*. Boston: Beacon Press.

Guthrie, William K. C. 1962–81. *A history of Greek philosophy*. 6 vols. Cambridge: Cambridge University Press.

Hackett, L. W. 1944. *Malaria in Europe: An ecological study*. London: Oxford University Press.

Hadzsits, G. D. 1936. "The *vera historia* of the Palatine *Ficus ruminalis*." *Classical Philology* 31: 305–19.

Haemoglobinopathies and allied disorders. (1966). Report of a WHO Scientific Group. World Health Organization Technical Report Series, 338. Geneva: World Health Organization.

Hanelt, Peter. 1972a. "Die infraspezifische Variabilität von *Vicia faba* L. und ihre Gliederung." *Die Kulturpflanze* 20: 75–128.

Hanelt, Peter. 1972b. "Zur Geschichte des Anbaues von *Vicia faba* L. und ihrer verschiedenen Formen." *Die Kulturpflanze* 20: 209–23.

Hanelt, Peter, Helga Schäfer, and Jürgen Schultze-Motel. 1972. "Die Stellung von *Vicia faba* L. in der Gattung *Vicia* L. und Betrachtungen zur Entstehung dieser Kulturart." *Die Kulturpflanze* 20: 263–75.

Hara, Hiroshi. 1970. "On the Asiatic species of the genus *Panax*." *Journal of Japanese Botany* 45: 197–212.

Hara, Hiroshi. 1971. *The flora of eastern Himalaya: Second report*. Tokyo: University of Tokyo Press.

Hardie, Margaret M. 1981. "The evil eye in some Greek villages of the Upper Haliakmon Valley in West Macedonia." Pp. 107–23 in Alan Dundes (ed.), *The evil eye: A folklore casebook*. Garland Folklore Casebooks, 2. New York and London: Garland.

Hardy, R. Spence. 1880. *A manual of Buddhism*. 2d ed. London and Edinburgh: Williams and Norgate.

Hardy, R. Spence. 1989. *Eastern monachism*. Bibliotheca Indo-Buddhica Series, 49. Delhi: Sri Satguru Publications.

Harfouche, Jamal Karam. 1981. "The evil eye and infant health in Lebanon." Pp. 86–106 in Alan Dundes (ed.), *The evil eye: A folklore casebook*. Garland Folklore Casebooks, 2. New York and London: Garland.

Harington, Sir John. 1970. *The Englishmans doctor: Or, the schoole of Salerne*. Pp. 67–156 in *The school of Salernum: Regimen sanitatis Salernitanum*. New York: Augustus M. Kelley.

Harlan, Lindsey. 1992. *Religion and Rajput women*. Berkeley, Los Angeles, Oxford: University of California Press.

Harper, Edward B. 1959. "A Hindu village pantheon." *Southwestern Journal of Anthropology* 15: 227–34.

Harper, Edward B. 1961. "Cultural factors in food consumption: An example from India." *Economic Botany* 15: 289–95.

Harper, Edward B. 1964. "Ritual pollution as an integrator of caste and religion." Pp. 151–96 in Edward B. Harper (ed.), *Religion in South Asia*. Seattle: University of Washington Press.

Harris, J. Rendel. 1917a. *The ascent of Olympus*. Manchester: Manchester University Press; London: Longmans, Green; and London: Bernard Quaritch.

Harris, J. Rendel. 1917b. "The origin of the cult of Aphrodite." *Bulletin, John Rylands Library, Manchester England* 3: 354–81.

Harris, William C. 1844. *The highlands of Aethiopia*. 3 vols. London: Longman, Brown, Green, and Longmans.

Harrison, Jane. 1955. *Prolegomena to the study of Greek religion*. New York: Meridian Books.

Hart, Donn V. 1969. *Bisayan Filipino and Malayan humoral pathologies: Folk medicine*

490　　　BIBLIOGRAPHY

and ethnohistory in Southeast Asia. Data Paper 76. Ithaca, N.Y.: Southeast Asia Program, Department of Asian Studies, Cornell University.

Hart, Gerald D. 1980. "Ancient diseases of the blood." Pp. 32–55 in Maxwell M. Wintrobe (ed.), *Blood, pure and eloquent: A story of discovery, of people, and of ideas.* New York: McGraw-Hill Book Company.

Hartland, Edwin Sidney. 1894–96. *The legend of Perseus: A study of tradition in story, custom and belief.* 3 vols. London: David Nutt.

Hartland, Edwin Sidney. 1908–26. "Phallism." Pp. 815–31 in Vol. 9 of *Encyclopaedia of religion and ethics.* 13 vols. Ed. James Hastings. Edinburgh: T. and T. Clark.

Hartland, Edwin Sidney. 1971. *Primitive paternity: The myth of supernatural birth in relation to the history of the family.* 2 vols. in 1. New York: Benjamin Blom.

Hasan, Khwaja A. 1971. "The Hindu dietary practices and culinary rituals in a North Indian village: An ethnomedical and structural analysis." *Ethnomedicine* 1: 43–70.

Hasan, S. B., and P. G. Deo. 1994. "*Ocimum sanctum* seeds for mosquito control." *International Pest Control* 36: 20–21.

Hassan, Mahmoud Mohamed. 1971. "Glucose-6-phosphate dehydrogenase deficiency in the Sudan." *Journal of Tropical Medicine and Hygiene* 74: 187–88.

Haug, Martin. 1922. *The Aitareya Brahmanam of the Rigveda.* Extra volume, 4, of *The sacred books of the Hindus.* Allahabad: Panini Office.

Haug, Martin. 1978. *The Parsis: Essays on their sacred language, writings and religion.* Rev. by K. W. West. New Delhi: Cosmo Publications.

Haupt, Karl. 1862–63. *Sagenbuch der Lausitz.* 2 parts in 1 vol. Leipzig: Wilhelm Engelmann.

Havell, E. B. 1905. *Benares: The sacred city.* London: Blackie and Son.

Hävernick, W. 1966. "Wunderwurzeln, Alraunen und Hausgeister im deutschen Volksglauben." *Beiträge zur deutschen Volks- und Altertumskunde* 10: 17–34.

Hawkes, J. G. 1972. "Solanaceae. *Mandragora officinarum* L." Pp. 356–57 in V. H. Heywood (ed.), "Flora Europaea: Notulae systematicae ad floram Europaeam, No. 13." *Botanical Journal of the Linnean Society* 65: 341–58.

Hayes, W. B. 1966. *Fruit growing in India.* Allahabad: Kitabistan.

Hazlitt, W. Carew. 1905. *Faiths and folklore.* 2 vols. London: Reeves and Turner.

Hedayat, Sh., D. D. Farhud, K. Montazami, and P. Ghadirian. 1981. "The pattern of bean consumption, laboratory findings in patients with favism, G-6-P-D deficient, and a control group." *Journal of Tropical Pediatrics* 27: 110–12.

Hedayat, Sh., S. Rahbar, E. Mahboobi, M. Ghaffarpour, and N. Sobhi. 1971. "Favism in the Caspian littoral area of Iran." *Tropical and Geographical Medicine* 23: 149–57.

Hegazy, Mohamed Ihab, and Ronald R. Marquardt. 1983. "Development of a simple procedure for the complete extraction of vicine and convicine from fababeans (*Vicia faba* L.)." *Journal of the Science of Food and Agriculture* 34: 100–108.

Hehn, Victor. 1888. *The wanderings of plants and animals from their first home*. Ed. James Steven Stallybrass. London: Swan Sonnenschein and Company.

Hellbom, Anna-Britta. 1963. "The creation egg." *Ethnos* 28: 63–105.

Henderson, William. 1866. *Notes on the folk-lore of the northern counties of England and the borders*. London: Longmans, Green, and Company.

Heras, H. 1938. "Tree worship in Mohenjo Daro." Pp. 31–39 in *Journal of the Anthropological Society of Bombay, Jubilee Volume*. Bombay: Anthropological Society of Bombay.

Herbarium of Apuleius. 1864. Pp. 1–325 in Vol. 1 of Thomas Oswald Cockayne (ed.), *Leechdoms, worthcunning, and starcraft of early England*. Chronicles and Memorials of Great Britain and Ireland during the Middle Ages, No. 35. London: Longman, Green, Longman, Roberts, and Green.

Herbelot, Barthelemy d'. 1777–79. *Bibliothèque orientale, ou dictionnaire universel*. 4 vols. La Haye: J. Neaulme and N. Van Daalen.

Herklots, G. A. C. 1972. *Vegetables in South-East Asia*. London: George Allen & Unwin.

Herodotus. 1880. *History*. 4th ed. 4 vols. Trans. George Rawlinson. London: John Murray.

Hertz, Wilhelm. 1905. "Die Sage vom Giftmädchen." Pp. 156–277 in his *Gesammelte Abhandlungen*. Stuttgart and Berlin: J. G. Cotta'sche Buchhandlung.

Heyne, K. 1950. *Die nuttige planten van Indonesië*. 2 vols. 's-Gravenhage and Bandung: W. van Hoeve.

Hildegard. 1882. *Physica*. Cols. 1125–1352 in Vol. 1 of Jacques Paul Migne, *S. Hildegardis abbatissae opera omnia, ad optimorum librorum fidem edita*. Patrologiae cursus completus, Series Latina, 197. Paris: Garnier Frères and J.-P. Migne.

Hiltebeitel, Alf. 1978. "The Indus Valley 'Proto-Śiva,' re-examined through reflections on the goddess, the buffalo, and the symbol of vāhanas." *Anthropos* 73: 767–97.

Hippocrates. 1957–95a. *Aphorisms*. Trans. W. H. S. Jones. Pp. 97–221 in Vol. 4 of *Hippocrates*. 10 vols. Trans. W. H. S. Jones, E. T. Withington, Paul Potter, and Wesley D. Smith. Loeb Classical Library. London: William Heinemann; Cambridge, Mass. and London: Harvard University Press.

Hippocrates. 1957–95b. *Diseases II*. Trans. Paul Potter. Pp. 185–333 in Vol. 5 of *Hippocrates*. 10 vols. Trans. W. H. S. Jones, E. T. Withington, Paul Potter, and Wesley D. Smith. Loeb Classical Library. London: William Heinemann; Cambridge, Mass. and London: Harvard University Press.

Hippocrates. 1957–95c. *Epidemics I and III*. Trans. W. H. S. Jones. Pp. 139–287 in

Vol. 1 of *Hippocrates*. 10 vols. Trans. W. H. S. Jones, E. T. Withington, Paul Potter, and Wesley D. Smith. Loeb Classical Library. London: William Heinemann; Cambridge, Mass. and London: Harvard University Press.

Hippocrates. 1957–95d. *Epidemics II, IV–VII*. Trans. Wesley D. Smith. Vol. 7 of *Hippocrates*. 10 vols. Trans. W. H. S. Jones, E. T. Withington, Paul Potter, and Wesley D. Smith. Loeb Classical Library. London: William Heinemann; Cambridge, Mass. and London: Harvard University Press.

Hippocrates. 1957–95e. *Fistulas*. Trans. Paul Potter. Pp. 390–407 in Vol. 8 of *Hippocrates*. 10 vols. Trans. W. H. S. Jones, E. T. Withington, Paul Potter, and Wesley D. Smith. Loeb Classical Library. London: William Heinemann; Cambridge, Mass. and London: Harvard University Press.

Hippocrates. 1957–95f. *Places in man*. Trans. Paul Potter. Pp. 13–101 in Vol. 8 of *Hippocrates*. 10 vols. Trans. W. H. S. Jones, E. T. Withington, Paul Potter, and Wesley D. Smith. Loeb Classical Library. London: William Heinemann; Cambridge, Mass. and London: Harvard University Press.

Hippocrates. 1957–95g. *Regimen*. Trans. W. H. S. Jones. Pp. 223–447 in Vol. 4 of *Hippocrates*. 10 vols. Trans. W. H. S. Jones, E. T. Withington, Paul Potter, and Wesley D. Smith. Loeb Classical Library. London: William Heinemann; Cambridge, Mass. and London: Harvard University Press.

Hippocrates. 1957–95h. *Regimen in acute diseases (appendix)*. Trans. Paul Potter. Pp. 257–327 in Vol. 6 of *Hippocrates*. 10 vols. Trans. W. H. S. Jones, E. T. Withington, Paul Potter, and Wesley D. Smith. Loeb Classical Library. London: William Heinemann; Cambridge, Mass. and London: Harvard University Press.

Hippocrates. 1957–95i. *The sacred disease*. Trans. W. H. S. Jones. Pp. 127–83 in Vol. 2 of *Hippocrates*. 10 vols. Trans. W. H. S. Jones, E. T. Withington, Paul Potter, and Wesley D. Smith. Loeb Classical Library. London: William Heinemann; Cambridge, Mass. and London: Harvard University Press.

Hippocrates. 1961–62. *Diseases of women*. Trans. É. Littré as *Des maladies des femmes*. Pp. 1–407 in Vol. 8 of *Oeuvres complètes d'Hippocrate*. 10 vols. Trans. É. Littré. Amsterdam: Adolf M. Hakkert.

Hippolytus, Saint. 1921. *Philosophumena, or the refutation of all heresies*. 2 vols. Trans. from the text of Cruice by F. Legge. London: Society for Promoting Christian Knowledge; New York: Macmillan.

Hira Lal. 1925. "III. Some notes about marriage, food, drink, and occupations of castes affecting social status in the Central Provinces." *Man in India* 5: 56–68.

Hoernle, A. F. R. (ed.). 1893–1912. *The Bower manuscript*. Archaeological Survey of India, New Imperial Series, 22. Calcutta: Superintendent, Government Printing.

Hoffner, Harry A., Jr. 1974. *Alimenta Hethaeorum: Food production in Hittite Asia Minor.* American Oriental Series, 55. New Haven: American Oriental Society.

Hoffpauir, Robert. 1982. "The water buffalo: India's other bovine." *Anthropos* 77: 217–38.

Höfler, M. 1899. "Krankheits-Dämonen." *Archiv für Religionswissenschaft* 2: 86–164.

Hole, Christina. 1976. *British folk customs.* London: Hutchinson.

Homer. 1887. *Odyssey.* Trans. as *The "Odyssey" of Homer* by William Morris. London: Reeves and Turner.

Homer. 1898. *Iliad.* Trans. as *The "Iliad" of Homer* by Samuel Butler. London: Longmans, Green, and Co.

Hone, William. 1845. *The year book of daily recreation and information.* London: Thomas Tegg.

Hong, Moon-wha. 1978. "A history of ginseng." Pp. 13–44 in Bae, Hyo-won (ed.), *Korean ginseng.* 2d ed. Seoul: Korea Ginseng Research Institute, Republic of Korea.

Hong, Soon-keun. 1982. "Ginseng cultivation." Pp. 418–35 in C. K. Atal and B. M. Kapur (eds.), *Cultivation and utilization of medicinal plants.* Jammu-Tawi (India): Regional Research Laboratory, Council of Scientific and Industrial Research.

Hooker, Joseph Dalton. 1872–97. *The flora of British India.* 7 vols. London: L. Reeve.

Hopf, Maria. 1969. "Plant remains and early farming in Jericho." Pp. 355–59 in Peter J. Ucko and G. W. Dimbleby (eds.), *The domestication and exploitation of plants and animals.* Chicago: Aldine.

Hopfner, Theodor. 1974. *Griechisch-ägyptischer Offenbarungszauber.* Vol. 1. Amsterdam: Adolf M. Hakkert.

Hopkins, E. Washburn. 1906. "The Buddhistic rule against eating meat." *Journal of the American Oriental Society* 27: 455–64.

Hopkins, E. Washburn. 1969. *Epic mythology.* New York: Biblio and Tannen.

Hopkins, Thomas J., and Alf Hiltebeitel. 1987. "Indus Valley religion." Pp. 215–23 in Vol. 7 of *The encyclopedia of religion.* 16 vols. Ed. Mircea Eliade. New York: Macmillan; London: Collier Macmillan.

Horace. 1895a. *The epistles.* Pp. 163–200 in *The works of Horace.* Trans. James Lonsdale and Samuel Lee. London and New York: Macmillan.

Horace. 1895b. *The satires.* Pp. 107–58 in *The works of Horace.* Trans. James Lonsdale and Samuel Lee. London and New York: Macmillan.

Horace. 1934. *The epodes.* Pp. 359–413 in *Horace, the odes and epodes.* Trans. C. E. Bennett. Loeb Classical Library. Cambridge, Mass.: Harvard University Press; London: William Heinemann.

Hou, Joseph P. 1978. *The myth and truth about ginseng.* South Brunswick: A. S. Barnes and Company; London: Thomas Yoseloff.

Howey, M. Oldfield. 1955. *The encircled serpent: A study of serpent symbolism in all countries and ages.* New York: Arthur Richmond.

Hoyland, J. S., and S. N. Banerjee (trans. and annotat.). 1922. *The commentary of Father Monserrate, S. J., on his journey to the court of Akbar.* London, Bombay, Madras, Calcutta: Oxford University Press.

Hu, Shiu-ying. 1976. "The genus *Panax* (ginseng) in Chinese medicine." *Economic Botany* 30: 11–28.

Hugot, H. J. 1968. "The origins of agriculture: Sahara." *Current Anthropology* 9: 483–88, 494–509.

Huheey, J. E., and D. L. Martin. 1975. "Malaria, favism and glucose-6-phosphate dehydrogenase deficiency." *Experientia* 31: 1145–47.

Humbert, Aimé. 1870. *Le Japon illustré.* 2 vols. Paris: Librairie de Hachette et cie.

Huntingford, G. W. B. (trans. and ed.). 1980. *The Periplus of the Erythraean Sea.* Hakluyt Society Works, 2d ser., 151. London: Hakluyt Society.

Hutton, J. H. 1933. "Hinduism in its relation to primitive religion in India." Pp. 392–417 in pt. 1, "Report," in Vol. 1, India, *Census of India, 1931.* Delhi: Manager of Publications.

Hutton, J. H. 1963. *Caste in India.* 4th ed. London: Oxford University Press.

Hutton, J. H. 1968. *The Sema Nagas.* 2d ed. Bombay: Oxford University Press.

Hutton, J. H. 1969. *The Angami Nagas.* 2d ed. Bombay: Oxford University Press.

Hyde, Walter Woodburn. 1923. *Greek religion and its survivals.* Boston: Marshall Jones.

Iamblichus. 1991. *On the Pythagorean life.* Trans. as *On the Pythagorean way of life* by John Dillon and Jackson Hershbell. Society for Biblical Literature, Texts and Translations 29, Graeco-Roman Religion Series 11. Atlanta, Georgia: Scholars Press.

Ibn el-Beïthar. 1877–83. *Traité des simples.* 3 vols. Trans. Lucien Leclerc. Notices et extraits des manuscrits de la Bibliothèque Nationale et autres bibliothèques, 23, 25, 26. Paris: Imprimerie Nationale.

Ignacimuthu, S., and C. R. Babu. 1987. "*Vigna radiata* var. *sublobata* (Fabaceae): Economically useful wild relative of urd and mung beans." *Economic Botany* 41: 418–22.

Isaac, Erich. 1959. "Influence of religion on the spread of citrus." *Science* 129: 179–86.

Iyer, A. Padmanabha. 1938–39. "Serpent worship in Travancore: Special temples or kavus (groves of trees)." *Quarterly Journal of the Mythic Society* 29: 326–28.

Iyer, L. K. Ananthakrishna. 1909–12. *The Cochin tribes and castes.* 2 vols. Madras: Government of Cochin; London: Luzac.

Jackson, Betty P., and Michael I. Berry. 1979. "Mandragora—taxonomy and chemistry of the European species." Pp. 505–12 in J. G. Hawkes, R. N. Lester, and A. D. Skelding (eds.), *The biology and taxonomy of the Solanaceae*. Linnean Society Symposium Series, 7. London: Academic Press.

Jacob, Dorothy. 1965. *A witch's guide to gardening*. New York: Taplinger.

Jacobi, Hermann (trans.). 1884. *Gaina sûtras*, part. 1. Volume 22 of *The sacred books of the East*. Ed. F. Max Müller. Oxford: Clarendon Press.

Jacoby, F. 1944. "Genesia: A forgotten festival of the dead." *Classical Quarterly* 38: 65–75.

Jaini, Padmanabh S. 1979. *The Jaina path of purification*. Berkeley, Los Angeles, London: University of California Press.

Jaini, Padmanabh S. 1987. "Indian perspectives on the spirituality of animals." Pp. 169–78 in David J. Kalupahana and W. G. Weeraratne (eds.), *Buddhist philosophy and culture: Essays in honour of N. A. Jayawickrema*. Colombo: N. A. Jayawickrema Felicitation Volume Committee.

Jamalian, Jalal. 1978. "Favism-inducing toxins in broad beans (*Vicia faba*): Determination of vicine content and investigation of other non-protein nitrogenous compounds in different broad bean cultivars." *Journal of the Science of Food and Agriculture* 29: 136–40.

Jamalian, Jalal, and Abdollah Bassiri. 1978. "Variation in vicine concentration during pod development in broad bean (*Vicia faba* L.)." *Journal of Agricultural and Food Chemistry* 26: 1454–56.

Jamalian, Jalal, Francis Aylward, and Bertram J. F. Hudson. 1976. "Favism-inducing toxins in broad beans (*Vicia faba*): Examination of bean extracts for pyrimidine glucosides." *Qualitas Plantarum. Plant Foods for Human Nutrition* 26: 331–39.

Jamalian, Jalal, Francis Aylward, and Bertram J. F. Hudson. 1977a. "Favism-inducing toxins in broad beans (*Vicia faba*): Biological activities of broad beans extracts in favism-sensitive subjects." *Qualitas Plantarum. Plant Foods for Human Nutrition* 27: 213–19.

Jamalian, Jalal, Francis Aylward, and Bertram J. F. Hudson. 1977b. "Favism inducing toxins in broad beans (*Vicia faba*): Estimation of the vicine contents of broad bean and other legume samples." *Qualitas Plantarum. Plant Foods for Human Nutrition* 27: 207–11.

James, E. O. 1966. *The Tree of Life: An archaeological study*. Leiden: E. J. Brill.

Jastrow, Morris. 1898. *The religion of Babylonia and Assyria*. Boston: Ginn.

Jathar, V. S., R. Hirwe, S. Desai, and R. S. Satoskar. 1976. "Dietetic habits and quality of semen in Indian subjects." *Andrologia* 8: 355–58.

Jaworskij, Juljan. 1896. "Die Mandragora im südrussischen Volksglauben." *Zeitschrift für osterreichische Volkskunde* 2: 353–61.

Jeffery, Patricia, Roger Jeffery, and Andrew Lyon. 1990. "Ethnic contrasts and parallels in the post-partum period: Some evidence from Bijnor, North India."

Pp. 7–33 in Gabriella Eichinger Ferro-Luzzi (ed.), *Rites and beliefs in modern India*. New Delhi: Manohar Publications.

Jelliffe, D. B. 1957. "Cultural blocks and protein malnutrition in early childhood in rural West Bengal." *Pediatrics* 20: 128–38.

Jerome. 1983. *Apology against Rufinus*. Trans. as *Saint Jérôme: Apologie contre Rufin* by Pierre Lardet. Paris: Éditions du Cerf.

Jindel, Rajendra. 1976. *Culture of a sacred town: A sociological study of Nathdwara*. Bombay: Popular Prakashan.

Joannes Lydus. 1898. *On months*. Ed. Richard Wuensch. Leipzig: Teubner.

Johnston, S. I. 1991. "Crossroads." *Zeitschrift für Papyrologie und Epigraphik* 88: 217–24.

Jolly, Julius (trans.). 1880. *The institutes of Vishnu*. Vol. 7 of *The sacred books of the East*. Ed. F. Max Müller. Oxford: Clarendon Press.

Jolly, Julius (trans.). 1889. *The minor law-books*. Vol. 33 of *The sacred books of the East*. Ed. F. Max Müller. Oxford: Clarendon Press.

Jones, W. H. S. 1909. *Malaria and Greek history*. University of Manchester Publications, 43. Manchester: Manchester University Press.

Jood, S., B. M. Chauhan, and A. C. Kapoor. 1989. "Protein digestibility (in vitro) of chickpea and blackgram seeds as affected by domestic processing and cooking." *Plant Foods for Human Nutrition* 39: 149–54.

Joret, Charles. 1976. *Les Plantes dans l'antiquité et au moyen âge*. 2 vols. Geneva: Statkine Reprints.

Josephus. 1926–65. *The Jewish war*. Vols. 2 and 3 in *Josephus*. 9 vols. Trans. H. St. J. Thackeray, Ralph Marcus, Allen Wikgren, and L. H. Feldman. Loeb Classical Library. London: William Heinemann; Cambridge, Mass.: Harvard University Press.

Julian. 1923. *Epistles*. Pp. 1–293 in Vol. 3 of *The works of the emperor Julian*. Trans. William Cave Wright. Loeb Classical Library. London: William Heinemann; New York: Macmillan.

Juvenal. 1965. *Satires*. Trans. Jerome Mazzaro. Ann Arbor: University of Michigan Press.

Kabiraj, Sibnarayan. 1965. "Fertility cult and trees." Pp. 148–55 in Sankar Sen Gupta (ed.), *Tree symbol worship in India*. Calcutta: Indian Publications.

Kachroo, P., and M. Arif (eds.). 1970. *Pulse crops of India*. New Delhi: Indian Council of Agricultural Research.

Kajale, M. D. 1977. "Ancient grains from excavations at Nevasa, Maharashtra." *Geophytology* 7: 93–106.

Kakar, D. N. 1977. *Folk and modern medicine (a North Indian case study)*. Delhi: New Asian Publishers.

Kantak, N. M., and M. G. Gogate. 1992. "Effect of short term administration of tulsi (*Ocimum sanctum* Linn.) on reproductive behavior of adult male rats." *Indian Journal of Physiology and Pharmacology* 36: 109–11.

Kantha, S. S. 1990. "Nutrition and health in China, 1949 to 1989." *Progress in Food and Nutrition Science* 14: 93–137.

Karmarkar, A. P. 1950. *The religions of India.* Vol. 1: *The Vrātya or Dravidian Systems.* Lonavla: Mira Publishing House.

Katona-Apte, Judit. 1975. "Dietary aspects of acculturation: Meals, feasts, and fasts in a minority community in South Asia." Pp. 315–26 in Margaret L. Arnott (ed.), *Gastronomy: The anthropology of food and food habits.* The Hague and Paris: Mouton.

Katona-Apte, Judit, and Mahadev L. Apte. 1977. "The significance of food in religious ideology and behavior in Marathi myths." Paper presented at the Third International Conference of Ethnological Food Research at Cardiff, August 22–27, 1977. 15 pp.

Kattamis, Christos. 1971. "Favism in breast-fed infants." *Archives of Disease in Childhood* 46: 741.

Kattamis, Christos. 1986. "Favism: Epidemiological and clinical aspects." Pp. 25–43 in Akira Yoshida and Ernest Beutler (eds.), *Glucose-6-phosphate dehydrogenase.* London: Academic Press.

Kattamis, Christos A., Athanasios Chaidas, and Stavros Chaidas. 1969a. "G6PD deficiency and favism in the island of Rhodes (Greece)." *Journal of Medical Genetics* 6: 286–90.

Kattamis, Christos A., Maria Kyriazakou, and Stavros Chaidas. 1969b. "Favism: Clinical and biochemical data." *Journal of Medical Genetics* 6: 34–41.

Kattamis, Christos, Katerina Karambula, Anna Metaxotou-Mavromati, and Nicolas Matsaniotis. 1971. "G.-6-P.D. deficiency and age." *Lancet* 1: 235.

Katz, Solomon H. 1987. "Fava bean consumption: A case for the co-evolution of genes and culture." Pp. 133–59 in Marvin Harris and Eric B. Ross (eds.), *Food and evolution.* Philadelphia: Temple University Press.

Kay, Daisy E. 1979. *Food legumes.* TPI Crop and Product Digest, 3. London: Tropical Products Institute.

Keats, John. 1899. *The complete poetical works and letters of John Keats.* Cambridge ed. Ed. Horace E. Scudder. Boston and New York: Houghton Mifflin; Cambridge: Riverside Press.

Keimer, Ludwig. 1933. "Materialien zum altägyptischen Zwiebelkult." *Egyptian Religion* 1: 52–60.

Keimer, Ludwig. 1967. *Die Gartenpflanzen im alten Ägypten.* Hildesheim: Georg Olms.

Keith, Arthur Berriedale. 1909. "Pythagoras and the doctrine of transmigration." *Journal of the Royal Asiatic Society,* 569–606.

Keith, Arthur Berriedale. 1914. *The Veda of the Black Yajus school entitled Taittiriya Sanhita*. 2 vols. Harvard Oriental Series, 18 and 19. Cambridge, Mass.: Harvard University Press.

Kendler, B. S. 1987. "Garlic (*Allium sativum*) and onion (*Allium cepa*): A review of their relationship to cardiovascular disease." *Preventive Medicine* 16: 670–85.

Kendrick, T. D. 1966. *The druids: A study in Keltic prehistory*. 2d ed. New York: Barnes and Noble.

Kerényi, C. (1976). *Dionysos: Archetypal image of indestructible life*. Trans. Ralph Manheim. Bollingen Series 65, Archetypal Images in Greek Religion, 2. Princeton: Princeton University Press.

Kern, Otto. 1922. *Orphicorum fragmenta*. Berlin: Weidmann.

Ketkar, Shridhar V. 1909. *The history of caste in India*. Vol. 1. Ithaca, N.Y.: Taylor and Carpenter.

Keyes, Charles F. 1987. "Buddhist pilgrimage in South and Southeast Asia." Pp. 347–49 in Vol. 11 of *The encyclopedia of religion*. 16 vols. Ed. Mircea Eliade. New York: Macmillan; London: Collier Macmillan.

Keys, John D. 1976. *Chinese herbs: Their botany, chemistry, and pharmacodynamics*. Rutland, Vt.: Charles E. Tuttle Company.

Khare, Dhirendra, N. K. Sharma, and C. B. Singh. 1984. "Faba bean—a promising pulse crop." *Indian Farming* 34, 6 (September): 7–8, 21.

Khare, R. S. 1966. "A case of anomalous values in Indian civilization: Meat-eating among the Kanya-Kubja Brahmans of Katyayan Gotra." *Journal of Asian Studies* 25: 229–40.

Khare, R. S. 1967. "Prediction of death among the Kanya-Kubja Brahmans: A study of predictive narratives." *Contributions to Indian Sociology*, n. s. 1: 1–25.

Khare, R. S. 1976a. *Culture and reality: Essays on the Hindu system of managing foods*. Simla: Indian Institute of Advanced Study.

Khare, R. S. 1976b. *The Hindu hearth and home*. New Delhi: Vikas.

Khory, Rustomjee Naserwanjee, and Nanabhai Navrosji Katrak. 1981. *Materia medica of India and their therapeutics*. Delhi: Neeraj Publishing House.

Kilmer, Fred B. 1932. "The mandragora." *American Journal of Pharmacy* 104: 79–82.

Kincaid, Charles Augustus. 1908. *The tale of the tulsi plant and other studies*. Bombay and London: The Times of India Office.

Kinsley, David. 1986. *Hindu goddesses: Visions of the divine feminine in the Hindu religious tradition*. Berkeley, Los Angeles, London: University of California Press.

Kipling, John Lockwood. 1892. *Beast and man in India*. 2d ed. London and New York: Macmillan.

Kirk, Geoffrey S., and John E. Raven. 1957. *The presocratic philosophers: A critical history with a selection of texts*. Cambridge: Cambridge University Press.

Kirtikar, K. R. 1912. "The use of saffron and turmeric in Hindu marriage cere-monies." *Journal of the Anthropological Society of Bombay* 9: 439–54.

Kirtikar, K. R., B. D. Basu, and An I. C. S. (retired). 1975. *Indian medicinal plants.* 2d ed. 4 vols. Ed., rev., enl. and mostly rewritten by E. Blatter, J. F. Caius, and K. S. Mhaskar. Dehra Dun: M/S Bishen Singh Mahendra Pal Singh; Delhi: M/S Periodical Experts.

Kirzner, E. W. (trans.). 1935. *Baba Ḳamma.* Vol. 1 of pt. 4 (Seder Neziḳin) of *The Babylonian Talmud.* Ed. Isidore Epstein. London: Soncino Press.

Kislev, M. E., and O. Bar-Yosef. 1988. "The legumes: The earliest domesticated plants in the Near East?" *Current Anthropology* 29: 175–79.

Kitayaporn, Dwip, Pricha Charoenlarp, Junya Pattaraarechachai, and Tian Phol-poti. 1991. "G6PD deficiency and fava bean consumption do not produce he-molysis in Thailand." *Southeast Asian Journal of Tropical Medicine and Public Health* 22: 176–82.

Knasmüller, Siegfried, Rainer de Martin, Gyula Domjan, and Akos Szakmary. 1989. "Studies on the antimutagenic activities of garlic extract." *Environmental and Molecular Mutagenesis* 13: 357–65.

Knox, Robert. 1911. *An historical relation of Ceylon.* Glasgow: James MacLehose and Sons.

Krishnaswamy, S. Y. 1974. "Food and drinks in ancient India." *Swarajya* (Madras) 19, 21 (November 23): 9–10.

Kuhn, Adalbert. 1886. *Die Herabkunft des Feuers und des Göttertranks.* Vol. 1 of his *Mythologische Studien.* Gütersloh: G. Bertelsmann.

Laderman, Carol. 1975. "Malaria and progress: Some historical and ecological considerations." *Social Science and Medicine* 9: 587–94.

Ladizinsky, G. 1975. "On the origin of the broad bean, *Vicia faba* L." *Israel Journal of Botany* 24: 80–88.

La Fontaine, Jean de. 1883–97. *Oeuvres de J. de la Fontaine.* New ed. 12 vols. Rev. Henri Regnier. Paris: Hachette.

Laisnel de la Salle, Germaine. 1875. *Croyances et legendes du centre de la France.* 2 vols. Paris: A. Chaix.

Lal, Shiv Darshan, and Kamlesh Lata. 1980. "Plants used by the Bhat community for regulating fertility." *Economic Botany* 34: 273–75.

Lamberg-Karlovsky, C. C. 1972. "Trade mechanisms in Indus-Mesopotamian in-terrelations." *Journal of the American Oriental Society* 92: 222–30.

Lang, Andrew. 1885. *Custom and myth.* New York: Harper and Brothers.

Lang, Andrew. 1901. *Myth, ritual and religion.* 2 vols. London: Longmans, Green.

Langdon-Brown, Walter. 1941. *From witchcraft to chemotherapy.* The Linacre Lec-tures 1941. Cambridge: Cambridge University Press.

Lassen, Christian. 1858–74. *Indische Alterthumskunde.* 2d ed. 4 vols. Leipzig: L. A. Kittler; London: Williams and Norgate.

Latham, James E. 1982. *The religious symbolism of salt.* Théologie historique, 64. Paris: Éditions Beauchesne.

Lau, B. H. S., M. A. Adetumbi, and A. Sanchez. 1983. *"Allium sativum* (garlic) and atherosclerosis: A review." *Nutrition Research* 3: 119–28.

Laufer, Berthold. 1917. "La Mandragore." *T'oung Pao* 18: 1–30.

Laufer, Berthold. 1919. "Sino-Iranica: Chinese contributions to the history of civilization in ancient Iran." *Field Museum of Natural History, Anthropological Series* 15: 185–630.

Lawless, Harry, Paul Rozin, and Joel Shenker. 1985. "Effects of oral capsaicin in gustatory, olfactory and irritant sensations and flavor identification in humans who regularly or rarely consume chili pepper." *Chemical Senses* 10: 579–89.

Lawson, John Cuthbert. 1964. *Modern Greek folklore and ancient Greek religion: A study in survivals.* New Hyde Park, N.Y.: University Books.

Leach, Maria (ed.). 1949–50. *Standard dictionary of folklore.* 2 vols. New York: Funk and Wagnalls.

Lefkowitz, Mary. 1995. *Not out of Africa: How afrocentrism became an excuse to teach myth as history.* New York: Basic Books.

Legge, James (trans.). 1886. *A record of the Buddhistic kingdoms, being an account by the Chinese monk Fâ-hien of his travels in India and Ceylon (A.D. 399–414) in search of the Buddhistic books of discipline.* Oxford: Clarendon Press.

Lehner, Ernst, and Johanna Lehner. 1960. *Folklore and symbolism of flowers, plants and trees.* New York: Tudor.

Lehner, Ernst, and Johanna Lehner. 1962. *Folklore and odysseys of food and medicinal plants.* New York: Tudor.

Levey, Martin. 1966. "Materia medica in al-Kindi's Medical Formulary." Pp. 223–377 in Martin Levey (trans.), *The medical formulary or Aqrābādhīn of Al-Kindī.* Madison, Milwaukee, and London: University of Wisconsin Press.

Lévi-Strauss, Claude. 1979. "Pythagoras in America." Pp. 33–41 in R. H. Hook (ed.), *Fantasy and symbol: Studies in anthropological interpretation.* London, New York, San Francisco: Academic Press.

Lewis, Oscar. 1958. *Village life in northern India: Studies in a Delhi village.* Urbana: University of Illinois Press.

Lewis, Y. S. 1984. *Spices and herbs for the food industry.* Orpington, England: Food Trade Press.

Leyel, Mrs. C. F. 1926. *The magic of herbs: A modern book of secrets.* New York: Harcourt, Brace.

Li, Hui-lin. 1979. *Nan-fang ts'ao-mu chuang: A fourth century flora of Southeast China.* Hong Kong: Chinese University Press.

Lieber, Elinor. 1970. "Favism in antiquity." *Koroth* 5: 331–35 and LIV–LV. (In Hebrew with English summary).

Lieber, Elinor. 1973. "The Pythagorean community as a sheltered environment for the handicapped." Pp. 33–41 in H. Karplus (ed.), *International Symposium on Society, Medicine, and Law, Jerusalem, March 1972.* Amsterdam, London, New York: Elsevier.

Limet, Henri. 1987. "The cuisine of ancient Sumer." *Biblical Archaeologist* 50: 132–40, 144–47.

Lindenbaum, Shirley. 1977. "The 'last course': Nutrition and anthropology in Asia." Pp. 141–55 in Thomas K. Fitzgerald (ed.), *Nutrition and anthropology in action.* Studies in Developing Countries, 21. Assen/Amsterdam: van Gorcum.

Linforth, Ivan M. 1941. *The arts of Orpheus.* Berkeley and Los Angeles: University of California Press.

Littré, Émile. 1863–72. *Dictionnaire de la langue française.* 4 vols. Paris: Librairie de L. Hachette et Cie.

Livingstone, Frank B. 1964. "Aspects of the population dynamics of the abnormal hemoglobin and glucose-6-phosphate dehydrogenase deficiency genes." *American Journal of Human Genetics* 16: 435–50.

Livingstone, Frank B. 1967. *Abnormal hemoglobins in human populations.* Chicago: Aldine.

Livingstone, Frank B. 1971. "Malaria and human polymorphisms. Pp. 33–64 in Herschel L. Roman, Laurence M. Sandler, and Allan Campbell (eds.), *Annual review of genetics.* Vol. 5. Palo Alto: Annual Reviews.

Livingstone, Frank B. 1973. *Data on the abnormal hemoglobins and glucose-6-phosphate dehydrogenase deficiency in human populations 1967–1973.* Technical Reports, 3. Contributions to Human Biology, 1. Ann Arbor: Museum of Anthropology, University of Michigan.

Livingstone, Frank B. 1983. "The malaria hypothesis." Pp. 15–44 in James E. Bowman (ed.), *Distribution and evolution of hemoglobin and globin loci.* New York, Amsterdam, Oxford: Elsevier.

Livingstone, Frank B. 1984. "The Duffy blood groups, vivax malaria, and malaria selection in human populations: A review." *Human Biology* 56: 413–25.

Livingstone, Frank B. 1985. *Frequencies of hemoglobin variants.* New York and Oxford: Oxford University Press.

Livingstone, Frank B. 1989. "Simulation of the diffusion of the β-globin variants in the Old World." *Human Biology* 61: 297–309.

Lloyd, G. E. R. 1964. "The hot and the cold, the dry and the wet in Greek philosophy." *Journal of Hellenic Studies* 84: 92–106.

Lodrick, Deryck O. 1981. *Sacred cows, sacred places: Origins and survivals of animal homes in India.* Berkeley, Los Angeles, London: University of California Press.

Lodrick, Deryck O. 1982. "Man and mongoose in Indian culture." *Anthropos* 77: 191–214.

Loewenfeld, Claire, and Philippa Back. 1978. *The complete book of herbs and spices.* 2d, rev. ed. Newton Abbot and London: David and Charles.

Logan, Michael H. 1977. "Anthropological research on the hot-cold theory of disease: Some methodological suggestions." *Medical Anthropology* 1, 4 (Fall): 87–112.

Lonsdale, Steven H. 1979. "Attitudes towards animals in ancient Greece." *Greece and Rome* 26: 146–59.

Lord, J. Henry. 1908–26. "Bene-Israel." Pp. 469–74 in Vol. 2 of *Encyclopaedia of religion and ethics*. 13 vols. Ed. James Hastings. Edinburgh: T. and T. Clark.

Lovett, E. 1913. "Folk medicine in London." *Folk-Lore* (London) 24: 120–21.

Löw, Immanuel. 1967. *Die Flora der Juden*. 4 vols. Hildesheim: Georg Olms.

Lu An-ming. 1986. "Solanaceae in China." Pp. 79–85 in William G. D'Arcy (ed.), *Solanaceae: Biology and systematics*. New York: Columbia University Press.

Lucan. 1928. *The civil war*, Books 1–9. Trans. as *Lucan* by J. D. Duff. Loeb Classical Library. Cambridge, Mass.: Harvard University Press; London: William Heinemann.

Lucian. 1913. *A true story*. Trans. A. M. Harmon. Pp. 247–357 in Vol. 1 of *Lucian*. 8 vols. Trans. A. M. Harmon, K. Kilburn, and M. D. Macleod. Loeb Classical Library. London: William Heinemann; Cambridge, Mass.: Harvard University Press.

Lucian. 1915. *Timon*. Trans. as *Timon, or the Misanthrope* by A. M. Harmon. Pp. 325–93 in Vol. 2 of *Lucian*. 8 vols. Trans. A. M. Harmon, K. Kilburn, and M. D. Macleod. Loeb Classical Library. London: William Heinemann; Cambridge, Mass.: Harvard University Press.

Lucian. 1960a. *The dream, or the cock*. Trans. A. M. Harmon. Pp. 171–239 in Vol. 2 of *Lucian*. 8 vols. Trans. A. M. Harmon, K. Kilburn, and M. D. Macleod. Loeb Classical Library. London: William Heinemann; Cambridge, Mass.: Harvard University Press.

Lucian. 1960b. *Philosophies for sale*. Trans. A. M. Harmon. Pp. 449–511 in Vol. 2 of *Lucian*. 8 vols. Trans. A. M. Harmon, K. Kilburn, and M. D. Macleod. Loeb Classical Library. London: William Heinemann; Cambridge, Mass.: Harvard University Press.

Lucian. 1960c. *Zeus rants*. Trans. A. M. Harmon. Pp. 89–169 in Vol. 2 of *Lucian*. 8 vols. Trans. A. M. Harmon, K. Kilburn, and M. D. Macleod. Loeb Classical Library. London: William Heinemann; Cambridge, Mass.: Harvard University Press.

Lucian. 1961. *Dialogues of the dead*. Trans. M. D. Macleod. Pp. 1–175 in Vol. 7 of *Lucian*. 8 vols. Trans. A. M. Harmon, K. Kilburn, and M. D. Macleod. Loeb Classical Library. London: William Heinemann; Cambridge, Mass.: Harvard University Press.

Ludowyk, E. F. C. 1958. *The footprint of the Buddha*. London: George Allen and Unwin.

Luisada, Aldo. 1941. "Favism: A singular disease chiefly affecting the red blood cells." *Medicine* (Baltimore) 20: 229–50.

Lupton, Thomas. 1612. *A thousand notable things of sundrie sorts.* London: Edward White.

Luzzatto, Lucio. 1979. "Genetics of red cells and susceptibility to malaria." *Blood* 54: 961–76.

Luzzatto, Lucio, and Atul Mehta. 1989. "Glucose-6-phosphate dehydrogenase deficiency." Pp. 2237–65 in Vol. 2 of Charles R. Scriver, Arthur L. Beaudet, William S. Sly, and David Valle (eds.), *The metabolic basis of inherited disease.* 6th ed. New York: McGraw-Hill.

Luzzatto, Lucio, and G. Battistuzzi. 1985. "Glucose-6-phosphate dehydrogenase." Pp. 217–329 in Harry Harris and Kurt Hirschhorn (eds.), *Advances in human genetics,* 14. New York and London: Plenum Press.

Luzzatto, Lucio, and U. Bienzle. 1979. "The malaria/G.-6-P.D. hypothesis." *Lancet* 1: 1183–84.

Luzzatto, Lucio, Essien A. Usanga, and G. Modiano. 1985. "Genetic resistance to *Plasmodium falciparum:* Studies in the field and in cultures *in vitro.*" Pp. 205–14 in D. Rollinson and R. M. Anderson (eds.), *Ecology and genetics of host-parasite interactions.* Linnean Society Symposium Series, 11. London: Academic Press.

Luzzatto, Lucio, Essien A. Usanga, and Shunmugam Reddy. 1969. "Glucose-6-phosphate dehydrogenase deficient red cells: Resistance to infection by malarial parasites." *Science* 164: 839–42.

Luzzatto, Lucio, O. Sodeinde, and G. Martini. 1983. "Genetic variation in the host and adaptive phenomena in *Plasmodium falciparum* infection." Pp. 159–73 in *Malaria and the red cell.* Ciba Foundation Symposium 94. London: Pitman.

Luzzatto, Lucio, Stella O'Brien, Essien Usanga, and Wanchai Wanachiwanawin. 1986. "Origin of G6PD polymorphism: Malaria and G6PD deficiency." Pp. 181–93 in Akira Yoshida and Ernest Beutler (eds.), *Glucose-6-phosphate dehydrogenase.* London: Academic Press.

McClure, F. A. 1933. "Methods and materials of Chinese table plant culture." *Lingnan Science Journal* 12, Supplement: 119–49.

McCrindle, John Watson. 1973. *The commerce and navigation of the Erythraean Sea; and ancient India as described by Ktesias the Knidian.* Amsterdam: Philo Press.

McCurdy, Paul R., and Laviza Mahmood. 1970. "Red cell glucose-6-phosphate dehydrogenase deficiency in Pakistan." *Journal of Laboratory and Clinical Medicine* 76: 943–48.

McDonald, Hamish. 1992. "India: A Hindu-Buddhist row." *Far-Eastern Economic Review* 155, 33 (August 20): 28–29.

Macdonell, Arthur A. 1897. *Vedic mythology.* Grundriss der Indo-Arischen Philologie und Altertumskunde. Band 3, Heft 1A. Strassburg: Karl J. Trübner.

Macdonell, Arthur A. 1968. *A history of Sanskrit literature*. New York: Haskell House Publishers.

Macdonell, Arthur Anthony, and Arthur Berriedale Keith. 1912. *Vedic index of names and subjects*. 2 vols. London: John Murray.

Machiavelli, Niccolò. 1957. *Mandragola*. Trans. Anne and Henry Paolucci. Indianapolis and New York: Bobbs-Merrill.

Mack, Ronald B. 1992. "Mortals run mad: Mandrake (Polophyllum) poisoning." *North Carolina Medical Journal* 53: 98–99.

McKay, A. M. 1992. "Hydrolysis of vicine and convicine from fababeans by microbial β-glucosidase enzymes." *Journal of Applied Bacteriology* 72: 475–78.

Mackay, Ernest J. H. 1937–38. *Further excavations at Mohenjo-daro*. 2 vols. Delhi: Manager of Publications.

Mackay, Ernest J. H. 1943. *Chanhu-daro excavations 1935–36*. American Oriental Series, 10. Boston and New Haven: American School of Indic and Iranian Studies and the Museum of Fine Arts.

Mackay, Ernest J. H., and Dorothy Mackay. 1948. *Early Indus civilizations*. London: Luzac.

Mackenzie, J. S. F. 1875. "Tree and serpent worship." *Indian Antiquary* 10: 5–6.

McLean, R. C., and W. R. Ivimey-Cook. 1956. *Textbook of theoretical botany*. Vol. 2. London, New York, Toronto: Longmans, Green.

McNeill, William H. 1976. *Plaques and peoples*. Garden City, N.Y.: Anchor Press/ Doubleday.

Macrobius. 1969. *Saturnalia*. Trans. Percival Vaughan Davies. New York and London: Columbia University Press.

Madan, T. N. 1975. "The gift of food." Pp. 84–96 in Balakrishna N. Nair (ed.), *Culture and society: A festschrift to Dr. A. Aiyappan*. Delhi: Thomson Press (India).

Mager, J., M. Chevion, and G. Glaser. 1980. "Favism." Pp. 265–94 in Irvin E. Liener (ed.), *Toxic constituents of plant foodstuffs*. 2d ed. New York: Academic Press.

Mahadevan, Indira. 1961. "Belief systems in food of the Telugu-speaking people of the Telengana region." *Indian Journal of Social Work* 21: 387–96.

Mahapatra, Piyushkanti. 1965. "Tree-symbol worship in Bengal." Pp. 125–39 in Sankar Sen Gupta (ed.), *Tree symbol worship in India*. Calcutta: Indian Publications.

Mahindru, S. N. 1982. *Spices in Indian life*. New Delhi: Sultan Chand & Sons.

Maimonides, Moses. 1904. *The guide for the perplexed*. Trans. M. Friedlander. 2d ed. London: Routledge and Kegan Paul.

Maimonides, Moses. 1966. *On poisons and their antidotes*. Ed. by Suessman Muntner as *Treatise on poisons and their antidotes*. The Medical Writings of Moses Maimonides, 2. Philadelphia and Montreal: J. B. Lippincott Company.

Maity, Pradyot Kumar. 1965. "Tree worship and its association with the snake cult in India." Pp. 47–53 in Sankar Sen Gupta (ed.), *Tree symbol worship in India.* Calcutta: Indian Publications.

Mandal, S., D. N. Das, K. De, K. Ray, G. Roy, S. B. Chaurhuri, C. C. Sahana, and M. K. Chowdhuri. 1993. "*Ocimum sanctum* Linn.—a study on gastric ulceration and gastric secretion in rats." *Indian Journal of Physiology and Pharmacology* 37: 91–92.

Mandelbaum, Allen (trans.). 1990. *The "Odyssey" of Homer.* Berkeley, Los Angeles, London: University of California Press.

Manderson, Lenore. 1987. "Hot-cold food and medical theories: Overview and introduction." *Social Science and Medicine* 25: 329–30.

"Mandragore." 1816–19. Pp. 174–77 in Vol. 19 of *Nouveau dictionnaire d'histoire naturelle, appliquée aux arts, à l'agriculture, à l'économie rurale et domestique, à la médecine, etc.* New ed. 36 vols. Paris: Déterville.

"Mandrake." 1893–96. P. 476 in Vol. 15 of *The Encyclopaedia Britannica.* 9th ed. 25 vols. Chicago: Werner Company.

Mani, S. B. 1981. "From marriage to child conception: An ethnomedical study in rural Tamil Nadu." Pp. 194–220 in Giri Raj Gupta (ed.), *The social and cultural context of medicine in India.* Main Currents in Indian Sociology, 4. New Delhi: Vikas.

Mani, Vettam. 1975. *Puranic encyclopaedia: A comprehensive dictionary with special reference to the epic and Puranic literature.* Delhi: Motilal Benarsidass.

Marcovich, Miroslav. 1964. "Pythagorica." *Philologus* 108: 29–44.

Marriott, McKim. 1966. "The feast of love." Pp. 200–212, 229–31 in Milton Singer (ed.), *Krishna: Myths, rites, and attitudes.* Honolulu: East-West Center Press.

Marshall, John. 1931. *Mohenjo-daro and the Indus civilization.* 3 vols. London: Arthur Probsthain.

Martin, Robert Montgomery. 1838. *The history, antiquities, topography and statistics of eastern India.* 3 vols. London: Wm. H. Allen.

Martin, Yan-kit. 1984. *Chinese cooking: Step by step techniques.* New York: Random House.

Maspero, Henri. 1981. *Taoism and Chinese religion.* Trans. Frank A. Kierman, Jr. Amherst: University of Massachusetts Press.

Massé, Henri. 1954. *Persian beliefs and customs.* Behavior Science Translations. New Haven: Human Relations Area Files.

Mathon, Claude-Charles. 1981. *L'Origine des plantes cultivées.* Collection Écologie appliquée et sciences de l'environnement, No. 5. Paris: Masson.

Mathur, K. S. 1964. *Caste and ritual in a Malwa village.* New York: Asia Publishing House.

Mattioli, Pietro Andrea. 1554. *Commentarii, in libros sex Pedacii Dioscoridis Anazarbei, De medica materia: Adiectis quam plurimis plantarum et animalium imaginibus, eodem authorej*. Venice: In Officina Erasmiana apud Vincentum Valgrisium.

Maundrell, Henry. 1963. *A journey from Aleppo to Jerusalem in 1697*. Beirut: Khayats.

Meera Khan, P. 1964. "Glucose-6-phosphate dehydrogenase deficiency in an Indian rural area." *Journal of Genetics* 59: 14–18.

Meera Khan, P., and J. Th. Wijnen. 1986. "G6PD variation in India." Pp. 245–59 in Akira Yoshida and Ernest Beutler (eds.), *Glucose-6-phosphate dehydrogenase*. London: Academic Press.

Megas, George A. 1963. *Greek calendar customs*. Athens: Press and Information Department, Prime Minister's Office.

Mehendale, M. A. 1970. "Ahimsa and the spread of vegetarianism in India." *Humanist Review* (Bombay) 2: 419–26.

Mehra, K. L. 1967. "History of sesame in India and its cultural significance." *Vishveshvaranad Indological Journal* 5: 93–107.

Mehra, K. L., K. C. Kanodia, and R. N. Srivastava. 1975. "Folk uses of plants for adornment in India." *Economic Botany* 29: 39–46.

Mehta, Atul B. 1994. "Review article: Glucose-6-phosphate dehydrogenase deficiency." *Postgraduate Medical Journal* 70: 871–77.

Meigs, Anna S. 1978. "A Papuan perspective on pollution." *Man*, n. s. 13: 304–18.

Meloni, Tullio, Gavino Forteleoni, and Gian Franco Meloni. 1992. "Marked decline of favism after neonatal glucose-6-phosphate dehydrogenase screening and health education: The northern Sardinian experience." *Acta Haematologica* 87: 29–31.

Meloni, Tullio, Gavino Forteleoni, Angelo Dore, and Stefano Cutillo. 1983. "Favism and hemolytic anemia in glucose-6-phosphate dehydrogenase-deficient subjects in North Sardinia." *Acta Haematologica* 70: 83–90.

Mennell, Stephen. 1985. *All manners of food: Eating and taste in England and France from the Middle Ages to the present*. Oxford and New York: Basil Blackwell.

Meyer, Frank N. 1911. *Agricultural explorations in the fruit and nut orchards of China*. U.S. Department of Agriculture, Bureau of Plant Industry, Bulletin No. 204. Washington, D.C.: U.S. Government Printing Office.

Meyer, Johann Jacob. 1929. "Einen Scheidenden bis an ein Wasser begleitin." *Zeitschrift für Indologie und Iranistik* 7: 71–88.

Meyer, Johann Jacob. 1937. *Trilogie altindischer Mächte und Feste der Vegetation*. 3 vols. Zürich and Leipzig: Max Niehans.

Miller, R. L., S. Ikram, G. J. Armelagos, R. Walker, W. B. Harer, C. J. Shiff, D. Baggett, M. Carrigan, and S. M. Maret. 1994. "Diagnosis of *Plasmodium falciparum* infections in mummies using the rapid manual *Para*Sight™–F test." *Transactions of the Royal Society of Tropical Medicine and Hygiene* 88: 31–32.

Mills, J. P. 1922. *The Lhota Nagas.* London: Macmillan.

Milne Edwards, Alphonse. 1864. *De la famille des solanacées.* Thèse, École Supérieure de Pharmacie de Paris. Paris: E. Martinet.

Minakata, Kumagusu. 1894–95. "The mandrake." *Nature* (London) 51: 608.

Minakata, Kumagusu. 1896. "The mandrake." *Nature* (London) 54: 343–44.

Minturn, Leigh, and John T. Hitchcock. 1966. *The Rājpūts of Khalapur, India.* Six Cultures Series, 3. New York, London, Sydney: John Wiley.

Mitchell, Robert D. 1971. "The grass pea: Distribution, diet, and disease." *Yearbook of the Association of Pacific Coast Geographers* 33: 29–46.

Mitra, Kalipada. 1925. "Impressions of the five fingers: The hand in magic." *Journal of the Bihar and Orissa Research Society* 11: 54–65.

Mitra, Rájendralála. 1873. "Spiritous drinks in ancient India." *Journal of the Royal Asiatic Society of Bengal* 41: 1–23.

Mitra, Rajendralala. 1972. *Buddha Gaya. The great Buddhist temple. The hermitage of Sakya Muni.* Delhi, Varanasi: Indological Book House.

Mitra, Sarat Chandra. 1939–40. "On the cult of the banyan and the pipal trees." *Quarterly Journal of the Mythic Society* 30: 446–50.

Modiano, G., A. S. Benerecetti-Santachiara, F. Gonano, G. Zei, A. Capaldo, and L. L. Cavalli-Sforza. 1965. "An analysis of ABO, MN, Rh, Tf and G-6-PD types in a sample from the human population of the Lecce province." *Annals of Human Genetics* 29: 19–31.

Moldenke, Harold N., and Alma L. Moldenke. 1952. *Plants of the Bible.* Waltham, Mass.: Chronica Botanica.

Money-Kyrle, Monica. 1934. "Mandrakes." *Folk-Lore* (London) 45: 192.

Monier-Williams, Monier. 1883. *Religious thought and life in India.* London: John Murray.

Monier-Williams, Monier. 1887. *Brāhmanism and Hindūsm, or religious thought and life in India.* 3d ed. London: John Murray.

Monier-Williams, Monier. 1889. *Buddhism, in its connexion with Brāhmanism and Hinduism and its contrast with Christianity.* New York: Macmillan.

Moor, Edward. 1834. *Oriental fragments.* London: Smith, Elder.

Moor, Edward. 1968. *The Hindu pantheon.* New ed. Varanasi and Delhi: Indological Book House.

Moore, Thomas. 1895. "Lalla Rookh." Pp. 369–479 in *Thomas Moore's complete poetical works.* Vol. 2. 2 vols. New York and Boston: Thomas Y. Crowell.

More, T. N. 1989. "Morphological study of *Ocimum sanctum* Linn. Pp. 15–20 in Bhaskar R. Mardikar, Subhash Ranada, Madhukar Paranjpe, and Bhushan Patwardhan (eds.), *Krishna tulas (Ocimum sanctum): A monograph.* Pune: Interdisciplinary School of Ayurvedic Medicine, University of Poona.

Motulsky, Arno G. 1960. "Metabolic polymorphisms and the role of infectious diseases in human evolution." *Human Biology* 32: 28–62.

Motulsky, Arno G. 1965. "Theoretical and clinical problems of glucose-6-phosphate dehydrogenase deficiency." Pp. 143–96 in J. H. P. Jonxis (ed.), *Abnormal haemoglobins in Africa*. Philadelphia: F. A. Davis Company.

Motulsky, Arno G., and Jean M. Campbell-Kraut. 1961. "Population genetics of glucose-6-phosphate dehydrogenase deficiency of the red cell." Pp. 159–91 in B. S. Blumberg (ed.), *Proceedings of the Conference on Genetic Polymorphisms and Geographic Variations in Disease*. New York: Grune and Stratton.

Mourant, A. E., Ada C. Kopeć, and Kazimiera Domaniewska-Sobczak. 1976. *The distribution of the human blood groups and other polymorphisms*. 2d ed. London Oxford University Press.

Mourant, A. E., Ada C. Kopeć, and Kazimiera Domaniewska-Sobczak. 1978. *The genetics of the Jews*. Oxford: Clarendon Press.

Mukhopadhyay, Amarendra. 1965. "A glossary of botanical names and their Indian synonyms." Pp. 156–64 in Sankar Sen Gupta (ed.), *Tree symbol worship in India*. Calcutta: Indian Publications.

Müller, F. Max (trans.). 1879–84. *The Upaniṣads*. 2 vols. Vols. 1 and 15 of *The sacred books of the East*. Ed. F. Max Müller. Oxford: Clarendon Press.

Müller, F. Max. 1886–92. "Âpastamba's Yagña-Paribhâshâ-Sûtras." Pp. 309–64 in Vol. 2 of Hermann Oldenberg and F. Max Müller (trans.), *Grihya-Sūtras: Rules of Vedic domestic ceremonies*. 2 vols. Vols. 29 and 30 of The sacred books of the East. Ed. F. Max Müller. Oxford: Clarendon Press.

Mundkur, Balaji. 1976. "The cult of the serpent in the Americas: Its Asian background." *Current Anthropology* 17: 429–40, 446–55.

Mundkur, Balaji. 1983. *The cult of the serpent: An interdisciplinary survey of its manifestations and origins*. Albany: State University of New York Press.

Murgoci, A. 1981. "The evil eye in Roumania and its antidotes." Pp. 124–29 in Alan Dundes (ed.), *The evil eye: A folklore casebook*. Garland Folklore Casebooks, 2. New York and London: Garland.

Murr, Josef. 1890. *Die Planzenwelt in der griechischen Mythologie*. Innsbruck: Wagner'schen Universitäts Buchhandlung.

Murray-Aynsley, Mrs. 1900. *Symbolism of the East and West*. London: George Redway.

Musil, Alois. 1907–8. *Arabia Petraea*. 3 vols in 4. Vienna: A. Holder.

Muthmann, Friedrich. 1982. *Der Granatapfel: Symbol des Lebens in der Alten Welt*. Schriften der Abegg-Stiftung Bern, Band 6. Fribourg: Office du livre.

Nadkarni, A. K. 1976. *Dr. K. M. Nadkarni's Indian materia medica*. 2 vols. Rev. and enl. by A. K. Nadkarni. Bombay: Popular Prakashan.

Naidu, Sarojini. 1912. *The bird of time: Songs of life, death and the spring*. New York: John Lane; London: W. Heinemann.

Naik, K. C. 1949. *South Indian fruits and their culture*. Madras: P. Varadachary.

Nair, P. Thankappan. 1965. "Tree-symbol worship among the Nairs of Kerala."

Pp. 93–103 in Sankar Sen Gupta (ed.), *Tree symbol worship in India*. Calcutta: Indian Publications.

Nanjundayya, H. V., and L. K. Ananthakrishna Iyer. 1930. *The Mysore tribes and castes*. 4 vols. Mysore: Mysore University.

Nayak, H. M. 1965. "Tree-cult in Karnataka." Pp. 120–24 in Sankar Sen Gupta (ed.), *Tree symbol worship in India*. Calcutta: Indian Publications.

Nayar, N. M. 1976. "Sesame: *Sesamum indicum* (Pedaliaceae)." Pp. 231–33 in N. W. Simmonds (ed.), *Evolution of crop plants*. London and New York: Longman.

Nayar, N. M., and K. L. Mehra. 1970. "Sesame: Its uses, botany, cytogenetics, and origin." *Economic Botany* 24: 20–31.

Neusner, Jacob (trans.). 1985. *Nedarim*. Vol. 23 of *The Talmud of the land of Israel*. Ed. Jacob Neusner. Chicago Studies in the History of Judaism. Chicago and London: University of Chicago Press.

Neusner, Jacob (trans.). 1987. *Megillah*. Vol. 19 of *The Talmud of the land of Israel*. Ed. Jacob Neusner. Chicago Studies in the History of Judaism. Chicago and London: University of Chicago Press.

Nichter, Mark. 1986. "Modes of food classification and the diet-health contingency: A South Indian case study." Pp. 185–221 in R. S. Khare and M. S. A. Rao (eds.), *Food, society, and culture*. Durham, N.C.: Carolina Academic Press.

Nilsson, Martin P. 1908. "Das Ei im Totenkult der Alten." *Archiv für Religionswissenschaft* 11: 530–46.

Nilsson, Martin P. 1949. *A history of Greek religion*. 2d ed. Trans. F. J. Fielden. Oxford: Clarendon Press.

Nilsson, Martin P. 1957. *The Dionysiac mysteries of the Hellenistic and Roman age*. Lund: C. W. K. Gleerup.

Nishino, H., A. Iwashima, Y. Itakura, H. Matsuura, and T. Fuwa. 1989. "Antitumor-promoting activity of garlic extracts." *Oncology* 46: 277–80.

Niukian, Khadjik, Joel Schwartz, and Gerald Shklar. 1987. "In vitro inhibitory effect of onion extract on hamster buccal pouch carcinogenesis." *Nutrition and Cancer* 10: 137–44.

Noehden, George Henry. 1827. "Account of the banyan-tree, or *Ficus indica*, as found in the ancient Greek and Roman authors." *Transactions of the Royal Asiatic Society of Great Britain and Ireland* 1: 119–32.

Norman, B. 1972. *Tales of the table: A history of Western cuisine*. Englewood Cliffs, N.J.: Prentice-Hall.

Oberhelman, Steven M. 1991. *The Oneirocriticon of Achmet: A medieval Greek and Arabic treatise on the interpretation of dreams*. Lubbock: Texas Technological University Press.

O'Flaherty, Wendy Doniger. 1981. *Śiva: The erotic ascetic*. Oxford, New York, Toronto, Melbourne: Oxford University Press.

Olck, Franz. 1897. "Bohne." Cols. 609–27 in Vol. 3 of *Paulys Realencyclopädie der classischen Altertumswissenschaft.* Ed. August Friedrich von Pauly and Georg Wissowa. Neue Bearbeitung. Stuttgart: J. B. Metzlersche Verlagsbuchhandlung.

Oldenberg, Hermann. 1988. *The religion of the Veda.* Trans. Shridhar B. Shrotri. Delhi: Motilal Banarsidass.

Oldenberg, Hermann, and F. Max Müller (trans.). 1886–92. *The Gṛihya-sūtras: Rules of Vedic domestic ceremonies.* 2 vols. Vols. 29 and 30 of *The sacred books of the East.* Ed. F. Max Müller. Oxford: Clarendon Press.

Oldham, C. F. 1901. "The Nāgas: A contribution to the history of serpent-worship." *Journal of the Royal Asiatic Society of Great Britain and Ireland,* 461–73.

Oldham, C. F. 1905. *The sun and the serpent: A contribution to the history of serpent-worship.* London: Archibald Constable.

Olsen, H. Sejr, and J. Hinge Andersen. 1978. "The estimation of vicine and convicine in fababeans (*Vicia faba* L.) and isolated fababean proteins." *Journal of the Science of Food and Agriculture* 29: 323–31.

O'Malley, L. S. S. 1935. *Popular Hinduism: The religion of the masses.* Cambridge: Cambridge University Press.

Onians, Richard Broxton. 1973. *The origins of European thought.* New York: Arno Press.

Ophiolatreia, or serpent worship 1889. N.p.: Privately printed.

Orekhov, A. N., V. V. Tertov, I. A. Sobenin, and E. M. Pivovarova. 1995. "Direct anti-atherosclerosis-related effects of garlic." *Annals of Medicine* 27: 63–65.

Ossendowski, Ferdinand. 1924. *Man and mystery in Asia.* New York: E. P. Dutton.

Ostermann, Velentino. 1940. *La vita in Friuli: Usi—costumi—credenze popolari.* 2d ed. 2 vols. Udine: Istituto delle Edizioni Accademiche.

Overbeck, H. 1926. "Note on the word 'selaseh.'" *Journal of the Malayan Branch of the Royal Asiatic Society* 4: 420–21.

Ovid. 1929. *Fasti.* Trans. as *Plublii ovidii nasonis fastorum libri sex: The Fasti of Ovid* by James George Frazer. 5 vols. London: Macmillan.

Owen, John. 1970. "The medico-social and cultural significance of *Adansonia digitata* (baobab) in African communities." *African Notes* (Ibadan) 6: 24–36.

Padmanaban, G. 1980. "Lathyrogens." Pp. 239–63 in Irvin E. Liener (ed.), *Toxic constituents of plant foodstuffs.* 2d ed. New York: Academic Press.

Palange, M. P. 1989. "Dravya guna vidnyan of Krishna tulas plant." Pp. 21–26 in Bhaskar R. Mardikar, Subhash Ranada, Madhukar Paranjpe, and Bhushan Patwardhan (eds.), *Krishna tulas (Ocimum sanctum): A monograph.* Pune: Interdisciplinary School of Ayurvedic Medicine, University of Poona.

Pande, Trilochan. 1965. "Tree-worship in ancient India." Pp. 35–46 in Sankar Sen Gupta (ed.), *Tree symbol worship in India.* Calcutta: Indian Publications.

Pandey, Brahma Prakash. 1989. *Sacred plants of India: Plants for human kind.* New Delhi: Shree Publishing House.

Panich, Vicharn. 1986. "G6PD variants in southern Asian populations." Pp. 195–

241 in Akira Yoshida and Ernest Beutler (eds.), *Glucose-6-phosphate dehydroge-nase*. London: Academic Press.

"Panjab—red food forbidden—Hindus." 1886. *Indian Notes and Queries* 4, 39 (December): 51.

Paranjpe, M. H., and Meera Paranjpe. 1989. "Compilation of folklore uses of Krishna tulas." Pp. 117–21 in Bhaskar R. Mardikar, Subhash Ranada, Madhukar Paranjpe, and Bhushan Patwardhan (eds.), *Krishna tulas (Ocimum sanctum): A monograph*. Pune: Interdisciplinary School of Ayurvedic Medicine, University of Poona.

Parke, H. W. 1967. *The oracles of Zeus: Dodona. Olympia. Ammon*. Oxford: Basil Blackwell.

Parke, H. W., and D. E. W. Wormell. 1956. *The Delphic oracle*. 2 vols. Oxford: Basil Blackwell.

Parker, Robert. 1983. *Miasma: Pollution and purification in early Greek religion*. Oxford: Clarendon Press.

Parkinson, John. 1976. *A garden of pleasant flowers (Paradisi in Sole: Paradisus Terrestris)*. New York: Dover Publications. (Reprint of edition published by Humphrey Lownes and Robert Young in London, 1629).

Parlby, Fanny (Parks). 1850. *Wanderings of a pilgrim, in search of the picturesque, during four-and-twenty years in the East*. 2 vols. London: Pelham Richardson.

Parry, John W. 1945. *The spice handbook*. Brooklyn, N.Y.: Chemical Publishing Company.

Patrick, Adam. 1967. "Disease in antiquity: Ancient Greece and Rome." Pp. 238–46 in Don Brothwell and A. T. Sandison (eds.), *Diseases in antiquity*. Springfield, Ill.: Charles C. Thomas.

Paul, Gemini. 1958. "Sherdukpens. IV: Village council, land, taxes and food." *Vanyajati* 1958: 153–56.

Pausanias. 1898. *Description of Greece*. 6 vols. Trans. J. G. Frazer. London: Macmillan.

Payne, Joseph Frank. 1904. *English medicine in the Anglo-Saxon times*. The Fitz-Patrick Lectures for 1903. Oxford: Clarendon Press.

Peck, Harry Thurston. 1896. *Harper's dictionary of classical literature and antiquities*. New York: American Book Company.

Pellini, S. 1894–95. "Usanze delle Marche." *Rivista delle tradizioni popolari italiane* 2: 65.

Penzer, N. M. (ed.). 1924–28. *The ocean of story, being C. H. Tawney's translation of Somadeva's Kathā Sarit Sāgara*. 10 vols. London: Privately printed.

Perry, Lily M. 1980. *Medicinal plants of East and Southeast Asia: Attributed properties and uses*. Cambridge, Mass. and London: MIT Press.

Persius. 1967. *The satires*. Trans. as *The satires of A. Persius Flaccus*, by John Conington; ed. H. Nettleship. 3d ed. Hildesheim: Georg Olms.

Phallic tree worship: Cultus arborum. 1971. Varanasi: Bharat-Bharati.

Philip, J. A. 1966. *Pythagoras and early Pythagoreanism.* Phoenix, Journal of the Classical Association of Canada, Supplementary Volume 7. Toronto: University of Toronto Press.

Phillips, Henry. 1827. *History of cultivated vegetables.* 2d ed. 2 vols. London: Henry Colburn.

Phillips, Walter Alison. 1910–11. "Vestments." Pp. 1056–62 in Vol. 27 of *The Encyclopaedia Britannica.* 11th ed. 29 vols. New York: Encyclopaedia Britannica.

Philo Judaeus. 1954. *On the contemplative life.* Trans. F. H. Colson. Pp. 103–11 in *Philo.* 10 vols. Loeb Classical Library. London: William Heinemann; Cambridge, Mass.: Harvard University Press.

Philpot, Mrs. J. H. 1897. *The sacred tree, or the tree in religion and myth.* London and New York: Macmillan.

Pickering, Charles. 1879. *Chronological history of plants.* Boston: Little, Brown.

Pillsbury, Barbara L. K. 1978. "'Doing the month': Confinement and convalescence of Chinese women after childbirth." *Social Science and Medicine* 12: 11–22.

Piomelli, Sergio. 1986. "G6PD-related neonatal jaundice." Pp. 95–108 in Akira Yoshida and Ernest Beutler (eds.), *Glucose-6-phosphate dehydrogenase.* London: Academic Press.

Pitre, Giuseppe. 1981. "The jettatura and the evil eye." Pp. 130–42 in Alan Dundes (ed.), *The evil eye: A folklore casebook.* Garland Folklore Casebooks, 2. New York and London: Garland.

Pitz, Walter J., and Frank W. Sosulski. 1979. "Determination of vicine and convicine in fababean cultivars by gas-liquid chromatography." *Journal, Canadian Institute of Food Science and Technology* 12: 93–97.

Pitz, Walter, Frank W. Sosulski, and Gordon G. Rowland. 1981. "Effect of genotype and environment on vicine and convicine levels in fababeans (*Vicia faba minor*)." *Journal of the Science of Food and Agriculture* 32: 1–8.

Plato. 1935–37. *The republic.* 2 vols. Trans. Paul Shorey. Loeb Classical Library. Cambridge, Mass.: Harvard University Press; London: William Heinemann.

Plato. 1968. *Laws.* 2 vols. Trans. R. G. Bury. Loeb Classical Library. Cambridge, Mass.: Harvard University Press.; London: William Heinemann.

Plato, C. C., D. L. Rucknagel, and H. Gershowitz. 1964. "Studies in the distribution of glucose-6-phosphate dehydrogenase deficiency, thalassemia, and other genetic traits in the coastal and mountain villages of Cyprus." *American Journal of Human Genetics* 16: 267–83.

Pliny. 1938–62. *Natural history.* 10 vols. Trans. H. Rackham et al. Loeb Classical Library. London: William Heinemann; Cambridge, Mass.: Harvard University Press.

Ploss, Hermann Heinrich. 1899. *Das Weib in der Natur- und Völkerkunde.* 2 vols. Leipzig: Th. Grieben's Verlag.

Plutarch. 1914a. *Aristides*. Trans. Bernadotte Perrin. Pp. 209–99 in Vol. 2 of *Plutarch's Lives*. Loeb Classical Library. London: William Heinemann; Cambridge, Mass.: Harvard University Press.

Plutarch. 1914b. *Romulus*. Trans. Bernadotte Perrin. Pp. 90–187 in Vol. 1 of *Plutarch's Lives*. Loeb Classical Library. London: William Heinemann; Cambridge, Mass.: Harvard University Press.

Plutarch. 1927. *How the young man should study poetry*. Trans. Frank Cole Babbitt. Pp. 71–197 in Vol. 1 of *Plutarch's Moralia*. Loeb Classical Library. London: William Heinemann; Cambridge, Mass.: Harvard University Press.

Plutarch. 1936. *Isis and Osiris*. Trans. Frank Cole Babbitt. Pp. 1–191 in Vol. 5 of *Plutarch's Moralia*. Loeb Classical Library. London: William Heinemann; Cambridge, Mass.: Harvard University Press.

Plutarch. 1957a. *The Roman questions*. Trans. F. C. Babbitt. Pp. 1–171 in Vol. 4 of *Plutarch's Moralia*. Loeb Classical Library. London: William Heinemann; Cambridge, Mass.: Harvard University Press.

Plutarch. 1957b. *Whether land or sea animals are cleverer*. Trans. Harold Cherniss and William C. Helmbold. Pp. 309–479 in Vol. 12 of *Plutarch's Moralia*. Loeb Classical Library. London: William Heinemann; Cambridge, Mass.: Harvard University Press.

Plutarch. 1959. *On love of wealth*. Trans. Phillip H. De Lacy and Benedict Einarson. Pp. 1–39 in Vol. 7 of *Plutarch's Moralia*. Loeb Classical Library. London: William Heinemann; Cambridge: Harvard University Press.

Plutarch. 1961–69. *Table-talk*. Trans. Paul A. Clement, H. B. Hoffleit, E. L. Minar, Jr., F. H. Sandbach, and W. C. Helmbold. Vols. 8 and 9 of *Plutarch's Moralia*. Loeb Classical Library. London: William Heinemann; Cambridge, Mass.: Harvard University Press.

Pollard, John. 1965. *Seers, shrines and sirens: The Greek religious revolution of the sixth century B.C.* South Brunswick and New York: A. S. Barnes and Company.

Polyaenus. 1974. *Stratagems of war*. Trans. R. Shepherd. Chicago: Ares Publishers.

Pool, Robert. 1987. "Hot and cold as an explanatory model: The example of Bharuch District in Gujarat, India." *Social Science and Medicine* 25: 389–99.

Porphyry. 1965. *On abstinence from animal food*. Trans. Thomas Taylor. New York: Barnes and Noble.

Porphyry. 1969. *The cave of the nymphs in the "Odyssey."* A revised text with translation. Arethusa Monographs, 1. Buffalo: Department of Classics, State University of New York.

Porphyry. 1982. *Life of Pythagoras*. Pp. 36–66 in Édouard des Places (trans.), *Porphyre: Vie de Pythagore. Lettre à Marcella*. Paris: Société d'Édition 'Les Belle Lettres.'

Porta, John Baptista. 1658. *Natural magick*. London: Thomas Young and Samuel Speed.

Possehl, Gregory L. (ed.). 1979. *Ancient cities of the Indus*. Durham, N.C.: Carolina Academic Press.

Post, George E. 1932–33. *Flora of Syria, Palestine and Sinai*. 2d ed. 2 vols. Rev. and enl. by John Edward Dinsmore. Beirut: Amiercan Press.

Powell, Claire. 1979. *The meaning of flowers: A garland of plant lore and symbolism from popular custom and literature*. Boulder, Colo.: Shambhala.

Powell, Harold Clark. 1930. *The culture of the orange and allied fruits*. South African Agricultural Series, 8. Johannesburg: Central News Agency.

Prakash, Om. 1961. *Food and drinks in ancient India*. Delhi: Munshi Ram Manohar Lal.

Prashar, R., A. Kumar, S. Banerjee, and A. R. Rao. 1994. "Chemopreventive action by an extract from *Ocimum sanctum* on mouse skin papillomagenesis and its enhancement of skin glutathione s-transferase activity and acid soluble sulfydryl level." *Anti-Cancer Drugs* 5: 567–72.

Pruthi, J. S. 1976. *Spices and condiments*. New Delhi: National Book Trust, India.

Quicherat, Jules. 1841–49. *Procès de condamnation et de réhabilitation de Jeanne d'Arc*. 5 vols. Paris: Jules Renouard.

Rabino Massa, E. 1997. "La malaria nell'antico Egitto." Abstract of a paper presented at the session "Antropologia Contemporanea," XII Congresso della Associazióne Antropológica Italiana, Palermo–Alia, September 16–20.

Radhakrishnan, Sarvepalli, and Charles A. Moore. 1957. *A source book in Indian philosophy*. Princeton: Princeton University Press.

Ragab, A. H., O. S. El-Alfi, and M. A. Abboud. 1966. "Incidence of glucose-6-phosphate dehydrogenase deficiency in Egypt." *American Journal of Human Genetics* 18: 21–25.

Ragozin, Zénaïde. 1902. *Vedic India*. New York: G. P. Putnam's Sons; London: T. Fisher Unwin.

Rahner, Hugo. 1955. "The Christian mystery and the pagan mysteries." Pp. 337–401 in Joseph Campbell (ed.), *The mysteries*. Papers from the Eranos Yearbooks. Bollingen Series, 30, 2. New York: Bollingen Foundation.

Rahner, Hugo. 1963. *Greek myths and Christian mystery*. New York and Evanston: Harper and Row.

Rai, Yash. 1992. *Holy basil: Tulsi (a herb). A unique medicinal plant*. Trans. K. K. Sata. Ahmedabad and Bombay: Gala Publishers.

Ramban (Nachmanides). 1971. *Commentary on the Torah: Genesis*. Trans. Charles B. Chavel. New York: Shilo Publishing House.

Randolph, Charles Brewster. 1905. "The mandragora of the ancients in folk-lore and medicine." *Proceedings of the American Academy of Arts and Sciences* 40: 487–537.

Rao, M. S. A. 1986. "Conservatism and change in food habits among the migrants in India: A study in gastrodynamics." Pp. 121–40 in R. S. Khare and M. S. A.

Rao (eds.), *Food, society, and culture*. Durham, N.C.: Carolina Academic Press.

Rao, S. L. N., K. Malathi, and P. S. Sarma. 1969. "Lathyrism." *World Review of Nutrition and Dietetics* 10: 214–38.

Rao, T. A. Gopinatha. 1985. *Elements of Hindu iconography*. 2 vols. in 4. Delhi: Motilal Banarsidass.

Ravenstein, E. G. (trans. and ed.). 1898. *A journal of the first voyage of Vasco da Gama. 1497–1499*. Hakluyt Society Works, 99. London: Hakluyt Society.

Ray, Joges-Chandra. 1933. "I. Food and drink in ancient India." *Man in India* 13: 217–39.

Ray, Joges-Chandra. 1934. "II. Food and drink in ancient India." *Man in India* 14: 15–35.

Ray, Joges-Chandra. 1939. "The soma plant." *Indian Historical Quarterly* 15: 197–207.

Ray, Sudhansu Kumar. 1961. *The ritual art of the Bratas of Bengal*. Calcutta: Firma K. L. Mukhopadhyay.

Reeves, P. D. (ed.). 1971. *Sleeman in Oudh: An abridgement of W. H. Sleeman's A Journey through the Kingdom of Oudh in 1849–50*. Cambridge: Cambridge University Press.

Reghunandanan, R., S. Sood, V. Reghunandanan, R. M. Mehta, and G. P. Singh. 1995. "The effect of *Ocimum sanctum* Linn (tulsi) extract on testicular function." *Indian Journal of Medical Sciences* 49, 4 (April): 83–87.

Reinach, Salomon. 1942. *Orpheus, a history of religions*. Rev. and enl. ed. Trans. Florence Simmonds. New York: Liveright Publishing Corp.

Reiner, Erica. 1956. "Lipšur litanies." *Journal of Near Eastern Studies* 15: 129–49.

Reitzenstein, Richard. 1978. *Hellenistic mystery-religions: Their basic ideas and significance*. Trans. John E. Steely. Pittsburgh: Pickwick Press.

Renfrew, Jane M. 1973. *Palaeoethnobotany: The prehistoric food plants of the Near East and Europe*. London: Methuen.

Renga, G., P. Nocerino, and A. Vitale. 1968. "Frequenza del deficit enzimatico di glucosio-6-fosfato deidrogenasi in gruppi di popolazioni della Campania." *Igiene Moderna* 61: 222–34.

Resch, K. L., and E. Ernst. 1995. ["Garlic (*Allium sativum*)—a potent medical plant"]. *Fortschritte der Medizin* 113: 311–15. (Original article in German).

Rheede, tot Drakestein, Hendrik van. 1673–1703. *Hortus Indicus Malabaricus*. 12 vols. Amsterdam: Sumptibus J. van Someren and J. van Dyck.

Rhind, William. [1840]. *A history of the vegetable kingdom*. London: Blackie and Son.

Rice, B. Lewis. 1897. *Mysore: A gazetteer compiled for government*. Rev. ed. 2 vols. Westminster: Archibald Constable.

Richardson, John. 1984. *Dictionary, Persian, Arabic and English*. New ed. Ed. Francis Johnson. Lahore: Sang-e-Meel Publications.

Rickards, O., G. Biondi, G. F. De Stefano, and G. Battistuzzi. 1988. "Distribution of genetically determined deficient variants of glucose-6-phosphate dehydrogenase (G6PD) in southern Italy." Pp. 570–73 in W. R. Mayr (ed.), *Advances in forensic haemogenetics 2.* 12th Congress of the Society for Forensic Haemogenetics, Vienna, August 26–29, 1987. Berlin, Heidelberg, New York, London, Paris, Tokyo: Springer-Verlag.

Ridley, Henry N. 1922–25. *The flora of the Malay Peninsula.* 5 vols. London: L. Reeve.

Riepl, R. L., J. Schreiner, B. Müller, S. Hildemann, and K. Loeschke. 1993. "'Dicke Bohnen' als Auslöser einer akuten hämolytischen Anämie." *Deutsche Medizinische Wochenschrift* 118: 932–35.

Risley, Herbert Hope. 1891. *The tribes and castes of Bengal.* 2 vols. Calcutta: Bengal Secretariat Press.

Ritter, Edith K. 1965. "Magical-expert (= āšipu), and physician (= asû): Notes on two complementary professions in Babylonian medicine." Pp. 299–321 in Hans G. Güterbock and Thorkild Jacobsen (eds.), *Studies in honor of Benno Landsberger on his seventy-fifth birthday, April 21, 1965.* Oriental Institute of the University of Chicago, Assyriological Studies, 16. Chicago: University of Chicago Press.

Rivett-Carnac, J. H. 1879. "The snake symbol in India, especially in connection with the worship of Śiva." *Journal of the Asiatic Society of Bengal* 48, pt. 1: 17–30.

Rizvi, Najma. 1986. "Food categories in Bangladesh and Its relationship to food beliefs and practices of vulnerable groups." Pp. 223–51 in R. S. Khare and M. S. A. Rao (eds.), *Food, society, and culture.* Durham, N.C.: Carolina Academic Press.

Robbins, Emmet. 1982. "Famous Orpheus." Pp. 3–24 in John Warden (ed.), *Orpheus: The metamorphoses of a myth.* Toronto, Buffalo, London: University of Toronto Press.

Robert, Paul. 1953–64. *Dictionnaire alphabétique et analogique de la langue française.* 6 vols. Paris: Société du Nouveau Littré.

Robert-Tornow, Walter Heinrich. 1893. *De apium mellisque apud veteres significatione et symbolica et mythologica.* Berlin: Weidmann.

Rohde, Erwin. 1925. *Psyche: The cult of souls and belief in immortality among the Greeks.* Trans. W. B. Hillis. London: Routledge and Kegan Paul.

Róheim, Géza. 1981. "The evil eye." Pp. 211–22 in Alan Dundes (ed.), *The evil eye: A folklore casebook.* Garland Folklore Casebooks, 2. New York and London: Garland.

Roscher, Wilhelm H. 1890. *Über Selene und Verwandtes.* Leipzig: B. G. Teubner.

Rose, H. J. 1908–26. "Divination (Greek)." Pp. 796–99 in Vol. 4 of *Encyclopaedia of religion and ethics.* 13 vols. Ed. James Hastings. Edinburgh: T. and T. Clark.

Rose, H. J. 1941. "Manes exite paterni." *University of California Publications in Classical Philology* 12, 6: 89–94.

Rose, H. J. 1943. "Review of *The Arts of Orpheus* by Ivan M. Linforth." *Classical Review* 57: 33–34.

Rosin, Susanna, Hely Tuorila, and Antti Uutela. 1992. "Garlic: A sensory pleasure or a social nuisance?" *Appetite: Journal for Intake Research* 19: 133–43.

Rosner, Victor. 1955. "The battle of spurs." *March of India* 8, 1 (November): 25–27.

Ross, Floyd Hiatt. 1965. *Shinto: The way of Japan.* Boston: Beacon Press.

Roth, Eugene F., Jr., and Seymour Schulman. 1989. "The parasite derived glucose-6-phosphate dehydrogenase of *P. falciparum:* What is its role?" Pp. 83–93 in John W. Eaton, Steven R. Meshnick, and George J. Brewer (eds.), *Malaria and the red cell-2.* New York: Alan R. Liss.

Roth, Eugene F., Jr., Carmen Raventos-Suarez, Antioniettina Rinaldi, and Ronald L. Nagel. 1983. "Glucose-6-phosphate dehydrogenase deficiency inhibits in vitro growth of *Plasmodium falciparum.*" *Proceedings of the National Academy of Sciences of the United States of America* 80: 298–99.

Rousselet, Louis. 1878. *India and its native princes.* London: Bickers and Son.

Rousselet, Louis. 1975. *India and its native princes: Travels in Central India and in the presidencies of Bombay and Bengal.* New ed. Rev. and ed. by Lieut.-Col. Buckle. Delhi: B. R. Publishing Corporation.

Roxburgh, William. 1971. *Flora Indica; or descriptions of Indian plants.* New Delhi: Today and Tomorrow's Printers and Publishers.

Roy, Pratap Chandra (trans.). 1919–30. *The Mahabharata of Krishna-Dwaipayana Vyasa.* 11 vols. Calcutta: Datta Bose and Co.

Roy, Shibani. 1983. *Koli culture.* New Delhi: Cosmo Publications.

Roy, Susanta K. 1985. "Bael." Pp. 498–504 in T. K. Bose (ed.), *Fruits of India, tropical and subtropical.* Calcutta: Naya Prokash.

Rozin, Paul. 1982. "Human food selection: The interaction of biology, culture and individual experience." Pp. 225–54 in Lewis M. Barker (ed.), *The psychobiology of human food selection.* Westport, Conn.: AVI.

Rozin, Paul. 1984. "The acquisition of food habits and preferences." Pp. 590–607 in Joseph D. Matarazzo, S. M. Weiss, J. A. Herd, N. E. Miller, and S. M. Weiss (eds.), *Behavioral health: A handbook of health enhancement and disease prevention.* New York: John Wiley.

Rozin, Paul. 1988a. "Cultural approaches to human food preferences." Pp. 137–53 in John E. Morley, M. Barry Sterman, and John H. Walsh (eds.), *Nutritional modulation of neural function.* San Diego: Academic Press.

Rozin, Paul. 1988b. "Social learning about food by humans." Pp. 165–87 in Thomas R. Zentall and Bennett G. Galef, Jr. (eds.), *Social learning: Psychological and biological perspectives.* Hillsdale, N.J., Hove, and London: Lawrence Erlbaum Associates.

Rozin, Paul. 1990. "Getting to like the burn of chili pepper: Biological, psychological, and cultural perspectives." Pp. 231–69 in Barry G. Green, J. Russell Mason, and Morley R. Kare (eds.), *Chemical senses*. Vol. 2: *Irritation*. New York and Basel: Marcel Dekker.

Rozin, Paul, and April E. Fallon. 1987. "A perspective on disgust." *Psychological Review* 94: 23–41.

Rozin, Paul, and Carol Nemeroff. 1990. "The laws of sympathetic magic: A psychological analysis of similarity and contagion." Pp. 205–32 in James W. Stigler, Richard A. Shweder, and Gilbert Herdt (eds.), *Cultural psychology: Essays on comparative human development*. Cambridge: Cambridge University Press.

Rozin, Paul, and Deborah Schiller. 1980. "The nature and acquisition of a preference for chili pepper by humans." *Motivation and Emotion* 4: 77–101.

Rozin, Paul, and T. A. Vollmecke. 1986. "Food likes and dislikes." *Annual Review of Nutrition* 6: 433–56.

Rozin, Paul, Jonathan Haidt, and Clark R. McCauley. 1993. "Disgust." Pp. 575–94 in Michael Lewis and Jeannette M. Haviland (eds.), *Handbook of emotions*. New York and London: Guilford Press.

Rozin, Paul, Lori Ebert, and Jonathan Schull. 1982. "Some like it hot: A temporal analysis of hedonic responses to chili pepper." *Appetite: Journal for Intake Research* 3: 13–22.

Rozin, Paul, Maureen Markwith, and Caryn Stoess. 1997. "Moralization and becoming a vegetarian: The transformation of preferences into values and the recruitment of disgust." *Psychological Science* 8: 67–73.

Rubin, Stanley. 1974. *Medieval English medicine*. Newton Abbot, London, Vancouver: David and Charles; New York: Barnes and Noble.

Russ, Jennifer M. 1982. *German festivals and customs*. London: Oswald Wolff.

Russell, Paul F. 1955. *Man's mastery of malaria*. London, New York, Toronto: Oxford University Press.

Russell, Paul F., Luther S. West, Reginald D. Manwell, and George MacDonald. 1963. *Practical malariology*. London, New York, Toronto: Oxford University Press.

Russell, R. V. 1908–26. "Central provinces." Pp. 311–16 in Vol. 3 of *Encyclopaedia of religion and ethics*. 13 vols. Ed. James Hastings. Edinburgh: T. and T. Clark.

Russell, R. V., and Hira Lal. 1916. *The tribes and castes of the central provinces of India*. 4 vols. London: Macmillan.

Russell, W. M. S. 1980. "Plutarch as a folklorist." Pp. 371–78 in Venetia Newall (ed.), *Folklore studies in the twentieth century*. Proceedings of the Centenary Conference of the Folklore Society. Woodbridge, Suffolk: D. S. Brewer; Totowa, N.J.: Rowman and Littlefield.

Russell, W. M. S., and Claire Russell. 1983. "Evolutionary and social aspects of disease." *Ecology of Disease* 2: 95–106.

Russo, G. 1967. "II favismo in Sicilia." *Rivista Pediatricia Siciliano* 22: 317–43.

Russo, Guiseppe, Florindo Mollica, Lorenzo Pavone, and Gino Schilirò. 1972. "Hemolytic crises of favism in Sicilian females heterozygous for G-6-PD deficiency." *Pediatrics* 49: 854–59.

Rusten, Jeffrey, I. C. Cunningham, and A. D. Knox. 1993. *Theophrastus, characters. Herodas, mimes. Cercidas and the choliambic poets.* Loeb Classical Library. Cambridge, Mass., and London: Harvard University Press.

"The sacred Bo." 1948. *Time: The Weekly Magazine* 52, 6 (August 9): 49.

Saggs, H. W. F. 1965. *Everyday life in Babylonia and Assyria.* New York: Dorset Press.

Saletore, Rajaram Narayan. 1943. *Life in the Gupta age.* Bombay: Popular Book Depot.

Salvidio, E., I. Pannacciulli, A. Tizianello, G. Gaetani, and G. Paravidino. 1969. "Glucose-6-phosphate dehydrogenase deficiency in Italy." *Acta Haematologica* 41: 331–40.

Sansone, G., A. M. Piga, and G. Segni. 1958. *Il favismo.* Turin: Edizioni Minerva Medica.

Sansone, G., G. Segni, and C. de Cecco. 1958. "II difetto biochimico eritrocitario predisponente all'emolisi favica. Ricerche sulla popolazione liguri e su quella sarda." *Bollettino della Società italiana di Biologia sperimentale* 34: 1558–61.

Sarkar, A., S. C. Lavania, D. N. Pandey, and M. C. Pant. 1994. "Changes in the blood lipid profile after administration of *Ocimum sanctum* (Tulsi) leaves in the normal albino rabbits." *Indian Journal of Physiology and Pharmacology* 38: 311–12.

Sartori, Ernesto. 1971. "On the pathogenesis of favism." *Journal of Medical Genetics* 8: 462–67.

Satyavati, G. V., Ashok K. Gupta, and Neeraj Tandon. 1987. *Medicinal plants of India.* Vol. 2. New Delhi: Indian Council of Medical Research.

Scarborough, John. 1981–82. "Beans, Pythagoras, taboos, and ancient dietetics." *Classical World* 75: 355–58.

Schachter, Jacob, and H. Freedman (trans.). 1987. *Sanhedrin.* Vol. 19 of *The Hebrew-English edition of the Babylonian Talmud.* Ed. Isidore Epstein. New Edition. London: Soncino Press.

Schafer, Edward H. 1954. *The empire of Min.* Rutland, Vt., and Tokyo, Japan: Charles E. Tuttle Company.

Schafer, Edward H. 1977. "T'ang." Pp. 85–140 in K. C. Chang (ed.), *Food in Chinese culture.* New Haven and London: Yale University Press.

Schilirò, G., A. Russo, R. Curreri, S. Marino, A. Sciotto, and G. Russo. 1979. "Glucose-6-phosphate dehydrogenase deficiency in Sicily. Incidence, biochemical characteristics and clinical implications." *Clinical Genetics* 15: 183–88.

Schilling, Robert. 1987a. "Parentalia." Pp. 198–99 in Vol. 11 of *The encyclopedia of religion.* 16 vols. Ed. Mircea Eliade. New York: Macmillan; London: Collier Macmillan.

Schilling, Robert. 1987b. "Roman religion: The early period." Pp. 445–61 in Vol. 12 of *The encyclopedia of religion*. 16 vols. Ed. Mircea Eliade. New York: Macmillan; London: Collier Macmillan.

Schimmel, Annemarie. 1987. "Cats." Pp. 121–23 in Vol. 3 of *The encyclopedia of religion*. 16 vols. Ed. Mircea Eliade. New York: Macmillan; London; Collier Macmillan.

Schlosser, Alfred. 1912. *Die Sage vom Galgenmännlein im Volksglauben und in der Literatur.* Inaugural-Dissertation, Westfälischen Wilhelms-Universität. Münster i. W.: Theissingschen Buchhandlung.

Schmidt, Albert-Marie. 1958. *La Mandragore.* Paris: Flammarion, Éditeur.

Schmitt, Paul. 1955. "The ancient mysteries in the society of their time, their transformation and most recent echoes." Pp. 93–118 in Joseph Campbell (ed.), *The mysteries.* Papers from the Eranos Yearbooks. Bollingen Series, 30, 2. New York: Bollingen Foundation.

Schrader, O. 1908–26. "Aryan religion." Pp. 11–57 in Vol. 2 of *The encyclopaedia of religion and ethics.* 13 vols. Ed. James Hastings. Edinburgh: T. and T. Clark.

Schram, Louis M. J. 1954. *The Monguors of the Kansu-Tibetan frontier: Their origin, history, and social organization.* Transactions of the American Philosophical Society, n. s. 44, pt. 1. Philadelphia: American Philosophical Society.

Schultze-Motel, Jürgen. 1972. "Die archäologischen Reste der Ackerbohne, *Vicia faba* L., und die Genese der Art." *Die Kulturpflanze* 19: 321–58.

Schweinfurth, Georg. 1884. "Neue Funde auf dem Gebiete der Flora des alten Ägyptens." *Botanische Jahrbücher für Systematik, Pflanzengeschichte und Pflanzengeographie* 5: 189–202.

Schwimmer, Erik. 1973. *Exchange in the social structure of the Orokaiva.* New York: St. Martin's Press.

Scullard, H. H. 1981. *Festivals and ceremonies of the Roman Republic.* Ithaca, N.Y.: Cornell University Press.

Sébillot, Paul. 1968. *Le Folk-lore de France.* 4 vols. Paris: Éditions G.-P. Maisonneuve et Larose.

Seeley, J. R. 1881. *Livy,* Book 1. 3d ed. Oxford: Clarendon Press.

Senart, Émile. 1930. *Caste in India: The facts and the system.* London: Methuen.

Sen Gupta, Sankar. 1965a. "Introduction by the editor." Pp. xi–xxvii in his *Tree symbol worship in India.* Calcutta: Indian Publications.

Sen Gupta, Sankar (ed.). 1965b. *Tree symbol worship in India.* Calcutta: Indian Publications.

Sen Gupta, Sankar. 1980. *Sacred trees across cultures and nations.* Indian Publications Folklore Series, 27. Calcutta: Indian Publications.

Sermini, Gentile. 1911. *Novelle.* 3 vols. Lanciano: R. Carabba.

Sextus Empiricus. 1933. *Outlines of Pyrrhonism.* Vol. 1 of *Sextus Empiricus.* Trans.

R. G. Bury. Loeb Classical Library. London: William Heinemann; Cambridge, Mass.: Harvard University Press.

Seyffert, Oskar. 1895. *A dictionary of classical antiquities, mythology, religion, literature and art*. Rev. and ed. by Henry Nettleship and J. E. Sandys. London: William Glaisher.

Sharma, K. N. 1961. "Hindu sects and food patterns in North India." Pp. 45–58 in L. P. Vidyarthi (ed.), *Aspects of religion in Indian society*. Meerut: Kedar Nath Ram Nath.

Sharma, P. V. 1973. "On the word 'tulasī.'" *Annals of the Bhandarkar Oriental Research Institute* 54: 232–33.

Sharma, Priyavrat (trans. and ed.). 1981. *Caraka-Saṃhitā*, Vol. 1. Agniveśa's treatise refined and annotated by Caraka and redacted by Dṛḍhabala. Jaikrishnadas Ayurveda Series, 36. Varanasi, Delhi: Chaukhambha Orientalia.

Sharpe, William D. 1964. *Isidore of Seville: The medical writings*. Transactions of the American Philosophical Society, n. s. 54, pt. 2. Philadelphia: American Philosophical Society.

Shastri, Hari Prasad (trans.). 1957–62. *The Ramayana of Valmiki*. 3 vols. London: Shanti Sadan.

Shea, David, and Anthony Troyer (trans.). 1843. *The Dabistán, or School of manners*. 3 vols. Paris: Oriental Translation Fund of Great Britain and Ireland.

Shea, David, and Anthony Troyer (trans.). 1901. *The Dabistán, or School of manners*. Abridged ed. Washington, D.C., and London: M. Walter Dunne.

Sheba, Chaim. 1963. "Environmental vs. ethnic factors determining the frequency of G6PD deficiency." Pp. 100–106 in Elisabeth Goldschmidt (ed.), *The genetics of migrant and isolate populations*. Baltimore: Williams and Wilkins Company.

Sheba, Chaim. 1971. "Jewish migration in its historical perspective." *Israel Journal of Medical Sciences* 7: 1333–41.

Sheriff, Mohideen. 1869. *Supplement to the pharmacopoeia of India; or, A catalogue of Indian synonymes of the medicinal plants, products, inorganic and organic substances included in that work* . . . Madras: H. Morgan.

Shipley, Graham. 1987. *A history of Samos—800–188 B.C.* Oxford: Clarendon Press.

Shourie, K. L. 1945. "An outbreak of lathyrism in Central India." *Indian Journal of Medical Research* 33: 239–47.

Sibthorp, John. 1806–13. *Florae Graecae prodromus*. 2 vols. London: Richard Taylor.

Sices, David, and James B. Atkinson (eds. and trans.). 1985. *The comedies of Machiavelli: The Woman from Andros. The Mandrake. Clizia*. Hanover, N. H., and London: University Press of New England.

Siegel, Ronald K. 1979. "Ginseng abuse syndrome: Problems with the panacea." *Journal of the American Medical Association* 241: 1614–15.

Silius Italicus. 1927–34. *Punica.* 2 vols. Trans. J. D. Duff. Loeb Classical Library. London; William Heinemann; Cambridge, Mass.: Harvard University Press.

Simon, Maurice (trans.). 1984. *Berakoth.* Vol. 1 of *The Hebrew-English edition of the Babylonian Talmud.* Ed. Isidore Epstein. London: Soncino Press.

Simoons, Frederick J. 1954. "The non-milking area of Africa." *Anthropos* 49: 58–66.

Simoons, Frederick J. 1960. *Northwest Ethiopia: Peoples and economy.* Madison: University of Wisconsin Press.

Simoons, Frederick J. 1970. "The traditional limits of milking and milk use in southern Asia." *Anthropos* 65: 547–93.

Simoons, Frederick J. 1974. "The purificatory role of 'the five products of the cow' in Hinduism." *Ecology of Food and Nutrition* 3: 21–34.

Simoons, Frederick J. 1991. *Food in China: A cultural and historical inquiry.* Boca Raton, Ann Arbor, Boston: CRC Press.

Simoons, Frederick J. 1994. *Eat not this flesh: Food avoidances from prehistory to the present.* Rev. ed. Madison: University of Wisconsin Press.

Simoons, Frederick J., and Deryck O. Lodrick. 1981. "Background to understanding the cattle situation of India: The sacred cow concept in Hindu religion and folk culture." *Zeitschrift für Ethnologie* 106: 121–37.

Sinclair, W. F. 1875. "Notes on the central tâlukâs of the Ṭhâṇâ Collectorate." *Indian Antiquary* 4: 65–69.

Singer, Charles. 1975. "Greek biology and its relation to the rise of modern biology." Pp. 1–101 in Vol. 2 of Charles Singer (ed.), *Studies in the history and method of science.* New York: Arno Press. 2 vols.

Singh, Indrajit. 1944. *The Gondwana and the Gonds.* Lucknow: Universal Publishers.

Singh, Kunjabihari. 1965. "The vestiges of tree-cult among the Meiteis." Pp. 86–88 in Sankar Sen Gupta (ed.), *Tree symbol worship in India.* Calcutta: Indian Publications.

Singh, Madan Mohan. 1967. *Life in north-eastern India in pre-Mauryan times.* Delhi, Varanasi, Patna: Motilal Banarsidass.

Singh, S., D. K. Majumdar, and H. M. Rehan. 1996. "Evaluation of anti-inflammatory potential of fixed oil of *Ocimum sanctum* (Holybasil) and its possible mechanism of action." *Journal of Ethnopharmacology* 54: 19–26.

Sinha, Binod Chandra. 1979. *Tree worship in ancient India.* New Delhi: Books Today.

Sinha, Surajit. 1966. "Vaiṣṇava influence on a tribal culture." Pp. 64–89 in Milton Singer (ed.), *Krishna: Myths, rites, and attitudes.* Honolulu: East-West Center Press.

Siniscalco, M., L. Bernini, B. Latte, and A. G. Motulsky. 1961. "Favism and thalassaemia in Sardinia and their relationship to malaria." *Nature* 190: 1179–80.

Siniscalco, M., L. Bernini, G. Filippi, B. Latte, P. Meera Khan, S. Piomelli, and M. Rattazzi. 1966. "Population genetics of haemoglobin variants, thalassaemia and glucose-6-phosphate dehydrogenase deficiency, with particular reference to the malaria hypothesis." *Bulletin of the World Health Organization* 34: 379–93.

Sirks, M. J. 1931. "Beiträge zu einer Genotypischen Analyse der Ackerbohne *Vicia faba*." *Genetica* 13: 209–631.

Sisini, A., A. Spanu, and P. Arese. 1981. "Miglioramento genetico in *Vicia faba* e favismo—I. Distribuzione e livelli di metaboliti presumibilmente emolitici." *Bollettino della Società italiana di Biologia sperimentale* 57: 1496–1502.

Sivarajan, V. V., and Indira Balachandran. 1994. *Ayurvedic drugs and their plant sources*. New Delhi, Bombay, Calcutta, Oxford: Oxford and IBH Publishing Company.

Skinner, Charles M. 1911. *Myths and legends of flowers, trees, fruits, and plants, in all ages and in all climes*. Philadelphia and London: J. B. Lippincott.

Sleeman, William H. 1973. *Rambles and recollections of an Indian official*. Rev. annotated ed. Ed. Vincent A. Smith. Karachi, London, New York, Delhi: Oxford University Press.

Smartt, J. 1976. *Tropical pulses*. London: Longman.

Smith, F. Porter. 1969. *Chinese materia medica*. 2d rev. ed. Ed. Ph. Daven Wei. Taipei: Ku T'ing Book House.

Smith, H. Daniel, and M. Narasimha Chary. 1991. *Handbook of Hindu gods, goddesses and saints*. Delhi: Sundeep Prakashan.

Smith, Kirby Flower. 1908–26. "Hecate's suppers." Pp. 565–67 in Vol. 6 of *Encyclopaedia of religion and ethics*. 13 vols. Ed. James Hastings. Edinburgh: T. and T. Clark.

Smith, Sir William. 1896. *A dictionary of the Bible*. Hartford, Conn.: S. S. Scranton.

Smith, William Robertson, and Owen Charles Whitehouse. 1910–11. "Priest." Pp. 316–22 in Vol. 22 of *The Encyclopaedia Britannica*. 11th ed. 29 vols. New York: Encyclopaedia Britannica.

Sokolov, Raymond. 1975. "A plant of ill repute." *Natural History* 84, 2 (February): 70–71.

Soler, Jean. 1979. "The dietary prohibitions of the Hebrews." *New York Review of Books* 26, 10 (June 14): 24–30. Trans. R. Forster from "Sémiotique de la nourriture dans la Bible." *Annales: Économies, sociétés, civilisations* 28 (1973): 943–55. (Also published as "The semiotics of food in the Bible," pp. 126–38 in R. Forster and O. Ranum (eds.) *Food and drink in history*. Baltimore and London: Johns Hopkins University Press, 1979).

"Some notes about mandrakes." 1891. *Chambers's Journal of Popular Literature* 68: 59–61.

Sontheimer, Joseph von (trans.). 1840–42. *Grosse Zusammenstellung über Kräfte der bekannten einfachen Heil- und Nahrungsmittel, von Abu Mohammed Abdallah ben Ahmed aus Malaga bekannt unter dem namen Ebn Baithar.* 2 vols. Stuttgart: Hallberger'sche Verlagshandlung.

Sopher, David E. 1964. "Indigenous uses of turmeric (*Curcuma domestica*) in Asia and Oceania." *Anthropos* 59: 93–127.

Sowerby, Arthur de C. 1940. *Nature in Chinese art.* New York: John Day.

Spence, Lewis. 1945. *The magic arts of Celtic Britain.* London: Rider and Company.

Squire, Charles. 1905. *The mythology of the British islands.* New York: Charles Scribner's Sons; London: Blackie and Son.

Srinivas, M. N. 1952. *Religion and society among the Coorgs of South India.* Oxford: Clarendon Press.

Srinivas, M. N. 1956. "Sanskritisation and Westernisation." Pp. 73–115 in A. Aiyappan and L. K. Bala Ratnam (eds.), *Society in India.* Madras: Social Sciences Association.

Srinivas, M. N. 1961. "Sociological aspects of Indian diet." *Agricultural Situation in India* 16: 246–48.

Srinivasan, Doris. 1975–76. "The so-called Proto-Śiva seal from Mohenjo-Daro: An iconological assessment." *Archives of Asian Art* 29: 47–58.

Srinivasan, Doris. 1984. "Unhinging Śiva from the Indus civilization." *Journal of the Royal Asiatic Society,* pt. 1: 77–89.

Stadler, Hermann. 1924. "Lauch (Allium)." Cols. 986–91 in Vol. 12, pt. 1, of August Friedrich von Pauly and Georg Wissowa (eds.), *Paulys Realencyclopädie der classischen Altertumswissenschaft.* Neue Bearbeitung. Stuttgart: J. B. Metzlersche Verlagsbuchhandlung.

Stamatoyannopoulos, G., and Ph. Fessas. 1964. "Thalassaemia, glucose-6-phosphate dehydrogenase deficiency, sickling, and malarial endemicity in Greece: A study of five areas." *British Medical Journal* 1: 875–79.

Stamatoyannopoulos, G., A. Panayotopoulos, and A. G. Motulsky. 1966. "The distribution of glucose-6-phosphate dehydrogenase deficiency in Greece." *American Journal of Human Genetics* 18: 296–308.

Starck, Adolf Taylor. 1917. *Der Alraun: Ein Beitrag zur Pflanzensagenkunde.* Baltimore: J. H. Furst.

Starr, Frederick. 1901. "Notes upon the mandrake." *American Antiquarian and Oriental Journal* 23: 258–68.

"The state religion of China." 1831–35. *Chinese Repository* 3: 49–53.

Statius. 1928–34. *Thebaid.* Pp. 339–571 in Vol. 1 and pp. 1–505 in Vol. 2 of *Statius.* 2 vols. Trans. J. H. Mozley. Loeb Classical Library. London: William Heinemann; Cambridge, Mass.: Harvard University Press.

Stavroulakis, Nicholas. 1986. *Cookbook of the Jews of Greece.* Athens: Lycabettus Press.

Steier, August. 1928. "Mandragoras." Cols. 1028–37 in Vol. 14, pt. 1, of *Paulys*

Realencyclopädie der classischen Altertumswissenschaft. New revision begun by Georg Wissowa. Stuttgart: Alfred Druckenmuller.

Stein, M. A. (trans.). 1900. *Kalhaṇa's Rājataraṅginī: A chronicle of the kings of Kashmir.* 2 vols. London: A. Constable.

Stevenson, H. N. C. 1954. "Status evaluation in the Hindu caste system." *Journal of the Royal Anthropological Institute of Great Britain and Ireland* 84: 45–65.

Stevenson, Margaret (Mrs. Sinclair). 1915. *The heart of Jainism.* London: Oxford University Press.

Stevenson, Margaret (Mrs. Sinclair). 1920. *The rites of the twice-born.* London: Oxford University Press.

Storniello, A. 1893–94. "Gli oracoli delle zitelle." *Rivista delle Tradizioni popolari italiane* 1: 865–66.

Strabo. 1960–69. *The geography of Strabo.* 8 vols. Trans. Horace Leonard Jones. London: W. Heinemann; Cambridge, Mass.: Harvard University Press.

Stuart, G. A. 1911. *Chinese materia medica: Vegetable kingdom.* Shanghai: American Presbyterian Mission Press.

Stutley, Margaret. 1985. *The illustrated dictionary of Hindu iconography.* London: Routledge and Kegan Paul.

Stutley, Margaret, and James Stutley. 1977. *Harper's dictionary of Hinduism: Its mythology, folklore, philosophy, literature, and history.* New York, Hagerstown, San Francisco, and London: Harper and Row.

Sullivan, H. P. 1964. "A re-examination of the religion of the Indus Civilization." *History of Religions* 4: 114–25.

Sundararaj, D. Daniel, and Girija Balasubramanyam. 1986. *Guide to the economic plants of South India.* Delhi: Periodical Expert Book Agency.

Swingle, Walter T., and Philip C. Reece. 1967. "The botany of Citrus and its wild relatives." Pp. 190–430 in Vol. 1 of Walter Reuther, Herbert John Webber, and Leon Dexter Batchelor (eds.), *The citrus industry.* Rev. ed. Berkeley: Division of Agricultural Sciences, University of California.

Symon, David E. 1991. "Gondwanan elements of the Solanaceae." Pp. 139–50 in J. G. Hawkes, R. N. Lester, M. Nee, and N. Estrada (eds.), *Solanaceae III: Taxonomy. Chemistry. Evolution.* Kew: The Royal Botanic Gardens.

Symons, Van Jay. 1981. *Ch'ing ginseng management: Ch'ing monopolies in microcosm.* Occasional Paper No. 13. Tempe: Center for Asian Studies, Arizona State University.

Szeinberg, Aryeh. 1963. "G6PD deficiency among Jews—Genetic and anthropological considerations." Pp. 69–72 in Elisabeth Goldschmidt (ed.), *The genetics of migrant and isolate populations.* Baltimore: Williams and Wilkins Company.

Szeinberg, Aryeh, and Chaim Sheba. 1958. "Hemolytic trait in oriental Jews connected with an hereditary enzymatic abnormality of erythrocytes." *Israel Medical Journal* 17: 158–68.

Szeinberg, Aryeh, Chaim Sheba, Nina Hirshorn, and Eva Bodonyi. 1957. "Studies on erythrocytes in cases with past history of favism and drug-induced acute hemolytic anemia." *Blood* 12: 603–13.

Tachard, Guy. 1981. *A relation of the voyage to Siam, performed by six Jesuits sent by the French king, to the Indies and China in the year 1685.* Bangkok: White Orchid Press.

Tacitus. 1889. *A treatise on the situation, manners, and inhabitants of Germany.* Pp. 286–342 in Vol. 2 of *The works of Tacitus.* Oxford trans. London: George Bell and Sons.

Täckholm, Vivi, and Mohammed Drar. 1973. *Flora of Egypt.* 3 vols. Koenigstein–Ts./B.R.D.: Otto Koeltz Antiquariat.

Tagare, G. V. (trans.). 1987–88. *The Vāyu Purāṇa.* Ancient Indian Tradition and Mythology, 37–38. 2 vols. Delhi: Motilal Banarsidass; Paris: UNESCO.

Tagarelli, Antonio. 1997. "La malaria nella storia antica." Pp. 77–79 in Antonio Tagarelli (ed.), *La malaria in Calabria.* Mangone (Cosenza): Comitato per gli Studi Storici e Scientifici della Malaria in Calabria.

Tagarelli, Antonio, and Carlo Brancati. N. d. *G6PD deficiency on the Calabrian population and on the Albanian ethnic minority of northern Calabria: Relationship with orographic features.* Cosenza, Italy: Istituto di Medicina sperimentale e Biotecnologie–CNR.

Tagarelli, Antonio, Anna Piro, and Giuseppe Tagarelli. 1997a. "Favismo e malaria in provincia di Cosenza." Pp. 205–7 in Antonio Tagarelli (ed.), *La malaria in Calabria.* Mangone (Cosenza): Comitato per gli Studi Storici e Scientifici della Malaria in Calabria.

Tagarelli, Antonio, Anna Piro, and Giuseppe Tagarelli. 1997b. "Talassemia e malaria." Pp. 201–3 in Antonio Tagarelli (ed.), *La malaria in Calabria.* Mangone (Cosenza): Comitato per gli Studi Storici e Scientifici della Malaria in Calabria.

Tagarelli, Antonio, R. Cittadella, M. Bria, and Carlo Brancati. 1992. "Glucose-6-phosphate dehydrogenase (G6PD) deficiency in the Albanian ethnic minority of Cosenza Province, Italy." *Gene Geography* 6: 71–78.

Tagarelli, Antonio, D. Civitelli, R. Cittadella, L. Bastone, and C. Brancati. 1995. "A social-demographic, isonymic and genetic investigation on an isolated Calabrian village." *International Journal of Anthropology* 10: 249–57.

Tagarelli, Antonio, L. Bastone, R. Cittadella, V. Calabrò, M. Bria, and C. Brancati. 1991. "Glucose-6-phosphate dehydrogenase (G6PD) deficiency in southern Italy: A study on the population of the Cosenza Province." *Gene Geography* 5: 141–50.

Tagarelli, Antonio, R. Mazzei, A. Bagalà, L. Bastone, A. Qualtieri, and C. Brancati. 1991. "Genetic polymorphism at the phosphoglucomutase 1 (PGM1) locus in Cosenza Province (Calabria-southern Italy)." *Gene Geography* 5: 107–12.

Taj-Eldin, Salman. 1971. "Favism in breast-fed infants." *Archives of Disease in Childhood* 46: 121–23.

Takakusu, J. (trans.). 1896. *A record of the Buddhist religion as practised in India and the Malay archipelago (A.D. 671–695), by I-Tsing.* Oxford: Clarendon Press.

Talley, Jeannine E. 1974. "Runes, mandrakes, and gallows." Pp. 157–68 in Gerald James Larson, C. Scott Littleton, and Jaan Puhvel (eds.), *Myth in Indo-European antiquity.* Berkeley, Los Angeles, London: University of California Press.

Taran, Mikhael. 1975. "Early records of the domestic fowl in ancient Judea." *Ibis* (London) 117: 109–10.

Taylor, Meadows. 1971. "Memorandum on snake worship." Pp. 236–37 in James Fergusson, *Tree and serpent worship: Or illustrations of mythology and art in India in the first and fourth centuries after Christ.* 1st Indian rep. Delhi: Oriental Publishers.

Taylor, Meadows. 1986. *Tara: A Mahratta tale.* New Delhi: Asian Educational Services.

Taylor, Norman. 1965. *Plant drugs that changed the world.* New York: Dodd, Mead.

Telang, Kāshināth Trimbak (trans.). 1882. *The Bhagavadgītā, with the Sanatsugātiya and the Anugītā.* Vol. 8 of *The sacred books of the East.* Ed. F. Max Müller. 2d ed. Oxford: Clarendon Press.

Tennent, James Emerson. 1859. *Ceylon: An account of the island, physical, historical, and topographical.* 5th ed. 2 vols. London: Longman, Green, Longman, and Roberts.

Tertullian. 1947. *On the soul.* Ed. with introduction and commentary by J. H. Waszink. Amsterdam: J. M. Meulenhoff.

Testa, U., T. Meloni, A. Lania, G. Battistuzzi, S. Cutillo, and L. Luzzatto. 1980. "Genetic heterogeneity of glucose 6-phosphate dehydrogenase deficiency in Sardinia." *Human Genetics* 56: 99–105.

Thakur, Upendra, Naseem Akhtar, and Naresh Banerjee (eds.). 1981. *Glories of Gaya: Glimpses of history and archaeology.* Bodh Gaya: Magadh University.

Theal, George McCall. 1886. *Kaffir folk-lore.* 2d ed. London: Swan Sonnenschein, Le Bas and Lowry.

Theophrastus. 1916. *Enquiry into plants.* Trans. Arthur Hort as *Enquiry into plants and other minor works on odours and weather signs.* 2 vols. Loeb Classical Library. London: William Heinemann; Cambridge, Mass.: Harvard University Press.

Theophrastus. 1929. *The characters.* Trans. J. M. Edmonds. London: William Heinemann; Cambridge, Mass.: Harvard University Press.

Theophrastus. 1990. *Causes of plants.* Books 5 and 6. Trans. and ed. Benedict Einarson and George K. K. Link. Loeb Classical Library. Cambridge, Mass. and London: Harvard University Press.

Thiselton-Dyer, T. F. 1898. *The folk-lore of plants.* New York: D. Appleton.

Thomas, Paul. 1960. *Hindu religion, customs and manners.* 4th rev. ed. Bombay: D. B. Taraporevala Sons.

Thomas, Paul. 1961. *Epics, myths and legends of India.* 12th ed. Bombay: D. B. Taraporevala Sons.

Thompson, Charles J. S. 1968. *The mystic mandrake*. New Hyde Park, N.Y.: University Books.

Thompson, D'Arcy W. 1966. *A glossary of Greek birds*. Hildesheim: Georg Olms.

Thompson, L. G. 1973. "Funeral rites in Taiwan." Pp. 160–69 in Laurence G. Thompson (ed.), *The Chinese way in religion*. Encino, California and Belmont, California: Dickenson.

Thompson, R. Campbell. 1903–4. *The devils and evil spirits of Babylonia*. 2 vols. London: Luzac.

Thompson, R. Campbell. 1926. "On mandrake and tragacanth in cuneiform." *Journal of the Royal Asiatic Society of Great Britain and Ireland* 1926: 100–103.

Thompson, R. Campbell. 1949. *A dictionary of Assyrian botany*. London: British Academy.

Thompson, Stuart E. 1988. "Death, food, and fertility." Pp. 71–108 in James L. Watson and Evelyn S. Rawski (eds.), *Death ritual in late imperial and modern China*. Berkeley, Los Angeles, London: University of California Press.

Thomson, William McClure. [1911]. *The land and the book*. 2 vols. in 1. New York and London: Harper and Brothers.

Thonger, Richard. 1968. *A calendar of German customs*. Chester Springs, Penna: Dufour Editions.

Thurston, Edgar. 1906. *Ethnographic notes in southern India*. Madras: Government Press.

Thurston, Edgar. 1909. *Castes and tribes of southern India*. 7 vols. Madras: Government Press.

Thurston, Edgar. 1912. *Omens and superstitions of southern India*. London: T. Fisher Unwin.

"To Apollo." 1914. Homeric Hymns 3. Pp. 324–63 in *Hesiod, the Homeric hymns and Homerica*. Trans. Hugh G. Evelyn-White. Loeb Classical Library. Cambridge, Mass.: Harvard University Press; London: William Heinemann.

Tod, James. 1971. *Annals and antiquities of Rajasthan*. 3 vols. Ed. William Crooke. Delhi, Varanasi, Patna: Motilal Banarsidass.

Tolkowsky, S. 1938. *Hesperides: A history of the culture and use of citrus fruits*. London: John Bale, Sons & Curnow.

Toomey, Paul M. 1986. "Food from the mouth of Krishna: Socio-religious aspects of sacred food in two Krishnaite sects." Pp. 55–83 in R. S. Khare and M. S. A. Rao (eds.), *Food, society, and culture*. Durham, N.C.: Carolina Academic Press.

Trevelyan, Marie. 1909. *Folk-lore and folk-stories of Wales*. London: E. Stock.

Trimen, Henry. 1893–1900. *A hand-book to the flora of Ceylon*. 5 pts. London: Dulau and Company.

Tripathi, Narayan. 1936. "A few fasts, festivities and observances in Orissa." *Man in India* 16: 156–82.

Tristram, H. B. 1873. *The natural history of the Bible.* 3d ed. London: Society for Promoting Christian Knowledge.

Trumbull, H. Clay. 1899. *The covenant of salt.* New York: Charles Scribner's Sons.

Tun Li-Ch'en. 1965. *Annual customs and festivals in Peking.* 2d ed. Trans. Derk Bodde. Hong Kong: Hong Kong University Press.

Turner, Victor. 1967. *The forest of symbols: Aspects of Ndembu ritual.* Ithaca, N.Y.: Cornell University Press.

Turner, William. 1568. *The first and secondes partes of the herbal of William Turner.* 4 pts. Collen: Arnold Birckman.

Tylor, Edward Burnett. 1958. *The origins of culture.* New York: Harper and Brothers.

Underhill, Muriel Marion. 1921. *The Hindu religious year.* Calcutta: Association Press; London: Oxford University Press.

Upadhyaya, K. D. 1965. "Indian botanical folklore." Pp. 1–18 in Sankar Sen Gupta (ed.), *Tree symbol worship in India.* Calcutta: Indian Publications.

Uphof, J. C. Th. 1959. *Dictionary of economic plants.* Weinheim (Bergstrasse): H. R. Engelmann (J. Cramer); New York: Hafner; Codicote: Wheldon and Wesley.

The useful plants of India. 1986. New Delhi: Publications and Information Directorate, Council of Scientific and Industrial Research.

Ussher, R. G. 1960. *The Characters of Theophrastus.* London: Macmillan; New York: St. Martin's Press.

Valaes, T., A. Karaklis, D. Stravrakakis, K. Bavela-Stravrakakis, A. Perakis, and S. A. Doxiadis. 1969. "Incidence and mechanism of neonatal jaundice related to glucose-6-phosphate dehydrogenase deficiency." *Pediatric Research* 3: 448–58.

Valle, Pietro della. 1892. *The travels of Pietro della Valle in India.* 2 vols. Trans. G. Havers. Ed. Edward Gray. Hakluyt Society Works, 84–85. London: Hakluyt Society.

van Buitenen, J. A. B. (trans. and ed.). 1973–78. *The Mahābhārata.* 3 vols. Chicago and London: University of Chicago Press.

van der Toorn, K. 1985. *Sin and sanction in Israel and Mesopotamia: A comparative study.* Studia Semitica Neerlandica, 22. Assen/Maastricht: Van Gorcum.

Varro. 1934. *On agriculture.* Pp. 159–529 in *Marcus Porcius Cato, On Agriculture. Marcus Terentius Varro, On Agriculture.* Trans. William Davis Hooper and Harrison Boyd Ash. Loeb Classical Library. Cambridge, Mass.: Harvard University Press; London: William Heinemann.

Vartak, V. D., and Anuradha Upadhye. 1989. "Floristic studies on Genus Ocimum L. from Western Maharashtra and Goa." Pp. 3–14 in Bhaskar R. Mardikar, Subhash Ranada, Madhukar Paranjpe, and Bhushan Patwardhan (eds.), *Krishna tulas (Ocimum sanctum): A monograph.* Pune: Interdisciplinary School of Ayurvedic Medicine, University of Poona.

Vats, Madho Sarup. 1940. *Excavations at Harappa.* 2 vols. Calcutta: Manager, Government of India Press.

Vavilov, N. I. 1949–50. *The origin, variation, immunity and breeding of cultivated plants.* Trans. K. S. Chester. Chronica Botanica, Vol. 13. Waltham, Mass.: Chronica Botanica Co.

Vayda, Andrew P. 1987. "Explaining what people eat: A review article." *Human Ecology* 15: 493–510.

Venzmer, Gerhard. 1972. *Five thousand years of medicine.* New York: Taplinger.

Veras, Solon. 1958. "II favismo era conosciuto dai Greci antichi?" Pp. 5–6 in G. Sansone, A. M. Piga, and G. Segni, *II favismo.* Trans. from the *Bulletin de la Société hellénique de Pédiatrie,* 1939. Turin: Edizioni Minerva Medica.

Veras, Solon. 1961. "Considerations sur 73 cas de favisme." *Archives françaises de Pédiatrie* 18: 345–51.

Verjee, Z. H. 1993. "Glucose 6-phosphate dehydrogenase deficiency in Africa—Review." *East African Medical Journal* 70, 4 (Supplement): 40–47.

Vernaleken, Theodor. 1859. *Mythen und Bräuche des Volkes in Oesterreich.* Vienna: Wilhelm Braumüller.

Veth, P. J. 1894. "De Mandragora." *Internationales Archiv für Ethnographie* 7: 199–205.

Vidyârṇava, Śriṣa Chandra. 1918. *Yajnavalkya Smriti.* Book 1: *The Āchâra adhyâya.* Vol. 21 of *The sacred books of the Hindus.* Allahabad: Pàninî Office.

Vidyarthi, L. P., R. K. Prasad, and V. S. Upadhyay. 1979. *Changing dietary patterns and habits: A socio-cultural study of Bihar.* New Delhi: Concept Publishing Company.

Vidyarthi, Lalita Prasad. 1961. *The sacred complex of Hindu Gaya.* London: Asia Publishing House.

Viennot, Odette. 1954. *Le culte de l'arbre dans l'Inde ancienne; textes et monuments brahmaniques et bouddhiques.* Paris: Presses Universitaires de France.

Viennot, Odette. 1964. *Les divinités fluviales Ganga et Yamunā.* Paris: Presses Universitaires de France.

Viglietto, G., V. Montanaro, V. Calabrò, D. Vallone, M. D'Urso, M. G. Persico, and G. Battistuzzi. 1990. "Common glucose-6-phosphate dehydrogenase (G6PD) variants from the Italian population: Biochemical and molecular characterization." *Annals of Human Genetics* 54: 1–15.

Vishnu-Mittre. 1968. "Protohistoric records of agriculture in India." *Transactions of the Bose Research Institute* (Calcutta) 31: 87–106.

Vishnu-Mittre. 1974. "Palaeobotanical evidence in India." Pp. 3–30 in Joseph Hutchinson (ed.), *Evolutionary studies in world crops.* London: Cambridge University Press.

Vishnu-Mittre. 1977. "Changing economy in ancient India." Pp. 569–88 in Charles A. Reed (ed.), *Origins of agriculture.* The Hague, Paris: Mouton.

Vogel, Friedrich, and Arno G. Motulsky. 1986. *Human genetics: Problems and approaches*. 2d ed. Berlin, Heidelberg, New York, Tokyo: Springer-Verlag.

Vogel, Jean Philippe. 1920. "The sign of the spread hand or 'Five-finger Token' (*pañcaṅgulika*) in Pali literature." *Mededeelingen, Akademie van Wetenschappen (Amsterdam), Afdeeling Letterkunde*, ser. 5, Vol. 4: 218–35.

Vogel, Jean Philippe. 1926. *Indian serpent-Lore; or, The Nāgas in Hindu legend and art*. London: A. Probsthain.

Vogel, Jean Philippe. 1929. "The woman and tree or *śālabhañjikā* in Indian literature and art." *Acta Orientalia* 7: 201–31.

Volčok, B. Y. 1976. "Images on objects with proto-Indian inscriptions." Pp. 73–87 in Arlene R. K. Zide and Kamil V. Zvelebil (eds.), *The Soviet decipherment of the Indus Valley script: Translation and critique*. Janua Linguarum, Series Practica, 156. The Hague, Paris: Mouton.

von Luschan, Felix. 1891. "Sechs Mandragora-Wurzeln." *Zeitschrift für Ethologie* 23: 726–28.

von Schiefner, F. Anton (trans.). 1926. *Tibetan tales derived from Indian sources*. Trans. from the German by W. R. S. Ralston. New ed. London: George Routledge and Sons; New York: E. P. Dutton.

von Schroeder, Leopold. 1884. *Pythagoras und die Inder*. Leipzig: Otto Schulze.

von Schroeder, Leopold. 1901. "Das Bohnenverbot bei Pythagoras und im Veda." *Wiener Zeitschrift für Kunde des Morgenländes* 15: 187–212.

Vural, Nevin, and Semra Sardas. 1984. "Biological activities of broad bean (*Vicia faba* L.) extracts cultivated in south Anatolia in favism sensitive subjects." *Toxicology* 31: 175–79.

Wachsmuth, Kurt. 1864. *Das alte Griechenland im neuen*. Bonn: M. Cohen.

Waddell, L. Austine. 1971. *The Buddhism of Tibet or Lamaism*. 2d ed. Cambridge: W. Heffer and Sons.

Wakil, H. N. 1895–96. "Surat: Marriage of doves and tulasi tree." *North Indian Notes and Queries* 5: 76.

Waldron, H. A. 1973. "Mediterranean anaemia in antiquity." *British Medical Journal* 2: 667.

Walker, Benjamin. 1968. *The Hindu world*. 2 vols. New York: Frederick A. Praeger.

Walker, Deryck G., and James E. Bowman. 1960. "In vitro effect of *Vicia faba* extracts upon reduced glutathione of erythrocytes." *Proceedings of the Society for Experimental Biology and Medicine* 103: 476–77.

Wandel, Margareta, Padmi Guna Wardena, Arne Oshaug, and Nils Wandel. 1984. "Heaty and cooling foods in relation to food habits in a southern Sri Lanka community." *Ecology of Food and Nutrition* 14: 93–104.

Ward, William. 1970. *A view of the history, literature, and mythology of the Hindoos*. New ed. 3 vols. Port Washington, N. Y., and London: Kennikat Press.

Wasson, R. Gordon. 1968. *Soma: Divine mushroom of immortality.* Ethno-Mycological Studies, 1. New York: Harcourt, Brace, and World.

Wasson, R. Gordon. 1982. "The last meal of the Buddha." *Journal of the American Oriental Society* 102: 591–603.

Watanabe, Tadashi. 1974. *Garlic therapy.* Tokyo: Japan Publications, Inc.

Watt, George. 1889–96. *A dictionary of the economic products of India.* 6 vols. London: W. H. Allen and Co.

Watt, George. 1908. *The commercial products of India.* London: John Murray.

Watt, John Mitchell. 1972. "Magic and witchcraft in relation to plants and folk medicine." Pp. 67–102 in Tony Swain (ed.), *Plants in the development of modern medicine.* Cambridge, Mass.: Harvard University Press.

Watters, Thomas. 1904–5. *On Yuan Chwang's travels in India, 629–645 A.D.* 2 vols. Oriental Translation Fund, n. s. 14. London: Royal Asiatic Society.

Webber, Herbert John. 1943. "History and development of the citrus industry." Pp. 1–40 in Vol. 1 of Herbert John Webber and Leon Dexter Batchelor (eds.), *The citrus industry.* Berkeley and Los Angeles: University of California Press.

Weiser, Francis X. 1952. *Handbook of Christian feasts and customs.* New York: Harcourt, Brace.

Welch, Holmes. 1958. *The parting of the way: Lao Tzu and the Taoist movement.* London: Methuen.

Welch, Holmes. 1967. *The practice of Chinese Buddhism, 1900–1950.* Harvard East Asian Series, 26. Cambridge, Mass.: Harvard University Press.

Wensinck, A. J. 1960. *A handbook of early Mohammedan tradition.* Leiden: E. J. Brill.

Werblowsky, R. J. Zwi. 1987. "Transmigration." Pp. 21–26 in Vol. 15 of *The encyclopedia of religion.* 16 vols. Ed. Mircea Eliade. New York: Macmillan; London: Collier Macmillan.

Wernsdorfer, Walther H. 1980. "The importance of malaria in the world." Pp. 1–93 in Vol. 1 of Julius P. Kreier (ed.), *Malaria.* New York: Academic Press.

West, Edward William (trans.). 1880–97. *Pahlavi texts.* 5 vols. Vols. 5, 18, 24, 37, and 47 of *The sacred books of the East.* Ed. F. Max Müller. Oxford: Clarendon Press.

West, M. L. 1983. *The Orphic poems.* Oxford: Clarendon Press.

Westermarck, Edward. 1906–8. *The origin and development of the moral ideas.* 2 vols. London: Macmillan.

Westermarck, Edward. 1920. *The belief in spirits in Morocco.* Acta Academiae Aboensis, Humaniora I: 1. Åbo: Åbo Akademi.

Westermarck, Edward. 1922. *The history of human marriage.* 5th ed. 3 vols. New York: Allerton Book Company.

Westermarck, Edward. 1926. *Ritual and belief in Morocco.* 2 vols. London: Macmillan.

Westermarck, Edward. 1973. *Pagan survivals in Mohammedan civilisation.* Amsterdam: Philo Press.

Wheatley, Paul. 1961. *The golden Khersonese: Studies in the historical geography of the Malay Peninsula before A. D. 1500.* Kuala Lumpur: University of Malaya Press.

Whitehead, H. 1908–26. "Madras and Coorg." Pp. 237–39 in Vol. 8 of *Encyclopaedia of religion and ethics.* 13 vols. Ed. James Hastings. Edinburgh: T. and T. Clark.

Whitlock, Ralph. 1979. *In search of lost gods: A guide to British folklore.* Oxford: Phaidon.

Wili, W. 1955. "The Orphic mysteries and the Greek spirit." Pp. 64–92 in Joseph Campbell (ed.), *The mysteries.* Papers from the Eranos Yearbooks. Bollingen Series, 30, 2. New York: Bollingen Foundation.

Wilkins, Augustus S. (ed.). 1937. *The "Epistles" of Horace.* London: Macmillan.

Wilkinson, J. Gardner. 1883. *The manners and customs of the ancient Egyptians.* 3 vols. Boston: S. E. Cassino.

Wilkinson, R. J. 1924. *Malay Literature.* Part 1: *Romance. History. Poetry.* Papers on Malay Subjects. Kuala Lumpur: F. M. S. Government Press.

Williams, C. A. S. 1941. *Outlines of Chinese symbolism and art motives.* 3d rev. ed. Shanghai: Kelly and Walsh.

Williams, Robert. 1963. *Jaina yoga: A survey of the mediaeval Śrāvakācāras.* London: Oxford University Press.

Willoughby, Harold R. 1929. *Pagan regeneration: A study of mystery initiations in the Graeco-Roman world.* Chicago: University of Chicago Press.

Willoughby-Meade, Gerald. 1929. *Chinese ghouls and goblins.* New York: Frederick A. Stokes.

Wilson, Horace Hayman. 1958. *Religious sects of the Hindus.* Ed. Ernst R. Rost. Calcutta: Susil Gupta.

Wilson, Horace Hayman (trans.). 1961. *The Vishṇu Purāṇa.* 3d ed. Calcutta: Punthi Pustak.

Wiser, Charlotte Viall. 1955. "The foods of a Hindu village of North India." *Annals of the Missouri Botanical Garden* 42: 303–412.

Woodburne, A. Stewart. 1981. "The evil eye in South Indian folklore." Pp. 55–65 in Alan Dundes (ed.), *The evil eye: A folklore casebook.* Garland Folklore Casebooks, 2. New York and London: Garland.

Woodward, Marcus. 1969. *Leaves from Gerard's Herball.* New York: Dover Publications.

Wright, Elizabeth Mary. 1914. *Rustic speech and folklore.* London: Oxford University Press.

Wright, Thomas (ed.). 1845. *The archaeological album: or, Museum of National Antiquities.* London: Chapman and Hall.

Wünsch, R. 1908–26. "Charms and amulets (Roman)." Pp. 461–65 in Vol. 3 of *Encyclopaedia of religion and ethics.* 13 vols. Ed. James Hastings. Edinburgh: T. and T. Clark.

Wünsch, Richard. 1902. *Das Frühlingsfest der Insel Malta.* Leipzig: B. G. Teubner.

Xenophon. 1922. *The banquet.* Trans. O. J. Todd. Pp. 373–481 in Vol. 3 of *Xenophon: "Hellenica," "Anabasis," "Symposium," and "Apology."* Loeb Classical Library. London: William Heinemann; Cambridge, Mass.: Harvard University Press.

Yahya, Hassan I., and Nasir A. S. Al-Allawi. 1993. "Acute haemolytic episodes and fava bean consumption in G6PD deficient Iraqis." *Indian Journal of Medical Research* (Section B) 98: 290–92.

Yetts, W. Perceval. 1912. *Symbolism in Chinese art.* [Leiden: E. J. Brill].

You, Wei-cheng, William J. Blot, Yuan-sheng Chang, Abby Ershow, Zhu-tian Yang, Qi An, Brian E. Henderson, Joseph F. Fraumeni, Jr., and Tian-gen Wang. 1989. "Allium vegetables and reduced risk of stomach cancer." *Journal of the National Cancer Institute* 81: 162–64.

Young, Mark C. (ed.). 1996. *The Guinness book of world records, 1997.* Stamford, Conn.: Guinness Media.

Yule, Henry (trans. and ed.). 1913–16. *Cathay and the way thither.* New ed. 4 vols. Rev. Henri Cordier. Hakluyt Society Works, Second Series, 33, 37, 38, 41. London: Hakluyt Society.

Yule, Henry. 1968. *A narrative of the mission to the court of Ava in 1855.* Kuala Lumpur, London, New York: Oxford University Press.

Yule, Henry, and A. C. Burnell. 1903. *Hobson-Jobson: A glossary of colloquial Anglo-Indian words and phrases, and of kindred terms, etymological, historical, geographical and discursive.* New ed. Ed. William Crooke. London: John Murray.

Zannos-Mariolea, Leda, and Christos Kattamis. 1961. "Glucose-6-phosphate deficiency in Greece." *Blood* 18: 34–47.

Zee, S. Y., and L. H. Hui. 1981. *Hong Kong food plants.* Hong Kong: Urban Council.

Zeven, A. C., and J. M. J. de Wet. 1982. *Dictionary of cultivated plants and their regions of diversity.* Wageningen: Centre for Agricultural Publishing and Documentation.

Zeven, A. C., and P. M. Zhukovsky. 1975. *Dictionary of cultivated plants and their centres of diversity.* Wageningen: Centre for Agricultural Publishing and Documentation.

Zhang, Yue-sheng, Xing-ruo Chen, and Ying-nian Yu. 1989. "Antimutagenic effect of garlic (*Allium sativum* L.) on 4NQO-induced mutagenesis in *Escherichia coli* WP2." *Mutation Research* 227: 215–19.

Zimmer, Heinrich. 1946. *Myths and symbols in Indian art and civilization.* Ed. Joseph Campbell. Bollingen Series, 6. Princeton: Princeton University Press.

Zimmer, Heinrich. 1955. *The art of Indian Asia: Its mythology and transformations.* 2 vols. Completed and ed. by Joseph Campbell. Bollingen Series, 39. New York: Pantheon Books.

Zohary, Daniel. 1977. "Comments on the origin of cultivated broad bean, *Vicia faba* L." *Israel Journal of Botany* 26: 39–40.

Zohary, Daniel, and Maria Hopf. 1973. "Domestication of pulses in the Old World." *Science* 182: 887–94.

Zohary, Daniel, and Maria Hopf. 1988. *Domestication of plants in the Old World.* Oxford: Clarendon Press.

Zohary, Daniel, and Pinhas Spiegel-Roy. 1975. "Beginnings of fruit growing in the Old World." *Science* 187: 319–27.

Zohary, Michael. 1982. *Plants of the Bible.* Cambridge: Cambridge University Press.

INDEX

537